The Art of the Essay

The Art of the Essay

Lydia Fakundiny
Cornell University

Houghton Mifflin Company **Boston**

Dallas Geneva, Illinois Palo Alto Princeton, New Jersey

Printed in the U.S.A.

Library of Congress Catalog Card Number: 90-83060

ISBN: 0-395-54441-6
DEFGHIJ-AM-9876

ACKNOWLEDGMENTS

Chinua Achebe. "Language and the Destiny of Man." Excerpt(s) from *Morning Yet on Creation Day* by Chinua Achebe, copyright © 1975 by Chinua Achebe. Used by permission of Doubleday, a division of Bantam Doubleday Dell Publishing Group, Inc. "Language and the Destiny of Man" is here reprinted in its entirety.

Joseph Addison. "The Royal Exchange: *Spectator* No. 69" and "The Tombs at Westminster Abbey: *Spectator* No. 26" by Joseph Addison from *The Spectator*, Donald Bond, ed., Oxford University Press, 1965. Reprinted by permission of the Oxford University Press.

Margaret Atwood. "Happy Endings" from *Murder in the Dark.* Copyright by Margaret Atwood, 1983, in "Murder in the Dark."

Sir Francis Bacon. "Of Boldness" and "Of Studies." Reprinted by permission of the publishers from *The Essayes or Counsels, Civill and Morall* by Sir Francis Bacon, edited by Michael Kiernan, Cambridge, Mass.: Harvard University Press, Copyright © 1985 by Michael Kiernan.

Acknowledgments continue on p. 745

For my parents, Elisabeth and Albert Fakundiny

Contents

Preface xv

Introduction: On Approaching the Essay 1

The Essays

Sir Francis Bacon (1561–1626)
Of Studies 22
Of Boldness 24

John Donne (1572–1631)
The Physician is Sent For: *Meditation* No. 4 26
I Sleep Not Day Nor Night: *Meditation* No. 15 28

Sir William Cornwallis (1579–1614)
Of Entertainment 30

John Earle (1601?–1665)
A Detractor 32
Paul's Walk 34

Abraham Cowley (1618–1667)
The Dangers of an Honest Man in Much Company 35

Jonathan Swift (1667–1745)
A Modest Proposal 41

Joseph Addison (1672–1719)
The Tombs at Westminster Abbey: *Spectator* No. 26 49
The Royal Exchange: *Spectator* No. 69 51

Benjamin Franklin (1706–1790)
The Ephemera 54

Henry Fielding (1707–1754)
An Essay on Nothing 57

Samuel Johnson (1709–1784)
On Spring: *Rambler* No. 5 66
In Pursuit of Fame: *Rambler* No. 146 70

David Hume (1711–1776)
Of the Delicacy of Taste and Passion 73

Oliver Goldsmith (1728–1774)
National Prejudices 77

Charles Lamb (1775–1834)
Grace Before Meat 81
The Convalescent 87

William Hazlitt (1778–1830)
On Going a Journey 93
On the Feeling of Immortality in Youth 101

Washington Irving (1783–1859)
The Voyage 111

Thomas De Quincey (1785–1859)
On the Knocking at the Gate in *Macbeth* 116

Thomas Macaulay (1800–1859)
On the Royal Society of Literature 122

Ralph Waldo Emerson (1803–1882)
Illusions 129

Nathaniel Hawthorne (1804–1864)
Foot-prints on the Sea-shore 138

Charles Dickens (1812–1870)
Night Walks 147

Henry David Thoreau (1817–1862)
Life Without Principle 156

Mark Twain (1835–1910)
Corn-pone Opinions 173

Alice Meynell (1847–1922)
Solitudes 177

Robert Louis Stevenson (1850–1894)
An Apology for Idlers 182

W. E. B. Du Bois (1868–1963)
On Being Black 191
The Guilt of the Cane 195

Hilaire Belloc (1870–1953)
The Mowing of a Field 199

Max Beerbohm (1872–1956)
A Relic 206

E. M. Forster (1879–1970)
What I Believe 213

Virginia Woolf (1882–1941)
How Should One Read a Book? 222
The Death of the Moth 231

D. H. Lawrence (1885–1930)
Whistling of Birds 235

Aldo Leopold (1886–1948)
Marshland Elegy 239

T. S. Eliot (1888–1965)
Tradition and the Individual Talent 245

Katherine Anne Porter (1890–1980)
St. Augustine and the Bullfight 253

Aldous Huxley (1894–1963)
Hyperion to a Satyr 264

Elizabeth Bowen (1899–1973)
Out of a Book 278

E. B. White (1899–1985)
A Slight Sound at Evening 284

Zora Neale Hurston (1901?–1960)
How It Feels to Be Colored Me 293

George Orwell (1903–1950)
Reflections on Gandhi 298

Nancy Mitford (1904–1973)
A Bad Time 306

Loren Eiseley (1907–1977)
The Winter of Man 318

M. F. K. Fisher (*b.* 1908)
Moment of Wisdom 322

Eudora Welty (*b.* 1909)
A Sweet Devouring 328

Lewis Thomas (*b.* 1913)
An Earnest Proposal 334

Doris Lessing (*b.* 1919)
My Father 337

James McConkey (*b.* 1921)
In Praise of Chekhov 345

William Manchester (*b.* 1922)
Okinawa: The Bloodiest Battle of All 357

James Baldwin (1924–1987)
Equal in Paris 367

Russell Baker (*b.* 1925)
The Flag 381

Margaret Laurence (1926–1987)
The Very Best Intentions 387

Jan Morris (*b.* 1926)
Fun City: Las Vegas, U.S.A. 396

Franklin Russell (*b.* 1926)
A Madness of Nature 408

Cynthia Ozick (*b.* 1928)
The Riddle of the Ordinary 416
A Drugstore in Winter 423

Richard Selzer (*b.* 1928)
An Absence of Windows 430
A Worm from My Notebook 434

Martin Luther King, Jr. (1929–1968)
Letter from Birmingham Jail 441

George Steiner (*b.* 1929)
A Kind of Survivor 457

Chinua Achebe (*b.* 1930)
Language and the Destiny of Man 471

Carol Bly (*b.* 1930)
Getting Tired 480

Donald Barthelme (1931–1989)
Not-Knowing 485

Caroline Blackwood (*b.* 1931)
Portrait of a Beatnik 499

John McPhee (*b.* 1931)
The Search for Marvin Gardens 508

Edward Hoagland (*b.* 1932)
City Walking 519

Joan Didion (*b.* 1934)
On Morality 522
On Going Home 525

N. Scott Momaday (*b.* 1934)
The Way to Rainy Mountain 529

Richard Rhodes (*b.* 1937)
The Death of the Everglades 535

Margaret Atwood (*b.* 1939)
Happy Endings 555

Stephen Jay Gould (*b.* 1941)
Of Wasps and WASPs 560

Paul Theroux (*b.* 1941)
Cowardice 570

Phyllis Rose (*b.* 1942)
Tools of Torture: An Essay on Beauty and Pain 579

Alice Walker (*b.* 1944)
Looking for Zora 584

Annie Dillard (*b.* 1945)
Life on the Rocks: The Galápagos 601

Shiva Naipaul (1945–1985)
City by the Sea 615

Scott Russell Sanders (*b.* 1945)
Doing Time in the Thirteenth Chair 632

Gretel Ehrlich (*b.* 1946)
The Smooth Skull of Winter 649

David Quammen (*b.* 1948)
Thinking About Earthworms: A Meditation on Darwin's Silent Choir 653

Kenneth McClane (*b.* 1951)
Walls: A Journey to Auburn 659

Resources for Readers and Writers 671

Montaigne and the Essay 673
Essayists on Their Art 689
Talking About Style 713

Index of Authors and Titles 741

Preface

This book on the essay's art evolved through the improvisations of the classroom. In spirit, and in many of its actual parts, it has been rehearsed again and again. The essays collected and the apparatus that accompanies them are, so to speak, the cumulative script of those rehearsals, a tribute to what the essay can do by showing what it has done during the course of its literary life in a single, widely distributed modern language: English. My aim has not been to trace the essay's development or to anatomize it by kinds, though this chronologically arranged, richly diversified selection lends itself to such studies and others. Rather, I have sought to choose from the wealth of some four centuries essays so accomplished in themselves yet so various in form, style, tone, aim, length, scope, subject, and effect, that their sum would illustrate as broad a rhetorical range, as large a generic terrain, as I could identify. There are no excerpts here, no edited chunks of originally longer works; and, although some of these essays began life as talks, none of them is, to my knowledge, a mere transcript of an address to a live audience. Every piece is, in that sense, a *written* text, composed *as* a short, independent, self-contained prose discourse: an essay. Literary distinction, insofar as I know it when I see it, has been my principal guide. In the tenth issue of his *Covent Garden Journal* (February 4, 1754), Henry Fielding proposed, as a first step in the formation of literary taste, "a total abstinence from all bad books." Without presuming to lay down rules of taste I can say only that, if I have failed in the eyes of some readers to choose only the very best essays for their enjoyment, I feel reasonably sure of having succeeded at promoting abstinence from any very bad ones.

Anthologies are for accommodating under one roof some family or tribe of discourses to be read, enjoyed, and studied together; and they are for whetting appetites, for signposting the vast countries beyond. In my own commentaries—an introduction, seventy-five headnotes, and an appended three-part discussion—I have tried to extend both functions of anthologies: to gather and order on the one hand, to suggest and point elsewhere on the other.

My introductory piece, "On Approaching the Essay," considers, in something of the spirit of the creature itself, the beginnings and the character of this fascinating genre. I try, in other words, to draw as close as I can manage to what the essay *is*; in the process, a serviceable trail may have been cut here and there for exploring the essays in this book and elsewhere.

The headnotes that precede each selection (or two by the same writer) are offered as brief guides along the way; like many such guides, they probably take on more meaning the farther in one ventures. In keeping with my aim to collect not a group of great *essayists* but a diverse range of distinguished *essays* (some by famous practitioners, some by writers known mainly for work of other kinds), I have not dwelled on biographical details. Instead, I have situated each selection in what I hope is a suggestive context, whether in respect to the essay as genre or, more narrowly, to the writer's personal and artistic concerns. Bibliographic sources are noted parenthetically in the headnotes to point interested readers, critics, and essayists in the right direction.

Following these eighty-seven essays in English, from Bacon to our contemporaries, are three perspectives on the essay under the heading "Resources for Readers and Writers." First, I take up the French inventor of the essay, Michel de Montaigne, without whom any foray into the tradition, in whatever language, seems unthinkable; Donald Frame's fine translation of Montaigne's essay "Of Practice" serves to lead readers and writers to this great and perhaps most influential of all essayists. Montaigne and a goodly number of his successors in English have their say in the second section, "Essayists on Their Art," a loosely linked series of excerpts intended to supplement my own intoductory essay. The wealth of ideas and beauties of language to be found in these comments on the essay by accomplished practitioners cannot but enhance any reader's appreciation of the form, any writer's own attempts. The last and longest part, "Talking about Style," seeks to engage readers and writers alike in the verbal artistry of essayistic prose, specifically the prose collected in this book. The scope of my discussion, its use of technical language, its range and degree of detail are, I hope, adequate to the dual task of introducing the fun and value of stylistic analysis to those who have never tried it and of reinforcing and refining the skill of those who have.

I am indebted to all who have variously incited, encouraged, facilitated, and supported the making of this book, especially:

The late Alistair Campbell, Bosworth-Rawlinson Professor of Anglo-Saxon, Oxford University, England, for compelling me to look at Early English sentences;

Scott B. Elledge, Goldwin Smith Professor of English Literature Emeritus, Cornell University, for getting me hooked on modern essayistic prose;

Joyce Elbrecht, Professor of Philosophy, Ithaca College (retired), friend and collaborator in teaching and in writing fiction, for all the hours of talk about language, literature, and theory, and for being my most steadfast, my most exacting and responsive reader and critic;

Henry Louis Gates, Jr., John Spencer Bassett Professor of English & Literature, Duke University, for his abiding interest in my course on the essay and for telling me more than once to write my own textbook and get a proposal out, fast;

My editors at Houghton Mifflin Company, women of skill and courage, for paying attention to my proposal, for shepherding it and ensuing manuscripts through their institutional phases with professional good sense, and, not least of all, for devising a production schedule that made reasonable and possible what might otherwise have been out of the question;

The following reviewers of my proposal to write this book and of its table of contents, for the generous gift of their time and for their discerning responses: Sylvan Barnet of Tufts University (retired), Neil Daniel of Texas Christian University, Miriam Dow of The George Washington University, David Espey of the University of Pennsylvania, Doug Hunt of the University of Missouri, Roger D. Lund of LeMoyne College, Michael Meyer of the University of Connecticut, Scott Russell Sanders of Indiana University, Patricia L. Skarda of Smith College, Robert Wiltenberg of Washington University;

The John S. Knight Writing Program and the College of Arts & Sciences, Cornell University, for their financial support during my teaching leave in the spring semester of 1990, and Dorothy Mermin, then Chair of the Department of English, for arranging that leave with merciful speed;

The staff of the Department of Rare Books, Cornell University, for generous access to Benjamin Franklin's handwritten draft, dated September 20, 1778, of "The Ephemera," and for permitting me to edit the manuscript for inclusion in this book;

Phillis Molock, who keeps typing up the much-edited pages I hand her into faultless manuscripts and does so with friendly good humor, however pressed she may be, and with wit and time to spare;

My colleagues, Ann Boehm, Stuart Davis, and Kenneth McClane, for our ongoing conversations about teaching writing of all kinds from "creative" and "critical" to "composition";

And to some two hundred veterans of a decade of English 388/89, "The Art of the Essay," who could always be counted on to put in my way questions, problems, and essays I needed to think up this book.

To all of these and, of course, to the essay, I give thanks.

Lydia Fakundiny
Cornell University

On Approaching the Essay

For some years I have been teaching a course called "The Art of the Essay," in which this book had its beginning. Each term gathers a new set of students, and that alone redraws the configuration of the possible: what people around the table know and don't know, how they think aloud and on paper, what moves them as readers, as writers. But something more prevents each time from becoming a comfortable reprise of the last, and that something has to do with our subject. The truth is that I'm never able to describe, let alone prescribe, where we're going. I have no syllabus, as such, to offer. It's always possible to make these things up, but, apprehensive as I may get, I try not to. From the outset, and most especially *at* the outset, I resist definition. I hold out against the need, all around, to pin down what the art of the essay is—what, at the very least, an essay is; for the problem of "art" will take care of itself, we imagine, as time goes on. Art, perhaps, is nothing more than success, and we think we can all smell that though hard put to define it. But the essay—ah, the essay must be some kind of a thing, if not exactly like a buttercup or a chair, then surely a taxonomic slot, as the schoolbooks say, a sort of plan, scheme, design for production. A set of instructions; a program. Tell me what it is, or failing that, show me how to make one.

Everyone learns for herself, we say, in one of those educational pieties so commonplace it hardly bears thinking about and so profound one never gets to the bottom of it even in a lifetime of teaching. There's the transfer of information, to be sure, and the enabling (since all education goes on in the cultural sphere) to learn again what someone somewhere already knows. But thinking your way through an essay, whether as reader or writer, gains little from being led by the hand, however adroitly, however strategically, to some preinscribed end. What I find myself becoming as a teacher is something more like a pointing finger.

"There," I say, "there's an essay, a good one, as far as I can tell. Read it. Follow it. Ask how it's done. Take Virginia Woolf's advice: 'Do not dictate to your author; become him' " ("How Should One Read a Book?"). Learn to read, she means, not like an opinionated censor, not even like a dispassionate critic, but like an interested party, a writer.

"And write. Keep on writing, daily if you can. There—now you're starting to make something that looks to me like an essay." For the duration of our course, I am this pointing finger, this arrow hovering over who knows what wilderness of hope and frustration. Still, as the days and weeks pass, more and more essays, valued as such by the people around the table, do get written and take their place beside those in the books. Now and then there will be one as good as those—"good all the way through," as Eudora Welty wrote of Mark Twain in "A Sweet Devouring": art.

How do I know, since I resist definition, where to point myself, which direction to list in and when, and where to pull back? By reading essays, and, of course, reading all around; a long habit of "becoming" this author and that one, including the ones before me in the class; studying each essay's craft by asking just how it is that this particular discourse can manage to elaborate a voice, an "I" for the occasion, a characteristic way of inhabiting the world. Or turn that view of the essayistic self around: call it a way of making, by words, a world to inhabit.

The essay class becomes a communal effort to apprehend, as we go, something of what everyone desired at the outset and could not have pinned down. What this says is that it proceeds in something of the way that writing an essay itself does. Every essay is the only one of its kind. There are no rules for making beginnings, or middles, or endings; it is a harder, a more original discipline than that. The eye that "takes in" what is "out there" and the "I" that makes sense of it persist from moment to moment in that unconscious symbiosis we experience as being alive: "the individual," as Walter Pater wrote, "in his isolation, each mind keeping as a solitary prisoner its own dream of a world" (Conclusion, *The Renaissance*). Suppose, then, I am engaged in what is called "writing." Somehow the "I" behind my eyes, as it were, always looking "out," aware of itself, remembering and dismembering, doubting, probing, speculating, savoring, strives to concentrate and steady itself in a phrase, a sentence, to elaborate itself in the run of words, there, on the page, the screen, paragraph by paragraph. Discourse. Somehow "I" am forming myself right there in front of my very eyes: my "self" forms itself in and as discourse. And if I keep it up, really stick to this exacting business of writing myself out—not with any finality, no more than a self occasioned by whatever set it writing, whether a morning headline, a conversation half-overheard, a dog crossing a street, a fleeting dissatisfaction with my own laziness—eventually, what I will have is an essay, or the raw makings of one.

Say you are wandering—without a map, because no satisfactory one comes to hand—in what you believe to be a neighborhood. Wandering about, you come to know it and locate yourself in it only as you keep on traversing it. Here is a fire station, a corner drugstore, a spot of green space, a row of turreted Victorian homes, a canal. As you pass and repass any one of these landmarks, you see where you are in relation to all the others; you map the place out *as* a neighborhood. Note: it is your own movement that brings into being the map that tells you what kind of terrain you are in. Your orientation is of your own making. You know where you are by having gone there.

So it is with coming to understand the essay as a genre, a way of writing prose, in a class on the essay; so it is, too, with any solitary effort to work through some particular essay, whether your own or someone else's. Essays discover themselves in the writing. (I am not the first to remark that even when you try, in any concentrated fashion, to talk about the essay, you will more than likely find yourself composing one; essays, it seems, insist on being thought about only in essays.) Every essay worth writing is, in the words of a great contemporary essayist, Cynthia Ozick, "heir to nothing, and sets out with empty pockets from scratch" (Foreword, *Art & Ardor*). When I am inside an airplane, dizzily high above ground, I both imagine and avoid imagining myself suspended there, inside the roar and hum of that hurtling bubble of steel and plastic. If I can get past the breathtaking terror of the image, I may begin to sense the freedom, the lightness, the sheer irresponsibility of being carried so swiftly, so involuntarily, to one's destination—just. As for writing essays: who doesn't experience at least a twinge of terror at sight of the white page, the blank screen, the huge uncertainty of where you are going, how you will end up? What and who you might become (or fail to become) in the process? I have always wondered at the faith of people who experience only the freedom of flying without its terror, their inexplicable certitude about being set down, firmly on the ground, at journey's end: the right place, a friend or a clean-swept rental car to meet them. Maybe such people simply don't care, and their freedom surges from that. Much of essay writing could not go on except for this learning not to mind that you are "heir to nothing." Whole passages must go by like that, the "I" neither startled nor uneasy at seeing itself so delicately spun out there, in bare words.

If you are writing a letter to your boss to ask for a raise or to complain about conditions of work, or if you are going to write a user's manual, or even a letter to the editor supporting a particular candidate for mayor, you had better think about your audience—that scrutinizing other "I"—from the start; you had better work out your argument beforehand and know exactly who you are talking to and what for. You had better care, in other words, exactly where and when you are going to come down. But an essayist, disposed though she may be to instruct or convert or entertain, has as her first task coming into being in the wilds of the occasion that sets her writing—her topic, subject, hunch, idea, concern, question, puzzle. Whatever in the wide world interests her.

Over the centuries of its life in English, the essay has hoarded the memorabilia of individual responsiveness to all that is, like a vast and variegated treasure. Any number of stories, so to speak, could be woven out of this sheer diversity of subject matter, the continuities, the gaps, the shifts of vision. So, too, the possibilities for amplification within essays seem to be boundless—the many ways, for instance, an essay can pack narrative inside itself, or meld it with any or all the other modes of discoursing: description, explanation, analysis, definition, argument. The fluid rhetorical textures so created have sustained the essay's liveliness, its capacity for renewal, from generation to generation. Then there is the variable timbre of essayistic prose—the human figure evoked by a particular way with language, a style—that we try to capture under metaphors like "voice" or "tone." And there is style itself: the register of the words, the shape and run of the sentences; and how taste in these matters has undergone its fascinating changes through the centuries, always proclaiming its own inventions and preferences superior to what came before.

Here, immediately, a sort of paradox of the trade comes into view. Setting out to write an essay, you have no predetermined course to follow, no generic mold to fill or rules of composition to draw on—pockets empty. And yet, like it or not, as an essayist your pockets are weighed down by the accumulated wealth of four hundred years.

More or less. For if you date the beginning in France with Michel de Montaigne's first edition of his *Essais* in 1580, our pliant and prolific genre is now safely over the four-century mark. Most people do, in fact, make this the starting point of the modern essay, though all acknowledge its classical precursors in the meditative and epistolary prose of writers like Seneca, Plutarch, Cicero, or Horace (to whose inspiration Montaigne and other early European essayists pay tribute). If, on the other hand, you consider the essay in English only, the usual practice is to begin with Francis Bacon's ten brief *Essays* of 1597, barely more than ripe aphorisms stacked under headings like "Studies" or "Negotiating" that might have come out of Bacon's commonplace book; from that earliest edition, the quadricentennial of the essay lies a few years in the future still. It's even farther off if the much longer 1625 edition counts as the real start of what English essay writing, at least of the terse and unadorned Baconian kind, was up to. By then, however, there have been several appearances of the somewhat more Montaignesque *Essays* of William Cornwallis, the first in 1600; John Donne has been ravaged by fever and survived to meditate on it in his *Devotions* of 1624, which graft on the earliest, deliberately plain, shoots of English essayistic prose the opulencies of thought and imagery that characterize Donne's "metaphysical" poetic corpus. If the English essay began with Bacon as most people would claim—for the reason, at least, that he succeeded incomparably well at what he attempted—it did so at its leisure, under repeated revision and feeding on the first fruits of other writers.

Increase followed upon increase and made its way eventually across oceans and continents, wherever English and essays came to be read and written. Riches may embarrass, especially inherited riches, when every day appalls us by every kind of terrible destitution far and near. Yet there are no two ways about it: to entertain the tradition of the essay in English, as reader or writer, is to become heir to treasure, a splendid accretion of prose that shows off the language in some of its rarest moments.

The question is what to do with such an inheritance—how one will have it. T. S. Eliot insisted that a tradition "cannot be inherited" anyway, that "if you want it you must obtain it by great labor" ("Tradition and the Individual Talent"). A labor of love, it's to be hoped. And of self-love, too; after all, you have to think reasonably well of your own resourcefulness to take on a rich legacy in good faith. One may, of course, forfeit an inheritance unknowingly, or refuse it outright, dispossess oneself sight unseen. Or squander it. One may insist on making a clean break with history out of sheer boredom with the past, or alienation, or to preserve a sense of starting afresh with no baggage beyond the present moment. It would have to be a tenuous sense at best, because for a human being no present moment is ever pure and simple. Language is inscribed with the cultural past of those who speak and write it, even as I myself am inscribed in my memory of myself. There cannot be, for a writer, anything so clean and fresh as a language or a form untouched by others. (Even to recognize a cliché as such, you must have a feel for what has been used so much and handed down so often that weaknesses of thought poke through the threadbare words like elbows and kneecaps.)

The essay is a remembering form, whether in the narratives of personal reminiscence we call autobiographical or in the affectionate awareness essayists have always shown of their predecessors. Even casual browsing will catch, let's say, Bacon, Cornwallis, Donne, Cowley, Addison somewhere in their work thinking of Montaigne; Lamb of Cowley; Johnson and Franklin of Addison; Macaulay of Bacon and, again, of Addison; Emerson once more of Montaigne; Meynell of Johnson; Eiseley of Emerson; White of Thoreau and Montaigne; Dillard of Eiseley; Hoagland of Mark Twain; Porter, Ozick, and Walker of Woolf; Thomas of Swift and Montaigne, yet again; and Virginia Woolf of almost everybody from Montaigne to Max Beerbohm (not always with unqualified affection). And that's merely a sampling. The going back of essayists to other essayists, whether centrally or casually in the midst of other business, seems as natural as tracing your blood ancestry. Much of the time such knowledge may be no more than gratuitous, mere data on a genealogical chart; then comes a day when it turns critical to the account we make of ourselves, to the story we tell ourselves and the world about who we think we are. This is what happens to E. B. White when he commemorates Thoreau, in "A Slight Sound at Evening," and to Alice Walker when she goes looking for Zora Neale Hurston's grave. As for the essay *per se*—a form as idiosyncratic, as open-ended, as supple as any that has been devised in the language—remembrance comes close to being everything.

It is through practice that the possibilities of the form have mapped themselves in a history. The essays that come to us from the past, that are available to us now in the present moment, are themselves memorials. We know what the essay is by looking at what has been made of it—and even that is only the beginning of all it can do. Each attempt breaks fresh ground, even if what it's doing is turning over previously cultivated ground in new and changed times; for every age has its own concerns and its different ear for how language should resonate on the page.

The thing is to read all the essays you can get hold of, studying the permutations. Read not to acquire what Elizabeth Bowen called "a bookish attitude towards books," which is a little bit like just sitting on your inheritance (the old dragon in *Beowulf*, remember, one of the greatest dragons ever, sits on his treasure hoard, fast asleep), but to glean from each essay what each can give: the maturity of its unique achievement. Study of that kind is incremental. Reading, says Bowen, "gave bias to my observations of everything in the between-times when I was not reading" ("Out of a Book"). If it is essays you read, you train yourself to see things in the way peculiar to essay writing. To read widely, attentively, in the rich tradition of the essay in English is to come into possession not only of human thoughts linked across four centuries in a chain of famous names, but of the very habits of thought that create essays rather than fictions, or poems, or news reports, or journal articles, or telephone directories. It is to grasp, essay by essay, how to do what has been done again and again, differently every time, by starting out "from scratch." And it is to find your motive closing in on some version of the question at the heart of it all: what sets—has set—writers to discoursing in the kind of prose we call an essay? Put another way: where does the essay begin and where does it take you? Or simply: what, in the economy of prose literature, are essays for?

"My thoughts reach all, comprehend all," John Donne wrote in his fourth Meditation; "I their creator am in a closed prison, a sick bed. . . .

O miserable abundance! O beggarly riches!" Donne's *Devotions Upon Emergent Occasions* (1624) portray the paradoxes of the human estate through the loose narrative of a bout with physical illness. For Donne the Renaissance thinker, man is both everything and nothing, encompassing the universe yet housed in a self-destroying body: "What's become of man's great extent and proportion when himself shrinks himself, and consumes himself to a handful of dust?" The times, the metaphors, change, but some version of the predicament persists. In the last quarter of the eighteenth century, Benjamin Franklin dryly allegorized human grandiosity in the character of a gravely philosophical but insignificant, because so very short-lived, fly ("The Ephemera"). "How comically puffed up a thing man is, how pitiable," he seems to say. In our own urbanized and technological age, Richard Selzer draws "mortal lessons" (the title of his first book of essays) from his practice as a teaching surgeon, the mundane and occasionally heroic operations on diseased, imperilled human flesh. How this work—and perhaps all work—is to be not only done but accomplished with a measure of beauty that can alone sustain it past mere endurance is the subject of his essay "An Absence of Windows." Living as we must, doing the things we now do for a living, how are we to remain human? How become so in the first place?

The question of man—if I may call it that, being a woman and all too aware of how slippery that indispensable category "man" is, how it now includes, now excludes, whom it wishes—the question, I'll say, of what it means to be human pervades not only essays but every kind of literature, all the arts. We are as a species not so much deformed as somehow unformed, not fit for living as other creatures seem to be from the outset, and whatever finish we may acquire by living makes us, in the temporal order of things, fit only for death. Malleable, indeterminate, we are a species with one eye forever fixed in the mirror, inquiring after ourselves. Art, in whatever medium, is just the triumph of craft and insight that makes the old question always fresh, gives it urgency in the idioms of successive ages.

The essay was a child of the later Renaissance. Scholars were assimilating and, in the process, testing the revived learning of ancient classical literature with its still powerful formulations of man and the world. Explorers and adventurers were charting new transoceanic territories peopled by exotic strangers to be at once idealized and colonized (not, in other words, comfortably assimilated to the human picture). The modern vernacular languages of Europe, challenged and enriched by the demands of classical rhetoric, were, in turn, challenging the old universality of Latin and its reigning literary models; the English prose of Bacon, like the French of Montaigne, is in important ways a new instrument for thinking your way down a piece of paper. Alongside all that, and inseparable from it, was a fresh interest in the ordinary bustle of living—people getting sick, deluding themselves, having friends, behaving like fools or like sharks, finding others (or themselves) unbearable at times, growing old, acting up, and all the rest, often in the most baffling combinations. What motives, what ends, drive such a creature? Montaigne set out to study the whole matter by means of the repeated, inconclusive prose forays he called *essais.* Bacon borrowed the word for English but acknowledged no other debt. Certainly he can't be accused of having imitated Montaigne, though Bacon, too, studied man very closely and shrewdly, and a perusal of their respective tables of contents reveals their common concern.

One way to go at this problem of being human is to consider it piecemeal: draw up, in the fashion of Bacon, an empirical typology of the values, beliefs, institutions by and through which people live. Another way is to catalogue the human constitution itself. John Earle, then a young teacher at Oxford who was to become an eminent divine, wrote, apparently for his friends' entertainment, what was to appear in 1628 as the *Microcosmography.* The title compounds the idea of world mapping (cosmography), aired by European exploration of the New World, with the conventional Renaissance image of man as "the little world," the microcosm embodying in miniature the great universal Creation itself, the macrocosm. Earle's book is, thus, both a "little map of the world" (micro-cosmography) and a "map of the little world" (microcosmography). It is, in other words, a scheme of "the world" conceived completely in human terms, what we might today call "society," with its demographics of age, assets, profession, temperament, outlook, moral disposition. There's young and old; poor and sordidly rich; surgeon, attorney, constable, entertainer, baker, student, cook; the contemplative, the conceited, the discontented, the empty-headed, the insolent, the rash; the religious skeptic, the upstart, the pretender to learning, the hypocrite. Man has no single nature but is a collectivity of "characters," each with its identifying marks, its brands of recognition. So, too, the worldly stage on which these Earlean characters have their being is marked off into tavern, bowling alley, prison, church. Charactery was an old device, with origins in late classical Greece, that acquired new depth and range through early assimilation to the essay; there, attention to the type made way for the person, the individual.

The fascination with delineating human character, and thereby exploring human motive, flows through the seventeenth-century essay into the eighteenth and beyond. It enlivened the prose of periodical writers such as Addison, Steele, Johnson, and Goldsmith. (Some of its energy spilled into the swelling courses of fiction, where it met up with the essay again, in the novels, most strikingly, of Henry Fielding.) Swift adapted it to powerful satiric ends. In "A Modest Proposal," he projects a character who is at once imaginary and all too real, driven by indignation and despair into moral regions that betray their all too human topography even as they render it monstrous. If ever an essay savaged the indeterminacy of being human—our capacity to become almost anything at all—this is it. In a gentler frame of mind, Charles Lamb revived what seems to be an old-fashioned seventeenth-century character—"The Convalescent"—to draw an early nineteenth-century self-portrait, an ironically inflated alter ego for none other than his writing self: your "insignificant essayist." The preoccupation with human character has undergone all manner of excavation. Caroline Blackwood's "Portrait of a Beatnik" is a deft social caricature that exploits the perverse comedy of individuality surrendering to type in mid-twentieth-century America. In a searching modern memoir, Lessing's "My Father," the very elusiveness of the dead man's character is realized through the scraps of him that remain in the essaying daughter's possession and memory. Other kinds of elusiveness impel Alice Walker's "Looking for Zora," her search for the character of a woman and a great writer consigned to obscurity, and Margaret Laurence's "The Very Best Intentions," a foray into the mystifications of character across cultural differences. And, still, in the twentieth century as in the seventeenth, character is entwined with place. For the places we live in and pass through characterize us in a double sense: they show us up for what we are even as they help mold us into who we are. Witness Morris's "Fun City," a portrait of corruption Las Vegas style, and Shiva Naipaul's improbably persevering Bombay, "City by the Sea."

One can't read very far into the essay without observing how the tireless old question narrows. To study "man," Montaigne studied himself: "a particular one, very ill-formed" ("Of Repentance"). Yet here he must begin, and begin he does, over and over again for three whole books and some twenty-odd years counting revisions. For Bacon, his own little "essayes," expanded and revised over as many years and more, had value insofar as they were "the best fruits" ("Epistle Dedicatory," 1625) of personal experience and observation: these terse Baconian "counsels moral and political" proceed from the trials and errors of a single life. Donne made the vulnerable human body a device for spiritual introspection and saw in its lonely materiality a figure of the whole human makeup; but it was his own diseased body that drew him to it. Only by way of personal ordeal—in what he called "this imaginary half-nothing, time" (*Meditation* XIV)—does he come to the realization that "no man is an island . . . any man's death diminishes me because I am involved in mankind" (XVII).

The essay did not invent what I've uneasily called "the question of man." But it is as if this discourse had to be invented, not in the learned tongues of systematic philosophy, Greek and Latin, and not in the elevated rhetoric of traditional oratory, but in the still largely untried prose vernaculars—French, English—precisely for the purpose of wrestling the problem of being human into the foreground where each of us, singly, makes his or her own habitat.

A generation after Bacon and his contemporaries, Abraham Cowley, with a public career behind him and a considerable reputation as a poet, re-enacted the move of many an ancient thinker and of Montaigne himself: he retired to the country, to take up botany and essay writing. "To learn the art and get the habit of thinking" ("Of Solitude"). It is a motive that Thoreau himself would have recognized—a properly human motive he would have considered it. Cowley was interested in what becomes of a decent person in the ubiquitous company of the world's "knaves"—the "fawning Dog . . . roaring Lion . . . thieving Fox . . . robbing Wolf . . . dissembling Crocodile . . . rapacious Vulture." Even rural retreat, finally, offers no guarantee against this charactery of moral regress. "Whither shall we fly then?" he asks ("The Dangers of an Honest Man in Much Company"). The problem of where to go, where to live (city? country? alone? with others?) resolves itself into how to inhabit wherever you are, not as a lion or a vulture but as a human being. You want a place for looking at it all, taking it all in somehow: the shifting human scene and yourself perilously in it.

The sheer momentum of the passing that is one's whole existence demands to be, if not arrested, somehow perpetually sorted out. Addison's Spectator (the mask under which he wrote essays in the periodical of that name from 1710–1714) roams the man-infested streets and coffeehouses of a great city, London, its cemeteries and places of commerce, looking and listening and making gently ironic good sense of whatever turns up—"every useful subject that falls in my way" (*Spectator* No. 556). This writing mask is none other than the man *as* essayist, someone defined by the activity of "speculation," with its old dual sense of seeing and of reflecting on what is seen. And, since the Spectator has a daily column to turn out, reflecting means writing essays on a regular schedule. In the Spectator mask, Addison (with help from his collaborator, Richard Steele) made the essayist that dimension of the self that inhabits the world so attentively, so responsively, it becomes the best of all ways of being alive, almost as if at your leisure while going about your business. One thinks of E. B. White composing his memorial essay on *Walden* in a state he calls "semi-detached": there he is in a secluded little one-room building not unlike Thoreau's cabin in the woods, turning out an essay for a magazine editor who is waiting.

Essay writing becomes a means for training one's capacity to be in two places at once: both doing and watching. You attend to your worldly business, its deadlines and disorders, while absorbed in the peculiarly human work of speculating—observing, reflecting, seeing how it is and could be. The essay claims no authority but that of life lived under such scrutiny, meaning, in the long run, self-scrutiny.

The aim of Addisonian speculation is to be "let into the knowledge of oneself" (*Spectator* No. 10). The words straggling across the page and my absorption in them as I write are proof twice over: they are evidence of how I regard whatever I regard and, in the same stroke, implements of the mind testing itself, trying out what it can do, how well or how feebly it works in discoursing on something or other—whatever interests it. "If it is a subject I do not understand at all," writes Montaigne, "even on that I essay my judgment" ("Of Democritus and Heraclitus"). For Montaigne, to "essay" is to create a text that tests—probes and measures—the writer's faculties. Cornwallis saw his own writing as an apprenticeship in self-knowledge. He uses paper "as a painter's boy a board, that is trying to bring his hand and his fancy acquainted" ("Of Essays and Books"). As Donald Barthelme was to put it in a recent year, "Writing is a process of not-knowing." What is "in" the mind does not readily translate to words, not only because my verbal craft may be deficient, a mere beginner's tool, but also because I do not yet know my mind, cannot be sure of its "fancy" except as I haltingly form it—except, using the imagery of Cornwallis, in the moment of acquaintance when the written word reflects back to me myself being born.

Or what comes to the same thing: the world as I see and experience it. The whole wide world of ephemeral and perennial things, of rocks and wasps and injustices and drugstores and adventure and cruelty and cowardice and reproduction and commerce and work and time; and of books, poets, stories, traditions, illusions, lost ways of life. The microcosm—if we can imagine ourselves, for a moment in the old way—is forever swallowing up the macrocosm. Processing it, as we might say. I know myself by how I ruminate on all that I experience as not-myself, the "world" I am always moving in and through.

Addison's Spectator stays on the move; speculating goes hand in hand with "rambling." His admirer, Samuel Johnson, while at work on his monumental *Dictionary*, wrote an essay periodical called the *Rambler* (later on an *Adventurer*, then an *Idler*) in which to "range," twice weekly, "where-e'er occasion points the way" (Epigram, *Rambler*); in the process, he dashed off the most famous collection of moral essays in English. Washington Irving, native New Yorker, speaks of his own "rambling propensity" and of the "sauntering gaze" with which he studies the "shifting scenes of life" on two continents in the early nineteenth century ("The Author's Account of Himself"). In "The Voyage," observations of clouds, ocean waves, "monsters of the deep at their gambols" mingle with the sometimes delightful, sometimes fearful "reveries" in which he loses himself on board ship. Irving's essay is as much an attempt at portraying how he came to arrive as "a stranger in the land" of his "forefathers" as it is a narrative of a sea-crossing from the New World to the Old. When Edward Hoagland writes about the perils of taking a walk in a place like today's New York City, the muggers and other hunters that cramp your style and your movements, he lets his essay amble, like an afterthought, into the lost America of another time. The trouble—unsaid, yet wonderfully intimated—is how to live in freedom amid the impoverishment of contemporary life ("City Walking"). It is not in a paralysis of introspection that essayists pose the imponderable question of being human; the thing surfaces so variously, with as much particularity and contingency, as there are eyes to look and words to chain end to end, the moment we live in and through informing both gaze and language. We know ourselves by studying our pasts and presents and futures, individual and collective, our society, our cultural productions—all that we have made to make us what we are.

And the things we have not made, that predate and condition our existences here. This, we have called variously: macrocosm, nature, the natural world, the environment. Each name tells its own complicated story of our mutual relations. At the beginning of this century, D. H. Lawrence ("The Whistling of Birds") could still experience nature somewhat as Johnson did in the eighteenth ("Of Spring"), even as Chaucer had experienced it centuries before: perennially dying, perennially reborn, a cosmic emblem of our own perpetual senescences and renewals. One of the great wrenching insights of our own day concerns the dissolution of that ancient poetic and spiritual truth. For everywhere, now, nature is shrinking, dying. What Eiseley calls "the winter of the heedless ones" ("The Winter of Man") is far advanced. If physical nature, as Eiseley's forerunner Emerson had it, is "the symbol of spirit," how shall each solitary one of us calculate for herself or himself the destruction of such a symbol? Thoreau's "wildness" has been domesticated, trapped, gutted, consumed, poisoned, crushed under "infrastructure." These appalling violations of our natural environment have complicated the problem as he saw it: how rightly to pass our time in this world. Essays with ecological concerns, like Leopold's "Marshland Elegy" or Rhodes's "The Death of the Everglades," give a somber and hard urgency to Thoreau's problem and, hauntingly, to Cowley's three-hundred-year-old conundrum: "Whither shall we fly then?"

How to spend our time; where to go; who to be. The Galapagos Islands spread nearly three thousand miles across the Pacific, several hundred miles from the Ecuadorian mainland. Their most famous association is with Darwin, the tortoises and finches that helped him puzzle out his theory of natural selection. "Being here," writes Annie Dillard, "is being here on the rocks." She means the Galapagonian rocks under her feet—and, by extension, the geographically separate "chunks of chaos" on which earthly life depends, on which it evolves in its infinite particularity and which it in turn transforms ("Life on the Rocks"). Then, too, taking life straight on the Galapagos, "on the rocks," confirms the destitution of individual consciousness in a cosmos that makes all kinds of lively noises but does not answer in a human voice.

This is the destitution within which the essay takes its characteristic outings, has a look around, rambles on in its multiplicity of voices about this and that. Pockets empty, the essayist gets on with his or her business, "resolved," as Addison's Spectator says, "to do it in writing" (*Spectator* No. 1). If the essay has seemed at times slight or ephemeral, somehow lacking the artifactual self-sufficiency of a statue or a poem, that may be because it stays closer to the largely tentative movements by which we make our individual ways through time. The resourcefulness of the essay lies in its ability to make the language of the day do this rudimentary labor of saying where we are in the moment of writing.

Walking, rambling, sauntering, strolling, wandering are more than recurrent topics of essay writing; they're images by which essayists like to figure their particular mode of discoursing, tropes of essaying itself. A jog around and around a track is a kind of kinetic geometry produced by an enforced regularity and singlemindedness of bodily effort; so, too, are what we call power walking and aerobic walking. We do them for exercise, and all have in common with the soldier's sustained march the idea of training the body as a machine. In a dash to the mailbox or down to the corner store for a bottle of milk, the body is no more than such a machine of locomotion; like the car or bicycle that often replaces it, it's a mere vehicle for seeing letters or milk to their proper destinations. For maximal effect and efficiency, these several activities brook no distractions, no lapse in purpose or pace. Walking, on the other hand, implies free time. Sauntering and strolling carry this sense more amply, freed as they are from any association with hurrying, exercising, executing, and other behaviors of that ilk. Rambling and wandering create an imagery of aimless, uneven, unregulated movement; the leisurely pace, in them, can dilate into something very much like idling.

In the essay's long preoccupation with these figures, rambling, sauntering, and the rest stake out the broader idea of walking as if to preserve its sense of leisure, of not keeping to a straight path in a predetermined amount of time. Although the walker necessarily strikes out in some one direction rather than another—you must go east or west, as Thoreau says in "Walking"—the route is not planned beforehand, or if planned, then only in a general way. There is room for being dilatory, time for digression. There is the prospect, too, of an occasional sally: a spirited little foray to some appealing spot ahead or sideways, some object or sight that calls for a closer look. The route is mapped in the going. And except for a general familiarity with the terrain to be walked, there's no anticipating what will come your way; you set out to see what is out there to be seen.

Responsiveness is the rambler's watchword. The unhurried pace, the dilations and digressions are in the service of alertness, not lethargy. The rambler is always there, ready. Hazlitt says that "the soul of a journey is liberty," and that he likes, therefore, to walk by himself ("On Going a Journey"). With a good talker like Lamb at his side, his faculties are not at liberty to take in whatever comes up. When Johnson says that "few men know how to take a walk," he means that most stay absorbed in their fantasies at the expense of reflections derived "from the objects around" (*Rambler* No. 5). Fantasy (like interesting conversation) closes off, and in. It takes some doing to remain alert to external stimuli, to cultivate the knack of it in the first place; walking doesn't come naturally. The ramble has its own discipline by which mind and sense liberate themselves for receptiveness to "the objects around." Paying attention, working the mind on whatever moves into its ambit—these are nothing other than ways of using our time and, as such, they speak to our moment-by-moment formation as human selves: what to do, who to be. You are what you do with your time. The responsiveness that is, in one sense, an aesthetic posture belongs inextricably and most deeply to our moral life.

The term "moral essay," long associated with Johnson (and Addison and Bacon before him), has been used to designate a subtype, a kind of essay said to be concerned with correcting the error of our ways. But consider the walk as a figure of essaying itself and you perceive the moral ground of the whole genre: the habit of attention, of receptivity to the unanticipated, marks the essayistic stance, whether as a way of living in the world or as an approach to discoursing on paper. "Moral" becomes a dimension of the tradition, not merely an attribute of certain essays that take questions of right and wrong, good and evil, as their subject. So it is, too, with terms like "reflective," "informal," "familiar"—and, most especially, "personal"—all of which tend to function for us like a nomenclature of subtypes. One imagines the essay as a bagful of more or less kindred but distinguishable things—fruits, perhaps, to be sorted out into unmistakable apples, oranges, bananas, kiwis, and so on, each with its own shape, color, texture, taste, place of origin, and nutritional content. Like "moral," these other epithets are more illuminating as ways of regarding the practice of the essay than they are either useful or viable as categories, however fluid or flexible.

Keeping eyes and ears open in her passage through life, the essayist is able to "lay in," as Hazlitt put it, "a stock of ideas" ("On Going a Journey"). And writing the essay becomes a matter of sauntering through, rambling among, ambling around that store—the things seen, felt, thought, imagined, learned, understood, tried, believed, that make up her mental life (and perhaps her journal or commonplace book, if she keeps one). The genre is "reflective" in the sense that essaying is characteristically such a process of second sight, of the writing "I" looking back, or looking again. The discipline of writing essays emerges from this exercise of second sight, not from any ready logical or rhetorical design. A general direction having been struck, the receptivity to whatever turns up meets the imperative to select—to exclude, to follow through, to divide, to join; in short, to shape.

It's impossible to say everything all at once, and what we call "spontaneity" in writing is not an unmonitored spilling out of whatever comes to mind (thought that may sometimes help as a way of getting going, acquiring a feel for where you want to strike out). It's not possible, in any case, to say everything; the essay is a relatively short form, not exhaustive or systematic, never more than an attempt, a go at something that might be tried yet again on another occasion, in quite a different way. Every essay is, thus, necessarily incomplete—"I do not see the whole of anything," said Montaigne. "Of a hundred members and faces that each thing has, I take one, sometimes only to pick it, sometimes to brush the surface, sometimes to pinch it to the bone" ("Of Democritus and Heraclitus"). "These are but grains of salt," said Bacon of his *Essays* in 1612, "that will rather give you an appetite than offend you with satiety." Although the essay may be vitally moral, the roughly four hundred years of its practice have produced no system of ethics; the essay is not part of what is called "moral philosophy." It is not part of any formal system whatever, adheres to the methodologies, the discovery procedures, the criteria for proof of no established discipline. In this way, the essay is "informal." It steers away from logically or conventionally ordered sequences of elaboration, from introduction and conclusion, from the overly explicit transition; it obeys no compulsion to tie up what may look like loose ends, tolerates a fair amount of inconclusiveness and indeterminacy.

Although the rhetoric of essays is not tied to that of any formal discipline, though the knowledge in them is not the narrow erudition of the specialist, yet the essayist must know things. He must have the knowledge, precisely, of the rambler: the intellectual "stock" of an alert transit through life—and books. There's no mistaking it: essayists read, avidly and widely. The testimony is plain, whether in the easy habit of quotation of a Bacon or a Hazlitt, the literary self-immersions of a Woolf, Welty, or Walker, the scientific training of a Thomas or Gould, or, less directly, in an essay's range of reference and allusion. What makes specialists like Gould and Thomas essayists is their ability to work out the implications of their training in the framework of general intellectual concerns; like all essayists, they are—in Lamb's memorable phrase—"writers on common life" ("Books with One Idea in Them"). The essay, then, is "familiar" not because it's necessarily chatty and intimate, but because it moves over intellectual common ground, ranges over a topography of concerns and interests familiar to any person whose faculties are engaged in the absorbing business of being human and alive in history. The essayist, as Macaulay remarked of Bacon, writes "in language which everybody understands, about things in which everybody is interested." "Everybody," then as now, means the generally educated individual who reads widely and avidly.

At the beginning of *Walden*, Thoreau states, "We commonly do not remember that it is, after all, always the first person that is speaking." The essay comes along to make us "remember" that self-evident yet curiously elusive fact of human communication, and it is in this sense that the essay is radically "personal." This is not to say that it makes the writer's personality its business. The personal, essayistic voice need not be autobiographical or self-referential, though it often enough is, either dominantly or in snatches. (Reminiscence and self-reference may turn up in an essay at the most unexpected moment). Whatever its topic and however amplified, an essay brings not only a singular perspective but a characteristic sensibility to the "common life" of which the genre makes continual survey. Whether thinking about earthworms, or royal societies, or torture, or taste, or ordinariness, or cities, or canes, or walls, an essayist whose work is "moral," "reflective," "informal," "familiar," cannot fail to speak in a "personal" voice. It is the person speaking that formal disciplines suppress; the individual adrift in time marking her place by words is an obstacle to the success of scholarly and technical discourses. But if you are a rambler, which is to say an essayist, you count on the fact that "every movement reveals us"—even as it creates us. Like Montaigne, you come to take a certain delight and satisfaction in that truth of psychic life and human utterance. The text I spin out spins out myself. "I have no more made my book than my book has made me" ("Of Giving the Lie"). What could be more elegant?

The essay is "personal" because it is in my every movement on paper that "I" come into being and, thereby, exist for my reader. I can't, as I said before, describe, let alone prescribe, where we're going; your own eyes will tell you. The reader, too, must get the habit of responsiveness. A reader of essays learns to listen for "the first person . . . speaking," to hear the "I" pushing to become "we"—pushing toward something like a mutuality of personhood, a conversation between friends, equals. Reading an essay is not a feat of information-gathering; it is not like running down to the corner store for a quart of milk. It is following the motions and paces of another mind, alert and open to whatever they reveal. Reading essays and writing them have this in common: either way you must "know how to take a walk." The art of it is one of the great pleasures a person can cultivate.

L. F.

The Essays

Sir Francis Bacon

(1561–1626)

Thirteen editions of Bacon's essays appeared in his lifetime and countless more thereafter. The dedicatory preface to the first (1597) describes its slender contents as "these fragments of my conceits." By 1612, the ten original pieces had been revised and as many new ones added; "grains of salt," he called them, "that will rather give you an appetite than offend with satiety." In 1625, a year before the death of their author, now Viscount St. Albans, the Essays and Counsels, *Civil and Moral numbered fifty-eight, including all the earlier attempts expanded and renovated. "I have as vast contemplative ends as I have moderate civil ones," Bacon wrote in his late twenties to Lord Burghley, an uncle by marriage with powerful influence at Elizabeth's court. Even as the little book of essays was growing, acquiring more polish and—Bacon's own word—"weight," success in public life passed well beyond "moderate," taking him from King's Counsel, to Attorney-General, to Lord Chancellor of England; Bacon the statesman was formed even as the thinker and writer pursued his "vast contemplative ends," challenging received philosophical and scientific thought in such books as* The Advancement of Learning *(1605),* The New Atlantis *(1613), and the* Novum Organum *(1620). What gives all these activities—political, philosophical, literary—their focus is Bacon's belief that he was "born for the service of mankind" (Preface,* De Interpretatione Naturae*). The English* Essays *are, in the imagery that Bacon himself liked to use, the "best fruits" (1625 Preface) of a fully active life, a mind as vitally engaged in the world as in books, the man himself the tree on which these fruits ripen for our moral sustenance and delectation. "Of Studies," one of the original ten essays, appears here in its 1625 version, its sententious analysis polished and amplified to nearly twice the initial length. "Of Boldness," which suggests something of the "character" sketch of writers like John Earle, was new in the 1625 edition and illustrates the Baconian essay at its compressed yet fluid best.*

Of Studies

Studies serve for delight, for ornament, and for ability. Their chief use for delight, is in privateness and retiring; for ornament, is in discourse;

and for ability, is in the judgment and disposition of business. For expert men can execute, and perhaps judge of particulars, one by one; but the general counsels, and the plots, and marshaling of affairs, come best from those that are learned. To spend too much time in studies, is sloth; to use them too much for ornament, is affectation; to make judgment wholly by their rules is the humor of a scholar. They perfect nature, and are perfected by experience: for natural abilities, are like natural plants, that need pruning by study: and studies themselves, do give forth directions too much at large, except they be bounded in by experience. Crafty men contemn studies; simple men admire them; and wise men use them: for they teach not their own use; but that is a wisdom without them, and above them, won by observation. Read not to contradict, and confute; nor to believe and take for granted; nor to find talk and discourse; but to weigh and consider. Some books are to be tasted, others to be swallowed, and some few to be chewed and digested: that is, some books are to be read only in parts; others to be read but not curiously; and some few to be read wholly, and with diligence and attention. Some books also may be read by deputy, and extracts made of them by others: but that would be, only in the less important arguments, and the meaner sort of books: else distilled books, are like common distilled waters, flashy things. Reading maketh a full man; conference a ready man; and writing an exact man. And therefore, if a man write little, he had need have a great memory; if he confer little, he had need have a present wit; and if he read little, he had need have much cunning, to seem to know that, he doth not. Histories make men wise; poets witty; the mathematics subtle; natural philosophy deep; moral grave; logic and rhetoric able to contend. *Abeunt studia in mores.*[1] Nay there is no stand[2] or impediment in the wit, but may be wrought out by fit studies: like as diseases of the body, may have appropriate exercises. Bowling is good for the stone and reins; shooting for the lungs and breast; gentle walking for the stomach; riding for the head; and the like. So if a man's wit be wandering, let him study the mathematics; for in demonstrations, if his wit be called away never so little, he must begin again: if his wit be not apt to distinguish or find differences, let him study the schoolmen; for they are *cymini sectores.*[3] If he be not apt to beat over matters, and to call up one thing, to prove and illustrate another, let him study the lawyers' cases: so every defect of the mind, may have a special receipt.[4]

[1] Studies culminate in manners (Ovid).

[2] Stoppage.

[3] Dividers of cumin seed (*i.e.*, hair-splitters).

[4] Remedy.

Of Boldness

It is a trivial grammar school text, but yet worthy a wise man's consideration. Question was asked of Demosthenes; what was the chief part of an orator? He answered, *Action;*[1] what next? "Action"; what next again? "Action." He said it, that knew it best; and had by nature, himself, no advantage, in that he commended. A strange thing, that that part of an orator, which is but superficial, rather the virtue of a player; should be placed so high, above those other noble parts, of invention, elocution, and the rest: nay almost alone, as if it were all in all. But the reason is plain. There is in human nature, generally, more of the fool, than of the wise; and therefore those faculties, by which the foolish part of men's minds is taken, are most potent. Wonderful like is the case of boldness, in civil business; what first? Boldness; what second, and third? Boldness. And yet boldness is a child of ignorance, and baseness, far inferior to other parts. But nevertheless, it doth fascinate, and bind hand and foot, those, that are either shallow in judgment; or weak in courage, which are the greatest part; yea and prevaileth with wise men, at weak times. Therefore, we see it hath done wonders, in popular states; but with senates and princes less; and more, ever upon the first entrance of bold persons into action, then soon after; for boldness is an ill keeper of promise. Surely, as there are mountebanks for the natural body: so are there mountebanks for the politic body: men that undertake great cures; and perhaps have been lucky, in two or three experiments, but want the grounds of science; and therefore cannot hold out. Nay you shall see a bold fellow, many times, do Mahomet's miracle. Mahomet made the people believe, that he would call an hill to him; and from the top of it, offer up his prayers, for the observers of his law. The people assembled; Mahomet called the hill to come to him, again, and again; and when the hill stood still, he was never a whit abashed, but said; "if the hill will not come to Mahomet, Mahomet will go to the hill." So these men, when they have promised great matters, and failed most shamefully, (yet if they have the perfection of boldness) they will but slight it over, and make a turn, and no more ado. Certainly, to men of great judgment, bold persons, are a sport to behold; nay and to the vulgar also, boldness is seldom without some absurdity. Especially, it is a sport to see, when a

[1] Delivery (performance) of an oration.

bold fellow is out of countenance; for that puts his face, into a most shrunken and wooden posture; as needs it must; for in bashfulness, the spirits do a little go and come; but with bold men, upon like occasion, they stand at a stay; like a stale at chess, where it is no mate, but yet the game cannot stir. But this last, were fitter for a satire, than for a serious observation. This is well to be weighed; that boldness is ever blind: for it seeth not dangers, and inconveniences. Therefore, it is ill in counsel, good in execution: so that the right use of bold persons is, that they never command in chief, but be seconds, and under the direction of others. For in counsel, it is good to see dangers; and in execution, not to see them, except they be very great.

John Donne
(1572–1631)

"Variable, and therefore miserable condition of man; this minute I am well, and am ill, this minute." So opens the first Meditation of Donne's Devotions upon Emergent Occasions *published in 1624, shortly after his recovery from a fever, perhaps typhus, that had ravaged London in the final months of the previous year. The twenty-three Meditations (each followed by an "Expostulation with God" and a "Prayer") trace the course of that illness. When "the senses and other faculties change and fail" (II) he takes to his bed (III), and, though as a man he is "diminutive to nothing" in the created cosmos, he has no recourse but to ask for help, to send for his physician (IV). Sick animals have the means to heal themselves; yet a human being, far greater, Donne reasons, than the "little world" or microcosmic model of the universe familiar to the imagery of his age, must submit to another's uncertain care and cure. Caught up in fear, he observes that even "the physician is afraid" (VI). Other medical men come to consult (VII–VIII), propose diagnoses and subject him to outlandish treatments (IX–XII), with the result only that the "sickness declares the infection and malignity thereof by spots" (XIII). Desolate, comfortless, he sleeps "not day nor night" (XV); in the incessant tolling of nearby church bells (XVI–XVIII) he hears his own human fate ("never send to know for whom the bell tolls; it tolls for thee . . ."). Gradually, he starts to recover, is purged (XX), as was medical practice at the time, and, like "Lazarus out of his tomb," is released from his sickbed (XXI) but warned "of the fearful danger of relapsing" (XXIII). In the* Devotions, *a great English poet gives an autobiographical account in prose of the body's frailty, changeability; it is, at the same time, a meditation on the paradox of human grandeur and nothingness, and on the profound isolation that is the common lot of all of us mortals.*

The Physician is Sent For

Meditation No. 4

It is too little to call man a little world; except God, man is a diminutive to nothing. Man consists of more pieces, more parts, than the world; than the world doeth, nay than the world is. And if those pieces were extended, and stretched out in man, as they are in the world, man would be the giant, and the world the dwarf, the world but the map, and the man the world. If all the veins in our bodies, were extended to rivers, and all the sinews, to veins of mines, and all the muscles, that lie upon one another, to hills, and all the bones to quarries of stones, and all the other pieces, to the proportion of those which correspond to them in the world, the air would be too little for this orb of man to move in, the firmament would be but enough for this star; for, as the whole world hath nothing, to which something in man doth not answer, so hath man many pieces, of which the whole world hath no representation. Enlarge this meditation upon this great world, man, so far, as to consider the immensity of the creatures this world produces; our creatures are our thoughts, creatures that are born giants: that reach from east to west, from earth to heaven, that do not only bestride all the sea, and land, but span the sun and firmament at once; my thoughts reach all, comprehend all. Inexplicable mystery; I their creator am in a close prison, in a sickbed, anywhere, and any one of my creatures, my thoughts, is with the sun, and beyond the sun, overtakes the sun, and overgoes the sun in one pace, one step, everywhere. And then as the other world produces serpents, and vipers, malignant, & venomous creatures, and worms, and caterpillars, that endeavor to devour the world which produces them, and monsters compiled and complicated of diverse parents, & kinds, so this world, our selves, produces all these in us, in producing diseases, & sicknesses, of all those sorts; venomous, and infectious diseases, feeding & consuming diseases, and manifold, and entangled diseases, made up of many several ones. And can the other world name so many venomous, so many consuming, so many monstrous creatures, as we can diseases, of all these kinds? O miserable abundance, O beggarly riches! how much do we lack of having remedies for every disease, when as yet we have not names for them? But we have a Hercules against these giants, these monsters; that is, the physician; he musters up all the forces of the other world, to succor this; all nature to relieve man. We have the physician, but we are not the physician. Here we shrink in our proportion, sink in our dignity, in respect of very mean creatures, who are physicians to themselves. The hart that is pursued and wounded, they say, knows an herb, which being eaten, throws off the arrow: a strange kind of vomit. The dog that pursues it, though he be subject to sickness, even proverbially, knows his grass that recovers him. And it may be true, that the drugger is as near to man, as to other creatures, it may be that obvious and present simples,[1] easy to be had, would cure him; but the apothecary is not so near him, nor the physician so near him, as they two are to other creatures; man hath not that innate instinct, to apply those natural med-

[1] Medicinal plants, or the medicines prepared from them.

icines to his present danger, as those inferior creatures have; he is not his own apothecary, his own physician, as they are. Call back therefore thy meditations again, and bring it down; what's become of man's great extent & proportion, when himself shrinks himself, and consumes himself to a handful of dust; what's become of his soaring thoughts, his compassing thoughts, when himself brings himself to the ignorance, to the thoughtlessness of the grave? His diseases are his own, but the physician is not; he hath them at home, but must send for the physician.

I Sleep Not Day Nor Night

Meditation No. 15

Natural men have conceived a twofold use of sleep; that it is a refreshing of the body in this life; that it is a feast, and it is the grace at that feast; that it is our recreation, and cheers us, and it is our catechism, and instructs us; we lie down in a hope, that we shall rise stronger; and we lie down in a knowledge that we may rise no more. Sleep is an opiate which gives us rest, but such an opiate, as perchance, being under it, we shall wake no more. But though natural men, who have induced secondary and figurative considerations, have found out this second, this emblematical use of sleep, that it should be a representation of death, God, who wrought and perfected his work, before nature began, (for nature was but his apprentice, to learn in the first seven days, and now is his foreman, and works next under him) God, I say, intended sleep only for the refreshing of man by bodily rest, and not for a figure of death, for he intended not death itself then. But man having induced death upon himself, God hath taken man's creature, death, into his hand, and mended it; and whereas it hath in itself a fearful form and aspect, so that man is afraid of his own creature, God presents it to him, in a familiar, in an assiduous, in an agreeable, and acceptable form, in sleep, that so when he awakes from sleep, and says to himself, shall I be no otherwise when I am dead, than I was even now, when I was asleep, he may be ashamed of his waking dreams, and of his melancholic fancying out a horrid and an affrightful figure of that death which is so like sleep. As then we need sleep to live out our threescore and ten years, so we need death, to live that life which we cannot outlive. And as death being our enemy, God allows us to defend ourselves against it (for we victual ourselves against death, twice every day, as often as we eat) so God having so sweetened death unto us, as he hath in sleep, we put ourselves into our enemy's hands once every day, so far, as sleep is death; and sleep is as much death, as meat is life. This then is the misery of my sickness, that death as it is produced from me, and is mine own creature, is now before mine eyes, but in that form, in which God hath mollified it to us, and made it acceptable, in sleep, I cannot see it: how many prisoners, who have even hollowed themselves their graves upon that earth, on which they have lain long under heavy fetters, yet at this hour, are asleep, though they be yet working upon their own graves, by their own weight? he that hath seen his friend die today, or knows he shall see it tomorrow, yet will sink into a sleep between. I cannot; and oh, if I be entering now into eternity, where there shall be no more distinction of hours, why is it all my business now to tell clocks? why is none of the heaviness of my heart, dispensed into mine eyelids, that they might fall as my heart doth? And why, since I have lost my delight in all objects, cannot I discontinue the faculty of seeing them, by closing mine eyes in sleep? But why rather, being entering into that presence, where I shall wake continually and never sleep more, do I not interpret my continual waking here, to be a parasceve,[1] and a preparation to that?

[1] The eve of the Sabbath.

Sir William Cornwallis

(1579–1614)

Cornwallis called his shortest essay—barely a page long—"Of Alehouses," and he starts it off like this: "I write this in an alehouse, into which I am driven by night . . . I am without any company but ink and paper and them I use instead of talking to myself." This and the piece printed here must have been written some time between ages fifteen and twenty-one. If there is some question about the exact year of Cornwallis's birth, as well as the extent of his formal education, there is none about the textual history of his Essays, *first published in 1600. There were twenty-four of them (a larger collection than Bacon's of 1597), growing by another twenty-five the next year, and reaching, after revisions, a total of fifty-two by 1610. Casually fresh and immediate at their best, they are the ruminations of a young man who regards his own youth as a kind of "malady . . . that wishes for what would hurt it, is dangerously sick and yet will take no physic" ("Of Youth"). He is at pains, everywhere, to puzzle out the bafflements of this, his particular human situation, but claims (or so he says) no special authority for his views: "I present thee, reader, with no excellences," he wrote in a preface, "To do thee no harm is my commendation." In his self-consciousness about his project as an essayist—as intense, on occasion, as that of Montaigne himself, whom he admired—Cornwallis deserves a more visible place among the seventeenth-century founders of the English essay.*

Of Entertainment

There are but two causes that pull on guests:[1] love and business. I must in good nature make much of the former, and the latter necessity enforceth me to entertain. But I like not to dwell upon these. A short time may satisfy visitation, and business not hindered by compliment cannot last long.

Methinks, I should have done now. It is tedious to meet with a fellow that will stay today and tomorrow and the next day on purpose to say he

[1] There are only two reasons to be a guest.

loveth. If he fear my memory that he thus reiterateth love, let him give me some token of remembrance. This tarrying persuades me rather the contrary; he is my enemy that thus eats up my meat and time without any cause that persuadeth his stay. Truly, the name of a good fellow is so dear[2] a title that I had rather traffic with coarser stuff and be called parsimonious, yea, miserable, if they will; it smarts not half so ill as the phrase, "everybody's friend but his own." I know some whom modesty restraineth from telling impudency their faults. Alas, good virtue, that thou art grown a coward and darest not discover thyself. Well, I have a medicine for these people; I will not be consumed living by these worms. "What's your pleasure?" This is my answer, "Farewell."

These words have an excellent virtue in them; they deliver you to solitariness, the mother of contemplation; they keep your house sweet; and at dinner if you like a dish, it is your own fault if you have it not cold. When my occasions[3] grow so desperately mad as, in despite of me, they will hale me abroad into throngs and great assemblies, he that entertains me, I will him speak to all,[4] reserve a strange familiarity for the best, and my good word and courtesy generally. I have known some affecting courtesy overthrow their labours with not having choice of compliments,[5] but confounding a gentleman and a peasant with the likeness of salutation and farewell. They were to blame to set up shop so ill furnished. As men differ, so must their usages and respects; not to all, "I am the servant of your servant's servant." In truth, I am naturally kind and pitiful and would gladly give every man a testimony that I neither hate nor contemn them. I will speak and pity and lament with all; and to some give my time without a fee, but not destroy myself for their sakes. They are no gods; I need not sacrifice myself. There is cruelty in this courtesy; I must not do thus. Marry, any kindness that shortens not in the spending, that makes not the purse empty, and the household book rich in items. I am ready to be their host and to entertain all, but to keep open house, until I shall be compelled to shut up my doors, must be pardoned me. I have a purse and a life, and all that I am for some few; but they are, indeed, but a few. *Non omnibus dormio.*[6]

[2] Costly, expensive.

[3] Affairs (business).

[4] I'll speak to him as I do to all.

[5] Not choosing their compliments; *i.e.*, flattering indiscriminately.

[6] Not to all am I asleep (Cicero).

John Earle
(1601?–1665)

Sir Walter Raleigh notes in his History of the World *(1614): "because in the little frame of man's body there is a representation of the universal . . . therefore was man called microcosmos, or the little world." John Earle's finely scaled map of the human scene entitled* Microcosmography *made its way into print in 1628, though not under the name of its author—fellow of Merton College, tutor to young gentlemen in high places, eventually Doctor of Divinity and Bishop of Worcester. Earle was not the first to write the pointed sketch known as the "character." The general idea goes back to Aristotle's pupil Theophrastus, whose extant works were translated into Latin and English in the late sixteenth century and variously imitated and modified in both England and France during the seventeenth. A "character," wrote Thomas Overbury (1581–1613), is "a short emblem, in little comprehending much." Earle's characters are no mere abstractions of virtues and vices, nor caricatures honed solely for the display of wit; they are closely observed particulars—people, interactions, places—drawn with an eye to their wider human import. Their verbal economy recalls Bacon. Here, for instance, on "The World's Wise Man" (he is very much with us still): "an able and sufficient wicked man. It is a proof of his sufficiency that he is not called wicked, but wise." "The Detractor," printed below, is an incisively worked portrait of this sort. "Paul's Walk" characterizes the main aisle of St. Paul's Cathedral (abode of Dr. John Donne's magnificent sermons), long notorious as a scene of newsmongering and assignations of every kind, morning and afternoon, innocent and shady. Money or goods might be exchanged, deals made, gossip passed along. Here, in miniature, is what was to become the essay of moral and social criticism, with tongue already in cheek.*

A Detractor

Is one of a more cunning and active envy, wherewith he gnaws not foolishly himself, but throws it abroad and would have it blister others. He is commonly some weak-parted fellow, and worse minded, yet is strangely ambitious to match others, not by mouthing their worth, but bringing them down with his tongue to his own poorness. He is indeed like the red dragon that pursued the woman, for when he cannot overreach another, he opens his mouth and throws a flood after to drown him. You cannot anger him worse than to do well, and he hates you more bitterly for this, than if you had cheated him of his patrimony with your own discredit. He is always slighting the general opinion, and wondering why such and such men should be applauded. Commend a good divine, he cries "Postilling";[1] a philologer "Pedantry"; a poet, "Rhyming"; a schoolman "Dull wrangling"; a sharp conceit, "Boyishness"; an honest man "Plausibility." He comes to public things not to learn, but to catch, and if there be but one solecism, that's all he carries away. He looks on all things with a prepared sourness, and is still furnished with a "Pish" beforehand, or some musty proverb that disrelishes all things whatsoever. If the fear of the company make him second a commendation, it is like a law written, always with a clause of exception, or to smooth the way to some greater scandal. He will grant you something, and debate more; and this debating shall in conclusion take away all he granted. His speech concludes still with an "Oh but," and "I could wish one thing amended"; and this one thing shall be enough to deface all his former commendations. He will be very inward[2] with a man to fish some bad out of him, and make his slanders hereafter more authentic, when it is said "A friend reported it." He will inveigle you to naughtiness to get your good name into his clutches, and make you drunk to show you reeling. He passes the more plausibly because all men have a smatch of his humor, and it is thought freeness which is malice.[3] If he can say nothing of a man, he will seem to speak riddles, as if he could tell strange stories if he would: and when he has racked his invention to the uttermost, he ends: "But I wish him well, and therefore must hold my peace." He is always listening and enquiring after men, and suffers not a cloak to pass him by unexamined. In brief, he is one that has lost all good himself, and is loath to find it in another.

[1] Scribbling notes in margins.

[2] Intimate.

[3] All men have a touch of his disposition, and what is (really) malice passes for candor.

Paul's Walk

Is the land's epitome, or you may call it the lesser isle[1] of Great Britain. It is more than this, the whole world's map, which you may here discern in its perfectest motion, jostling and turning. It is a heap of stones and men, with a vast confusion of languages, and were the steeple not sanctified, nothing liker Babel. The noise in it is like that of bees, a strange humming or buzz, mixed of walking, tongues and feet: it is a kind of still roar or loud whisper. It is the great Exchange of all discourse, and no business whatsoever but is here stirring and afoot. It is the synod of all pates politic,[2] jointed and laid together in most serious posture, and they are not half so busy at the Parliament. It is the antic of tails to tails, and backs to backs, and for vizards[3] you need go no further than faces. It is the market of young lecturers,[4] whom you may cheapen here at all rates and sizes. It is the general mint of all famous lies, which are here like the legends of popery, first coined and stamped in the church. All inventions are emptied here, and not a few pockets. The best sign of a temple in it is, that it is the thieves' sanctuary, which rob more safely in the crowd than a wilderness, whilst every searcher is a bush to hide them. It is the other expense of the day, after plays, tavern, and a bawdy house, and men have still some oaths left to swear here. . . . The visitants are all men without exceptions, but the principal inhabitants and possessors are stale knights, and captains out of service, men of long rapiers and breeches, which after all turn merchants here, and traffic for news. Some make it a preface to their dinner, and travel for a stomach:[5] but thriftier men make it their ordinary:[6] and board here very cheap. Of all such places it is least haunted with hobgoblins, for if a ghost would walk more, he could not.

[1] Pun on "aisle," which was then sometimes spelled "isle."

[2] Politicians.

[3] Visors, masks.

[4] Lecturers were preachers supported by public contributions; for "cheapen," read "bargain for."

[5] Walk for an appetite.

[6] Table d'hôtel; *i.e.*, meal table or menu.

Abraham Cowley
(1618–1667)

In a letter to Coleridge of January 10, 1797, Charles Lamb asked his old schoolfriend's opinion of "the now out of fashion Cowley." "Tell me," he writes, "if his prose essays, in particular . . . be not delicious." He himself prefers them to the essays of the great Addison, because of their "graceful rambling." Cowley, better known in his own time as a courtier and poet (the subject in the later eighteenth century of one of Samuel Johnson's Lives*), was indeed among the first English essayists to "ramble"—to amplify his topic more in the ruminative fashion of Montaigne than in the terse cogitations of his countryman Francis Bacon. By the time Cowley, then in his early forties, had made his retreat to the tranquil solitude of the countryside near London (first Barn Elms, then the Chertsea mentioned in the present selection), the earliest essayists were names on books, the "Sieur de Montagne," as he liked to call him, more than seventy years gone. The essay offered itself as an occasion to mull over the pleasures and values of life lived "incognito" (Of Solitude"), making gardens, growing fruit trees, pondering the corruptions of urban existence. Already in boyhood, Cowley reports, he was an "enemy of all constraint" ("Of Myself"). The youthful disposition to find his own way "through reading and observation" turns up in the associative, rambling indirection of his essays—the work of his last years—and renders them at once spontaneous and insistently searching. They appeared posthumously in 1668, as part of* The Works of Mr. Abraham Cowley, *edited by his literary executor and biographer, Thomas Sprat.*

The Dangers of an Honest Man in Much Company

If twenty thousand naked Americans were not able to resist the assaults of but twenty well-armed Spaniards, I see little possibility for one honest man to defend himself against twenty thousand knaves, who are all furnished *cap-a pie*,[1] with the defensive arms of worldly prudence, and

[1] From head to foot.

the offensive too of craft and malice. He will find no less odds than this against him, if he have much to do in human affairs. The only advice therefore which I can give him, is, to be sure not to venture his person any longer in the open campaign, to retreat and entrench himself, to stop up all avenues, and draw up all bridges against so numerous an enemy. The truth of it is, that a man in much business must either make himself a knave, or else the world will make him a fool: and if the injury went no farther than the being laughed at, a wise man would content himself with the revenge of retaliation; but the case is much worse, for these civil cannibals too, as well as the wild ones, not only dance about such a taken stranger, but at last devour him. A sober man cannot get too soon out of drunken company, though they be never so kind and merry among themselves, 'tis not unpleasant only, but dangerous to him. Do ye wonder that a virtuous man should love to be alone? It is hard for him to be otherwise; he is so, when he is among ten thousand: neither is the solitude so uncomfortable to be alone without any other creature, as it is to be alone, in the midst of wild beasts. Man is to man all kind of beasts, a fawning Dog, a roaring Lion, a thieving Fox, a robbing Wolf, a dissembling Crocodile, a treacherous Decoy, and a rapacious Vulture. The civilest, methinks, of all nations, are those whom we account the most barbarous, there is some moderation and good nature in the Toupinambaltians[2] who eat no men but their enemies, whilst we learned and polite and Christian Europeans, like so many Pikes and Sharks prey upon everything that we can swallow. It is the great boast of eloquence and philosophy, that they first congregated men dispersed, united them into societies, and built up the houses and the walls of cities. I wish they could unravel all they had woven; that we might have our woods and our innocence again instead of our castles and our policies. They have assembled many thousands of scattered people into one body; 'tis true, they have done so, they have brought them together into cities, to cozen, and into armies to murder one another: they found them hunters and fishers of wild creatures, they have made them hunters and fishers of their brethren; they boast to have reduced them to a state of peace, when the truth is, they have only taught them an art of war; they have framed, I must confess, wholesome laws for the restraint of vice, but they rais'd first that devil which now they conjure and cannot bind; though there were before no punishments for wickedness, yet there was less committed because there were no rewards for it. But the men who praise philosophy from this topic are much deceived; let oratory answer for itself, the tinkling perhaps of that may unite a swarm: it never was the work of philosophy to assemble multitudes, but to regulate only, and govern

[2] A northern Brazilian people.

them when they were assembled, to make the best of an evil, and bring them, as much as is possible, to unity again. Avarice and ambition only were the first builders of towns, and founders of empire; they said, "Go to, let us build us a city and a tower whose top may reach unto heaven, and let us make us a name, lest we be scattered abroad upon the face of the earth."[3] What was the beginning of Rome, the metropolis of all the world? What was it, but a concourse of thieves, and a sanctuary of criminals? It was justly named by the augury of no less then twelve vultures, and the founder cemented his walls with the blood of his brother; not unlike to this was the beginning even of the first town too in the world, and such is the original sin of most cities: their actual increase daily with their age and growth; the more people, the more wicked all of them; everyone brings in his part to inflame the contagion, which becomes at last so universal and so strong, that no precepts can be sufficient preservatives, nor anything secure our safety, but flight from among the infected. We ought in the choice of a situation to regard above all things the healthfulness of the place, and the heathfulness of it for the mind rather than for the body. But suppose (which is hardly to be supposed) we had antidote enough against this poison; nay, suppose farther, we were always and at all pieces armed and provided both against the assaults of hostility, and the mines of treachery, 'twill yet be but an uncomfortable life to be ever in alarms; though we were compassed round with fire, to defend ourselves from wild beasts, the lodging would be unpleasant, because we must always be obliged to watch that fire, and to fear no less the defects of our guard, than the diligences of our enemy. The sum of this is, that a virtuous man is in danger to be trod upon and destroyed in the crowd of his contraries, nay, which is worse, to be changed and corrupted by them, and that 'tis impossible to escape both these inconveniences without so much caution, as will take away the whole quiet, that is, the happiness of his life. Ye see then, what he may lose, but, I pray, What can he get there? *Quid Romæ faciam? Mentiri nescio.*[4] What should a man of truth and honesty do at Rome? he can neither understand, nor speak the language of the place; a naked man may swim in the sea, but 'tis not the way to catch fish there; they are likelier to devour him, than he them, if he bring no nets, and use no deceits. I think therefore it was wise and friendly advice which Martial gave to Fabian, when he met him newly arrived at Rome.

Honest and poor, faithful in word and thought;
What has thee, Fabian, to the city brought?
Thou neither the buffoon, nor bawd canst play,

[3] Genesis 11:4.

[4] What would I do in Rome? I know not how to lie (Juvenal, *Satires*).

Nor with false whispers th'innocent betray:
Nor corrupt wives, nor from rich beldams get
A living by thy industry and sweat;
Nor with vain promises and projects cheat,
Nor bribe or flatter any of the great.
But you'r a man of learning, prudent, just;
A man of courage, firm, and fit for trust.
Why you may stay, and live unenvyed here;
But (faith) go back, and keep you where you were.

Nay, if nothing of all this were in the case, yet the very sight of uncleanness is loathsome to the cleanly; the sight of folly and impiety vexatious to the wise and pious.

Lucretius, by his favor, though a good poet; was but an ill-natur'd man, when he said, it was delightful to see other men in a great storm: And no less ill-natur'd should I think Democritus, who laughed at all the world, but that he retired himself so much out of it, that we may perceive he took no great pleasure in that kind of mirth. I have been drawn twice or thrice by company to go to Bedlam, and have seen others very much delighted with the fantastical extravagance of so many various madnesses, which upon me wrought so contrary an effect, that I always returned, not only melancholy, but ev'n sick with the sight. My compassion there was perhaps too tender, for I meet a thousand madmen abroad, without any perturbation; though, to weigh the matter justly, the total loss of reason is less deplorable than the total depravation of it. An exact judge of human blessings, of riches, honors, beauty, even of wit itself, should pity the abuse of them more than the want.

Briefly, though a wise man could pass never so securely through the great roads of human life, yet he will meet perpetually with so many objects and occasions of compassion, grief, shame, anger, hatred, indignation, and all passions but envy (for he will find nothing to deserve that) that he had better strike into some private path; nay, go so far, if he could, out of the common way, *Ut nec facta audiat Pelopidarum;* that he might not so much as hear of the actions of the sons of Adam. But, whither shall we fly then? into the deserts, like the ancient hermits?

Qua terra patet fera regnat Erynnis,
In facinus jurasse putes.[5]

One would think that all mankind had bound themselves by an oath to do all the wickedness they can; that they had all (as the Scripture speaks) sold themselves to sin: the difference only is, that some are a little more crafty (and but a little God knows) in making of the bargain. I

[5] Far as earth reaches, Furies rule the land/All men have joined in Hell's conspiracy (Ovid).

thought when I went first to dwell in the country, that without doubt I should have met there with the simplicity of the old poetical Golden Age: I thought to have found no inhabitants there, but such as the shepherds of Sir Philip. Sydney in Arcadia, or in Monsieur d'Urfe upon the banks of Lignon; and began to consider with myself, which way I might recommend no less to posterity the happiness and innocence of the men of Chertsea: but to confess the truth, I perceived quickly, by infallible demonstrations, that I was still in old England, and not in Arcadia, or La Forrest; that if I could not content myself with anything less than exact fidelity in human conversation, I had almost as good go back and seek for it in the Court, or the Exchange, or Westminster Hall. I ask again then whither shall we fly, or what shall we do? The world may so come in a man's way, that he cannot choose but salute it, he must take heed though not to go a'whoring after it. If by any lawful vocation, or just necessity men happen to be married to it, I can only give them St. Paul's advice. "Brethren, the time is short, it remains that they that have wives be as though they had none. But I would that all men were even as I myself."

In all cases they must be sure that they do *Mundum ducere*, and not *Mundo nubere*.[6] They must retain the superiority and headship over it: happy are they who can get out of the sight of this deceitful beauty, that they may not be led so much as into temptation; who have not only quitted the metropolis, but can abstain from ever seeing the next market town of their country.

[6] Lead the world, not marry it.

Jonathan Swift

(1667-1745)

When the author of Gulliver's Travels *and other powerful satires, the renowned political journalist and Dean of St. Patrick's Cathedral, returned from his last English sojourn in 1727, he appeared inclined to renounce politics and live quietly at his Deanery in Dublin, Ireland. "Here," he wrote to a correspondent, "it is a shame to be in [politics], unless by way of laughter and ridicule, for both which my taste is gone." Nonetheless, the very next year saw yet another political pamphlet entitled "A Short View of the State of Ireland." It set forth by straightforward analysis and impassioned argument what was to be conveyed so trenchantly and far-reachingly in "A Modest Proposal" of October 1729: the economic and human misery of a fertile land ransacked and shackled not only by the absent English but by its own collaborating gentry and parliament. "A Short View" falls in among those "vain, idle, visionary thoughts" repudiated by the confident projector of the new scheme to institutionalize cannibalism as the best remedy for Ireland's wretchedness. The summer of 1729 had brought yet another "dearth of corn" with attendant food shortages. But "our evils here lie much deeper," Swift told his English friend Alexander Pope in August. "Imagine a nation the two thirds of whose revenues are spent out of it [in England], and who are not permitted to trade with the other third [because of restrictive laws]. . . . These evils operate more every day, and the kingdom is absolutely undone, as I have been telling often in print these years past." "A Modest Proposal," perhaps the most enigmatic and widely read essay in English, emerged from the rage of frustrated effort to impel sensible economic reforms. Beyond "politics" and even beyond "laughter and ridicule," Swift's savagely sustained irony creates a satire whose targets move outward from the specific conditions of Ireland in the 1720s to those perennial misappropriations of rationality and feeling that taint human communities and that have been a hallmark of our own horrific century.*

A Modest Proposal

For Preventing the Children of Poor People in Ireland, *from Being a Burden to Their Parents or Country; and for Making Them Beneficial to the Public.*

It is a melancholy object to those, who walk through this great town, or travel in the country; when they see the streets, the roads, and cabin-doors crowded with beggars of the female sex, followed by three, four, or six children, all in rags, and importuning every passenger for an alms. These mothers, instead of being able to work for their honest livelihood, are forced to employ all their time in strolling to beg sustenance for their helpless infants; who, as they grow up, either turn thieves for want of work; or leave their dear native country, to fight for the Pretender in Spain, or sell themselves to the Barbados.

I think it is agreed by all parties, that this prodigious number of children in the arms, or on the backs, or at the heels of their mothers, and frequently of their fathers, is in the present deplorable state of the kingdom, a very great additional grievance; and therefore, whoever could find out a fair, cheap, and easy method of making these children sound and useful members of the Commonwealth, would deserve so well of the public, as to have his statue set up for a preserver of the nation.

But my intention is very far from being confined to provide only for the children of professed beggars: it is of a much greater extent, and shall take in the whole number of infants at a certain age, who are born of parents, in effect as little able to support them, as those who demand our charity in the streets.

As to my own part, having turned my thoughts for many years, upon this important subject, and maturely weighed the several schemes of other projectors, I have always found them grossly mistaken in their computation. It is true a child, just dropped from its dam, may be supported by her milk, for a solar year with little other nourishment; at most not above the value of two shillings; which the mother may certainly get or the value in scraps, by her lawful occupation of begging: and, it is exactly at one year old, that I propose to provide for them in such a manner, as, instead of being a charge upon their parents, or the parish, or wanting food and raiment for the rest of their lives; they shall, on the contrary, contribute to the feeding, and partly to the clothing, of many thousands.

There is likewise another great advantage in my scheme, that it will prevent those voluntary abortions, and that horrid practice of women murdering their bastard children; alas! too frequent among us; sacrificing the poor innocent babes, I doubt, more to avoid the expense than the shame; which would move tears and pity in the most savage and inhuman breast.

The number of souls in Ireland being usually reckoned one million and a half; of these I calculate there may be about two hundred thousand couples whose wives are breeders; from which number I subtract thirty thousand couples, who are able to maintain their own children; although I apprehend there cannot be so many, under the present distresses of the kingdom; but this being granted, there will remain an hundred and seventy thousand breeders. I again subtract fifty thousand, for those women who miscarry, or whose children die by accident, or disease, within the year. There only remain an hundred and twenty thousand children of poor parents, annually born: the question therefore is, how this number shall be reared, and provided for? Which, as I have already said, under the present situation of affairs, is utterly impossible, by all the methods hitherto proposed: for we can neither employ them in handicraft or agriculture; we neither build houses, (I mean in the country) nor cultivate land: they can very seldom pick up a livelihood by stealing until they arrive at six years old; except where they are of towardly parts; although, I confess, they learn the rudiments much earlier; during which time, they can, however, be properly looked upon only as probationers; as I have been informed by a principal gentleman in the country of Cavan, who protested to me, that he never knew above one or two instances under the age of six, even in a part of the kingdom so renowned for the quickest proficiency in that art.

I am assured by our merchants, that a boy or a girl before twelve years old, is no saleable commodity; and even when they come to this age, they will not yield above three pounds, or three pounds and half a crown at most, on the Exchange; which cannot turn to account either to the parents or the kingdom; the charge of nutriment and rags, having been at least four times that value.

I shall now therefore humbly propose my own thoughts; which I hope will not be liable to the least objection.

I have been assured by a very knowing American of my acquaintance in London; that a young healthy child, well nursed, is, at a year old, a most delicious, nourishing, and wholesome food; whether stewed, roasted, baked, or boiled; and I make no doubt, that it will equally serve in a fricasee, or ragout.

I do therefore humbly offer it to public consideration, that of the hundred and twenty thousand children, already computed, twenty thousand may be reserved for breed; whereof only one fourth part to be males; which is more than we allow to sheep, black cattle, or swine; and my reason is, that these children are seldom the fruits of marriage, a circumstance not much regarded by our savages; therefore, one male will be sufficient to serve four females. That the remaining hundred thousand, may, at a year old, be offered in sale to the persons of quality and fortune, through the kingdom; always advising the mother to let them suck plentifully in the last month, so as to render them plump, and fat for a good table. A child will make two dishes at an entertainment for friends; and when the family dines alone, the fore or hind quarter will make a reasonable dish; and seasoned with a little pepper or salt, will be very good boiled on the fourth day, especially in winter.

I have reckoned upon a medium, that a child just born will weigh twelve pounds; and in a solar year, if tolerably nursed, increaseth to twenty eight pounds.

I grant this food will be somewhat dear, and therefore very proper for landlords; who, as they have already devoured most of the parents, seem to have the best title to the children.

Infants' flesh will be in season throughout the year; but more plentiful in March, and a little before and after: for we are told by a grave author, an eminent French physician, that fish being a prolific diet, there are more children born in Roman Catholic countries about nine months after Lent, than at any other season: therefore reckoning a year after Lent, the markets will be more glutted than usual; because the number of Popish infants, is, at least, three to one in this kingdom; and therefore it will have one other collateral advantage by lessening the number of Papists among us.

I have already computed the charge of nursing a beggar's child (in which list I reckon all cottagers, labourers, and four-fifths of the farmers) to be about two shillings per annum, rags included; and I believe no gentleman would repine to give ten shillings for the carcass of a good fat child; which, as I have said, will make four dishes of excellent nutritive meat, when he hath only some particular friend, or his own family, to dine with him. Thus the squire will learn to be a good landlord, and grow popular among his tenants; the mother will have eight shillings net profit, and be fit for work until she produceth another child.

Those who are more thrifty (as I must confess the times require) may flay the carcass; the skin of which, artificially dressed, will make admirable gloves for ladies, and summer boots for fine gentlemen.

As to our city of Dublin; shambles[1] may be appointed for this purpose, in the most convenient parts of it; and butchers we may be assured will not be wanting; although I rather recommend buying the children alive, and dressing them hot from the knife, as we do roasting pigs.

A very worthy person, a true lover of his country, and whose virtues I highly esteem, was lately pleased, in discoursing on this matter, to offer

[1] Slaughterhouses.

a refinement upon my scheme. He said, that many gentlemen of this kingdom, having of late destroyed their deer; he conceived, that the want of venison might be well supplied by the bodies of young lads and maidens, not exceeding fourteen years of age, nor under twelve; so great a number of both sexes in every county being now ready to starve, for want of work and service: and these to be disposed of by their parents, if alive, or otherwise by their nearest relations. But with due deference to so excellent a friend, and so deserving a patriot, I cannot be altogether in his sentiments. For as to the males, my American acquaintance assured me from frequent experience, that their flesh was generally tough and lean, like that of our schoolboys, by continual exercise, and their taste disagreeable; and to fatten them would not answer the charge. Then, as to the females, it would, I think, with humble submission, be a loss to the public, because they soon would become breeders themselves: and besides it is not improbable, that some scrupulous people might be apt to censure such a practice (although indeed very unjustly) as a little bordering upon cruelty; which, I confess, hath always been with me the strongest objection against any project, how wellsoever intended.

But in order to justify my friend; he confessed, that this expedient was put into his head by the famous Salmanaazor, a native of the island Formosa, who came from thence to London, above twenty years ago, and in conversation told my friend, that in his country, when any young person happened to be put to death, the executioner sold the carcass to persons of quality, as a prime dainty; and that, in his time, the body of a plump girl of fifteen, who was crucified for an attempt to poison the emperor, was sold to his imperial Majesty's prime minister of state, and other great mandarins of the court, in joints from the gibbet, at four hundred crowns. Neither indeed can I deny, that if the same use were made of several plump young girls in this town, who, without one single groat to the fortunes, cannot stir abroad without a chair, and appear at the playhouse, and assemblies in foreign fineries, which they never will pay for; the kingdom would not be the worse.

Some persons of a desponding spirit are in great concern about that vast number of poor people, who are aged, diseased, or maimed; and I have been desired to employ my thoughts what course may be taken, to ease the nation of so grievous an encumbrance. But I am not in the least pain upon that matter; because it is very well known, that they are every day dying, and rotting, by cold and famine, and filth, and vermin, as fast as can be reasonably expected. And as the younger labourers, they are now in almost as hopeful a condition: they cannot get work, and consequently pine away for want of nourishment, to a degree, that if at any time they are accidentally hired to common labor, they have not strength to perform it; and thus the country, and themselves, are in a fair way of being soon delivered from the evils to come.

I have too long digressed; and therefore shall return to my subject. I think the advantages by the proposal which I have made, are obvious, and many, as well as of the highest importance.

For, first, as I have already observed, it would greatly lessen the number of Papists, with whom we are yearly overrun; being the principal breeders of the nation, as well as our most dangerous enemies; and who stay at home on purpose, with a design to deliver the kingdom to the Pretender; hoping to take their advantage by the absence of so many good Protestants, who have chosen rather to leave their country, than stay at home, and pay tithes against their conscience, to an idolatrous Episcopal curate.

Secondly, the poorer tenants will have something valuable of their own, which, by law, may be made liable to distress,[2] and help to pay their landlord's rent; their corn and cattle being already seized, and money a thing unknown.

Thirdly, whereas the maintenance of an hundred thousand children, from two years old, and upwards, cannot be computed at less than ten shillings a piece per annum, the nation's stock will be thereby increased fifty thousand pounds per annum; besides the profit of a new dish, introduced to the tables of all gentlemen of fortune in the kingdom, who have any refinement in taste; and the money will circulate among ourselves, the goods being entirely of our own growth and manufacture.

Fourthly, the constant breeders, besides the gain of eight shillings sterling per annum, by the sale of their children, will be rid of the charge of maintaining them after the first year.

Fifthly, this food would likewise bring great custom to taverns, where the vintners will certainly be so prudent, as to produce the best receipts for dressing it to perfection; and consequently, have their houses frequented by all the fine gentlemen, who justly value themselves upon their knowledge in good eating; and a skillful cook, who understands how to oblige his guests, will contrive to make it as expensive as they please.

Sixthly, this would be a great inducement to marriage, which all wise nations have either encouraged by rewards, or enforced by laws and penalties. It would increase the care and tenderness of mothers towards their children, when they were sure of a settlement for life, to the poor babes, provided in some sort by the public, to their annual profit instead of expense. We should soon see an honest emulation among the married women, which of them could bring the fattest child to the market. Men

[2] Seizure for paying off a debt.

would become as fond of their wives, during the time of their pregnancy, as they are now of their mares in foal, their cows in calf, or sows when they are ready to farrow; nor offer to beat or kick them, (as it is too frequent a practice) for fear of a miscarriage.

Many other advantages might be enumerated. For instance, the addition of some thousand carcasses in our exportation of barrelled beef: the propagation of swines' flesh, and improvement in the art of making good bacon; so much wanted among us by the great destruction of pigs, too frequent at our tables, and are no way comparable in taste, or magnificence, to a well-grown fat yearling child; which roasted whole, will make a considerable figure at a Lord Mayor's feast, or any other public entertainment. But this, and many others, I omit; being studious of brevity.

Supposing that one thousand families in this city, would be constant customers for infants' flesh; besides others who might have it at merry meetings, particularly weddings and christenings; I compute that Dublin would take off, annually, about twenty thousand carcasses; and the rest of the kingdom (where probably they will be sold somewhat cheaper) the remaining eighty thousand.

I can think of no one objection, that will possibly be raised against this proposal; unless it should be urged, that the number of people will be thereby much lessened in the kingdom. This I freely own; and it was indeed one principal design in offering it to the world. I desire the reader will observe, that I calculate my remedy for this one individual kingdom of Ireland, and for no other that ever was, is, or I think can be upon earth. Therefore, let no man talk to me of other expedients: *of taxing our absentees at five shillings a pound: of using neither clothes, nor household furniture except what is of our own growth and manufacture: of utterly rejecting the materials and instruments that promote foreign luxury: of curing the expensiveness of pride, vanity, idleness, and gaming in our women: of introducing a vein of parsimony, prudence and temperance: of learning to love our country, wherein we differ even from* Laplanders, *and the inhabitants of* Topinamboo: *of quitting our animosities, and factions; nor act any longer like the* Jews, *who were murdering one another at the very moment their city was taken: of being a little cautious not to sell our country and consciences for nothing; of teaching landlords to have, at least, one degree of mercy towards their tenants.* Lastly, *of putting a spirit of honesty, industry, and skill into our shopkeepers; who, if a resolution could now be taken to buy only our native goods, would immediately unite to cheat and exact upon us in the price, the measure, and the goodness; nor could ever yet be brought to make one fair proposal of just dealing, though often and earnestly invited to it.*

Therefore I repeat, let no man talk to me of these and the like expedients; 'till he hath, at least, a glimpse of hope, that there will ever be some hearty and sincere attempt to put them in practice.

But, as to myself; having been wearied out for many years with offering vain, idle, visionary thoughts; and at length utterly despairing of success, I fortunately fell upon this proposal; which, as it is wholly new, so it hath something solid and real, of no expense, and little trouble, full in our own power; and whereby we can incur no danger in disobliging England: for, this kind of commodity will not bear exportation; the flesh being of too tender a consistency, to admit a long continuance in salt; *although, perhaps, I could name a country, which would be glad to eat up our whole nation without it.*

After all, I am not so violently bent upon my own opinion, as to reject any offer proposed by wise men, which shall be found equally innocent, cheap, easy, and effectual. But before something of that kind shall be advanced, in contradiction to my scheme, and offering a better; I desire the author, or authors, will be pleased maturely to consider two points. First, as things now stand, how they will be able to find food and raiment, for a hundred thousand useless mouths and backs? And secondly, there being a round million of creatures in human figure, throughout this kingdom; whose whole subsistence, put into a common stock, would leave them in debt two millions of pounds sterling; adding those, who are beggars by profession, to the bulk of farmers, cottagers, and laborers, with their wives and children, who are beggars in effect; I desire those politicians, who dislike my overture, and may perhaps be so bold to attempt an answer, that they will first ask the parents of these mortals, whether they would not, at this day, think it a great happiness to have been sold for food at a year old, in the manner I prescribe; and thereby have avoided such a perpetual scene of misfortunes, as they have since gone through; by the oppression of landlords; the impossibility of paying rent, without money or trade; the want of common sustenance, with neither house nor clothes, to cover them from the inclemencies of weather; and the most inevitable prospect of entailing the like, or greater miseries upon their breed for ever.

I profess, in the sincerity of my heart, that I have not the least personal interest, in endeavoring to promote this necessary work; having no other motive than the public good of my country, by advancing our trade, providing for infants, relieving the poor, and giving some pleasure to the rich. I have no children, by which I can propose to get a single penny; the youngest being nine years old, and my wife past childbearing.

Joseph Addison

(1672–1719)

The Spectator, *a collaborative project of Joseph Addision and Richard Steele, appeared daily (except Sunday) between March 1, 1711, and December 7, 1712; then again from June 18, 1714, to December 20 of that year. Unlike most periodicals of its time and before, it did not report news and avoided current politics; its aim was to print a single essay on a single sheet, front and back, on some social, cultural, or moral topic. In the tenth number, a wide readership already assured, Addison proposed to bring "philosophy out of the closets and libraries, schools and colleges, to dwell in clubs and assemblies, at tea-tables and coffee-houses." By "philosophy," he meant an examined life, somewhat in the Socratic spirit: "I shall leave it to my readers' consideration," he wrote, "whether it is not much better to be let into the knowledge of oneself than to hear what passes in Moscovy and Poland." Because one is essentially a social being, "knowledge of oneself" necessarily entails "speculation" (a favorite Addisonian word for what he considered himself to be doing) on our social existence in all its variety and perversity. What has kept Addison's early eighteenth-century moral vision so active in the essay these many years is perhaps his insight that what is "good" for us should give us pleasure; the best of his* Spectator *papers do, indeed, "enliven morality with wit," as he strove to do. Even when he is speculating on tombs and the decay of the body, Addison creates not a grim Good Friday sermon but a "serious amusement" appropriate to the season (No. 26). The pleasure, on the other hand, of "mixing" and being "jostled among" the polyglot crowd at the Royal Exchange (No. 69) is of a purer kind. Here was a feast for the speculating eye: a vast two-story structure, contemporaries say, around a central courtyard, with galleries and porticos housing two hundred shops on the top floor alone—offering the world's goods for appreciation and purchase. Built in 1669 after the Great Fire destroyed an earlier structure, it too burned down in 1838, to be replaced a few years later by the Royal Exchange that still stands today, across the street from the modern London Stock Exchange.*

The Tombs at Westminster Abbey

Spectator No. 26: Good Friday, 30 March 1711

When I am in a serious humour, I very often walk by myself in Westminster Abbey; where the gloominess of the place, and the use to which it is applied, with the solemnity of the building, and the condition of the people who lie in it, are apt to fill the mind with a kind of melancholy, or rather thoughtfulness, that is not disagreeable. I yesterday pass'd a whole afternoon in the churchyard, the cloisters, and the church, amusing myself with the tombstones and inscriptions that I met with in those several regions of the dead. Most of them recorded nothing else of the buried person, but that he was born upon one day and died upon another: the whole history of his life, being comprehended in those two circumstances that are common to all mankind. I could not but look upon these registers of existence, whether of brass or marble, as a kind of satire upon the departed persons; who had left no other memorial of them, but that they were born and that they died. They put me in mind of several persons mentioned in the battles of heroic poems, who have sounding names given them, for no other reason but that they may be killed, and are celebrated for nothing but being knocked on the head.

> *Γλαῦκόν τε Μέδοντά τε Θερσιλοχόν τε.* Hom.
> *Glaucumque, Medontaque, Thersilochumque.* Virg.[1]

The life of these men is finely described in Holy Writ, by the path of an arrow which is immediately closed up and lost.

Upon my going into the church, I entertain'd myself with the digging of a grave; and saw in every shovelful of it that was thrown up, the fragment of a bone or skull intermixed with a kind of fresh mouldering earth that some time or other had a place in the composition of a human body. Upon this, I began to consider with myself what innumerable multitudes of people lay confus'd together under the pavement of that ancient cathedral; how men and women, friends and enemies, priests and soldiers, monks and prebendaries, were crumbled amongst one another, and blended together in the same common mass; how beauty, strength, and youth, with old age, weakness, and deformity, lay undistinguish'd in the same promiscuous heap of matter.

After having thus surveyed this great magazine of mortality, as it were in the lump, I examined it more particularly by the accounts which I found on several of the monuments which are raised in every quarter

[1] Glaucus, Medon, and Thersilochus are epic heroes, given here first in the Greek of Homer's *Iliad*, then in the Latin of Virgil's *Aeneid*.

of that ancient fabric. Some of them were covered with such extravagant epitaphs, that, if it were possible for the dead person to be acquainted with them, he would blush at the praises which his friends have bestow'd upon him. There are others so excessively modest, that they deliver the character of the person departed in Greek or Hebrew, and by that means are not understood once in a twelve-month. In the poetical quarter, I found there were poets who had no monuments, and monuments which had no poets. I observed indeed that the present war had filled the church with many of these uninhabited monuments, which had been erected to the memory of persons whose bodies were perhaps buried in the plains of Blenheim or in the bosom of the ocean.

I could not but be very much delighted with several modern epitaphs, which are written with great elegance of expression and justness of thought, and therefore do honor to the living as well as to the dead. As a foreigner is very apt to conceive an idea of the ignorance or politeness of a nation from the turn of their public monuments and inscriptions, they should be submitted to the perusal of men of learning and genius before they are put in execution. Sir Cloudesly Shovel's monument has very often given me great offense: instead of the brave rough English admiral, which was the distinguishing character of that plain gallant man, he is represented on his tomb by the figure of a beau, dress'd in a long perriwig, and reposing himself upon velvet cushions under a canopy of state. The inscription is answerable to the monument; for instead of celebrating the many remarkable actions he had performed in the service of his country, it acquaints us only with the manner of his death, in which it was impossible for him to reap any honor. The Dutch, whom we are apt to despise for want of genius, show an infinitely greater taste of antiquity and politeness in their buildings and works of this nature, than what we meet with in those of our own country. The monuments of their admirals, which have been erected at the public expence, represent 'em like themselves; and are adorn'd with rostral crowns and naval ornaments, with beautiful festoons of seaweed, shells, and coral.

But to return to our subject. I have left the repository of our English kings for the contemplation of another day, when I shall find my mind disposed for so serious an amusement. I know that entertainments of this nature, are apt to raise dark and dismal thoughts in timorous minds and gloomy imaginations; but for my own part, though I am always serious, I do not know what it is to be melancholy; and can therefore take a view of nature in her deep and solemn scenes, with the same pleasure as in her most gay and delightful ones. By this means I can improve myself with those objects, which others consider with terror. When I look upon the tombs of the great, every emotion of envy dies in me; when I read the epitaphs of the beautiful, every inordinate desire goes out; when I meet with the grief of parents upon a tombstone, my heart melts with compassion; when I see the tomb of the parents themselves, I consider the vanity of grieving for those whom we must quickly follow: when I see kings lying by those who deposed them, when I consider rival wits plac'd side by side, or the holy men that divided the world with their contests and disputes, I reflect with sorrow and astonishment on the little competitions, fractions, and debates of mankind. When I read the several dates of the tombs, of some that died yesterday, and some six hundred years ago, I consider that great day when we shall all of us be contemporaries, and make our appearance together.

The Royal Exchange

Spectator No. 69: Saturday, 19 May 1711

There is no place in the town which I so much love to frequent as the Royal Exchange. It gives me a secret satisfaction, and, in some measure, gratifies my vanity, as I am an Englishman, to see so rich an assembly of countrymen and foreigners consulting together upon the private business of mankind, and making this metropolis a kind of emporium for the whole earth. I must confess I look upon High-Change to be a great council, in which all considerable nations have their representatives. Factors in the trading world are what ambassadors are in the politic world; they negotiate affairs, conclude treaties, and maintain a good correspondence between those wealthy societies of men that are divided from one another by seas and oceans, or live on the different extremities of a continent. I have often been pleased to hear disputes adjusted between an inhabitant of Japan and an alderman of London, or to see a subject of the Great Mogul entering into a league with one of the Czar of Muscovy. I am infinitely delighted in mixing with these several ministers of commerce, as they are distinguished by their different walks and different languages: sometimes I am justled among a body of Armenians: sometimes I am lost in a crowd of Jews, and sometimes make one in a group of Dutchmen. I am a Dane, Swede, or Frenchman at different times, or rather fancy myself like the old philosopher, who upon being asked what countryman he was, replied, that he was a citizen of the world.

Though I very frequently visit this busy multitude of people, I am known to nobody there but my friend, Sir Andrew, who often smiles upon me as he sees me bustling in the crowd, but at the same time connives at my presence without taking any further notice of me. There is indeed a merchant of Egypt, who just knows me by sight, having formerly remitted me some money to Grand Cairo; but as I am not versed in the Modern Coptic, our conferences go no further than a bow and a grimace.

This grand scene of business gives me an infinite variety of solid and substantial entertainments. As I am a great lover of mankind, my heart naturally overflows with pleasure at the sight of a prosperous and happy multitude, insomuch that at many public solemnities I cannot forbear expressing my joy with tears that have stolen down my cheeks. For this reason I am wonderfully delighted to see such a body of men thriving in their own private fortunes, and at the same time promoting the public stock; or in other words, raising estates for their own families, by bringing into their country whatever is wanting, and carrying out of it whatever is superfluous.

Nature seems to have taken a particular care to disseminate her blessings among the different regions of the world, with an eye to this mutual intercourse and traffic among mankind, that the natives of the several parts of the globe might have a kind of dependence upon one another and be united together by their common interest. Almost every degree produces something peculiar to it. The food often grows in one country, and the sauce in another. The fruits of Portugal are corrected by the products of Barbados: the infusion of a China plant sweetened with the pith of an Indian cane: the Philippic Islands give a flavor to our European bowls. The single dress of a woman of quality is often the product of an hundred climates. The muff and the fan come together from the different ends of the earth. The scarf is sent from the torrid zone, and the tippet from beneath the Pole. The brocade petticoat rises out of the mines of Peru, and the diamond necklace out of the bowels of Indostan.

If we consider our own country in its natural prospect, without any of the benefits and advantages of commerce, what a barren uncomfortable spot of earth falls to our share! Natural historians tells us, that no fruit grows originally among us, besides hips and haws, acorns and pig nuts, with other delicacies of the like nature; that our climate of itself, and without the assistances of art, can make no further advances towards a plumb than to a sloe, and carries an apple to no greater a perfection than a crab: that our melons, our peaches, our figs, our apricots, and cherries, are strangers among us, imported in different ages, and naturalized in our English gardens; and that they would all degenerate and fall away into the trash of our own country, if they were wholly neglected by the planter, and left out to the mercy of our sun and soil. Nor has traffic more enriched our vegetable world, than it has improved the whole face of nature among us. Our ships are laden with the harvest of every climate: our tables are stored with spices, and oils, and wines: our rooms are filled with pyramids of China, and adorned with the workmanship of Japan: our morning's draught comes to us from the remotest corners of the earth: we repair our bodies by the drugs of America, and repose ourselves under Indian canopies. My friend Sir Andrew calls the vineyards of France our gardens; the spice islands our hotbeds; the Persians our silk weavers, and the Chinese our potters. Nature indeed furnishes us with the bare necessaries of life, but traffic gives us a great variety of what is useful, and at the same time supplies us with everything that is convenient and ornamental. Nor is it the least part of this our happiness, that whilst we enjoy the remotest products of the north and south, we are free from those extremities of weather which give them birth; that our eyes are refreshed with the green fields of Britain, at the same time that our palates are feasted with fruits that rise between the tropics.

For these reasons there are not more useful members in a commonwealth than merchants. They knit mankind together in a mutual intercourse of good offices, distribute the gifts of nature, find work for the poor, add wealth to the rich, and magnificence to the great. Our English merchant converts the tin of his own country into gold, and exchanges his wool for rubies. The Mohammedans are clothed in our British manufacture, and the inhabitants of the frozen zone warmed with the fleeces of our sheep.

When I have been upon the 'Change, I have often fancied one of our old kings standing in person, where he is represented in effigy, and looking down upon the wealthy concourse of people with which that place is every day filled. In this case, how would he be surprised to hear all the languages of Europe spoken in this little spot to his former dominions, and to see so many private men, who in his time would have been the vassals of some powerful baron, negotiating like princes for greater sums of money than were formerly to be met with in the Royal Treasury! Trade, without enlarging the British territories, has given us a kind of additional empire: it has multiplied the number of the rich, made our landed estates infinitely more valuable than they were formerly, and added to them an accession of other estates as valuable as the lands themselves.

Benjamin Franklin

(1706–1790)

"The Ephemera" is the most famous of the short essays, circulated among friends and hand-printed on his private press, to which Franklin gave the name Bagatelles. *He was in his seventies when he composed them, distant in both time and place from the teenaged printer's apprentice who sat in his room in Boston "reading the greatest part of the night" and teaching himself, by imitating old numbers of the* Spectator, *to become "a tolerable English writer" (*The Autobiography of Benjamin Franklin*). Now he was an eminent man, widely loved, representing the new United States of America at the French court. At Passy, then a quiet village on the outskirts of Paris—the nearby Bois de Boulogne still a real forest—he socialized with neighbors and studied French with one of them, the attractive and much younger Mme. Brillon, who addressed him as* "mon cher papa." *She is the "Brillante" of the essay, and it is for her he composed "The Ephemera" some time in August or September 1778. A letter of Franklin's to William Carmichael, some two years later, provides an informative gloss. Mme. Brillon, he writes, "kindly entertains me and my grandson with little concerts, a dish of tea and a game of chess." The Moulin Joli, the essay's setting, he identifies as "a little island in the Seine about two leagues from hence . . . where we visit every summer and spend a day in the pleasing society of the ingenious learned and very politic persons who inhabit it"; the overheard spat about "two foreign musicians" refers to controversies then raging in Paris about the relative merit of the German composer Glück and the Italian Piccinni. As for "the thought" in his essay, he credits that to "a little piece of some unknown writer which I met with fifty years since in a newspaper and which the sight of the Ephemera brought to my recollection." Scholars have suggested that Franklin may have been thinking (among others) of an article published in* The Free Thinker, *in 1719, called "The Vanity and Ambition of the Human Mind." In fifty years, that mind can work marvelous and witty transformations.*

The Ephemera

You may remember, my dear friend, that when we lately spent that happy day in the delightful garden and sweet society of the Moulin Joli,

I stopt a little in one of our walks, and stayed some time behind the company. We had been shewn numberless skeletons of a kind of little fly, called an ephemeron, all whose successive generations we were told were bred and expired within the day. I happen'd to see a living company of them on a leaf, who appear'd to be engag'd in conversation. You know I understand all the inferior animal tongues: my too great application to the study of them is the best excuse I can give for the little progress I have made in your charming language. I listened thro' curiosity to the discourse of these little creatures, but as they in their national vivacity spoke three or four together, I could make but little of their discourse. I found, however, by some broken expressions that I caught now and then, they were disputing warmly the merit of two foreign musicians, one a *Cousin*,[1] the other a *Musketo*, in which dispute they spent their time seemingly as regardless of the shortness of life, as if they had been sure of living a month. Happy people! thought I, you live certainly under a wise, just and mild government, since you have no public grievances to complain of, nor any subject of contention but the perfections or imperfections of foreign music. I turned from them to an old greyheaded one, who was single on another leaf, and talking to himself. Being amus'd with his soliloquy, I have put it down in writing, in hopes it will likewise amuse her to whom I am so much indebted for the most pleasing of all amusements, her delicious company, and her heavenly harmony.

"It was," says he, "the opinion of learned philosophers of our race, who lived and flourished long before my time, that this vast world, the Moulin Joli, could not itself subsist more than eighteen hours; and I think there was some foundation for that opinion, since by the apparent motion of the great luminary that gives life to all nature, and which in my time has evidently declin'd considerably towards the ocean at the end of our earth, it must then finish its course, be extinguish'd in the waters that surround us, and leave the world in cold and darkness, necessarily producing universal death and destruction. I have lived seven of those hours; a great age, being no less than 420 minutes of time. How very few of us continue so long! I have seen generations born, flourish, and expire. My present friends are the children and grandchildren of the friends of my youth, who are now, alas, no more! And I must soon follow them; for by the course of nature, tho' still in health, I cannot expect to live above seven or eight minutes longer. What now avails all my toil and labor in amassing honey dew on this leaf, which I cannot live to enjoy! What the political struggles I have been engag'd in for the good of my compatriots, inhabitants of this bush; or my philosophical studies for the benefit of our race in general! For in politics, what can laws do without

[1] A midge, gnatlike fly.

morals? Our present race of ephemera will in a course of minutes, become corrupt like those of other and older bushes, and consequently as wretched. And in philosophy how small our progress! Alas, art is long, and life is short! My friends would comfort me with the idea of a name they say I shall leave behind me; and they tell me I have lived long enough, to nature and to glory: but what will fame be to an ephemeron who no longer exists? And what will become of all history, in the eighteenth hour, when the world itself, even the whole Moulin Joli, shall come to its end, and be buried in universal ruin? To me, after all my eager pursuits, no solid pleasures now remain, but the reflection of a long life spent in meaning well, the sensible conversation of a few good lady ephemera and now and then a kind smile, and a tune from the ever-amiable Brillante."

Henry Fielding

(1707–1754)

By the mid-eighteenth century, periodicals—and, therefore, outlets for essays of all kinds—were proliferating and competing for attention. In the start-off issue of his Covent-Garden Journal, *a project of the early 50s, Fielding promised to be as entertaining as he could: "to avoid with the utmost care all kind of encroachment on that spacious field . . . which from time immemorial hath been called the land of dullness." "The Essay on Nothing" of about ten years earlier (*Miscellanies, *1743) found a way, as it were, to have fun with "dullness." Dilating on its subject with "utmost care," it drags in the whole machinery of dullness: grandiose formal divisions, dead-earnest definitions, finicky logic, belabored examples and the like, smartly undercut by all manner of semantic shiftiness. Here, among other parodic delights, is something noteworthy (not to mention salubrious) for the student of the essay: an essay chuckling, in the guise of pseudo-philosophical speculation, at the whole essay-writing enterprise. And by one who had written, and was still to write, many an essay, including the sometimes ironic, sometimes astutely critical essays embedded in novels like* Tom Jones *and others of Fielding's long fictions. One of these is entitled "An Essay to Prove That an Author Will Write the Better for Having Some Knowledge of the Subject on Which He Writes" (*Tom Jones, *XIV, i). Familiar advice? What* does *the author of "An Essay on Nothing" "know"? He, who has "confessedly sat down to write this essay with Nothing in my head, or, which is the same thing, to write about Nothing. . . ." Does an essayist transcribe what he or she "knows" about a subject, or is what we call the essay's "subject" formed—invented—in the very dilation of writing?*

An Essay on Nothing

The Introduction

It is surprising, that while such trifling matters employ the masterly pens of the present age, the great and noble subject of this essay should have passed totally neglected; and the rather, as it is a subject to which the genius of many of those writers who have unsuccessfully applied themselves to politics, religion, etc., is most peculiarly adapted.

Perhaps their unwillingness to handle what is of such importance may not improperly be ascribed to their modesty; though they may not be remarkably addicted to this vice on every occasion. Indeed I have heard it predicated of some, whose assurance in treating other subjects hath been sufficiently notable, that they have blushed at this. For such is the awe with which this Nothing inspires mankind, that I believe it is generally apprehended of many persons of very high character among us, that were title, power, or riches to allure them, they would stick at it.

But whatever be the reason, certain it is, that except a hardy wit in the reign of Charles II, none ever hath dared to write on this subject. I mean openly and avowedly; for it must be confessed, that most of our modern authors, however foreign the matter which they endeavour to treat may seem at their first setting out, they generally bring the work to this in the end.

I hope, however, this attempt will not be imputed to me as an act of immodesty; since I am convinced there are many persons in this kingdom who are persuaded of my fitness for what I have undertaken. But as talking of a man's self is generally suspected to arise from vanity, I shall, without any more excuse or preface, proceed to my essay.

Section I. Of the Antiquity of Nothing

There is nothing falser than that old proverb which (like many other falsehoods) is in everyone's mouth:

> "Ex nihilo nihil fit."

Thus translated by Shakespeare, in *Lear:*

> "Nothing can come of nothing."

Whereas in fact from Nothing proceeds everything. And this is a truth confessed by the philosophers of all sects: the only point in controversy between them being, whether Something made the world out of Nothing, or Nothing out of Something. A matter not much worth debating at present, since either will equally serve our turn. Indeed the wits of all ages seem to have ranged themselves on each side of this question, as their genius tended more or less to the spiritual or material substance. For those of the more spiritual species have inclined to the former, and those whose genius hath partaken more of the chief properties of matter, such as solidity, thickness, etc., have embraced the latter.

But whether Nothing was the *artifex* or *materies* only,[1] it is plain in either case, it will have a right to claim to itself the origination of all things.

And farther, the great antiquity of Nothing is apparent from its being so visible in the accounts we have of the beginning of every nation. This is very plainly to be discovered in the first pages, and sometimes books, of all general historians; and indeed, the study of this important subject fills up the whole life of an antiquary, it being always at the bottom of his inquiry, and is commonly at last discovered by him with infinite labour and pains.

Section II. Of the Nature of Nothing

Another falsehood which we must detect in the pursuit of this essay is an assertion, *That no one can have an idea of nothing;* but men who thus confidently deny us this idea, either grossly deceive themselves, or would impose a downright cheat on the world: for, so far from having none, I believe there are few who have not many ideas of it; though perhaps they may mistake them for the idea of something.

For instance, is there any one who hath not an idea of immaterial* substance?—Now what is immaterial substance, more than Nothing? But here we are artfully deceived by the use of words: for were we to ask another what idea he had of immaterial matter, or unsubstantial substance, the absurdity of affirming it to be Something would shock him, and he would immediately reply, it was *Nothing*.

Some persons perhaps will say, then we have no idea of it; but, as I can support the contrary by such undoubted authority, I shall, instead of trying to confute such idle opinions, proceed to show; first, what Nothing is: secondly, I shall disclose the various kinds of Nothing; and, lastly shall prove its great dignity, and that it is the end of everything.

It is extremely hard to define Nothing in positive terms, I shall therefore do it in negative. Nothing then is not Something. And here I must object to a third error concerning it, which is, that it is in no place; which is an indirect way of depriving it of its existence; whereas indeed it possesses the greatest and noblest place on this earth; *viz.*, the human brain. But indeed this mistake had been sufficiently refuted by many very wise men; who, having spent their whole lives in the contemplation

[1] Maker or matter (*i.e.*, material) only.

* The author would not be here understood to speak against the doctrine of immateriality, to which he is a hearty well-wisher; but to point at the stupidity of those, who instead of immaterial *essence*, which would convey a rational meaning, have substituted immaterial *substance*, which is a contradiction in terms [Fielding].

and pursuit of nothing, have at last gravely concluded—*That there is Nothing in this world.*

Farther, as Nothing is not Something, so everything which is not Something is Nothing; and wherever Something is not Nothing is: a very large allowance in its favour, as must appear to persons well skilled in human affairs.

For instance, when a bladder is full of wind, it is full of Something; but when that is let out, we aptly say, there is Nothing in it.

The same may be as justly asserted of a man as of a bladder. However well he may be bedaubed with lace, or with title, yet if he have not Something in him, we may predicate the same of him as of an empty bladder.

But if we cannot reach an adequate knowledge of the true essence of Nothing, no more than we can of matter, let us, in imitation of the experimental philosophers, examine some of its properties or accidents.

And here we shall see the infinite advantages which Nothing hath over Something; for, while the latter is confined to one sense, or two perhaps at the most, Nothing is the object of them all.

For, first, Nothing may be seen, as is plain from the relation of persons who have recovered from high fevers; and perhaps may be suspected from some (at least) of those who have seen apparitions, both on earth and in the clouds. Nay, I have often heard it confessed by men, when asked what they saw at such a place and time, that they saw Nothing. Admitting then that there are two sights, *viz.* a first and second sight, according to the firm belief of some, Nothing must be allowed to have a very large share of the first; and as to the second, it hath it all entirely to itself.

Secondly, Nothing may be heard: of which the same proofs may be given as of the foregoing. The Argive mentioned by Horace is a strong instance of this.

—"Fuit haud ignobilis Argis
Qui se credebat miros aydire Tragœdos
In vacuo lœtos sessor, Plausorque Theatro."[2]

That Nothing may be tasted and smelt is not only known to persons of delicate palates and nostrils. How commonly do we hear, that such a thing smells or tastes of nothing? The latter I have heard asserted of a dish compounded of five or six savoury ingredients. And as to the former, I remember an elderly gentlewoman who had a great antipathy to the smell of apples; who, upon discovering that an idle boy had fastened some mellow apple to her tail, contracted a habit of smelling

[2] Once at Argos there was a man of some rank, who used to fancy that he was listening to wonderful tragic actors, while he sat happy and applauded in the empty theater (Horace, H.R. Fairclough, trans.).

them whenever that boy came within her sight, though there were then none within a mile of her.

Lastly, feeling; and sure if any sense seems more particularly the object of matter only, which must be allowed to be Something, this doth. Nay, I have heard it asserted (and with a colour of truth) of several persons that they can feel nothing but a cudgel. Notwithstanding which some have felt the motions of the spirit; and others have felt very bitterly the misfortunes of their friends, without endeavouring to relieve them. Now these seem two plain instances, that Nothing is an object of this sense. Nay, I have heard a surgeon declare, while he was cutting off a patient's leg, that *he was sure he felt nothing*.

Nothing is as well the object of our passions as our senses. Thus there are many who love Nothing, some who hate Nothing, and some who fear Nothing, etc.

We have already mentioned three of the properties of a noun to belong to Nothing; we shall find the fourth likewise to be as justly claimed by it: and that Nothing is as often the object of the understanding as of the senses.

Indeed some have imagined that knowledge, with the adjective *human* placed before it, is another word for Nothing. And one of the wisest men in the world declared he knew nothing.

But, without carrying it so far, this I believe may be allowed, that it is at least possible for a man to know Nothing. And whoever hath read over many works of our ingenious moderns, with proper attention and emolument, will, I believe, confess, that if he understands them right, he understands *Nothing*.

This is a secret not known to all readers; and want of this knowledge hath occasioned much puzzling; for where a book, or chapter, or paragraph, hath seemed to the reader to contain Nothing, his modesty hath sometimes persuaded him, that the true meaning of the author hath escaped him, instead of concluding, as in reality the fact was, that the author, in the said book, etc., did truly, and *bonà fide*, mean nothing. I remember once, at the table of a person of great eminence, and one no less distinguished by superiority of wit than fortune, when a very dark passage was read out of a poet famous for being so sublime that he is often out of the sight of his reader, some persons present declared they did not understand the meaning. The gentleman himself, casting his eye over the performance, testified a surprise at the dullness of his company; seeing Nothing could, he said, possibly be plainer than the meaning of the passage which they stuck at. This set all of us to puzzling again; but with like success; we frankly owned we could not find it out, and desired he would explain it.—Explain it! said the gentleman, why he means *Nothing*.

In fact, this mistake arises from a too vulgar error among persons unacquainted with the mystery of writing, who imagine it impossible that a man should sit down to write without any meaning at all; whereas, in reality, nothing is more common: for, not to instance in myself, who have confessedly set down to write this essay with Nothing in my head, or, which is much the same thing, to write about Nothing, it may be incontestably proved, *ab effectu*,[3] that nothing is commoner among the moderns. The inimitable author of a preface to the Posthumous Eclogues of a late ingenious young gentleman, says,—"There are men who sit down to write what they think, and others to think what they shall write." But indeed there is a third, and much more numerous sort, who never think either before they sit down or afterwards; and who, when they produce on paper what was before in their heads, are sure to produce Nothing.

Thus we have endeavoured to demonstrate the nature of Nothing, by showing first, definitively, *what it is not;* and, secondly, by describing *what it is.* The next thing therefore proposed is to show its various kinds.

Now some imagine these several kinds differ in name only. But without endeavouring to confute so absurd an opinion, especially as these different kinds of Nothing occur frequently in the best authors, I shall content myself with setting them down, and leave it to the determination of the distinguished reader, whether it is probable, or indeed possible, that they should all convey one and the same meaning.

These are, Nothing *per se* Nothing; Nothing at all; Nothing in the least; Nothing in nature; Nothing in the world; Nothing in the whole world; Nothing in the whole universal world. And perhaps many others of which we say—*Nothing*.

Section III. Of the Dignity of Nothing; and an Endeavour to Prove, That It Is the End as Well as Beginning of All Things

Nothing contains so much dignity as Nothing. Ask an infamous worthless nobleman (if any such be) in what his dignity consists? It may not be perhaps consistent with his dignity to give you an answer, but suppose he should be willing to condescend so far, what could he in effect say. Should he say he had it from his ancestors, I apprehend a lawyer would oblige him to prove that the virtues to which his dignity was annexed descended to him. If he claims it as inherent in the title, might he not be told, that a title originally implied dignity, as it implied the presence of those virtues to which dignity is inseparably annexed; but

[3] From the effect, *i.e.*, by way of the deed.

that no implication will fly in the face of downright positive proof to the contrary. In short, to examine no farther, since his endeavour to derive it from any other fountain would be equally impotent, his dignity arises from Nothing, and in reality is Nothing. Yet, that this dignity really exists, that it glares in the eyes of men, and produces much good to the person who wears it, is, I believe, incontestable.

Perhaps this may appear in the following syllogism.

The respect paid to men on account of their titles is paid at least to the supposal of their superior virtues and abilities, or it is paid to *Nothing*.

But when a man is a notorious knave or fool it is impossible there should be any such supposal.

The conclusion is apparent.

Now that no man is ashamed of either paying or receiving this respect I wonder not, since the great importance of Nothing seems, I think, to be pretty apparent: but that they should deny the Deity worshipped, and endeavour to represent Nothing as Something, is more worthy reprehension. This is a fallacy extremely common. I have seen a fellow, whom all the world knew to have Nothing in him, not only pretend to Something himself, but supported in that pretension by others who have been less liable to be deceived. Now whence can this proceed but from their being ashamed of Nothing? A modesty very peculiar to this age.

But, notwithstanding all such disguises and deceit, a man must have very little discernment who can live very long in courts, or populous cities, without being convinced of the great dignity of Nothing; and though he should, through corruption or necessity, comply with the vulgar worship and adulation, he will know to what it is paid; namely, to *Nothing*.

The most astonishing instance of this respect, so frequently paid to Nothing, is when it is paid (if I may so express myself) to Something less than Nothing; when the person who receives it is not only void of the quality for which he is respected, but is in reality notoriously guilty of the vices directly opposite to the virtues whose applause he receives. This is, indeed, the highest degree of Nothing, or (if I may be allowed the word), the *Nothingest of all Nothings*.

Here it is to be known, that respect may be aimed at Something and really light on Nothing. For instance, when mistaking certain things called gravity, canting, blustering, ostentation, pomp, and such like, for wisdom, piety, magnanimity, charity, true greatness, etc., we give to the former the honour and reverence due to the latter. Not that I would be understood so far to discredit my subject as to insinuate that gravity, canting, etc. are really Nothing; on the contrary, there is much more reason to suspect (if we judge from the practice of the world) that wisdom, piety, and other virtues, have a good title to that name. But we do not, in fact, pay our respect to the former, but to the latter: in other words, we pay it to that which is not, and consequently pay it to Nothing.

So far then for the dignity of the subject on which I am treating. I am now to show, that Nothing is the end as well as beginning of all things.

That everything is resolvable, and will be resolved into its first principles, will be, I believe, readily acknowledged by all philosophers. As, therefore, we have sufficiently proved the world came from Nothing, it follows that it will likewise end in the same: but as I am writing to a nation of Christians, I have no need to be prolix on this head; since every one of my readers, by his faith acknowledges that the world is to have an end, *i.e.* is to come to Nothing.

And, as Nothing is the end of the world, so is it of everything in the world. Ambition, the greatest, highest, noblest, finest, most heroic and godlike of all passions, what doth it end in?—Nothing. What did Alexander, Caesar, and all the rest of that heroic band, who have plundered and massacred so many millions, obtain by all their care, labour, pain, fatigue, and danger?—Could they speak for themselves, must they not own, that the end of all their pursuit was Nothing? Nor is this the end of private ambition only. What is become of that proud mistress of the world,— the *Caput triumphati orbis?* that Rome, of which her own flatterers so liberally prophesied the immortality. In what hath all her glory ended? Surely in Nothing.

Again, what is the end of avarice? Not power, or pleasure, as some think, for the miser will part with a shilling for neither: not ease or happiness; for the more he attains of what he desires, the more uneasy and miserable he is. If every good in this world was put to him, he could not say he pursued one. Shall we say then he pursues misery only? That surely would be contradictory to the first principles of human nature. May we not therefore, nay, must we not confess, that he aims at Nothing? especially if he be himself unable to tell us what is the end of all this bustle and hurry, this watching and toiling, this self-denial and self- constraint?

It will not, I apprehend, be sufficient for him to plead that his design is to amass a large fortune, which he never can nor will use himself, nor would willingly quit to any other person; unless he can show us some substantial good which this fortune is to produce, we shall certainly be justified in concluding, that his end is the same with that of ambition.

The great Mr. Hobbes so plainly saw this, that as he was an enemy to that notable immaterial substance which we have here handled, and therefore unwilling to allow it the large province we have contended for, he advanced a very strange doctrine, and asserted truly,—That in all these grand pursuits the means themselves were the end proposed, *viz.*

to ambition, plotting, fighting, danger, difficulty, and such like:—to avarice, cheating, starving, watching, and the numberless painful arts by which this passion proceeds.

However easy it may be to demonstrate the absurdity of this opinion it will be needless to my purpose, since, if we are driven to confess that the means are the only end attained, I think we must likewise confess, that the end proposed is absolutely Nothing.

As I have shown the end of our two greatest and noblest pursuits, one or other of which engages almost every individual of the busy part of mankind, I shall not tire the reader with carrying him through all the rest, since I believe the same conclusion may be easily drawn from them all.

I shall therefore finish this essay with an inference, which aptly enough suggests itself from what hath been said: seeing that such is its dignity and importance, and that it is really the end of all those things which are supported with so much pomp and solemnity, and looked on with such respect and esteem, surely it becomes a wise man to regard Nothing with the utmost awe and adoration; to pursue it with all his parts and pains; and to sacrifice to it his ease, his innocence, and his present happiness. To which noble pursuit we have this great incitement, that we may assure ourselves of never being cheated or deceived in the end proposed. The virtuous, wise, and learned, may then be unconcerned at all the changes of ministries and of government; since they may be well satisfied, that while ministers of state are rogues themselves, and have inferior knavish tools to bribe and reward; true virtue, wisdom, learning, wit, and integrity, will most certainly bring their possessors—Nothing.

Samuel Johnson

(1709–1784)

The Rambler *seems to have been undertaken mainly for money, three issues per week, to support Johnson's immense project, the* Dictionary of the English Language. *He later told a friend that he had been "at a loss to name it." But, as in the case of the earlier* Spectator, *Johnson's nearest model, it is the name itself—* Rambler*—that holds the key to the work. One hears Johnson the moralist described (and even, in a curiously inverted compliment, dismissed) as "magisterial" or "solemn," one of those overly dignified voices from the past that anyone truly serious about building character cannot afford to tune out. But a receptive ear picks up in the* Rambler's *wonderful sonorities of style a mind not easily made up and far from neat moral pronouncements. Even as Bacon's "counsels" always follow the ramifications of thought rooted in complex experience, so the* Rambler *essays, created under the constant pressure of deadlines, trace the motions of an intellect far too restless, too implicated in it all, to stand aloof pontificating on the human spectacle of jostling for status, approval, money, happiness, fame—all the "snares," as Johnson called them, of living. "Very few men know how to take a walk," according to* Rambler *No. 5. The "walk" makes concrete "this habit of turning every new object to [our] entertainment"—the rambling habit, in short, of paying attention to whatever turns up wherever we happen to be, and to what it may all portend for the soul's health. The absurdly frantic author of* Rambler *No. 146, obsessed with finding out what the world thinks of him, rushing about "from one indifferent setting to the next," has, in a sense, foregone the proper pace of living. He is like those who, preoccupied only with future fantasies, "lose their hours" (No. 5). To practice these "arts of voluntary delusion" is only to achieve "forgetfulness of [one's] own reality." The art of the essay entails learning "how to take a walk."*

On Spring

Rambler No. 5: Tuesday, 3 April 1750

Every man is sufficiently discontented with some circumstances of his present state, to suffer his imagination to range more or less in quest of future happiness, and to fix upon some point of time, in which, by the removal of the inconvenience which now perplexes him, or acquisition of the advantage which he at present wants, he shall find the condition of his life very much improved.

When this time, which is too often expected with great impatience, at last arrives, it generally comes without the blessing for which it was desired; but we solace ourselves with some new prospect, and press forward again with equal eagerness.

It is lucky for a man, in whom this temper prevails, when he turns his hopes upon things wholly out of his own power; since he forbears then to precipitate his affairs, for the sake of the great event that is to complete his felicity, and waits for the blissful hour with less neglect of the measures necessary to be taken in the meantime.

I have long known a person of this temper, who indulged his dream of happiness with less hurt to himself than such chimerical wishes commonly produce, and adjusted his scheme with such address, that his hopes were in full bloom three parts of the year, and in the other part never wholly blasted. Many, perhaps, would be desirous of learning by what means he procured to himself such a cheap and lasting satisfaction. It was gained by a constant practice of referring the removal of all his uneasiness to the coming of the next spring; if his health was impaired, the spring would restore it; if what he wanted was at a high price, it would fall its value in the spring.

The spring indeed did often come without any of these effects, but he was always certain that the next would be more propitious; nor was ever convinced that the present spring would fail him before the middle of summer; for he always talked of the spring as coming 'till it was past, and when it was once past, everyone agreed with him that it was coming.

By long converse with this man, I am, perhaps, brought to feel immoderate pleasure in the contemplation of this delightful season; but I have the satisfaction of finding many, whom it can be no shame to resemble, infected with the same enthusiasm; for there is, I believe, scarce any poet of eminence, who has not left some testimony of his fondness for the flowers, the zephyrs, and the warblers of the spring. Nor has the most luxuriant imagination been able to describe the serenity and happiness of the golden age, otherwise than by giving a perpetual spring, as the highest reward of uncorrupted innocence.

There is, indeed, something inexpressibly pleasing in the annual renovation of the world, and the new display of the treasures of nature. The cold and darkness of winter, with the naked deformity of every object on which we turn our eyes, make us rejoice at the succeeding season, as well for what we have escaped as for what we may enjoy; and every budding flower, which a warm situation brings early to our view, is considered by us as a messenger to notify the approach of more joyous days.

The spring affords to a mind, so free from the disturbance of cares or passions as to be vacant to calm amusements, almost everything that our present state makes us capable of enjoying. The variegated verdure of the fields and woods, the succession of grateful odours, the voice of pleasure pouring out its notes on every side, with the gladness apparently conceived by every animal, from the growth of his food, and the clemency of the weather, throw over the whole earth an air of gaiety, significantly expressed by the smile of nature.

Yet there are men to whom these scenes are able to give no delight, and who hurry away from all the varieties of rural beauty, to lose their hours and divert their thoughts by cards or assemblies, a tavern dinner, or the prattle of the day.

It may be laid down as a position which will seldom deceive, that when a man cannot bear his own company, there is something wrong. He must fly from himself, either because he feels a tediousness in life from the equipoise of an empty mind, which, having no tendency to one motion more than another, but as it is impelled by some external power, must always have recourse to foreign objects; or he must be afraid of the intrusion of some unpleasing ideas, and perhaps is struggling to escape from the remembrance of a loss, the fear of a calamity, or some other thought of greater horror.

Those whom sorrow incapacitates to enjoy the pleasures of contemplation, may properly apply to such diversions, provided they are innocent, as lay strong hold on the attention; and those, whom fear of any future affliction chains down to misery, must endeavour to obviate the danger.

My considerations shall, on this occasion, be turned on such as are burdensome to themselves, merely because they want subjects for reflection, and to whom the volume of nature is thrown open without affording them pleasure or instruction, because they never learned to read the characters.

A French author has advanced this seeming paradox, that "very few men know how to take a walk"; and, indeed, it is true, that few know how to take a walk with a prospect of any other pleasure, than the same company would have afforded them at home.

There are animals that borrow their colour from the neighbouring body, and consequently vary their hue as they happen to change their place. In like manner, it ought to be the endeavour of every man to derive his reflections from the objects about him; for it is to no purpose that he alters his position, if his attention continues fixed to the same point. The mind should be kept open to the access of every new idea, and so far disengaged from the predominance of particular thoughts as easily to accommodate itself to occasional entertainment.

A man that has formed his habit of turning every new object to his entertainment, finds in the productions of nature an inexhaustible stock of materials upon which he can employ himself, without any temptations to envy or malevolence; faults, perhaps seldom totally avoided by those, whose judgment is much exercised upon the works of art. He has always a certain prospect of discovering new reasons for adoring the sovereign author of the universe, and probable hopes of making some discovery of benefit to others, or of profit to himself. There is no doubt but many vegetables and animals have qualities that might be of great use, to the knowledge of which there is not required much force of penetration, or fatigue of study, but only frequent experiments, and close attention. What is said by the chemists of their darling mercury, is, perhaps, true of every body through the whole creation, that if a thousand lives should be spent upon it, all its properties would not be found out.

Mankind must necessarily be diversified by various tastes, since life affords and requires such multiplicity of employments, and a nation of naturalists is neither to be hoped or desired; but it is surely not improper to point out a fresh amusement to those who languish in health, and repine in plenty, for want of some source of diversion that may be less easily exhausted, and to inform the multitudes of both sexes, who are burdened with every new day, that there are many shows which they have not seen.

He that enlarges his curiosity after the works of nature, demonstrably multiplies the inlets to happiness; and, therefore, the younger part of my readers, to whom I dedicate this vernal speculation, must excuse me for calling upon them, to make use at once of the spring of the year, and the spring of life; to acquire, while their minds may be yet impressed with new images, a love of innocent pleasures, and an ardor for useful knowledge; and to remember, that a blighted spring makes a barren year, and that the vernal flowers, however beautiful and gay, are only intended by nature as preparatives to autumnal fruits.

In Pursuit of Fame

Rambler No. 146: Saturday 10, August 1751

None of the projects or designs which exercise the mind of man are equally subject to obstructions and disappointments with the pursuit of fame. Riches cannot easily be denied to them who have something of greater value to offer in exchange; he whose fortune is endangered by litigation, will not refuse to augment the wealth of the lawyer; he whose days are darkened by languor, or whose nerves are excruciated by pain, is compelled to pay tribute to the science of healing. But praise may be always omitted without inconvenience. When once a man has made celebrity necessary to his happiness, he has put it in the power of the weakest and most timorous malignity, if not to take away his satisfaction, at least to withhold it. His enemies may indulge their pride by airy negligence, and gratify their malice by quiet neutrality. They that could never have injured a character by invectives, may combine to annihilate it by silence; as the women of Rome threatened to put an end to conquest and dominion, by supplying no children to the commonwealth.

When a writer has with long toil produced a work intended to burst upon mankind with unexpected lustre, and withdraw the attention of the learned world from every other controversy or enquiry, he is seldom contented to wait long without the enjoyment of his new praises. With an imagination full of his own importance, he walks out like a monarch in disguise to learn the various opinions of his readers. Prepared to feast upon admiration; composed to encounter censures without emotion; and determined not to suffer his quiet to be injured by a sensibility too exquisite of praise or blame, but to laugh with equal contempt at vain objections and injudicious commendations, he enters the places of mingled conversation, sits down to his tea in an obscure corner, and while he appears to examine a file of antiquated journals, catches the conversation of the whole room. He listens, but hears no mention of his book, and therefore supposes that he has disappointed his curiosity by delay; and that as men of learning would naturally begin their conversation with such a wonderful novelty, they had digressed to other subjects before his arrival. The company disperses, and their places are supplied by others equally ignorant, or equally careless. The same expectation hurries him to another place, from which the same disappointment drives him soon away. His impatience then grows violent and tumultuous; he ranges over the town with restless curiosity, and hears in one quarter of a cricket-match, in another of a pick-pocket; is told by some of an unexpected bankruptcy, by others of a turtle-feast; is sometimes provoked by importunate enquiries after the white bear, and sometimes with praises of the dancing dog; he is afterwards entreated to give his judgment upon a wager about the height of the monument; invited to see a foot-race in the adjacent villages; desired to read a ludicrous advertisement; or consulted about the most effectual method of making enquiry after a favourite cat. The whole world is busied in affairs, which he thinks below the notice of reasonable creatures, and which are nevertheless sufficient to withdraw all regard from his labours and his merits.

He resolves at last to violate his own modesty, and to recall the talkers from their folly by an enquiry after himself. He finds every one provided with an answer; one has seen the work advertised, but never met with any that had read it; another has been so often imposed upon by specious titles, that he never buys a book till its character is established; a third wonders what any man can hope to produce after so many writers of greater eminence; the next has enquired after the author, but can hear no account of him, and therefore suspects the name to be fictitious; and another knows him to be a man condemned by indigence to write too frequently what he does not understand.

Many are the consolations with which the unhappy author endeavours to allay his vexation, and fortify his patience. He has written with too little indulgence to the understanding of common readers; he has fallen upon an age in which solid knowledge, and delicate refinement, have given way to low merriment, and idle buffoonery, and therefore no writer can hope for distinction, who has any higher purpose than to raise laughter. He finds that his enemies, such as superiority will always raise, have been industrious, while his performance was in the press, to vilify and blast it; and that the bookseller, whom he had resolved to enrich, has rivals that obstruct the circulation of his copies. He at last reposes upon the consideration, that the noblest works of learning and genius have always made their way slowly against ignorance and prejudice; and that reputation, which is never to be lost, must be gradually obtained, as animals of longest life are observed not soon to attain their full stature and strength.

By such arts of voluntary delusion does every man endeavour to conceal his own unimportance from himself. It is long before we are convinced of the small proportion which every individual bears to the collective body of mankind; or learn how few can be interested in the fortune of any single man; how little vacancy is left in the world for any new object of attention; to how small extent the brightest blaze of merit can be spread amidst the mists of business and of folly; and how soon it is clouded by the intervention of other novelties. Not only the writer of books, but the commander of armies, and the deliverer of nations, will easily outlive all noisy and popular reputation; he may be celebrated for a time by the public voice, but his actions and his name will soon be considered as remote and unaffecting, and be rarely mentioned but by those whose alliance gives them some vanity to gratify by frequent commemoration.

It seems not to be sufficiently considered how little renown can be admitted in the world. Mankind are kept perpetually busy by their fears or desires, and have not more leisure from their own affairs, than to acquaint themselves with the accidents of the current day. Engaged in contriving some refuge from calamity, or in shortening the way to some new possession, they seldom suffer their thoughts to wander to the past or future; none but a few solitary students have leisure to enquire into the claims of ancient heroes or sages; and names which hoped to range over kingdoms and continents, shrink at last into cloisters or colleges.

Nor is it certain, that even of these dark and narrow habitations, these last retreats of fame, the possession will be long kept. Of men devoted to literature, very few extend their views beyond some particular science, and the greater part seldom enquire, even in their own profession, for any authors but those whom the present mode of study happens to force upon their notice; they desire not to fill their minds with unfashionable knowledge, but contentedly resign to oblivion those books which they now find censured or neglected.

The hope of fame is necessarily connected with such considerations as must abate the ardour of confidence, and repress the vigour of pursuit. Whoever claims renown from any kind of excellence, expects to fill the place which is now possessed by another; for there are already names of every class sufficient to employ all that will desire to remember them; and surely he that is pushing his predecessors into the gulf of obscurity, cannot but sometimes suspect, that he must himself sink in like manner, and, as he stands upon the same precipice, be swept away with the same violence.

It sometimes happens that fame begins when life is at an end; but far the greater number of candidates for applause have owed their reception to the world to some favourable casualties, and have therefore immediately sunk into neglect, when death stripped them of their casual influence, and neither fortune nor patronage operated in their favour. Among those who have better claims to regard, the honour paid to their memory is commonly proportionate to the reputation which they enjoyed in their lives, though still growing fainter, as it is at a greater distance from the first emission; and since it is so difficult to obtain the notice of contemporaries, how little is to be hoped from future times? What can merit effect by its own force, when the help of art or friendship can scarcely support it?

David Hume

(1711–1776)

Oliver Goldsmith has a fanciful incomplete essay about literary fame in The Bee *for November 3, 1759, called "A Reverie." In it he imagines a coachyard crowded with vehicles. The Pleasure Stage-Coach is there, the Wagon of Industry, the Landau of Riches, and a smaller carriage, the Fame Machine, whose driver informs him that he has recently conveyed to "the temple of fame" the likes of Addison and Swift. In the stream of new passengers is Dr. Johnson, carrying his* Dictionary, *but admitted only when, by a piece of luck, the sharp-eyed coachman spies a copy of the* Rambler *"peeping from one of [Johnson's] pockets." Close behind, comes one "willing to enter yet afraid to ask"; in his hand he has "a bundle of essays." It is the Scotsman David Hume, essayist indeed, but better known to us as a philosopher and historian. In one of his essays, "Of Essay Writing," he deplores "the separation of the learned from the conversable worlds." Learning, he says (echoing Addison?), has been "shut up in colleges and cells"; it is "a moping recluse method of study." Our general and social discourses, on the other hand, descend to "gossiping stories and idle remarks." He offers his essays in the spirit of one trying to forge a "league" between the methodical approach of the erudite treatise and the intellectual casualness of something like a popular periodical essay. The Humean essay, therefore—whether fairly long, like "Of the Standards of Taste" and "Of Tragedy," or as brief as the one presented here—is an intricately wrought argument in limpid, deft English, unfolding a beautifully trained mind and a discriminating sensibility, not to the learned, the specialist, the philosopher, but to any reader who cares to take the trouble to pay attention and follow.*

Of the Delicacy of Taste and Passion

Some people are subject to a certain delicacy of passion, which makes them extremely sensible to all the accidents of life, and gives them a lively joy upon every prosperous event, as well as a piercing grief, when they meet with misfortunes and adversity. Favours and good offices easily engage their friendship; while the smallest injury provokes their resentment. Any honour or mark of distinction elevates them above measure; but they are as sensibly touched with contempt. People of this character have, no doubt, more lively enjoyments, as well as more pungent sorrows, than men of cool and sedate tempers: but, I believe, when everything is balanced, there is no one, who would not rather be of the latter character, were he entirely master of his own disposition. Good or ill fortune is very little at our disposal: and when a person, that has this sensibility of temper, meets with any misfortune, his sorrow or resentment takes entire possession of him, and deprives him of all relish in the common occurrences of life; the right enjoyment of which forms the chief part of our happiness. Great pleasures are much less frequent than great pains; so that a sensible temper must meet with fewer trials in the former way than in the latter. Not to mention, that men of such lively passions are apt to be transported beyond all bounds of prudence and discretion, and to take false steps in the conduct of life, which are often irretrievable.

There is a delicacy of taste observable in some men, which very much resembles this delicacy of passion, and produces the same sensibility to beauty and deformity of every kind, as that does to prosperity and adversity, obligations and injuries. When you present a poem or a picture to a man possessed of this talent, the delicacy of his feeling makes him be sensibly touched with every part of it; nor are the masterly strokes perceived with more exquisite relish and satisfaction, than the negligences or absurdities with disgust and uneasiness. A polite and judicious conversation affords him the highest entertainment; rudeness or impertinence is as great a punishment to him. In short, delicacy of taste has the same effect as delicacy of passion: it enlarges the sphere both of our happiness and misery, and makes us sensible to pains as well as pleasures, which escape the rest of mankind.

I believe, however, everyone will agree with me, that, notwithstanding this resemblance, delicacy of taste is as much to be desired and cultivated as delicacy of passion is to be lamented, and to be remedied, if possible. The good or ill accidents of life are very little at our disposal; but we are pretty much masters what books we shall read, what diversions we shall partake of, and what company we shall keep. Philosophers have endeavoured to render happiness entirely independent of everything external. That degree of perfection is impossible to be attained: but every wise man will endeavour to place his happiness on such objects chiefly as depend upon himself: and that is not to be attained so much by any other means as by this delicacy of sentiment. When a man is possessed of that talent, he is more happy by what pleases his taste, than by what gratifies his appetites, and receives more enjoyment from a poem or a piece of reasoning than the most expensive luxury can afford.[1]

Whatever connexion there may be originally between these two species of delicacy, I am persuaded, that nothing is so proper to cure us of this delicacy of passion, as the cultivating of that higher and more refined taste, which enables us to judge of the characters of men, of compositions of genius, and of the productions of the nobler arts. A greater or less relish for those obvious beauties, which strike the senses, depends entirely upon the greater or less sensibility of the temper: but with regard to the sciences and liberal arts, a fine taste is, in some measure, the same with strong sense, or at least depends so much upon it, that they are inseparable. In order to judge aright of a composition of genius, there are so many views to be taken in, so many circumstances to be compared, and such a knowledge of human nature requisite, that no man, who is not possessed of the soundest judgment, will ever make a tolerable critic in such performances. And this is a new reason for cultivating a relish in the liberal arts. Our judgment will strengthen by this exercise: we shall form juster notions of life: many things, which please or afflict others, will appear to us too frivolous to engage our attention: and we shall lose by degrees that sensibility and delicacy of passion, which is so incommodious.

But perhaps I have gone too far in saying, that a cultivated taste for the polite arts extinguishes the passions, and renders us indifferent to those objects, which are so fondly pursued by the rest of mankind. On farther reflection, I find, that it rather improves our sensibility for all the tender and agreeable passions; at the same time that it renders the mind incapable of the rougher and more boisterous emotions.

> Ingenuas didicisse fideliter artes,
> Emollit mores, nec sinit esse feros.[2]

For this, I think there may be assigned two very natural reasons. In the first place, nothing is so improving to the temper as the study of the beauties, either of poetry, eloquence, music, or painting. They give a certain elegance of sentiment to which the rest of mankind are strangers. The emotions which they excite are soft and tender. They draw off the

[1] How far delicacy of taste, and that of passion, are connected together in the original frame of the mind, it is hard to determine. To me there appears a very considerable connexion between them. For we may observe that women, who have more delicate passions than men, have also a more delicate taste of the ornaments of life, of dress, equipage, and the ordinary decencies of behaviour. [Hume]

[2] A faithful study of the liberal arts humanizes character and permits it not to be cruel (Ovid, A. L. Wheeler, trans.).

mind from the hurry of business and interest; cherish reflection; dispose to tranquillity; and produce an agreeable melancholy, which, of all dispositions of the mind, is the best suited to love and friendship.

In the second place, a delicacy of taste is favourable to love and friendship, by confining our choice to few people, and making us indifferent to the company and conversation of the greater part of men. You will seldom find, that mere men of the world, whatever strong sense they may be endowed with, are very nice in distinguishing characters, or in marking those insensible differences and gradations, which make one man preferable to another. Anyone, that has competent sense, is sufficient for their entertainment: they talk to him, of their pleasure and affairs, with the same frankness that they would to another; and finding many, who are fit to supply his place, they never feel any vacancy or want in his absence. But to make use of the allusion of a celebrated French author, the judgment may be compared to a clock or watch, where the most ordinary machine is sufficient to tell the hours; but the most elaborate alone can point out the minutes and seconds, and distinguish the smallest differences of time. One that has well digested his knowledge both of books and men, has little enjoyment but in the company of a few select companions. He feels too sensibly, how much all the rest of mankind fall short of the notions which he has entertained. And, his affections being thus confined within a narrow circle, no wonder he carries them further, than if they were more general and undistinguished. The gaiety and frolic of a bottle companion improves with him into a solid friendship: and the ardours of a youthful appetite become an elegant passion.

Oliver Goldsmith

(1728–1774)

*Told by the driver of the Fame Machine (**see p. 73**) to wait until it can be determined whether there will be a seat to spare, poor Goldsmith watches the coach fill up with literary celebrities and ends up, not among them, but "mounted behind." What happened afterwards will never be known, strictly speaking. "The Reverie" breaks off with those famous last words, "To Be Continued"; three Saturdays later,* The Bee *made its last appearance. Goldsmith kept writing essays for various other periodicals, including his popular "Chinese Letters" for* The Public Ledger, *reissued in 1762 as* The Citizen of the World. *Here he writes about English life and manners, inventively and satirically, behind an expatriate Chinese philosopher's mask. "National Prejudices," printed anonymously in* The British Magazine *for August 1760, links the "citizen of the world" with the essayist as self-described "saunterer," the contemplative student of life whose rambles through the world have enlarged both his judgment and his capacity for fellow feeling. Goldsmith did not include the piece in his collected* Essays *of 1765–1766, admittedly a fraction of his periodical output. Although later collectors and editors, from the time of his death, have routinely counted it among his works, its authenticity has been questioned by modern scholars. In the preface to his essay collection, Goldsmith notes the unscrupulous appropriation by others of his universally unsigned journalism. By claiming these chosen essays as his own, he purports to be following the shipwrecked fat man "who, when the sailors, pressed by famine, were taking slices from his posteriors to satisfy their hunger, insisted, with great justice, on having the first cut for himself." The persistent and continuing attribution of "National Prejudices" to Oliver Goldsmith, essayist, novelist, playwright, and poet, is perhaps no more than a bit of posthumous corporeal restitution—and as fine a "slice" of eighteenth-century periodical essay writing as anyone could ask for.*

National Prejudices

As I am one of that sauntering tribe of mortals, who spend the greatest part of their time in taverns, coffee-houses, and other places of public resort, I have thereby an opportunity of observing an infinite variety of characters, which, to a person of a contemplative turn, is a much higher entertainment than a view of all the curiosities of art or nature. In one of these my late rambles, I accidentally fell into the company of half-a-dozen gentlemen, who were engaged in a warm dispute about some political affair; the decision of which, as they were equally divided in their sentiments, they thought proper to refer to me, which naturally drew me in for a share of the conversation.

Amongst a multiplicity of other topics, we took occasion to talk of the different characters of the several nations of Europe; when one of the gentlemen, cocking his hat, and assuming such an air of importance as if he had possessed all the merit of the English nation in his own person, declared that the Dutch were a parcel of avaricious wretches; the French a set of flattering sycophants; that the Germans were drunken sots, and beastly gluttons; and the Spaniards proud, haughty, and surly tyrants: but that in bravery, generosity, clemency, and in every other virtue, the English excelled all the world.

This very learned and judicious remark was received with a general smile of approbation by all the company—all, I mean, but your humble servant; who, endeavouring to keep my gravity as well as I could, and reclining my head upon my arm, continued for some time in a posture of affected thoughtfulness, as if I had been musing on something else, and did not seem to attend to the subject of conversation; hoping, by this means, to avoid the disagreeable necessity of explaining myself, and thereby depriving the gentleman of his imaginary happiness.

But my pseudo-patriot had no mind to let me escape so easily: not satisfied that his opinion should pass without contradiction, he was determined to have it ratified by the suffrage of everyone in the company; for which purpose, addressing himself to me with an air of inexpressible confidence, he asked me if I was not of the same way of thinking. As I am never forward in giving my opinion, especially when I have reason to believe that it will not be agreeable; so, when I am obliged to give it, I always hold it for a maxim to speak my real sentiments. I therefore told him, that, for my own part, I should not have ventured to talk in such peremptory strain, unless I had made the tour of Europe, and examined the manners of the several nations with great care and accuracy; that, perhaps a more impartial judge would not scruple to affirm, that the Dutch were more frugal and industrious, the French more temperate and polite, the Germans more hardy and patient of labour and fatigue, and the Spaniards more staid and sedate, than the English; who, though undoubtedly brave and generous, were at the same time rash, headstrong, and impetuous, too apt to be elated with prosperity, and to despond in adversity.

I could easily perceive, that all the company began to regard me with a jealous eye before I had finished my answer; which I had no sooner done than the patriotic gentleman observed, with a contemptuous sneer, that he was greatly surprised how some people could have the conscience to live in a country which they did not love, and to enjoy the protection of a government, to which in their hearts they were inveterate enemies. Finding that by this modest declaration of my sentiments, I had forfeited the good opinion of my companions, and given them occasion to call my political principles in question, and well knowing that it was in vain to argue with men who were so very full of themselves, I threw down my reckoning, and retired to my own lodgings, reflecting on the absurd and ridiculous nature of national prejudice and prepossession.

Among all the famous sayings of antiquity, there is none that does greater honour to the author, or affords greater pleasure to the reader (at least if he be a person of a generous and benevolent heart), than that of the philosopher, who being asked what countryman he was, replied that he was a citizen of the world. How few are there to be found in modern times who can say the same, or whose conduct is consistent with such a profession! We are now become so much Englishmen, Frenchmen, Dutchmen, Spaniards, or Germans, that we are no longer citizens of the world; so much the natives of one particular spot, or members of one petty society, that we no longer consider ourselves as the general inhabitants of the globe, or members of that grand society which comprehends the whole human kind.

Did these prejudices prevail only among the meanest and lowest of the people, perhaps they might be excused, as they have few, if any opportunities of correcting them by reading, travelling, or conversing with foreigners; but the misfortune is, that they infect the minds, and influence the conduct even of our gentlemen; of those, I mean, who have every title to this appellation but an exemption from prejudice, which, however, in my opinion, ought to be regarded as the characteristical mark of a gentleman: for let a man's birth be ever so high, his station ever so exalted, or his fortune ever so large, yet, if he is not free from the national and all other prejudices, I should make bold to tell him, that he had a low and vulgar mind, and had no just claim to the character of a gentleman. And, in fact, you will always find, that those are most apt to boast of national merit, who have little or no merit of their own to depend on, than which, to be sure, nothing is more natural: the slender vine twists around the sturdy oak for no other reason in the world, but because it has not strength sufficient to support itself.

Should it be alleged in defense of national prejudice, that it is the natural and necessary growth of love to our country, and that therefore the former cannot be destroyed without hurting the latter; I answer that this is a gross fallacy and delusion. That it is the growth of love to our country, I will allow; but that it is the natural and necessary growth of it, I absolutely deny. Superstition and enthusiasm too are the growth of religion; but whoever took it in his head to affirm, that they are the necessary growth of this noble principle? They are, if you will, the bastard sprouts of this heavenly plant; but not its natural and genuine branches, and may safely enough be lopt off, without doing any harm to the parent stock: nay, perhaps, 'till once they are lopt off, this goodly tree can never flourish in perfect health and vigour.

Is it not very possible that I may love my own country, without hating the natives of other countries? That I may exert the most heroic bravery, the most undaunted resolution, in defending its laws and liberty, without despising all the rest of the world as cowards and poltroons? Most certainly it is: and if it were not—but what need I suppose what is absolutely impossible?—but if it were not I must own I should prefer the title of the ancient philosopher, namely, a citizen of the world, to that of an Englishman, a Frenchman, an European, or to any other appellation whatever.

Charles Lamb

(1775–1834)

Fielding, Johnson, Goldsmith struggled—sometimes on the edge of poverty—to make a living by writing; Lamb was one of the first periodical writers to hold an ordinary humdrum job earning him the steady kind of income that creates small spaces for leisure and the psychological freedom to write. For thirty-three years, six days a week, he clerked in the accounting office of East India House. When he wrote, it was in the evening and on Sunday, in the apartment he shared with his sister Mary. His best essays appeared during the early 1820's in the London Magazine *under the penname "Elia" borrowed from an old Italian clerk Lamb had known as a youth, on his first job. More than a periodical convention and a handy pseudonym, "Elia" was for Lamb a self-conscious prose style and a way of being truthful as an essayist. In contrast to the colloquial ease of his personal letters, the Elia essays have the lovingly cultivated archaic air of one who delighted in what he termed "the beautiful obloquies" ("Mackery End") of old writers like Sir Thomas Browne and Margaret Newcastle. Lamb was not by temperament a periodical writer eagerly turned to the currents of social and political life. "Public affairs," he wrote to a friend, "except as they touch upon me, and so turn into private, I cannot whip up my mind to feel any interest in." Yet, as his fellow essayist, William Hazlitt, said of Lamb, "he occupies that nice point between egotism and disinterested humanity" ("Elia and Geoffrey Crayon"). If "The Convalescent" is admissible evidence, Lamb considered self-inflating egotism, especially his own, both a fine butt of humor and a pathology. In his Preface to* The Last Essays of Elia, *he describes Elia's essays as "villainously pranked out in an affected array of antique modes and phrases." And yet, he says, "They had not been* his *if they had been other than such; and better it is that a writer should be natural in a self-pleasing quaintness than affect a naturalness (so called) that should be strange to him." During his leisure hours, Lamb the essayist crafted a voice to fit the person he felt himself to be.*

Grace Before Meat

The custom of saying grace at meals had, probably, its origin in the early times of the world, and the hunter-state of man, when dinners were precarious things, and a full meal was something more than a common blessing; when a bellyfull was a windfall, and looked like a special providence. In the shouts and triumphal songs with which, after a season of sharp abstinence, a lucky booty of deer's or goat's flesh would naturally be ushered home, existed, perhaps, the germ of the modern grace. It is not otherwise easy to be understood, why the blessing of food—the act of eating—should have had a particular expression of thanksgiving annexed to it, distinct from that implied and silent gratitude with which we are expected to enter upon the enjoyment of the many other various gifts and good things of existence.

I own that I am disposed to say grace upon twenty other occasions in the course of the day besides my dinner. I want a form for setting out upon a pleasant walk, for a moonlight ramble, for a friendly meeting, or a solved problem. Why have we none for books, those spiritual repasts—a grace before Milton—a grace before Shakespeare—a devotional exercise proper to be said before reading the Faery Queen?—but, the received ritual having prescribed these forms to the solitary ceremony of manducation, I shall confine my observations to the experience which I have had of the grace, properly so-called; commending my new scheme for extension to a niche in the grand philosophical, poetical, and perchance in part heretical, liturgy, now compiling by my friend Homo Humanus, for the use of a certain snug congregation of Utopian Rabelaisian Christians,[1] no matter where assembled.

The form then of the benediction before eating has its beauty at a poor man's table, or at the simple and unprovocative repasts of children. It is here that the grace becomes exceedingly graceful. The indigent man, who hardly knows whether he shall have a meal the next day or not, sits down to his fare with a present sense of the blessing, which can be but feebly acted by the rich, into whose minds the conception of wanting a dinner could never, but by some extreme theory, have entered. The proper end of food—the animal sustenance—is barely contemplated by them. The poor man's bread is his daily bread, literally his bread for the day. Their courses are perennial.

Again, the plainest diet seems the fittest to be preceded by the grace. That which is least stimulative to appetite, leaves the mind most free for foreign considerations. A man may feel thankful, heartily thankful, over a dish of plain mutton with turnips, and have leisure to reflect upon the ordinance and institution of eating; when he shall confess a perturbation of mind, inconsistent with the purposes of the grace, at the presence of venison or turtle. When I have sate (a *rarus hospes*[2]) at rich

[1] Lamb is thinking of the Abbey of Thelema, a utopian monastery for men and women in Rabelais' *Gargantua and Pantagruel*. Its motto is "Do what you like."

[2] Uncommon guest.

men's tables, with the savoury soup and messes steaming up the nostrils, and moistening the lips of the guests with desire and a distracted choice, I have felt the introduction of that ceremony to be unseasonable. With the ravenous orgasm upon you, it seems impertinent to interpose a religious sentiment. It is a confusion of purpose to mutter out praises from a mouth that waters. The heats of epicurism put out the gentle flame of devotion. The incense which rises round is pagan, and the belly-god intercepts it for his own. The very excess of the provision beyond the needs, takes away all sense of proportion between the end and means. The giver is veiled by his gifts. You are startled at the injustice of returning thanks—for what?—for having too much, while so many starve. It is to praise the Gods amiss.

I have observed this awkwardness felt, scarce consciously perhaps, by the good man who says the grace. I have seen it in clergymen and others—a sort of shame—a sense of the co-presence of circumstances which unhallow the blessing. After a devotional tone put on for a few seconds, how rapidly the speaker will fall into his common voice, helping himself or his neighbour, as if to get rid of some uneasy sensation of hypocrisy. Not that the good man was a hypocrite, or was not most conscientious in the discharge of the duty; but he felt in his inmost mind the incompatibility of the scene and the viands before him with the exercise of a calm and rational gratitude.

I hear somebody exclaim—Would you have Christians sit down at table, like hogs to their troughs, without remembering the Giver?—no—I would have them sit down as Christians, remembering the Giver, and less like hogs. Or if their appetites must run riot, and they must pamper themselves with delicacies for which east and west are ransacked, I would have them postpone their benediction to a fitter season, when appetite is laid; when the still small voice can be heard, and the reason of the grace returns—with temperate diet and restricted dishes. Gluttony and surfeiting are no proper occasions for thanksgiving. When Jeshurun waxed fat, we read that he kicked. Virgil knew the harpy-nature better, when he put into the mouth of Celæno anything but a blessing.[3] We may be gratefully sensible of the deliciousness of some kinds of food beyond others, though that is a meaner and inferior gratitude: but the proper object of the grace is sustenance, not relishes; daily bread, not delicacies; the means of life, and not the means of pampering the carcass. With what frame or composure, I wonder, can a city chaplain pronounce his benediction at some great hall feast, when he knows that his last concluding pious word—and that, in all probability, the sacred name which he preaches—is but the signal for so many impatient

[3] Calæno, the harpy, curses Aeneas in *Aeneid* III, 247–257.

harpies to commence their foul orgies, with as little sense of true thankfulness (which is temperance) as those Virgilian fowl! It is well if the good man himself does not feel his devotions a little clouded, those foggy sensuous steams mingling with and polluting the pure altar sacrifice.

The severest satire upon full tables and surfeits is the banquet which Satan, in the *Paradise Regained*, provides for a temptation in the wilderness:

> A table richly spread in regal mode,
> With dishes piled, and meats of noblest sort
> And savour; beasts of chase, or fowl of game,
> In pastry build, or from the spit, or boiled,
> Gris-amber-steamed; all fish from sea or shore,
> Freshet or purling brook, for which was drained
> Pontus, and Lucrine bay, and Afric coast.[4]

The Tempter, I warrant you, thought these cates would go down without the recommendatory preface of a benediction. They are like to be short graces where the devil plays the host.—I am afraid the poet wants his usual decorum in this place. Was he thinking of the old Roman luxury, or of a gaudy day at Cambridge?[5] This was a temptation fitter for a Heliogabalus. The whole banquet is too civic and culinary, and the accompaniments altogether a profanation of that deep, abstracted, holy scene. The mighty artillery of sauces, which the cook-fiend conjures up, is out of proportion to the simple wants and plain hunger of the guest. He that disturbed him in his dreams, from his dreams might have been taught better. To the temperate fantasies of the famished Son of God, what sort of feasts presented themselves?—He dreamed indeed,

> —As appetite is wont to dream,
> Of meats and drinks, nature's refreshment sweet.

But what meats?—

> Him thought, he by the brook of Cherith stood,
> And saw the ravens with their horny beaks
> Food to Elijah bringing, even and morn
> Though ravenous, taught to abstain from what they brought:
> He saw the prophet also how he fled
> Into the desert, and how there he slept
> Under a juniper; then how awaked
> He found his supper on the coals prepared,
> And by the angel was bid rise and eat,
> And ate the second time after repose,

[4] Milton's *Paradise Regained*, II, 340–347.

[5] A feast day, the annual university dinner.

> The strength whereof sufficed him forty days:
> Sometimes, that with Elijah he partook,
> Or as a guest with Daniel at his pulse.[6]

Nothing in Milton is finelier fancied than these temperate dreams of the divine Hungerer. To which of these two visionary banquets, think you, would the introduction of what is called the grace have been most fitting and pertinent?

Theoretically I am no enemy to graces; but practically I own that (before meat especially) they seem to involve something awkward and unseasonable. Our appetites, of one or another kind, are excellent spurs to our reason, which might otherwise but feebly set about the great ends of preserving and continuing the species. They are fit blessings to be contemplated at a distance with a becoming gratitude; but the moment of appetite (the judicious reader will apprehend me) is, perhaps, the least fit season for that exercise. The Quakers who go about their business, of every description, with more calmness than we, have more title to the use of these benedictory prefaces. I have always admired their silent grace, and the more because I have observed their application to the meat and drink following to be less passionate and sensual than ours. They are neither gluttons nor wine-bibbers as a people. They eat, as a horse bolts his chopt hay, with indifference, calmness, and cleanly circumstances. They neither grease nor slop themselves. When I see a citizen in his bib and tucker, I cannot imagine it a surplice.

I am no Quaker at my food. I confess I am not indifferent to the kinds of it. Those unctuous morsels of deer's flesh were not made to be received with dispassionate services. I hate a man who swallows it, affecting not to know what he is eating. I suspect his taste in higher matters. I shrink instinctively from one who professes to like minced veal. There is a physiognomical character in the tastes for food. C——[7] holds that a man cannot have a pure mind who refuses apple-dumplings. I am not certain but he is right. With the decay of my first innocence, I confess a less and less relish daily for those innocuous cates. The whole vegetable tribe have lost their gust with me. Only I stick to asparagus, which still seems to inspire gentle thoughts. I am impatient and querulous under culinary disappointments, as to come home at the dinner hour, for instance, expecting some savoury mess, and to find one quite tasteless and sapidless. Butter ill melted—that commonest of kitchen failures—puts me beside my tenour.—The author of the *Rambler* used to make inarticulate animal noises over a favourite food. Was this the music quite proper to be preceded by the grace? or would the pious man have

[6] *Paradise Regained*, II, 246–278.

[7] Samuel Taylor Coleridge, Lamb's friend since schooldays.

done better to postpone his devotions to a season when the blessing might be contemplated with less perturbation? I quarrel with no man's tastes, nor would set my thin face against those excellent things, in their way, jollity and feasting. But as these exercises, however laudable, have little in them of grace or gracefulness, a man should be sure, before he ventures so to grace them, that while he is pretending his devotions otherwise, he is not secretly kissing his hand to some great fish—his Dagon—with a special consecration of no ark but the fat tureen before him. Graces are the sweet preluding strains to the banquets of angels and children; to the roots and severer repasts of the Chartreuse; to the slender, but not slenderly acknowledged, refection of the poor and humble man: but at the heaped-up boards of the pampered and the luxurious they become of dissonant mood, less timed and tuned to the occasion, methinks, than the noise of those better befitting organs would be, which children hear tales of, at Hog's Norton.[8] We sit too long at our meals, or are too curious in the study of them, or too disordered in our application to them, or engross too great a portion of those good things (which should be common) to our share, to be able with any grace to say grace. To be thankful for what we grasp exceeding our proportion is to add hypocrisy to injustice. A lurking sense of this truth is what makes the performance of this duty so cold and spiritless a service at most tables. In houses where the grace is as indispensable as the napkin, who has not seen that never settled question arise, as to *who shall say it;* while the good man of the house and the visitor clergyman, or some other guest belike of next authority from years or gravity, shall be bandying about the office between them as a matter of compliment, each of them not unwilling to shift the awkward burden of an equivocal duty from his own shoulders?

I once drank tea in company with two Methodist divines of different persuasions, whom it was my fortune to introduce to each other for the first time that evening. Before the first cup was handed round, one of these reverend gentlemen put it to the other, with all due solemnity, whether he chose to *say anything*. It seems it is the custom with some sectaries to put up a short prayer before this meal also. His reverend brother did not at first quite apprehend him, but upon an explanation, with little less importance he made answer, that it was not a custom known in his church: in which courteous evasion the other acquiescing for good manners' sake, or in compliance with a weak brother, the supplementary or tea-grace was waived altogether. With what spirit might not Lucian have painted two priests, of *his* religion, playing into

[8] Lamb is punning on "organs" by way of an old proverb: "I think thou wast born at Hog's Norton, where piggs play upon the organs." "Pigg" may have been the name of one of the villagers.

each other's hands the compliment of performing or omitting a sacrifice,—the hungry God meantime, doubtful of his incense, with expectant nostrils hovering over the two flamens, and (as between two stools) going away in the end without his supper.

A short form upon these occasions is felt to want reverence; a long one, I am afraid, cannot escape the charge of impertinence. I do not quite approve of the epigrammatic conciseness with which that equivocal wag (but my pleasant school-fellow) C.V.L., when importuned for a grace, used to inquire, first slyly leering down the table, "Is there no clergyman here?"—significantly adding, "thank G—." Nor do I think our old form at school quite pertinent, where we were used to preface our bald bread and cheese suppers with a preamble, connecting with that humble blessing a recognition of benefits the most awful and overwhelming to the imagination which religion has to offer. *Non tunc illis erat locus.*[9] I remember we were put to it to reconcile the phrase "good creatures," upon which the blessing rested, with the fare set before us, wilfully understanding that expression in a low and animal sense,—'till someone recalled a legend, which told how in the golden days of Christ's, the young Hospitallers were wont to have smoking joints of roast meat upon their nightly boards, till some pious benefactor, commiserating the decencies, rather than the palates, of the children, commuted our flesh for garments, and gave us—*horresco referens*[10]—trousers instead of mutton.

The Convalescent

A pretty severe fit of indisposition which, under the name of a nervous fever, has made a prisoner of me for some weeks past, and is but slowly leaving me, has reduced me to an incapacity of reflecting upon any topic foreign to itself. Expect no healthy conclusions from me this month, reader; I can offer you only sick men's dreams.

And truly the whole state of sickness is such; for what else is it but a magnificent dream for a man to lie a-bed, and draw day-light curtains about him; and, shutting out the sun, to induce a total oblivion of all the

[9] But that was not the occasion for such things (Horace).

[10] I tremble at the recollection (Virgil, *Aeneid*).

works which are going on under it? To become insensible to all the operations of life, except the beatings of one feeble pulse?

If there be a regal solitude, it is a sick bed. How the patient lords it there; what caprices he acts without control! how king-like he sways his pillow—tumbling, and tossing, and shifting, and lowering, and thumping, and flatting, and moulding it, to the ever varying requisitions of his throbbing temples.

He changes sides oftener than a politician. Now he lies full length, then half-length, obliquely, transversely, head and feet quite across the bed; and none accuses him of tergiversation. Within the four curtains he is absolute. They are his *mare clausum.*[1]

How sickness enlarges the dimensions of a man's self to himself! he is his own exclusive object. Supreme selfishness is inculcated upon him as his only duty. 'Tis the Two Tables of the Law to him. He has nothing to think of but how to get well. What passes out of doors, or within them, so he hear not the jarring of them, affects him not.

A little while ago he was greatly concerned in the event of a lawsuit, which was to be the making or the marring of his dearest friend. He was to be seen trudging about upon this man's errand to fifty quarters of the town at once, jogging this witness, refreshing that solicitor. The cause was to come on yesterday. He is absolutely as indifferent to the decision, as if it were a question to be tried at Pekin. Peradventure from some whispering, going on about the house, not intended for his hearing, he picks up enough to make him understand, that things went cross-grained in the court yesterday, and his friend is ruined. But the word "friend," and the word "ruin," disturb him no more than so much jargon. He is not to think of anything but how to get better.

What a world of foreign cares are merged in that absorbing consideration!

He has put on the strong armour of sickness, he is wrapped in the callous hide of suffering, he keeps his sympathy, like some curious vintage, under trusty lock and key, for his own use only.

He lies pitying himself, honing and moaning to himself; he yearneth over himself; his bowels are even melted within him, to think what he suffers; he is not ashamed to weep over himself.

He is forever plotting how to do some good to himself; studying little stratagems and artificial alleviations.

He makes the most of himself; dividing himself, by an allowable fiction, into as many distinct individuals, as he hath sore and sorrowing members. Sometimes he meditates—as of a thing apart from him—

[1]A closed sea.

upon his poor aching head, and that dull pain which, dozing or waking, lay in it all the past night like a log, or palpable substance of pain, not to be removed without opening the very skull, as it seemed, to take it thence. Or he pities his long, clammy, attenuated fingers. He compassionates himself all over; and his bed is a very discipline of humanity, and tender heart.

He is his own sympathiser; and instinctively feels that none can so well perform that office for him. He cares for few spectators to his tragedy. Only that punctual face of the old nurse pleases him, that announces his broths, and his cordials. He likes it because it is so unmoved, and because he can pour forth his feverish ejaculations before it as unreservedly as to his bed-post.

To the world's business he is dead. He understands not what the callings and occupations of mortals are; only he has a glimmering conceit of some such thing, when the doctor makes his daily call: and even in the lines of that busy face he reads no multiplicity of patients, but solely conceives of himself as *the sick man*. To what other uneasy couch the good man is hastening, when he slips out of his chamber, folding up his thin douceur so carefully for fear of rustling—is no speculation which he can at present entertain. He thinks only of the regular return of the same phenomenon at the same hour to-morrow.

Household rumours touch him not. Some faint murmur, indicative of life going on within the house, soothes him, while he knows not distinctly what it is. He is not to know anything, not to think of anything. Servants gliding up or down the distant staircase, treading as upon velvet, gently keep his ear awake, so long as he troubles not himself further than with some feeble guess at their errands. Exacter knowledge would be a burden to him: he can just endure the pressure of conjecture. He opens his eye faintly at the dull stroke of the muffled knocker, and closes it again without asking "Who was it?" He is flattered by a general notion that inquiries are making after him, but he cares not to know the name of the inquirer. In the general stillness, and awful hush of the house, he lies in state, and feels his sovereignty.

To be sick is to enjoy monarchal prerogatives. Compare the silent tread, and quiet ministry, almost by the eye only, with which he is served—with the careless demeanour, the unceremonious goings in and out (slapping of doors, or leaving them open) of the very same attendants, when he is getting a little better—and you will confess, that from the bed of sickness (throne let me rather call it) to the elbow chair of convalescence, is a fall from dignity, amounting to a deposition.

How convalescence shrinks a man back to his pristine stature! Where is now the space, which he occupied so lately, in his own, in the family's eye?

The scene of his regalities, his sick room, which was his presence chamber, where he lay and acted his despotic fancies—how is it reduced to a common bed-room! The trimness of the very bed has something petty and unmeaning about it. It is made every day. How unlike to that wavy many-furrowed, oceanic surface, which it presented so short a time since, when to make it was a service not to be thought of at oftener than three or four day revolutions, when the patient was with pain and grief to be lifted for a little while out of it, to submit to the encroachments of unwelcome neatness, and decencies which his shaken frame deprecated; then to be lifted into it again, for another three or four days' respite, to flounder it out of shape again, while every fresh furrow was a historical record of some shifting posture, some uneasy turning, some seeking for a little ease; and the shrunken skin scarce told a truer story than the crumpled coverlid.

Hushed are those mysterious sighs—those groans—so much more awful, while we knew not from what caverns of vast hidden suffering they proceeded. The Lernean pangs are quenched. The riddle of sickness is solved; and Philoctetes is become an ordinary personage.

Perhaps some relic of the sick man's dream of greatness survives in the still lingering visitations of the medical attendant. But how is he too changed with everything else! Can this be he—this man of news—of chat—of anecdotes—of everything but physic—can this be he, who so lately came between the patient and his cruel enemy, as on some solemn embassy from Nature, erecting herself into a high mediating party?—Pshaw! 'tis some old woman.

Farewell with him all that made sickness pompous—the spell that hushed the household—the desertlike stillness, felt throughout its inmost chambers—the mute attendance—the enquiry by looks—the still softer delicacies of self-attention—the sole and single eye of distemper alonely fixed upon itself—world-thoughts excluded—the man a world unto himself—his own theatre—

What a speck is he dwindled into!

In this flat swamp of convalescence, left by the ebb of sickness, yet far enough from the terra firma of established health, your note, dear editor, reached me, requesting—an article. *In articulo mortis*,[2] thought I; but it is something hard—and the quibble, wretched as it was, relieved me. The summons, unreasonable as it appeared, seemed to link me on again to the petty businesses of life, which I had lost sight of; a gentle call to activity, however trivial; a wholesome weaning from that preposterous dream of self-absorption—the puffy state of sickness—in which I con-

[2] At the moment of death.

fess to have lain so long, insensible to the magazines and monarchies, of the world alike; to its laws, and to its literature. The hypochondriac flatus is subsiding; the acres, which in imagination I had spread over—for the sick man swells in the sole contemplation of his single sufferings, till he becomes a Tityus to himself—are wasting to a span; and for the giant of self-importance, which I was so lately, you have me once again in my natural pretensions—the lean and meagre figure of your insignificant essayist.

William Hazlitt

(1778–1830)

Here is Virginia Woolf, whose writings on other essayists still hit the mark:

> *There can be no question that Hazlitt the thinker is an admirable companion. He is strong and fearless; he knows his mind and he speaks his mind forcibly yet brilliantly too. . . . But besides Hazlitt the thinker there is Hazlitt the artist . . . with his sensibility to all those emotions which disturb the reason and make it often seem futile enough to spend one's time slicing things up finer and finer with the intellect when the body of the world is so firm and so warm and demands so imperatively to be pressed to the heart. ("William Hazlitt,"* Common Reader *II)*

And wrenched from the heart, she might have said, cut away live, with the intensity of hate and hurt still clinging to the words, the energetic reach of the sentences. The range of feeling in Hazlitt's essays is unprecedented in the English tradition, as is the length to which he often amplifies whatever moves him. The publications for which he was writing were no longer the single-essay periodicals of Addison's or Johnson's time, but the heftier literary magazines that had begun to attract new kinds of readers, making new kinds of demands on them and delivering new kinds of pleasures. An essay by Hazlitt draws one into a mercurial, recollective, digressive intellectual movement more reminiscent of Montaigne's longer essays than anything that had come before. The complexities of feeling and the "sinewy textures" of his ideas ("A Farewell to Essay Writing") surprise and engage at every turn. Woolf considered Hazlitt the essayist, the critic of literature, politics, art, and the drama, the best prose writer of his generation. Hazlitt both advocated and himself practiced superbly well what he called "a genuine familiar style." To write such a style, according to him, is "to write as anyone would speak in common conversation who had the thorough command and choice of words, or who could discourse with ease, force, and perspicuity, setting aside all pedantic and oratorical flourishes" ("On Familiar Style"). However transformed by a Romantic sensibility, its affinities are with the prose of Addison rather than of Hazlitt's contemporary and good friend Charles Lamb or their great predecessor Samuel Johnson. The two essays presented here were both published originally in New Monthly Magazine, *the first in 1822, the second in 1827.*

On Going a Journey

One of the pleasantest things in the world is going a journey; but I like to go by myself. I can enjoy society in a room; but out of doors, nature is company enough for me. I am then never less alone than when alone.

> The fields his study, nature was his book.

I cannot see the wit of walking and talking at the same time. When I am in the country, I wish to vegetate like the country. I am not for criticising hedge-rows and black cattle. I go out of town in order to forget the town and all that is in it. There are those who for this purpose go to watering-places, and carry the metropolis with them. I like more elbow-room, and fewer incumbrances. I like solitude, when I give myself up to it, for the sake of solitude; nor do I ask for

> —a friend in my retreat,
> Whom I may whisper solitude is sweet.

The soul of a journey is liberty, perfect liberty, to think, feel, do just as one pleases. We go a journey chiefly to be free of all impediments and of all inconveniences; to leave ourselves behind, much more to get rid of others. It is because I want a little breathing-space to muse on indifferent matters, where Contemplation

> May plume her feathers and let grow her wings,
> That in the various bustle of resort
> Were all too ruffled, and sometimes impair'd,

that I absent myself from the town for a while, without feeling at a loss the moment I am left by myself. Instead of a friend in a postchaise or in a tilbury, to exchange good things with, and vary the same stale topics over again, for once let me have a truce with impertinence. Give me the clear blue sky over my head, and the green turf beneath my feet, a winding road before me, and a three hours' march to dinner—and then to thinking! It is hard if I cannot start some game on these lone heaths. I laugh, I run, I leap, I sing for joy. From the point of yonder rolling cloud, I plunge into my past being, and revel there, as the sun-burnt Indian plunges headlong into the wave that wafts him to his native shore. Then long-forgotten things, like "sunken wrack and sumless treasuries," burst upon my eager sight, and I begin to feel, think, and be myself again. Instead of an awkward silence, broken by attempts at wit or dull common-places, mine is that undisturbed silence of the heart which alone is perfect eloquence. No one likes puns, alliterations, antitheses, argument, and analysis better than I do; but I sometimes had rather be without them. "Leave, oh, leave me to my repose!" I have just now other business in hand, which would seem idle to you, but is with me "the very stuff of the conscience." Is not this wild rose sweet without a comment? Does not this daisy leap to my heart, set in its coat of emerald? Yet if I were to explain to you the circumstance that has so endeared it to me, you would only smile. Had I not better then keep it to myself, and let it serve me to brood over, from here to yonder craggy point, and from thence onward to the far-distant horizon? I should be but bad company all that way, and therefore prefer being alone. I have heard it said that you may, when the moody fit comes on, walk or ride on by yourself, and indulge your reveries. But this looks like a breach of manners, a neglect of others, and you are thinking all the time that you ought to rejoin your party. "Out upon such half-faced fellowship," say I. I like to be either entirely to myself, or entirely at the disposal of others; to talk or be silent, to walk or sit still, to be sociable or solitary. I was pleased with an observation of Mr. Cobbett's, that "he thought it a bad French custom to drink our wine with our meals, and that an Englishman ought to do only one thing at a time." So I cannot talk and think, or indulge in melancholy musing and lively conversation by fits and starts. "Let me have a companion of my way," says Sterne, "were it but to remark how the shadows lengthen as the sun goes down." It is beautifully said: but in my opinion, this continual comparing of notes interferes with the involuntary impression of things upon the mind, and hurts the sentiment. If you only hint what you feel in a kind of dumb show, it is insipid: if you have to explain it, it is making a toil of a pleasure. You cannot read the book of nature, without being perpetually put to the trouble of translating it for the benefit of others. I am for the synthetical method on a journey, in preference to the analytical. I am content to lay in a stock of ideas then, and to examine and anatomise them afterwards. I want to see my vague notions float like the down of the thistle before the breeze, and not to have them entangled in the briars and thorns of controversy. For once, I like to have it all my own way; and this is impossible unless you are alone, or in such company as I do not covet. I have no objection to argue a point with anyone for twenty miles of measured road, but not for pleasure. If you remark the scent of a beanfield crossing the road, perhaps your fellow-traveller has no smell. If you point to a distant object, perhaps he is short-sighted, and has to take out his glass to look at it. There is a feeling in the air, a tone in the colour of a cloud which hits your fancy, but the effect of which you are unprepared to account for. There is then no sympathy, but an uneasy craving after it, and a dissatisfaction which pursues you on the way, and in the end probably produces ill humour. Now I never quarrel with myself, and take all my own conclusions for granted 'till I find it necessary to defend them against objections. It is not merely that you may not be of accord on the objects and circumstances that present themselves before you—they may recall a number of ideas, and lead to associations too delicate and refined to be possibly communicated to others. Yet these I love to cherish, and sometimes still fondly clutch them, when I can escape from the throng to do so. To give way to our feelings before company, seems extravagance or affectation; on the other hand, to have to unravel this mystery of our being at every turn, and to make others take an equal interest in it (otherwise the end is not answered) is a task to which few are competent. We must "give it an understanding, but no tongue." My old friend C———,[1] however, could do both. He could go on in the most delightful explanatory way over hill and dale, a summer's day, and convert a landscape into a didactic poem or a Pindaric ode. "He talked far above singing." If I could so clothe my ideas in sounding and flowing words, I might perhaps wish to have someone with me to admire the swelling theme; or I could be more content, were it possible for me still to hear his echoing voice in the woods of All-Foxden. They had "that fine madness in them which our first poets had"; and if they could have been caught by some rare instrument, would have breathed such strains as the following.

—Here be woods as green
As any, air likewise as fresh and sweet
As when smooth Zephyrus plays on the fleet
Face of the curled stream, with flow'rs as many
As the young spring gives, and as choice as any;
Here be all new delights, cool streams and wells,
Arbours o'ergrown with woodbine, caves and dells:
Choose where thou wilt, while I sit by and sing,
Or gather rushes to make many a ring
For thy long fingers; tell thee tales of love,
How the pale Phœbe, hunting in a grove,
First saw the boy Endymion, from whose eyes
She took eternal fire that never dies;
How she convey'd him softly in a sleep,
His temples bound with poppy, to the steep
Head of old Latmos, where she stoops each night,
Gilding the mountain with her brother's light,
To kiss her sweetest.—[2]

Had I words and images at command like these, I would attempt to wake the thoughts that lie slumbering on golden ridges in the evening clouds: but at the sight of nature my fancy, poor as it is, droops and closes up

[1] Samuel Taylor Coleridge.

[2] Fletcher, *The Faithful Shepherdess*, Act I, Scene 3.

its leaves, like flowers at sunset. I can make nothing out on the spot:—I must have time to collect myself.

In general, a good thing spoils out-of-door prospects: it should be reserved for table-talk. L———[3] is for this reason, I take it, the worst company in the world out of doors; because he is the best within. I grant, there is one subject on which it is pleasant to talk on a journey; and that is, what one shall have for supper when we get to our inn at night. The open air improves this sort of conversation or friendly altercation, by setting a keener edge on appetite. Every mile of the road heightens the flavour of the viands we expect at the end of it. How fine it is to enter some old town, walled and turreted, just at the approach of night-fall, or to come to some straggling village, with the lights streaming through the surrounding gloom; and then after inquiring for the best entertainment that the place affords, to "take one's ease at one's inn"! These eventful moments in our lives are in fact too precious, too full of solid, heartfelt happiness to be frittered and dribbled way in imperfect sympathy. I would have them all to myself, and drain them to the last drop: they will do to talk of or to write about afterwards. What a delicate speculation it is, after drinking whole goblets of tea,

> The cups that cheer, but not inebriate,

and letting the fumes ascend into the brain, to sit considering what we shall have for supper—eggs and a rasher, a rabbit smothered in onions, or an excellent veal-cutlet! Sancho in such a situation once fixed upon cow-heel; and his choice, though he could not help it, is not to be disparaged. Then in the intervals of pictured scenery and Shandean contemplation, to catch the preparation and the stir in the kitchen—*Procul, O procul este profani!*[4] These hours are sacred to silence and to musing, to be treasured up in the memory, and to feed the source of smiling thoughts hereafter. I would not waste them in idle talk; or if I must have the integrity of fancy broken in upon, I would rather it were by a stranger than a friend. A stranger takes his hue and character from the time and place; he is a part of the furniture and costume of an inn. If he is a Quaker, or from the West Riding of Yorkshire, so much the better. I do not even try to sympathise with him, and he breaks no squares. I associate nothing with my travelling companion but present objects and passing events. In his ignorance of me and my affairs, I in a manner forget myself. But a friend reminds one of other things, rips up old grievances, and destroys the abstraction of the scene. He comes in ungraciously between us and our imaginary character. Something is

[3] Charles Lamb.

[4] "Away, o away all who are unblessed!" (*Aeneid VI*)

dropped in the course of conversation that gives a hint of your profession and pursuits; or from having someone with you that knows the less sublime portions of your history, it seems that other people do. You are no longer a citizen of the world: but your "unhoused free condition is put into circumscription and confine." The *incognito* of an inn is one of its striking privileges—"lord of oneself, uncumber'd with a name." Oh! it is great to shake off the trammels of the world and of public opinion—to lose our importunate, tormenting, everlasting personal identity in the elements of nature, and become the creature of the moment, clear of all ties—to hold to the universe only by a dish of sweet-breads, and to owe nothing but the score of the evening—and no longer seeking for applause and meeting with contempt, to be known by no other title than *the Gentleman in the parlour!* One may take one's choice of all characters in this romantic state of uncertainty as to one's real pretensions, and become indefinitely respectable and negatively right-worshipful. We baffle prejudice and disappoint conjecture; and from being so to others, begin to be objects of curiosity and wonder even to ourselves. We are no more those hackneyed commonplaces that we appear in the world: an inn restores us to the level of nature, and quits scores with society! I have certainly spent some enviable hours at inns—sometimes when I have been left entirely to myself, and have tried to solve some metaphysical problem, as once at Witham-common, where I found out the proof that likeness is not a case of the association of ideas—at other times, when there have been pictures in the room, as at St. Neot's, (I think it was) where I first met with Gribelin's engravings of the Cartoons, into which I entered at once; and at a little inn on the border of Wales, where there happened to be hanging some of Westall's drawings, which I compared triumphantly (for a theory that I had, not for the admired artist) with the figure of a girl who had ferried me over the Severn, standing up in the boat between me and the fading twilight—at other times I might mention luxuriating in books, with a peculiar interest in this way, as I remember sitting up half the night to read *Paul and Virginia*, which I picked up at an inn at Bridgewater, after being drenched in the rain all day; and at the same place I got through two volumes of Madame D'Arblay's *Camilla*. It was on the tenth of April, 1798, that I sat down to a volume of the *New Eloise*, at the inn at Llangollen, over a bottle of sherry and a cold chicken. The letter I chose was that in which St. Preux describes his feelings as he first caught a glimpse from the heights of the Jura of the Pays de Vaud, which I had brought with me as a *bonne bouche*[5] to crown the evening with. It was my birthday, and I had for the first time come from a place in the neighbourhood to visit this delightful spot. The road

[5] Literally, "good mouth"; here, a kiss or seal.

to Llangollen turns off between Chirk and Wrexham; and on passing a certain point, you come all at once upon the valley, which opens like an amphitheatre, broad, barren hills rising in majestic state on either side, with "green upland swells that echo to the bleat of flocks" below, and the river Dee babbling over its stony bed in the midst of them. The valley at this time "glittered green with sunny showers," and a budding ash-tree dipped its tender branches in the chiding stream. How proud, how glad I was to walk along the high road that commanded the delicious prospect, repeating the lines which I have just quoted from Mr. Coleridge's poems! But besides the prospect which opened beneath my feet, another also opened to my inward sight, a heavenly vision, on which were written, in letters large as Hope could make them, these four words, *Liberty*, *Genius*, *Love*, *Virtue;* which have since faded into the light of common day, or mock my idle gaze.

> The beautiful is vanished, and returns not.

Still I would return sometime or other to this enchanted spot; but I would return to it alone. What other self could I find to share that influx of thoughts, of regret, and delight, the traces of which I could hardly conjure up to myself, so much have they been broken and defaced! I could stand on some tall rock, and overlook the precipice of years that separates me from what I then was. I was at that time going shortly to visit the poet whom I have above named. Where is he now? Not only I myself have changed; the world, which was then new to me, has become old and incorrigible. Yet will I turn to thee in thought, O sylvan Dee, as then thou wert, in joy, in youth and gladness; and thou shalt always be to me the river of Paradise, where I will drink of the waters of life freely!

There is hardly anything that shows the short-sightedness or capriciousness of the imagination more than travelling does. With change of place we change our ideas; nay, our opinions and feelings. We can by an effort indeed transport ourselves to old and long-forgotten scenes, and then the picture of the mind revives again; but we forget those that we have just left. It seems that we can think but of one place at a time. The canvas of the fancy has only a certain extent, and if we paint one set of objects upon it, they immediately efface every other. We cannot enlarge our conceptions; we only shift our point of view. The landscape bares its bosom to the enraptured eye; we take our fill of it; and seem as if we could form no other image of beauty or grandeur. We pass on, and think no more of it: the horizon that shuts it from our sight also blots it from our memory like a dream. In travelling through a wild barren country, I can form no idea of a woody and cultivated one. It appears to me that all the world must be barren, like what I see of it. In the country we forget the town, and in town we despise the country. "Beyond Hyde Park," says Sir Fopling Flutter, "all is a desert." All that part of the map that we do not see before us is a blank. The world in our conceit of it is not much bigger than a nutshell. It is not one prospect expanded into another, county joined to county, kingdom to kingdom, lands to seas, making an image voluminous and vast;—the mind can form no larger idea of space than the eye can take in at a single glance. The rest is a name written on a map, a calculation of arithmetic. For instance, what is the true signification of that immense mass of territory and population, known by the name of China to us? An inch of paste-board on a wooden globe, of no more account than a China orange! Things near us are seen of the size of life: things at a distance are diminished to the size of the understanding. We measure the universe by ourselves, and even comprehend the texture of our own being only piece-meal. In this way, however, we remember an infinity of things and places. The mind is like a mechanical instrument that plays a great variety of tunes, but it must play them in succession. One idea recalls another, but it at the same time excludes all others. In trying to renew old recollections,we cannot as it were unfold the whole web of our existence; we must pick out the single threads. So in coming to a place where we have formerly lived and with which we have intimate associations, everyone must have found that the feeling grows more vivid the nearer we approach the spot, from the mere anticipation of the actual impression: we remember circumstances, feelings, persons, faces, names, that we had not thought of for years; but for the time all the rest of the world is forgotten!—To return to the question I have quitted above.

I have no objection to go to see ruins, aqueducts, pictures, in company with a friend or a party, but rather the contrary, for the former reason reversed. They are intelligible matters, and will bear talking about. The sentiment here is not tacit, but communicable and overt. Salisbury Plain is barren of criticism, but Stonehenge will bear a discussion antiquarian, picturesque, and philosophical. In setting out on a party of pleasure, the first consideration always is where we shall go: in taking a solitary ramble, the question is what we shall meet with by the way. The mind then is "its own place"; nor are we anxious to arrive at the end of our journey. I can myself do the honours indifferently well to works of art and curiosity. I once took a party to Oxford with no mean *éclat*—showed them the seat of the Muses at a distance,

> With glistering spires and pinnacles adorn'd—

descanted on the learned air that breathes from the grassy quadrangles and stone walls of halls and colleges—was at home in the Bodleian; and at Blenheim quite superseded the powdered Ciceroni that attended us, and that pointed in vain with his wand to common-place beauties in matchless pictures.—As another exception to the above reasoning, I should not feel confident in venturing on a journey in a foreign country without a companion. I should want at intervals to hear the sound of my own language. There is an involuntary antipathy in the mind of an Englishman to foreign manners and notions that requires the assistance of social sympathy to carry it off. As the distance from home increases, this relief, which was at first a luxury, becomes a passion and an appetite. A person would almost feel stifled to find himself in the deserts of Arabia without friends and countrymen: there must be allowed to be something in the view of Athens or old Rome that claims the utterance of speech; and I own that the Pyramids are too mighty for any single contemplation. In such situations, so opposite to all one's ordinary train of ideas, one seems a species by oneself, a limb torn off from society, unless one can meet with instant fellowship and support.—Yet I did not feel this want or craving very pressing once, when I first set my foot on the laughing shores of France. Calais was peopled with novelty and delight. The confused, busy murmur of the place was like oil and wine poured into my ears; nor did the mariners' hymn, which was sung from the top of an old crazy vessel in the harbour, as the sun went down, send an alien sound into my soul. I breathed the air of general humanity. I walked over "the vine-covered hills and gay regions of France," erect and satisfied; for the image of man was not cast down and chained to the foot of arbitrary thrones. I was at no loss for language, for that of all the great schools of painting was open to me. The whole is vanished like a shade. Pictures, heroes, glory, freedom, all are fled: nothing remains but the Bourbons and the French people!—There is undoubtedly a sensation in travelling into foreign parts that is to be had nowhere else: but it is more pleasing at the time than lasting. It is too remote from our habitual associations to be a common topic of discourse or reference, and, like a dream or another state of existence, does not piece into our daily modes of life. It is an animated but a momentary hallucination. It demands an effort to exchange our actual for our ideal identity; and to feel the pulse of our old transports revive very keenly, we must "jump" all our present comforts and connexions. Our romantic and itinerant character is not to be domesticated. Dr. Johnson remarked how little foreign travel added to the facilities of conversation in those who had been abroad. In fact, the time we have spent there is both delightful and in one sense instructive; but it appears to be cut out of our substantial, downright existence, and never to join kindly on to it. We are not the same, but another, and perhaps more enviable individual, all the time we are out of our own country. We are lost to ourselves, as well as to our friends. So the poet somewhat quaintly sings,

> Out of my country and myself I go.

Those who wish to forget painful thoughts, do well to absent themselves for a while from the ties and objects that recall them: but we can be said only to fulfill our destiny in the place that gave us birth. I should on this account like well enough to spend the whole of my life in travelling abroad, if I could anywhere borrow another life to spend afterwards at home!

On the Feeling of Immortality in Youth

Life is a pure flame, and we live by an invisible sun within us.
—Sir Thomas Browne

No young man believes he shall ever die. It was a saying of my brother's, and a fine one. There is a feeling of Eternity in youth, which makes us amends for everything. To be young is to be as one of the Immortal Gods. One half of time indeed is flown—the other half remains in store for us with all its countless treasures; for there is no line drawn, and we see no limit to our hopes and wishes. We make the coming age our own.——

> The vast, the unbounded prospect lies before us.

Death, old age, are words without a meaning, that pass by us like the idle air which we regard not. Others may have undergone, or may still be liable to them—we "bear a charmed life," which laughs to scorn all such sickly fancies. As in setting out on a delightful journey, we strain our eager gaze forward——

> Bidding the lovely scenes at distance hail,—

and see no end to the landscape, new objects presenting themselves as we advance; so, in the commencement of life, we set no bounds to our inclinations, nor to the unrestricted opportunities of gratifying them. We have as yet found no obstacle, no disposition to flag; and it seems that we can go on so forever. We look round in a new world, full of life, and motion, and ceaseless progress; and feel in ourselves all the vigour and spirit to keep pace with it, and do not foresee from any present symptoms how we shall be left behind in the natural course of things, decline into old age, and drop into the grave. It is the simplicity, and as it were abstractedness of our feelings in youth, that (so to speak) identifies us with nature, and (our experience being slight and our passions strong) deludes us into a belief of being immortal like it. Our short-lived connection with existence, we fondly flatter ourselves, is an indissoluble and lasting union—a honey-moon that knows neither coldness, jar, nor separation. As infants smile and sleep, we are rocked in the cradle of our wayward fancies, and lulled into security by the roar of the universe around us—we quaff the cup of life with eager haste without draining it, instead of which it only overflows the more—objects press around us, filling the mind with their magnitude and with the throng of desires that wait upon them, so that we have no room for the thoughts of death. From that plenitude of our being, we cannot change all at once to dust and ashes, we cannot imagine "this sensible, warm motion, to become a kneaded clod"—we are too much dazzled by the brightness of the waking dream around us to look into the darkness of the tomb. We no more see our end than our beginning: the one is lost in oblivion and vacancy, as the other is hid from us by the crowd and hurry of approaching events. Or the grim shadow is seen lingering in the horizon, which we are doomed never to overtake, or whose last, faint, glimmering outline touches upon Heaven and translates us to the skies! Nor would the hold that life has taken of us permit us to detach our thoughts from present objects and pursuits, even if we would. What is there more opposed to health, than sickness; to strength and beauty, than decay and dissolution; to the active search of knowledge than mere oblivion? Or is there none of the usual advantage to bar the approach of Death, and mock his idle threats; Hope supplies their place, and draws a veil over the abrupt termination of all our cherished schemes. While the spirit of youth remains unimpaired, ere the "wine of life is drank up," we are like people intoxicated or in a fever, who are hurried away by the violence of their own sensations: it is only as present objects begin to pall upon the sense, as we have been disappointed in our favourite pursuits, cut off from our closest ties, that passion loosens its hold upon the breast, that we by degrees become weaned from the world, and allow ourselves to contemplate, "as in a glass, darkly," the possibility of parting with it for good. The example of others, the voice of experience, has no effect upon us whatever. Casualties we must avoid: the slow and deliberate advances of age we can play at hide-and-seek with. We think ourselves too lusty and too nimble for that blear-eyed decrepit old gentleman to catch us. Like the foolish fat scullion, in Sterne, when she hears that Master Bobby is dead, our only reflection is—"So am not I!" The idea of death, instead of staggering our confidence, rather seems to strengthen and enhance our possession and our enjoyment of life. Others may fall around us like leaves, or be mowed down like flowers by the scythe of Time: these are but tropes and figures to the unreflecting ears and overweening presumption of youth. It is not till we see the flowers of Love, Hope, and Joy, withering around us, and our own pleasures cut up by the roots, that we bring the moral home to ourselves, that we abate something of the wanton extravagance of our pretensions, or that the emptiness and dreariness of the prospect before us reconciles us to the stillness of the grave!

> Life! thou strange thing, that hast a power to feel
> Thou art, and to perceive that others are.

Well might the poet begin his indignant invective against an art, whose professed object is its destruction, with this animated apostrophe to life. Life is indeed a strange gift, and its privileges are most miraculous. Nor is it singular that when the splendid boon is first granted us, our gratitude, our admiration, and our delight should prevent us from reflecting on our own nothingness, or from thinking it will ever be recalled. Our first and strongest impressions are taken from the mighty scene that is opened to us, and we very innocently transfer its durability as well as magnificence to ourselves. So newly found, we cannot make up our minds to parting with it yet and at least put off that consideration to an indefinite term. Like a clown at a fair, we are full of amazement and rapture, and have no thoughts of going home, or that it will soon be night. We know our existence only from external objects, and we measure it by them. We can never be satisfied with gazing; and nature will still want us to look on and applaud. Otherwise, the sumptuous entertainment, "the feast of reason and the flow of soul," to which we were invited, seems little better than a mockery and a cruel insult. We do not go from a play till the scene is ended, and the lights are ready to be extinguished. But the fair face of things still shines on; shall we be called away, before the curtain falls, or ere we have scarce had a glimpse of what is going on? Like children, our step-mother Nature holds us up to see the raree-show of the universe; and then, as if life were a burthen to support, lets us instantly down again. Yet in that short interval, what "brave sublunary things" does not the spectacle unfold; like a bubble, at one minute reflecting the universe, and the next, shook to air!—To see the golden sun and the azure sky, the outstretched ocean, to walk upon the green earth, and to be lord of a thousand creatures, to look down giddy precipices or over distant flowery vales, to see the world spread out under one's finger in a map, to bring the stars near, to view the smallest insects in a microscope, to read history, and witness the revolutions of empires and the succession of generations, to hear of the glory of Sidon and Tyre, of Babylon and Susa, as of a faded pageant, and to say all these were, and are now nothing, to think that we exist in such a point of time, and in such a corner of space, to be at once spectators and a part of the moving scene, to watch the return of the seasons, of spring and autumn, to hear

> —The stockdove plain amid the forest deep,
> That drowsy rustles to the sighing gale—

to traverse desert wildernesses, to listen to the midnight choir, to visit lighted halls, or plunge into the dungeon's gloom, or sit in crowded theatres and see life itself mocked, to feel heat and cold, pleasure and pain, right and wrong, truth and falsehood, to study the works of art and refine the sense of beauty to agony, to worship fame and to dream of immortality, to have read Shakespear [sic] and belong to the same species as Sir Isaac Newton; to be and to do all this, and then in a moment to be nothing, to have it all snatched from one like a juggler's ball or a phantasmagoria; there is something revolting and incredible to sense in the transition, and no wonder that, aided by youth and warm blood, and the flush of enthusiasm, the mind contrives for a long time to reject it with disdain and loathing as a monstrous and improbable fiction, like a monkey on a house-top, that is loath, amidst its fine discoveries and specious antics, to be tumbled head-long into the street, and crushed to atoms, the sport and laughter of the multitude!

The change, from the commencement to the close of life, appears like a fable, after it has taken place; how should we treat it otherwise than as a chimera before it has come to pass? There are some things that happened so long ago, places or persons we have formerly seen, of which such dim traces remain, we hardly know whether it was sleeping or waking they occurred; they are like dreams within the dream of life, a mist, a film before the eye of memory, which, as we try to recall them more distinctly, elude our notice altogether. It is but natural that the lone interval that we thus look back upon, should have appeared long and endless in prospect. There are others so distinct and fresh, they seem but of yesterday—their very vividness might be deemed a pledge of their permanence. Then, however far back our impressions may go, we find others still older (for our years are multiplied in youth); descriptions of scenes that we had read, and people before our time, Priam and the Trojan war; and even then, Nestor was old and dwelt delighted on his youth, and spoke of the race of heroes that were no more;—what wonder that, seeing this long line of being pictured in our minds, and reviving as it were in us, we should give ourselves involuntary credit for an indeterminate period of existence? In the Cathedral at Peterborough there is a monument to Mary, Queen of Scots, at which I used to gaze when a boy, while the events of the period, all that had happened since, passed in review before me. If all this mass of feeling and imagination could be crowded into a moment's compass, what might not the whole of life be supposed to contain? We are heirs of the past; we count upon the future as our natural reversion. Besides, there are some of our early impressions so exquisitely tempered, it appears that they must always last—nothing can add to or take away from their sweetness and purity—the first breath of spring, the hyacinth dipped in dew, the mild lustre of the evening-star, the rainbow after a storm—while we have the full enjoyment of these, we must be young; and what can ever alter us in this respect? Truth, friendship, love, books, are also proof against the canker of time; and while we live, but for them, we can never grow old. We take out a new lease of existence from the objects on which we set our affections, and become abstracted, impassive, immortal in them. We cannot conceive how certain sentiments should ever decay or grow cold in our breasts; and, consequently, to maintain them in their first youthful glow and vigour, the flame of life must continue to burn as bright as ever, or rather, they are the fuel that feed the sacred lamp, that kindle "the purple light of love," and spread a golden cloud around our heads! Again, we not only flourish and survive in our affections (in which we will not listen to the possibility of a change, any more than we foresee the wrinkles on the brow of a mistress), but we have a farther guarantee against the thoughts of death in our favourite studies and pursuits, and in their continual advance. Art we know is long; life, we feel, should be so too. We see no end of the difficulties we have to encounter: perfection is slow of attainment, and we must have time to accomplish it in. Rubens complained that when he had just learnt his art, he was snatched away from it: we trust we shall be more fortunate! A wrinkle in an old head takes whole days to finish it properly: but to catch "the Raphael grace, the Guido air," no limit should be put to our endeavours. What a prospect for the future! What a task we have entered upon! and shall we be arrested in the middle of it? We do not reckon our time thus employed lost, or our pains thrown away, or our progress slow—we do not droop or grow tired, but "gain new vigour at our endless task";—and shall Time grudge us the opportunity to finish what we have auspiciously begun, and have formed a sort of compact with nature to achieve? The fame of the great names we look up to is also imperishable; and shall not we, who contemplate it with such intense yearnings, imbibe a portion of ethereal fire, the *divinæ particula auræ*, which nothing can extinguish? I remember to have looked at a print of Rembrandt for hours together, without being conscious of the flight of time, trying to resolve it into its component parts, to connect its strong and sharp gradations, to learn the secret of its reflected lights, and found neither satiety nor pause in the prosecution of my studies. The print over which I was poring would last long enough; why should the idea in my mind, which was finer, more impalpable, perish before it? At this, I redoubled the ardour of my pursuit, and by the very subtlety and refinement of my inquiries, seemed to bespeak for them an exemption from corruption and the rude grasp of Death.*

Objects, on our first acquaintance with them, have that singleness and integrity of impression that it seems as if nothing could destroy or obliterate them, so firmly they are stamped and rivetted on the brain. We repose on them with a sort of voluptuous indolence, in full faith and boundless confidence. We are absorbed in the present moment, or return to the same point—idling away a great deal of time in youth, thinking we have enough and to spare. There is often a local feeling in the air, which is as fixed as if it were of marble; we loiter in dim cloisters, losing ourselves in thought and in their glimmering arches; a winding road before us seems as long as the journey of life, and as full of events. Time and experience dissipate this illusion; and by reducing them to detail, circumscribe the limits of our expectations. It is only as the pageant of life passes by and the masques turn their backs upon us, that we see through the deception, or believe that the train will have an end. In many cases, the slow progress and monotonous texture of our lives, before we mingle with the world and are embroiled in its affairs, has a tendency to aid the same feeling. We have a difficulty, when left to ourselves, and without the resource of books or some more lively pursuit, to "beguile the slow and creeping hours of time," and argue that if it moves on always at this tedious snail's-pace, it can never come to an end. We are willing to skip over certain portions of it that separate us from favourite objects, that irritate ourselves at the unnecessary delay. The young are prodigal of life from a superabundance of it; the old are tenacious on the same score, because they have little left, and cannot enjoy even what remains of it.

For my part, I set out in life with the French Revolution, and that event had considerable influence on my early feelings, as on those of others. Youth was then doubly such. It was the dawn of a new era, a new impulse had been given to men's minds, and the sun of Liberty rose upon the sun of Life in the same day, and both were proud to run their race together. Little did I dream, while my first hopes and wishes went hand in hand with those of the human race, that long before my eyes should close, that dawn would be overcast, and set once more in the night of despotism—"total eclipse"! Happy that I did not. I felt for years, and

* Is it not this that frequently keeps artists alive so long, *viz*, the constant occupation of their minds with vivid images, with little of the *wear-and-tear* of the body? [Hazlitt]

during the best parts of my existence, heart-whole in that cause, and triumphed in the triumphs over the enemies of man! At that time, while the fairest aspirations of the human mind seemed about to be realised, ere the image of man was defaced and his breast mangled in scorn, philosophy took a higher, poetry could afford a deeper range. At that time, to read the "Robbers" was indeed delicious, and to hear

> From the dungeon of the tower time-rent,
> That fearful voice, a famish'd father's cry,

could be borne only amidst the fullness of hope, the crash of the fall of the strong holds of power, and the exulting sounds of the march of human freedom. What feelings the death-scene in *Don Carlos* sent into the soul! In that headlong career of lofty enthusiasm, and the joyous opening of the prospects of the world and our own, the thought of death crossing it, smote doubly cold upon the mind; there was a stifling sense of oppression and confinement, an impatience of our present knowledge, a desire to grasp the whole of our existence in one strong embrace, to sound the mystery of life and death, and in order to put an end to the agony of doubt and dread, to burst through our prison-house, and confront the King of Terrors in his grisly palace! . . . As I was writing out this passage, my miniature-picture when a child lay on the mantle-piece, and I took it out of the case to look at it. I could perceive few traces of myself in it; but there was the same placid brow, the dimpled mouth, the same timid, inquisitive glance as ever. But its careless smile did not seem to reproach me with having become a recreant to the sentiments that were then sown in my mind, or with having written a sentence that could call up a blush in this image of ingenuous youth!

"That time is past with all its giddy raptures." Since the future was barred to my progress, I have turned for consolation to the past, gathering up the fragments of my early recollections, and putting them into a form that might live. It is thus, that when we find our personal and substantial identity vanishing from us, we strive to gain a reflected and substituted one in our thoughts: we do not like to perish wholly, and wish to bequeath our names at least to posterity. As long as we can keep alive our cherished thoughts and nearest interests in the minds of others, we do not appear to have retired altogether from the stage, we still occupy a place in the estimation of mankind, exercise a powerful influence over them, and it is only our bodies that are trampled into dust or dispersed to air. Our darling speculations still find favour and encouragement, and we make as good a figure in the eyes of our descendants, nay, perhaps, a better than we did in our life-time. This is one point gained; the demands of our self-love are so far satisfied. Besides, if by the proofs of intellectual superiority we survive ourselves in this world, by exemplary virtue or unblemished faith, we are taught to ensure an interest in another and a higher state of being, and to anticipate at the same time the applauses of men and angels.

> Even from the tomb the voice of nature cries;
> Even in our ashes live their wonted fires.

As we advance in life, we acquire a keener sense of the value of time. Nothing else, indeed, seems of any consequence; and we become misers in this respect. We try to arrest its few last tottering steps, and to make it linger on the brink of the grave. We can never leave off wondering how that which has ever been should cease to be, and would still live on, that we may wonder at our own shadow, and when "all the life of life is flown," dwell on the retrospect of the past. This is accompanied by a mechanical tenaciousness of whatever we possess, by a distrust and a sense of fallacious hollowness in all we see. Instead of the full, pulpy feeling of youth, everything is flat and insipid. The world is a painted witch, that puts us off with false shows and tempting appearances. The ease, the jocund gaiety, the unsuspecting security of youth are fled: nor can we, without flying in the face of common sense,

> From the last dregs of life, hope to receive
> What its first sprightly runnings could not give.

If we can slip out of the world without notice or mischance, can tamper with bodily infirmity, and frame our minds to the becoming composure of still-life, before we sink into total insensibility, it is as much as we ought to expect. We do not in the regular course of nature die all at once: we have mouldered away gradually long before; faculty after faculty, attachment after attachment, we are torn from ourselves piece-meal while living; year after year takes something from us; and death only consigns the last remnant of what we were to the grave. The revulsion is not so great, and a quiet euthanasia is a winding-up of the plot, that is not out of reason or nature.

That we should thus in a manner outlive ourselves, and dwindle imperceptibly into nothing, is not surprising, when even in our prime the strongest impressions leave so little traces of themselves behind, and the last object is driven out by the succeeding one. How little effect is produced on us at any time by the books we have read, the scenes we have witnessed, the sufferings we have gone through! Think only of the variety of feelings we experience in reading an interesting romance, or being present at a fine play—what beauty, what sublimity, what soothing, what heart-rending emotions! You would suppose these would last forever, or at least subdue the mind to a correspondent tone and harmony—while we turn over the page, while the scene is passing before us, it seems as if nothing could ever after shake our resolution, that "treason domestic, foreign levy, nothing could touch us farther"! The first splash of mud we get, on entering the street, the first pettifogging shop-keeper that cheats us out of two-pence, and the whole vanishes clean out of our remembrance, and we become the idle prey of the most petty and annoying circumstances. The mind soars by an effort to the grand and lofty; it is at home in the grovelling, the disagreeable, and the little. This happens in the height and hey-day of our existence, when novelty gives a stronger impulse to the blood and takes a faster hold of the brain, (I have known the impression on coming out of a gallery of pictures then last half a day)—as we grow old, we become more feeble and querulous, every object "reverbs its own hollowness," and both worlds are not enough to satisfy the peevish importunity and extravagant presumption of our desires! There are a few superior, happy beings, who are born with a temper exempt from every trifling annoyance. This spirit sits serene and smiling as in its native skies, and a divine harmony (whether heard or not) plays around them. This is to be at peace. Without this, it is in vain to fly into deserts, or to build a hermitage on the top of rocks, if regret and ill-humour follow us there: and with this, it is needless to make the experiment. The only true retirement is that of the heart; the only true leisure is the repose of the passions. To such persons it makes little difference whether they are young or old; and they die as they have lived, with graceful resignation.

Washington Irving
(1783–1859)

In 1806, the young Washington Irving, just back from Europe, started up a semi-monthly publication with a few friends called Salmagundi. *It aimed "to instruct the young, inform the old, correct the town, and castigate the age." It was, quite deliberately, a* Spectator *come back to life, but with this difference: the "town" was New York, then numbering about 25,000 inhabitants, and the "age" was not England's but that of the young United States. In 1815, Irving crossed the ocean again, on business, not to return for seventeen years. During that time, he travelled and lived in England, Germany, Spain, and produced seven books, including his best known,* The Sketchbook *(New York, 1819), from which "The Voyage" is taken. William Hazlitt, man of the modern Romantic temper, considered the popular Irving very fine in his way, but arrested (as bookish Americans are bound to be) in the England of a bygone literary era, that of "Addison and other approved authors" ("Elia and Geoffrey Crayon"). And while it is true enough that Irving's English models are primarily eighteenth century—essays such as his "Westminster Abbey," "The Boar's Head Tavern, Eastcheap," and the fancifully satirical "The Art of Bookmaking" lovingly recreate Addison and Goldsmith—he was also, as Thackeray was to say of him, "the first ambassador whom the New World of letters sent to the Old." Irving's "The Voyage" marks the literal passage between these two worlds and suggests, by descriptive and narrative indirection, something of the personal anxiety in store for the American abroad. In the first essay of* The Sketchbook, *"The Author's Account of Himself," Irving likens his method to that of the tourists of the time who (not yet outfitted with camera and film) "travel pencil in hand and bring home their portfolios filled with sketches." His essays and stories are drawings in words of what he termed "the shifting scenes of life." In his single most famous sketch, the tale of "Rip van Winkle," the scenery is American, as it is in his powerful, long, largely forgotten essay in historical revisionism, "Philip of Pokanoket."*

The Voyage

Ships, ships, I will descrie you
Amidst the main,
I will come and try you,
What you are protecting,
And projecting,
What's your end and aim.
One goes abroad for merchandise and trading,
Another stays to keep his country from invading,
A third is coming home with rich and wealthy lading.
Halloo! my fancie, whither wilt thou go?
Old Poem

To an American visiting Europe, the long voyage he has to make is an excellent preparative. The temporary absence of worldly scenes and employments produces a state of mind peculiarly fitted to receive new and vivid impressions. The vast space of waters that separates the hemispheres is like a blank page in existence. There is no gradual transition by which, as in Europe, the features and population of one country blend almost imperceptibly with those of another. From the moment you lose sight of the land you have left, all is vacancy until you step on the opposite shore, and are launched at once into the bustle and novelties of another world.

In traveling by land there is a continuity of scene, and a connected succession of persons and incidents, that carry on the story of life, and lessen the effect of absence and separation. We drag, it is true, "a lengthening chain" at each remove of our pilgrimage; but the chain is unbroken: we can trace it back link by link; and we feel that the last still grapples us to home. But a wide sea voyage severs us at once. It makes us conscious of being cast loose from the secure anchorage of settled life, and sent adrift upon a doubtful world. It interposes a gulf, not merely imaginary, but real, between us and our homes—a gulf subject to tempest, and fear, and uncertainty, rendering distance palpable, and return precarious.

Such, at least, was the case with myself. As I saw the last blue line of my native land fade away like a cloud in the horizon, it seemed as if I had closed one volume of the world and its concerns, and had time for meditation, before I opened another. That land, too, now vanishing from my view, which contained all most dear to me in life; what vicissitudes might occur in it—what changes might take place in me, before I should visit it again! Who can tell, when he sets forth to wander, whither he may be driven by the uncertain currents of existence; or when he may return; or whether it may ever be his lot to revisit the scenes of his childhood?

I said that at sea all is vacancy; I should correct the expression. To one given to day-dreaming, and fond of losing himself in reveries, a sea voyage is full of subjects for meditation; but then they are the wonders of the deep, and of the air, and rather tend to abstract the mind from worldly themes. I delighted to loll over the quarter-railing, or climb to the main-top, of a calm day, and muse for hours together on the tranquil bosom of a summer's sea; to gaze upon the piles of golden clouds just peering above the horizon, fancy them some fairy realms, and people them with a creation of my own;—to watch the gentle undulating billows, rolling their silver volumes, as if to die away on those happy shores.

There was a delicious sensation of mingled security and awe with which I looked down, from my giddy height, on the monsters of the deep at their uncouth gambols. Shoals of porpoises tumbling about the bow of the ship; the grampus slowly heaving his huge form above the surface; or the ravenous shark, darting, like a spectre, through the blue waters. My imagination would conjure up all that I had heard or read of the watery world beneath me; of the finny herds that roam its fathomless valleys; of the shapeless monsters that lurk among the very foundations of the earth; and of those wild phantasms that swell the tales of fishermen and sailors.

Sometimes a distant sail, gliding along the edge of the ocean, would be another theme of idle speculation. How interesting this fragment of a world, hastening to rejoin the great mass of existence! What a glorious monument of human invention; which has in a manner triumphed over wind and wave; has brought the ends of the world into communion; has established an interchange of blessings, pouring into the sterile regions of the north all the luxuries of the south; has diffused the light of knowledge and the charities of cultivated life; and has thus bound together those scattered portions of the human race, between which nature seemed to have thrown an insurmountable barrier.

We one day descried some shapeless object drifting at a distance. At sea, everything that breaks the monotony of the surrounding expanse attracts attention. It proved to be the mast of a ship that must have been completely wrecked; for there were the remains of handkerchiefs, by which some of the crew had fastened themselves to this spar, to prevent their being washed off by the waves. There was no trace by which the name of the ship could be ascertained. The wreck had evidently drifted about for many months; clusters of shell-fish had fastened about it, and long sea-weeds flaunted at its sides. But where, thought I, is the crew? Their struggle has long been over—they have gone down amidst the roar of the tempest—their bones lie whitening among the caverns of the deep.

Silence, oblivion, like the waves, have closed over them, and no one can tell the story of their end. What sighs have been wafted after that ship! what prayers offered up at the deserted fireside of home! How often has the mistress, the wife, the mother, pored over the daily news, to catch some casual intelligence of this rover of the deep! How has expectation darkened into anxiety—anxiety into dread—and dread into despair! Alas! not one memento may ever return for love to cherish. All that may ever be known, is, that she sailed from her port, "and was never heard of more!"

The sight of this wreck, as usual, gave rise to many dismal anecdotes. This was particularly the case in the evening, when the weather, which had hitherto been fair, began to look wild and threatening, and gave indications of one of those sudden storms which will sometimes break in upon the serenity of a summer voyage. As we sat round the dull light of a lamp in the cabin, that made the gloom more ghastly, everyone had his tale of shipwreck and disaster. I was particularly struck with a short one related by the captain.

"As I was once sailing," said he, "in a fine stout ship across the banks of Newfoundland, one of those heavy fogs which prevail in those parts rendered it impossible for us to see far ahead even in the daytime; but at night the weather was so thick that we could not distinguish any object at twice the length of the ship. I kept lights at the mast-head, and a constant watch forward to look out for fishing smacks, which are accustomed to lie at anchor on the banks. The wind was blowing a smacking breeze, and we were going at a great rate through the water. Suddenly the watch gave the alarm of 'a sail ahead!'—it was scarcely uttered before we were upon her. She was a small schooner, at anchor, with her broadside towards us. The crew were all asleep, and had neglected to hoist a light. We struck her just amid-ships. The force, the size, and weight of our vessel bore her down below the waves; we passed over her and were hurried on our course. As the crashing wreck was sinking beneath us, I had a glimpse of two or three half-naked wretches rushing from her cabin; they just started from their beds to be swallowed shrieking by the waves. I heard their drowning cry mingling with the wind. The blast that bore it to our ears swept us out of all farther hearing. I shall never forget that cry! It was some time before we could put the ship about, she was under such headway. We returned, as nearby as we could guess, to the place where the smack had anchored. We cruised about for several hours in the dense fog. We fired signal guns, and listened if we might hear the halloo of any survivors: but all was silent—we never saw or heard anything of them more."

I confess these stories, for a time, put an end to all my fine fancies. The storm increased with the night. The sea was lashed into tremendous confusion. There was a fearful, sullen sound of rushing waves, and broken surges. Deep called unto deep. At times the black volume of clouds over head seemed rent asunder by flashes of lightning which quivered along the foaming billows, and made the succeeding darkness doubly terrible. The thunders bellowed over the wild waste of waters, and were echoed and prolonged by the mountain waves. As I saw the ship staggering and plunging among these roaring caverns, it seemed miraculous that she regained her balance, or preserved her buoyancy. Her yards would dip into the water: her bow was almost buried beneath the waves. Sometimes an impending surge appeared ready to overwhelm her, and nothing but a dexterous movement of the helm preserved her from the shock.

When I retired to my cabin, the awful scene still followed me. The whistling of the wind through the rigging sounded like funeral wailings. The creaking of the masts, the straining and groaning of bulk-heads, as the ship labored in the weltering sea, were frightful. As I heard the waves rushing along the sides of the ship, and roaring in my very ear, it seemed as if Death were raging round this floating prison, seeking for his prey: the mere starting of a nail, the yawning of a seam, might give him entrance.

A fine day, however, with a tranquil sea and favoring breeze, soon put all these dismal reflections to flight. It is impossible to resist the gladdening influence of fine weather and fair wind at sea. When the ship is decked out in all her canvas, every sail swelled, and careering gayly over the curling waves, how lofty, how gallant she appears—how she seems to lord it over the deep!

I might fill a volume with the reveries of a sea voyage, for with me it is almost a continual reverie—but it is time to get to shore.

It was a fine sunny morning when the thrilling cry of "land!" was given from the mast-head. None but those who have experienced it can form an idea of the delicious throng of sensations which rush into an American's bosom, when he first comes in sight of Europe. There is a volume of associations with the very name. It is the land of promise, teeming with everything of which his childhood has heard, or on which his studious years have pondered.

From that time until the moment of arrival, it was all feverish excitement. The ships of war, that prowled like guardian giants along the coast; the headlands of Ireland, stretching out into the channel; the Welsh mountains, towering into the clouds; all were objects of intense interest. As we sailed up the Mersey, I reconnoitred the shores with a telescope. My eye dwelt with delight on neat cottages, with their trim shrubberies and green grass plots. I saw the mouldering ruin of an abbey overrun with ivy, and the taper spire of a village church rising from the brow of a neighboring hill—all were characteristic of England.

The tide and wind were so favorable that the ship was enabled to come at once to the pier. It was thronged with people; some, idle lookers-on, others, eager expectants of friends or relatives. I could distinguish the merchant to whom the ship was consigned. I knew him by his calculating brow and restless air. His hands were thrust into his pockets; he was whistling thoughtfully, and walking to and fro, a small space having been accorded him by the crowd, in deference to his temporary importance. There were repeated cheerings and salutations interchanged between the shore and the ship, as friends happened to recognize each other. I particularly noticed one young woman of humble dress, but interesting demeanor. She was leaning forward from among the crowd; her eye hurried over the ship as it neared the shore, to catch some wished-for countenance. She seemed disappointed and agitated; when I heard a faint voice call her name. It was from a poor sailor who had been ill all the voyage, and had excited the sympathy of everyone on board. When the weather was fine, his messmates had spread a mattress for him on deck in the shade, but of late his illness had so increased, that he had taken to his hammock, and only breathed a wish that he might see his wife before he died. He had been helped on deck as we came up the river, and was now leaning against the shrouds, with a countenance so wasted, so pale, so ghastly, that it was no wonder even the eye of affection did not recognize him. But at the sound of his voice, her eye darted on his features; it read, at once, a whole volume of sorrow; she clasped her hands, uttered a faint shriek, and stood wringing them in silent agony.

All now was hurry and bustle. The meetings of acquaintances—the greetings of friends—the consultations of men of business. I alone was solitary and idle. I had no friend to meet, no cheering to receive. I stepped upon the land of my forefathers—but felt that I was a stranger in the land.

Thomas De Quincey

(1785–1859)

De Quincey is most widely known for his Confessions of an Opium Eater *(originally subtitled "Being an Extract from the Life of a Scholar"). To a lesser extent, because it has been anthologized from time to time, he is remembered for the present essay, one of the most engaging short literary studies in English. Both were works of the early 1820s and both appeared in the* London Magazine *(where Lamb's Elia was already flourishing). They show different sides of a complex prose writer who was, among other things, a youthful prodigy, a teenage runaway and vagrant, an erudite bibliophile, a perpetual debtor often forced to hide from creditors, and an opium addict. It was as the latter that De Quincey, destitute and with a growing family to support, appeared on the literary scene in his mid-thirties; he managed by way of the success of* The Confessions, *and the audience they created for him, to go on eking out a tenuous income writing for magazines the rest of his life. De Quincey himself valued most what he called "impassioned prose," the visionary and lyrical passages of works like* The Confessions *and his later* Suspiria de Profundis *("Sighs from the Depths"). Essays as such were for him essentially a means of solving particular intellectual problems addressed, in his words, to "the understanding as an insulated faculty." Yet this address, as the present essay so brilliantly demonstrates, can itself be impassioned. Setting out to explore a single moment in* Macbeth*—the knocking at the gate after Duncan's murder—the essay unfolds an effective mystery which, the author claims, has perplexed him since childhood, at the same time that it clarifies for him his passion for the dramatic genius of Shakespeare.*

On the Knocking at the Gate in *Macbeth*

From my boyish days I had always felt a great perplexity on one point in *Macbeth:* it was this: the knocking at the gate, which succeeds to the murder of Duncan, produced to my feelings an effect for which I never could account: the effect was—that it reflected back upon the murder a peculiar awfulness and a depth of solemnity: yet, however obstinately I endeavoured with my understanding to comprehend this, for many years I could never see *why* it should produce such an effect.—

Here I pause for one moment to exhort the reader never to pay any attention to his understanding when it stands in opposition to any other faculty of his mind. The mere understanding, however useful and indispensable, is the meanest faculty in the human mind and the most to be distrusted: and yet the great majority of people trust to nothing else; which may do for ordinary life, but not for philosophic purposes. Of this, out of ten thousand instances that I might produce, I will cite one. Ask of any person whatsoever, who is not previously prepared for the demand by a knowledge of perspective, to draw in the rudest way the commonest appearance which depends upon the laws of that science—as for instance, to represent the effect of two walls standing at right angles to each other, or the appearance of the houses on each side of a street, as seen by a person looking down the street from one extremity. Now in all cases, unless the person has happened to observe in pictures how it is that artists produce these effects, he will be utterly unable to make the smallest approximation to it. Yet why?—For he has actually seen the effect every day of his life. The reason is—that he allows his understanding to overrule his eyes. His understanding, which includes no intuitive knowledge of the laws of vision, can furnish him with no reason why a line which is known and can be proved to be a horizontal line, should not *appear* a horizontal line: a line, that made any angle with the perpendicular less than a right angle, would seem to him to indicate that his houses were all tumbling down together. Accordingly he makes the line of his houses a horizontal line, and fails of course to produce the effect demanded. Here then is one instance out of many, in which not only the understanding is allowed to overrule the eyes, but where the understanding is positively allowed to obliterate the eyes as it were: for not only does the man believe the evidence of his understanding in opposition to that of his eyes, but (which is monstrous!) the idiot is not aware that his eyes ever gave such evidence. He does not know that he has seen (and therefore *quoad* his consciousness has *not* seen) that which he *has* seen every day of his life. But to return from this digression,—my understanding could furnish no reason why the knocking at the gate in *Macbeth* should produce any effect direct or reflected: in fact, my understanding said positively that it could *not* produce any effect. But I knew better: I felt that it did: and I waited and clung to the problem until further knowledge should enable me to solve it.—At length, in 1812, Mr. Williams made his *début* on the stage of Ratcliffe Highway, and executed those unparalleled murders which have procured for him such a brilliant and undying reputation. On which murders, by the way, I must observe, that in one respect they have had an ill effect, by making the connoisseur in murder very fastidious in his taste, and dissatisfied with any thing that has been since done in that line. All other murders look pale by the deep crimson of his: and, as an amateur once said to me in a querulous tone, "There has been absolutely nothing *doing* since his time, or nothing that's worth speaking of." But this is wrong: for it is unreasonable to expect all men to be great artists, and born with the genius of Mr. Williams.—Now it will be remembered that in the first of these murders (that of the Marrs) the same incident (of a knocking at the door soon after the work of extermination was complete) did actually occur which the genius of Shakespeare has invented: and all good judges and the most eminent dilettanti acknowledged the felicity of Shakespeare's suggestion as soon as it was actually realized. Here then was a fresh proof that I had been right in relying on my own feeling in opposition to my understanding; and again I set myself to study the problem: at length I solved it to my own satisfaction; and my solution is this. Murder in ordinary cases, where the sympathy is wholly directed to the case of the murdered person, is an incident of coarse and vulgar horror; and for this reason—that it flings the interest exclusively upon the natural but ignoble instinct by which we cleave to life; an instinct which, as being indispensable to the primal law of self-preservation, is the same in kind (though different in degree) amongst all living creatures; this instinct therefore, because it annihilates all distinctions, and degrades the greatest of men to the level of "the poor beetle that we tread on," exhibits human nature in its most abject and humiliating attitude. Such an attitude would little suit the purpose of the poet. What then must he do? He must throw the interest on the murderer: our sympathy must be with *him* (of course I mean a sympathy of comprehension, a sympathy by which we enter into his feelings, and are made to understand them,—not a sympathy* of pity or approbation): in the murdered person all strife of thought, all flux and reflux of passion and of purpose, are crushed by one overwhelming panic: the fear of instant death smites him "with its petrific mace." But in the murderer, such a murderer as a poet will condescend to, there must be raging some great storm of passion,—jealousy, ambition, vengeance, hatred,—which will create a hell within him; and into this hell we are to look. In *Macbeth*, for the sake of gratifying his own enormous and teeming faculty of creation, Shakespeare has introduced two murderers: and, as usual in his hands, they are remarkably discriminated; but though in Macbeth the strife of mind is greater than in his wife, the tiger spirit not so awake, and his feelings

* It seems almost ludicrous to guard and explain my use of a word in a situation where it should naturally explain itself. But it has become necessary to do so, in consequence of the unscholarlike use of the word sympathy, at present so general, by which, instead of taking it in its proper use, as the act of reproducing in our minds the feelings of another, whether for hatred, indignation, love, pity, or approbation, it is made a mere synonym of the word *pity;* and hence, instead of saying "sympathy *with* another," many writers adopt the monstrous barbarism of "sympathy *for* another." [De Quincey]

caught chiefly by contagion from her,—yet, as both were finally involved in the guilt of murder, the murderous mind of necessity is finally to be presumed in both. This was to be expressed; and on its own account, as well as to make it a more proportionable antagonist to the unoffending nature of their victim, "the gracious Duncan," and adequately to expound "the deep damnation of his taking off," this was to be expressed with peculiar energy. We were to be made to feel that the human nature, *i.e.*, the divine nature of love and mercy, spread through the hearts of all creatures and seldom utterly withdrawn from man,—was gone, vanished, extinct; and that the fiendish nature had taken its place. And, as this effect is marvellously accomplished in the dialogues and soliloquies themselves, so it is finally consummated by the expedient under consideration; and it is to this that I now solicit the reader's attention. If the reader has ever witnessed a wife, daughter, or sister, in a fainting fit, he may chance to have observed that the most affecting moment in such a spectacle, is *that* in which a sigh and a stirring announce the recommencement of suspended life. Or, if the reader has ever been present in a vast metropolis on the day when some great national idol was carried in funeral pomp to his grave, and chancing to walk near to the course through which it passed, has felt powerfully in the silence and desertion of the streets and in the stagnation of ordinary business, the deep interest which at that moment was possessing the heart of man,—if all at once he should hear the death-like stillness broken up by the sound of wheels rattling away from the scene, and making known that the transitory vision was dissolved, he will be aware that at no moment was his sense of the complete suspension and pause in ordinary human concerns so full and affecting as at that moment when the suspension ceases, and the goings-on of human life are suddenly resumed. All action in any direction is best expounded, measured, and made apprehensible, by reaction. Now apply this to the case in *Macbeth.* Here, as I have said, the retiring of the human heart and the entrance of the fiendish heart was to be expressed and made sensible. Another world has stepped in; and the murderers are taken out of the region of human things, human purposes, human desires. They are transfigured: Lady Macbeth is "unsexed"; Macbeth has forgot that he was born of woman; both are conformed to the image of devils; and the world of devils is suddenly revealed. But how shall this be conveyed and made palpable? In order that a new world may step in, this world must for a time disappear. The murderers, and the murder, must be insulated—cut off by an immeasurable gulf from the ordinary tide and succession of human affairs locked up and sequestered in some deep recess: we must be made sensible that the world of ordinary life is suddenly arrested—laid asleep—tranced—racked into a dread armistice: time must be annihilated; relation to things without abolished; and all must pass self-withdrawn into a deep syncope and suspension of earthly passion. Hence it is that when the deed is done—when the work of darkness is perfect, then the world of darkness passes away like a pageantry in the clouds: the knocking at the gate is heard; and it makes known audibly that the reaction has commenced: the human has made its reflux upon the fiendish: the pulses of life are beginning to beat again: and the re-establishment of the goings-on of the world in which we live, first makes us profoundly sensible of the awful parenthesis that had suspended them.

Oh! mighty poet!—Thy works are not as those of other men, simply and merely great works of art; but are also like the phenomena of nature, like the sun and the sea, the stars and the flowers,—like frost and snow, rain and dew, hail-storm and thunder, which are to be studied with entire submission of our own faculties, and in the perfect faith that in them there can be no too much or too little, nothing useless or inert—but that, the further we press in our discoveries, the more we shall see proofs of design and self-supporting arrangement where the careless eye had seen nothing but accident!

N.B. In the above specimen of psychological criticism, I have purposely omitted to notice another use of the knocking at the gate, *viz.* the opposition and contrast which it produces in the porter's comments to the scenes immediately preceding; because this use is tolerably obvious to all who are accustomed to reflect on what they read.

Thomas Macaulay

(1800–1859)

Appearing in 1823, this essay marked the playful beginning of what was to become one of the most distinguished literary careers in Victorian England. That beginning, however, is usually placed two years later, with the publication in The Edinburgh Review *of Macaulay's essay "Milton," to be followed by some twenty years of writing for this most prestigious of the literary reviews founded in the early nineteenth century. Here he published polemical articles championing such causes, early on, as the antislavery movement, and the lifting of civil restrictions against English Jews; and here, in biographical essays on figures like Bacon, Addison, Johnson, and Fannie Burney, he earned his reputation as a compelling narrative writer and judicial critic, as well as a great stylist. Macaulay's reputation soared with the* History of England *(1848 and 1855) whose narrative richness made it the rival, in sales and readership, of the most successful novels of the day. But it was his several contributions made at age twenty-three to* Knight's Quarterly *that first brought Macaulay to the public's attention. The Royal Society of Literature, against which he mounts his spirited polemic in our essay's first half, was the only learned organization of its kind directly under the king's patronage, with moneys set aside for pensioning ten "Royal Associates" and an additional sum for prizes. Its aims were at first ill-defined, as Macaulay's needling about the Dartmoor project implies. His comparison of a "prize poem" to a "prize sheep" takes a jab at organized encouragement of literary art and also, perhaps, turns a wry gaze on his own youthful prize-winning accomplishments at Cambridge University. The "apologue," or fable, about King Gomer Chephoraod of Babylon appears to be a fabrication—early evidence of the author's flair for apt narrative—to moralize and balance the preceding argument. Macaulay's "excellent sovereign" bears a partly Biblical name: Gomer turns up in Genesis 10:2 as one of the descendants of Noah, whose three sons, including Gomer's father Japheth, "begat" the races of mankind after the great Deluge.*

On the Royal Society of Literature

This is the age of societies. There is scarcely one Englishman in ten who has not belonged to some association for distributing books, or for prosecuting them; for sending invalids to the hospital, or beggars to the treadmill; for giving plate to the rich or blankets to the poor. To be the most absurd institution among so many institutions is no small distinction; it seems, however, to belong indisputably to the Royal Society of Literature. At the first establishment of that ridiculous academy, every sensible man predicted that, in spite of regal patronage and episcopal management, it would do nothing, or do harm. And it will scarcely be denied that those expectations have hitherto been fulfilled.

I do not attack the founders of the association. Their characters are respectable; their motives, I am willing to believe, were laudable. But I feel, and it is the duty of every literary man to feel, a strong jealousy of their proceedings. Their society can be innocent only while it continues to be despicable. Should they ever possess the power to encourage merit, they must also possess the power to depress it. Which power will be more frequently exercised, let everyone who has studied literary history, let everyone who has studied human nature, declare.

Envy and faction insinuate themselves into all communities. They often disturb the peace, and pervert the decisions, of benevolent and scientific associations. But it is in literary academies that they exert the most extensive and pernicious influence. In the first place, the principles of literary criticism, though equally fixed with those on which the chemist and the surgeon proceed, are by no means equally recognised. Men are rarely able to assign a reason for their approbation or dislike on questions of taste; and therefore they willingly submit to any guide who boldly asserts his claim to superior discernment. It is more difficult to ascertain and establish the merits of a poem than the powers of a machine or the benefits of a new remedy. Hence it is in literature, that quackery is most easily puffed, and excellence most easily decried.

In some degree this argument applies to academies of the fine arts; and it is fully confirmed by all that I have ever heard of that institution which annually disfigures the walls of Somerset-House with an acre of spoiled canvass. But a literary tribunal is incomparably more dangerous. Other societies, at least, have no tendency to call forth any opinions on those subjects which most agitate and inflame the minds of men. The sceptic and the zealot, the revolutionist and the placeman, meet on common ground in a gallery of paintings or a laboratory of science. They can praise or censure without reference to the differences which exist between them. In a literary body this can never be the case. Literature is, and always must be, inseparably blended with politics and theology; it is the great engine which moves the feelings of a people on the most momentous questions. It is, therefore, impossible that any society can be formed so impartial as to consider the literary character of an individual abstracted from the opinions which his writings inculcate. It is not to be hoped, perhaps it is not to be wished, that the feelings of the man should be so completely forgotten in the duties of the academician. The consequences are evident. The honours and censures of this Star-chamber of the Muses will be awarded according to the prejudices of the particular sect or faction which may at the time predominate. Whigs would canvass against a Southey, Tories against a Byron. Those who might at first protest against such conduct as unjust would soon adopt it on the plea of retaliation; and the general good of literature, for which the society was professedly instituted, would be forgotten in the stronger claims of political and religious partiality.

Yet even this is not the worst. Should the institution ever acquire any influence, it will afford most pernicious facilities to every malignant coward who may desire to blast a reputation which he envies. It will furnish a secure ambuscade, behind which the Maroons of literature may take a certain and deadly aim. The editorial *we* has often been fatal to rising genius; though all the world knows that it is only a form of speech, very often employed by a single needy blockhead. The academic *we* would have a far greater and more ruinous influence. Numbers, while they increased the effect, would diminish the shame, of injustice. The advantages of an open and those of an anonymous attack would be combined; and the authority of avowal would be united to the security of concealment. The serpents in Virgil, after they had destroyed Laocoön, found an asylum from the vengeance of the enraged people behind the shield of the statue of Minerva. And, in the same manner, every thing that is grovelling and venomous, every thing that can hiss, and every thing that can sting, would take sanctuary in the recesses of this new temple of wisdom.

The French academy was, of all such associations, the most widely and the most justly celebrated. It was founded by the greatest of ministers; it was patronised by successive kings; it numbered in its lists most of the eminent French writers. Yet what benefit has literature derived from its labours? What is its history but an uninterrupted record of servile compliances—of paltry artifices—of deadly quarrels—of perfidious friendships? Whether governed by the court, by the Sorbonne, or by the philosophers, it was always equally powerful for evil, and equally impotent for good. I might speak of the attacks by which it attempted to depress the rising fame of Corneille; I might speak of the reluctance with which it gave its tardy confirmation to the applauses which the whole civilised world had bestowed on the genius of Voltaire. I might prove by overwhelming evidence that, to the latest period of its existence, even under the superintendence of the all-accomplished D'Alembert, it continued to be a scene of the fiercest animosities and the basest intrigues. I might cite Piron's epigrams, and Marmontel's memoirs, and Montesquieu's letters. But I hasten on to another topic.

One of the modes by which our Society proposes to encourage merit is the distribution of prizes. The munificence of the king has enabled it to offer an annual premium of a hundred guineas for the best essay in prose, and another fifty guineas for the best poem, which may be transmitted to it. This is very laughable. In the first place the judges may err. Those imperfections of human intellect to which, as the articles of the church tell us, even general councils are subject may possibly be found even in the Royal Society of Literature. The French academy, as I have already said, was the most illustrious assembly of the kind, and numbered among its associates men much more distinguished than ever will assemble at Mr. Hatchard's to rummage the box of the English Society. Yet this famous body gave a poetical prize, for which Voltaire was a candidate, to a fellow who wrote some verses about "the frozen and the burning pole."

Yet, granting that the prizes were always awarded to the best composition, that composition, I say without hesitation, will always be bad. A prize poem is like a prize sheep. The object of the competitor for the agricultural premium is to produce an animal fit, not to be eaten, but to be weighed. Accordingly he pampers his victim into morbid and unnatural fatness; and, when it is in such a state that it would be sent away in disgust from any table, he offers it to the judges. The object of the poetical candidate, in like manner, is to produce, not a good poem, but a poem of that exact degree of frigidity or bombast which may appear to his censors to be correct or sublime. Compositions thus constructed will always be worthless. The few excellences which they may contain will have an exotic aspect and flavour. In general, prize sheep are good for nothing but to make tallow candles, and prize poems are good for nothing but to light them.

The first subject proposed by the Society to the poets of England was Dartmoor. I thought that they intended a covert sarcasm at their own projects. Their institution was a literary Dartmoor scheme;—a plan for forcing into cultivation the waste lands of intellect,—for raising poetical produce, by means of bounties, from soil too meagre to have yielded any returns in the natural course of things. The plan for the cultivation of Dartmoor has, I hear, been abandoned. I hope that this may be an omen of the fate of the Society.

In truth, this seems by no means improbable. They have been offering for several years the rewards which the king placed at their disposal, and have not, as far as I can learn, been able to find in their box one composition which they have deemed worthy of publication. At least no publication has taken place. The associates may perhaps be astonished at this. But I will attempt to explain it, after the manner of ancient times, by means of an apologue.

About four hundred years after the deluge, King Gomer Chephoraod reigned in Babylon. He united all the characteristics of an excellent sovereign. He made good laws, won great battles, and white-washed long streets. He was, in consequence, idolised by his people, and panegyrised by many poets and orators. A book was then a serious undertaking. Neither paper nor any similar material had been invented. Authors were therefore under the necessity of inscribing their compositions on massive bricks. Some of these Babylonian records are still preserved in European museums; but the language in which they are written has never been deciphered. Gomer Chephoraod was so popular that the clay of all the plains round the Euphrates could scarcely furnish brick-kilns enough for his eulogists. It is recorded in particular that Pharonezzar, the Assyrian Pindar, published a bridge and four walls in his praise.

One day the king was going in state from his palace to the temple of Belus. During this procession it was lawful for any Babylonian to offer any petition or suggestion to his sovereign. As the chariot passed before a vintner's shop, a large company, apparently half-drunk, sallied forth into the street; and one of them thus addressed the king:

"Gomer Chephoraod, live forever! It appears to thy servants that of all the productions of the earth good wine is the best, and bad wine is the worst. Good wine makes the heart cheerful, the eyes bright, the speech ready. Bad wine confuses the head, disorders the stomach, makes us quarrelsome at night, and sick the next morning. Now therefore let my lord the king take order that thy servants may drink good wine."

"And how is this to be done?" said the good-natured prince.

"Oh, King," said his monitor, "this is most easy. Let the king make a decree, and seal it with his royal signet: and let it be proclaimed that the king will give ten she-asses, and ten slaves, and ten changes of raiment, every year, unto the man who shall make ten measures of the best wine. And whosoever wishes for the she-asses, and the slaves, and the raiment, let him send the ten measures of wine to thy servants, and we will drink thereof and judge. So shall there be much good wine in Assyria."

The project pleased Gomer Chephoraod. "Be it so," said he. The people shouted. The petitioners prostrated themselves in gratitude. The same night heralds were despatched to bear the intelligence to the remotest districts of Assyria.

After a due interval the wines began to come in; and the examiners assembled to adjudge the prize. The first vessel was unsealed. Its odour was such that the judges, without tasting it, pronounced unanimous condemnation. The next was opened: it had a villainous taste of clay. The third was sour and vapid. They proceeded from one cask of execrable liquor to another, 'till at length, in absolute nausea, they gave up the investigation.

The next morning they all assembled at the gate of the king, with pale faces and aching heads. They owned that they could not recommend any competitor as worthy of the rewards. They swore that the wine was little better than poison, and intreated permission to resign the office of deciding between such detestable potions.

"In the name of Belus, how can this have happened?" said the king.

Merolchazzar, the high-priest, muttered something about the anger of the gods at the toleration shown to a sect of impious heretics who ate pigeons broiled, "whereas," said he, "our religion commands us to eat them roasted. Now therefore, oh King," continued this respectable divine, "give command to thy men of war, and let them smite the disobedient people with the sword, them, and their wives, and their children, and let their houses, and their flocks, and their herds, be given to thy servants the priests. Then shall the land yield its increase, and the fruits of the earth shall be no more blasted by the vengeance of heaven."

"Nay," said the King, "the ground lies under no general curse from heaven. The season has been singularly good. The wine which thou didst thyself drink at the banquet a few nights ago, oh venerable Merolchazzar, was of this year's vintage. Dost thou not remember how thou didst praise it? It was the same night that thou wast inspired by Belus, and didst reel to and fro, and discourse sacred mysteries. These things are too hard for me. I comprehend them not. The only wine which is bad is that which is sent to my judges. Who can expound this to us?"

The king scratched his head. Upon which all the courtiers scratched their heads.

He then ordered proclamation to be made, that a purple robe and a golden chain should be given to the man who could solve this difficulty.

An old philosopher, who had been observed to smile rather disdainfully when the prize had first been instituted, came forward and spoke thus:—

"Gomer Chephoraod, live forever! Marvel not at that which has happened. It was no miracle, but a natural event. How could it be otherwise? It is true that much good wine has been made this year. But who would send it in for thy rewards? Thou knowest Ascobaruch who hath the great vineyards in the north, and Cohahiroth who sendeth wine every year from the south over the Persian gulf. Their wines are so delicious that ten measures thereof are sold for an hundred talents of silver. Thinkest thou that they will exchange them for thy slaves and thine asses? What would thy prize profit any who have vineyards in rich soils?"

"Who then," said one of the judges, "are the wretches who sent us this poison?"

"Blame them not," said the sage, "seeing that you have been the authors of the evil. They are men whose lands are poor, and have never yielded them any returns equal to the prizes which the king proposed. Wherefore, knowing that the lords of the fruitful vineyards would not enter into competition with them, they planted vines, some on rocks, and some in light sandy soil, and some in deep clay. Hence their wines are bad. For no culture or reward will make barren land bear good vines. Know therefore, assuredly, that your prizes have increased the quantity of bad but not of good wine."

There was a long silence. At length the king spoke.

"Give him the purple robe and the chain of gold. Throw the wines into the Euphrates; and proclaim that the Royal Society of Wines is dissolved."

Ralph Waldo Emerson

(1803–1882)

"There is but one completely human voice to me in the world, and you are it." So wrote Thomas Carlyle in 1860 to Emerson, his American friend of nearly thirty years. We learn, too early perhaps, to tag the ideas of influential older writers—"transcendentalist," in Emerson's case—and forego listening to the "human voice," nuanced as it inevitably is by the rhetoric of its own age. Yet in an essay, that listening is close to everything. If I cannot hear the "completely human voice" of the dead writer, his or her essay can have no other kind of life in it. One way to listen for the humanity of a difficult nineteenth-century writer like Emerson is to begin by hearing what one can—the occasional crystalline utterances, let us say, breaking the pace of silent reading: "We live by our imaginations, by our admirations, by our sentiments. . . . Even the prose of the streets is full of refractions. . . . The world rolls, the din of life is never hushed. . . . Society does not love its unmaskers. . . ." The solidity, the truthfulness, of such sentences startle and involve us. Yet it would be self-impoverishment to stop there, refuse to explore how these "lightning-gleams of meaning" (Carlyle) gather conceptual force across paragraphs from the essay's wondrous yet sensible narrative opening, through the intricately illustrated meditations on the pervasiveness of illusion, to the gently didactic moral resolve of "Whatever games are played with us, we must play no games with ourselves. . . ," and all the way to Emerson's grand concluding paragraph. Loren Eiseley, physical anthropologist and essayist, was profoundly attuned to the timbre of Emerson's thought-world, his sense of "the weary slipping . . . the ebbing away of the human spirit into fox and weasel as it struggled upward while all its [evolutionary] past tugged upon it from below." To this, says Eiseley, Emerson counterposed his sense of the "infinitude of the private man" ("Man Against the Universe"). It was always the individual, private listener as moral locus that Emerson was trying to rouse in his famous lectures, which, by much reading aloud before audiences and subsequent revisions, became his essays and books. And the "completely human voice" still sounding through them claims to be no more than the voice of another such individual in his "strict and faithful dealing at home."

Illusions

Some years ago, in company with an agreeable party, I spent a long summer day in exploring the Mammoth Cave in Kentucky. We traversed, through spacious galleries affording a solid masonry foundation for the town and county overhead, the six or eight black miles from the mouth of the cavern to the innermost recess which tourists visit,—a niche or grotto made of one seamless stalactite, and called, I believe, Serena's Bower. I lost the light of one day. I saw high domes, and bottomless pits; heard the voice of unseen waterfalls; paddled three quarters of a mile in the deep Echo River, whose waters are peopled with the blind fish; crossed the streams "Lethe" and "Styx"; plied with music and guns the echoes in these alarming galleries; saw every form of stalagmite and stalactite in the sculptured and fretted chambers,—icicle, orange-flower, acanthus, grapes, and snowball. We shot Bengal lights into the vaults and groins of the sparry cathedrals, and examined all the masterpieces which the four combined engineers, water, limestone, gravitation, and time, could make in the dark.

The mysteries and scenery of the cave had the same dignity that belongs to all natural objects, and which shames the fine things to which we foppishly compare them. I remarked, especially, the mimetic habit, with which Nature, on new instruments, hums her old tunes, making night to mimic day, and chemistry to ape vegetation. But I then took notice, and still chiefly remember, that the best thing which the cave had to offer was an illusion. On arriving at what is called the "Star-Chamber," our lamps were taken from us by the guide, and extinguished or put aside, and, on looking upwards, I saw or seemed to see the night heaven thick with stars glimmering more or less brightly over our heads, and even what seemed a comet flaming among them. All the party were touched with astonishment and pleasure. Our musical friends sung with much feeling a pretty song, "The stars are in the quiet sky," etc., and I sat down on the rocky floor to enjoy the serene picture. Some crystal specks in the black ceiling high overhead, reflecting the light of a half-hid lamp, yielded this magnificent effect.

I own, I did not like the cave so well for eking out its sublimities with this theatrical trick. But I have had many experiences like it, before and since; and we must be content to be pleased without too curiously analyzing the occasions. Our conversation with Nature is not just what it seems. The cloud-rack, the sunrise and sunset glories, rainbows and northern lights, are not quite so spheral as our childhood thought them; and the part our organization plays in them is too large. The senses interfere everywhere, and mix their own structure with all they report of. Once, we fancied the earth a plane, and stationary. In admiring the sunset, we do not yet deduct the rounding, co-ordinating, pictorial powers of the eye.

The same interference from our organization creates the most of our pleasure and pain. Our first mistake is the belief that the circumstance gives the joy which we give to the circumstance. Life is an ecstasy. Life is sweet as nitrous oxide; and the fisherman dripping all day over a cold pond, the switchman at the railway intersection, the farmer in the field, the negro in the rice-swamp, the fop in the street, the hunter in the woods, the barrister with the jury, the belle at the ball, all ascribe a certain pleasure to their employment, which they themselves give it. Health and appetite impart the sweetness to sugar, bread, and meat. We fancy that our civilization has got on far, but we still come back to our primers.

We live by our imaginations, by our admirations, by our sentiments. The child walks amid heaps of illusions, which he does not like to have disturbed. The boy, how sweet to him is his fancy! how dear the story of barons and battles! What a hero he is, whilst he feeds on his heroes! What a debt is his to imaginative books! He has no better friend or influence, than Scott, Shakespeare, Plutarch, and Homer. The man lives to other objects, but who dare affirm that they are more real? Even the prose of the streets is full of refractions. In the life of the dreariest alderman, fancy enters into all details, and colors them with rosy hue. He imitates the air and actions of people whom he admires, and is raised in his own eyes. He pays a debt quicker to a rich man than to a poor man. He wishes the bow and compliment of some leader in the state, or in society; weighs what he says; perhaps he never comes nearer to him for that, but dies at last better contented for this amusement of his eyes and his fancy.

The world rolls, the din of life is never hushed. In London, in Paris, in Boston, in San Francisco, the carnival, the masquerade, is at its height. Nobody drops his domino. The units, the fictions of the piece, it would be an impertinence to break. The chapter of fascinations is very long. Great is paint; nay, God is the painter; and we rightly accuse the critic who destroys too many illusions. Society does not love its unmaskers. It was wittily, if somewhat bitterly, said by D'Alembert, *"qu'un état de vapeur était un état très fâcheux, parcequ'il nous faisait voir les choses comme elles sont."*[1] I find men victims of illusion in all parts of life. Children, youths, adults, and old men, all are led by one bawble or another. Yoganidra, the goddess of illusion, Proteus, or Momus, or Gylfi's Mocking,—for the Power has many names,—is stronger than the Titans, stronger than

[1] . . . that a vaporous (illusory) condition was very unfortunate because it made us see things as they are.

Apollo. Few have overheard the gods, or surprised their secret. Life is a succession of lessons which must be lived to be understood. All is riddle, and the key to a riddle is another riddle. There are as many pillows of illusion as flakes in a snow-storm. We wake from one dream into another dream. The toys, to be sure, are various, and are graduated in refinement to the quality of the dupe. The intellectual man requires a fine bait; the sots are easily amused. But everybody is drugged with his own frenzy, and the pageant marches at all hours, with music and banner and badge.

Amid the joyous troop who give in to the charivari comes now and then a sad-eyed boy, whose eyes lack the requisite refractions to clothe the show in due glory, and who is afflicted with a tendency to trace home the glittering miscellany of fruits and flowers to one root. Science is a search after identity, and the scientific whim is lurking in all corners. At the State Fair, a friend of mine complained that all the varieties of fancy pears in our orchards seem to have been selected by somebody who had a whim for a particular kind of pear, and only cultivated such as had that perfume; they were all alike. And I remember the quarrel of another youth with the confectioners, that, when he racked his wit to choose the best comfits in the shops, in all the endless varieties of sweetmeat he could only find three flavors, or two. What then? Pears and cakes are good for something; and because you, unluckily, have an eye or nose too keen, why need you spoil the comfort which the rest of us find in them? I knew a humorist, who, in a good deal of rattle, had a grain or two of sense. He shocked the company by maintaining that the attributes of God were two,—power and risibility; and that it was the duty of every pious man to keep up the comedy. And I have known gentlemen of great stake in the community, but whose sympathies were cold,—presidents of colleges, and governors, and senators,—who held themselves bound to sign every temperance pledge, and act with Bible societies, and missions, and peacemakers, and cry "Hist-a-boy!" to every good dog. We must not carry comity too far, but we all have kind impulses in this direction. When the boys come into my yard for leave to gather horse-chestnuts, I own I enter into Nature's game, and affect to grant the permission reluctantly, fearing that any moment they will find out the imposture of that showy chaff. But this tenderness is quite unnecessary; the enchantments are laid on very thick. Their young life is thatched with them. Bare and grim to tears is the lot of the children in the hovel I saw yesterday; yet not the less they hung it round with frippery romance, like the children of the happiest fortune, and talked of "the dear cottage where so many joyful hours had flown." Well, this thatching of hovels is the custom of the country. Women, more than all, are the element and kingdom of illusion. Being fascinated, they fascinate. They see through Claude-Lorraines.[2] And how dare anyone, if he could, pluck away the *coulisses*, stage effects, and ceremonies, by which they live? Too pathetic, too pitiable, is the region of affection, and its atmosphere always liable to *mirage*.

We are not very much to blame for our bad marriages. We live amid hallucinations; and this especial trap is laid to trip up our feet with, and all are tripped up first or last. But the mighty Mother who had been so sly with us, as if she felt that she owed us some indemnity, insinuates into the Pandora-box of marriage some deep and serious benefits, and some great joys. We find a delight in the beauty and happiness of children, that makes the heart too big for the body. In the worst-assorted connections there is ever some mixture of true marriage. Teague and his jade get some just relations of mutual respect, kindly observation, and fostering of each other, learn something, and would carry themselves wiselier, if they were now to begin.

'T is fine for us to point at one or another fine madman, as if there were any exempts. The scholar in his library is none. I, who have all my life heard any number of orations and debates, read poems and miscellaneous books, conversed with many geniuses, am still the victim of any new page; and, if Marmaduke, or Hugh, or Moosehead, or any other, invent a new style or mythology, I fancy that the world will be all brave and right, if dressed in these colors, which I had not thought of. Then at once I will daub with this new paint; but it will not stick. 'T is like the cement which the peddler sells at the door; he makes broken crockery hold with it, but you can never buy of him a bit of cement which will make it hold when he is gone.

Men who make themselves felt in the world avail themselves of a certain fate in their constitution, which they know how to use. But they never deeply interest us, unless they lift a corner of the curtain, or betray never so slightly their penetration of what is behind it. 'T is the charm of practical men, that outside of their practicality are a certain poetry and play, as if they led the good horse Power by the bridle, and preferred to walk, though they can ride so fiercely. Bonaparte is intellectual, as well as Caesar; and the best soldiers, sea-captains, and railway men, have a gentleness, when off duty; a good-natured admission that there are illusions, and who shall say that he is not their sport? We stigmatize the cast-iron fellows, who cannot so detach themselves, as "dragon-ridden," "thunder-stricken," and fools of fate, with whatever powers endowed.

Since our tuition is through emblems and indirections, 't is well to know that there is method in it, a fixed scale, and rank above rank in the

[2] Claude Lorraine (1600–1682) was a French painter whose light-infused works were typical of the "ideal landscape" school, which held that representations of nature could be more beautiful than nature itself.

phantasms. We begin low with coarse masks, and rise to the most subtle and beautiful. The red men told Columbus, "they had an herb which took away fatigue"; but he found the allusion of "arriving from the east at the Indies" more composing to his lofty spirit than any tobacco. Is not our faith in the impenetrability of matter more sedative than narcotics? You play with jack-straws, balls, bowls, horse and gun, estates and politics; but there are finer games before you. Is not time a pretty toy? Life will show you masks that are worth all your carnivals. Yonder mountain must migrate into your mind. The fine star-dust and nebulous blur in Orion, "the portentous year of Mizar and Alcor," must come down and be dealt with in your household thought. What if you shall come to discern that the play and playground of all this pompous history are radiations from yourself, and that the sun borrows his beams? What terrible questions we are learning to ask! The former men believed in magic, by which temples, cities, and men were swallowed up, and all trace of them gone. We are coming on the secret of a magic which sweeps out of men's minds all vestige of theism and beliefs which they and their fathers held and were framed upon.

There are deceptions of the senses, deceptions of the passions, and the structural, beneficent illusions of sentiment and of the intellect. There is the illusion of love, which attributes to the beloved person all which that person shares with his or her family, sex, age, or condition, nay with the human mind itself. 'T is these which the lover loves, and Anna Matilda gets the credit of them. As if one shut up always in a tower, with one window, through which the face of heaven and earth could be seen, should fancy that all the marvels he beheld belonged to that window. There is the illusion of time, which is very deep; who has disposed of it? or come to the conviction that what seems the succession of thought is only the distribution of wholes into causal series? The intellect sees that every atom carries the whole of Nature; that the mind opens to omnipotence; that, in the endless striving and ascents, the metamorphosis is entire, so that the soul doth not know itself in its own act, when that act is perfected. There is illusion that shall deceive even the elect. There is illusion that shall deceive even the performer of the miracle. Though he make his body, he denies that he makes it. Though the world exist from thought, thought is daunted in presence of the world. One after the other we accept the mental laws, still resisting those which follow, which however must be accepted. But all our concessions only compel us to new profusion. And what avails it that science has come to treat space and time as simply forms of thought, and the material world as hypothetical, and withal our pretension of property and even of selfhood are fading with the rest, if, at last, even our thoughts are not finalities; but the incessant flowing and ascension reach these also, and each thought which yesterday was a finality, to-day is yielding to a larger generalization?

With such volatile elements to work in, 't is no wonder if our estimates are loose and floating. We must work and affirm, but we have no guess of the value of what we say or do. The cloud is now as big as your hand, and now it covers a county. That story of Thor, who was set to drain the drinking-horn in Asgard, and to wrestle with the old woman, and to run with the runner Lok, and presently found that he had been drinking up the sea, and wrestling with Time, and racing with Thought, describes us who are contending, amid these seeming trifles, with the supreme energies of Nature. We fancy we have fallen into bad company and squalid condition, low debts, shoe-bills, broken glass to pay for, pots to buy, butcher's meat, sugar, milk, and coal. "Set me some great task, ye gods! and I will show my spirit." "Not so," says the good Heaven; "plod and plough, vamp your old coats and hats, weave a shoe-string; great affairs and the best wine by and by." Well 't is all phantasm; and if we weave a yard of tape in all humility, and as well as we can, long hereafter we shall see it was no cotton tape at all, but some galaxy which we braided, and that the threads were Time and Nature.

We cannot write the order of the variable winds. How can we penetrate the law of our shifting moods and susceptibility? Yet they differ as all and nothing. Instead of the firmament of yesterday, which our eyes require, it is to-day an eggshell which coops us in; we cannot even see what or where our stars of destiny are. From day to day, the capital facts of human life are hidden from our eyes. Suddenly the mist rolls up, and reveals them, and we think how much good time is gone, that might have been saved, had any hint of these things been shown. A sudden rise in the road shows us the system of mountains, and all the summits, which have been just as near us all the year, but quite out of mind. But these alternations are not without their order, and we are parties to our various fortune. If life seem a succession of dreams, yet poetic justice is done in dreams also. The visions of good men are good; it is the undisciplined will that is whipped with bad thoughts and bad fortunes. When we break the laws, we lose our hold on the central reality. Like sick men in hospitals, we change only from bed to bed, from one folly to another; and it cannot signify much what becomes of such castaways,—wailing, stupid, comatose creatures,—lifted from bed to bed, from the nothing of life to the nothing of death.

In this kingdom of illusions we grope eagerly for stays and foundations. There is none but a strict and faithful dealing at home, and a severe barring out of all duplicity or illusion there. Whatever games are played with us, we must play no games with ourselves, but deal in our privacy with the last honesty and truth. I look upon the simple and childish virtues of veracity and honesty as the root of all that is sublime in character. Speak as you think, be what you are, pay your debts of all kinds. I prefer to be owned as sound and solvent, and my word as good as my bond, and to be what cannot be skipped, or dissipated, or undermined, to all the *éclat* in the universe. This reality is the foundation of friendship, religion, poetry, and art. At the top or at the bottom of all illusions, I set the cheat which still leads us to work and live for appearances, in spite of our conviction, in all sane hours, that it is what we really are that avails with friends, with strangers, and with fate or fortune.

One would think from the talk of men, that riches and poverty were a great matter; and our civilization mainly respects it. But the Indians say, that they do not think the white man with his brow of care, always toiling, afraid of heat and cold, and keeping within doors, has any advantage of them. The permanent interest of every man is, never to be in a false position, but to have the weight of Nature to back him in all that he does. Riches and poverty are a thick or thin costume; and our life—the life of all of us—identical. For we transcend the circumstance continually, and taste the real quality of existence; as in our employments, which only differ in the manipulations, but express the same laws; or in our thoughts, which wear no silks, and taste no ice-creams. We see God face to face every hour, and know the savor of Nature.

The early Greek philosophers Heraclitus and Xenophanes measured their force on this problem of identity. Diogenes of Apollonia said, that unless the atoms were made of one stuff, they could never blend and act with one another. But the Hindoos, in their sacred writings, express the liveliest feeling, both of the essential identity, and of that illusion which they conceive variety to be. "The notions, '*I am*,' and '*This is mine*,' which influence mankind, are but delusions of the mother of the world. Dispel, O Lord of all creatures! the conceit of knowledge which proceeds from ignorance." And the beatitude of man they hold to lie in being freed from fascination.

The intellect is stimulated by the statement of truth in a trope, and the will by clothing the laws of life in illusions. But the unities of Truth and of Right are not broken by the disguise. There need never be any confusion in these. In a crowded life of many parts and performers, on a stage of nations, or in the obscurest hamlet in Maine or California, the same elements offer the same choices to each new-comer, and, according to his election, he fixes his fortune in absolute Nature. It would be hard to put more mental and moral philosophy than the Persians have thrown into a sentence:—

Fooled thou must be, though wisest of the wise:
Then be the fool of virtue, not of vice.

There is no chance, and no anarchy, in the universe. All is system and gradation. Every god is there sitting in his sphere. The young mortal enters the hall of the firmament; there is he alone with them alone, they pouring on him benedictions and gifts, and beckoning him up to their thrones. On the instant, and incessantly, fall snow-storms of illusions. He fancies himself in a vast crowd which sways this way and that, and whose movement and doings he must obey: he fancies himself poor, orphaned, insignificant. The mad crowd drives hither and thither, now furiously commanding this thing to be done, now that. What is he that he should resist their will, and think or act for himself? Every moment, new changes, and new showers of deceptions, to baffle and distract him. And when, by and by, for an instant, the air clears, and the cloud lifts a little, there are the gods still sitting around him on their thrones,—they alone with him alone.

Nathaniel Hawthorne

(1804–1864)

Much has been said about Hawthorne and solitariness—as a personal trait, as a feature of his professional life, as a subject of his literary interest. There was the young Nathaniel rambling alone through the Maine woods, and there was the grown man of thirty-seven leaving Brook Farm (that idealistic nineteenth-century experiment in communal living) soon after he had arrived because, as he wrote to Sophia Peabody, his wife-to-be, "the real ME *was never an associate of the community." All the words, one feels, "associate," "community," and of course "*ME*," carry their fullest weight in this laconic sentence. Between leaving college in 1824 and his first collection of "twice-told" stories and essays in 1837, Hawthorne had been writing in Salem, Massachusetts—"the obscurest man of letters in America," he later described himself (Preface to third edition,* Twice-Told Tales). *His cool assessment of these early pieces in 1851, when* The Scarlet Letter *had made him famous, declared them "proper to the production of a person in retirement." And yet, he goes on to say, looking back, they "are not the talk of a secluded man with his own mind and heart . . . but the attempts, and very imperfectly successful ones, to open an intercourse with the world." "Foot-steps on the Sea-shore" was included in the second, expanded edition of* Twice-Told Tales *(1842), though originally published in a periodical, like others of the sketches from his early years of "retirement." The essay amplifies and focuses material from Hawthorne's* American Notebooks, *especially the entries for June 18, 1835, and October 16, 1837. In the former, he tells of his encounter with three little girls bathing, who reappear in the essay; in the later entry, he records what became controlling images of the essay: the companionable shorebirds and the fascinated retracing of his own footprints in the sand. These signs of his "own nature on its wayward course" are laid out again for the reader of the essay, through its sunny, or lyrical, or dreamy, or uncanny moments, all the way to its unexpected close. And this close, one quickly realizes, is no more than fitting after the phantasms of solitude, no more than ordinary—a kind of unlooked-for blessedness at day's end.*

Foot-prints on the Sea-shore

It must be a spirit much unlike my own, which can keep itself in health and vigor without sometimes stealing from the sultry sunshine of the world, to plunge into the cool bath of solitude. At intervals, and not infrequent ones, the forest and the ocean summon me—one with the roar of its waves, the other with the murmur of its boughs—forth from the haunts of men. But I must wander many a mile, ere I could stand beneath the shadow of even one primeval tree, much less be lost among the multitude of hoary trunks, and hidden from earth and sky by the mystery of darksome foliage. Nothing is within my daily reach more like a forest than the acre or two of woodland near some suburban farm-house. When, therefore, the yearning for seclusion becomes a necessity within me, I am drawn to the sea-shore, which extends its line of rude rocks and seldom-trodden sands, for leagues around our bay. Setting forth, at my last ramble, on a September morning, I bound myself with a hermit's vow, to interchange no thoughts with man or woman, to share no social pleasure, but to derive all that day's enjoyment from shore, and sea, and sky,—from my soul's communion with these, and from fantasies, and recollections, or anticipated realities. Surely here is enough to feed a human spirit for a single day. Farewell, then, busy world! 'Till your evening lights shall shine along the street—'till they gleam upon my sea-flushed face, as I tread homeward—free me from your ties, and let me be a peaceful outlaw.

Highways and cross-paths are hastily traversed; and, clambering down a crag, I find myself at the extremity of a long beach. How gladly does the spirit leap forth, and suddenly enlarge its sense of being to the full extent of the broad, blue, sunny deep! A greeting and a homage to the Sea! I descend over its margin, and dip my hand into the wave that meets me, and bathe my brow. That far-resounding roar is Ocean's voice of welcome. His salt breath brings a blessing along with it. Now let us pace together—the reader's fancy arm in arm with mine—this noble beach, which extends a mile or more from that craggy promontory to yonder rampart of broken rocks. In front, the sea; in the rear, a precipitous bank, the grassy verge of which is breaking away, year after year, and flings down its tufts of verdure upon the barrenness below. The beach itself is a broad space of sand, brown and sparkling, with hardly any pebbles intermixed. Near the water's edge there is a wet margin, which glistens brightly in the sunshine, and reflects objects like a mirror; and as we tread along the glistening border, a dry spot flashes around each footstep, but grows moist again, as we lift our feet. In some spots, the sand receives a complete impression of the sole—square toe and all;

elsewhere, it is of such marble firmness, that we must stamp heavily to leave a print even of the iron-shod heel. Along the whole of this extensive beach gambols the surf-wave; now it makes a feint of dashing onward in a fury, yet dies away with a meek murmur, and does but kiss the strand; now, after many such abortive efforts, it rears itself up in an unbroken line, heightening as it advances, without a speck of foam on its green crest. With how fierce a roar it flings itself forward, and rushes far up the beach!

As I threw my eyes along the edge of the surf, I remember that I was startled, as Robinson Crusoe might have been, by the sense that human life was within the magic circle of my solitude. Afar off in the remote distance of the beach, appearing like sea-nymphs, or some airier things, such as might tread upon the feathery spray, was a group of girls. Hardly had I beheld them, when they passed into the shadow of the rocks and vanished. To comfort myself—for truly I would fain have gazed a while longer—I made acquaintance with a flock of beach-birds. These little citizens of the sea and air preceded me by about a stone's-throw along the strand, seeking, I suppose, for food upon its margin. Yet, with a philosophy which mankind would do well to imitate, they drew a continual pleasure from their toil for a subsistence. The sea was each little bird's great playmate. They chased it downward as it swept back, and again ran up swiftly before the impending wave, which sometimes overtook them and bore them off their feet. But they floated as lightly as one of their own feathers on the breaking crest. In their airy flutterings, they seemed to rest on the evanescent spray. Their images,—long-legged little figures, with grey backs and snowy bosoms,—were seen as distinctly as the realities in the mirror of the glistening strand. As I advanced, they flew a score or two of yards, and, again alighting, recommenced their dalliance with the surf-wave; and thus they bore me company along the beach, the types of pleasant fantasies, 'till, at its extremity, they took wing over the ocean, and were gone. After forming a friendship with these small surf-spirits, it is really worth a sigh, to find no memorial of them save their multitudinous little tracks in the sand.

When we have paced the length of the beach, it is pleasant, and not unprofitable, to retrace our steps, and recall the whole mood and occupation of the mind during the former passage. Our tracks, being all discernible, will guide us with an observing consciousness through every unconscious wandering of thought and fancy. Here we followed the surf in its reflux, to pick up a shell which the sea seemed loath to relinquish. Here we found a sea-weed, with an immense brown leaf, and trailed it behind us by its long snake-like stalk. Here we seized a live horse-shoe by the tail, and counted the many claws of that queer monster. Here we dug into the sand for pebbles, and skipped them upon the surface of the water. Here we wet our feet while examining a jelly-fish, which the waves, having just tossed it up, now sought to snatch away again. Here we trod along the brink of a fresh-water brooklet, which flows across the beach, becoming shallower and more shallow, 'till at last it sinks into the sand, and perishes in the effort to bear its little tribute to the main. Here some vagary appears to have bewildered us; for our tracks go round and round, and are confusedly intermingled, as if we had found a labyrinth upon the level beach. And here, amid our idle pastime, we sat down upon almost the only stone that breaks the surface of the sand, and were lost in an unlooked-for and overpowering conception of the majesty and awfulness of the great deep. Thus, by tracking our foot-prints in the sand, we track our own nature in its wayward course, and steal a glance upon it, when it never dreams of being so observed. Such glances always make us wiser.

This extensive beach affords room for another pleasant pastime. With your staff, you may write verses—love-verses, if they please you best—and consecrate them with a woman's name. Here, too, may be inscribed thoughts, feelings, desires, warm outgushings from the heart's secret places, which you would not pour upon the sand without the certainty that, almost ere the sky has looked upon them, the sea will wash them out. Stir not hence, till the record be effaced. Now—for there is room enough on your canvass—draw huge faces—huge as that of the Sphynx on Egyptian sands—and fit them with bodies of corresponding immensity, and legs which might stride half-way to yonder island. Child's play becomes magnificent on so grand a scale. But, after all, the most fascinating employment is simply to write your name in the sand. Draw the letters gigantic, so that two strides may barely measure them, and three for the long strokes! Cut deep, that the record may be permanent! Statesmen, and warriors, and poets, have spent their strength in no better cause than this. Is it accomplished? Return, then, in an hour or two, and seek for this mighty record of a name. The sea will have swept over it, even as time rolls its effacing waves over the names of statesmen, and warriors, and poets. Hark, the surf-wave laughs at you!

Passing from the beach, I begin to clamber over the crags, making my difficult way among the ruins of a rampart, shattered and broken by the assaults of a fierce enemy. The rocks rise in every variety of attitude; some of them have their feet in the foam, and are shagged half-way upward with sea-weed; some have been hollowed almost into caverns by the unwearied toil of the sea, which can afford to spend centuries in wearing away a rock, or even polishing a pebble. One huge rock ascends in monumental shape, with a face like a giant's tombstone, on which the veins resemble inscriptions, but in an unknown tongue. We will fancy them the forgotten characters of an antediluvian race; or else that nature's own hand has here recorded a mystery, which, could I read her language, would make mankind the wiser and the happier. How many a thing has troubled me with that same idea! Pass on, and leave it unexplained. Here is a narrow avenue, which might seem to have been hewn through the very heart of an enormous crag, affording passage for the rising sea to thunder back and forth, filling it with tumultuous foam, and then leaving its floor of black pebbles bare and glistening. In this chasm there was once an intersecting vein of softer stone, which the waves have gnawed away piecemeal, while the granite walls remain entire on either side. How sharply, and with what harsh clamor, does the sea rake back the pebbles, as it momentarily withdraws into its own depths! At intervals, the floor of the chasm is left nearly dry; but anon, at the outlet, two or three great waves are seen struggling to get in at once; two hit the walls athwart, which one rushes straight through, and all three thunder, as if with rage and triumph. They heap the chasm with a snow-drift of foam and spray. While watching this scene, I can never rid myself of the idea, that a monster, endowed with life and fierce energy, is striving to burst his way through the narrow pass. And what a contrast, to look through the stormy chasm, and catch a glimpse of the calm bright sea beyond!

Many interesting discoveries may be made among these broken cliffs. Once, for example, I found a dead seal, which a recent tempest had tossed into a nook of the rocks, where his shaggy carcass lay rolled in a heap of eel-grass, as if the sea-monster sought to hide himself from my eye. Another time, a shark seemed on the point of leaping from the surf to swallow me; nor did I, wholly without dread, approach near enough to ascertain that the man-eater had already met his own death from some fisherman in the bay. In the same ramble, I encountered a bird—a large grey bird—but whether a loon, or a wild goose, or the identical albatross of the Ancient Mariner, was beyond my ornithology to decide. It reposed so naturally on a bed of dry sea-weed, with its head beside its wing, that I almost fancied it alive, and trod softly lest it should suddenly spread its wings skyward. But the sea-bird would soar among the clouds no more, nor ride upon its native waves; so I drew near, and pulled out one of its mottled tail-feathers for a remembrance. Another day, I discovered an immense bone, wedged into a chasm of the rocks; it was at least ten feet long, curved like a scimitar, bejewelled with barnacles and small shell-fish, and partly covered with a growth of sea-weed. Some leviathan of former ages had used this ponderous mass as a jaw-bone. Curiosities of a minuter order may be observed in a deep reservoir, which is replenished with water at every tide, but becomes a lake among the crags, save when the sea is at its height. At the bottom of this rocky basin grow marine plants, some of which tower high beneath the water, and cast a shadow in the sunshine. Small fishes dart to and fro, and hide themselves among the sea-weed; there is also a solitary crab, who appears to lead the life of a hermit, communing with none of the other denizens of the place; and likewise several five-fingers—for I know no other name than that which children give them. If your imagination be at all accustomed to such freaks, you may look down into the depths of this pool, and fancy it the mysterious depth of ocean. But where are the hulks and scattered timbers of sunken ships?—where the treasures that old Ocean hoards?—where the corroded cannon?—where the corpses and skeletons of seamen, who went down in storm and battle?

On the day of my last ramble, (it was a September day, yet as warm as summer,) what should I behold as I approached the above described basin but three girls sitting on its margin, and—yes, it is veritably so—laving their snowy feet in the sunny water! These, these are the warm realities of those three visionary shapes that flitted from me on the beach. Hark! their merry voices, as they toss up the water with their feet! They have not seen me. I must shrink behind this rock, and steal away again.

In honest truth, vowed to solitude as I am, there is something in the encounter that makes the heart flutter with a strangely pleasant sensation. I know these girls to be realities of flesh and blood, yet, glancing at them so briefly, they mingle like kindred creatures with the ideal beings of my mind. It is pleasant, likewise, to gaze down from some high crag, and watch a group of children, gathering pebbles and pearly shells, and playing with the surf, as with old Ocean's hoary beard. Nor does it infringe upon my seclusion, to see yonder boat at anchor off the shore, swinging dreamily to and fro, and rising and sinking with the alternate swell; while the crew—four gentlemen in round-about jackets—are busy with their fishing-lines. But, with an inward antipathy and a headlong flight, do I eschew the presence of any meditative stroller like myself, known by his pilgrim staff, his sauntering step, his shy demeanour, his observant yet abstracted eye. From such a man, as if another self had scared me, I scramble hastily over the rocks and take refuge in a nook which many a secret hour has given me a right to call my own. I would do battle for it even with the churl that should produce the title-deeds. Have not my musings melted into its rocky walls and sandy floor, and made them a portion of myself?

It is a recess in the line of cliffs, walled round by a rough, high precipice, which almost encircles and shuts in a little space of sand. In front, the sea appears as between the pillars of a portal. In the rear, the precipice is broken and intermixed with earth, which gives nourishment not only to clinging and twining shrubs, but to trees, that grip the rock with their naked roots, and seem to struggle hard for footing and for soil enough to live upon. These are fir trees; but oaks hang their heavy branches from above, and throw down acorns on the beach, and shed their withering foliage upon the waves. At this autumnal season, the precipice is decked with variegated splendor; trailing wreaths of scarlet flaunt from the summit downward; tufts of yellow-flowering shrubs, and rose bushes, with their reddened leaves and glossy seed-berries, sprout from each crevice; at every glance, I detect some new light or shade of beauty, all contrasting with the stern, grey rock. A rill of water trickles down the cliff and fills a little cistern near the base. I drain it at a draught, and find it fresh and pure. This recess shall be my dining-hall. And what the feast? A few biscuits, made savory by soaking them in sea-water, a tuft of samphire gathered from the beach, and an apple for the dessert. By this time, the little rill has filled its reservoir again; and, as I quaff it, I thank God more heartily than for a civic banquet, that He gives me the healthful appetite to make a feast of bread and water.

Dinner being over, I throw myself at length upon the sand, and basking in the sunshine, let my mind disport itself at will. The walls of this my hermitage have no tongue to tell my follies, though I sometimes fancy that they have ears to hear them, and a soul to sympathize. There is a magic in this spot. Dreams haunt its precincts, and flit around me in broad sunlight, nor require that sleep shall blindfold me to real objects, ere these be visible. Here can I frame a story of two lovers, and make their shadows live before me, and be mirrored in the tranquil water, as they tread along the sand, leaving no foot-prints. Here, should I will it, I can summon up a single shade, and be myself her lover. Yes, dreamer,—but your lonely heart will be the colder for such fancies. Sometimes, too, the Past comes back, and finds me here, and in her train come faces which were gladsome, when I knew them, yet seem not gladsome now. Would that my hiding place were lonelier, so that the Past might not find me! Get ye all gone, old friends, and let me listen to the murmur of the sea,—a melancholy voice, but less sad than yours. Of what mysteries is it telling? Of sunken ships, and whereabouts they lie? Of islands afar and undiscovered, whose tawny children are unconscious of other islands and of continents. and deem the stars of heaven their nearest neighbours? Nothing of all this. What then? Has it talked for so many ages, and meant nothing all the while? No; for those ages find utterance in the sea's unchanging voice, and warn the listener to withdraw his interest from mortal vicissitudes, and let the infinite idea of eternity pervade his soul. This is wisdom; and, therefore, will I spend the next half-hour in shaping little boats of drift-wood, and launching them on voyages across the cove, with the feather of a sea-gull for a sail. If the voice of ages tell me true, this is as wise an occupation as to build ships of five hundred tons, and launch them forth upon the main, bound to "far Cathay." Yet, how would the merchant sneer at me!

And, after all, can such philosophy be true? Methinks I could find a thousand arguments against it. Well, then, let yonder shaggy rock, mid-deep in the surf—see! he is somewhat wrathful,—he rages and roars and foams—let that tall rock be my antagonist, and let me exercise my oratory like him of Athens, who bandied words with an angry sea and got the victory. My maiden speech is a triumphant one; for the gentleman in sea-weed has nothing to offer in reply, save an immitigable roaring. His voice, indeed, will be heard a long while after mine is hushed. Once more I shout, and the cliffs reverberate the sound. Oh, what joy for a shy man to feel himself so solitary, that he may lift his voice to its highest pitch without hazard of a listener! But, hush!—be silent, my good friend!—whence comes that stifled laughter? It was musical,—but how should there be such music in my solitude? Looking upwards, I catch a glimpse of three faces, peeping from the summit of the cliff, like angels between me and their native sky. Ah, fair girls, you may make yourselves merry at my eloquence,—but it was my turn to smile when I saw your white feet in the pool! Let us keep each other's secrets.

The sunshine has now passed from my hermitage, except a gleam upon the sand just where it meets the sea. A crowd of gloomy fantasies will come and haunt me, if I tarry longer here, in the darkening twilight of these grey rocks. This is a dismal place in some moods of the mind. Climb we, therefore, the precipice, and pause a moment on the brink, gazing down into that hollow chamber by the deep, where we have been, what few can be, sufficient to our own pastime—yes, say the word outright!—self-sufficient to our own happiness. How lonesome looks the recess now, and dreary too,—like all other spots where happiness has been! There lies my shadow in the departing sunshine with its head upon the sea. I will pelt it with pebbles. A hit! a hit! I clap my hands in triumph, and see my shadow clapping its unreal hands, and claiming the triumph for itself. What a simpleton must I have been all day, since my own shadow makes a mock of my fooleries!

Homeward! homeward! It is time to hasten home. It is time; it is time; for as the sun sinks over the western wave, the sea grows melancholy, and the surf has a saddened tone. The distant sails appear astray, and not of earth, in their remoteness amid the desolate waste. My spirit wanders forth afar, but finds no resting place, and comes shivering back. It is time that I were hence. But grudge me not the day that has been spent in seclusion, which yet was not solitude, since the great sea has been my companion, and the little sea-birds my friends, and the wind has told me his secrets, and airy shapes have flitted around me in my hermitage. Such companionship works an effect upon a man's character, as if he had been admitted to the society of creatures that are not mortal. And when, at noontide, I tread the crowded streets, the influence of this day will still be felt; so that I shall walk among men kindly and as a brother, with affection and sympathy, but yet shall not melt into the indistinguishable mass of humankind. I shall think my own thoughts, and feel my own emotions, and possess my individuality unviolated.

But it is good, at the eve of such a day, to feel and know that there are men and women in the world. That feeling and that knowledge are mine, at this moment; for, on the shore, far below me, the fishing-party have landed from their skiff, and are cooking their scaly prey by a fire of drift-wood, kindled in the angle of two rude rocks. The three visionary girls are likewise there. In the deepening twilight, while the surf is dashing near their hearth, the ruddy gleam of the fire throws a strange air of comfort over the wild cove, bestrewn as it is with pebbles and sea-weed, and exposed to the "melancholy main." Moreover, as the smoke climbs up the precipice, it brings with it a savory smell from a pan of fried fish, and a black kettle of chowder, and reminds me that my dinner was nothing but bread and water, and a tuft of samphire, and an apple. Methinks the party might find room for another guest, at that flat rock which serves them for a table; and if spoons be scarce, I could pick up a clam-shell on the beach. They see me now; and—the blessing of a hungry man upon him!—one of them sends up a hospitable shout—halloo, Sir Solitary! come down and sup with us! The ladies wave their handkerchiefs. Can I decline? No; and be it owned, after all my solitary joys, that this is the sweetest moment of a Day by the Sea-Shore.

Charles Dickens

(1812–1870)

During much of 1860, between the serial publication of A Tale of Two Cities *and* Great Expectations, *Dickens wrote a series of essays and autobiographic sketches called* The Uncommercial Traveller *for his weekly magazine* All the Year Round. *Like its popular predecessor,* Household Words, *this journal had its editorial offices at 26 Wellington, the street bordering the old Flower Market at Covent Garden. Dickens's Traveller is "Uncommercial" (sometimes called just "The Uncommercial") because his affiliation is with "the great house of Human Interest Brothers." "Literally speaking," he explains in the brief opening piece of the series, "I am always wandering here and there from my rooms in Covent Garden . . . seeing many little things, and some great things, which, because they interest me, I think may interest others" ("His General Line of Business"). What interests him in "Night Walks" is the desolate nocturnal scenery of Victorian London: from Covent Garden to "dreary" Waterloo Bridge, then eastward past infamous Newgate Prison with its sleeping inmates and its wretched ghosts of public hangings, on to the Bank of England and down to old Billingsgate Fishmarket, then across London Bridge to the south shore of the Thames, past King's Bench prison for debtors and the enclosed hell of Bethlehem Hospital for the insane (the "bedlam" of ordinary language), across the river again on Westminster Bridge to Parliament and Westminster Abbey, and, finally, by way of Christopher Wren's St. Martin's in the Fields, back to Covent Garden for early coffee and toast, or to a railway terminal for a bit of company as dawn is about to break. One can read Dickens's essay with an old London map in hand—or let his perambulations draw and shade the terrain of the city he knew best. In his lamp-lit look at the dark orchestra pit of an empty theater ("like a great grave dug for a time of pestilence"), or in the macabre "thing" of rags met with on the steps of St. Martin's, one feels the pull into Dickensian fiction. Yet such moments, far from dispersing the essay's speculative impact, energize and concentrate it. One explicitly speculative turn—on how the sane and the insane are levelled at night "as the sane lie dreaming"—not only recalls another essayist, Cowley, on the subject of "Bedlam," but suggests a thematic focus for the Uncommercial's insomniac wanderings through his evocative, haunted and haunting urban landscape.*

Night Walks

Some years ago, a temporary inability to sleep, referable to a distressing impression, caused me to walk about the streets all night, for a series of several nights. The disorder might have taken a long time to conquer, if it had been faintly experimented on in bed; but, it was soon defeated by the brisk treatment of getting up directly after lying down, and going out, and coming home tired at sunrise.

In the course of those nights, I finished my education in a fair amateur experience of houselessness. My principal object being to get through the night, the pursuit of it brought me into sympathetic relations with people who have no other object every night in the year.

The month was March, and the weather damp, cloudy, and cold. The sun not rising before half-past five, the night perspective looked sufficiently long at half-past twelve: which was about my time for confronting it.

The restlessness of a great city, and the way in which it tumbles and tosses before it can get to sleep, formed one of the first entertainments offered to the contemplation of us houseless people. It lasted about two hours. We lost a great deal of companionship when the late public-houses turned their lamps out, and when the potmen thrust the last brawling drunkards into the street; but stray vehicles and stray people were left us, after that. If we were very lucky, a policeman's rattle sprang and a fray turned up; but, in general, surprisingly little of this diversion was provided. Except in the Haymarket, which is the worst kept part of London, and about Kent-street in the Borough, and along a portion of the line of the Old Kent-road, the peace was seldom violently broken. But, it was always the case that London, as if in imitation of individual citizens belonging to it, had expiring fits and starts of restlessness. After all seemed quiet, if one cab rattled by, half-a-dozen would surely follow; and Houselessness even observed that intoxicated people appeared to be magnetically attracted towards each other; so that we knew when we saw one drunken object staggering against the shutters of a shop, that another drunken object would stagger up before five minutes were out, to fraternise or fight with it. When we made a divergence from the regular species of drunkard, the thin-armed, puff-faced, leaden-lipped gin-drinker, and encountered a rarer specimen of a more decent appearance, fifty to one but that specimen was dressed in soiled mourning. As the street experience in the night, so the street experience in the day: the common folk who came unexpectedly into a little property, come unexpectedly into a deal of liquor.

At length these flickering sparks would die away, worn out—the last veritable sparks of waking life trailed from some late pieman or hot-potato man—and London would sink to rest. And then the yearning of the houseless mind would be for any sign of company, any lighted place, any movement, anything suggestive of anyone being up—nay, even so much as awake, for the houseless eye looked out for lights in windows.

Walking the streets under the pattering rain, Houselessness would walk and walk and walk, seeing nothing but the interminable tangle of streets, save at a corner, here and there, two policemen in conversation, or the sergeant or inspector looking after his men. Now and then in the night—but rarely—Houselessness would become aware of a furtive head peering out of a doorway a few yards before him, and, coming up with the head, would find a man standing bolt upright to keep within the doorway's shadow, and evidently intent upon no particular service to society. Under a kind of fascination, and in a ghostly silence suitable to the time, Houselessness and this gentleman would eye one another from head to foot, and so, without exchange of speech, part, mutually suspicious. Drip, drip, drip, from ledge and coping, splash from pipes and water-spouts, and by-and-by the houseless shadow would fall upon the stones that pave the way to Waterloo-bridge; it being in the houseless mind to have a halfpenny worth of excuse for saying "Good-night" to the toll-keeper, and catching a glimpse of his fire. A good fire and a good great-coat and a good woollen neck-shawl, were comfortable things to see in conjunction with the toll-keeper; also his brisk wakefulness was excellent company when he rattled the change of halfpence down upon that metal table of his, like a man who defied the night, with all its sorrowful thoughts, and didn't care for the coming of dawn. There was need of encouragement on the threshold of the bridge, for the bridge was dreary. The chopped-up murder man, had not been lowered with a rope over the parapet when those nights were; he was alive, and slept then quietly enough most likely, and undisturbed by any dream of where he was to come. But the river had an awful look, the buildings on the banks were muffled in black shrouds, and the reflected lights seemed to originate deep in the water, as if the spectres of suicides were holding them to show where they went down. The wild moon and clouds were as restless as an evil conscience in a tumbled bed, and the very shadow of the immensity of London seemed to lie oppressively upon the river.

Between the bridge and the two great theatres, there was but the distance of a few hundred paces, so the theatres came next. Grim and black within, at night, those great dry wells, and lonesome to imagine, with the rows of faces faded out, the lights extinguished, and the seats all empty. One would think that nothing in them knew itself at such a time but Yorick's skull. In one of my night walks, as the church steeples were shaking the March winds and rain with the strokes of Four, I passed the outer boundary of one of these great deserts, and entered it. With a dim lantern in my hand, I groped my well-known way to the stage and looked over the orchestra—which was like a great grave dug for a time of pestilence—into the void beyond. A dismal cavern of an immense aspect, with the chandelier gone dead like everything else, and nothing visible through mist and fog and space, but tiers of winding-sheets. The ground at my feet where, when last there, I had seen the peasantry of Naples dancing among the vines, reckless of the burning mountain which threatened to overwhelm them, was now in possession of a strong serpent of engine-hose, watchfully lying in wait for the serpent Fire, and ready to fly at it if it showed its forked tongue. A ghost of a watchman, carrying a faint corpse candle, haunted the distant upper gallery and flitted away. Retiring within the proscenium, and holding my light above my head towards the rolled-up curtain—green no more, but black as ebony—my sight lost itself in a gloomy vault, showing faint indications in it of a shipwreck of canvas and cordage. Methought I felt much as a diver might, at the bottom of the sea.

In those small hours when there was no movement in the streets, it afforded matter for reflection to take Newgate in the way, and, touching its rough stone, to think of the prisoners in their sleep, and then to glance in at the lodge over the spiked wicket, and see the fire and light of the watching turnkeys, on the white wall. Not an inappropriate time either, to linger by that wicked little Debtors' Door—shutting tighter than any other door one ever saw—which has been Death's Door to so many. In the days of the uttering of forged one-pound notes by people tempted up from the country, how many hundreds of wretched creatures of both sexes—many quite innocent—swung out of a pitiless and inconsistent world, with the tower of yonder Christian church of Saint Sepulchre monstrously before their eyes! Is there any haunting of the Bank Parlour, by the remorseful souls of old directors, in the nights of these later days, I wonder, or is it as quiet as this degenerate Aceldama of an Old Bailey?

To walk on to the Bank, lamenting the good old times and bemoaning the present evil period, would be an easy next step, so I would take it, and would make my houseless circuit of the Bank, and give a thought to the treasure within; likewise to the guard of soldiers passing the night there, and nodding over the fire. Next, I went to Billingsgate, in some hope of market-people, but it proving as yet too early, crossed London-bridge and got down by the water-side on the Surrey shore among the buildings of the great brewery. There was plenty going on at the brewery; and the reek, and the smell of grains, and the rattling of the plump dray horses at their mangers, were capital company. Quite refreshed by having mingled with this good society, I made a new start with a new heart, setting the old King's Bench prison before me for my next object, and resolving, when I should come to the wall, to think of poor Horace Kinch, and the Dry Rot in men.

A very curious disease the Dry Rot in men, and difficult to detect the beginning of. It had carried Horace Kinch inside the wall of the old King's Bench prison, and it had carried him out with his feet foremost. He was a likely man to look at, in the prime of life, well to do, as clever as he needed to be, and popular among many friends. He was suitably married, and had healthy and pretty children. But, like some fair-looking horses or fair-looking ships, he took the Dry Rot. The first strong external revelation of the Dry Rot in men, is a tendency to lurk and lounge; to be at street-corners without intelligible reason; to be going anywhere when met; to be about many places rather than at any; to do nothing tangible, but to have an intention of performing a variety of intangible duties to-morrow or the day after. When this manifestation of the disease is observed, the observer will usually connect it with a vague impression once formed or received, that the patient was living a little too hard. He will scarcely have had leisure to turn it over in his mind and form the terrible suspicion "Dry Rot," when he will notice a change for the worse in the patient's appearance: a certain slovenliness and deterioration, which is not poverty, nor dirt, nor intoxication, nor ill-health, but simply Dry Rot. To this, succeeds a smell as of strong waters, in the morning; to that, a looseness respecting money; to that, a stronger smell as of strong waters, at all times; to that, a looseness respecting everything; to that, a trembling of the limbs, somnolency, misery, and crumbling to pieces. As it is in wood, so it is in men. Dry Rot advances at a compound usury quite incalculable. A plank is found infected with it, and the whole structure is devoted.[1] Thus it had been with the unhappy Horace Kinch, lately buried by a small subscription. Those who knew him had not nigh done saying, "So well off, so comfortably established, with such hope before him—and yet, it is feared, with a slight touch of Dry Rot!" when lo! the man was all Dry Rot and dust.

From the dead wall associated on those houseless nights with this too common story, I chose next to wander by Bethlehem Hospital; partly, because it lay on my road round to Westminster; partly, because I had a night fancy in my head which could be best pursued within sight of its walls and dome. And the fancy was this: Are not the sane and the insane equal at night as the sane lie a dreaming? Are not all of us outside this hospital, who dream, more or less in the condition of those inside it, every night of our lives? Are we not nightly persuaded, as they daily are,

[1] Doomed.

that we associate preposterously with kings and queens, emperors and empresses, and notabilities of all sorts? Do we not nightly jumble events and personages and times and places, as these do daily? Are we not sometimes troubled by our own sleeping inconsistencies, and do we not vexedly try to account for them or excuse them, just as these do sometimes in respect of their waking delusions? Said an afflicted man to me, when I was last in a hospital like this, "Sir, I can frequently fly." I was half ashamed to reflect that so could I—by night. Said a woman to me on the same occasion, "Queen Victoria frequently comes to dine with me, and her Majesty and I dine off peaches and macaroni in our night-gowns, and his Royal Highness the Prince Consort does us the honour to make a third on horseback in a field-marshal's uniform." Could I refrain from reddening with consciousness when I remembered the amazing royal parties I myself had given (at night), the unaccountable viands I had put on table, and my extraordinary manner of conducting myself on those distinguished occasions? I wonder that the great master who knew everything, when he called Sleep the death of each day's life, did not call Dreams the insanity of each day's sanity.

By this time I had left the Hospital behind me, and was again setting towards the river; and in a short breathing space I was on Westminster-bridge, regaling my houseless eyes with the external walls of the British Parliament—the perfection of a stupendous institution, I know, and the admiration of all surrounding nations and succeeding ages, I do not doubt, but perhaps a little the better now and then for being pricked up to its work. Turning off into Old Palace-yard, the Courts of Law kept me company for a quarter of an hour; hinting in low whispers what numbers of people they were keeping awake, and how intensely wretched and horrible they were rendering the small hours to unfortunate suitors. Westminster Abbey was fine gloomy society for another quarter of an hour; suggesting a wonderful procession of its dead among the dark arches and pillars, each century more amazed by the century following it than by all the centuries going before. And indeed in those houseless night walks—which even included cemeteries where watchmen went round among the graves at stated times, and moved the tell-tale handle of an index which recorded that they had touched it at such an hour—it was a solemn consideration what enormous hosts of dead belong to one old great city, and how, if they were raised while the living slept, there would not be the space of a pin's point in all the streets and ways for the living to come out into. Not only that, but the vast armies of dead would overflow the hills and valleys beyond the city, and would stretch away all round it, God knows how far.

When a church clock strikes, on houseless ears in the dead of the night, it may be at first mistaken for company and hailed as such. But, as the spreading circles of vibration, which you may perceive at such a time with great clearness, go opening out, for ever and ever afterwards widening perhaps (as the philosopher has suggested) in eternal space, the mistake is rectified and the sense of loneliness is profounder. Once—it was after leaving the Abbey and turning my face north—I came to the great steps of St. Martin's church as the clock was striking Three. Suddenly, a thing that in a moment more I should have trodden upon without seeing, rose up at my feet with a cry of loneliness and houselessness, struck out of it by the bell, the like of which I never heard. We then stood face to face looking at one another, frightened by one another. The creature was like a beetle-browed hair-lipped youth of twenty, and it had a loose bundle of rags on, which it held together with one of its hands. It shivered from head to foot, and its teeth chattered, and as it stared at me—persecutor, devil, ghost, whatever it thought me—it made with its whining mouth as if it were snapping at me, like a worried dog. Intending to give this ugly object money, I put out my hand to stay it—for it recoiled as it whined and snapped—and laid my hand upon its shoulder. Instantly, it twisted out of its garment, like the young man in the New Testament, and left me standing alone with its rags in my hands.

Covent-garden Market, when it was market morning, was wonderful company. The great waggons of cabbages, with growers' men and boys lying asleep under them, and with sharp dogs from market-garden neighbourhoods looking after the whole, were as good as a party. But one of the worst night sights I know in London, is to be found in the children who prowl about this place; who sleep in the baskets, fight for the offal, dart at any object they think they can lay their thieving hands on, dive under the carts and barrows, dodge the constables, and are perpetually making a blunt pattering of the pavement of the Piazza with the rain of their naked feet. A painful and unnatural result comes of the comparison one is forced to institute between the growth of corruption as displayed in the so much improved and cared for fruits of the earth, and the growth of corruption as displayed in these all uncared for (except inasmuch as ever-hunted) savages.

There was early coffee to be got about Covent-garden Market, and that was more company—warm company, too, which was better. Toast of a very substantial quality, was likewise procurable: though the tousled-headed man who made it, in an inner chamber within the coffee-room, hadn't got his coat on yet, and was so heavy with sleep that in every interval of toast and coffee he went off anew behind the partition into complicated cross-roads of choke and snore, and lost his way directly. Into one of these establishments (among the earliest) near Bow-street, there came one morning as I sat over my houseless cup, pondering where to go next, a man in a high and long snuff-coloured coat, and shoes, and, to the best of my belief, nothing else but a hat, who took out of his hat a large cold meat pudding; a meat pudding so large that it was a very tight fit, and brought the lining of the hat out with it. This mysterious man was known by his pudding, for on his entering, the man of sleep brought him a pint of hot tea, a small loaf, and a large knife and fork and plate. Left to himself in his box, he stood the pudding on the bare table, and, instead of cutting it, stabbed it, overhand, with the knife, like a mortal enemy; then took the knife out, wiped it on his sleeve, tore the pudding asunder with his fingers, and ate it all up. The remembrance of this man with the pudding remains with me as the remembrance of the most spectral person my houselessness encountered. Twice only was I in that establishment, and twice I saw him stalk in (as I should say, just out of bed, and presently going back to bed), take out his pudding, stab his pudding, wipe the dagger, and eat his pudding all up. He was a man whose figure promised cadaverousness, but who had an excessively red face, though shaped like a horse's. On the second occasion of my seeing him, he said huskily to the man of sleep, "Am I red to-night?" "You are," he uncompromisingly answered. "My mother," said the spectre, "was a red-faced woman that liked drink, and I looked at her hard when she laid in her coffin, and I took the complexion." Somehow, the pudding seemed an unwholesome pudding after that, and I put myself in its way no more.

When there was no market, or when I wanted variety, a railway terminus with the morning mails coming in, was remunerative company. But like most of the company to be had in this world, it lasted only a very short time. The station lamps would burst out ablaze, the porters would emerge from places of concealment, the cabs and trucks would rattle to their places (the post-office carts were already in theirs), and, finally, the bell would strike up, and the train would come banging in. But there were few passengers and little luggage, and everything scuttled away with the greatest expedition. The locomotive post-offices, with their great nets—as if they had been dragging the country for bodies—would fly open as to their doors, and would disgorge a smell of lamp, an exhausted clerk, a guard in a red coat, and their bags of letters; the engine would blow and heave and perspire, like an engine wiping its forehead and saying what a run it had had; and within ten minutes the lamps were out, and I was houseless and alone again.

But now, there were driven cattle on the high road near, wanting (as cattle always do) to turn into the midst of stone walls, and squeeze themselves through six inches' width of iron railing, and getting their heads down (also as cattle always do) for tossing-purchase at quite imaginary dogs, and giving themselves and every devoted creature associated with them a most extraordinary amount of unnecessary trouble. Now, too, the conscious gas began to grow pale with the knowledge that daylight was coming, and straggling work-people were already in the streets, and, as waking life had become extinguished with the last pieman's sparks, so it began to be rekindled with the fires of the first street-corner breakfast-sellers. And so by faster and faster degrees, until the last degrees were very fast, the day came, and I was tired and could sleep. And it is not, as I used to think, going home at such times, the least wonderful thing in London, that in the real desert region of the night, the houseless wanderer is alone there. I knew well enough where to find Vice and Misfortune of all kinds, if I had chosen; but they were put out of sight, and my houselessness had many miles upon miles of streets in which it could, and did, have its own solitary way.

Henry David Thoreau
(1817–1862)

> *I thought of you the other afternoon as I was approaching Concord doing fifty on Route 62. . . . As I say, it was a delicious evening. The snake had come out to die in a bloody S on the highway, the wheel upon its head, its bowels flat now and exposed. . . . The evening was full of sounds. . . . Automobiles, skirting a village green, are like flies that have gained the inner ear—they buzz, cease, pause, start, shift, stop, halt, brake, and the whole effect is a nervous polytone curiously disturbing. . . . A fire engine, out for a trial spin, roared past Emerson's house hot with readiness for public duty.*
>
> —*E. B. White, "Walden"*

That was 1939 in Concord, Massachusetts, Thoreau's town and Emerson's, and for some years Hawthorne's residence too. In his imaginary "Dear Henry" letter (half a busy century old by now) White was writing a sardonic endnote to what he called Thoreau's "tale of individual simplicity" of two years' living in the woods near Concord, as reported in the classic Walden. *What he was noting was the triumph of precisely that degradation of life which Thoreau understood as the consequence of "our loose and expensive way of living" (Journal, November 5, 1855) and against which his writing and his life raised their protest. "Let your life be a counter-friction to stop the machine," he had urged in his influential essay "On the Duty of Civil Disobedience" (1849)—meaning by "machine" not only the engine of state, its politics and processes and laws, but also the technological apparatus of a new industrial age and its human cost. More fundamentally, the "machine" suggests the mechanization of living that in "Life Without Principle," he terms "this incessant business" whereby "a man may be very industrious and yet not spend his time well." Thoreau based his essay on his Journal for the years 1850–1854 and was still revising it in the final weeks of his life, weak and dying from tuberculosis. Like the longer magnificent essay of his last years, "Walking," "Life Without Principle" was published posthumously in 1863. It is unmistakably a personal manifesto: an energetic piece of scolding about our unthinking forfeiture of freedom, an inspired "lesson of value" about the human use of time.*

Life Without Principle

At a lyceum, not long since, I felt that the lecturer had chosen a theme too foreign to himself, and so failed to interest me as much as he might have done. He described things not in or near to his heart, but toward his extremities and superficies. There was, in this sense, no truly central or centralizing thought in the lecture. I would have had him deal with his privatest experience, as the poet does. The greatest compliment that was ever paid me was when one asked me what *I thought*, and attended to my answer. I am surprised, as well as delighted, when this happens, it is such a rare use he would make of me, as if he were acquainted with the tool. Commonly, if men want anything of me, it is only to know how many acres I make of their land—since I am a surveyor—or, at most, what trivial news I have burdened myself with. They never will go to law for my meat; they prefer the shell. A man once came a considerable distance to ask me to lecture on slavery; but on conversing with him, I found that he and his clique expected seven eighths of the lecture to be theirs, and only one eighth mine; so I declined. I take it for granted, when I am invited to lecture anywhere—for I have had a little experience in that business—that there is a desire to hear what *I think* on some subject, though I may be the greatest fool in the country—and not that I should say pleasant things merely, or such as the audience will assent to; and I resolve, accordingly, that I will give them a strong dose of myself. They have sent for me, and engaged to pay for me, and I am determined that they shall have me, though I bore them beyond all precedent.

So now I would say something similar to you, my readers. Since *you* are my readers, and I have not been much of a traveller, I will not talk about people a thousand miles off, but come as near home as I can. As the time is short, I will leave out all the flattery, and retain all the criticism.

Let us consider the way in which we spend our lives.

This world is a place of business. What an infinite bustle! I am awaked almost every night by the panting of the locomotive. It interrupts my dreams. There is no sabbath. It would be glorious to see mankind at leisure for once. It is nothing but work, work, work. I cannot easily buy a blank-book to write thoughts in; they are commonly ruled for dollars and cents. An Irishman, seeing me making a minute in the fields, took it for granted that I was calculating my wages. If a man was tossed out of a window when an infant, and so made a cripple for life, or scared out of his wits by the Indians, it is regretted chiefly because he was thus incapacitated for—business! I think that there is nothing, not even crime, more opposed to poetry, to philosophy, ay, to life itself, than this incessant business.

There is a coarse and boisterous money-making fellow in the outskirts of our town, who is going to build a bank-wall under the hill along the edge of his meadow. The powers have put this into his head to keep him out of mischief, and he wishes me to spend three weeks digging there with him. The result will be that he will perhaps get some more money to hoard, and leave for his heirs to spend foolishly. If I do this, most will commend me as an industrious and hard-working man; but if I choose to devote myself to certain labors which yield more real profit, though but little money, they may be inclined to look on me as an idler. Nevertheless, as I do not need the police of meaningless labor to regulate me, and do not see anything absolutely praiseworthy in this fellow's undertaking any more than in many an enterprise of our own or foreign governments, however amusing it may be to him or them, I prefer to finish my education at a different school.

If a man walk in the woods for love of them half of each day, he is in danger of being regarded as a loafer; but if he spends his whole day as a speculator, shearing off those woods and making earth bald before her time, he is esteemed an industrious and enterprising citizen. As if a town had no interest in its forests but to cut them down!

Most men would feel insulted if it were proposed to employ them in throwing stones over a wall, and then in throwing them back, merely that they might earn their wages. But many are no more worthily employed now. For instance: just after sunrise, one summer morning, I noticed one of my neighbors walking beside his team, which was slowly drawing a heavy hewn stone swung under the axle, surrounded by an atmosphere of industry—his day's work begun—his brow commenced to sweat—a reproach to all sluggards and idlers—pausing abreast the shoulders of his oxen, and half turning round with a flourish of his merciful whip, while they gained their length on him. And I thought, Such is the labor which the American Congress exists to protect—honest, manly toil—honest as the day is long—that makes his bread taste sweet, and keeps society sweet—which all men respect and have consecrated; one of the sacred band, doing the needful but irksome drudgery. Indeed, I felt a slight reproach, because I observed this from a window, and was not abroad and stirring about a similar business. The day went by, and at evening I passed the yard of another neighbor, who keeps many servants, and spends much money foolishly, while he adds nothing to the common stock, and there I saw the stone of the morning lying beside a whimsical structure intended to adorn this Lord Timothy Dexter's premises, and the dignity forthwith departed from the teamster's labor, in my eyes. In my opinion, the sun was made to light worthier toil than this. I may add that his employer has since run off, in debt to a good part of the town, and, after passing through Chancery, has settled somewhere else, there to become once more a patron of the arts.

The ways by which you may get money almost without exception lead downward. To have done anything by which you earned money *merely* is to have been truly idle or worse. If the laborer gets no more than the wages which his employer pays him, he is cheated, he cheats himself. If you would get money as a writer or lecturer, you must be popular, which is to go down perpendicularly. Those services which the community will most readily pay for, it is most disagreeable to render. You are paid for being something less than a man. The State does not commonly reward a genius any more wisely. Even the poet laureate would rather not have to celebrate the accidents of royalty. He must be bribed with a pipe of wine; and perhaps another poet is called away from his muse to gauge that very pipe. As for my own business, even the kind of surveying which I could do with most satisfaction my employers do not want. They would prefer that I should do my work coarsely and not too well, ay, not well enough. When I observe that there are different ways of surveying, my employer commonly asks which will give him the most land, not which is most correct. I once invented a rule for measuring cord-wood, and tried to introduce it in Boston; but the measurer there told me that the sellers did not wish to have their wood measured correctly—that he was already too accurate for them, and therefore they commonly got their wood measured in Charlestown before crossing the bridge.

The aim of the laborer should be, not to get his living, to get "a good job," but to perform well a certain work; and, even in a pecuniary sense, it would be economy for a town to pay its laborers so well that they would not feel that they were working for low ends, as for a livelihood merely, but for scientific, or even moral ends. Do not hire a man who does your work for money, but him who does it for love of it.

It is remarkable that there are few men so well employed, so much to their minds, but that a little money or fame would commonly buy them off from their present pursuit. I see advertisements for *active* young men, as if activity were the whole of a young man's capital. Yet I have been surprised when one has with confidence proposed to me, a grown man, to embark in some enterprise of his, as if I had absolutely nothing to do, my life having been a complete failure hitherto. What a doubtful compliment this to pay me! As if he had met me half-way across the ocean beating up against the wind, but bound nowhere, and proposed to me to go along with him! If I did, what do you think the underwriters would say? No, no! I am not without employment at this stage of the voyage. To tell the truth, I saw an advertisement for able-bodied seamen, when I was a boy, sauntering in my native port, and as soon as I came of age I embarked.

The community has no bribe that will tempt a wise man. You may raise money enough to tunnel a mountain, but you cannot raise money enough to hire a man who is minding *his own* business. An efficient and valuable man does what he can, whether the community pay him for it or not. The inefficient offer their inefficiency to the highest bidder, and are forever expecting to be put into office. One would suppose that they were rarely disappointed.

Perhaps I am more than usually jealous with respect to my freedom. I feel that my connection with and obligation to society are still very slight and transient. Those slight labors which afford me a livelihood, and by which it is allowed that I am to some extent serviceable to my contemporaries, are as yet commonly a pleasure to me, and I am not often reminded that they are a necessity. So far I am successful. But I foresee that if my wants should be much increased, the labor required to supply them would become a drudgery. If I should sell both my forenoons and afternoons to society, as most appear to do, I am sure that for me there would be nothing left worth living for. I trust that I shall never thus sell my birthright for a mess of pottage. I wish to suggest that a man may be very industrious, and yet not spend his time well. There is no more fatal blunderer than he who consumes the greater part of his life getting his living. All great enterprises are self-supporting. The poet, for instance, must sustain his body by his poetry, as a steam planing-mill feeds its boilers with the shavings it makes. You must get your living by loving. But as it is said of the merchants that ninety-seven in a hundred fail, so the life of men generally, tried by this standard, is a failure, and bankruptcy may be surely prophesied.

Merely to come into the world the heir of a fortune is not to be born, but to be still-born, rather. To be supported by the charity of friends, or a government pension—provided you continue to breathe—by whatever fine synonyms you describe these relations, is to go into the almshouse. On Sundays the poor debtor goes to church to take an account of stock, and finds, of course, that his outgoes have been greater than his income. In the Catholic Church, especially, they go into chancery, make a clean confession, give up all, and think to start again. Thus men will lie on their backs, talking about the fall of man, and never make an effort to get up.

As for the comparative demand which men make on life, it is an important difference between two, that the one is satisfied with a level success, that his marks can all be hit by point-blank shots, but the other, however low and unsuccessful his life may be, constantly elevates his aim, though at a very slight angle to the horizon. I should much rather be the last man—though, as the Orientals say, "Greatness doth not approach him who is forever looking down; and all those who are looking high are growing poor."

It is remarkable that there is little or nothing to be remembered written on the subject of getting a living; how to make getting a living not merely honest and honorable, but altogether inviting and glorious; for if *getting* a living is not so, then living is not. One would think, from looking at literature, that this question had never disturbed a solitary individual's musings. Is it that men are too much disgusted with their experience to speak of it? The lesson of value which money teaches, which the Author of the Universe has taken so much pains to teach us, we are inclined to skip altogether. As for the means of living, it is wonderful how indifferent men of all classes are about it, even reformers, so called—whether they inherit, or earn, or steal it. I think that Society has done nothing for us in this respect, or at least has undone what she has done. Cold and hunger seem more friendly to my nature than those methods which men have adopted and advise to ward them off.

The title *wise* is, for the most part, falsely applied. How can one be a wise man, if he does not know any better how to live than other men?—if he is only more cunning and intellectually subtle? Does Wisdom work in a tread-mill? or does she teach how to succeed *by her example?* Is there such a thing as wisdom not applied to life? Is she merely the miller who grinds the finest logic? It is pertinent to ask if Plato got his *living* in a better way or more successfully than his contemporaries—or did he succumb to the difficulties of life like other men? Did he seem to prevail over some of them merely by indifference, or by assuming grand airs? or find it easier to live, because his aunt remembered him in her will? The ways in which most men get their living, that is, live, are mere makeshifts, and a shirking of the real business of life—chiefly because they do not know, but partly because they do not mean, any better.

The rush to California, for instance, and the attitude, not merely of the merchants, but of philosophers and prophets, so called, in relation to it, reflect the greatest disgrace on mankind. That so many are ready to live by luck, and so get the means of commanding the labor of others less lucky, without contributing any value to society! And that is called enterprise! I know of no more startling development of the immorality of trade, and all the common modes of getting a living. The philosophy and poetry and religion of such a mankind are not worth the dust of a puffball. The hog that gets his living by rooting, stirring up the soil so, would be ashamed of such company. If I could command the wealth of all the worlds by lifting a finger, I would not pay *such* a price for it. Even Mahomet knew that God did not make this world in jest. It makes God to be a moneyed gentleman who scatters a handful of pennies in order to see mankind scramble for them. The world's raffle! A subsistence in the domains of Nature a thing to be raffled for! What a comment, what a satire, on our institutions! The conclusion will be, that mankind will hang itself upon a tree. And have all the precepts in all the Bibles taught men only this? and is the last and most admirable invention of the human race only an improved muck-rake? Is this the ground on which Orientals and Occidentals meet? Did God direct us so to get our living, digging where we never planted—and He would, perchance, reward us with lumps of gold?

God gave the righteous man a certificate entitling him to food and raiment, but the unrighteous man found a facsimile of the same in God's coffers, and appropriated it, and obtained food and raiment like the former. It is one of the most extensive systems of counterfeiting that the world has seen. I did not know that mankind was suffering for want of gold. I have seen a little of it. I know that it is very malleable, but not so malleable as wit. A grain of gold will gild a great surface, but not so much as a grain of wisdom.

The gold-digger in the ravines of the mountains is as much a gambler as his fellow in the saloons of San Francisco. What difference does it make whether you shake dirt or shake dice? If you win, society is the loser. The gold-digger is the enemy of the honest laborer, whatever checks and compensations there may be. It is not enough to tell me that you worked hard to get your gold. So does the Devil work hard. The way of transgressors may be hard in many respects. The humblest observer who goes to the mines sees and says that gold-digging is of the character of a lottery; the gold thus obtained is not the same thing with the wages of honest toil. But, practically, he forgets what he has seen, for he has seen only the fact, not the principle, and goes into trade there, that is, buys a ticket in what commonly proves another lottery, where the fact is not so obvious.

After reading Howitt's account of the Australian gold-diggings one evening, I had in my mind's eye, all night, the numerous valleys, with their streams, all cut up with foul pits, from ten to one hundred feet deep, and half a dozen feet across, as close as they can be dug, and partly filled with water—the locality to which men furiously rush to probe for their fortunes—uncertain where they shall break ground—not knowing but the gold is under their camp itself—sometimes digging one hundred and sixty feet before they strike the vein, or then missing it by a foot—turned into demons, and regardless of each others' rights, in their thirst for riches—whole valleys, for thirty miles, suddenly honeycombed by the pits of the miners, so that even hundreds are drowned in them—standing in water, and covered with mud and clay, they work night and day, dying of exposure and disease. Having read this, and partly forgotten it, I was thinking, accidentally, of my own unsatisfactory life, doing as others do; and with that vision of the diggings still before me, I asked myself why *I* might not be washing some gold daily, though it were only the finest particles—why *I* might not sink a shaft down to the gold within me, and work that mine. *There* is a Ballarat, a Bendigo for you—what though it were a sulky-gully? At any rate, I might pursue some path, however solitary and narrow and crooked, in which I could walk with love and reverence. Wherever a man separates from the multitude, and goes his own way in this mood, there indeed is a fork in the road, though ordinary travellers may see only a gap in the paling. His solitary path across lots will turn out the *higher way* of the two.

Men rush to California and Australia as if the true gold were to be found in that direction; but that is to go to the very opposite extreme to where it lies. They go prospecting farther and farther away from the true lead, and are most unfortunate when they think themselves most successful. Is not our *native* soil auriferous? Does not a stream from the golden mountains flow through our native valley? and has not this for more than geologic ages been bringing down the shining particles and forming the nuggets for us? Yet, strange to tell, if a digger steal away, prospecting for this true gold, into the unexplored solitudes around us, there is no danger that any will dog his steps, and endeavor to supplant him. He may claim and undermine the whole valley even, both the cultivated and the uncultivated portions, his whole life long in peace, for no one will ever dispute his claim. They will not mind his cradles or his toms. He is not confined to a claim twelve feet square, as at Ballarat, but may mine anywhere, and wash the whole wide world in his tom.

Howitt says of the man who found the great nugget which weighed twenty-eight pounds, at the Bendigo diggings in Australia: "He soon began to drink; got a horse, and rode all about, generally at full gallop, and, when he met people, called out to inquire if they knew who he was, and then kindly informed them that he was 'the bloody wretch that had found the nugget.' At last he rode full speed against a tree, and nearly knocked his brains out." I think, however, there was no danger of that, for he had already knocked his brains out against the nugget. Howitt adds, "He is a hopelessly ruined man." But he is a type of the class. They are all fast men. Hear some of the names of the places where they dig: "Jackass Flat"—"Sheep's-Head Gully"—"Murderer's Bar," etc. Is there no satire in these names? Let them carry their ill-gotten wealth where they will, I am thinking it will still be "Jackass Flat," if not "Murderer's Bar," where they live.

The last resource of our energy has been the robbing of graveyards on the Isthmus of Darien, an enterprise which appears to be but in its infancy; for, according to late accounts, an act has passed its second reading in the legislature of New Granada, regulating this kind of mining; and a correspondent of the "*Tribune*" writes: "In the dry season, when the weather will permit of the country being properly prospected, no doubt other rich *guacas*[1] will be found." To emigrants he says: "do not come before December; take the Isthmus route in preference to the Boca del Toro one; bring no useless baggage, and do not cumber yourself with a tent; but a good pair of blankets will be necessary; a pick, shovel, and axe of good material will be almost all that is required": advice which might have been taken from the "Burker's Guide." And he concludes with this line in italics and small capitals: "*If you are doing well at home,* STAY THERE," which may fairly be interpreted to mean, "If you are getting a good living by robbing graveyards at home, stay there."

But why go to California for a text? She is a child of New England, bred at her own school and church.

It is remarkable that among all the preachers there are so few moral teachers. The prophets are employed in excusing the ways of men. Most reverend seniors, the *illuminati* of the age, tell me, with a gracious, reminiscent smile, betwixt an aspiration and a shudder, not to be too tender about these things—to lump all that, that is, make a lump of gold of it. The highest advice I have heard on these subjects was grovelling. The burden of it was—It is not worth your while to undertake to reform the world in this particular. Do not ask how your bread is buttered; it will make you sick, if you do—and the like. A man had better starve at once than lose his innocence in the process of getting his bread. If within the sophisticated man there is not an unsophisticated one, then he is but one of the devil's angels. As we grow old, we live more coarsely, we relax a little in our disciplines, and, to some extent, cease to obey our finest instincts. But we should be fastidious to the extreme of sanity, disregarding the gibes of those who are more unfortunate than ourselves.

In our science and philosophy, even, there is commonly no true and absolute account of things. The spirit of sect and bigotry has planted its hoof amid the stars. You have only to discuss the problem, whether the stars are inhabited or not, in order to discover it. Why must we daub the heavens as well as the earth? It was an unfortunate discovery that Dr. Kane was a Mason, and that Sir John Franklin was another. But it was a more cruel suggestion that possibly that was the reason why the former went in search of the latter. There is not a popular magazine in this country that would dare to print a child's thought on important subjects without comment. It must be submitted to the D.D.'s. I would it were the chickadee-dees.

You come from attending the funeral of mankind to attend to a natural phenomenon. A little thought is sexton to all the world.

I hardly know an *intellectual* man, even, who is so broad and truly liberal that you can think aloud in his society. Most with whom you

[1] Graveyards.

endeavor to talk soon come to a stand against some institution in which they appear to hold stock—that is, some particular, not universal, way of viewing things. They will continually thrust their own low roof, with its narrow skylight, between you and the sky, when it is the unobstructed heavens you would view. Get out of the way with your cobwebs; wash your windows, I say! In some lyceums they tell me that they have voted to exclude the subject of religion. But how do I know what their religion is, and when I am near to or far from it? I have walked into such an arena and done my best to make a clean breast of what religion I have experienced, and the audience never suspected what I was about. The lecture was as harmless as moonshine to them. Whereas, if I had read to them the biography of the greatest scamps in history, they might have thought that I had written the lives of the deacons of their church. Ordinarily, the inquiry is, Where did you come from? or, Where are you going? That was a more pertinent question which I overheard one of my auditors put to another one—"What does he lecture for?" It made me quake in my shoes.

To speak impartially, the best men that I know are not serene, a world in themselves. For the most part, they dwell in forms, and flatter and study effect only more finely than the rest. We select granite for the underpinning of our houses and barns; we build fences of stone; but we do not ourselves rest on an underpinning of granitic truth, the lowest primitive rock. Our sills are rotten. What stuff is the man made of who is not coexistent in our thought with the purest and subtlest truth? I often accuse my finest acquaintances of an immense frivolity; for, while there are manners and compliments we do not meet, we do not teach one another the lessons of honesty and sincerity that the brutes do, or of steadiness and solidity that the rocks do. The fault is commonly mutual, however; for we do not habitually demand any more of each other.

That excitement about Kossuth, consider how characteristic, but superficial, it was!—only another kind of politics or dancing. Men were making speeches to him all over the country, but each expressed only the thought, or the want of thought, of the multitude. No man stood on truth. They were merely banded together, as usual one leaning on another, and all together on nothing; as the Hindoos made the world rest on an elephant, the elephant on a tortoise, and the tortoise on a serpent, and had nothing to put under the serpent. For all fruit of that stir we have the Kossuth hat.

Just so hollow and ineffectual, for the most part, is our ordinary conversation. Surface meets surface. When our life ceases to be inward and private, conversation degenerates into mere gossip. We rarely meet a man who can tell us any news which he has not read in a newspaper, or been told by his neighbor; and, for the most part, the only difference between us and our fellow is that he has seen the newspaper, or been out to tea, and we have not. In proportion as our inward life fails, we go more constantly and desperately to the post-office. You may depend on it, that the poor fellow who walks away with the greatest number of letters, proud of his extensive correspondence, has not heard from himself this long while.

I do not know but it is too much to read one newspaper a week. I have tried it recently, and for so long it seems to me that I have not dwelt in my native region. The sun, the clouds, the snow, the trees say not so much to me. You cannot serve two masters. It requires more than a day's devotion to know and to possess the wealth of the day.

We may well be ashamed to tell what things we have read or heard in our day. I did not know why my news should be so trivial—considering what one's dreams and expectations are, why the developments should be so paltry. The news we hear, for the most part, is not news to our genius. It is the stalest repetition. You are often tempted to ask why such stress is laid on a particular experience which you have had—that, after twenty-five years, you should meet Hobbins, Registrar of Deeds, again on the sidewalk. Have you not budged an inch, then? Such is the daily news. Its facts appear to float in the atmosphere, insignificant as the sporules of fungi, and impinge on some neglected *thallus*, or surface of our minds, which affords a basis for them, and hence a parasitic growth. We should wash ourselves clean of such news. Of what consequence, though our planet explode, if there is no character involved in the explosion? In health we have not the least curiosity about such events. We do not live for idle amusement. I would not run round a corner to see the world blow up.

All summer, and far into the autumn, perchance, you unconsciously went by the newspapers and the news, and now you find it was because the morning and the evening were full of news to you. Your walks were full of incidents. You attended, not to the affairs of Europe, but to your own affairs in Massachusetts fields. If you chance to live and move and have your being in that thin stratum in which the events that make the news transpire—thinner than the paper on which it is printed—then these things will fill the world for you; but if you soar above or dive below that plane, you cannot remember nor be reminded of them. Really to see the sun rise or go down every day, so to relate ourselves to a universal fact, would preserve us sane forever. Nations! What are nations? Tartars, and Huns, and Chinamen! Like insects, they swarm. The historian strives in vain to make them memorable. It is for want of a man that there are so many men. It is individuals that populate the world. Any man thinking may say with the Spirit of Lodin—

I look down from my height on nations,
And they become ashes before me;—
Calm is my dwelling in the clouds;
Pleasant are the great fields of my rest.

Pray, let us live without being drawn by dogs, Esquimaux-fashion, tearing over hill and dale, and biting each other's ears.

Not without a slight shudder at the danger, I often perceive how near I had come to admitting into my mind the details of some trivial affair—the news of the street; and I am astonished to observe how willing men are to lumber their minds with such rubbish—to permit idle rumors and incidents of the most insignificant kind to intrude on ground which should be sacred to thought. Shall the mind be a public arena, where the affairs of the street and the gossip of the tea-table chiefly are discussed? Or shall it be a quarter of heaven itself—an hypæthral temple, consecrated to the service of the gods? I find it so difficult to dispose of the few facts which to me are significant, that I hesitate to burden my attention with those which are insignificant, which only a divine mind could illustrate. Such is, for the most part, the news in newspapers and conversation. It is important to preserve the mind's chastity in this respect. Think of admitting the details of a single case of the criminal court into our thoughts, to stalk profanely through their very *sanctum sanctorum* for an hour, ay, for many hours! to make a very barroom of the mind's inmost apartment, as if for so long the dust of the street had occupied us—the very street itself, with all its travel, its bustle, and filth, had passed through our thoughts' shrine! Would it not be an intellectual and moral suicide? When I have been compelled to sit spectator and auditor in a court-room for some hours, and have seen my neighbors, who were not compelled, stealing in from time to time, and tiptoeing about with washed hands and faces, it has appeared to my mind's eye, that, when they took off their hats, their ears suddenly expanded into vast hoppers for sound, between which even their narrow heads were crowded. Like the vanes of windmills, they caught the broad but shallow stream of sound, which, after a few titillating gyrations in their coggy brains, passed out the other side. I wondered if, when they got home, they were as careful to wash their ears as before their hands and faces. It has seemed to me, at such a time, that the auditors and the witnesses, the jury and the counsel, the judge and the criminal at the bar—if I may presume him guilty before he is convicted—were all equally criminal, and a thunderbolt might be expected to descend and consume them all together.

By all kinds of traps and signboards, threatening the extreme penalty of the divine law, exclude such trespassers from the only ground which can be sacred to you. It is so hard to forget what it is worse than useless to remember! If I am to be a thoroughfare, I prefer that it be of the mountain brooks, the Parnassian streams, and not the town sewers. There is inspiration, that gossip which comes to the ear of the attentive mind from the courts of heaven. There is the profane and sale revelation of the barroom and the police court. The same ear is fitted to receive both communications. Only the character of the hearer determines to which it shall be open, and to which closed. I believe that the mind can be permanently profaned by the habit of attending to trivial things, so that all our thoughts shall be tinged with triviality. Our very intellect shall be macadamized, as it were—its foundation broken into fragments for the wheels of travel to roll over; and if you would know what will make the most durable pavement, surpassing rolled stones, spruce blocks, and asphaltum, you have only to look into some of our minds which have been subjected to this treatment for so long.

If we have thus desecrated ourselves—as who has not?—the remedy will be by wariness and devotion to reconsecrate ourselves, and make once more a fane of the mind. We should treat our minds, that is, ourselves, as innocent and ingenuous children, whose guardians we are, and be careful what objects and what subjects we thrust on their attention. Read not the Times. Read the Eternities. Conventionalities are at length as bad as impurities. Even the facts of science may dust the mind by their dryness, unless they are in a sense effaced each morning, or rather rendered fertile by the dews of fresh and living truth. Knowledge does not come to us by details, but in flashes of light from heaven. Yes, every thought that passes through the mind helps to wear and tear it, and to deepen the ruts, which, as in the streets of Pompeii, evince how much it has been used. How many things there are concerning which we might well deliberate whether we had better know them—had better let their peddling-carts be driven, even at the slowest trot or walk, over that bridge of glorious span by which we trust to pass at last from the farthest brink of time to the nearest shore of eternity! Have we no culture, no refinement—but skill only to live coarsely and serve the Devil?—to acquire a little worldly wealth, or fame, or liberty, and make a false show with it, as if we were all husk and shell, with no tender and living kernel to us? Shall our institutions be like those chestnut burs which contain abortive nuts, perfect only to prick the fingers?

America is said to be the arena on which the battle of freedom is to be fought, but surely it cannot be freedom in a merely political sense that is meant. Even if we grant that the American has freed himself from a political tyrant, he is still the slave of an economical and moral tyrant. Now that the republic—the *res-publica*—has been settled, it is time to look after these *res-privata*—the private state—to see, as the Roman senate charged its consuls, "*ne quid res*-privata *detrimenti caperet*," that the *private* state receive no detriment.

Do we call this the land of the free? What is it to be free from King George and continue the slaves of King Prejudice? What is it to be born free and not to live free? What is the value of any political freedom, but as a means to moral freedom? Is it a freedom to be slaves, or a freedom to be free, of which we boast? We are a nation of politicians, concerned about the outmost defences only of freedom. It is our children's children who may perchance be really free. We tax ourselves unjustly. There is a part of us which is not represented. It is taxation without representation. We quarter troops, we quarter fools and cattle of all sorts upon ourselves. We quarter our gross bodies on our poor souls, till the former eat up all the latter's substance.

With respect to a true culture and manhood, we are essentially provincial still, not metropolitan—mere Jonathans. We are provincial, because we do not find at home our standards; because we do not worship truth, but the reflection of truth; because we are warped and narrowed by an exclusive devotion to trade and commerce and manufactures and agriculture and the like, which are but means, and not the end.

So is the English Parliament provincial. Mere country bumpkins, they betray themselves, when any important question arises for them to settle, the Irish question, for instance—the English question why did I not say? Their natures are subdued to what they work in. Their "good breeding" respects only secondary objects. The finest manners in the world are awkwardness and fatuity when contrasted with a finer intelligence. They appear but as the fashions of past days—mere courtliness, knee-buckles and small-clothes, out of date. It is the vice, but not the excellence of manners, that they are continually being deserted by the character; they are cast-off-clothes or shells, claiming the respect which belonged to the living creature. You are presented with the shells instead of the meat, and it is no excuse generally, that, in the case of some fishes, the shells are of more worth than the meat. The man who thrusts his manners upon me does as if he were to insist on introducing me to his cabinet of curiosities, when I wished to see himself. It was not in this sense that the poet Decker called Christ "the first true gentleman that ever breathed." I repeat that in this sense the most splendid court in Christendom is provincial, having authority to consult about Transalpine interests only, and not the affairs of Rome. A prætor or proconsul would suffice to settle the questions which absorb the attention of the English Parliament and the American Congress.

Government and legislation! these I thought were respectable professions. We have heard of heaven-born Numas, Lycurguses, and Solons, in the history of the world, whose *names* at least may stand for ideal legislators; but think of legislating to *regulate* the breeding of slaves, or the exportation of tobacco! What have divine legislators to do with the exportation or the importation of tobacco? what humane ones with the breeding of slaves? Suppose you were to submit the question to any son of God—and has He no children in the nineteenth century? is it a family which is extinct?—in what condition would you get it again? What shall a state like Virginia say for itself at the last day, in which these have been the principal, the staple productions? What ground is there for patriotism in such a state? I derive my facts from statistical tables which the states themselves have published.

A commerce that whitens every sea in quest of nuts and raisins, and makes slaves of its sailors for this purpose! I saw, the other day, a vessel which had been wrecked, and many lives lost, and her cargo of rags, juniper berries, and bitter almonds were strewn along the shore. It seemed hardly worth the while to tempt the dangers of the sea between Leghorn and New York for the sake of a cargo of juniper berries and bitter almonds. America sending to the Old World for her bitters! Is not the sea-brine, is not shipwreck, bitter enough to make the cup of life go down here? Yet such, to a great extent, is our boasted commerce; and there are those who style themselves statesmen and philosophers who are so blind as to think that progress and civilization depend on precisely this kind of interchange and activity—the activity of flies about a molasses-hogshead. Very well, observes one, if men were oysters. And very well, answer I, if men were mosquitoes.

Lieutenant Herndon, whom the government sent to explore the Amazon, and, it is said, to extend the area of slavery, observed that there was wanting there "an industrious and active population, who know what the comforts of life are, and who have artificial wants to draw out the great resources of the country." But what are the "artificial wants" to be encouraged? Not the love of luxuries, like the tobacco and slaves of, I believe, his native Virginia, nor the ice and granite and other material wealth of our native New England; nor are "the great resources of a country" that fertility or barrenness of soil which produces these. The chief want, in every state that I have been into, was a high and earnest purpose in its inhabitants. This alone draws out "the great resources" of Nature, and at last taxes her beyond her resources; for man naturally dies out of her. When we want culture more than potatoes, and illumination more than sugar-plums, then the great resources of a world are taxed and drawn out, and the result, or staple production, is, not slaves, nor operatives, but men—those rare fruits called heroes, saints, poets, philosophers, and redeemers.

In short, as a snow-drift is formed where there is a lull in the wind, so, one would say, where there is a lull of truth, an institution springs up. But the truth blows right on over it, nevertheless, and at length blows it down.

What is called politics is comparatively something so superficial and inhuman, that practically I have never fairly recognized that it concerns me at all. The newspapers, I perceive, devote some of their columns specially to politics or government without charge; and this, one would say, is all that saves it; but as I love literature and to some extent the truth also, I never read those columns at any rate. I do not wish to blunt my sense of right so much. I have not got to answer for having read a single President's Message. A strange age of the world this, when empires, kingdoms, and republics come a-begging to a private man's door, and utter their complaints at his elbow! I cannot take up a newspaper but I find that some wretched government or other, hard pushed and on its last legs, is interceding with me, the reader, to vote for it—more importunate than an Italian beggar; and if I have a mind to look at its certificate, made, perchance, by some benevolent merchant's clerk, or the skipper that brought it over, for it cannot speak a word of English itself, I shall probably read of the eruption of some Vesuvius, or the overflowing of some Po, true or forged, which brought it into this condition. I do not hesitate, in such a case, to suggest work, or the almshouse; or why not keep its castle in silence, as I do commonly? The poor president, what with preserving his popularity and doing his duty, is completely bewildered. The newspapers are the ruling power. Any other government is reduced to a few marines at Fort Independence. If a man neglects to read the Daily Times, government will go down on its knees to him, for this is the only treason these days.

Those things which now most engage the attention of men, as politics and the daily routine, are, it is true, vital functions of human society, but should be unconsciously performed, like the corresponding functions of the physical body. They are *infra*-human, a kind of vegetation. I sometimes awake to a half-consciousness of them going on about me, as a man may become conscious of some of the processes of digestion in a morbid state, and so have the dyspepsia, as it is called. It is as if a thinker submitted himself to be rasped by the great gizzard of creation. Politics is, as it were, the gizzard of society, full of grit and gravel, and the two political parties are its two opposite halves—sometimes split into quarters, it may be, which grind on each other. Not only individuals, but states, have thus a confirmed dyspepsia, which expresses itself, you can imagine by what sort of eloquence. Thus our life is not altogether a forgetting, but also, alas! to a great extent, a remembering, of that which we should never have been conscious of, certainly not in our waking hours. Why should we not meet, not always as dyspeptics, to tell our bad dreams, but sometimes as *eu*peptics, to congratulate each other on the ever-glorious morning? I do not make an exorbitant demand, surely.

Mark Twain

(1835–1910)

It's unusual to come upon an essay whose opening sentence situates it so pointedly in its author's life and times as this one: "Fifty years ago, when I was a boy of fifteen and helping to inhabit a Missourian village on the banks of the Mississippi. . . ." The village was the Hannibal of Samuel Clemens's (alias Mark Twain's) youth, a little farmers' market town "drowsing in the sunshine of a summer's morning" on the western bank of "the great Mississippi, the majestic, the magnificent Mississippi, rolling its mile-wide tide along, shining in the sun." In "Old Times on the Mississippi," the early autobiographical essay (1875) from which this luminous snapshot comes, Mark Twain recounts his boyhood fantasy of piloting a steamboat on the great river. His reminiscence evokes all the hopeful ardor of life in a pre-industrial, freewheeling, unbounded America dreaming its way westward. By 1900, the United States had passed through its hungrily expansionist century and closed it with a measure of doubt and disenchantment; Mark Twain, beloved American funny man, satirist, traveler, and talker, author of Tom Sawyer, Huckleberry Finn, *and much else, was sixty-five years old. After half a century, this writer who had championed democracy, even seemed to embody it in its peculiarly American version, was hammering away at what looked to him like the rotten foundation not only of democracy but all rational human endeavor: human nature itself. "This grotesque folly," he called it in a letter to his friend, the novelist William Dean Howells. "Why was the human race created? Or at least why wasn't something creditable created in place of it?" (January 25, 1900). We live by no law of reason (not even rational self-interest of the kind preached by Hannibal's young "corn-pone" philosopher), but by the "petrified habit" that drives us like instinct, by a thought that "walks in its sleep" ("What Is Man?" 1906). Nor were these just the formulae of misanthropy precipitated by old age. "I can snip out of the* Times," *Twain added in a chipper postscript to his Howell letter, "various examples and sidelights that bring the race down to date and expose it as of yesterday." This happened to be the London* Times.

Corn-pone Opinions

Fifty years ago, when I was a boy of fifteen and helping to inhabit a Missourian village on the banks of the Mississippi, I had a friend whose society was very dear to me because I was forbidden by my mother to partake of it. He was a gay and impudent and satirical and delightful young black man—a slave—who daily preached sermons from the top of his master's woodpile, with me for sole audience. He imitated the pulpit style of the several clergymen of the village, and did it well, and with fine passion and energy. To me he was a wonder. I believed he was the greatest orator in the United States and would someday be heard from. But it did not happen; in the distribution of rewards he was overlooked. It is the way, in this world.

He interrupted his preaching, now and then, to saw a stick of wood; but the sawing was a pretense—he did it with his mouth; exactly imitating the sound the bucksaw makes in shrieking its way through the wood. But it served its purpose; it kept his master from coming out to see how the work was getting along. I listened to the sermons from the open window of a lumber room at the back of the house. One of his texts was this:

"You tell me whar a man gits his corn pone, en I'll tell you what his 'pinions is."

I can never forget it. It was deeply impressed upon me. By my mother. Not upon my memory, but elsewhere. She had slipped in upon me while I was absorbed and not watching. The black philosopher's idea was that a man is not independent, and cannot afford views which might interfere with his bread and butter. If he would prosper, he must train with the majority; in matters of large moment, like politics and religion, he must think and feel with the bulk of his neighbors, or suffer damage in his social standing and in his business prosperities. He must restrict himself to corn-pone opinions—at least on the surface. He must get his opinions from other people; he must reason out none for himself; he must have no first-hand views.

I think Jerry was right, in the main, but I think he did not go far enough.

1. It was his idea that a man conforms to the majority view of his locality by calculation and intention.

This happens, but I think it is not the rule.

2. It was his idea that there is such a thing as a first-hand opinion; an original opinion; an opinion which is coldly reasoned out in a man's head, by a searching analysis of the facts involved, with the heart unconsulted, and the jury room closed against outside influences. It may be that such an opinion has been born somewhere, at some time or other,

but I suppose it got away before they could catch it and stuff it and put it in the museum.

I am persuaded that a coldly-thought-out and independent verdict upon a fashion in clothes, or manners, or literature, or politics, or religion, or any other matter that is projected into the field of our notice and interest, is a most rare thing—if it has indeed ever existed.

A new thing in costume appears—the flaring hoopskirt, for example—and the passers-by are shocked, and the irreverent laugh. Six months later everybody is reconciled; the fashion has established itself; it is admired, now, and no one laughs. Public opinion resented it before, public opinion accepts it now, and is happy in it. Why? Was the resentment reasoned out? Was the acceptance reasoned out? No. The instinct that moves to conformity did the work. It is our nature to conform; it is a force which not many can successfully resist. What is its seat? The inborn requirement of self-approval. We all have to bow to that; there are no exceptions. Even the woman who refuses from the first to last to wear the hoopskirt comes under that law and is its slave; she could not wear the skirt and have her own approval; and that she *must* have, she cannot help herself. But as a rule our self-approval has its source in but one place and not elsewhere—the approval of other people. A person of vast consequences can introduce any kind of novelty in dress and the general world will presently adopt it—moved to do it, in the first place, by the natural instinct to passively yield to that vague something recognized as authority, and in the second place by the human instinct to train with the multitude and have its approval. An empress introduced the hoopskirt, and we know the result. A nobody introduced the bloomer, and we know the result. If Eve should come again, in her ripe renown, and reintroduce her quaint styles—well, we know what would happen. And we should be cruelly embarrassed, along at first.

The hoopskirt runs its course and disappears. Nobody reasons about it. One woman abandons the fashion; her neighbor notices this and follows her lead; this influences the next woman; and so on and so on, and presently the skirt has vanished out of the world, no one knows how nor why, nor cares, for that matter. It will come again, by and by; and in due course will go again.

Twenty-five years ago, in England, six or eight wine glasses stood grouped by each person's plate at a dinner party, and they were used, not left idle and empty; to-day there are but three or four in the group, and the average guest sparingly uses about two of them. We have not adopted this new fashion yet, but we shall do it presently. We shall not think it out; we shall merely conform, and let it go at that. We get our notions and habits and opinions from outside influences; we do not have to study them out.

Our table manners, and company manners, and street manners change from time to time, but the changes are not reasoned out; we merely notice and conform. We are creatures of outside influences; as a rule we do not think, we only imitate. We cannot invent standards that will stick; what we mistake for standards are only fashions, and perishable. We may continue to admire them, but we drop the use of them. We notice this in literature. Shakespeare is a standard, and fifty years ago we used to write tragedies which we couldn't tell from—from somebody else's; but we don't do it anymore, now. Our prose standard, three quarters of a century ago, was ornate and diffuse; some authority or other changed it in the direction of compactness and simplicity, and conformity followed, without argument. The historical novel starts up suddenly, and sweeps the land. Everybody writes one, and the nation is glad. We had historical novels before; but nobody read them, and the rest of us conformed—without reasoning it out. We are conforming in the other way, now, because it is another case of everybody.

The outside influences are always pouring in upon us, and we are always obeying their orders and accepting their verdicts. The Smiths like the new play; the Joneses go to see it, and they copy the Smith verdict. Morals, religions, politics, get their following from surrounding influences and atmospheres, almost entirely; not from study, not from thinking. A man must and will have his own approval first of all, in each and every moment and circumstance of his life—even if he must repent of a self-approved act the moment after its commission, in order to get his self-approval *again:* but, speaking in general terms, a man's self-approval in the large concerns of life has its source in the approval of the peoples about him, and not in a searching personal examination of the matter. Mohammedans are Mohammedans because they are born and reared among that sect, not because they have thought it out and can furnish sound reasons for being Mohammedans; we know why Catholics are Catholics; why Presbyterians are Presbyterians; why Baptists are Baptists; why Mormons are Mormons; why thieves are thieves; why monarchists are monarchists; why Republicans are Republicans and Democrats, Democrats. We know it is a matter of association and sympathy, not reasoning and examination; that hardly a man in the world has an opinion upon morals, politics, or religion which he got otherwise than through his associations and sympathies. Broadly speaking, there are none but corn-pone opinions. And broadly speaking, corn-pone stands for self-approval. Self-approval is acquired mainly from the approval of other people. The result is conformity. Sometimes conformity has a sordid business interest—the bread-and-butter interest—but not in most cases, I think. I think that in the majority of cases it is unconscious and not calculated; that it is born of the human being's natural yearning to stand well with his fellows and have their inspiring approval and praise—a yearning which is commonly so strong and so insistent that it cannot be effectually resisted, and must have its way.

A political emergency brings out the corn-pone opinion in fine force in its two chief varieties—the pocketbook variety, which has its origin in self-interest, and the bigger variety, the sentimental variety—the one which can't bear to be outside the pale; can't bear to be in disfavor; can't endure the averted face and the cold shoulder; wants to stand well with his friends, wants to be smiled upon, wants to be welcome, wants to hear the precious words, "*He's* on the right track!" Uttered, perhaps by an ass, but still an ass of high degree, an ass whose approval is gold and diamonds to a smaller ass, and confers glory and honor and happiness, and membership in the herd. For these gauds many a man will dump his life-long principles into the street, and his conscience along with them. We have seen it happen. In some millions of instances.

Men think they think upon great political questions, and they do; but they think with their party, not independently; they read its literature, but not that of the other side; they arrive at convictions, but they are drawn from a partial view of the matter in hand and are of no particular value. They swarm with their party, they feel with their party, they are happy in their party's approval; and where the party leads they will follow, whether for right and honor, or through blood and dirt and a mush of mutilated morals.

In our late canvass half of the nation passionately believed that in silver lay salvation, the other half as passionately believed that that way lay destruction. Do you believe that a tenth part of the people, on either side, had any rational excuse for having an opinion about the matter at all? I studied that mighty question to the bottom—came out empty. Half of our people passionately believe in high tariff, the other half believe otherwise. Does this mean study and examination, or only feeling? The latter, I think. I have deeply studied that question, too—and didn't arrive. We all do no end of feeling, and we mistake it for thinking. And out of it we get an aggregation which we consider a boon. Its name is Public Opinion. It is held in reverence. It settles everything. Some think it the Voice of God.

Alice Meynell

(1847–1922)

Like friendship, truth, and the other timeless subjects, solitude has been a standby of essay writing. Alice Meynell's subject differs by a single letter: "Solitudes" (1928). Her plurality of solitudes implies a conceptual shift; the ready structural path (enumeration by kind) is discarded without a second look. So, too, the occasionally dense sentence, the elliptical summation, the startlingly chosen word, force a more careful pace, a dislocation from the preconceived and the obvious. The language of this neglected writer—poet, essayist, editor, mother of seven forever ducking under and around the table on which she wrote—has been described as having the "elaborate finish" of works wrought "with an etching pen" (Victoria Sackville-West, introducing Alice Meynell: Prose and Poetry). *It is a language to be read close up, as she read others. Charlotte Brontë, for instance, whom she admired but whom she saw as sometimes guarding, to her own detriment, the high latinisms of august male predecessors in the realm of style: "She practiced those verbs 'to evince,' 'to reside,' 'to intimate,' 'to peruse.' . . . She wrote 'communicating instruction' for teaching" ("The Brontës"). Meynell studies writing as minutely as eyelids, "beautiful, eloquent, full of secrets" ("Eyes"). Even the clichés of language may be teased back into vitality, as she does here, in the case of that favorite vague slur on another's style, "thin": "If it is true that in many of Christina Rossetti's lighter poems the fine quality is thin, you do not call the thinnest beaten gold a cheap thing" ("Christina Rossetti"). Writing, she knows, may serve needs greater than those of stylistic effect, as in the case of the man who authored the* Rambler: *"Johnson feared death. Did his noble English control postpone the terror?" ("Composure"). Yet, if writing has power to tender such comforts in and to all our solitudes, it also partakes of the violence of "life broken open, edited, and published" ("The Colors of Life").*

Solitudes

The wild man is alone when he wills, and so is the man for whom civilization has been kind. But there are the multitudes to whom civilization has given little but its reaction, its rebound, its chips, its refuse, its shavings, sawdust, and waste, its failures; to them solitude is a right forgone or a luxury unattained; a right forgone, we may name it, in the case of the nearly savage, and a luxury unattained in the case of the nearly refined. These has the movement of the world thronged together into some blind by-way. Their share in the enormous solitude which is the common, unbounded, and virtually illimitable possession of all mankind has lapsed, unclaimed. They do not know it is theirs. Of many of their kingdoms they are ignorant, but of this most ignorant. They have not guessed that they own for every man a space inviolate, a place of unhidden liberty and of no obscure enfranchisement. They do not claim even the solitude of closed corners, the narrow privacy of lock and key. Nor could they command so much.

For the solitude that has a sky and a horizon they do not know how to wish. It lies in a perpetual distance. England has leagues of it, landscapes of it, verge beyond verge, a thousand thousand places in the woods, and on uplifted hills. Or rather, solitudes are not to be measured by miles; they are to be numbered by days. They are freshly and freely the dominion of every man for the day of his possession. There is loneliness for innumerable solitaries. As many days as there are in all the ages, so many solitudes are there for men. This is the open house of the earth. No one is refused. Nor is the space shortened or the silence marred because, one by one, men in multitudes have been alone there before. Solitude is separate experience. Nay, solitudes are not to be numbered by days, but by men themselves. Every man of the living and every man of the dead might have had his "privacy of light."

It needs no park. It is to be found in the merest working country; and a thicket may be as secret as a forest. It is not so difficult to get for a time out of sight and earshot. Even if your solitude be enclosed, it is still an open solitude, so there be "no cloister for the eyes," and a space of far country or a cloud in the sky be privy to your hiding-place. But the best solitude does not hide at all. This the people who have drifted together into the streets live whole lives and never know. Do they suffer from their deprivation of even the solitude of the hiding-place? There are many who never have a whole hour alone. They live in reluctant or indifferent companionship, as people do in a boarding-house, by paradoxical choice, familiar with one another and not intimate. They live under careless observation and subject to a cold curiosity. Theirs is the involuntary and perhaps the unconscious loss which is futile and barren.

One knows the men, and the many women, who have sacrificed all their solitude to the perpetual society of the school, the cloister, or the hospital-ward. They walk without secrecy, candid, simple, visible, without moods, unchangeable, in a constant communication and practice of action and speech. Theirs assuredly is no barren or futile loss, and they have a conviction, and they bestow the conviction, of solitude deferred.

Who has painted solitude so that the solitary seemed to stand alone and inaccessible? There is the loneliness of the shepherdess in many a drawing of Millet. The little figure is away, aloof. The girl stands so when the painter is gone. She waits so on the sun for the closing of the hours of pasture. Millet has her as she looks, out of sight.

And, although solitude is a prepared, secured, defended, elaborate possession of the rich, they too deny themselves the natural solitude of a woman with a child. A newly born child is often so nursed and talked about, handled and jolted and carried about by aliens, and there is so much importunate service going forward, that a woman is hardly alone long enough to feel; in silence and recollection, how her own blood moves separately, beside her, with another rhythm and different pulses. All is commonplace until the doors are closed upon the two. This unique intimacy is a profound retreat, an absolute seclusion. It is more than single solitude, it is a multiplied isolation more remote than mountains, safer than valleys, deeper than forests, and further than mid-sea. That solitude partaken—the only partaken solitude in the world—is the Point of Honour of ethics. Treachery to that obligation and a betrayal of that confidence might well be held to be the least pardonable of all crimes. There is no innocent sleep so innocent as sleep shared between a woman and a child, the little breath hurrying beside the longer, as a child's foot runs. But the favourite crime of the modern sentimentalist is that of a woman against her child. Her power, her intimacy, her opportunity, that should be her accusers, excuse her.

A conventional park is by no means necessary for the preparation of a country solitude. Indeed, to make those far and wide and long approaches and avenues to peace seems to be a denial of the accessibility of what should be so simple. A step, a pace or so aside, is enough to lead thither. Solitude is not for a lifetime, but for intervals. A park insists too much, and, besides, does not insist very sincerely. In order to fulfill the apparent professions and to keep the published promise of a park, the owner thereof should be a lover of long seclusion or of a very life of loneliness. He should have gained the state of solitariness which is a condition of life quite unlike any other. The traveller who may have gone astray in countries where there is an almost lifelong solitude possible is aware how invincibly apart are the lonely figure he has seen in desert places there. Their loneliness is broken by his passage, it is true, but hardly so to them. They look at him, but they are not aware that he looks at them. Nay, they look at him as though they were invisible. Their un-selfconsciousness is absolute; it is in the wild degree. They are solitaries, body and soul. Even when they are curious, and turn to watch the passer-by, they are essentially alone. Now, no one ever found that attitude in a squire's figure, or that look in any country gentleman's eyes. The squire is not a lifelong solitary. He never bore himself as though he were invisible. He never had the impersonal ways of a herdsman in the remoter Apennines, with a blind, blank hut in the rocks for his dwelling. Millet would not even have taken him as a model for a solitary in the briefer and milder sylvan solitudes of France. And yet nothing but a life-long, habitual, and wild solitariness would be quite proportionate to a park of any magnitude.

If there is a look of human eyes that tells of perpetual loneliness, so there is also the familiar look that is the sign of perpetual crowds. It is the London expression, and, in its way, the Paris expression. It is the quickly caught, though not interested look, the dull but ready glance of those who do not know of their forfeited place apart; who have neither the open secret nor the close, neither liberty nor the right of lock and key; no reserve, no need of refuge, no flight nor impulse of flight; no moods but what they may brave out in the street, no hope of news from solitary counsels. Even in many men and women who have all their rights over all the solitudes—solitudes of closed doors and territorial soliltudes of sward and forest—even in these who have enough solitudes to fulfill the wants of a city, even in these is found, not seldom, the look of the street.

Robert Louis Stevenson

(1850-1894)

*An interesting study might be made of essay titles. Some, like Bacon's "Of Studies" or Forster's "What I Believe," are straightforward, informative tags. A title like Didion's "On Morality" foils ready assumptions about just such tagging. Dillard's "Life on the Rocks" and Selzer's "A Worm from My Notebook" stand in yet a subtler relation to their essays. "An Apology for Idlers," a widely anthologized essay turned classic since it was first published (*Virginibus Puerisque, *1876), announces by its title that it leans on a grave tradition—that of the apologetic oration or treatise—with which it has, in one sense, nothing in common, yet from whose alien dignity it borrows some of its own moral seriousness, however amiably and playfully forwarded. The ordinary meaning of "apology" in Stevenson's time was, as in ours, acknowledgment of having offended, with expression of regret. It is precisely against this familiar sense of the word that the essay's wandering, seemingly casual argument accumulates. Because, of course, Stevenson does not regret being an "idler," far from it. His essay is an "apology" in the ancient Greek sense:* apologia, *meaning a defense of oneself, one's acts, one's way of life. The sort of vindication most famously undertaken by Socrates in Plato's* Apology. *The tradition turns up variously in English works such as More's* Apology for Sir Thomas More, Knight *(1533), Robert Barclay's* Apology for the People Called Quakers *(1678), and Cardinal Newman's* Apologia Pro Vita Sua *(1864)—all of them deeply serious, considered responses to actual or implied attacks. (A great modern example is King's "Letter from Birmingham Jail.") To rise up against the unexamined reigning consensus about the moral turpitude of "idlers" can be no easy task for one of that species—to do the thing well, that is—"therefore," says Stevenson right near the start, "please to remember this is an apology." How so? Yet another meaning of the word current in the writer's day was "excuse," in the sense of "a poor substitute." What, then, is this playful "Apology" an "apology" for? If you are not Socrates on trial for your life, or writing about personal morality with the exemplary conviction of a Thoreau, can anything very vital hang on your words?*

An Apology for Idlers

Boswell: We grow weary when idle.
Johnson: That is, sir, because others being busy, we want company; but if we were idle, there would be no growing weary; we should all entertain one another.

Just now, when everyone is bound, under pain of a decree in absence convicting them of *lèse*-respectability,[1] to enter on some lucrative profession, and labour therein with something not far short of enthusiasm, a cry from the opposite party who are content when they have enough, and like to look on and enjoy in the meanwhile, savours a little of bravado and gasconade. And yet this should not be. Idleness so called, which does not consist in doing nothing, but in doing a great deal not recognised in the dogmatic formularies of the ruling class, has as good a right to state its position as industry itself. It is admitted that the presence of people who refuse to enter in the great handicap race of sixpenny pieces, is at once an insult and a disenchantment for those who do. A fine fellow (as we see so many) takes his determination, votes for the sixpences, and in the emphatic Americanism, "goes for" them. And while such an one is ploughing distressfully up the road, it is not hard to understand his resentment, when he perceives cool persons in the meadows by the wayside, lying with a handkerchief over their ears and a glass at their elbow. Alexander is touched in a very delicate place by the disregard of Diogenes. Where was the glory of having taken Rome for these tumultuous barbarians, who poured into the Senate house, and found the Fathers sitting silent and unmoved by their success? It is a sore thing to have laboured along and scaled the arduous hilltops, and when all is done, find humanity indifferent to your achievement. Hence physicists condemn the unphysical; financiers have only a superficial toleration for those who know little of stocks; literary persons despise the unlettered; and people of all pursuits combine to disparage those who have none.

But though this is one difficulty of the subject, it is not the greatest. You could not be put in prison for speaking against industry, but you can be sent to Coventry for speaking like a fool. The greatest difficulty with most subjects is to do them well; therefore, please to remember this is an apology. It is certain that much may be judiciously argued in favour of diligence; only there is something to be said against it, and that is what, on the present occasion, I have to say. To state one argument is not necessarily to be deaf to all others, and that a man

[1] A play on *lèse-majesté*, a crime or offense committed against a sovereign, such as a king.

has written a book of travels in Montenegro, is no reason why he should never have been to Richmond.

It is surely beyond a doubt that people should be a good deal idle in youth. For though here and there a Lord Macaulay may escape from school honours with all his wits about him, most boys pay so dear for their medals that they never afterwards have a shot in their locker, and begin the world bankrupt. And the same holds true during all the time a lad is educating himself, or suffering others to educate him. It must have been a very foolish old gentleman who addressed Johnson at Oxford in these words: "Young man, ply your book diligently now, and acquire a stock of knowledge; for when years come upon you, you will find that poring upon books will be but an irksome task." The old gentleman seems to have been unaware that many other things besides reading grow irksome, and not a few become impossible, by the time a man has to use spectacles and cannot walk without a stick. Books are good enough in their own way, but they are a mighty bloodless substitute for life. It seems a pity to sit, like the Lady of Shalott, peering into a mirror, with your back turned on all the bustle and glamour of reality. And if a man reads very hard, as the old anecdote reminds us, he will have little time for thought.

If you look back on your own education, I am sure it will not be the full, vivid, instructive hours of truantry that you regret; you would rather cancel some lack-lustre periods between sleep and waking in the class. For my own part, I have attended a good many lectures in my time. I still remember that the spinning of a top is a case of Kinetic Stability. I still remember that Emphyteusis is not a disease, nor Stillicide a crime. But though I would not willingly part with such scraps of science, I do not set the same store by them as by certain other odds and ends that I came by in the open street while I was playing truant. This is not the moment to dilate on that mighty place of education, which was the favourite school of Dickens and of Balzac, and turns out yearly many inglorious masters in the Science of the Aspects of Life. Suffice it to say this: if a lad does not learn in the streets, it is because he has no faculty of learning. Nor is the truant always in the streets, for if he prefers, he may go out by the gardened suburbs into the country. He may pitch on some tuft of lilacs over a burn, and smoke innumerable pipes to the tune of the water on the stones. A bird will sing in the thicket. And there he may fall into a vein of kindly thought, and see things in a new perspective. Why, if this be not education, what is? We may conceive Mr. Worldly Wiseman accosting such an one, and the conversation that should thereupon ensue:—

"How now, young fellow, what dost thou here?"

"Truly, sir, I take mine ease."

"Is not this the hour of the class? and should'st thou not be plying thy Book with diligence, to the end thou mayest obtain knowledge?"

"Nay, but thus also I follow after Learning, by your leave."

"Learning, quotha! After what fashion, I pray thee? Is it mathematics?"

"No, to be sure."

"Is it metaphysics?"

"Nor that."

"Is it some language?"

"Nay, it is no language."

"Is it a trade?"

"Nor a trade neither."

"Why, then, what is't?"

"Indeed, sir, as a time may soon come for me to go upon Pilgrimage, I am desirous to note what is commonly done by persons in my case, and where are the ugliest Sloughs and Thickets on the Road; as also, what manner of Staff is of the best service. Moreover, I lie here, by this water, to learn by root-of-heart a lesson which my master teaches me to call Peace, or Contentment."

Hereupon Mr. Worldly Wiseman was much commoved with passion, and shaking his cane with a very threatful countenance, broke forth upon this wise: "Learning, quotha!" said he; "I would have all such rogues scourged by the Hangman!"

And so he would go his way, ruffling out his cravat with a crackle of starch, like a turkey when it spread its feathers.

Now this, of Mr. Wiseman's, is the common opinion. A fact is not called a fact, but a piece of gossip, if it does not fall into one of your scholastic categories. An inquiry must be in some acknowledged direction, with a name to go by; or else you are not inquiring at all, only lounging; and the workhouse is too good for you. It is supposed that all knowledge is at the bottom of a well, or the far end of a telescope. Sainte-Beuve, as he grew older, came to regard all experience as a single great book, in which to study for a few years ere we go hence; and it seemed all one to him whether you should read in Chapter xx, which is the differential calculus, or in Chapter xxxix, which is hearing the band play in the gardens. As a matter of fact, an intelligent person, looking out of his eyes and hearkening in his ears, with a smile on his face all the time, will get more true education than many another in a life of heroic vigils. There is certainly some chill and arid knowledge to be found upon the summits of formal and laborious science; but it is all round about you, and for the trouble of looking, that you will acquire the warm and palpitating facts of life. While others are filling their memory with a lumber of words, one-half of which they will forget before the week be out, your truant may learn some really useful art: to play the fiddle, to know a good cigar, or to speak with ease and opportunity to all varieties of men. Many who have "plied their book diligently," and know all about some one branch or another of accepted lore, come out of the study with an ancient and owl-like demeanour, and prove dry, stockish, and dyspeptic in all the better and brighter parts of life. Many make a large fortune, who remain underbred and pathetically stupid to the last. And meantime there goes the idler, who began life along with them—by your leave, a different picture. He has had time to take care of his health and his spirits; he has been a great deal in the open air, which is the most salutary of all things for both body and mind; and if he has never read the great Book in very recondite places, he has dipped into it and skimmed it over to excellent purpose. Might not the student afford some Hebrew roots, and the business man some of his half-crowns, for a share of the idler's knowledge of life at large, and Art of Living? Nay, and the idler has another and more important quality than these. I mean his wisdom. He who has much looked on at the childish satisfaction of other people in their hobbies, will regard his own with only a very ironical indulgence. He will not be heard among the dogmatists. He will have a great and cool allowance for all sorts of people and opinions. If he finds no out-of-the-way truths, he will identify himself with no very burning falsehood. His way takes him along a by-road, not much frequented, but very even and pleasant, which is called Commonplace Lane, and leads to the Belvedere of Commonsense. Thence he shall command an agreeable, if no very noble prospect; and while others behold the East and West, the Devil and the Sunrise, he will be contentedly aware of a sort of morning hour upon all sublunary things, with an army of shadows running speedily and in many different directions into the great daylight of Eternity. The shadows and the generations, the shrill doctors and the plangent wars, go by into ultimate silence and emptiness; but underneath all this, a man may see, out of the Belvedere windows, much green and peaceful landscape; many firelit parlours; good people laughing, drinking, and making love as they did before the Flood or the French Revolution; and the old shepherd telling his tale under the hawthorn.

Extreme *busyness*, whether at school or college, kirk or market, is a symptom of deficient vitality; and a faculty for idleness implies a catholic appetite and a strong sense of personal identity. There is a sort of dead-alive, hackneyed people about, who are scarcely conscious of living except in the exercise of some conventional occupation. Bring these fellows into the country, or set them aboard ship, and you will see how they pine for their desk or their study. They have no curiosity; they cannot give themselves over to random provocations; they do not take pleasure in the exercise of their faculties for its own sake; and unless Necessity lays about them with a stick, they will even stand still. It is no good speaking to such folk: they *cannot* be idle, their nature is not generous enough; and they pass those hours in a sort of coma, which are not dedicated to furious moiling in the gold-mill. When they do not require to go to the office, when they are not hungry and have no mind to drink, the whole breathing world is blank to them. If they have to wait an hour or so for a train, they fall into a stupid trance with their eyes open. To see them, you would suppose there was nothing to look at and no one to speak with; you would imagine they were paralysed or alienated; and yet very possibly they are hard workers in their own way, and have good eyesight for a flaw in a deed or a turn of the market. They have been to school and college, but all the time they had their eye on the medal; they have gone about in the world and mixed with clever people, but all the time they were thinking of their own affairs. As if a man's soul were not too small to begin with, they have dwarfed and narrowed theirs by a life of all work and no play; until here they are at forty, with a listless attention, a mind vacant of all material of amusement, and not one thought to rub against another, while they wait for the train. Before he was breeched, he might have clambered on the boxes; when he was twenty, he would have stared at the girls; but now the pipe is smoked out, the snuffbox empty, and my gentleman sits bolt upright upon a bench, with lamentable eyes. This does not appeal to me as being Success in Life.

But it is not only the person himself who suffers from his busy habits, but his wife and children, his friends and relations, and down to the very people he sits with in a railway carriage or an omnibus. Perpetual devotion to what a man calls his business, is only to be sustained by perpetual neglect of many other things. And it is not by any means certain that a man's business is the most important thing he has to do. To an impartial estimate it will seem clear that many of the wisest, most virtuous, and most beneficent parts that are to be played upon the Theatre of Life are filled by gratuitous performers, and pass, among the world at large, as phases of idleness. For in that Theatre, not only the walking gentlemen, singing chambermaids, and diligent fiddlers in the orchestra, but those who look on and clap their hands from the benches, do really play a part and fulfill important offices towards the general result. You are no doubt very dependent on the care of your lawyer and stockbroker, of the guards and signalmen who convey you rapidly from place to place, and the policemen who walk the streets for your protection; but is there not a thought of gratitude in your heart for certain other benefactors who set you smiling when they fall in your way, or season your dinner with good company? Colonel Newcome helped to lose his friend's money; Fred Bayham had an ugly trick of borrowing shirts; and yet they were better people to fall among than Mr. Barnes. And though Falstaff was neither sober nor very honest, I think I could name one or two long-faced Barabbases whom the world could better have done without. Hazlitt mentions that he was more sensible of obligation to Northcote, who had never done him anything he could call a service, than to his whole circle of ostentatious friends; for he thought a good companion emphatically the greatest benefactor. I know there are people in the world who cannot feel grateful unless the favour has been done them at the cost of pain and difficulty. But this is a churlish disposition. A man may send you six sheets of letter-paper covered with the most entertaining gossip, or you may pass half an hour pleasantly, perhaps profitably, over an article of his; do you think the service would be greater, if he had made the manuscript in his heart's blood, like a compact with the devil? Do you really fancy you should be more beholden to your correspondent, if he had been damning you all the while for your importunity? Pleasures are more beneficial than duties because, like the quality of mercy, they are not strained, and they are twice blest. There must always be two to a kiss, and there may be a score in a jest; but wherever there is an element of sacrifice, the favour is conferred with pain, and, among generous people, received with confusion. There is no duty we so much underrate as the duty of being happy. By being happy, we sow anonymous benefits upon the world, which remain unknown even to ourselves, or when they are disclosed, surprise nobody so much as the benefactor. The other day, a ragged, barefoot boy ran down the street after a marble, with so jolly an air that he set everyone he passed into a good humour; one of these persons, who had been delivered from more than usually black thoughts, stopped the little fellow and gave him some money with this remark: "You see what sometimes comes of looking pleased." If he had looked pleased before, he had now to look both pleased and mystified. For my part, I justify this encouragement of smiling rather than tearful children; I do not wish to pay for tears anywhere but upon the stage; but I am prepared to deal largely in the opposite commodity. A happy man or woman is a better thing to find than a five-pound note. He or she is a radiating focus of goodwill; and their entrance into a room is as though another candle had been lighted. We need not care whether they could prove the forty-seventh proposition; they do a better thing than that, they practically demonstrate the great Theorem of the Liveableness of Life. Consequently, if a person cannot be happy without remaining idle, idle he should remain. It is a revolutionary precept; but thanks to hunger and the workhouse, one not easily to be abused; and within practical limits, it is one of the most incontestable truths in the whole Body of Morality. Look at one of your industrious fellows for a moment, I beseech you. He sows hurry and reaps indigestion; he puts a vast deal of activity out to interest, and receives a large measure of nervous derangement in return. Either he absents himself entirely from all fellowship, and lives a recluse in a garret, with carpet slippers and a leaden inkpot; or he comes among people swiftly and bitterly, in a contraction of his whole nervous system, to discharge some temper before he returns to work. I do not care how much or how well he works, this fellow is an evil feature in other people's lives. They would be happier if he were dead. They could easier do without his services in the Circumlocution Office, than they can tolerate his fractious spirits. He poisons life at the well-head. It is better to be beggared out of hand by a scapegrace nephew, than daily hag-ridden by a peevish uncle.

And what, in God's name, is all this pother about? For what cause do they embitter their own and other people's lives? That a man should publish three or thirty articles a year, that he should finish or not finish his great allegorical picture, are questions of little interest to the world. The ranks of life are full; and although a thousand fall, there are always some to go into the breach. When they told Joan of Arc she should be at home minding women's work, she answered there were plenty to spin and wash. And so, even with your own rare gifts! When nature is "so careless of the single life," why should we coddle ourselves into the fancy that our own is of exceptional importance? Suppose Shakespeare had been knocked on the head some dark night in Sir Thomas Lucy's preserves, the world would have wagged on better or worse, the pitcher gone to the well, the scythe to the corn, and the student to his book; and no one been any the wiser of the loss. There are not many works extant, if you look the alternative all over, which are worth the price of a pound of tobacco to a man of limited means. This is a sobering reflection for the proudest of our earthly vanities. Even a tobacconist may, upon consideration, find no great cause for personal vainglory in the phrase; for although tobacco is an admirable sedative, the qualities necessary for retailing it are neither rare nor precious in themselves. Alas and alas! you may take it how you will, but the services of no single individual are indispensable. Atlas was just a gentleman with a protracted nightmare! And yet you see merchants who go and labour themselves into a great fortune and thence into the bankruptcy court; scribblers who keep scribbling at little articles until their temper is a cross to all who come about them, as though Pharaoh should set the Israelites to make a pin instead of a pyramid; and fine young men who work themselves into a decline, and are driven off in a hearse with white plumes upon it. Would you not suppose these persons had been whispered, by the Master of Ceremonies, the promise of some momentous destiny? and that this lukewarm bullet on which they play their farces was the bull's-eye and centrepoint of all the universe? And yet it is not so. The ends for which they give away their priceless youth, for all they know, may be chimerical or hurtful; the glory and riches they expect may never come, or may find them indifferent; and they and the world they inhabit are so inconsiderable that the mind freezes at the thought.

W. E. B. Du Bois

(1868–1963)

As different from each other in feeling and method as any two essays in this book, "On Being Black" and "The Guilt of the Cane" are the work of a man born three years after the end of the Civil War, who died only the day before the great March on Washington, August 28, 1963. A life of ninety-five years—"doing what must be done," as Du Bois told his great-grandson in 1958. He was a scholar, a teacher in both the professional and the widest social sense, a great American intellectual and activist, a passionately engaged critic of "the disgraceful denial of human brotherhood" to Americans of color, a journalist, the distinguished and influential editor for twenty-four years of the NAACP's journal Crisis, *an innovative social historian, a founding Pan-Africanist, a novelist, a writer of essays. The earliest of these, such as the moving account of his little son's death, "Of the Passing of the First-Born" (*The Souls of Black Folk, *1897), retain the poetic elegance of late Victorian prose. Less than fifteen years later, his searing editorials against lynching have the perennial contemporaneity of English shorn to its rudiments: "We have crawled and pleaded for justice and we have been cheerfully spit upon and murdered and burned. We will not endure forever. If we are to die, in God's name let us perish like men and not like bales of hay"* (Crisis, *1911). Published in 1920, "On Being Black" is surely among the most eloquent polemics in English; its brilliantly formed narrative draws the reader like a fiction uttering the bitterest truths, experienced and thus irrefutable. The memory of World War I is still fresh in this essay, its lingering "rifts of battlesmoke" like a nightmarish token of the world's "dark and awful depths." Twenty-eight years and a second world slaughter separate this essay from the brief, half-comical, half-shattering "Guilt of the Cane." His long-ago years (1892–93) as a student at Berlin University, referred to at the essay's opening, had been for Du Bois a part of what he elsewhere described as the "Age of Miracles," a time of unlimited hope and achievement: "I seemed to ride in conquering might. . . . Distinctions of color faded. I felt myself just a man" ("The Shadow of Years"). This is the dream that was "born and died."*

On Being Black

My friend, who is pale and positive, said to me yesterday, as the tired sun was nodding: "You are too sensitive."

I admit, I am—sensitive. I am artificial. I cringe or am bumptious or immobile. I am intellectually dishonest, art-blind, and I lack humor.

"Why don't you stop all this?" she retorts triumphantly.

You will not let us.

"There you go, again. You know that I—"

Wait! I answer. Wait!

I arise at seven. The milkman has neglected me. He pays little attention to colored districts. My white neighbor glares elaborately. I walk softly, lest I disturb him. The children jeer as I pass to work. The women in the streetcar withdraw their skirts or prefer to stand. The policeman is truculent. The elevator man hates to serve Negroes. My job is insecure because the white union wants it and does not want me. I try to lunch, but no place near will serve me. I go forty blocks to Marshall's, but the Committee of Fourteen closes Marshall's; they say that white women frequent it.

"Do all eating places discriminate?"

No, but how shall I know which do not—except—

I hurry home through crowds. They mutter or get angry. I go to a mass-meeting. They stare. I go to church. "We don't admit niggers!"

Or perhaps I leave the beaten track. I seek new work. "Our employees would not work with you; our customers would object."

I ask to help in social uplift.

"Why—er—we will write you."

I enter the free field of science. Every laboratory door is closed and no endowments are available.

I seek the universal mistress, Art; the studio door is locked.

I write literature. "We cannot publish stories of colored folks of that type." It's the only type I know.

This is my life. It makes me idiotic. It gives me artificial problems. I hesitate, I rush, I waver. In fine—I am sensitive!

My pale friend looks at me with disbelief and curling tongue.

"Do you mean to sit there and tell me that this is what happens to you each day?"

Certainly not, I answer low.

"Then you only fear it will happen?"

I fear!

"Well, haven't you the courage to rise above a—almost a craven fear?"

Quite—quite craven is my fear, I admit; but the terrible thing is—these things do happen!

"But you just said—"

They do happen. Not all each day—surely not. But now and then—now seldom; now, sudden; now after a week, now in a chain of awful minutes; not everywhere, but anywhere—in Boston, in Atlanta. That's the hell of it. Imagine spending your life looking for insults or for hiding places from them—shrinking (instinctively and despite desperate bolsterings of courage) from blows that are not always, but ever; not each day, but each week, each month, each year. Just, perhaps, as you have choked back the craven fear and cried, "I am and will be the master of my—"

"No more tickets downstairs; here's one to the smoking gallery."

You hesitate. You beat back your suspicions. After all, a cigarette with Charlie Chaplin—then a white man pushes by—

"Three in the orchestra."

"Yes, sir." And in he goes.

Suddenly your heart chills. You turn yourself away toward the golden twinkle of the purple night and hesitate again. What's the use? Why not always yield—always take what's offered—always bow to force, whether of cannon or dislike? Then the great fear surges in your soul, the real fear—the fear beside which other fears are vain imaginings; the fear lest right there and then you are losing your own soul; that you are losing your own soul and the souls of a people; that millions of unborn children, black and gold and mauve, are being there and then despoiled by you because you are a coward and dare not fight!

Suddenly that silly orchestra seat and the cavorting of a comedian with funny feet become matters of life, death, and immortality; you grasp the pillars of the universe and strain as you sway back to that befilled ticket girl. You grip your soul for riot and murder. You choke and sputter, and she, seeing that you are about to make a "fuss" obeys her orders and throws the tickets at you in contempt. Then you slink to your seat and crouch in the darkness before the film, with every tissue burning! The miserable wave of reaction engulfs you. To think of compelling puppies to take your hard-earned money; fattening hogs to hate you and yours; forcing your way among cheap and tawdry idiots—God! What a night of pleasure!

Why do not those who are scarred in the world's battle and hurt by its hardness travel to these places of beauty and drown themselves in the utter joy of life? I asked this once sitting in a Southern home. Outside the spring of a Georgia February was luring gold to the bushes and languor to the soft air. Around me sat color in human flesh—brown that crimsoned readily; dim soft-yellow that escaped description; creamlike duskiness that shadowed to rich tints of autumn leaves. And yet a suggested journey in the world brought no response.

"I should think you would like to travel," said the white one.

But no, the thought of a journey seemed to depress them.

Did you ever see a Jim Crow waiting room? There are always exceptions, as at Greensboro—but usually there is no heat in winter and no air in summer; with undisturbed loafers and train hands and broken, disreputable settees; to buy a ticket is torture; you stand and stand and wait and wait until every white person at the "other window" is waited on. Then the tired agent yells across, because all the tickets and money are over there—

"What d' ye want? What? Where?"

The agent browbeats and contradicts you, hurries and confuses the ignorant, gives many persons the wrong change, compels some to purchase their tickets on the train at a higher price, and sends you and me out on the platform burning with indignation and hatred!

The Jim Crow car is up next the baggage car and engine. It stops out beyond the covering in the rain or sun dust. Usually there is no step to help you climb on, and often the car is a smoker cut in two, and you must pass through the white smokers or else they pass through your part, with swagger and noise and stares. Your compartment is a half or a quarter or an eighth of the oldest car in service on the road. Unless it happens to be a through express, the plush is caked with dirt, the floor is grimy, and the windows dirty. An impertinent white newsboy occupies two seats at the end of the car and importunes you to the point of rage to buy cheap candy, Coca-Cola, and worthless, if not vulgar, books. He yells and swaggers, while a continued stream of white men saunters back and forth from the smoker, to buy and hear. The white train crew from the baggage car uses the Jim Crow to lounge in and perform their toilet. The conductor appropriates two seats for himself and his papers and yells gruffly for your tickets before the train has scarcely started. It is best not to ask him for information even in the gentlest tones. His information is for white persons chiefly. It is difficult to get lunch or clean water. Lunch rooms either don't serve niggers or serve them at some dirty and ill-attended hole in the wall. As for toilet rooms—don't! If you have to change cars, be wary of junctions which are usually without accommodation and filled with quarrelsome white persons who hate a "darky dressed up." You are apt to have the company of a sheriff and a couple of meek or sullen black prisoners on part of your way, and dirty colored section hands will pour in toward night and drive you to the smallest corner.

"No," said the little lady in the corner (she looked like an ivory cameo and her dress flowed on her like a caress), "we don't travel much."

Pessimism is a cowardice. The man who cannot frankly acknowledge the Jim Crow car as a fact and yet live and hope is simply afraid either of himself or of the world. There is not in the world a more disgraceful denial of human brotherhood than the Jim Crow car of the Southern United States; but, too, just as true, there is nothing more beautiful in the universe than sunset and moonlight on Montego Bay in far Jamaica. And both things are true and both belong to this, our world, and neither can be denied.

High in the tower, where I sit above the loud complaining of the human sea, I know many souls that toss and whirl and pass, but none there are that intrigue me more than the Souls of White Folk.

Of them I am singularly clairvoyant. I see in and through them. I view them from unusual points of vantage. Not as a foreigner do I come, for I am native, not foreign, bone of their thought and flesh of their language. Mine is not the knowledge of the traveler or the colonial composite of dear memories, words, and wonder. Nor yet is my knowledge that which servants have of masters, or mass of class, or capitalist of artisan. Rather I see the working of their entrails. I know their thoughts and they know that I know. This knowledge makes them now embarrassed, now furious! They deny my right to live and be and call me misbirth! My word is to them mere bitterness and my soul, pessimism. And yet as they preach and strut and shout and threaten, crouching as they clutch at rags of facts and fancies to hide their nakedness, they go twisting, flying by my tired eyes and I see them ever stripped—ugly, human.

The discovery of personal whiteness among the world's peoples is a very modern thing—a nineteenth- and twentieth-century matter, indeed. The ancient world would have laughed at such a distinction. The Middle Ages regarded skin color with mild curiosity; and even up into the eighteenth century we were hammering our national manikins into one, great, Universal Man, with fine frenzy which ignored color and race even more than birth. Today we have changed all that, and the world in a sudden, emotional conversation has discovered that it is white and by that token, wonderful!

As we saw the dead dimly through rifts of battlesmoke and heard faintly the cursing and accusations of blood brothers, we darker men said: This is not Europe gone mad; this is not aberration nor insanity; this *is* Europe; this seeming Terrible is the real soul of white culture—back of all culture—stripped and visible today. This is where the world has arrived—these dark and awful depths, and not the shining and ineffable heights of which it boasted. Here is whither the might and energy of modern humanity has really gone.

But may not the world cry back at us and ask: "What better thing have you to show? What have you done or would do better than this if you had today the world rule? Paint with all riot of hateful colors the thin skin of European culture—is it not better than any culture that arose in Africa or Asia?"

It is. Of this there is no doubt and never has been; but why is it better? Is it better because Europeans are better, nobler, greater, and more gifted than other folk? It is not. Europe has never produced and never will in our day bring forth a single human soul who cannot be matched and overmatched in every line of human endeavor by Asia and Africa. Run the gamut, if you will, and let us have the Europeans who in sober truth overmatch Nefertari, Mohammed, Rameses, and Askia, Confucius, Buddha, and Jesus Christ. If we could scan the calendar of thousands of lesser men, in like comparison, the result would be the same; but we cannot do this because of the deliberately educated ignorance of white schools by which they remember Napoleon and forget Sonni Ali.

Why, then, is Europe great? Because of the foundations which the mighty past have furnished her to build upon: the iron trade of ancient black Africa, the religion and empire-building of yellow Asia, the art and science of the "dago" Mediterranean shore, east, south, and west, as well as north. And where she has builded securely upon this great past and learned from it, she has gone forward to greater and more splendid human triumph; but where she has ignored this past and forgotten and sneered at it, she has shown the cloven hoof of poor, crucified humanity—she has played, like other empires gone, the world fool!

The Guilt of the Cane

When I attended the Friedrich Wilhelm's University in Berlin in 1892 to 1893, the insignia of a student which were absolutely compulsory were gloves and cane. There I acquired the cane habit and have carried one ever since. It is useless and silly, but also harmless and cheap. So I still carry a cane, an incorrigible habit. Once as I was revisiting Germany, I found in a little shop on the Friedrichstrasse, now in ghastly ruins, an enticing umbrella cane. It was a thin silk umbrella with a removable wooden outer sheath. I bought it forthwith and carried it for years until it wore out.

Recently in an old umbrella shop on Forty-fifth street, New York, what did I see but an umbrella cane almost a replica of my old one! I inquired the price—it was much too high and I left. But the temptation was irresistible. Twice I returned, and finally I bought it at a ridiculous price, which I then increased by equipping it with a silver band engraved with name and address. I took singular satisfaction in this toy. It renewed my youth; it brought back a land and a culture forever dead; it healed and revived memories.

I fared west, talking to groups of varied complexions of mind and body; eating a delicious Thanksgiving dinner with my friends the Lochards; seeing Des Moines again fifty-one years after my wedding, at Cedar Rapids, and finally landing in Union Station, Chicago, on my way home. Here is a restaurant, where I have a favorite seat. Pushing the Third World War firmly into the background, I had a trout from the North Woods, an appetizing salad, a small bottle of sauterne (albeit Californian), and a demi-tasse in a dainty cup—not a bowl. I then strolled leisurely to my sleeping-car, at peace with a cockeyed world, until I laid my precious cane-umbrella on the bed: the cane sheath was missing! It was made of turned wood from Sweden and folded sweetly into a warm brown roll. I had the umbrella. I had the engraved silver address but the cane-cover was gone. I had dropped it! I had lost it! It was irreplaceable! I had the sick feeling which, whether it rises from the fall of the world or the flick of a finger, spells doom. Suddenly a whole group of memories, experiences, hopes, triumphs, and failures of fifty years, rose and curled themselves around that lost cane-cover. To the porter's astonishment, I rushed out and began to search the depot floors and platforms.

As you may know, the Chicago Union Station occupies upward of two acres, fairly full of feet and traveling bags. I threaded doggedly through passengers, looking in vain, and porters eyed me askance. I finally flew back to the Pullman and again searched there. It was still gone. Ah! I remembered, the restaurant! I hurried there. It was closed! The connecting lunch counter was open however. I rushed in there and laid my case feelingly before the pretty counter-girl and the sympathetic head waitress. I was led on to the closed restaurant and searched the check-room. No trace! "But," said the waitress brightly, "How about the Lost and Found?" In vain! There was nothing there but a yellow stick with a ribbon! My time was running short. I began to have the feeling, not simply of loss, but of loss of nothing, which still seemed of fundamental importance, because it linked to this world the dream of another that had been born and died—I was unbelievably and illogically dejected and disillusioned. After all, what was the use—and just then I saw it! It lay quietly folded in its soft, brown roll, cunningly hidden under the desk of the Pullman agent, where I had checked in an hour since.

I fell upon it. I rubbed it gently and slipped it carefully in place. I became suddenly quite voluble. I explained to the Pullman agent, the Gatemen, the Pullman porter—until finally I began to sense obscurely but definitely that to none of these did the matter seem of that cosmic importance which it did to me. Then I went to bed.

Hilaire Belloc

(1870–1953)

*In a humorous and somewhat abashed little essay called "A Conversation with a Reader" (*Short Talks with the Dead, *1926), Hilaire Belloc tells the story of sharing a railway compartment, from Birmingham to Oxford, with a man who happened to be reading one of Belloc's own "too numerous books of essays." "This is fame," he thinks happily to himself, "I am getting known." But the bored reader, unaware that he is in the presence of its author, puts down the book disgustedly as "silly stuff"—"a shilling wasted." What he really likes is writing that "stirs the blood," and proceeds to recite some of his favorites. "I wonder how it comes to 'em. It's genius, I suppose," he tells the miserable Belloc, who ends up pressing a shilling on the man as they part, in return for his own scorned book of essays. Belloc had a talent for self-criticism, especially in its ironic modes. In another funny, somewhat later piece, "A Guide to Boring" (*A Conversation with a Cat, *1931), he argues with dead-pan seriousness that even "Boring may properly be regarded as an Art," which only a writer of some ability can practice well—a writer like Belloc, whose best works are superbly crafted. An essay such as "The Mowing of a Field" (*Hills and the Sea, *1906) may not, indeed, "stir the blood" of many; it doesn't rouse the conscience or the passions. It reminisces, but not primarily for the sake of tugging at those chords of feeling that readily unite writer and reader. Its business is with how to do things and how to do them pleasurably and well: the aesthetics of work. It unfolds to the imaginative eye scenes and processes of such clarity one becomes absorbed not only in what is being described or explained but in the fine arts of describing and explaining themselves. Like the art of "mowing well" with which the essay concerns itself, these arts of language consist of part practice in the ancient know-how, part sheer hard, sweaty labor, and part delight in the thing itself. Not, be it noted, "genius"; nothing so mysterious or so special.*

The Mowing of a Field

There is a valley in South England remote from ambition and from fear, where the passage of strangers is rare and unperceived, and where the scent of the grass in summer is breathed only by those who are native to that unvisited land. The roads of the Channel do not traverse it; they choose upon either side easier passes over the range. One track alone leads up through it to the hills, and this is changeable: now green where men have little occasion to go, now a good road where it nears the homesteads and the barns. The woods grow steep above the slopes; they reach sometimes the very summit of the heights, or, when they cannot attain them, fill in and clothe the coombes. And, in between, along the floor of the valley, deep pastures and their silence are bordered by lawns of chalky grass and the small yew trees of the Downs.

The clouds that visit its sky reveal themselves beyond the one great rise, and sail, white and enormous, to the other, and sink beyond that other. But the plains above which they have travelled and the Weald to which they go, the people of the valley cannot see and hardly recall. The wind, when it reaches such fields, is no longer a gale from the salt, but fruitful and soft, an inland breeze; and those whose blood was nourished here feel in that wind the fruitfulness of our orchards and all the life that all things draw from the air.

In this place, when I was a boy, I pushed through a fringe of beeches that made a complete screen between me and the world, and I came to a glade called No Man's Land. I climbed beyond it, and I was surprised and glad, because from the ridge of that glade I saw the sea. To this place very lately I returned.

The many things that I recovered as I came up the countryside were not less charming than when a distant memory had enshrined them, but much more. Whatever veil is thrown by a longing recollection had not intensified nor even made more mysterious the beauty of that happy ground; not in my very dreams of morning had I, in exile, seen it more beloved or more rare. Much also that I had forgotten now returned to me as I approached—a group of elms, a little turn of the parson's wall, a small paddock beyond the graveyard close, cherished by one man, with a low wall of very old stone guarding it all round. And all these things fulfilled and amplified my delight, till even the good vision of the place, which I had kept so many years, left me and was replaced by its better reality. "Here," I said to myself, "is a symbol of what some say is reserved for the soul: pleasure of a kind which cannot be imagined save in a moment when at last it is attained."

When I came to my own gate and my own field, and had before me the house I knew, I looked around a little (though it was already evening), and I saw that the grass was standing as it should stand when it is ready for the scythe. For in this, as in everything that a man can do—of those things at least which are very old—there is an exact moment when they are done best. And it has been remarked of whatever rules us that it works blunderingly, seeing that the good things given to man are not given at the precise moment when they would have filled him with delight. But, whether this be true or false, we can choose the just turn of the seasons in everything we do of our own will, and especially in the making of hay. Many think that hay is best made when the grass is thickest; and so they delay until it is rank and in flower, and has already heavily pulled the ground. And there is another false reason for delay, which is wet weather. For very few will understand (though it comes year after year) that we have rain always in South England between the sickle and the scythe, or say just after the weeks of east wind are over. First we have a week of sudden warmth, as though the South had come to see us all; then we have the weeks of east and southeast wind; and then we have more or less of that rain of which I spoke, and which always astonishes the world. Now it is just before, or during, or at the very end of that rain—but not later—that grass should be cut for hay. True, upland grass, which is always thin, should be cut earlier than the grass in the bottoms and along the water meadows; but not even the latest, even in the wettest seasons, should be left (as it is) to flower and even to seed. For what we get when we store our grass is not a harvest of something ripe, but a thing just caught in its prime before maturity: as witness that our corn and straw are best yellow, but our hay is best green. So also Death should be represented with a scythe and Time with a sickle; for Time can take only what is ripe, but Death comes always too soon. In a word, then, it is always much easier to cut grass too late than too early; and I, under that evening and come back to these pleasant fields, looked at the grass and knew that it was time. June was in full advance: it was the beginning of that season when the night has already lost her foothold of the earth and hovers over it, never quite descending, but mixing sunset with the dawn.

Next morning, before it was yet broad day, I awoke, and thought of the mowing. The birds were already chattering in the trees beside my window, all except the nightingale, which had left and flown away to the Weald, where he sings all summer by day as well as by night in the oaks and the hazel spinneys, and especially along the little river Adur, one of the rivers of the Weald. The birds and the thought of the mowing had awakened me, and I went down the stairs and along the stone floors to where I could find a scythe; and when I took it from its nail, I remembered how, fourteen years ago, I had last gone out with my scythe, just so, into the fields at morning. In between that day and this were many things, cities and armies, and a confusion of books, mountains and the desert, and horrible great breadths of sea.

When I got out into the long grass the sun was not yet risen, but there were already many colours in the eastern sky, and I made haste to sharpen my scythe, so that I might get to the cutting before the dew should dry. Some say that it is best to wait 'till all the dew has risen, so as to get the grass quite dry from the very first. But, though it is an advantage to get the grass quite dry, yet it is not worthwhile to wait till the dew has risen. For, in the first place, you lose many hours of work (and those the coolest), and next—which is more important—you lose that great ease and thickness in cutting which comes of the dew. So I at once began to sharpen my scythe.

There is an art also in the sharpening of a scythe, and it is worth describing carefully. Your blade must be dry, and that is why you will see men rubbing the scythe-blade with grass before they whet it. Then also your rubber must be quite dry, and on this account it is a good thing to lay it on your coat and keep it there during all your day's mowing. The scythe you stand upright, with the blade pointing away from you, and you put your left hand firmly on the back of the blade, grasping it: then you pass the rubber first down one side of the blade-edge and then down the other, beginning near the handle and going on to the point and working quickly and hard. When you first do this you will, perhaps, cut your hand; but it is only at first that such an accident will happen to you.

To tell when the scythe is sharp enough this is the rule. First the stone clangs and grinds against the iron harshly; then it rings musically to one note; then, at last, it purrs as though the iron and stone were exactly suited. When you hear this, your scythe is sharp enough; and I, when I heard it that June dawn, with everything quite silent except the birds, let down the scythe and bent myself to mow.

When one does anything anew, after so many years, one fears very much for one's trick or habit. But all things once learnt are easily recoverable, and I very soon recovered the swing and power of the mower. Mowing well and mowing badly—or rather not mowing at all—are separated by very little; as is also true of writing verse, of playing the fiddle, and of dozens of other things, but of nothing more than of believing. For the bad or young or untaught mower without tradition, the mower Promethean, the mower original and contemptuous of the past, does all these things: He leaves great crescents of grass uncut. He digs the point of the scythe hard into the ground with a jerk. He loosens the handles and even the fastening of the blade. He twists the blade with his blunders, he blunts the blade, he chips it, dulls it, or breaks it clean off at the tip. If anyone is standing by he cuts him in the ankle. He sweeps up into the air wildly, with nothing to resist his stroke. He drags up earth with the grass, which is like making the meadow bleed. But the good mower who does things just as they should be done and have been for a hundred thousand years, falls into none of these fooleries. He goes forward very steadily, his scythe-blade just barely missing the ground, every grass falling; the swish and rhythm of his mowing are always the same.

So great an art can only be learnt by continual practice; but this much is worth writing down, that, as in all good work, to know the thing with which you work is the core of the affair. Good verse is best written on good paper with an easy pen, not with a lump of coal on a whitewashed wall. The pen thinks for you; and so does the scythe mow for you if you treat it honourably and in a manner that makes it recognize its service. The manner is this. You must regard the scythe as a pendulum that swings, not as a knife that cuts. A good mower puts no more strength into his stroke than into his lifting. Again, stand up to your work. The bad mower, eager and full of pain, leans forward and tries to force the scythe through the grass. The good mower, serene and able, stands as nearly straight as the shape of the scythe will let him, and follows up every stroke closely, moving his left foot forward. Then also let every stroke get well away. Mowing is a thing of ample gestures, like drawing a cartoon. Then, again, get yourself into a mechanical and repetitive mood: be thinking of anything at all but your mowing, and be anxious only when there seems some interruption to the monotony of the sound. In this mowing should be like one's prayers—all of a sort and always the same, and so made that you can establish a monotony and work them, as it were, with half your mind: that happier half, the half that does not bother.

In this way, when I had recovered the art after so many years, I went forward over the field, cutting lane after lane through the grass, and bringing out its most secret essences with the sweep of the scythe until the air was full of odours. At the end of every lane I sharpened my scythe and looked back at the work done, and then carried my scythe down again upon my shoulder to begin another. So, long before the bell rang in the chapel above me—that is, long before six o'clock, which is the time for the *Angelus*—I had many swathes already lying in order parallel like soldiery; and the high grass yet standing, making a great contrast with the shaven part, looked dense and high. As it says in the *Ballad of Val-és-Dunes*, where—

> The tall son of the Seven Winds
> Came riding out of Hither-hythe,

and his horse-hoofs (you will remember) trampled into the press and made a gap in it, and his sword (as you know)

> was like a scythe
> In Arcus when the grass is high
> And all the swathes in order lie,
> And there's the bailiff standing by
> A-gathering of the tithe.

So I mowed all the morning, 'till the houses awoke in the valley, and from some of them rose a little fragrant smoke, and men began to be seen.

I stood still and rested on my scythe to watch the awakening of the village, when I saw coming up to my field a man whom I had known in older times, before I had left the Valley.

He was of that dark silent race upon which all the learned quarrel, but which, by whatever meaningless name it may be called—Iberian, or Celtic, or what you will—is the permanent root of all England, and makes England wealthy and preserves it everywhere, except perhaps in the Fens and in a part of Yorkshire. Everywhere else you will find it active and strong. These people are intensive; their thoughts and their labours turn inward. It is on account of their presence in these islands that our gardens are the richest in the world. They also love low rooms and ample fires and great warm slopes of thatch. They have, as I believe, an older acquaintance with the English air than any other of all the strains that make up England. They hunted in the Weald with stones, and camped in the pines of the green-sand. They lurked under the oaks of the upper rivers, and saw the legionaries go up, up the straight paved road from the sea. They helped the few pirates to destroy the towns, and mixed with those pirates and shared the spoils of the Roman villas, and were glad to see the captains and priests destroyed. They remain; and no admixture of the Frisian pirates, or the Breton, or the Angevin and Norman conquerors, has very much affected their cunning eyes.

To this race, I say, belonged the man who now approached me. And he said to me, "Mowing?" And I answered, "Ar." Then he also said "Ar," as in duty bound; for so we speak to each other in the Stenes of the Downs.

Next he told me that, as he had nothing to do, he would lend me a hand; and I thanked him warmly, or, as we say, "kindly." For it is a good custom of ours always to treat bargaining as though it were a courteous pastime; and though what he was after was money, and what I wanted was his labour at the least pay, yet we both played the comedy that we were free men, the one granting a grace and the other accepting it. For the dry bones of commerce, avarice and method and need, are odious to the Valley; and we cover them up with a pretty body of fiction and observances. Thus, when it comes to buying pigs, the buyer does not begin to decry the pig and the vendor to praise it, as is the custom with lesser men; but tradition makes them do business in this fashion:—

First the buyer will go up to the seller when he sees him in his own steading, and, looking at the pig with admiration, the buyer will say that rain may or may not fall, or that we shall have snow or thunder, according to the time of year. Then the seller, looking critically at the pig, will agree that the weather is as his friend maintains. There is no haste at all; great leisure marks the dignity of their exchange. And the next step is, that the buyer says: "That's a fine pig you have there, Mr. —" (giving the seller's name). "Ar, powerful fine pig." Then the seller, saying also "Mr." (for twin brothers rocked in one cradle give each other ceremonious observance here), the seller, I say, admits, as though with reluctance, the strength and beauty of the pig, and falls into deep thought. Then the buyer says, as though moved by a great desire, that he is ready to give so much for the pig, naming half the proper price, or a little less. Then the seller remains in silence for some moments; and at last begins to shake his head slowly, 'till he says: "I don't be thinking of selling the pig, anyways." He will also add that a party only Wednesday offered him so much for the pig—and he names about double the proper price. Thus all ritual is duly accomplished; and the solemn act is entered upon with reverence and in a spirit of truth. For when the buyer uses this phrase: "I'll tell you what I *will* do," and offers within half a crown of the pig's value, the seller replies that he can refuse him nothing, and names half a crown above its value; the difference is split, the pig is sold, and in the quiet soul of each runs the peace of something accomplished.

Thus do we buy a pig or land or labour or malt or lime, always with elaboration and set forms; and many a London man has paid double and more for his violence and his greedy haste and very unchivalrous higgling. As happened with the land at Underwaltham, which the mortgagees had begged and implored the estate to take at twelve hundred and had privately offered to all the world at a thousand, but which a sharp direct man, of the kind that makes great fortunes, a man in a motor-car, a man in a fur coat, a man of few words, bought for two thousand three hundred before my very eyes, protesting that they might take his offer or leave it; and all because he did not begin by praising the land.

Well then, this man I spoke of offered to help me, and he went to get his scythe. But I went into the house and brought out a gallon jar of small ale for him and for me; for the sun was now very warm, and small ale goes well with mowing. When we had drunk some of this ale in mugs called "I see you," we took each a swathe, he a little behind me because he was the better mower; and so for many hours we swung, one before the other, mowing and mowing at the tall grass of the field. And the sun rose to noon and we were still at our mowing; and we ate food, but only for a little while, and we took again to our mowing. And at last there was nothing left but a small square of grass, standing like a square of linesmen who keep their formation, tall and unbroken, with all the dead lying around them when a battle is over and done.

Then for some little time I rested after all those hours; and the man and I talked together, and a long way off we heard in another field the musical sharpening of a scythe.

The sunlight slanted powdered and mellow over the breadth of the valley; for day was nearing its end. I went to fetch rakes from the steading; and when I had come back the last of the grass had fallen, and all the field lay flat and smooth, with the very green short grass in lanes between the dead and yellow swathes.

These swathes we raked into cocks to keep them from the dew against our return at daybreak; and we made the cocks as tall and steep as we could, for in that shape they best keep off the dew, and it is easier also to spread them after the sun has risen. Then we raked up every straggling blade, till the whole field was a clean floor for the tedding and the carrying of the hay next morning. The grass we had mown was but little over two acres; for that is all the pasture on my little tiny farm.

When we had done all this, there fell upon us the beneficent and deliberate evening; so that as we sat a little while together near the rakes, we saw the valley more solemn and dim around us, and all the trees and hedgerows quite still, and held by a complete silence. Then I paid my companion his wage, and bade him a good night, 'till we should meet in the same place before sunrise.

He went off with a slow and steady progress, as all our peasants do, making their walking a part of the easy but continual labour of their lives. But I sat on, watching the light creep around towards the north and change, and the waning moon coming up as though by stealth behind the woods of No Man's Land.

Max Beerbohm

(1872–1956)

A relic is a kind of remainder, something left over from another era either because times have changed and made the thing go hopelessly out of date, or, conversely, because someone has so cherished it as a memento that it takes on an aura of specialness, of sanctity. When people believed in miracles, relics of the holy dead were stored in precious coffers or shrines called reliquaries. All these notions come into play in Beerbohm's "A Relic." But push any of them too far and you disturb the lightness of this writer's touch—a lightness for which he was famous, one of the most admired and lovingly savored of English essayists around the turn of the century. "The incomparable Max," George Bernard Shaw called him, when he was succeeded by Beerbohm as drama critic of The Saturday Review *in 1898. Virginia Woolf, reviewing a five-volume collection of essays from 1870–1920, unkind as she could be to a Stevenson or a Belloc (as well as countless others), singled out Beerbohm's essays for unqualified praise; she considered him "without doubt the prince of his profession," because, she decided, he knew how to write ("The Modern Essay"). He himself was more modest, and the modesty sounds, in its precise way, genuine enough. In 1921, he wrote to a would-be biographer: "My gifts are small. I've used them very well and discreetly, never straining them: and the result is that I've made a charming little reputation." The self-amused tone of "A Relic" (included in his collection* And Even Now, *1921) does not belie that assessment. Indirectly, the essay comments on the character and the use of those "gifts," and the tempting possibilities for misuse of what one does not yet correctly value. It is a retrospective essay by a writer who loved retrospection, whether personal or cultural. Retrospection of the personal kind we quite naturally link with autobiography, the essay of self-origins: how I became X. Or, in this case perhaps, didn't.*

A Relic

Yesterday I found in a cupboard an old, small, battered portmanteau which, by the initials on it, I recognised as my own property. The lock appeared to have been forced. I dimly remembered having forced it myself, with a poker, in my hot youth, after some journey in which I had lost the key; and this act of violence was probably the reason why the trunk had so long ago ceased to travel. I unstrapped it, not without dust; it exhaled the faint scent of its long closure; it contained a tweed suit of Late Victorian pattern, some bills, some letters, a collar-stud, and—something which, after I had wondered for a moment or two what on earth it was, caused me suddenly to murmur, "Down below, the sea rustled to and fro over the shingle."

Strange that these words had, year after long year, been existing in some obscure cell at the back of my brain!—forgotten but all the while existing, like the trunk in that cupboard. What released them, what threw open the cell door, was nothing but the fragment of a fan; just the butt-end of an inexpensive fan. The sticks are of white bone, clipped together with a semicircular ring that is not silver. They are neatly oval at the base, but variously jagged at the other end. The longest of them measures perhaps two inches. Ring and all, they have no market value; for a farthing is the least coin in our currency. And yet, though I had so long forgotten them, for me they are not worthless. They touch a chord . . . Lest this confession raise false hopes in the reader, I add that I did not know their owner.

I did once see her, and in Normandy, and by moonlight, and her name was Angélique. She was graceful, she was even beautiful. I was but nineteen years old. Yet even so I cannot say that she impressed me favourably. I was seated at a table of a café on the terrace of a casino. I sat facing the sea, with my back to the casino. I sat listening to the quiet sea, which I had crossed that morning. The hour was late, there were few people about. I heard the swing-door behind me flap open, and was aware of a sharp snapping and crackling sound as a lady in white passed quickly by me. I stared at her erect thin back and her agitated elbows. A short fat man passed in pursuit of her—an elderly man in a black alpaca jacket that billowed. I saw that she had left a trail of little white things on the asphalt. I watched the efforts of the agonised short fat man to overtake her as she swept wraithlike away to the distant end of the terrace. What was the matter? What had made her so spectacularly angry with him? The three or four waiters of the café were exchanging cynical smiles and shrugs, as waiters will. I tried to feel cynical, but was thrilled with excitement, with wonder and curiosity. The woman out yonder had doubled on her tracks. She had not slackened her furious speed, but the man waddling contrived to keep pace with her now. With every moment they became more distinct, and the prospect that they would presently pass by me, back into the casino, gave me that physical tension which one feels on a wayside platform at the imminent passing of an express. In the rushingly enlarged vision I had of them, the wrath on the woman's face was even more saliently the main thing than I had supposed it would be. That very hard Parisian face must have been as white as the powder that coated it. "Écoute,[1] Angélique," gasped the perspiring bourgeois, "écoute, je te supplie—"[2] The swing-door received them and was left swinging to and fro. I wanted to follow, but had not paid for my bock. I beckoned my waiter. On his way to me he stooped down and picked up something which, with a smile and a shrug, he laid on my table: "Il semble que Mademoiselle ne s'en servira plus."[3] This is the thing I now write of, and at sight of it I understood why there had been that snapping and crackling, and what the white fragments on the ground were.

I hurried through the rooms, hoping to see a continuation of that drama—a scene of appeasement, perhaps, or of fury still implacable. But the two oddly-assorted players were not performing there. My waiter had told me he had not seen either of them before. I suppose they had arrived that day. But I was not destined to see either of them again. They went away, I suppose, next morning; jointly or singly; singly, I imagine.

They made, however, a prolonged stay in my young memory, and would have done so even had I not had that tangible memento of them. Who were they, those two of whom that one strange glimpse had befallen me? What, I wondered, was the previous history of each? What, in particular, had all that tragic pother been about? Mlle. Angélique I guessed to be thirty years old, her friend perhaps fifty-five. Each of their faces was as clear to me as in the moment of actual vision—the man's fat shiny bewildered face; the taut white face of the woman, the hard red line of her mouth, the eyes that were not flashing, but positively dull, with rage. I presumed that the fan had been a present from him, and a recent present—bought perhaps that very day, after their arrival in the town. But what, *what* had he done that she should break it between her hands, scattering the splinters as who should sow dragon's teeth? I could not believe he had done anything much amiss. I imagined her grievance a trivial one. But this did not make the case less engrossing. Again and again I would take the fan-stump from my pocket, examining it on the palm of my hand, or between finger and thumb, hoping to read the mystery it had been mixed up in, so that I might reveal that mystery to the world. To the world, yes; nothing less than that. I was determined to make a story of what I had seen—a *conte* in the manner of great Guy de Maupassant. Now and again, in the course of the past year of so, it had occurred to me that I might be a writer. But I had not felt the impulse to sit down and write something.

[1] Listen.

[2] Listen, I beg you—.

[3] It seems that Mademoiselle no longer needs this.

I did feel that impulse now. It would indeed have been an irresistible impulse if I had known just what to write.

I felt I might know at any moment, and had but to give my mind to it. Maupassant was an impeccable artist, but I think the secret of the hold he had on the young men of my day was not so much that we discerned his cunning as that we delighted in the simplicity which his cunning achieved. I had read a great number of his short stories, but none that had made me feel as though I, if I were a writer, mightn't have written it myself. Maupassant had an European reputation. It was pleasing, it was soothing and gratifying, to feel that one could at any time win an equal fame if one chose to set pen to paper. And now, suddenly, the spring had been touched in me, the time was come. I was grateful for the fluke by which I had witnessed on the terrace that evocative scene. I looked forward to reading the MS. of 'The Fan'—tomorrow, at latest. I was not wildly ambitious. I was not inordinately vain. I knew I couldn't ever, with the best will in the world, write like Mr. George Meredith. Those wondrous works of his, seething with wit, with poetry and philosophy and what not, never had beguiled me with the sense that I might do something similar. I had full consciousness of not being a philosopher, of not being a poet, and of not being a wit. Well, Maupassant was none of these things. He was just an observer like me. Of course he was a good deal older than I, and had observed a good deal more. But it seemed to me that he was not my superior in knowledge of life. I knew all about life through *him*.

Dimly, the initial paragraph of my tale floated in my mind. I—not exactly I myself, but rather that impersonal *je* familiar to me through Maupassant—was to be sitting at that table, with a bock before me, just as I *had* sat. Four or five short sentences would give the whole scene. One of these I had quite definitely composed. You have already heard it. "Down below, the sea rustled to and fro over the shingle."

These words, which pleased me much, were to do double duty. They were to recur. They were to be, by a fine stroke, the very last words of my tale, their tranquillity striking a sharp ironic contrast with the stress of what had just been narrated. I had, you see, advanced further in the form of my tale than in the substance. But even the form was as yet vague. What, exactly, was to happen after Mlle. Angélique and M. Joumand (as I provisionally called him) had rushed back past me into the casino? It was clear that I must hear the whole inner history from the lips of one or the other of them. Which? Should M. Joumand stagger out onto the terrace, sit down heavily at the table next to mine, bury his head in his hands, and presently, in broken words, blurt out to me all that might be of interest? . . .

" 'And I tell you I gave up everything for her—everything.' He stared at me with his old hopeless eyes. 'She is more than the fiend I have described to you. Yet I swear to you, monsieur, that if I had anything left to give, it should be hers.' "

"Down below, the sea rustled to and fro over the shingle."

Or should the lady herself be my informant? For a while, I rather leaned to this alternative. It was more exciting, it seemed to make the writer more signally a man of the world. On the other hand, it was less simple to manage. Wronged persons might be ever so communicative, but I surmised that persons in the wrong were reticent. Mlle. Angélique, therefore, would have to be modified by me in appearance and behaviour, toned down, touched up; and poor M. Joumand must look like a man of whom one could believe anything. . . .

"She ceased speaking. She gazed down at the fragments of her fan, and then, as though finding in them an image of her own life, whispered, 'To think what I once was, monsieur!—what, but for him, I might be, even now!' She buried her face in her hands, then stared out into the night. Suddenly she uttered a short, harsh laugh.

"Down below, the sea rustled to and fro over the shingle."

I decided that I must choose the first of these two ways. It was the less chivalrous as well as the less lurid way, but clearly it was the more artistic as well as the easier. The *chose vue*,[4] the *tranche de la vie*'[5]—this was the thing to aim at. Honesty was the best policy. I must be nothing if not merciless. Maupassant was nothing if not merciless. He would not have spared Mlle. Angélique. Besides, why should I libel M. Joumand? Poor—no, not *poor* M. Joumand! I warned myself against pitying him. One touch of 'sentimentality,' and I should be lost. M. Joumand was ridiculous. I must keep him so. But—what was his position in life? Was he a lawyer perhaps?—or the proprietor of a shop in the Rue de Rivoli? I toyed with the possibility that he kept a fan shop—that the business had once been a prosperous one, but had gone down, down, because of his infatuation for this woman to whom he was always giving fans—which she *always* smashed. . . ." 'Ah monsieur, cruel and ungrateful to me though she is, I swear to you that if I had anything left to give, it should be hers; but,' he stared at me with his old hopeless eyes, 'the fan she broke tonight was the last—the last, monsieur—of my stock.' Down below,"—but I pulled myself together, and asked pardon of my Muse.

It may be that I had offended her by my fooling. Or it may be that she had a sisterly desire to shield Mlle. Angélique from my mordant art. Or it may be that she was bent on saving M. de Maupassant from a

[4] Thing seen.

[5] Slice of life.

dangerous rivalry. Anyway, she withheld from me the inspiration I had so confidently solicited. I *could not* think what had led up to that scene on the terrace. I tried hard and soberly. I turned the *chose vue* over and over in my mind, day by day, and the fan-stump over and over in my hand. But the *chose à figurer*[6]—what, oh what, was that? Nightly I revisited the café, and sat there with an open mind—a mind wide-open to catch the idea that should drop into it like a ripe golden plum. The plum did not ripen. The mind remained wide-open for a week or more, but nothing except that phrase about the sea rustled to and fro in it.

A full quarter of a century has gone by. M. Joumand's death, so far too fat was he all those years ago, may be presumed. A temper so violent as Mlle. Angélique's must surely have brought its owner to the grave, long since. But here, all unchanged, the stump of her fan is; and once more I turn it over and over in my hand, not learning its secret—no, nor even trying to, now. The chord this relic strikes in me is not one of curiosity as to that old quarrel, but (if you will forgive me) one of tenderness for my first effort to write, and for my first hopes of excellence.

[6] Thing to be represented.

E. M. Forster

(1879–1970)

It is not easy, at any time, to manifest in writing the largely unspoken, even unformulated, values that govern one's individual life. It would have called for courage of an uncommon kind to essay such a personal manifesto in the time of "madness and cruelty" that was World War II and the years leading up to it. So E. M. Forster described the age in his anti-Nazi radio broadcasts. "During the present decade," he wrote at the close of the 1930s, "thousands and thousands of innocent people have been killed, robbed, mutilated, insulted, imprisoned" ("Post-Munich"). One of the earlier signs of things to come, he knew, had been the conflagration, in 1933, of 25,000 books outside the University of Berlin before a crowd of 40,000. "What I Believe" is just such a personal manifesto; the "today" of the essay is 1939, Hitler's "age of bloodshed" energized by a "creed of racial purity" (Radio Broadcasts). The dangerous route whereby creed becomes dogma of destruction was being engineered with awful precision. The courage of such an essay, if you are an eminent English author, lies not so much in opposing what is so patently evil, but in having the heart to engage in a discourse of belief at a time when belief itself has been so monstrously corrupted. To write an essay called "What I Believe" in an age terrorized by the spirit of Mein Kampf *takes, not least of all, a steadfast regard for the capacity of human language to cleanse and recreate itself. The essay was reprinted (as were the pieces cited earlier) in Forster's postwar collection* Two Cheers for Democracy; *"What I Believe" is, in the author's words, "the key to the book" (Prefatory Note). Now and again, by who knows what slip of tongue or typewriter, the title of Forster's book turns up as* "Three Cheers . . . ," *a small error, but an error of substance. The qualified name that Forster gave his book adjusts the volume, so to speak, of the central essay's own title. The quietly sane, steadfastly singular voice of this essay insists on addressing the individual reader even while all around the dictator–hero—the "Great Man"—and the mentality that sustains him are busy melting humanity down into "a single man."*

What I Believe

I do not believe in Belief. But this is an age of faith, and there are so many militant creeds that, in self-defence, one has to formulate a creed of one's own. Tolerance, good temper and sympathy are no longer enough in a world which is rent by religious and racial persecution, in a world where ignorance rules, and science, who ought to have ruled, plays the subservient pimp. Tolerance, good temper and sympathy—they are what matter really, and if the human race is not to collapse they must come to the front before long. But for the moment they are not enough, their action is no stronger than a flower, battered beneath a military jack-boot. They want stiffening, even if the process coarsens them. Faith, to my mind, is a stiffening process, a sort of mental starch, which ought to be applied as sparingly as possible. I dislike the stuff. I do not believe in it, for its own sake, at all. Herein I probably differ from most people, who believe in Belief, and are only sorry they cannot swallow even more than they do. My law-givers are Erasmus and Montaigne, not Moses and St. Paul. My temple stands not upon Mount Moriah but in that Elysian Field where even the immoral are admitted. My motto is: "Lord, I disbelieve—help thou my unbelief."

I have, however, to live in an Age of Faith—the sort of epoch I used to hear praised when I was a boy. It is extremely unpleasant really. It is bloody in every sense of the word. And I have to keep my end up in it. Where do I start?

With personal relationships. Here is something comparatively solid in a world full of violence and cruelty. Not absolutely solid, for Psychology has split and shattered the idea of a "Person," and has shown that there is something incalculable in each of us, which may at any moment rise to the surface and destroy our normal balance. We don't know what we are like. We can't know what other people are like. How, then, can we put any trust in personal relationships, or cling to them in the gathering political storm? In theory we cannot. But in practice we can and do. Though A is not unchangeably A or B unchangeably B, there can still be love and loyalty between the two. For the purpose of living one has to assume that the personality is solid, and the "self" is an entity, and to ignore all contrary evidence. And since to ignore evidence is one of the characteristics of faith, I certainly can proclaim that I believe in personal relationships.

Starting from them, I get a little order into the contemporary chaos. One must be fond of people and trust them if one is not to make a mess of life, and it is therefore essential that they should not let one down. They often do. The moral of which is that I must, myself, be as reliable as possible, and this I try to be. But reliability is not a matter of contract—that is the main difference between the world of personal relationships and the world of business relationships. It is a matter for the heart, which signs no documents. In other worlds, reliability is impossible unless there is a natural warmth. Most men possess this warmth, though they often have bad luck and get chilled. Most of them, even when they are politicians, *want* to keep faith. And one can, at all events, show one's own little light here, one's own poor little trembling flame, with the knowledge that it is not the only light that is shining in the darkness, and not the only one which the darkness does not comprehend. Personal relations are despised today. They are regarded as bourgeois luxuries, as products of a time of fair weather which is now past, and we are urged to get rid of them, and to dedicate ourselves to some movement or cause instead. I hate the idea of causes, and if I had to choose between betraying my country and betraying my friend, I hope I should have the guts to betray my country. Such a choice may scandalise the modern reader, and he may stretch out his patriotic hand to the telephone at once and ring up the police. It would not have shocked Dante, though. Dante places Brutus and Cassius in the lowest circle of Hell because they had chosen to betray their friend Julius Caesar rather than their country Rome. Probably one will not be asked to make such an agonising choice. Still, there lies at the back of every creed something terrible and hard for which the worshipper may one day be required to suffer, and there is even a terror and a hardness in this creed of personal relationships, urbane and mild though it sounds. Love and loyalty to an individual can run counter to the claims of the State. When they do—down with the State, say I, which means that the State would down me.

This brings me along to Democracy, "even Love, the Beloved Republic, which feeds upon Freedom and lives." Democracy is not a Beloved Republic really, and never will be. But it is less hateful than other contemporary forms of government, and to that extent it deserves our support. It does start from the assumption that the individual is important, and that all types are needed to make a civilisation. It does not divide its citizens into the bossers and the bossed—as an efficiency-regime tends to do. The people I admire most are those who are sensitive and want to create something or discover something, and do not see life in terms of power, and such people get more of a chance under a democracy than elsewhere. They found religions, great or small, or they produce literature and art, or they do disinterested scientific research, or they may be what is called "ordinary people," who are creative in their private lives, bring up their children decently, for instance, or help their neighbours. All these people need to express themselves; they cannot do so unless society allows them liberty to do so, and the society which allows them most liberty is a democracy.

Democracy has another merit. It allows criticism, and if there is not public criticism there are bound to be hushed-up scandals. That is why I believe in the Press, despite all its lies and vulgarity, and why I believe in Parliament. Parliament is often sneered at because it is a Talking Shop. I believe in it *because* it is a talking shop. I believe in the Private Member who makes himself a nuisance. He gets snubbed and is told that he is cranky or ill-informed, but he does expose abuses which would otherwise never have been mentioned, and very often an abuse gets put right just by being mentioned. Occasionally, too, a well-meaning public official starts losing his head in the cause of efficiency, and thinks himself God Almighty. Such officials are particularly frequent in the Home Office. Well, there will be questions about them in Parliament sooner or later, and then they will have to mind their steps. Whether Parliament is either a representative body or an efficient one is questionable, but I value it because it criticises and talks, and because its chatter gets widely reported.

So Two Cheers for Democracy: one because it admits variety and two because it permits criticism. Two cheers are quite enough: there is no occasion to give three. Only Love the Beloved Republic deserves that.

What about Force, though? While we are trying to be sensitive and advanced and affectionate and tolerant, an unpleasant question pops up: does not all society rest upon force? If a government cannot count upon the police and the army, how can it hope to rule? And if an individual gets knocked on the head or sent to a labour camp, of what significance are his opinions?

This dilemma does not worry me as much as it does some. I realise that all society rests upon force. But all the great creative actions, all the decent human relations, occur during the intervals when force has not managed to come to the front. These intervals are what matter. I want them to be as frequent and as lengthy as possible, and I call them "civilisation." Some people idealise force and pull it into the foreground and worship it, instead of keeping it in the background as long as possible. I think they make a mistake, and I think that their opposites, the mystics, err even more when they declare that force does not exist. I believe that it exists, and that one of our jobs is to prevent it from getting out of its box. It gets out sooner or later, and then it destroys us and all the lovely things which we have made. But it is not out all the time, for the fortunate reason that the strong are so stupid. Consider their conduct for a moment in the Niebelung's Ring. The giants there have the guns, or in other words the gold; but they do nothing with it, they do not realise that they are all-powerful, with the result that the catastrophe is delayed and the castle of Walhalla, insecure but glorious, fronts the storms. Fafnir, coiled round his hoard, grumbles and grunts; we can hear him under Europe today; the leaves of the wood already tremble, and the Bird calls its warnings uselessly. Fafnir will destroy us, but by a blessed dispensation he is stupid and slow, and creation goes on just outside the poisonous blast of his breath. The Nietzschean would hurry the monster up, the mystic would say he did not exist, but Wotan, wiser than either, hastens to create warriors before doom declares itself. The Valkyries are symbols not only of courage but of intelligence; they represent the human spirit snatching its opportunity while the going is good, and one of them even finds time to love. Brünnhilde's last song hymns the recurrence of love, and since it is the privilege of art to exaggerate, she goes even further, and proclaims the love which is eternally triumphant and feeds upon freedom, and lives.

So that is what I feel about force and violence. It is, alas! the ultimate reality on this earth, but it does not always get to the front. Some people call its absences "decadence"; I call them "civilisation" and find in such interludes the chief justification for the human experiment. I look the other way until fate strikes me. Whether this is due to courage or to cowardice in my own case I cannot be sure. But I know that if men had not looked the other way in the past, nothing of any value would survive. The people I respect most behave as if they were immortal and as if society was eternal. Both assumptions are false: both of them must be accepted as true if we are to go on eating and working and loving, and are to keep open a few breathing holes for the human spirit. No millennium seems likely to descend upon humanity; no better and stronger League of Nations will be instituted; no form of Christianity and no alternative to Christianity will bring peace to the world or integrity to the individual; no "change of heart" will occur. And yet we need not despair, indeed, we cannot despair; the evidence of history shows us that men have always insisted on behaving creatively under the shadow of the sword; that they have done their artistic and scientific and domestic stuff for the sake of doing it, and that we had better follow their example under the shadow of the aeroplanes. Others, with more vision or courage than myself, see the salvation of humanity ahead, and will dismiss my conception of civilisation as paltry, a sort of tip-and-run game. Certainly it is presumptuous to say that we *cannot* improve, and that Man, who has only been in power for a few thousand years, will never learn to make use of his power. All I mean is that, if people continue to kill one another as they do, the world cannot get better than it is, and that since there are more people than formerly, and their means for destroying one another superior, the world may well get worse. What is good in people—and consequently in the world—is their insistence on creation, their belief in friendship and loyalty for their own sakes; and though Violence remains and is, indeed, the major partner in this muddled establishment, I believe that creativeness remains too, and will always assume direction when violence sleeps. So, though I am not an optimist, I cannot agree with Sophocles that it were better never to have been born. And although, like Horace, I see no evidence that each batch of births is superior to the last, I leave the field open for the more complacent view. This is such a difficult moment to live in, one cannot help getting gloomy and also a bit rattled, and perhaps short-sighted.

In search of a refuge, we may perhaps turn to hero-worship. But here we shall get no help, in my opinion. Hero-worship is a dangerous vice, and one of the minor merits of a democracy is that it does not encourage it, or produce that unmanageable type of citizen known as the Great Man. It produces instead different kinds of small men—a much finer achievement. But people who cannot get interested in the variety of life, and cannot make up their own minds, get discontented over this, and they long for a hero to bow down before and to follow blindly. It is significant that a hero is an integral part of the authoritarian stock-in-trade today. An efficiency-regime cannot be run without a few heroes stuck about it to carry off the dullness—much as plums have to be put into a bad pudding to make it palatable. One hero at the top and a smaller one each side of him is a favourite arrangement, and the timid and the bored are comforted by the trinity, and, bowing down, feel exalted and strengthened.

No, I distrust Great Men. They produce a desert of uniformity around them and often a pool of blood too, and I always feel a little man's pleasure when they come a cropper. Every now and then one reads in the newspapers some such statement as: "The coup d'état appears to have failed, and Admiral Toma's whereabouts is at present unknown." Admiral Toma had probably every qualification for being a Great Man—an iron will, personal magnetism, dash, flair, sexlessness—but fate was against him, so he retires to unknown whereabouts instead of parading history with his peers. He fails with a completeness which no artist and no lover can experience, because with them the process of creation is itself an achievement, whereas with him the only possible achievement is success.

I believe in aristocracy, though—if that is the right word, and if a democrat may use it. Not an aristocracy of power, based upon rank and influence, but an aristocracy of the sensitive, the considerate and the plucky. Its members are to be found in all nations and classes, and all through the ages, and there is a secret understanding between them when they meet. They represent the true human tradition, the one permanent victory of our queer race over cruelty and chaos. Thousands of them perish in obscurity, a few are great names. They are sensitive for others as well as for themselves, they are considerate without being fussy, their pluck is not swankiness but the power to endure, and they can take a joke. I give no examples—it is risky to do that—but the reader may as well consider whether this is the type of person he would like to meet and to be, and whether (going farther with me) he would prefer that this type should *not* be an ascetic one. I am against asceticism myself. I am with the old Scotsman who wanted less chastity and more delicacy. I do not feel that my aristocrats are a real aristocracy if they thwart their bodies, since bodies are the instruments through which we register and enjoy the world. Still, I do not insist. This is not a major point. It is clearly possible to be sensitive, considerate and plucky and yet be an ascetic too, if anyone possesses the first three qualities, I will let him in! On they go—an invincible army, yet not a victorious one. The aristocrats, the elect, the chosen, the Best People—all the words that describe them are false, and all attempts to organise them fail. Again and again Authority, seeing their value, has tried to net them and to utilise them as the Egyptian Priesthood or the Christian Church or the Chinese Civil Service or the Group Movement, or some other worthy stunt. But they slip through the net and are gone; when the door is shut, they are no longer in the room; their temple, as one of them remarked, is the Holiness of the Heart's Affection, and their kingdom, though they never possess it, is the wide-open world.

With this type of person knocking about, and constantly crossing one's path if one has eyes to see or hands to feel, the experiment of earthly life cannot be dismissed as a failure. But it may well be hailed as a tragedy, the tragedy being that no device has been found by which these private decencies can be transmitted to public affairs. As soon as people have power they go crooked and sometimes dotty as well, because the possession of power lifts them into a region where normal honesty never pays. For instance, the man who is selling newspapers outside the Houses of Parliament can safely leave his papers to go for a drink and his cap beside them: anyone who takes a paper is sure to drop a copper into the cap. But the men who are inside the Houses of Parliament—they cannot trust one another like that, still less the Government they compose trust other governments. No caps upon the pavement here, but suspicion, treachery and armaments. The more highly public life is organised the lower does its morality sink; the nations of today behave to each other worse than they ever did in the past, they cheat, rob, bully and bluff, make war without notice, and kill as many women and children as possible; whereas primitive tribes were at all events restrained by taboos. It is a humiliating outlook—though the greater the darkness, the brighter shine the little lights, reassuring one another, signalling: "Well, at all events, I'm still here. I don't like it very much, but how are you?" Unquenchable lights of my aristocracy! Signals of the invincible army! "Come along—anyway, let's have a good time while we can." I think they signal that too.

The Saviour of the future—if ever he comes—will not preach a new Gospel. He will merely utilise my aristocracy, he will make effective the good will and the good temper which are already existing. In other words, he will introduce a new technique. In economics, we are told that if there was a new technique of distribution, there need be no poverty, and people would not starve in one place while crops were being ploughed under in another. A similar change is needed in the sphere of morals and politics. The desire for it is by no means new; it was expressed, for example, in theological terms by Jacopone da Todi over six hundred years ago. "Ordina questo amore, O tu che m'ami," he said; "O thou who lovest me—set this love in order." His prayer was not granted, and I do not myself believe that it ever will be, but here, and not through a change of heart, is our probable route. Not by becoming better, but by ordering and distributing his native goodness, will Man shut up Force into its box, and so gain time to explore the universe and to set his mark upon it worthily. At present he only explores it at odd moments, when Force is looking the other way, and his divine creativeness appears as a trivial by-product, to be scrapped as soon as the drums beat and the bombers hum.

Such a change, claim the orthodox, can only be made by Christianity, and will be made by it in God's good time: man always has failed and always will fail to organise his own goodness, and it is presumptuous of him to try. This claim—solemn as it is—leaves me cold. I cannot believe that Christianity will ever cope with the present world-wide mess, and I think that such influence as it retains in modern society is due to the money behind it, rather than to its spiritual appeal. It was a spiritual force once, but the indwelling spirit will have to be restated if it is to calm the waters again, and probably restated in a non-Christian form. Naturally a lot of people, and people who are not only good but able and intelligent, will disagree here; they will vehemently deny that Christianity has failed, or they will argue that its failure proceeds from the wickedness of men, and really proves its ultimate success. They have Faith, with a large F. My faith has a very small one, and I only intrude it because these are strenuous and serious days, and one likes to say what one thinks while speech is comparatively free: it may not be free much longer.

The above are the reflections of an individualist and a liberal who has found liberalism crumbling beneath him and at first felt ashamed. Then, looking around, he decided there was no special reason for shame, since other people, whatever they felt, were equally insecure. And as for individualism—there seems no way of getting off this, even if one wanted to. The dictator-hero can grind down his citizens till they are all alike, but he cannot melt them into a single man. That is beyond his power. He can order them to merge, he can incite them to mass-antics, but they are obliged to be born separately, and to die separately, and, owing to these unavoidable termini, will always be running off the totalitarian rails. The memory of birth and the expectation of death always lurk within the human being, making him separate from his fellows and consequently capable of intercourse with them. Naked I came into the world, naked I shall go out of it! And a very good thing too, for it reminds me that I am naked under my shirt, whatever its colour.

Virginia Woolf

(1882–1941)

*Virginia Woolf was a great reader, both in the colloquial British sense—one who is always reading and loves it—and in the weightier sense: a superbly good reader, a percipient reader. Katherine Anne Porter lauded her as "one of the glories of our time" ("Virginia Woolf"). Her friend E. M. Forster spoke soon after Woolf's death of "the breadth of her knowledge" as a critic and essayist, "and the depth of her literary sympathy" (Rede Lecture, 1941). Both attributes inform and enliven her essay, originally a talk, "How Should One Read a Book?" (*Common Reader, *1932). In the end, all you have to report about reading is what you yourself do when you read; Woolf's title—a question— captures the spirit of the whole, which at once explores how she reads and, with the assurance characteristic of this essayist, offers itself also as a model of reading. By very different means of form, style, and feeling, "The Death of the Moth" recounts another kind of reading, another occasion for training one's receptivity and making the difficult move from sympathy to judgment (*The Death of the Moth and Other Essays, *1942). But Forster's affectionate tribute continues in an oddly qualified way: "Improving the world," he observed with a hint of uneasiness, "she would not consider, on the ground that the world is man-made and that she, a woman, had no responsibility for the mess." Whether writers have the power to improve the world, or any piece of it, is open to question. Responsible or not, it is certain that Woolf did indeed change the world by writing in it as she did, as the woman she was. That she changed the novel, and therefore the way we read novels, few would dispute. She also transformed the essay; more precisely, she transformed the authorship of the essay: after Virginia Woolf, the essayist in English is no longer typically male. She had read them all and wrote about many of them with superb sympathy and discernment. She was, in Cynthia Ozick's suggestive phrase, "a courier for the past" ("Mrs. Virginia Woolf: A Madwoman and Her Nurse"), carrying the tradition of the essay by way of her reading into her writing, very conscious of what she was doing all the while. Not as Montaigne, the inventor of the essay, was conscious, but in the way of a writer who is also a great reader, whose reading is always a kind of collaboration with the other writer, whether novelist, memoirist, poet, or essayist. By way of such collaborations with the great practitioners, Woolf made the essay her own.*

How Should One Read a Book?

In the first place, I want to emphasise the note of interrogation at the end of my title. Even if I could answer the question for myself, the answer would apply only to me and not to you. The only advice, indeed, that one person can give another about reading is to take no advice, to follow your own instincts, to use your own reason, to come to your own conclusions. If this is agreed between us, then I feel at liberty to put forward a few ideas and suggestions because you will not allow them to fetter that independence which is the most important quality that a reader can possess. After all, what laws can be laid down about books? The battle of Waterloo was certainly fought on a certain day; but is *Hamlet* a better play than *Lear?* Nobody can say. Each must decide that question for himself. To admit authorities, however heavily furred and gowned, into our libraries and let them tell us how to read, what to read, what value to place upon what we read, is to destroy the spirit of freedom which is the breath of those sanctuaries. Everywhere else we may be bound by laws and conventions—there we have none.

But to enjoy freedom, if the platitude is pardonable, we have of course to control ourselves. We must not squander our powers, helplessly and ignorantly, squirting half the house in order to water a single rose-bush; we must train them, exactly and powerfully, here on the very spot. This, it may be, is one of the first difficulties that faces us in a library. What is "the very spot"? There may well seem to be nothing but a conglomeration and huddle of confusion. Poems and novels, histories and memoirs, dictionaries and blue-books; books written in all languages by men and women of all tempers, races, and ages jostle each other on the shelf. And outside the donkey brays, the women gossip at the pump, the colts gallop across the fields. Where are we to begin? How are we to bring order into this multitudinous chaos and so get the deepest and widest pleasure from what we read?

It is simple enough to say that since books have classes—fiction, biography, poetry—we should separate them and take from each what it is right that each should give us. Yet few people ask from books what books can give us. Most commonly we come to books with blurred and divided minds, asking of fiction that it shall be true, of poetry that it shall be false, of biography that it shall be flattering, of history that it shall enforce our own prejudices. If we could banish all such preconceptions when we read, that would be an admirable beginning. Do not dictate to your author; try to become him. Be his fellow-worker and accomplice. If you hang back, and reserve and criticise at first, you are preventing yourself from getting the fullest possible value from what you read. But if you open your mind as widely as possible, then signs and hints of almost imperceptible fineness, from the twist and turn of the first sentences, will bring you into the presence of a human being unlike any other. Steep yourself in this, acquaint yourself with this, and soon you will find that your author is giving you, or attempting to give you, something far more definite. The thirty-two chapters of a novel—if we consider how to read a novel first—are an attempt to make something as formed and controlled as a building: but words are more impalpable than bricks; reading is a longer and more complicated process than seeing. Perhaps the quickest way to understand the elements of what a novelist is doing is not to read, but to write; to make your own experiment with the dangers and difficulties of words. Recall, then, some event that has left a distinct impression on you—how at the corner of the street, perhaps, you passed two people talking. A tree shook; an electric light danced; the tone of the talk was comic, but also tragic; a whole vision, an entire conception, seemed contained in that moment.

But when you attempt to reconstruct it in words, you will find that it breaks into a thousand conflicting impressions. Some must be subdued; others emphasised; in the process you will lose, probably, all grasp upon the emotion itself. Then turn from your blurred and lettered pages to the opening pages of some great novelist—Defoe, Jane Austen, Hardy. Now you will be better able to appreciate their mastery. It is not merely that we are in the presence of a different person—Defoe, Jane Austen, or Thomas Hardy—but that we are living in a different world. Here, in *Robinson Crusoe*, we are trudging a plain highroad; one thing happens after another; the fact and the order of the fact is enough. But if the open air and adventure mean everything to Defoe they mean nothing to Jane Austen. Hers is the drawing-room, and people talking, and by the many mirrors of their talk revealing their characters. And if, when we have accustomed ourselves to the drawing-room with its reflections, we turn to Hardy, we are at once spun round. The moors are round us and the stars are above our heads. The other side of the mind is now exposed—the dark side that comes uppermost in solitude, not the light side that shows in company. Our relations are not towards people, but towards Nature and destiny. Yet different as these worlds are, each is consistent with itself. The maker of each is careful to observe the laws of his own perspective, and however great a strain they may put upon us they will never confuse us, as lesser writers so frequently do, by introducing two different kinds of reality into the same book. Thus to go from one great novelist to another—from Jane Austen to Hardy, from Peacock to Trollope, from Scott to Meredith—is to be wrenched and uprooted; to be thrown this way and then that. To read a novel is a difficult and complex art. You must be capable not only of great fineness of perception, but of great boldness of imagination if you are going to make use of all that the novelist—the great artist—gives you.

But a glance at the heterogeneous company on the shelf will show you that writers are very seldom "great artists"; far more often a book makes no claim to be a work of art at all. These biographies and autobiographies, for example, lives of great men, of men long dead and forgotten, that stand cheek by jowl with the novels and poems, are we to refuse to read them because they are not "art"? Or shall we read them, but read them in a different way, with a different aim? Shall we read them in the first place to satisfy that curiosity which possesses us sometimes when in the evening we linger in front of a house where the lights are lit and the blinds not yet drawn, and each floor of the house shows us a different section of human life in being? Then we are consumed with curiosity about the lives of these people—the servants gossiping, the gentlemen dining, the girl dressing for a party, the old woman at the window with her knitting. Who are they, what are they, what are their names, their occupations, their thoughts, and adventures?

Biographies and memoirs answer such questions, light up innumerable such houses; they show us people going about their daily affairs, toiling, failing, succeeding, eating, hating, loving, until they die. And sometimes as we watch, the house fades and the iron railings vanish and we are out at sea; we are hunting, sailing, fighting; we are among savages and soldiers; we are taking part in great campaigns. Or if we like to stay here in England, in London, still the scene changes; the street narrows; the house becomes small, cramped, diamond-paned, and malodorous. We see a poet, Donne, driven from such a house because the walls were so thin that when the children cried their voices cut through them. We can follow him, through the paths that lie in the pages of books, to Twickenham; to Lady Bedford's Park, a famous meeting-ground for nobles and poets; and then turn our steps to Wilton, the great house under the downs, and hear Sidney read the *Arcadia* to his sister; and ramble among the very marshes and see the very herons that figure in that famous romance; and then again travel north with that other Lady Pembroke, Anne Clifford, to her wild moors, or plunge into the city and control our merriment at the sight of Gabriel Harvey in his black velvet suit arguing about poetry with Spenser. Nothing is more fascinating than to grope and stumble in the alternate darkness and splendour of Elizabethan London. But there is no staying there. The Temples and the Swifts, the Harleys and the St. Johns beckon us on; hour upon hour can be spent disentangling their quarrels and deciphering their characters; and when we tire of them we can stroll on, past a lady in black wearing diamonds, to Samuel Johnson and Goldsmith and Garrick; or cross the channel, if we like, and meet Voltaire and Diderot, Madame du Deffand; and so back to England and Twickenham—how certain places repeat themselves and certain names!—where Lady Bedford had her Park once and Pope lived later, to Walpole's home at Strawberry Hill. But Walpole introduces us to such a swarm of new acquaintances, there are so many houses to visit and bells to ring that we may well hesitate for a moment, on the Miss Berrys' doorstep, for example, when behold, up comes Thackeray; he is the friend of the woman whom Walpole loved; so that merely by going from friend to friend, from garden to garden, from house to house, we have passed from one end of English literature to another and wake to find ourselves here again in the present, if we can so differentiate this moment from all that have gone before. This, then, is one of the ways in which we can read these lives and letters; we can make them light up the many windows of the past; we can watch the famous dead in their familiar habits and fancy sometimes that we are very close and can surprise their secrets, and sometimes we may pull out a play or a poem that they have written and see whether it reads differently in the presence of the author. But this again rouses other questions. How far, we must ask ourselves, is a book influenced by its writer's life—how far is it safe to let the man interpret the writer? How far shall we resist or give way to the sympathies and antipathies that the man himself rouses in us—so sensitive are words, so receptive of the character of the author? These are questions that press upon us when we read lives and letters, and we must answer them for ourselves, for nothing can be more fatal than to be guided by the preferences of others in a matter so personal.

But also we can read such books with another aim, not to throw light on literature, not to become familiar with famous people, but to refresh and exercise our own creative powers. Is there not an open window on the right hand of the bookcase? How delightful to stop reading and look out! How stimulating the scene is, in its unconsciousness, its irrelevance, its perpetual movement—the colts galloping round the field, the woman filling her pail at the well, the donkey throwing back his head and emitting his long, acrid moan. The greater part of any library is nothing but the record of such fleeting moments in the lives of men, women, and donkeys. Every literature, as it grows old, has its rubbish-heap, its record of vanished moments and forgotten lives told in flattering and feeble accents that have perished. But if you give yourself up to the delight of rubbish-reading you will be surprised, indeed you will be overcome, by the relics of human life that have been cast out to moulder. It may be one letter—but what a vision it gives! It may be a few sentences—but what vistas they suggest! Sometimes a whole story will come together with such beautiful humour and pathos and completeness that it seems as if a great novelist had been at work, yet it is only an old actor, Tate Wilkinson, remembering the strange story of Captain Jones; it is only a young subaltern serving under Arthur Wellesley and falling in love with a pretty girl at Lisbon; it is only Maria Allen letting fall her sewing in the empty drawing-room and sighing how she wishes she had taken Dr. Burney's good advice and had never eloped with her Rishy. None of this has any value; it is negligible in the extreme; yet how absorbing it is now and again to go through the rubbish-heaps and find rings and scissors and broken noses buried in the huge past and try to piece them together while the colt gallops round the field, the woman fills her pail at the well, and the donkey brays.

But we tire of rubbish-reading in the long run. We tire of searching for what is needed to complete the half-truth which is all that the Wilkinsons, the Bunburys, and the Maria Allens are able to offer us. They had not the artist's power of mastering and eliminating; they could not tell the whole truth even about their own lives; they have disfigured the story that might have been so shapely. Facts are all that they can offer us, and facts are a very inferior form of fiction. Thus the desire grows upon us to have done with half-statements and approximations; to cease from searching out the minute shades of human character, to enjoy the greater abstractness, the purer truth of fiction. Thus we create the mood, intense and generalised, unaware of detail, but stressed by some regular, recurrent beat, whose natural expression is poetry; and that is the time to read poetry when we are almost able to write it.

Western wind, when wilt thou blow?
The small rain down can rain.
Christ, if my love were in my arms,
And I in my bed again!

The impact of poetry is so hard and direct that for the moment there is no other sensation except that of the poem itself. What profound depths we visit then—how sudden and complete is our immersion! There is nothing here to catch hold of; nothing to stay us in our flight. The illusion of fiction is gradual; its effects are prepared; but who when they read these four lines stops to ask who wrote them, or conjures up the thought of Donne's house or Sidney's secretary; or enmeshes them in the intricacy of the past and the succession of generations? The poet is always our contemporary. Our being for the moment is centred and constricted, as in any violent shock of personal emotion. Afterwards, it is true, the sensation begins to spread in wider rings through our minds; remoter senses are reached; these begin to sound and to comment and we are aware of echoes and reflections. The intensity of poetry covers an immense range of emotion. We have only to compare the force and directness of

> I shall fall like a tree, and find my grave,
>   Only remembering that I grieve,

with the wavering modulation of

> Minutes are numbered by the fall of sands,
> As by an hour glass; the span of time
> Doth waste us to our graves, and we look on it;
> An age of pleasure, revelled out, comes home
> At last, and ends in sorrow; but the life,
> Weary of riot, numbers every sand,
> Wailing in sighs, until the last drop down,
> So to conclude calamity in rest,

or place the meditative calm of

>   whether we be young or old,
> Our destiny, our being's heart and home,
> Is with infinitude, and only there;
> With hope it is, hope that can never die,
> Effort, and expectation, and desire,
> And something evermore about to be,

beside the complete and inexhaustible loveliness of

> The moving Moon went up the sky,
> And no where did abide:
> Softly she was going up,
> And a star or two beside—

or the splendid fantasy of

> And the woodland haunter
> Shall not cease to saunter
>   When, far down some glade,
> Of the great world's burning,
> One soft flame upturning
> Seems, to his discerning,
>   Crocus in the shade.

to bethink us of the varied art of the poet; his power to make us at once actors and spectators; his power to run his hand into character as if it were a glove, and be Falstaff or Lear; his power to condense, to widen, to state, once and forever.

"We have only to compare"—with those words the cat is out of the bag, and the true complexity of reading is admitted. The first process, to receive impressions with the utmost understanding, is only half the process of reading; it must be completed, if we are to get the whole pleasure from a book, by another. We must pass judgment upon these multitudinous impressions; we must make of these fleeting shapes one that is hard and lasting. But not directly. Wait for the dust of reading to settle; for the conflict and the questioning to die down; walk, talk, pull the dead petals from a rose, or fall asleep. Then suddenly without our willing it, for it is thus that Nature undertakes these transitions, the book will return, but differently. It will float to the top of the mind as a whole. And the book as a whole is different from the book received currently in separate phrases. Details now fit themselves into their places. We see the shape from start to finish; it is a barn, a pig-sty, or a cathedral. Now then we can compare book with book as we compare building with building. But this act of comparison means that our attitude has changed; we are no longer the friends of the writer, but his judges; and just as we cannot be too sympathetic as friends, so as judges we cannot be too severe. Are they not criminals, books that have wasted our time and sympathy; are they not the most insidious enemies of society, corrupters, defilers, the writers of false books, faked books, books that fill the air with decay and disease? Let us then be severe in our judgments; let us compare each book with the greatest of its kind. There they hang in the mind the shapes of the books we have read solidified by the judgments we have passed on them—*Robinson Crusoe*, *Emma*, *The Return of the Native.* Compare the novels with these—even the latest and least of novels has a right to be judged with the best. And so with poetry—when the intoxication of rhythm has died down and the splendour of words has faded a visionary shape will return to us and this must be compared with *Lear*, with *Phèdre*, with *The Prelude;* or if not with these, with whatever is the best or seems to us to be the best in its own kind. And we may be sure that the newness of new poetry and fiction is its most superficial quality and that we have only to alter slightly, not to recast, the standards by which we have judged the old.

It would be foolish, then, to pretend that the second part of reading, to judge, to compare, is as simple as the first—to open the mind wide to the fast flocking of innumerable impressions. To continue reading without the book before you, to hold one shadow-shape against another, to have read widely enough and with enough understanding to make such comparisons alive and illuminating—that is difficult; it is still more difficult to press further and to say, "Not only is the book of this sort, but it is of this value; here it fails; here it succeeds; this is bad; that is good."

To carry out this part of a reader's duty needs such imagination, insight, and learning that it is hard to conceive any one mind sufficiently endowed; impossible for the most self-confident to find more than the seeds of such powers in himself. Would it not be wiser, then, to remit this part of reading and to allow the critics, the gowned and furred authorities of the library, to decide the question of the book's absolute value for us? Yet how impossible! We may stress the value of sympathy; we may try to sink our own identity as we read. But we know that we cannot sympathise wholly or immerse ourselves wholly; there is always a demon in us who whispers, "I hate, I love," and we cannot silence him. Indeed, it is precisely because we hate and we love that our relation with the poets and novelists is so intimate that we find the presence of another person intolerable. And even if the results are abhorrent and our judgments are wrong, still our taste, the nerve of sensation that sends shocks through us, is our chief illuminant; we learn through feeling; we cannot suppress our own idiosyncrasy without impoverishing it. But as time goes on perhaps we can train our taste; perhaps we can make it submit to some control. When it has fed greedily and lavishly upon books of all sorts—poetry, fiction, history, biography—and has stopped reading and looked for long spaces upon the variety, the incongruity of the living world, we shall find that it is changing a little; it is not so greedy, it is more reflective. It will begin to bring us not merely judgments on particular books, but it will tell us that there is a quality common to certain books. Listen, it will say, what shall we call *this?* And it will read us perhaps *Lear* and then perhaps the *Agamemnon* in order to bring out that common quality. Thus, with our taste to guide us, we shall venture beyond the particular book in search of qualities that group books together; we shall give them names and thus frame a rule that brings order into our perceptions. We shall gain a further and a rarer pleasure from that discrimination. But as a rule only lives when it is perpetually broken by contact with the books themselves—nothing is easier and more stultifying than to make rules which exist out of touch with facts, in a vacuum—now at last, in order to steady ourselves in this difficult attempt, it may be well to turn to the very rare writers who are able to enlighten us upon literature as an art. Coleridge and Dryden and Johnson, in their considered criticism, the poets and novelists themselves in their unconsidered sayings, are often surprisingly relevant; they light up and solidify the vague ideas that have been tumbling in the misty depths of our minds. But they are only able to help us if we come to them laden with questions and suggestions won honestly in the course of our own reading. They can do nothing for us if we herd ourselves under their authority and lie down like sheep in the shade of a hedge. We can only understand their ruling when it comes in conflict with our own and vanquishes it.

If this is so, if to read a book as it should be read calls for the rarest qualities of imagination, insight, and judgment, you may perhaps conclude that literature is a very complex art and that it is unlikely that we shall be able, even after a lifetime of reading, to make any valuable contribution to its criticism. We must remain readers; we shall not put on the further glory that belongs to those rare beings who are also critics. But still we have our responsibilities as readers and even our importance. The standards we raise and the judgments we pass steal into the air and become part of the atmosphere which writers breathe as they work. An influence is created which tells upon them even if it never finds its way into print. And that influence, if it were well instructed, vigorous and individual and sincere, might be of great value now when criticism is necessarily in abeyance; when books pass in review like the procession of animals in a shooting-gallery, and the critic has only one second in which to load and aim and shoot and may well be pardoned if he mistakes rabbits for tigers, eagles for barndoor fowls, or misses altogether and wastes his shot upon some peaceful cow grazing in a further field. If behind the erratic gunfire of the press the author felt that there was another kind of criticism, the opinion of people reading for the love of reading, slowly and unprofessionally, and judging with great sympathy and yet with great severity, might this not improve the quality of his work? And if by our means books were to become stronger, richer, and more varied, that would be an end worth reaching.

Yet who reads to bring about an end however desirable? Are there not some pursuits that we practise because they are good in themselves, and some pleasures that are final? And is not this among them? I have sometimes dreamt, at least, that when the Day of Judgment dawns and the great conquerors and lawyers and statesmen come to receive their rewards—their crowns, their laurels, their names carved indelibly upon imperishable marble—the Almighty will turn to Peter and will say, not without a certain envy when He sees us coming with our books under our arms, "Look, these need no reward. We have nothing to give them here. They have loved reading."

The Death of the Moth

Moths that fly by day are not properly to be called moths; they do not excite that pleasant sense of dark autumn nights and ivy-blossom which the commonest yellow-underwing asleep in the shadow of the curtain never fails to rouse in us. They are hybrid creatures, neither gay like butterflies nor sombre like their own species. Nevertheless the present specimen, with his narrow hay-coloured wings, fringed with a tassel of the same colour, seemed to be content with life. It was a pleasant morning, mid-September, mild, benignant, yet with a keener breath than that of the summer months. The plough was already scoring the field opposite the window, and where the share had been, the earth was pressed flat and gleamed with moisture. Such vigour came rolling in from the fields and the down beyond that it was difficult to keep the eyes strictly turned upon the book. The rooks too were keeping one of their annual festivities; soaring round the tree tops until it looked as if a vast net with thousands of black knots in it had been cast up into the air; which, after a few moments sank slowly down upon the trees until every twig seemed to have a knot at the end of it. Then, suddenly, the net would be thrown into the air again in a wider circle this time, with the utmost clamour and vociferation, as though to be thrown into the air and settle slowly down upon the tree tops were a tremendously exciting experience.

The same energy which inspired the rooks, the ploughmen, the horses, and even, it seemed, the lean bare-backed downs, sent the moth fluttering from side to side of his square window-pane. One could not help watching him. One was, indeed, conscious of a queer feeling of pity for him. The possibilities of pleasure seemed that morning so enormous and so various that to have only a moth's part in life, and a day moth's at that, appeared a hard fate, and his zest in enjoying his meagre opportunities to the full, pathetic. He flew vigorously to one corner of his compartment, and, after waiting there a second, flew across to the other. What remained for him but to fly to a third corner and then to a fourth? That was all he could do, in spite of the size of the downs, the width of the sky, the far-off smoke of houses, and the romantic voice, now and then, or a steamer out at sea. What he could do he did. Watching him, it seemed as if a fibre, very thin but pure, of the enormous energy of the world had been thrust into his frail and diminutive body. As often as he crossed the pane, I could fancy that a thread of vital light became visible. He was little or nothing but life.

Yet, because he was so small, and so simple a form of the energy that was rolling in at the open window and driving its way through so many narrow and intricate corridors in my own brain and in those of other human beings, there was something marvellous as well as pathetic about him. It was as if someone had taken a tiny bead of pure life and decking it as lightly as possible with down and feathers, had set it dancing and zigzagging to show us the true nature of life. Thus displayed one could not get over the strangeness of it. One is apt to forget all about life, seeing it humped and bossed and garnished and cumbered so that it has to move with the greatest circumspection and dignity. Again, the thought of all that life might have been had he been born in any other shape caused one to view his simple activities with a kind of pity.

After a time, tired by his dancing apparently, he settled on the window ledge in the sun, and, the queer spectacle being at an end, I forgot about him. Then, looking up, my eye was caught by him. He was trying to resume his dancing, but seemed either so stiff or so awkward that he could only flutter to the bottom of the window-pane; and when he tried to fly across it he failed. Being intent on other matters I watched these futile attempts for a time without thinking, unconsciously waiting for him to resume his flight, as one waits for a machine, that has stopped momentarily, to start again without considering the reason of its failure. After perhaps a seventh attempt he slipped from the wooden ledge and fell, fluttering his wings, onto his back on the window sill. The helplessness of his attitude roused me. It flashed upon me that he was in difficulties; he could no longer raise himself; his legs struggled vainly. But, as I stretched out a pencil, meaning to help him to right himself, it came over me that the failure and awkwardness were the approach of death. I laid the pencil down again.

The legs agitated themselves once more. I looked as if for the enemy against which he struggled. I looked out of doors. What had happened there? Presumably it was midday, and work in the fields had stopped. Stillness and quiet had replaced the previous animation. The birds had taken themselves off to feed in the brooks. The horses stood still. Yet the power was there all the same, massed outside indifferent, impersonal, not attending to anything in particular. Somehow it was opposed to the little hay-coloured moth. It was useless to try to do anything. One could only watch the extraordinary efforts made by those tiny legs against an oncoming doom which could, had it chosen, have submerged an entire city, not merely a city, but masses of human beings; nothing, I knew had any chance against death. Nevertheless after a pause of exhaustion the legs fluttered again. It was superb this last protest, and so frantic that he succeeded at last in righting himself. One's sympathies, of course, were all on the side of life. Also, when there was nobody to care or to know, this gigantic effort on the part of an insignificant little moth, against a power of such magnitude, to retain what no one else valued or desired to keep, moved one strangely. Again, somehow, one saw life, a pure bead.

I lifted the pencil again, useless though I knew it to be. But even as I did so, the unmistakable tokens of death showed themselves. The body relaxed, and instantly grew stiff. The struggle was over. The insignificant little creature now knew death. As I looked at the dead moth, this minute wayside triumph of so great a force over so mean an antagonist filled me with wonder. Just as life had been strange a few minutes before, so death was now as strange. The moth having righted himself now lay most decently and uncomplainingly composed. O yes, he seemed to say, death is stronger than I am.

D. H. Lawrence

(1885–1930)

During the early months of 1919, Lawrence's letters to friends are full of reports of winter snow. With a naturalist's knowledge and a poet's eye, he reads the marks that birds and other wild things leave on the snowy landscape: "beautiful ropes of rabbit prints, trailing away over the brows . . . birds with two feet that hop . . . splendid little leaping marks of weasel, coming along like a necklace chain of berries" (January 27). By early March, confined to bed with the flu, he laments, "I want to get on my legs and feel I am moving again—moving into a new phase." A few days later: "I have never felt so down in the mud in all my life." And, still, on about March 20: "It is snow, snow here—white, white, white. Yesterday was the endless silence of softly falling snow. I thought the world had come to an end." Near the letter's close he reports that "There is a pheasant comes and lies by the wall under the gooseberry bushes, for shelter. He is so cold he hardly notices us. We plan to catch him by throwing over him the netted hammock. But for the sake of his green head and his long pointed fingers I cannot." A week later, he ends a letter "I wish it was spring for us all." The story of the passage from winter to spring, and of the longing for that passage, has been told many times over. Samuel Johnson had it in mind when he remembered the line of English poets who have celebrated "the annual renovation of the world"—the world, be it noted, not only the natural environment (Rambler *No. 5, "On Spring"). In "Whistling of Birds," D. H. Lawrence too asserts that "the transit from the grip of death into new being" occurs "in us as well as outside us." Descriptive exactitude and profusion combine with an oracular simplicity of meditative utterance to catch in equal measure the horror and beauty of the great myth of death and rebirth. But it is the sudden, unwilled release of life from "the winter-mortified earth" that impels the essay, and to this it seems compelled to return again and again. "Whistling of Birds" opens the large posthumous collection of miscellaneous writings by D. H. Lawrence called* Phoenix. *It was originally published in* Atheneum *on April 11, 1919, Lawrence having recently recovered from his dangerous bout with influenza; in the world at large, the carnage of World War I had only just ended.*

Whistling of Birds

The frost held for many weeks, until the birds were dying rapidly. Everywhere in the fields and under the hedges lay the ragged remains of lapwings, starlings, thrushes, redwings, innumerable ragged bloody cloaks of birds, whence the flesh was eaten by invisible beasts of prey.

Then, quite suddenly, one morning, the change came. The wind went to the south, came off the sea warm and soothing. In the afternoon there were little gleams of sunshine, and the doves began, without interval, slowly and awkwardly to coo. The doves were cooing, though with a laboured sound, as if they were still winter-stunned. Nevertheless, all the afternoon they continued their noise, in the mild air, before the frost had thawed off the road. At evening the wind blew gently, still gathering a bruising quality of frost from the hard earth. Then, in the yellow-gleamy sunset, wild birds began to whistle faintly in the blackthorn thickets of the stream-bottom.

It was startling and almost frightening after the heavy silence of frost. How could they sing at once, when the ground was thickly strewn with the torn carcasses of birds? Yet out of the evening came the uncertain, silvery sounds that made one's soul start alert, almost with fear. How could the little silver bugles sound the rally so swiftly, in the soft air, when the earth was yet bound? Yet the birds continued their whistling, rather dimly and brokenly, but throwing the threads of silver, germinating noise into the air.

It was almost a pain to realize, so swiftly, the new world. *Le monde est mort. Vive le monde!*[1] But the birds omitted even the first part of the announcement, their cry was only a faint, blind, fecund *vive!*

There is another world. The winter is gone. There is a new world of spring. The voice of the turtle is heard in the land. But the flesh shrinks from so sudden a transition. Surely the call is premature while the clods are still frozen, and the ground is littered with the remains of wings! Yet we have no choice. In the bottoms of impenetrable blackthorn, each evening and morning now, out flickers a whistling of birds.

Where does it come from, the song? After so long a cruelty, how can they make it up so quickly? But it bubbles through them, they are like little well-heads, little fountain-heads whence the spring trickles and bubbles forth. It is not of their own doing. In their throats the new life distils itself into sound. It is the rising of silvery sap of a new summer, gurgling itself forth.

[1] The world is dead. Long live the world!

All the time, whilst the earth lay choked and killed and winter-mortified, the deep undersprings were quiet. They only wait for the ponderous encumbrance of the old order to give way, yield in the thaw, and there they are, a silver realm at once. Under the surge of ruin, unmitigated winter, lies the silver potentiality of all blossom. One day the black tide must spend itself and fade back. Then all-suddenly appears the crocus, hovering triumphant in the rear, and we know the order has changed, there is a new regime, sound of a new *vive! vive!*

It is no use anymore to look at the torn remnants of birds that lie exposed. It is no longer any use remembering the sullen thunder of frost and the intolerable pressure of cold upon us. For whether we will or not, they are gone. The choice is not ours. We may remain wintry and destructive for a little longer, if we wish it, but the winter is gone out of us, and willy-nilly our hearts sing a little at sunset.

Even whilst we stare at the ragged horror of the birds scattered broadcast, part-eaten, the soft, uneven cooing of the pigeon ripples from the outhouses, and there is a faint silver whistling in the bushes come twilight. No matter, we stand and stare at the torn and unsightly ruins of life, we watch the weary, mutilated columns of winter retreating under our eyes. Yet in our ears are the silver vivid bugles of a new creation advancing on us from behind, we hear the rolling of the soft and happy drums of the doves.

We may not choose the world. We have hardly any choice for ourselves. We follow with our eyes the bloody and horrid line of march of extreme winter, as it passes away. But we cannot hold back the spring. We cannot make the birds silent, prevent the bubbling of the wood-pigeons. We cannot stay the fine world of silver-fecund creation from gathering itself and taking place upon us. Whether we will or no, the daphne tree will soon be giving off perfume, the lambs dancing on two feet, the celandines will twinkle all over the ground, there will be a new heaven and new earth.

For it is in us, as well as without us. Those who can may follow the columns of winter in their retreat from the earth. Some of us, we have no choice, the spring is within us, the silver fountain begins to bubble under our breast, there is gladness in spite of ourselves. And on the instant we accept the gladness! The first day of change, out whistles an unusual, interrupted pæan, a fragment that will augment itself imperceptibly. And this in spite of the extreme bitterness of the suffering, in spite of the myriads of torn dead.

Such a long, long winter, and the frost only broke yesterday. Yet it seems, already, we cannot remember it. It is strangely remote, like a far-off darkness. It is as unreal as a dream in the night. This is the morning of reality, when we are ourselves. This is natural and real, the glimmering of a new creation that stirs in us and about us. We know there was winter, long, fearful. We know the earth was strangled and mortified, we know the body of life was torn and scattered broadcast. But what is this retrospective knowledge? It is something extraneous to us, extraneous to this that we are now. And what we are, and what, it seems, we always have been, is this quickening lovely silver plasm of pure creativity. All the mortification and tearing, ah yes, it was upon us, encompassing us. It was like a storm or a mist or a falling from a height. It was estrangled upon us, like bats in our hair, driving us mad. But it was never really our innermost self. Within, we were always apart, we were this, this limpid fountain of silver, then quiescent, rising and breaking now into the flowering.

It is strange, the utter incompatibility of death with life. Whilst there is death, life is not to be found. It is all death, one overwhelming flood. And then a new tide rises, and it is all life, a fountain of silvery blissfulness. It is one or the other. We are for life, or we are for death, one or the other, but never in our essence both at once.

Death takes us, and all is torn redness, passing into darkness. Life rises, and we are faint fine jets of silver running out to blossom. All is incompatible with all. There is the silver-speckled, incandescent-lovely thrush, whistling pipingly his first song in the blackthorn thicket. How is he to be connected with the bloody, feathered unsightliness of the thrush-remnants just outside the bushes? There is no connexion. They are not to be referred the one to the other. Where one is, the other is not. In the kingdom of death the silvery song is not. But where there is life, there is no death. No death whatever, only silvery gladness, perfect, the otherworld.

The blackbird cannot stop his song, neither can the pigeon. It takes place in him, even though all his race was yesterday destroyed. He cannot mourn, or be silent, or adhere to the dead. Of the dead he is not, since life had kept him. The dead must bury their dead. Life has now taken hold on him and tossed him into the new ether of a new firmament, where he bursts into song as if he were combustible. What is the past, those others, now he is tossed clean into the new, across the untranslatable difference?

In his song is heard the first brokenness and uncertainty of the transition. The transit from the grip of death into new being is a death from death, in its sheer metempsychosis a dizzy agony. But only for a second, the moment of trajectory, the passage from one state to the other, from the grip of death to the liberty of newness. In a moment he is a kingdom of wonder, singing at the centre of a new creation.

The bird did not hang back. He did not cling to his death and his dead. There is no death, and the dead have buried their dead. Tossed into the chasm between two worlds, he lifted his wings in dread, and found himself carried on the impulse.

We are lifted to be cast away into the new beginning. Under our hearts the fountain surges, to toss us forth. Who can thwart the impulse that comes upon us? It comes from the unknown upon us, and it behooves us to pass delicately and exquisitely upon the subtle new wind from heaven, conveyed like birds in unreasoning migrations from death to life.

Aldo Leopold

(1886–1948)

In his long posthumous essay "Walking," Thoreau contemplates man as "a part and parcel of Nature rather than a member of society." For Thoreau, nature meant wilderness—"wildness"; and so it did for Aldo Leopold, author of A Sand County Almanac, *a classic of naturalist writing and of ecology first published in 1949. But Leopold reminds us that to be a member of society is itself to be part of the human species inhabiting nature. The question is whether we will regard the land as "a commodity belonging to us" or as "a community to which we belong" (Foreword). Such a community of land joins rock, soil, water, plant, air, animal, any natural thing, living or nonliving, in a dependence on others. It is out of this natural community, out of wilderness, that "man hammered the artifact called civilization." We destroy nature by using it up, ignorant of how "wilderness gives definition to the human enterprise" ("Wilderness"). To lose the wild places is to be cut off in civilization: cut off from the knowledge of culture's origins in nature. In its purity, Leopold points out, wilderness can be entered only once by a member of our species; the place you go back to a second time is no longer wild. But "one makes shift with things as they are," and "these essays are my shifts" (Foreword). They call for "husbandry," the creation of sanctuaries for the return of the wild and for our leisure time. But, he warns, "recreational development is a job not of building roads into lovely country, but of building receptivity into the still unlovely human mind" ("Conservation Esthetic"). A founder of the Wilderness Society and the profession of game management during his distinguished career in forestry, Leopold writes with the detail, concreteness, and beauty of perception only to be acquired by the patient ecological eye. "Marshland Elegy" details the build-up of a marsh in geological and evolutionary time, and its loss in a century or two after man begins using it up.*

Marshland Elegy

A dawn wind stirs on the great marsh. With almost imperceptible slowness it rolls a bank of fog across the wide morass. Like the white ghost of a glacier the mists advance, riding over phalanxes of tamarack, sliding across bog-meadows heavy with dew. A single silence hangs from horizon to horizon.

Out of some far recess of the sky a tinkling of little bells falls soft upon the listening land. Then again silence. Now comes a baying of some sweet-throated hound, soon the clamor of a responding pack. Then a far clear blast of hunting horns, out of the sky into the fog.

High horns, low horns, silence, and finally a pandemonium of trumpets, rattles, croaks, and cries that almost shakes the bog with its nearness, but without yet disclosing whence it comes. At last a glint of sun reveals the approach of a great echelon of birds. On motionless wing they emerge from the lifting mists, sweep a final arc of sky, and settle in clangorous descending spirals to their feeding grounds. A new day has begun on the crane marsh.

A sense of time lies thick and heavy on such a place. Yearly since the ice age it has awakened each spring to the clangor of cranes. The peat layers that comprise the bog are laid down in the basin of an ancient lake. The cranes stand, as it were, upon the sodden pages of their own history. These peats are the compressed remains of the mosses that clogged the pools, of the tamaracks that spread over the moss, of the cranes that bugled over the tamaracks since the retreat of the ice sheet. An endless caravan of generations has built of its own bones this bridge into the future, this habitat where the oncoming host again may live and breed and die.

To what end? Out of the bog a crane, gulping some luckless frog, springs his ungainly hulk into the air and flails the morning sun with mighty wings. The tamaracks re-echo with his bugled certitude. He seems to know.

Our ability to perceive quality in nature begins, as in art, with the pretty. It expands through successive stages of the beautiful to values as yet uncaptured by language. The quality of cranes lies, I think, in this higher gamut, as yet beyond the reach of words.

This much, though, can be said: our appreciation of the crane grows with the slow unraveling of earthly history. His tribe, we now know, stems out of the remote Eocene. The other members of the fauna in which he originated are long since entombed within the hills. When we hear his call we hear no mere bird. We hear the trumpet in the orchestra of evolution. He is the symbol of our untamable past, of that incredible sweep of millennia which underlies and conditions the daily affairs of birds and men.

And so they live and have their being—these cranes—not in the constricted present, but in the wider reaches of evolutionary time. Their annual return is the ticking of the geologic clock. Upon the place of their return they confer a peculiar distinction. Amid the endless mediocrity of the commonplace, a crane marsh holds a paleontological patent of nobility, won in the march of aeons, and revocable only by shotgun. The sadness discernible in some marshes arises, perhaps, from their once having harbored cranes. Now they stand humbled, adrift in history.

Some sense of this quality in cranes seems to have been felt by sportsmen and ornithologists of all ages. Upon such quarry as this the Holy Roman Emperor Frederick loosed his gyrfalcons. Upon such quarry as this once swooped the hawks of Kublai Khan. Marco Polo tells us: "He derives the highest amusement from sporting with gyrfalcons and hawks. At Changanor the Khan has a great Palace surrounded by a fine plain where are found cranes in great numbers. He causes millet and other grains to be sown in order that the birds may not want."

The ornithologist Bengt Berg, seeing cranes as a boy upon the Swedish heaths, forthwith made them his life work. He followed them to Africa and discovered their winter retreat on the White Nile. He says of his first encounter: "It was a spectacle which eclipsed the flight of the roc in the Thousand and One Nights."

When the glacier came down out of the north, crunching hills and gouging valleys, some adventuring rampart of the ice climbed the Baraboo Hills and fell back into the outlet gorge of the Wisconsin River. The swollen waters backed up and formed a lake half as long as the state, bordered on the east by cliffs of ice, and fed by the torrents that fell from melting mountains. The shorelines of this old lake are still visible; its bottom is the bottom of the great marsh.

The lake rose through the centuries, finally spilling over east of the Baraboo range. There it cut a new channel for the river, and thus drained itself. To the residual lagoons came the cranes, bugling the defeat of the retreating winter, summoning the on-creeping host of living things to their collective task of marsh-building. Floating bogs of sphagnum moss clogged the lowered waters, filled them. Sedge and leatherleaf, tamarack and spruce successively advanced over the bog, anchoring it by their root fabric, sucking out its water, making peat. The lagoons disappeared, but not the cranes. To the moss-meadows that replaced the ancient waterways they returned each spring to dance and bugle and rear their gangling sorrel-colored young. These, albeit birds, are not properly called chicks, but *colts.* I cannot explain why. On some dewy June morning watch them gambol over their ancestral pastures at the heels of the roan mare, and you will see for yourself.

One year not long ago a French trapper in buckskins pushed his canoe up one of the moss-clogged creeks that thread the great marsh. At this attempt to invade their miry stronghold the cranes gave vent to loud and ribald laughter. A century or two later Englishmen came in covered wagons. They chopped clearings in the timbered moraines that border the marsh, and in them planted corn and buckwheat. They did not intend, like the Great Khan at Changanor, to feed the cranes. But the cranes do not question the intent of glaciers, emperors, or pioneers. They ate the grain, and when some irate farmer failed to concede their usufruct in his corn, they trumpeted a warning and sailed across the marsh to another farm.

There was no alfalfa in those days, and the hill-farms made poor hay land, especially in dry years. One dry year someone set a fire in the tamaracks. The burn grew up quickly to bluejoint grass, which, when cleared of dead trees, made a dependable hay meadow. After that, each August, men appeared to cut hay. In winter, after the cranes had gone South, they drove wagons over the frozen bogs and hauled the hay to their farms in the hills. Yearly they plied the marsh with fire and axe, and in two short decades hay meadows dotted the whole expanse.

Each August when the haymakers came to pitch their camps, singing and drinking and lashing their teams with whip and tongue, the cranes whinnied to their colts and retreated to the far fastnesses. "Red shitepokes" the haymakers called them, from the rusty hue which at that season often stains the battleship-gray crane plumage. After the hay was stacked and the marsh again their own, the cranes returned, to call down out of October skies the migrant flocks from Canada. Together they wheeled over the new-cut stubbles and raided the corn until frosts gave the signal for the winter exodus.

These haymeadow days were the Arcadian age for marsh dwellers. Man and beast, plant and soil lived on and with each other in mutual toleration, to the mutual benefit of all. The marsh might have kept on producing hay and prairie chickens, deer and muskrat, crane-music and cranberries forever.

The new overlords did not understand this. They did not include soil, plants, or birds in their ideas of mutuality. The dividends of such a balanced economy were too modest. They envisaged farms not only around, but *in* the marsh. An epidemic of ditch-digging and land-booming set in. The marsh was gridironed with drainage canals, speckled with new fields and farmsteads.

But crops were poor and beset by frosts, to which the expensive ditches added an aftermath of debt. Farmers moved out. Peat beds dried, shrank, caught fire. Sun-energy out of the Pleistocene shrouded the countryside in acrid smoke. No man raised his voice against the waste, only his nose against the smell. After a dry summer not even the winter snows could extinguish the smoldering marsh. Great pockmarks were burned into field and meadow, the scars reaching down to the sands of the old lake, peat-covered these hundred centuries. Rank weeds sprang out of the ashes, to be followed after a year or two by aspen scrub. The cranes were hard put, their numbers shrinking with the remnants of the unburned meadow. For them, the song of the power shovel came near being an elegy. The high priests of progress knew nothing of cranes, and cared less. What is a species more or less among engineers? What good is an undrained marsh anyhow?

For a decade or two crops grew poorer, fires deeper, wood-fields larger, and cranes scarcer, year by year. Only reflooding, it appeared, could keep the peat from burning. Meanwhile the cranberry growers had, by plugging drainage ditches, reflooded a few spots and obtained good yields. Distant politicians bugled about marginal land, overproduction, unemployment relief, conservation. Economists and planners came to look at the marsh. Surveyors, technicians, CCC's, buzzed about. A counter-epidemic of reflooding set in. Government bought land, resettled farmers, plugged ditches wholesale. Slowly the bogs are re-wetting. The fire-pocks become ponds. Grass fires still burn, but they can no longer burn the wetted soil.

All this, once the CCC camps were gone, was good for cranes, but not so the thickets of scrub popple that spread inexorably over the old burns, and still less the maze of new roads that inevitably follow governmental conservation. To build a road is so much simpler than to think of what the country really needs. A roadless marsh is seemingly as worthless to the alphabetical conservationist as an undrained one was to the empire-builders. Solitude, the one natural resource still undowered of alphabets, is so far recognized as valuable only by ornithologists and cranes.

Thus always does history, whether of marsh or market place, end in paradox. The ultimate value in these marshes is wildness, and the crane is wildness incarnate. But all conservation of wildness is self-defeating, for to cherish we must see and fondle, and when enough have seen and fondled, there is no wilderness left to cherish.

Someday, perhaps in the very process of our benefactions, perhaps in the fullness of geologic time, the last crane will trumpet his farewell and spiral skyward from the great marsh. High out of the clouds will fall the sound of hunting horns, the baying of the phantom pack, the tinkle of little bells, and then a silence never to be broken, unless perchance in some far pasture of the Milky Way.

T. S. Eliot
(1888–1965)

T.S. Eliot takes on the weighted word "tradition" and by the start of his third paragraph has translated it (via *etymology*) *into the colloquial, if equally weighted, "handing down." In the same space, he turns the formal word "criticism" into something as "inevitable as breathing"; "criticism," he says simply, is "articulating what passes in our mind when we read a book and feel an emotion about it." Soon he has made the defamiliarizing split between "the poet" and "the man," and in the second section of his essay stretches out the distinction by means of a richly alien analogy from inorganic chemistry: the poet as catalyst. Adopting the "we" of the theorizing stance throughout, he keeps disrupting its authority by a persistent, tentative "I": "And I do not mean . . . I mean this . . . I tried . . . I hinted . . . I am struggling to attack . . ." The short third section of the essay defers the expected linkage between parts I and II to the final sentence, as agile and concentrated a piece of wordplay as ever closed an essay. Eliot's "Tradition and the Individual Talent"* (The Sacred Wood, *1919*) *has not always been available to us in quite this way—as an essay, a prose discourse of a certain rhetorical texture and shape portraying a poet's struggle to say what it means to be a poet. For at least a generation after the end of the first World War, Eliot the non-academic man of letters dominated the institution of literature—the teaching of English in American universities and the writing of academic criticism. The fact that he was an "authority," as well as an important poet, seemed to obscure the essayistic character of his criticism. Only after successive waves of changed academic thinking about language, literature, and literary history is Eliot resurfacing gradually as a distinguished writer of prose, an essayist who happened to take as his subject the things that moved him as a poet, a poet alive not in some insular present but in history. "I was implicitly defending the sort of poetry that I and my friends wrote," he said late in his life; "this gave my essays a kind of urgency, the warmth of appeal of the advocate" ("To Criticize the Critic"). "Tradition and the Individual Talent" has some kinship with personal manifesto essays like "Life Without Principle" and "What I Believe." It is a modernist poet's manifesto whose relevance for essayists and their four hundred year-old practice makes for interesting speculation.*

Tradition and the Individual Talent

I

In English writing we seldom speak of tradition, though we occasionally apply its name in deploring its absence. We cannot refer to "the tradition" or to "a tradition"; at most, we employ the adjective in saying that the poetry of So-and-so is "traditional" or even "too traditional." Seldom, perhaps, does the word appear except in a phrase of censure. If otherwise, it is vaguely approbative, with the implication, as to the work approved, of some pleasing archaeological reconstruction. You can hardly make the word agreeable to English ears without this comfortable reference to the reassuring science of archaeology.

Certainly the word is not likely to appear in our appreciations of living or dead writers. Every nation, every race, has not only its own creative, but its own critical turn of mind; and is even more oblivious of the shortcomings and limitations of its critical habits than of those of its creative genius. We know, or think we know, from the enormous mass of critical writing that has appeared in the French language the critical method or habit of the French; we only conclude (we are such unconscious people) that the French are "more critical" than we, and sometimes even plume ourselves a little with the fact, as if the French were the less spontaneous. Perhaps they are; but we might remind ourselves that criticism is as inevitable as breathing, and that we should be none the worse for articulating what passes in our minds when we read a book and feel an emotion about it, for criticizing our own minds in their work of criticism. One of the facts that might come to light in this process is our tendency to insist, when we praise a poet, upon those aspects of his work in which he least resembles anyone else. In these aspects or parts of his work we pretend to find what is individual, what is the peculiar essence of the man. We dwell with satisfaction upon the poet's difference from his predecessors, especially his immediate predecessors; we endeavour to find something that can be isolated in order to be enjoyed. Whereas if we approach a poet without this prejudice we shall often find that not only the best, but the most individual parts of his work may be those in which the dead poets, his ancestors, assert their immortality most vigorously. And I do not mean the impressionable period of adolescence, but the period of full maturity.

Yet if the only form of tradition, of handing down, consisted in following the ways of the immediate generation before us in a blind or timid adherence to its successes, "tradition" should positively be discouraged.

We have seen many such simple currents soon lost in the sand; and novelty is better than repetition. Tradition is a matter of much wider significance. It cannot be inherited, and if you want it you must obtain it by great labour. It involves, in the first place, the historical sense, which we may call nearly indispensable to anyone who would continue to be a poet beyond his twenty-fifth year; and the historical sense involves a perception, not only of the pastness of the past, but of its presence; the historical sense compels a man to write not merely with his own generation in his bones, but with a feeling that the whole of the literature of Europe from Homer and within it the whole of the literature of his own country has a simultaneous existence and composes a simultaneous order. This historical sense, which is a sense of the timeless as well as of the temporal and of the timeless and of the temporal together, is what makes a writer traditional. And it is at the same time what makes a writer most acutely conscious of his place in time, of his own contemporaneity.

No poet, no artist of any art, has his complete meaning alone. His significance, his appreciation is the appreciation of his relation to the dead poets and artists. You cannot value him alone; you must set him, for contrast and comparison, among the dead. I mean this as a principle of aesthetic, not merely historical, criticism. The necessity that he shall conform, that he shall cohere, is not onesided; what happens when a new work of art is created is something that happens simultaneously to all the works of art which preceded it. The existing monuments form an ideal order among themselves, which is modified by the introduction of the new (the really new) work of art among them. The existing order is complete before the new work arrives; for order to persist after the supervention of novelty, the *whole* existing order must be, if ever so slightly, altered; and so the relations, proportions, values of each work of art toward the whole are readjusted; and this is conformity between the old and the new. Whoever has approved this idea of order, of the form of European, of English literature will not find it preposterous that the past should be altered by the present as much as the present is directed by the past. And the poet who is aware of this will be aware of great difficulties and responsibilities.

In a peculiar sense he will be aware also that he must inevitably be judged by the standards of the past. I say judged, not amputated, by them; not judged to be as good as, or worse or better than, the dead; and certainly not judged by the canons of dead critics. It is a judgment, a comparison, in which two things are measured by each other. To conform merely would be for the new work not really to conform at all; it would not be new, and would therefore not be a work of art. And we do not quite say that the new is more valuable because it fits in; but its fitting in is a test of its value—a test, it is true, which can only be slowly and cautiously applied, for we are none of us infallible judges of conformity. We say: it appears to conform, and is perhaps individual, or it appears individual, and may conform; but we are hardly likely to find that it is one and not the other.

To proceed to a more intelligible exposition of the relation of the poet to the past: he can neither take the past as a lump, an indiscriminate bolus, nor can he form himself wholly on one or two private admirations, nor can he form himself wholly upon one preferred period. The first course is inadmissible, the second is an important experience of youth, and the third is a pleasant and highly desirable supplement. The poet must be very conscious of the main current, which does not at all flow invariably through the most distinguished reputations. He must be quite aware of the obvious fact that art never improves, but that the material of art is never quite the same. He must be aware that the mind of Europe—the mind of his own country—a mind which he learns in time to be much more important than his own private mind—is a mind which changes, and that this change is a development which abandons nothing *en route*, which does not superannuate either Shakespeare, or Homer, or the rock drawing of the Magdalenian draughtsmen. That this development, refinement perhaps, complication certainly, is not, from the point of view of the artist, any improvement. Perhaps not even an improvement from the point of view of the psychologist or not to the extent which we imagine; perhaps only in the end based upon a complication in economics and machinery. But the difference between the present and the past is that the conscious present is an awareness of the past in a way and to an extent which the past's awareness of itself cannot show.

Someone said: "The dead writers are remote from us because we *know* so much more than they did." Precisely, and they are that which we know.

I am alive to a usual objection to what is clearly part of my programme for the *métier* of poetry. The objection is that the doctrine requires a ridiculous amount of erudition (pedantry), a claim which can be rejected by appeal to the lives of poets in any pantheon. It will even be affirmed that much learning deadens or perverts poetic sensibility. While, however, we persist in believing that a poet ought to know as much as will not encroach upon his necessary receptivity and necessary laziness, it is not desirable to confine knowledge to whatever can be put into a useful shape for examinations, drawing-rooms, or the still more pretentious modes of publicity. Some can absorb knowledge, the more tardy must sweat for it. Shakespeare acquired more essential history from Plutarch than most men could from the whole British Museum.

What is to be insisted upon is that the poet must develop or procure the consciousness of the past and that he should continue to develop this consciousness throughout his career.

What happens is a continual surrender of himself as he is at the moment to something which is more valuable. The progress of an artist is a continual self-sacrifice, a continual extinction of personality.

There remains to define this process of depersonalization and its relation to the sense of tradition. It is in this depersonalization that art may be said to approach the condition of science. I, therefore, invite you to consider, as a suggestive analogy, the action which takes place when a bit of finely filiated platinum is introduced into a chamber containing oxygen and sulphur dioxide.

II

Honest criticism and sensitive appreciation are directed not upon the poet but upon the poetry. If we attend to the confused cries of the newspaper critics and the *susurrus* of popular repetition that follows, we shall hear the names of poets in great numbers; if we seek not Blue-book knowledge but the enjoyment of poetry, and ask for a poem, we shall seldom find it. I have tried to point out the importance of the relation of the poem to other poems by other authors, and suggested the conception of poetry as a living whole of all the poetry that has ever been written. The other aspect of this Impersonal theory of poetry is the relation of the poem to its author. And I hinted, by an analogy, that the mind of the mature poet differs from that of the immature one not precisely in any valuation of "personality," not being necessarily more interesting, or having "more to say," but rather by being a more finely perfected medium in which special, or very varied, feelings are at liberty to enter into new combinations.

The analogy was that of the catalyst. When the two gasses previously mentioned are mixed in the presence of a filament of platinum, they form sulphurous acid. This combination takes place only if the platinum is present; nevertheless the newly formed acid contains no trace of platinum, and the platinum itself is apparently unaffected; has remained inert, neutral, and unchanged. The mind of the poet is the shred of platinum. It may partly or exclusively operate upon the experience of the man himself; but, the more perfect the artist, the more completely separate in him will be the man who suffers and the mind which creates; the more perfectly will the mind digest and transmute the passions which are its material.

The experience, you will notice, the elements which enter the presence of the transforming catalyst, are of two kinds: emotions and feelings. The effect of a work of art upon the person who enjoys it is an experience different in kind from any experience not of art. It may be formed out of one emotion, or may be a combination of several; and various feelings, inhering for the writer in particular words or phrases or images, may be added to compose the final result. Or great poetry may be made without the direct use of any emotion whatever: composed out of feelings solely. Canto XV of the *Inferno* (Brunetto Latini) is a working up of the emotion evident in the situation; but the effect, though single as that of any work of art, is obtained by considerable complexity of detail. The last quatrain gives an image, a feeling attaching to an image, which "came," which did not develop simply out of what precedes, but which was probably in suspension in the poet's mind until the proper combination arrived for it to add itself to. The poet's mind is in fact a receptacle for seizing and storing up numberless feelings, phrases, images, which remain there until all the particles which can unite to form a new compound are present together.

If you compare several representative passages of the greatest poetry you see how great is the variety of types of combination, and also how completely any semi-ethical criterion of "sublimity" misses the mark. For it is not the "greatness," the intensity, of the emotions, the components, but the intensity of the artistic process, the pressure, so to speak, under which the fusion takes place, that counts. The episode of Paolo and Francesca employs a definite emotion, but the intensity of the poetry is something quite different from whatever intensity in the supposed experience it may give the impression of. It is no more intense, furthermore, than Canto XXVI, the voyage of Ulysses, which has not the direct dependence upon an emotion. Great variety is possible in the process of transmutation of emotion: the murder of Agamemnon, or the agony of Othello, gives an artistic effect apparently closer to a possible original than the scenes from Dante. In the *Agamemnon*, the artistic emotion approximates to the emotion of an actual spectator; in *Othello* to the emotion of the protagonist himself. But the difference between art and the event is always absolute; the combination which is the murder of Agamemnon is probably as complex as that which is the voyage of Ulysses. In either case there has been a fusion of elements. The ode of Keats contains a number of feelings which have nothing particular to do with the nightingale, but which the nightingale, partly, perhaps, because of its attractive name, and partly because of its reputation, served to bring together.

The point of view which I am struggling to attack is perhaps related to the metaphysical theory of the substantial unity of the soul: for my meaning is, that the poet has, not a "personality" to express, but a particular medium, which is only a medium and not a personality, in which impressions and experiences combine in peculiar and unexpected ways. Impressions and experiences which are important for the man may take no place in the poetry, and those which become important in the poetry may play quite a negligible part in the man, the personality.

I will quote a passage which is unfamiliar enough to be regarded with fresh attention in the light—or darkness—of these observations:

> And now methinks I could e'en chide myself
> For doating on her beauty, though her death
> Shall be revenged after no common action.
> Does the silkworm expend her yellow labours
> For thee? For thee does she undo herself?
> Are lordships sold to maintain ladyships
> For the poor benefit of a bewildering minute?
> Why does yon fellow falsify highways,
> And put his life between the judge's lips,
> To refine such a thing—keeps horse and men
> To beat their valours for her? . . .

In this passage (as is evident if it is taken in its context) there is a combination of positive and negative emotions: an intensely strong attraction toward beauty and an equally intense fascination by the ugliness which is contrasted with it and which destroys it. This balance of contrasted emotion is in the dramatic situation to which the speech is pertinent, but that situation alone is inadequate to it. This is, so to speak, the structural emotion, provided by the drama. But the whole effect, the dominant tone, is due to the fact that a number of floating feelings, having an affinity to this emotion by no means superficially evident, have combined with it to give us a new art emotion.

It is not in his personal emotions, the emotions provoked by particular events in his life, that the poet is in any way remarkable or interesting. His particular emotions may be simple, or crude, or flat. The emotion in his poetry will be a very complex thing, but not with the complexity of the emotions of people who have very complex or unusual emotions in life. One error, in fact, of eccentricity in poetry is to seek for new human emotions to express; and in this search for novelty in the wrong place it discovers the perverse. The business of the poet is not to find new emotions, but to use the ordinary ones and, in working them up into poetry, to express feelings which are not in actual emotions at all. And emotions which he has never experienced will serve his turn as well as those familiar to him. Consequently, we must believe that "emotion recollected in tranquillity"[1] is an inexact formula. For it is neither emotion, nor recollection, nor, without distortion of meaning, tranquillity. It is a concentration, and a new thing resulting from the concentration, of a very great number of experiences which to the practical and active person would not seem to be experiences at all; it is a concentration which does not happen consciously or of deliberation. These experiences are not "recollected," and they finally unite in an atmosphere which is "tranquil" only in that it is a passive attending upon the event. Of course this is not quite the whole story. There is a great deal, in the writing of poetry, which must be conscious and deliberate. In fact, the bad poet is usually unconscious where he ought to be conscious, and conscious where he ought to be unconscious. Both errors tend to make him "personal." Poetry is not a turning loose of emotion, but an escape from emotion; it is not the expression of personality, but an escape from personality. But, of course, only those who have personality and emotions know what it means to want to escape from these things.

III

ὁ δὲ νοῦς ἴσως θειότερόν τι καὶ ἀπαθές ἐστιν.[2]

This essay proposes to halt at the frontier of metaphysics or mysticism, and confine itself to such practical conclusions as can be applied by the responsible person interested in poetry. To divert interest from the poet to the poetry is a laudable aim: for it would conduce to a juster estimation of actual poetry, good and bad. There are many people who appreciate the expression of sincere emotion in verse, and there is a smaller number of people who can appreciate technical excellence. But very few know when there is an expression of *significant* emotion, emotion which has its life in the poem and not in the history of the poet. The emotion of art is impersonal. And the poet cannot reach this impersonality without surrendering himself wholly to the work to be done. And he is not likely to know what is to be done unless he lives in what is not merely the present, but the present moment of the past, unless he is conscious, not of what is dead, but of what is already living.

[1] In his influential Preface to *Lyrical Ballads, With Other Poems* (1800), the Romantic poet William Wordsworth stated that poetry "takes its origin from emotion recollected in tranquillity."

[2] But the mind, perhaps, is more divine and indifferent.

Katherine Anne Porter

(1890–1980)

Written in the years 397–98, the Confessions *of St. Augustine is the first autobiography in Western literature and, doubtless, the most widely read. Augustine had become a Christian more than a decade earlier and was then Bishop of Hippo in North Africa. As the account, mainly, of his pre-conversion life, the book is an extended meditation on his own ignorance, his troubled and self-estranged immersion in a world "drunk with the invisible wine of its own perverted earthbound will" (II, 3). He is at pains to relate the details of that ignorance from infancy to manhood, and to understand his past actions. In one of his best known stories—about stealing pears with a gang of boys—he probes his own ignoble motives at fascinating length to "unravel this twisted tangle of knots" (II, 10). The title of Katherine Anne Porter's "St. Augustine and the Bullfight" (1955) acknowledges her literary debt even before she asserts, several paragraphs into the essay, that St. Augustine is a "clue" to what she calls "one of the most important and lasting experiences of my life." As the young Augustine, sent to Carthage to study law, "fell in with a set of sensualists" (III, 6), so the young American woman come to Mexico "for the express purpose of attending a Revolution, and studying Mayan people art, fell in with the most lordly gang of fashionable young hoodlums." Both are instances of "adventure" as Porter defines the term: acts engaged in "under powerful stimulus" but without understanding. In the turbulent second decade of the twentieth century, during Mexico's Madero Revolution, the world is again "drunk" with "invisible wine," the young adventurer's actions and motives still a "twisted tangle of knots." To write about "what really happened," therefore, as she sets out to do in this essay, is to write about herself in a state of ignorance. As she put it elsewhere: "I feel that to give a true testimony it is necessary to know and remember what I was, what I felt, and what I knew then, and not confuse it with what I know or think I know now" ("My First Speech"). We say that autobiographical writing is writing about ourselves, our experience. With St. Augustine's* Confessions *in mind, Porter rethinks the meaning of "experience" and its relationship to autobiography.*

St. Augustine and the Bullfight

Adventure. The word has become a little stale to me, because it has been applied too often to the dull physical exploits of professional "adventurers" who write books about it, if they know how to write; if not, they hire ghosts who quite often can't write either.

I don't read them, but rumors of them echo, and re-echo. The book business at least is full of heroes who spend their time, money and energy worrying other animals, manifestly their betters such as lions and tigers, to death in trackless jungles and deserts only to be crossed by the stoutest motorcar; or another feeds hooks to an inedible fish like the tarpon; another crosses the ocean on a raft, living on plankton and seaweed, why ever, I wonder? And always always, somebody is out climbing mountains, and writing books about it, which are read by quite millions of persons who feel, apparently, like the next best thing to going there yourself is to hear from somebody who went. And I have heard more than one young woman remark that, though she did not want to get married, still, she would like to have a baby, for the adventure: not lately though. That was a pose of the 1920s and very early '30s. Several of them did it, too, but I do not know of any who wrote a book about it—good for them.

W. B. Yeats remarked—I cannot find the passage now, so must say it in other words—that the unhappy man (unfortunate?) was one whose adventures outran his capacity for experience, capacity for experience being, I should say, roughly equal to the faculty for understanding what has happened to one. The difference then between mere adventure and a real experience might be this? That adventure is something you seek for pleasure, or even for profit, like a gold rush or invading a country; for the illusion of being more alive than ordinarily, the thing you will to occur; but experience is what really happens to you in the long run; the truth that finally overtakes you.

Adventure is sometimes fun, but not too often. Not if you can remember what really happened; all of it. It passes, seems to lead nowhere much, is something to tell friends to amuse them, maybe. "Once upon a time," I can hear myself saying, for I once said it, "I scaled a cliff in Boulder, Colorado, with my bare hands, and in Indian moccasins, bare-legged. And at nearly the top, after six hours of feeling for toe- and fingerholds, and the gayest feeling in the world that when I got to the top I should see something wonderful, something that sounded awfully like a bear growled out of a cave, and I scuttled down out of there in a hurry." This is a fact. I had never climbed a mountain in my life, never had the least wish to climb one. But there I was, for perfectly good reasons, in a hut on a mountainside in heavenly sunny though sometimes stormy weather, so I went out one morning and scaled a very minor cliff; alone, unsuitably clad, in the season when rattlesnakes are casting their skins; and if it was not a bear in that cave, it was some kind of unfriendly animal who growls at people; and this ridiculous escapade, which was nearly six hours of the hardest work I ever did in my life, toeholds and fingerholds on a cliff, put me to bed for just nine days with a complaint the local people called "muscle poisoning." I don't know exactly what they meant, but I do remember clearly that I could not turn over in bed without help and in great agony. And did it teach me anything? I think not, for three years later I was climbing a volcano in Mexico, that celebrated unpronounceably named volcano, Popocatepetl which everybody who comes near it climbs sooner or later; but was that any reason for me to climb it? No. And I was knocked out for weeks, and that finally did teach me: I am not supposed to go climbing things. Why did I not know in the first place? For me, this sort of thing must come under the head of Adventure.

I think it is pastime of rather an inferior sort; yet I have heard men tell yarns like this only a very little better: their mountains were higher, or their sea was wider, or their bear was bigger and noisier, or their cliff was steeper and taller, yet there was no point whatever to any of it except that it had happened. This is not enough. May it not be, perhaps, that experience, that is, the thing that happens to a person living from day to day, is anything at all that sinks in? is, without making any claims, a part of your growing and changing life? what it is that happens in your mind, your heart?

Adventure hardly ever seems to be that at the time it is happening: not under that name, at least. Adventure may be an afterthought, something that happens in the memory with imaginative trimmings if not downright lying, so that one should suppress it entirely, or go the whole way and make honest fiction of it. My own habit of writing fiction has provided a wholesome exercise to my natural, incurable tendency to try to wangle the sprawling mess of our existence in this bloody world into some kind of shape: almost any shape will do, just so it is recognizably made with human hands, one small proof the more of the validity and reality of the human imagination. But even within the most limited frame what utter confusion shall prevail if you cannot take hold firmly, and draw the exact line between what really happened, and what you have since imagined about it. Perhaps my soul will be saved after all in spite of myself because now and then I take some unmanageable, indigestible fact and turn it into fiction; cause things to happen with some kind of logic—my own logic, of course—and everything ends as I think it should end and no back talk, or very little, from anybody about it. Otherwise, and except for this safety advice, I should be the greatest liar unhung. (When was the last time anybody was hanged for lying?) What is Truth? I often ask myself. Who knows?

A publisher asked me a great while ago to write a kind of autobiography, and I was delighted to begin; it sounded very easy when he said, "Just start, and tell everything you remember until now!" I wrote about a hundred pages before I realized, or admitted, the hideous booby trap into which I had fallen. First place, I remember quite a lot of stupid and boring things: there were other times when my life seemed merely an endurance test, or a quite mysterious but not very interesting and often monotonous effort at survival on the most primitive terms. There are dozens of things that might be entertaining but I have no intention of telling them, because they are nobody's business; and endless little gossipy incidents that might entertain indulgent friends for a minute, but in print they look as silly as they really are. Then, there are the tremendous, unmistakable, life-and-death crises, the scalding, the bone-breaking events, the lightnings that shatter the landscape of the soul—who would write that by request? No, that is for a secretly written manuscript to be left with your papers, and if your executor is a good friend, who has probably been brought up on St. Augustine's *Confessions*, he will read it with love and attention and gently burn it to ashes for your sake.

Yet I intend to write something about my life, here and now, and so far as I am able without one touch of fiction, and I hope to keep it as shapeless and unforeseen as the events of life itself from day to day. Yet, look! I have already betrayed my occupation, and dropped a clue in what would be the right place if this were fiction, by mentioning St. Augustine when I hadn't meant to until it came in its right place in life, not in art. Literary art, at least, is the business of setting human events to rights and giving them meanings that, in fact, they do not possess, or not obviously, or not the meanings the artist feels they should have—we do understand so little of what is really happening to us in any given moment. Only by remembering, comparing, waiting to know the consequences can we sometimes, in a flash of light, see what a certain event really meant, what it was trying to tell us. So this will be notes on a fateful thing that happened to me when I was young and did not know much about the world or about myself. I had been reading St. Augustine's *Confessions* since I was able to read at all, and I thought I had read every word, perhaps because I did know certain favorite passages by heart. But then, it was something like having read the *Adventures of Gargantua* by Rabelais when I was twelve and enjoying it; when I read it again at thirty-odd, I was astounded at how much I had overlooked in the earlier reading, and wondered what I thought I had seen there.

So it was with St. Augustine and my first bullfight. Looking back nearly thirty-five years on my earliest days in Mexico, it strikes me that, for a fairly serious young woman who was in the country for the express purpose of attending a Revolution, and studying Mayan people art, I fell in with a most lordly gang of fashionable international hoodlums. Of course I had Revolutionist friends and artist friends, and they were gay and easy and poor as I was. This other mob was different: they were French, Spanish, Italian, Polish, and they all had titles and good names: a duke, a count, a marquess, a baron, and they all were in some flashy money-getting enterprise like importing cognac wholesale, or selling sports cars to newly rich politicians; and they all drank like fish and played fast games like polo or tennis or jai alai; they haunted the wings of theaters, drove slick cars like maniacs, but expert maniacs, never missed a bullfight or a boxing match; all were reasonably young and they had ladies to match, mostly imported and all speaking French. These persons stalked pleasure as if it were big game—they took their fun exactly where they found it, and the way they liked it, and they worked themselves to exhaustion at it. A fast, tough, expensive, elegant, high low-life they led, for the ladies and gentlemen each in turn had other friends you would have had to see to believe; and from time to time, without being in any way involved or engaged, I ran with this crowd of shady characters and liked their company and ways very much. I don't like gloomy sinners, but the merry ones charm me. And one of them introduced me to Shelley. And Shelley, whom I knew in the most superficial way, who remained essentially a stranger to me to the very end, led me, without in the least ever knowing what he had done, into one of the most important and lasting experiences of my life.

He was British, a member of the poet's family; said to be authentic great-great-nephew; he was rich and willful, and had come to Mexico young and wild, and mad about horses, of course. Coldly mad—he bred them and raced them and sold them with the stony detachment and merciless appraisal of the true horse lover—they call it love, and it could be that: but he did not like them. "What is there to like about a horse but his good points? If he has a vice, shoot him or send him to the bullring; that is the only way to work a vice out of the breed!"

Once, during a riding trip while visiting a ranch, my host gave me a stallion to ride, who instantly took the bit in his teeth and bolted down a steep mountain trail. I managed to stick on, held an easy rein, and he finally ran himself to a standstill in an open field. My disgrace with Shelley was nearly complete. Why? Because the stallion was not a good horse. I should have refused to mount him. I said it was a question how to refuse the horse your host offered you—Shelley thought it no question at all. "A lady," he reminded me, "can always excuse herself gracefully from anything she doesn't wish to do." I said, "I wish that were really true," for the argument about the bullfight was already well started. But the peak of his disapproval of me, my motives, my temperament, my ideas, my ways, was reached when, to provide a diversion and end a dull discussion, I told him the truth: that I had liked being run away with, it had been fun and the kind of thing that had to happen unexpectedly, you couldn't arrange for it. I tried to convey to him my exhilaration, my pure joy when this half-broken, crazy beast took off down that trail with just a hoofhold between a cliff on one side and a thousand-foot drop on the other. He said merely that such utter frivolity surprised him in someone whom he had mistaken for a well-balanced, intelligent girl; and I remember thinking how revoltingly fatherly he sounded, exactly like my own father in his stuffier moments.

He was a stocky, red-faced, muscular man with broad shoulders, hard-jowled, with bright blue eyes glinting from puffy lids; his hair was a grizzled tan, and I guessed him about fifty years old, which seemed a great age to me then. But he mentioned that his Mexican wife had "died young" about three years before, and that his eldest son was only eleven years old. His whole appearance was so remarkably like the typical horsy, landed-gentry sort of Englishman one meets in books by Frenchmen or Americans, if this were fiction I should feel obliged to change his looks altogether, thus falling into one stereotype to avoid falling into another. However, so Shelley did look, and his clothes were magnificent and right beyond words, and never new-looking and never noticeable at all except one could not help observing sooner or later that he was beyond argument the best-dressed man in America, North or South; it was that kind of typical British inconspicuous good taste: he had it, superlatively. He was evidently leading a fairly rakish life, or trying to, but he was of a cast-iron conventionality even in that. We did not fall in love—far from it. We struck up a hands-off, quaint, farfetched, tetchy kind of friendship which consisted largely of good advice about worldly things from him, mingled with critical marginal notes on my character—a character of which I could not recognize a single trait; and if I said, helplessly, "But I am not in the least like that," he would answer, "Well, you should be!" or "Yes, you are, but you don't know it."

This man took me to my first bullfight. I'll tell you later how St. Augustine comes into it. It was the first bullfight of that season; Covadonga Day; April; clear, hot blue sky; and a long procession of women in flower-covered carriages; wearing their finest lace veils and highest combs and gauziest fans; but I shan't describe a bullfight. By now surely there is no excuse for anyone who can read or even hear or see not to know pretty well what goes on in a bullring. I shall say only that Sánchez Mejías and Rudolfo Gaona each killed a bull that day; but before the Grand March of the toreros, Hattie Weston rode her thoroughbred High School gelding into the ring to thunders of shouts and brassy music.

She was Shelley's idol. "Look at that girl, for God's sake," and his voice thickened with feeling, "the finest rider in the world," he said in his dogmatic way, and it is true I have not seen better since.

She was a fine buxom figure of a woman, a highly colored blonde with a sweet, childish face; probably forty years old, and perfectly rounded in all directions; a big round bust, and that is the word, there was nothing plural about it, just a fine, warm-looking bolster straight across her front from armpit to armpit; fine firm round hips—again, why the plural? It was an ample seat born to a sidesaddle, as solid and undivided as the bust, only more of it. She was tightly laced and her waist was small. She wore a hard-brimmed dark gray Spanish sailor hat, sitting straight and shallow over her large golden knot of hair; a light gray bolero and a darker gray riding skirt—not a Spanish woman's riding dress, nor yet a man's, but something tight and fit and formal and appropriate. And there she went, the most elegant woman in the saddle I have ever seen, graceful and composed in her perfect style, with her wonderful, lightly dancing, learned horse, black and glossy as shoe polish, perfectly under control—no, not under control at all, you might have thought, but just dancing and showing off his paces by himself for his own pleasure.

"She makes the bullfight seem like an anticlimax," said Shelley, tenderly.

I had not wanted to come to this bullfight. I had never intended to see a bullfight at all. I do not like the slaughtering of animals as sport. I am carnivorous, I love all the red juicy meats and all the fishes. Seeing animals killed for food on the farm in summers shocked and grieved me sincerely, but it did not cure my taste for flesh. My family for as far back as I know anything about them, only about 450 years, were the huntin', shootin', fishin' sort: their houses were arsenals and their dominion over the animal kingdom was complete and unchallenged. When I was older, my father remarked on my tiresome timidity, or was I just pretending to finer feelings than those of the society around me? He hardly knew which was the more tiresome. But that was perhaps only a personal matter. Morally, if I wished to eat meat I should be able to kill the animal—otherwise it appeared that I was willing to nourish myself on other people's sins? For he supposed I considered it a sin. Otherwise why bother about it? Or was it just something unpleasant I wished to avoid? Maintaining my own purity—and a very doubtful kind of purity he found it, too—at the expense of the guilt of others? Altogether, my father managed to make a very sticky question of it, and for some years at intervals I made it a matter of conscience to kill an animal or bird, something I intended to eat. I gave myself and the beasts some horrible times, through fright and awkwardness, and to my shame, nothing cured me of my taste for flesh. All forms of cruelty offended me bitterly, and this repugnance is inborn, absolutely impervious to any arguments, or even insults, at which the red-blooded lovers of blood sports are very expert; they don't admire me at all, any more than I admire them. . . . Ah, me, the contradictions, the paradoxes! I was once perfectly capable of keeping a calf for a pet until he outgrew the yard in the country and had to be sent to the pastures. His subsequent fate I leave you to guess. Yes, it is all revoltingly sentimental and, worse than that, confused. My defense is that no matter whatever else this world seemed to promise me, never once did it promise to be simple.

So, for a great tangle of emotional reasons I had no intention of going to a bullfight. But Shelley was so persistently unpleasant about my cowardice, as he called it flatly, I just wasn't able to take the thrashing any longer. Partly,too, it was his natural snobbery: smart people of the world did not have such feelings; it was to him a peculiarly provincial if not downright Quakerish attitude. "I have some Quaker ancestors," I told him. "How absurd of you!" he said, and really meant it.

The bullfight question kept popping up and had a way of spoiling other occasions that should have been delightful. Shelley was one of those men, of whose company I feel sometimes that I have had more than my fair share, who simply do not know how to drop a subject, or abandon a position once they have declared it. Constitutionally incapable of admitting defeat, or even its possibility, even when he had not the faintest shadow of right to expect a victory—for why should he make a contest of my refusal to go to a bullfight?—he would start an argument during the theater intermissions, at the fronton, at a street fair, on a stroll in the Alameda, at a good restaurant over coffee and brandy; there was no occasion so pleasant that he could not shatter it with his favorite gambit: "If you would only see one, you'd get over this nonsense."

So there I was, at the bullfight, with cold hands, trembling innerly, with painful tinglings in the wrists and collarbone: yet my excitement was not altogether painful; and in my happiness at Hattie Weston's performance I was calmed and off guard when the heavy barred gate to the corral burst open and the first bull charged through. The bulls were from the Duke of Veragua's ranch, as enormous and brave and handsome as any I ever saw afterward. (This is not a short story, so I don't have to maintain any suspense.) This first bull was a beautiful monster of brute courage: his hide was a fine pattern of black and white, much enhanced by the goad with fluttering green ribbons stabbed into his shoulder as he entered the ring; this in turn furnished an interesting design in thin rivulets of blood, the enlivening touch of scarlet in his sober color scheme, with highly aesthetic effect.

He rushed at the waiting horse, blindfolded in one eye and standing at the proper angle for the convenience of his horns, the picador making only the smallest pretense of staving him off, and disemboweled the horse with one sweep of his head. The horse trod in his own guts. It happens at least once every bullfight. I could not pretend not to have expected it; but I had not been able to imagine it. I sat back and covered my eyes. Shelley, very deliberately and as inconspicuously as he could, took both my wrists and held my hands down on my knees. I shut my eyes and turned my face away, away from the arena, away from him, but not before I had seen in his eyes a look of real, acute concern and almost loving anxiety for me—he really believed that my feelings were the sign of a grave flaw of character, or at least an unbecoming, unworthy weakness that he was determined to overcome in me. He couldn't shoot me, alas, or turn me over to the bullring; he had to deal with me in human terms, and he did it according to his lights. His voice was hoarse and fierce: "Don't you dare come here and then do this! You must face it!"

Part of his fury was shame, no doubt, at being seen with a girl who would behave in such a pawky way. But at this point he was, of course, right. Only he had been wrong before to nag me into this, and I was altogether wrong to have let him persuade me. Or so I felt then. "You have got to face this!" By then he was right; and I did look and I did face it, though not for years and years.

During those years I saw perhaps a hundred bullfights, all in Mexico City, with the finest bulls from Spain and the greatest bullfighters—but not with Shelley—never again with Shelley, for we were not comfortable together after that day. Our odd, mismatched sort of friendship declined and neither made any effort to revive it. There was bloodguilt between us, we shared an evil secret, a hateful revelation. He hated what he had revealed in me to himself, and I hated what he had revealed to me about myself, and each of us for entirely opposite reasons; but there was nothing more to say or do, and we stopped seeing each other.

I took to the bullfights with my Mexican and Indian friends. I sat with them in the cafés where the bullfighters appeared; more than once went at two o'clock in the morning with a crowd to see the bulls brought into the city; I visited the corral back of the ring where they could be seen before the corrida. Always, of course, I was in the company of impassioned adorers of the sport, with their special vocabulary and mannerisms and contempt for all others who did not belong to their charmed and chosen cult. Quite literally there were those among them I never heard speak of anything else; and I heard then all that can be said—the topic is limited, after all, like any other—in love and praise of bullfighting. But it can be tiresome, too. And I did not really live in that world, so narrow and so trivial, so cruel and so unconscious; I was a mere visitor. There was something deeply, inseparably wrong with my being there at all, something against the grain of my life; except for this (and here was the falseness I had finally to uncover): I loved the spectacle of the bullfights, I was drunk on it, I was in a strange, wild dream from which I did not want to be awakened. I was now drawn irresistibly to the bullring as before I had been drawn to the race tracks and the polo fields at home. But this had death in it, and it was the death in it that I loved. . . . And I was bitterly ashamed of this evil in me, and believed it to be in me only—no one had fallen so far into cruelty as this! These bullfight buffs I truly believed did not know what they were doing—but I did, and I knew better because I had once known better; so that spiritual pride got in and did its deadly work, too. How could I face the cold fact that at heart I was just a killer, like any other, that some deep corner of my soul consented not just willingly but with rapture? I still clung obstinately to my flattering view of myself as a unique case, as a humane, blood-avoiding civilized being, somehow a fallen angel, perhaps? Just the same, what was I doing here? And why was I beginning secretly to abhor Shelley as if he had done me a great injury, when in fact he had done me the terrible and dangerous favor of helping me to find myself out?

In the meantime I was reading St. Augustine; and if Shelley had helped me find myself out, St. Augustine helped me find myself again. I read for the first time then his story of a friend of his, a young man from the provinces who came to Rome and was taken up by the gang of clever, wellborn young hoodlums Augustine then ran with; and this young man, also wellborn but severely brought up, refused to go with the crowd to the gladiatorial combat; he was opposed to them on the simple grounds that they were cruel and criminal. His friends naturally ridiculed such dowdy sentiments; they nagged him slyly, bedeviled him openly, and, of course, finally some part of him consented—but only to a degree. He would go with them, he said, but he would not watch the games. And he did not, until the time for the first slaughter, when the howling of the crowd brought him to his feet, staring: and afterward he was more bloodthirsty than any.

Why, of course: oh, it might be a commonplace of human nature, it might be it could happen to anyone! I longed to be free of my uniqueness, to be a fellow-sinner at least with someone: I could not bear my guilt alone—and there was this student, this boy at Rome in the fourth century, somebody I felt I knew well on sight, who had been weak enough to be led into adventure but strong enough to turn it into experience. For no matter how we both attempted to deceive ourselves, our acts had all the earmarks of adventure: violence of motive, events taking place at top speed, at sustained intensity, under powerful stimulus and a willful seeking for pure sensation; willful, I say, because I was not kidnapped and forced, after all, nor was that young friend of St. Augustine's. We both proceeded under the power of our own weakness. When the time came to kill the splendid black and white bull, I who had pitied him when he first came into the ring stood straining on tiptoe to see everything, yet almost blinded with excitement, and crying out when the crowd roared, and kissing Shelley on the cheekbone when he shook my elbow and shouted in the voice of one justified: "Didn't I? Didn't I?"

Aldous Huxley

(1894–1963)

In the preface to his Collected Essays, *Huxley calls the essay "a literary device for saying almost everything about almost anything" and proceeds to sketch a still useful taxonomy of the genre. The elasticity of the essay is due, he believes, to its "three-poled frame of reference": the pole of autobiography, whose art works mainly by narration and description; the "objective" pole of the "concrete-particular," which proceeds by explanation, analysis, and judgment; and the "abstract-universal" pole where moral speculation goes on. The most satisfying essays manage to link all three: "Freely, effortlessly, thought and feeling move in these consummate works of art, hither and thither . . . from the personal to the universal, from the abstract back to the concrete, from the objective datum to the inner experience." Huxley's essays at their best move precisely in these ways—essays like "The Olive Tree," "Music at Night," "Usually Destroyed," "Faith, Taste, and History," "Madness, Badness, and Sadness" all exhibit this mastery of range. "Hyperion To A Satyr" considers* homo sapiens*—man the thinker, purveyor of symbols—under the aspect of* homo pediculosus, *man the louse-ridden; and of* homo immundus, *man the unclean, the impure, the foul. It builds up a socio-moral history from a most ordinary part of our bodily lives: dirt. The effluvia of our organs and the parasites that breed in them and in us. The essay's autobiographical opening into this material is a familiar twentieth-century waste-product, more plentiful on the California beach where Huxley and friends found themselves strolling one day, early in the century, than the daffodils—"ten thousand at a glance"—that Wordsworth saw one spring day in the Lake District ("I Wandered Lonely As A Cloud"). If Wordsworth's poem gives a fine ironical incentive to Huxley's essay, Shakespeare's* Hamlet *(I, ii) provides the title and all that flows from it in the essay's speculative course. The majestic sun-god of the early Greeks, Hyperion, having undergone a technological theophany in California, one is left pondering the whereabouts of that rowdy, raunchy type, the satyr—more urgently today, in the 1990s, than at the time of the essay's appearance in 1956.*

Hyperion to a Satyr

A few months before the outbreak of the Second World War I took a walk with Thomas Mann on a beach some fifteen or twenty miles southwest of Los Angeles. Between the breakers and the highway stretched a broad belt of sand, smooth, gently sloping and (blissful surprise!) void of all life but that of the pelicans and godwits. Gone was the congestion of Santa Monica and Venice. Hardly a house was to be seen; there were no children, no promenading loincloths and brassiéres, not a single sunbather was practicing his strange obsessive cult. Miraculously, we were alone. Talking of Shakespeare and the musical glasses, the great man and I strolled ahead. The ladies followed. It was they, more observant than their all too literary spouses, who first remarked the truly astounding phenomenon. "Wait," they called, "wait!" And when they had come up with us, they silently pointed. At our feet, and as far as the eye could reach in all directions, the sand was covered with small whitish objects, like dead caterpillars. Recognition dawned. The dead caterpillars were made of rubber and had once been contraceptives of the kind so eloquently characterized by Mantegazza as *"una tela di ragno contro l'infezione, una corazza contro il piacere."*[1]

Continuous as the stars that shine
And twinkle in the milky way,
They stretched in never-ending line
Along the margin of a bay:
Ten thousand saw I at a glance . . .

Ten thousand? But we were in California, not the Lake District. The scale was American, the figures astronomical. Ten million saw I at a glance. Ten million emblems and mementoes of Modern Love.

O bitter barren woman! what's the name
The name, the name, the new name thou hast won?

And the old name, the name of the bitter fertile woman—what was that? These are questions that can only be asked and talked about, never answered in any but the most broadly misleading way. Generalizing about Woman is like indicting a Nation—an amusing pastime, but very unlikely to be productive either of truth or utility.

Meanwhile, there was another, a simpler and more concrete question: How on earth had these objects got here, and why in such orgiastic

[1] A cobweb against infection, a breastplate against pleasure.

profusion? Still speculating, we resumed our walk. A moment later our noses gave us the unpleasant answer. Offshore from this noble beach was the outfall through which Los Angeles discharged, raw and untreated, the contents of its sewers. The emblems of modern love and the other things had come in with the spring tide. Hence that miraculous solitude. We turned and made all speed towards the parked car.

Since that memorable walk was taken, fifteen years have passed. Inland from the beach, three or four large cities have leapt into existence. The bean fields and Japanese truck gardens of those ancient days are now covered with houses, drugstores, supermarkets, drive-in theaters, junior colleges, jet-plane factories, laundromats, six-lane highways. But instead of being, as one would expect, even more thickly constellated with Malthusian flotsam and unspeakable jetsam, the sands are now clean, the quarantine has been lifted. Children dig, well-basted sunbathers slowly brown, there is splashing and shouting in the surf. A happy consummation—but one has seen this sort of thing before. The novelty lies, not in the pleasantly commonplace end—people enjoying themselves—but in the fantastically ingenious means whereby that end has been brought about.

Forty feet above the beach, in a seventy-five-acre oasis scooped out of the sand dunes, stands one of the marvels of modern technology, the Hyperion Activated Sludge Plant. But before we start to discuss the merits of activated sludge, let us take a little time to consider sludge in its unactivated state, as plain, old-fashioned dirt.

Dirt, with all its concomitant odors and insects, was once accepted as an unalterable element in the divinely established Order of Things. In his youth, before he went into power politics as Innocent III, Lotario de' Conti found time to write a book on the *Wretchedness of Man's Condition*. "How filthy the father," he mused, "how low the mother, how repulsive the sister!" And no wonder! For "dead, human beings give birth to flies and worms; alive, they generate worms and lice." Moreover, "consider the plants, consider the trees. They bring forth flowers and leaves and fruits. But what do *you* bring forth? Nits, lice, vermin. Trees and plants exude oil, wine, balm—and *you*, spittle, snot, urine, ordure. *They* diffuse the sweetness of all fragrance—*you*, the most abominable stink." In the Age of Faith, Homo sapiens was also Homo pediculosus, also Homo immundus—a little lower than the angels, but dirty by definition, lousy, not *per accidens*, but in his very essence. And as for man's helpmate—*si nec extremis digitis flegma vel stercus tangere patimur, quomodo ipsum stercoris saccum amplecti desideramus?* "We who shrink from touching, even with the tips of our fingers, a gob of phlegm or a lump of dung, how is it that we crave for the embraces of this mere bag of night-soil?" But men's eyes are not, as Odo of Cluny wished they were, "like those of the lynxes of Boeotia"; they cannot see through the smooth and milky surfaces into the palpitating sewage within. That is why

> There swims no goose so grey but soon or late
> Some honest gander takes her for his mate.

That is why (to translate the notion into the language of medieval orthodoxy), every muck-bag ends by getting herself embraced—with the result that yet another stinker-with-a-soul finds himself embarked on a sea of misery, bound for a port which, since few indeed can hope for salvation, is practically certain to be Hell. The embryo of this future reprobate is composed of "foulest seed," combined with "blood made putrid by the heat of lust." And as though to make it quite clear what He thinks of the whole proceeding, God has decreed that "the mother shall conceive in stink and nastiness."

That there might be a remedy for stink and nastiness—namely soap and water—was a notion almost unthinkable in the thirteenth century. In the first place, there was hardly any soap. The substance was known to Pliny, as an import from Gaul and Germany. But more than a thousand years later, when Lotario de' Conti wrote his book, the burgesses of Marseilles were only just beginning to consider the possibility of manufacturing the stuff in bulk. In England no soap was made commercially until halfway through the fourteenth century. Moreover, even if soap had been abundant, its use for mitigating the "stink and nastiness," then inseparable from love, would have seemed, to every right-thinking theologian, an entirely illegitimate, because merely physical, solution to a problem in ontology and morals—an escape, by means of the most vulgarly materialistic trick, from a situation which God Himself had intended, from all eternity, to be as squalid as it was sinful. A conception without stink and nastiness would have the appearance—what a blasphemy!—of being Immaculate. And finally there was the virtue of modesty. Modesty, in that age of codes and pigeonholes, had its Queensberry Rules—no washing below the belt. Sinful in itself, such an offense against modesty in the present was fraught with all kinds of perils for modesty in the future. Havelock Ellis observed, when he was practicing obstetrics in the London slums, that modesty was due, in large measure, to a fear of being disgusting. When his patients realized that "I found nothing disgusting in whatever was proper and necessary to be done under the circumstances, it almost invariably happened that every sign of modesty at once disappeared." Abolish "stink and nastiness," and you abolish one of the most important sources of feminine modesty, along with one of the most richly rewarding themes of pulpit eloquence.

A contemporary poet has urged his readers not to make love to those who wash too much. There is, of course, no accounting for tastes; but there *is* an accounting for philosophical opinions. Among many other things, the greatly gifted Mr. Auden is a belated representative of the school which held that sex, being metaphysically tainted, ought also to be physically unclean.

Dirt, then, seemed natural and proper, and dirt in fact was everywhere. But, strangely enough, this all-pervading squalor never generated its own psychological antidote—the complete indifference of habit. Everybody stank, everybody was verminous; and yet, in each successive generation, there were many who never got used to these familiar facts. What has changed in the course of history is not the disgusted reaction to filth, but the moral to be drawn from that reaction. "Filth," say the men of the twentieth century, "is disgusting. Therefore let us quickly do something to get rid of filth." For many of our ancestors, filth was as abhorrent as it seems to almost all of us. But how different was the moral they chose to draw! "Filth is disgusting," they said. "Therefore the human beings who produce the filth are disgusting, and the world they inhabit is a vale, not merely of tears, but of excrement. This state of things has been divinely ordained, and all we can do is cheerfully to bear our vermin, loathe our nauseating carcasses and hope (without much reason, since we shall probably be damned) for an early translation to a better place. Meanwhile it is an observable fact that villeins are filthier even than lords. It follows, therefore, that they should be treated as badly as they smell." This loathing for the poor on account of the squalor in which they were condemned to live outlasted the Middle Ages and has persisted to the present day. The politics of Shakespeare's aristocratic heroes and heroines are the politics of disgust. "Footboys" and other members of the lower orders are contemptible because they are lousy—not in the metaphorical sense in which that word is now used, but literally; for the louse, in Sir Hugh Evans' words, "is a familiar beast to man, and signifies love." And the lousy were also the smelly. Their clothes were old and unclean, their bodies sweaty, their mouths horrible with decay. It made no difference that, in the words of a great Victorian reformer, "by no prudence on their part can the poor avoid the dreadful evil of their surroundings." They were disgusting and that, for the aristocratic politician, was enough. To canvass the common people's suffrages was merely to "beg their stinking breath." Candidates for elective office were men who "stand upon the breath of garlic eaters." When the citizens of Rome voted against him, Coriolanus told them that they were creatures,

whose breath I hate
As reek o' th' rotten fens, whose loves I prize
As the dead carcasses of unburied men
That do corrupt my air.

And, addressing these same citizens, "You are they," says Menenius,

You are they
That made the air unwholesome when you cast
Your stinking greasy caps in hooting at
Coriolanus' exile.

Again, when Caesar was offered the crown, "the rabblement shouted and clapped their chopped hands,and threw up their sweaty night-caps, and uttered such a deal of stinking breath, because Caesar had refused the crown, that it had almost choked Caesar; for he swounded and fell down at it; and for mine own part," adds Casca, "I durst not laugh for fear of opening my lips and receiving the bad air." The same "mechanic slaves, with greasy aprons" haunted Cleopatra's imagination in her last hours.

In their thick breaths,
Rank of gross diet, shall we be enclouded,
And forced to drink their vapours.

In the course of evolution man is supposed to have sacrificed the greater part of his olfactory center to his cortex, his sense of smell to his intelligence. Nevertheless, it remains a fact that in politics, no less than in love and social relations, smell judgments continue to play a major role. In the passages cited above, as in all the analogous passages penned or uttered since the days of Shakespeare, there is the implication of an argument, which can be formulated in some such terms as these. "Physical stink is a symbol, almost a symptom, of intellectual and moral inferiority. All the members of a certain group stink physically. Therefore, they are intellectually and morally vile, inferior and, as such, unfit to be treated as equals."

Tolstoy, who was sufficiently clear-sighted to recognize the undesirable political consequences of cleanliness in high places and dirt among the poor, was also sufficiently courageous to advocate, as a remedy, a general retreat from the bath. Bathing, he saw, was a badge of class distinction, a prime cause of aristocratic exclusiveness. For those who, in Mr. Auden's words, "wash too much," find it exceedingly distasteful to associate with those who wash too little. In a society where, let us say, only one in five can afford the luxury of being clean and sweet-smelling, Christian brotherhood will be all but impossible. Therefore, Tolstoy argued, the bathers should join the unwashed majority. Only where there is equality in dirt can there be genuine and unforced fraternity.

Mahatma Gandhi, who was a good deal more realistic than his Russian mentor, chose a different solution to the problem of differential cleanliness. Instead of urging the bathers to stop washing, he worked indefatigably to help the non-bathers to keep clean. Brotherhood was to be achieved, not by universalizing dirt, vermin and bad smells, but by building privies and scrubbing floors.

Spengler, Sorokin, Toynbee—all the philosophical historians and sociologists of our time have insisted that a stable civilization cannot be built except on the foundations of religion. But if man cannot live by bread alone, neither can he live exclusively on metaphysics and worship. The gulf between theory and practice, between the ideal and the real, cannot be bridged by religion alone. In Christendom, for example, the doctrines of God's fatherhood and the brotherhood of man have never been self-implementing. Monotheism has proved to be powerless against the divisive forces first of feudalism and then of nationalistic idolatry. And within these mutually antagonistic groups, the injunction to love one's neighbor as oneself has proved to be as ineffective, century after century, as the commandment to worship one God.

A century ago the prophets who formulated the theories of the Manchester School were convinced that commerce, industrialization and improved communications were destined to be the means whereby the age-old doctrines of monotheism and human brotherhood would at last be implemented. Alas, they were mistaken. Instead of abolishing national rivalries, industrialization greatly intensified them. With the march of technological progress, wars became bloodier and incomparably more ruinous. Instead of uniting nation with nation, improved communications merely extended the range of collective hatreds and military operations. That human beings will, in the near future, voluntarily give up their nationalistic idolatry, seems, in these middle years of the twentieth century, exceedingly unlikely. Nor can one see, from this present vantage point, any technological development capable, by the mere fact of being in existence, of serving as an instrument for realizing those religious ideals, which hitherto mankind has only talked about. Our best consolation lies in Mr. Micawber's hope that, sooner or later, "Something will Turn Up."

In regard to brotherly love within the mutually antagonistic groups, something *has* turned up. That something is the development, in many different fields, of techniques for keeping clean at a cost so low that practically everybody can afford the luxury of not being disgusting.

For creatures which, like most of the carnivores, make their home in a den or burrow, there is a biological advantage in elementary cleanliness.

To relieve nature in one's bed is apt, in the long run, to be unwholesome. Unlike the carnivores, the primates are under no evolutionary compulsion to practice the discipline of the sphincters. For these free-roaming nomads of the woods, one tree is as good as another and every moment is equally propitious. It is easy to house-train a cat or a dog, all but impossible to teach the same desirable habits to a monkey. By blood we are a good deal closer to poor Jocko that to Puss or Tray. Man's instincts were developed in the forest; but ever since the dawn of civilization, his life has been lived in the more elaborate equivalent of a rabbit warren. His notions of sanitation were not, like those of the cat, inborn, but had to be painfully acquired. In a sense the older theologians were quite right in regarding dirt as natural to man—an essential element in the divinely appointed order of his existence.

But in spite of its unnaturalness, the art of living together without turning the city into a dunghill has been repeatedly discovered. Mohenjodaro, at the beginning of the third millennium B.C., had a water-borne sewage system; so, several centuries before the siege of Troy, did Cnossos; so did many of the cities of ancient Egypt, albeit only for the rich. The poor were left to demonstrate their intrinsic inferiority by stinking, in their slums, to high heaven. A thousand years later Rome drained her swamps and conveyed her filth to the contaminated Tiber by means of the Cloaca Maxima. But these solutions to the problem of what we may politely call "unactivated sludge" were exceptional. The Hindus preferred to condemn a tithe of their population to untouchability and the daily chore of carrying slops. In China the thrifty householder tanked the family sludge and sold it, when mature, to the highest bidder. There was a smell, but it paid, and the fields recovered some of the phosphorus and nitrogen of which the harvesters had robbed them. In medieval Europe every alley was a public lavatory, every window a sink and garbage chute. Droves of pigs were dedicated to St. Anthony and, with bells round their necks, roamed the streets, battening on the muck. (When operating at night, burglars and assassins often wore bells. Their victims heard the reassuring tinkle, turned over in their beds and went to sleep again—it was only the blessed pigs.) And meanwhile there were cesspools (like the black hole into which that patriotic Franciscan, Brother Salimbene, deliberately dropped his relic of St. Dominic), there was portable plumbing, there were members of the lower orders, whose duty it was to pick up the unactivated sludge and deposit it outside the city limits. But always the sludge accumulated faster than it could be removed. The filth was chronic and, in the slummier quarters, appalling. It remained appalling until well into the nineteenth century. As late as the early years of Queen Victoria's reign sanitation in the East End of London consisted in dumping everything into the stagnant pools that still stood between the jerry-built houses. From the peak of their superior (but still very imperfect) cleanliness the middle and upper classes looked down with unmitigated horror at the Great Unwashed. "The Poor" were written and spoken about as though they were creatures of an entirely different species. And no wonder! Nineteenth-century England was loud with Non-Conformist and Tractarian piety; but in a society most of whose members stank and were unclean the practice of brotherly love was out of the question.

The first modern sewage systems, like those of Egypt before them, were reserved for the rich and had the effect of widening still further the gulf between rulers and ruled. But endemic typhus and several dangerous outbreaks of Asiatic cholera lent weight to the warnings and denunciations of the sanitary reformers. In self-defense the rich had to do something about the filth in which their less fortunate neighbors were condemned to live. Sewage systems were extended to cover entire metropolitan areas. The result was merely to transfer the sludge problem from one place to another. "The Thames," reported a Select Committee of 1836, "receives the excrementitious matter from nearly a million and a half of human beings; the washing of their foul linen; the filth and refuse of many hundred manufactories; the offal and decomposing vegetable substances from the markets; the foul and gory liquid from the slaughter-houses; and the purulent abominations from hospitals and dissecting rooms, too disgusting to detail. Thus that most noble river, which has been given us by Providence for our health, recreation and beneficial use, is converted into the Common sewer of London, and the sickening mixture it contains is daily pumped up into the water for the inhabitants of the most civilized capital of Europe."

In England the heroes of the long campaign for sanitation were a strangely assorted band. There was a bishop, Blomfield of London; there was the radical Edwin Chadwick, a disciple of Jeremy Bentham; there was a physician, Dr. Southwood Smith; there was a low-church man of letters, Charles Kingsley; and there was the seventh Earl of Shaftesbury, an aristocrat who had troubled to acquaint himself with the facts of working-class life. Against them were marshaled the confederate forces of superstition, vested interest and brute inertia. It was a hard fight; but the cholera was a staunch ally, and by the end of the century the worst of the mess had been cleared up, even in the slums. Writing in 1896, Lecky called it "the greatest achievement of our age." In the historian's estimation, the sanitary reformers had done more for general happiness and the alleviation of human misery than all the more spectacular figures of the long reign put together. Their labors, moreover, were destined to bear momentous fruit. When Lecky wrote, upper-class noses could still find plenty of occasions for passing olfactory judgments on the majority.

But not nearly so many as in the past. The stage was already set for the drama which is being played today—the drama whose theme is the transformation of the English caste system into an equalitarian society. Without Chadwick and his sewers, there might have been violent revolution, never that leveling by democratic process, that gradual abolition of untouchability, which are in fact taking place.

Hyperion—what joy the place would have brought to those passionately prosaic lovers of humanity, Chadwick and Bentham! And the association of the hallowed name with sewage, of sludge with the great god of light and beauty—what romantic furies it would have evoked in Keats and Blake! And Lotario de' Conti—how thunderously, in the name of religion, he would have denounced this presumptuous demonstration that Homo immundus can effectively modify the abjection of his predestined condition! And Dean Swift, above all—how deeply the spectacle would have disturbed him! For, if Celia could relieve nature without turning her lover's bowels, if Yahoos, footmen and even ladies of quality did not *have* to stink, then, obviously, his occupation was gone and his neurosis would be compelled to express itself in some other, some less satisfactory, because less excruciating, way.

An underground river rushes into Hyperion. Its purity of 99.7 per cent exceeds that of Ivory Soap. But two hundred million gallons are a lot of water; and the three thousandth part of that daily quota represents a formidable quantity of muck. But happily the ratio between muck and muckrakers remains constant. As the faecal tonnage rises, so does the population of aerobic and anaerobic bacteria. Busier than bees and infinitely more numerous, they work unceasingly on our behalf. First to attack the problem are the aerobes. The chemical revolution begins in a series of huge shallow pools, whose surface is perpetually foamy with the suds of Surf, Tide, Dreft and all the other monosyllables that have come to take the place of soap. For the sanitary engineers, these new detergents are a major problem. Soap turns very easily into something else; but the monosyllables remain intractably themselves, frothing so violently that it has become necessary to spray the surface of the aerobes' pools with overhead sprinklers. Only in this way can the suds be prevented from rising like the foam on a mug of beer and being blown about the countryside. And this is not the only price that must be paid for easier dishwashing. The detergents are greedy for oxygen. Mechanically and chemically, they prevent the aerobes from getting all the air they require. Enormous compressors must be kept working night and day to supply the needs of the suffocating bacteria. A cubic foot of compressed air to every cubic foot of sludgy liquid. What will happen when Zoom, Bang and Whiz come to replace the relatively mild monosyllables of today, nobody, in the sanitation business, cares to speculate.

When, with the assistance of the compressors, the aerobes have done all they are capable of doing, the sludge, now thickly concentrated, is pumped into the Digestion System. To the superficial glance, the Digestion System looks remarkably like eighteen very large Etruscan mausoleums. In fact it consists of a battery of cylindrical tanks, each more than a hundred feet in diameter and sunk fifty feet into the ground. Within these huge cylinders steam pipes maintain a cherishing heat of ninety-five degrees—the temperature at which the anaerobes are able to do their work with maximum efficiency. From something hideous and pestilential the sludge is gradually transformed by these most faithful of allies into sweetness and light—light in the form of methane, which fuels nine supercharged Diesel engines, each of seventeen hundred horsepower, and sweetness in the form of an odorless solid which, when dried, pelleted and sacked, sells to farmers at ten dollars a ton. The exhaust of the Diesels raises the steam which heats the Digestion System, and their power is geared either to electric generators or centrifugal blowers. The electricity works the pumps and the machinery of the fertilizer plant, the blowers supply the aerobes with oxygen. Nothing is wasted. Even the emblems of modern love contribute their quota of hydrocarbons to the finished products, gaseous and solid. And meanwhile another torrent, this time about 99.95 per cent pure, rushes down through the submarine outfall and mingles, a mile offshore, with the Pacific. The problem of keeping a great city clean without polluting a river or fouling the beaches, and without robbing the soil of its fertility, has been triumphantly solved.

But untouchability depends on other things besides the bad sanitation of slums. We live not merely in our houses, but even more continuously in our garments. And we live not exclusively in health, but very often in sickness. Where sickness rages unchecked and where people cannot afford to buy new clothes or keep their old ones clean, the occasions for being disgusting are innumerable.

Thersites, in *Troilus and Cressida*, lists a few of the commoner ailments of Shakespeare's time: "the rotten diseases of the south, the guts-griping, ruptures, catarrhs, loads o' gravel i' the back, lethargies, cold palsies, raw eyes, dirt-rotten livers, wheezing lungs, bladders full of imposthume, sciaticas, lime-kilns i' the palm, incurable bone-ache, and the rivelled fee-simple of the tetter." And there were scores of others even more repulsive. Crawling, flying, hopping, the insect carriers of infection swarmed uncontrollably. Malaria was endemic, typhus never absent, bubonic plague a regular visitor, dysentery, without benefit of plumbing, a commonplace. And meanwhile, in an environment that was uniformly septic, everything that *could* suppurate *did* suppurate. The Cook, in Chaucer's "Prologue," had a "mormal," or gangrenous sore, on his shin. The Summoner's face was covered with the "whelkes" and "knobbes" of a skin disease that would not yield to any known remedy. Every cancer was inoperable, and gnawed its way, through a hideous chaos of cellular proliferation and breakdown, to its foregone conclusion. The unmitigated horror surrounding illness explains the admiration felt, throughout the Middle Ages and early modern times, for those heroes and heroines of charity who voluntarily undertook the care of the sick. It explains, too, certain actions of the saints—actions which, in the context of modern life, seem utterly incomprehensible. In their filth and wretchedness, the sick were unspeakably repulsive. This dreadful fact was a challenge to which those who took their Christianity seriously responded by such exploits as the embracing of lepers, the kissing of sores, the swallowing of pus. The modern response to this challenge is soap and water, with complete asepsis as the ultimate ideal. The great gulf of disgust which used to separate the sick and the chronically ailing from their healthier fellows, has been, not indeed completely abolished, but narrowed everywhere and, in many places, effectively bridged. Thanks to hygiene, many who, because of their afflictions, used to be beyond the pale of love or even pity, have been re-admitted into the human fellowship. An ancient religious ideal has been implemented, at least in part, by the development of merely material techniques for dealing with problems previously soluble (and then how very inadequately, so far as the sick themselves were concerned!) only by saints.

"The essential act of thought is symbolization." Our minds transform experiences into signs. If these signs adequately represent the experiences to which they refer, and if we are careful to manipulate them according to the rules of a many-valued logic, we can deepen our understanding of experience and thereby achieve some control of the world and our own destiny. But these conditions are rarely fulfilled. In all too many of the affairs of life we combine ill-chosen signs in all kinds of irrational ways, and are thus led to unrealistic conclusions and inappropriate acts.

There is nothing in experience which cannot be transformed by the mind into a symbol—nothing which cannot be made to signify something else. We have seen, for example, that bad smells may be made to stand for social inferiority, dirt for a low IQ, vermin for immorality, sickness for a status beneath the human. No less important that these purely physiological symbols are the signs derived, not from the body itself, but from its coverings. A man's clothes are his most immediately perceptible attribute. Stinking rags or clean linen, liveries, uniforms, canonicals, the latest fashions—these are symbols in terms of which men and women have thought about the relations of class with class, of person with person. In the *Institutions of Athens*, written by an anonymous author of the fifth century B.C., we read that it was illegal in Athens to assault a slave even when he refused to make way for you in the street. "The reason why this is the local custom shall be explained. If it were legal for the slave to be struck by the free citizen, your Athenian citizen himself would always be getting assaulted through being mistaken for a slave. Members of the free proletariat of Athens are no better dressed than slaves or aliens and no more respectable in appearance." But Athens—a democratic city state with a majority of "poor whites"—was exceptional. In almost every other society the wearing of cheap and dirty clothes has been regarded (such is the power of symbols) as the equivalent of a moral lapse—a lapse for which the wearers deserved to be ostracized by all decent people. In *Les Précieuses Ridicules*[2] the high-flown heroines take two footmen, dressed up in their masters' clothes, for marquises. The comedy comes to its climax when the pretenders are stripped of their symbolic finery and the girls discover the ghastly truth. *Et eripitur persona, manet res*[3]—or, to be more precise, *manet altera persona.*[4] The mask is torn off and there remains—what? Another mask—the footman's.

In eighteenth-century England the producers of woolens were able to secure legislation prohibiting the import of cotton prints from the Orient and imposing an excise duty, not repealed until 1832, on the domestic product. But in spite of this systematic discouragement, the new industry prospered—inevitably; for it met a need, it supplied a vast and growing demand. Wool could not be cleaned, cotton was washable. For the first time in the history of Western Europe it began to be possible for all but the poorest women to look clean. The revolution then begun is still in progress. Garments of cotton and the new synthetic fibers have largely abolished the ragged and greasy symbols of earlier class distinctions. And meanwhile, for such fabrics as cannot be washed, the chemical industry has invented a host of new detergents and solvents. In the past, grease spots were a problem for which there was no solution. Proletarian garments were darkly shiny with accumulated fats and oils, and even the merchant's broadcloth, even the velvets and satins of lords and ladies displayed the ineradicable traces of last year's candle droppings, of yesterday's gravy. Dry cleaning is a modern art, a little younger than railway travel, a little older than the first Atlantic cable.

In recent years, and above all in America, the revolution in clothing has entered a new phase. As well as cleanliness, elegance is being placed within the reach of practically everyone. Cheap clothes are mass-

[2] A one-act comedy by Molière of 1659.
[3] And snatch away the mask, the thing remains.
[4] The other mask remains.

produced from patterns created by the most expensive designers. Unfashionableness was once a stigma hardly less damning, as a symbol of inferiority, than dirt. Fifty years ago a girl who wore cheap clothes proclaimed herself, by their obvious dowdiness, to be a person whom it was all but out of the question, if one were well off, to marry. Misalliance is still deplored; but, thanks to Sears and Ohrbach, it seems appreciably less dreadful than it did to our fathers.

Sewage systems and dry cleaning, hygiene and washable fabrics, DDT and penicillin—the catalogue represents a series of technological victories over two great enemies: dirt and that system of untouchability, that unbrotherly contempt, to which, in the past, dirt has given rise.

It is, alas, hardly necessary to add that these victories are in no sense definitive or secure. All we can say is that, in certain highly industrialized countries, technological advances have led to the disappearance of some of the immemorial symbols of class distinction. But this does not guarantee us against the creation of new symbols no less compulsive in their antidemocratic tendencies than the old. A man may be clean; but if, in a dictatorial state, he lacks a party card, he figuratively stinks and must be treated as an inferior at the best and, at the worst, an untouchable.

In the nominally Christian past two irreconcilable sets of symbols bedeviled the Western mind—the symbols, inside the churches, of God's fatherhood and the brotherhood of man; and the symbols, outside, of class distinction, mammon worship and dynastic, provincial or national idolatry. In the totalitarian future—and if we go on fighting wars, the future of the West is bound to be totalitarian—the time-hallowed symbols of monotheism and brotherhood will doubtless be preserved. God will be One and men will all be His children, but in a strictly Pickwickian sense. Actually there will be slaves and masters, and the slaves will be taught to worship a parochial Trinity of Nation, Party and Political Boss. Samuel Butler's Musical Banks will be even more musical than they are today, and the currency in which they deal will have even less social and psychological purchasing power than the homilies of the Age of Faith.

Symbols are necessary—for we could not think without them. But they are also fatal—for the thinking they make possible is just as often unrealistic as it is to the point. In this consists the essentially tragic nature of the human situation. There is no way out, except for those who have learned how to go beyond all symbols to a direct experience of the basic fact of the divine immanence. *Tat tvam asi*—thou are That. When this is perceived, the rest will be added. In the meantime we must be content with such real but limited goods as Hyperion, and such essentially precarious and mutable sources of good as are provided by the more realistic of our religious symbols.

Elizabeth Bowen

(1899–1973)

Elizabeth Bowen was seven years old when her father became mentally ill and she and her mother, on the advice of doctors, left their home in Ireland to live here and there in southern England. "Here we were, adventurers in this other country," she recalled in her unfinished autobiography which was to be entitled Pieces and Conversations. *Her mother died when she was thirteen. Loss and dislocation thread their way through her novels and short stories, particularly as felt in the lives of children. At age seven, too, she learned to read—unusually late, because her mother feared the exertion might make the child susceptible to the Bowen disease ("so that I should not burn out my eyes, she said"). But there had been and continued to be much reading aloud, to Elizabeth's perpetual delight. By age eight, she reports, "I entered upon a long phase in which I saw life as a non-stop historical novel." And coming to London at eighteen to work and write, she saw the great city as a place "out of books," Dickens, Galsworthy, Conan Doyle. It was more than a case of youthful literary romanticism, of literature coloring and embellishing life. The book—or "story," for Bowen was pre-eminently a writer of fiction—is at the center of life, what gives it continuity, shape, wholeness: "Nothing made full sense to me that was not in print. Life seemed to promise to be intolerable without full sense, authoritative imaginative knowledge. Feeling what a book could do and what indeed only a book* could *do made me wish to write: I conceived of nothing else worth doing" ("Coming to London," 1956). The autobiographical book undertaken during the last year of her life was to be an account of "the relationship (so far as that can be traceable, and perhaps it is most interesting when it is apparently not traceable) between living and writing." With its weave of reminiscences, impressions, and quotations from her own fiction, it would take up in another form material worked so elegantly and suggestively in "Out of a Book" (1946). For Bowen the fiction writer, the lifelong lure of autobiography—she returned to it again and again—was the possibility of tracing "the apparently not traceable": where the writer herself came from.*

Out of a Book

I know that I have in my make-up layers of synthetic experience, and that the most powerful of my memories are only half true.

Reduced to the minimum, to the what did happen, my life would be unrecognizable by me. Those layers of fictitious memory densify as they go deeper down. And this surely must be the case with everyone else who reads deeply, ravenously, unthinkingly, sensuously, as a child. The overlapping and haunting of life by fiction began, of course, before there was anything to be got from the printed page; it began from the day one was old enough to be told a story or shown a picture book. It went on up to the age when a bookish attitude towards books began to be inculcated by education. The young person is then thrown out of Eden; forevermore his brain is to stand posted between his self and the story. Appreciation of literature is the end of magic; in place of the virgin susceptibility to what is written he is given taste, something to be refined and trained.

Happily, the Eden, like a natal climate, can be unconsciously remembered, and the magic stored up in those years goes on secreting under today's chosen sensations and calculated thoughts. What entered the system during childhood remains; and remains indistinguishable from the life of those years because it *was* the greater part of life. Probably children, if they said what they thought, would be much franker about the insufficiency of so-called real life to the requirements of those who demand to be really alive. Nothing but the story can meet the untried nature's need and capacity for the whole. Of course one cannot narrow down children to the reading child; but I could not as a child, and I cannot now, conceive what the non-reading child must be like inside. Outdoor children were incomprehensible to me when I was their age, and I still find them dull; I could not, and cannot, find out what makes them do what they do, or why they like what they like; and of such children now they are grown up I can only say that I cannot conceive what they remember, if they do remember—for how can even the senses carry imprints when there was no story? The non-reading active children were not stupid; they had their senses. Nor was it the clever children who read most, or who were at any rate the ones who inhaled fiction—quite apart there were always the horrible little students, future grown-ups, who pursued knowledge. The light-headed reading child and the outdoor child had more in common (in fact, the life of sensation) than either had with the student. Readers of my kind were the heady ones, the sensationalists—recognizing one another at sight we were banded together inside a climate of our own. Landscapes or insides of houses or streets or gardens, outings or even fatigue duties all took the cast of the book we were circulating at the time; and the reading made of us an electric ring. Books were story or story-poetry books: we were unaware that there could be any others.

Some of the heady group remained wonderfully proof against education: having never graduated these are the disreputable grown-ups who snap up shiny magazines and garner and carry home from libraries fiction that the critics ignore. They read as we all once read—because they must: without fiction, either life would be insufficient or the winds from the north would blow too cold. They read as we all read when we were twelve; but unfortunately the magic has been adulterated; the dependence has become ignominious—it becomes an enormity, inside the full-sized body, to read without the brain. Now the stories they seek go on being children's stories, only with sex added to the formula; and somehow the addition queers everything. These readers, all the same, are the great malleable bulk, the majority, the greater public—hence best-sellers, with their partly artful, party unconscious play on a magic that has gone stale. The only above-board grown-up children's stories are detective stories.

No, it is not only our fate but our business to lose innocence, and once we have lost that it is futile to attempt a picnic in Eden. One kind of power to read, or power that reading had over us, is gone. And not only that: it is a mistake to as much as re-open the books of childhood—they are bare ruined choirs. Everything has evaporated from those words, leaving them meaningless on the page. This is the case, for me, even with Dickens—I cannot read him now because I read him exhaustively as a child. Though I did not in those years read all his books, I cannot now read any that I did not read then—there is no more oxygen left, for me, anywhere in the atmosphere of his writing. The boredom I seem to feel as I pursue the plots is, really, a flagging of my intellect in this (by me) forever used up and devitalized air. I came to an end with Dickens when I had absorbed him into myself.

Yes, one stripped bare the books of one's childhood to make oneself—it is inevitable that there should be nothing left when one goes back to them. The fickleness of children and very young persons shocks their elders—children abandon people, for instance, without a flicker, with a simplicity that really ought not to be hurting: the abandoned one has been either a "best" friend or an object of hero-worship and the more emotionally fruitful and fanciful the relationship, the more complete the break. "Where is So-and-so these days? I don't seem to have heard anything about him (or her) for a long time. Haven't you two got any more plans?"—"Oh, I can't be bothered." What applies to people applies to books, and for the same reason: everything that was wanted has been taken; only the husk or, still worse, mortifying repetition remains. The child is on the make—rapacious, mobile and single-minded. If the exhausted book survives physical abandonment—being given away or left out in the garden in the rain—it languishes on in its owner's indifferent keeping; however, once memory and sentiment have had time to set in and gather about it, it is safe. I still keep a row of books I loved as a child—but I neither wish nor dare to touch them.

What do I mean by those books making myself? In the first place, they were power-testing athletics for my imagination—cross-country runs into strange country, sprints, long and high jumps. It was exhilarating to discover what one could feel: the discovery itself was an advance. Then, by successively "being" a character in every book I read, I doubled the meaning of everything that happened in my otherwise constricted life. Books introduced me to, and magnified, desire and danger. They represented life, with a conclusiveness I had no reason to challenge, as an affair of mysteries and attractions, in which each object or place or face was in itself a volume of promises and deceptions, and in which nothing was impossible. Books made me see everything that I saw either as a symbol or as having its place in a mythology—in fact, reading gave bias to my observations of everything in the between-times when I was not reading. And obviously, the characters in the books gave prototypes under which, forevermore, to assemble all living people. This did not by any means simplify people for me; it had the reverse effect, and I was glad that it should—the characters who came out of my childish reading to obsess me were the incalculable ones, who always moved in a blur of potentialities. It appeared that nobody who mattered was capable of being explained. Thus was inculcated a feeling for the dark horse. I can trace in all people whom I have loved a succession from book characters—not from one only, from a fusion of many. "Millions of strange shadows on you tend."

Also the expectation, the search, was geographic. I was and I am still on the lookout for places where something happened: the quivering needle swings in turn to a prospect of country, a town unwrapping itself from folds of landscape or seen across water, or a significant house. Such places are haunted—scenes of acute sensation for someone, vicariously me. My identity, so far as I can pin it down at all, resides among these implacable likes or dislikes, these subjections to magnetism spaced out between ever-widening lacunæ of indifference. I feel certain that if I *could* read my way back, analytically, through the books of my childhood, the clues to everything could be found.

The child lives in the book; but just as much the book lives in the child. I mean that, admittedly, the process of reading is reciprocal; the book is no more than a formula, to be furnished out with images out of the reader's mind. At any age, the reader must come across: the child reader is the most eager and quick to do so; he not only lends to the story, he flings into the story the whole of his sensuous experience which from being limited is the more intense. Book dishes draw saliva to the mouth; book fears raise gooseflesh and make the palms clammy; book suspense makes the cheeks burn and the heart thump. Still more, at the very touch of a phrase there is a surge of brilliant visual images: the child rushes up the scenery for the story. When the story, as so often happens, demands what has not yet come into stock, indefatigable makeshifts are arrived at—as when a play that calls for elaborate staging is performed by an enterprising little company with scanty equipment and few drop-scenes. Extension (to draw an iceberg out of a fishmonger's ice-block) or multiplication (to make a thin, known wood into a trackless forest) goes on. For castles, gorges, or anything else spectacular out of art or nature, recollections of picture postcards, posters or travel albums are drawn on; and, of course, the child today has amassed a whole further scenic stock from the cinema. This provision of a convincing *where* for the story is a reflex.

For the child, any real-life scene that has once been sucked into the ambience of the story is affected, or infected, forever. The road, crossroads, corner of a wood, cliff, flight of steps, town square, quayside or door in a wall keeps a transmuted existence: it has not only given body to fiction, it has partaken of fiction's body. Such a thing, place or scene cannot again be walked past indifferently; it exerts a pull and sets up a tremor; and it is to indent the memory for life. It is at these points, indeed, that what I have called synthetic experience has its sources. Into that experience come relationships, involving valid emotion, between the child reader and book characters; a residuum of the book will be in all other emotions that are to follow.

In reverse, there are the real-life places—towns, seaports, suburbs of London—unknown to the child, though heard of, which become "real" through being also in books. For instance, after *David Copperfield* I could not hear either Dover or Yarmouth mentioned, in the most ordinary context, without excitement: I had a line on them. Towns that were in books, and the routes between them travelled by characters, stood out in relief on the neutral map of England. Not a Londoner, I was continuously filling in and starring my map of the environs—at Richmond lived Sir Percy, the Scarlet Pimpernel, and his wife Marguerite, who fainted into a bed of heliotrope in her riverside garden; at Highgate, the Steerforths and Rosa Dartle; at Blackheath and Lewisham, the E. Nesbit children. When I came to read "Kipps," I was made dizzy by the discovery that I had, for years, been living in two places, Hythe and Folkestone, that were in a book. Historic places one was taken to see meant no more and no less to me than this; history was fiction—it took me a long time to be able to see that it gained anything further from being "true."

Though not all reading children grow up to be writers, I take it that most creative writers must in their day have been reading children. All through creative writing there must run a sense of dishonesty and of debt. In fact, is there such a thing, anymore, as creative writing? The imagination, which may appear to bear such individual fruit, is rooted in a compost of forgotten books. The apparent choices of art are nothing but addictions, pre-dispositions: where did these come from, how were they formed? The æsthetic is nothing but a return to images that will allow nothing to take their place; the æsthetic is nothing but an attempt to disguise and glorify the enforced return. All susceptibility belongs to the age of magic, the Eden where fact and fiction were the same; the imaginative writer was the imaginative child, who relied for life upon being lied to—and how, now, is he to separate the lies from his consciousness of life? If he be a novelist, all his psychology is merely a new parade of the old mythology. We have relied on our childhoods, on the sensations of childhood, because we mistake vividness for purity; actually, the story was there first—one is forced to see that it was the story that apparelled everything in celestial light. It could lead to madness to look back and back for the true primary impression or sensation; those we did ever experience we have forgotten—we only remember that to which something was added. Almost no experience, however much simplified by the distance of time, is to be vouched for as being wholly my own—*did* I live through that, or was I told that it happened, or did I read it? When I write, I am re-creating what was created for me. The gladness of vision, in writing, is my own gladness, but not at my own vision. I may see, for instance, a road running uphill, a skyline, a figure coming slowly over the hill—the approach of the figure is momentous, accompanied by fear or rapture or fear of rapture or a rapture of fear. But who and how is this? Am I sure this is not a figure out of a book?

E. B. White

(1899–1985)

"Every man, I think, has one book in his life, and this one is mine," White wrote in a New Yorker *column in 1953; the book was* Walden. *White's most famous excursion into Thoreau's woods had been his 1939 essay "Walden," a wry account of trashing in motorized twentieth-century America that manages the unlikely fusion of elegy with comedy. The occasion for "A Slight Sound at Evening," written for* The Yale Review *as "Walden—1954," was the one hundredth anniversary of the publication of Thoreau's book about his experiment on Walden Pond. The fifteen years that separated White's two tributes had brought into being yet another new America, land of the McCarthy witch hunts and the Cold War. White's attempt, this time, at the significance of what Thoreau did and wrote, moves into a new terrain of feeling as well: it is a "short ramble" into the regions of "the remembering heart," a memorial essay. Remembering, of course, is what memorials are for, calling to mind what is past, what may have been forgotten in the "long stretches of [one's] trivial days"; commemorating, too, doing honor. The small, near-empty boathouse where he wrote the essay itself recalls the scene of* Walden, *hence confers upon the writing an air of ceremony, of ritual. White's own life and the times he must now inhabit are opened, thereby, to his predecessor's "wide-awake" moral scrutiny. The language of* Walden *resonates through the final section of the essay—"lifts us up by the ears"—so that we too might become more attentive to the dissonances of our times; and it captures us in another way as well, by making real* via *the page the sound of "the offbeat prose that Thoreau was master of, a prose at once strictly disciplined and wildly abandoned." If Thoreau wrote in "certified sentences," E.B. White did the same, though in his own uncluttered, deceptively easy, contemporary way. And as anyone who has looked in White's* Elements of Style *well knows, language and vision, style and self, are indissoluble: "Every writer, by the way he uses language, reveals something of his spirit, his habits, his capacities, his bias." For "writing is the Self escaping into the open." As for the essayist, "Each new excursion . . . each new 'attempt,' differs from the last and takes him into new country" (Foreword,* Collected Essays).

A Slight Sound at Evening

In his journal for July 10–12, 1841, Thoreau wrote: "A slight sound at evening lifts me up by the ears, and makes life seem inexpressibly serene and grand. It may be in Uranus, or it may be in the shutter." The book into which he later managed to pack both Uranus and the shutter was published in 1854, and now, a hundred years having gone by, *Walden*, its serenity and grandeur unimpaired, still lifts us up by the ears, still translates for us that language we are in danger of forgetting, "which all things and events speak without metaphor, which alone is copious and standard."

Walden is an oddity in American letters. It may very well be the oddest of our distinguished oddities. For many it is a great deal too odd, and for many it is a particular bore. I have not found it to be a well-liked book among my acquaintances, although usually spoken of with respect, and one literary critic for whom I have the highest regard can find no reason for anyone's giving *Walden* a second thought. To admire the book is, in fact, something of an embarrassment, for the mass of men have an indistinct notion that its author was a sort of Nature Boy.

I think it is of some adventage to encounter the book at a period in one's life when the normal anxieties and enthusiasms and rebellions of youth closely resemble those of Thoreau in that spring of 1845 when he borrowed an ax, went out to the woods, and began to whack down some trees for timber. Received at such a juncture, the book is like an invitation to life's dance, assuring the troubled recipient that no matter what befalls him in the way of success or failure he will always be welcome at the party—that the music is played for him, too, if he will but listen and move his feet. In effect, that is what the book is—an invitation, unengraved; and it stirs one as a young girl is stirred by her first big party bid. Many think it a sermon; many set it down as an attempt to rearrange society; some think it an exercise in nature-loving; some find it a rather irritating collection of inspirational puffballs by an eccentric show-off. I think it none of these. It seems to me the best youth's companion yet written by an American, for it carries a solemn warning against the loss of one's valuables, it advances a good argument for traveling light and trying new adventures, it rings with the power of positive adoration, it contains religious feeling without religious images, and it steadfastly refuses to record bad news. Even its pantheistic note is so pure as to be noncorrupting—pure as the flute-note blown across the pond on those faraway summer nights. If our colleges and universities were alert, they would present a cheap pocket edition of the book to every senior upon graduating, along with his sheepskin, or instead of it. Even if some senior were to take it literally and start felling trees, there could be worse mishaps: the ax is older than the Dictaphone and it is just as well for a young man to see what kind of chips he leaves before listening to the sound of his own voice. And even if some were to get no farther than the table of contents, they would learn how to name eighteen chapters by the use of only thirty-nine words and would see how sweet are the uses of brevity.

If Thoreau had merely left us an account of a man's life in the woods or if he had simply retreated to the woods and there recorded his complaints about society, or even if he had contrived to include both records in one essay, *Walden* would probably not have lived a hundred years. As things turned out, Thoreau, very likely without knowing quite what he was up to, took man's relation to Nature and man's dilemma in society and man's capacity for elevating his spirit and he beat all these matters together, in a wild free interval of self-justification and delight, and produced an original omelette from which people can draw nourishment in a hungry day. *Walden* is one of the first of the vitamin-enriched American dishes. If it were a little less good than it is, or even a little less queer, it would be an abominable book. Even as it is, it will continue to baffle and annoy the literal mind and all those who are unable to stomach its caprices and imbibe its theme. Certainly the plodding economist will continue to have rough going if he hopes to emerge from the book with a clear system of economic thought. Thoreau's assault on the Concord society of the mid-nineteenth century has the quality of a modern Western: he rides into the subject at top speed, shooting in all directions. Many of his shots ricochet and nick him on the rebound, and throughout the melee there is a horrendous cloud of inconsistencies and contradictions, and when the shooting dies down and the air clears, one is impressed chiefly by the courage of the rider and by how splendid it was that somebody should have ridden in there and raised all that ruckus.

When he went to the pond, Thoreau struck an attitude and did so deliberately, but his posturing was not to draw the attention of others to him but rather to draw his own attention more closely to himself. "I learned this at least by my experiment: that if one advances confidently in the direction of his dreams, and endeavors to live the life which he has imagined, he will meet with a success unexpected in common hours." The sentence has the power to resuscitate the youth drowning in his sea of doubt. I recall my exhilaration upon reading it, many years ago, in a time of hesitation and despair. It restored me to health. And now in 1954 when I salute Henry Thoreau on the hundredth birthday of his book, I am merely paying off an old score—or an installment on it.

In his journal for May 3–4, 1838—Boston to Portland—he wrote: "Midnight—head over the boat's side—between sleeping and waking—with glimpses of one or more lights in the vicinity of Cape Ann. Bright moonlight—the effect heightened by seasickness." The entry illuminates the man, as the moon the sea on that night in May. In Thoreau the natural scene was heightened, not depressed, by a disturbance of the stomach, and nausea met its match at last. There was a steadiness in at least one passenger if there was none in the boat. Such steadiness (which in some would be called intoxication) is at the heart of *Walden*—confidence, faith, the discipline of looking always at what is to be seen, undeviating gratitude for the life-everlasting that he found growing in his front yard. "There is nowhere recorded a simple and irrepressible satisfaction with the gift of life, any memorable praise of God." He worked to correct that deficiency. *Walden* is his acknowledgment of the gift of life. It is the testament of a man in a high state of indignation because (it seemed to him) so few ears heard the uninterrupted poem of creation, the morning wind that forever blows. If the man sometimes wrote as though all his readers were male, unmarried, and well-connected, it is because he gave his testimony during the callow years. For that matter, he never really grew up. To reject the book because of the immaturity of the author and the bugs in the logic is to throw away a bottle of good wine because it contains bits of the cork.

Thoreau said he required of every writer, first and last, a simple and sincere account of his own life. Having delivered himself of this chesty dictum, he proceeded to ingore it. In his books and even in his enormous journal, he withheld or disguised most of the facts from which an understanding of his life could be drawn. *Walden*, subtitled "Life in the Woods," is not a simple and sincere account of a man's life, either in or out of the woods; it is an account of a man's journey into the mind, a toot on the trumpet to alert the neighbors. Thoreau was well aware that no one can alert his neighbors who is not wide-awake himself, and he went to the woods (among other reasons) to make sure that he would stay awake during his broadcast. What actually took place during the years 1845–47 is largely unrecorded, and the reader is excluded from the private life of the author, who supplies almost no gossip about himself, a great deal about his neighbors and about the universe.

As for me, I cannot in this short ramble give a simple and sincere account of my own life, but I think Thoreau might find it instructive to know that this memorial essay is being written in a house that, through no intent on my part, is the same size and shape as his own domicile on the pond—about ten by fifteen, tight, plainly finished, and at a little distance from my Concord. The house in which I sit this morning was built to accommodate a boat, not a man, but by long experience I have learned that in most respects it shelters me better than the larger dwelling where my bed is, and which, by design, is a manhouse not a boathouse. Here in the boathouse I am a wilder and, it would appear, a healthier man, by a safe margin. I have a chair, a bench, a table, and I can walk into the water if I tire of the land. My house fronts a cove. Two fishermen have just arrived to spot fish from the air—an osprey and a man in a small yellow plane who works for the fish company. The man, I have noticed, is less well equipped than the hawk, who can dive directly on his fish and carry it away, without telephoning. A mouse and a squirrel share the house with me. The building is, in fact, a multiple dwelling, a semidetached affair. It is because I am semidetached while here that I find it possible to transact this private business with the fewest obstacles.

There is also a woodchuck here, living forty feet away under the wharf. When the wind is right, he can smell my house; and when the wind is contrary, I can smell his. We both use the wharf for sunning, taking turns, each adjusting his schedule to the other's convenience. Thoreau once ate a woodchuck. I think he felt he owed it to his readers, and that it was little enough, considering the indignities they were suffering at his hands and the dressing-down they were taking. (Parts of *Walden* are pure scold.) Or perhaps he ate the woodchuck because he believed every man should acquire strict business habits, and the woodchuck was destroying his market beans. I do not know. Thoreau had a strong experimental streak in him. It is probably no harder to eat a woodchuck than to construct a sentence that lasts a hundred years. At any rate, Thoreau is the only writer I know who prepared himself for his great ordeal by eating a woodchuck; also the only one who got a hangover from drinking too much water. (He was drunk the whole time, though he seldom touched wine or coffee or tea.)

Here in this compact house where I would spend one day as deliberately as Nature if I were not being pressed by the editor of a magazine, and with a woodchuck (as yet uneaten) for neighbor, I can feel the companionship of the occupant of the pond-side cabin in Walden woods, a mile from the village, near the Fitchburg right of way. Even my immediate business is no barrier between us: Thoreau occasionally batted out a magazine piece, but was always suspicious of any sort of purposeful work that cut into his time. A man, he said, should take care not to be thrown off the track by every nutshell and mosquito's wing that falls on the rails.

There has been much guessing as to why he went to the pond. To set it down to escapism is, of course, to misconstrue what happened. Henry went forth to battle when he took to the woods, and *Walden* is the report of a man torn by two powerful and opposing drives—the desire to enjoy the world (and not be derailed by a mosquito wing) and the urge to set the world straight. One cannot join these two successfully, but sometimes, in rare cases, something good or even great results from the attempt of the tormented spirit to reconcile them. Henry went forth to battle, and if he set the stage himself, if he fought on his own terms and with his own weapons, it was because it was his nature to do things differently from most men, and to act in a cocky fashion. If the pond and the woods seemed a more plausible site for a house than an in-town location, it was because a cowbell made for him a sweeter sound than a churchbell. *Walden*, the book, makes the sound of a cowbell, more than a churchbell, and proves the point, although both sounds are in it, and both remarkably clear and sweet. He simply preferred his churchbell at a little distance.

I think one reason he went to the woods was a perfectly simple and commonplace one—and apparently he thought so, too. "At a certain season of our life," he wrote, "we are accustomed to consider every spot as the possible site of a house." There spoke the young man, a few years out of college, who had not yet broken away from home. He hadn't married, and he had found no job that measured up to his rigid standards of employment, and like any young man, or young animal, he felt uneasy and on the defensive until he had fixed himself a den. Most young men, of course, casting about for a site, are content merely to draw apart from their kinfolks. Thoreau, convinced that the greater part of what his neighbors called good was bad, withdrew from a great deal more than family: he pulled out of everything for a while, to serve everybody right for being so stuffy, and to try his own prejudices on the dog.

The house-hunting sentence above, which starts the chapter called "Where I Lived, and What I Lived For," is followed by another passage that is worth quoting here because it so beautifully illustrates the offbeat prose that Thoreau was master of, a prose at once strictly disciplined and wildly abandoned. "I have surveyed the country on every side within a dozen miles of where I live," continued this delirious young man. "In imagination I have bought all the farms in succession, for all were to be bought, and I knew their price. I walked over each farmer's premises, tasted his wild apples, discoursed on husbandry with him, took his farm at his price, at any price, mortgaging it to him in my mind; even put a higher price on it—took everything but a deed of it—took his word for his deed, for I dearly love to talk—cultivated it, and him too to some extent, I trust, and withdrew when I had enjoyed it long enough, leaving him to carry it on." A copy-desk man would get a double hernia trying to clean up that sentence for the management, but the sentence needs no fixing, for it perfectly captures the meaning of the writer and the quality of the rumble.

"Wherever I sat, there I might live, and the landscape radiated from me accordingly." Thoreau, the home-seeker, sitting on his hummock with the entire State of Massachusetts radiating from him, is to me the most humorous of the New England figures, and *Walden* the most humorous of the books, though its humor is almost continuously subsurface and there is nothing deliberately funny anywhere, except a few weak jokes and bad puns that rise to the surface like the perch in the pond that rose to the sound of the maestro's flute. Thoreau tended to write in sentences, a feat not every writer is capable of, and *Walden* is, rhetorically speaking, a collection of certified sentences, some of them, it would now appear, as indestructible as they are errant. The book is distilled from the vast journals, and this accounts for its intensity: he picked out bright particles that pleased his eye, whirled them in the kaleidoscope of content and, produced the pattern that has endured—the color, the form, the light.

On this its hundredth birthday, Thoreau's *Walden* is pertinent and timely. In our uneasy season, when all men unconsciously seek a retreat from a world that has got almost completely out of hand, his house in the Concord woods is a haven. In our culture of gadgetry and the multiplicity of convenience, his cry "Simplicity, simplicity, simplicity!" has the insistence of a fire alarm. In the brooding atmosphere of war and the gathering radioactive storm, the innocence and serenity of his summer afternoons are enough to burst the remembering heart, and one gazes back upon that pleasing interlude—its confidence, its purity, its deliberateness—with awe and wonder, as one would look upon the face of a child asleep.

"This small lake was of most value as a neighbor in the intervals of a gentle rain-storm in August, when, both air and water being perfectly still, but the sky overcast, midafternoon had all the serenity of evening, and the wood-thrush sang around, and was heard from shore to shore." Now, in the perpetual overcast in which our days are spent, we hear with extra perception and deep gratitude that song, tying century to century.

I sometimes amuse myself by bringing Henry Thoreau back to life and showing him the sights. I escort him into a phone booth and let him dial Weather. "This is a delicious evening," the girl's voice says, "when the whole body is one sense, and imbibes delight through every pore." I show him the spot in the Pacific where an island used to be, before some magician made it vanish. "We know not where we are," I murmur. "The light which puts out our eyes is darkness to us. Only that day dawns to which we are awake." I thumb through the latest copy of *Vogue* with him. "Of two patterns which differ only by a few threads more or less of a particular color," I read, "the one will be sold readily, the other lie on the shelf, though it frequently happens that, after the lapse of the season, the latter becomes the most fashionable." Together we go outboarding on the Assabet, looking for what we've lost—a hound, a bay horse, a turtledove. I show him a distracted farmer who is trying to repair a hay baler before the thunder shower breaks. "This farmer," I remark, "is endeavoring to solve the problem of a livelihood by a formula more complicated than the problem itself. To get his shoestrings he speculates in herds of cattle."

I take the celebrated author to Twenty-One for lunch, so the waiters may study his shoes. The proprietor welcomes us. "The gross feeder," remarks the proprietor, sweeping the room with his arm, "is a man in the larva stage." After lunch we visit a classroom in one of those schools conducted by big corporations to teach their superannuated executives how to retire from business without serious injury to their health. (The shock to men's systems these days when relieved of the exacting routine of amassing wealth is very great and must be cushioned.) "It is not necessary," says the teacher to his pupils, "that a man should earn his living by the sweat of his brow, unless he sweats easier than I do. We are determined to be starved before we are hungry."

I turn on the radio and let Thoreau hear Winchell beat the red hand around the clock. "Time is but the stream I go a-fishing in," shouts Mr. Winchell, rattling his telegraph key. "Hardly a man takes a half hour's nap after dinner, but when he wakes he holds up his head and asks, 'What's the news?' If we read of one man robbed, or murdered, or killed by accident, or one house burned, or one vessel wrecked, or one steamboat blown up, or one cow run over on the Western Railroad, or one mad dog killed, or one lot of grasshoppers in the winter—we need never read of another. One is enough."

I doubt that Thoreau would be thrown off balance by the fantastic sights and sounds of the twentieth century. "The Concord nights," he once wrote, "are stranger than the Arabian nights." A four-engined air liner would merely serve to confirm his early views on travel. Everywhere he would observe, in new shapes and sizes, the old predicaments and follies of men—the desperation, the impedimenta, the meanness—along with the visible capacity for elevation of the mind and soul. "This curious world which we inhabit is more wonderful than it is convenient; more beautiful than it is useful; it is more to be admired and enjoyed than used." He would see that today ten thousand engineers are busy making sure that the world shall be convenient even if it is destroyed in the process, and others are determined to increase its usefulness even though its beauty is lost somewhere along the way.

At any rate, I'd like to stroll about the countryside in Thoreau's company for a day, observing the modern scene, inspecting today's snowstorm, pointing out the sights, and offering belated apologies for my sins. Thoreau is unique among writers in that those who admire him find him uncomfortable to live with—a regular hairshirt of a man. A little band of dedicated Thoreauvians would be a sorry sight indeed: fellows who hate compromise and have compromised, fellows who love wildness and have lived tamely, and at their side, censuring them and chiding them, the ghostly figure of this upright man, who long ago gave corroboration to impulses they perceived were right and issued warnings against the things they instinctively knew to be their enemies. I should hate to be called a Thoreauvian, yet I wince every time I walk into the barn I'm pushing before me, seventy-five feet by forty, and the author of *Walden* has served as my conscience through the long stretches of my trivial days.

Hairshirt or no, he is a better companion than most, and I would not swap him for a soberer or more reasonable friend even if I could. I can reread his famous invitation with undiminished excitement. The sad thing is that not more acceptances have been received, that so many decline for one reason or another, pleading some previous engagement or ill health. But the invitation stands. It will beckon as long as this remarkable book stays in print—which will be as long as there are August afternoons in the intervals of a gentle rainstorm, as long as there are ears to catch the faint sounds of the orchestra. I find it agreeable to sit here this morning, in a house of correct proportions, and hear across a century of time his flute, his frogs, and his seductive summons to the wildest revels of them all.

Zora Neale Hurston

(1901?–1960)

In 1927, anthropologist Franz Boaz sent Hurston from Barnard back home to Eatonville, Florida—"a pure Negro town," she describes it, "the first attempt at organized self-government on the part of Negroes in America"—to collect folklore. She took along his injunction not to try to prove anything but to record whatever she found, with no warping. The study of anthropology disciplined her capacity to suspend judgment and strengthened an independence of mind born in a "hard-hitting, rugged-individualistic setting" (Dust Tracks on the Road). *According to her autobiographical essay "How It Feels to Be Colored Me" (1928,* I Love Myself When I Am Laughing), *having color as a literal fact must be distinguished from being colored as a social construct. Color was no issue until she was exposed to it as a category devised by whites; but having become aware of how such a construct, a mere abstraction, can dominate the experience of all within its sphere, she "became a fast brown—warranted not to rub nor run." The ways of her own folk that had always been an unconscious norm for her became her conscious focus. Her fictions and folklore collections show that nothing, even the insidious wrongs of discrimination, distracts her from her people; their personalities, values, beliefs, the kind of world they create, their relationships not to whites but to each other are all dramatized in the language of their daily lives. In short, she made art out of everything that her own folk handed down. Far from being the naïf some took her to be, Zora Neale Hurston is the great pioneer of an African-American cultural integrity later associated with the Black Arts movement. Herself "a brown bag of miscellany," she sought to portray a wide spectrum of colored personalities, with the insight that what speaks most fervently to the substantial sameness of all humans is the cultural range of our differences: the various ways our species has fashioned to express "the jumble" inside all of us. Hurston speaks with the indomitable voice of a woman embodying the traditions of an African-American community. In her wit and her warmth, she refuses to sully that voice with the pomposities, the illusions of superiority, by which cultural violence against outsiders is usually justified.*

How It Feels to Be Colored Me

I am colored but I offer nothing in the way of extenuating circumstances except the fact that I am the only Negro in the United States whose grandfather on the mother's die was *not* an Indian chief.

I remember the very day that I became colored. Up to my thirteenth year I lived in the little Negro town of Eatonville, Florida. It is exclusively a colored town. The only white people I knew passed through the town going to or coming from Orlando. The native whites rode dusty horses, the Northern tourists chugged down the sandy village road in automobiles. The town knew the Southerners and never stopped cane chewing when they passed. But the Northerners were something else again. They were peered at cautiously from behind curtains by the timid. The more venturesome would come out on the porch to watch them go past and got just as much pleasure out of the tourists as the tourists got out of the village.

The front porch might seem a daring place for the rest of the town, but it was a gallery seat for me. My favorite place was atop the gate-post. Proscenium box for a born first-nighter. Not only did I enjoy the show, but I didn't mind the actors knowing that I liked it. I usually spoke to them in passing. I'd wave at them and when they returned my salute, I would say something like this: "Howdy-do-well-I-thank-you-where-you-goin'?" Usually automobile or the horse paused at this, and after a queer exchange of compliments, I would probably "go a piece of the way" with them, as we say in farthest Florida. If one of my family happened to come to the front in time to see me, of course negotiations would be rudely broken off. But even so, it is clear that I was the first "welcome-to-our-state" Floridian, and I hope the Miami Chamber of Commerce will please take notice.

During this period, white people differed from colored to me only in that they rode through town and never lived there. They liked to hear me "speak pieces" and sing and wanted to see me dance the parse-me-la,[1] and gave me generously of their small silver for doing these things, which seemed strange to me for I wanted to do them so much that I needed bribing to stop. Only they didn't know it. The colored people gave no dimes. They deplored any joyful tendencies in me, but I was their Zora nevertheless. I belonged to them, to the nearby hotels, to the county—everybody's Zora.

But changes came in the family when I was thirteen, and I was sent to school in Jacksonville. I left Eatonville, the town of the oleanders, as

[1] Parse-me-la may be a transformation of the "Possum-a-la," a dance-song of 1898, which itself goes back to "La Pas Ma La," a dance-song of 1895.

Zora. When I disembarked from the river-boat at Jacksonville, she was no more. It seemed that I had suffered a sea change. I was not Zora of Orange County anymore, I was now a little colored girl. I found it out in certain ways. In my heart as well as in the mirror, I became a fast brown—warranted not to rub nor run.

But I am not tragically colored. There is no great sorrow dammed up in my soul, nor lurking behind my eyes. I do not mind at all. I do not belong to the sobbing school of Negrohood who hold that nature somehow has given them a lowdown dirty deal and whose feelings are all hurt about it. Even in the helter-skelter skirmish that is my life, I have seen that the world is to the strong regardless of a little pigmentation more or less. No, I do not weep at the world—I am too busy sharpening my oyster knife.

Someone is always at my elbow reminding me that I am the granddaughter of slaves. It fails to register depression with me. Slavery is sixty years in the past. The operation was successful and the patient is doing well, thank you. The terrible struggle that made me an American out of a potential slave said "On the line!" The Reconstruction said "Get set!"; and the generation before said "Go!" I am off to a flying start and I must not halt in the stretch to look behind and weep. Slavery is the price I paid for civilization, and the choice was not with me. It is a bully adventure and worth all that I have paid through my ancestors for it. No one on earth ever had a greater chance for glory. The world to be won and nothing to be lost. It is thrilling to think—to know that for any act of mine, I shall get twice as much praise or twice as much blame. It is quite exciting to hold the center of the national stage, with the spectators not knowing whether to laugh or to weep.

The position of my white neighbor is much more difficult. No brown specter pulls up a chair beside me when I sit down to eat. No dark ghost thrusts its leg against mine in bed. The game of keeping what one has is never so exciting as the game of getting.

I do not always feel colored. Even now I often achieve the unconscious Zora of Eatonville before the Hegira. I feel most colored when I am thrown against a sharp white background.

For instance at Barnard. "Beside the waters of the Hudson" I feel my race. Among the thousand white persons, I am a dark rock surged upon, and overswept, but through it all, I remain myself. When covered by the waters, I am; and the ebb but reveals me again.

Sometimes it is the other way around. A white person set down in our midst, but the contrast is just as sharp for me. For instance, when I sit in the drafty basement that is The New World Cabaret with a white person, my color comes. We enter chatting about any little nothing that we have in common and are seated by the jazz waiters. In the abrupt way that jazz orchestras have, this one plunges into a number. It loses no time in circumlocutions, but gets right down to business. It constricts the thorax and splits the heart with its tempo and narcotic harmonies. This orchestra grows rambunctious, rears on its hind legs and attacks the tonal veil with primitive fury, rending it, clawing it until it breaks through to the jungle beyond. I follow those heathen—follow them exultingly. I dance wildly inside myself; I yell within, I whoop; I shake my assegai above my head, I hurl it true to the mark *yeeeeooww!* I am in the jungle and living in the jungle way. My face is painted red and yellow and my body is painted blue. My pulse is throbbing like a war drum. I want to slaughter something—give pain, give death to what, I do not know. But the piece ends. The men of the orchestra wipe their lips and rest their fingers. I creep back slowly to the veneer we call civilization with the last tone and find the white friend sitting motionless in his seat, smoking calmly.

"Good music they have here," he remarks, drumming the table with his fingertips.

Music. The great blobs of purple and red emotion have not touched him. He has only heard what I felt. He is far away and I see him but dimly across the ocean and the continent that have fallen between us. He is so pale with his whiteness then and I am *so* colored.

At certain times I have no race, I am *me*. When I set my hat at a certain angle and saunter down Seventh Avenue, Harlem City, feeling as snooty as the lions in front of the Forty-Second Street Library, for instance. So far as my feelings are concerned, Peggy Hopkins Joyce on the Boule Mich[2] with her gorgeous raiment, stately carriage, knees knocking together in a most aristocratic manner, has nothing on me. The cosmic Zora emerges. I belong to no race nor time. I am the eternal feminine with its string of beads.

I have no separate feeling about being an American citizen and colored. I am merely a fragment of the Great Soul that surges within the boundaries. My country, right or wrong.

Sometimes, I feel discriminated against, but it does not make me angry. It merely astonishes me. How *can* any deny themselves the pleasure of my company? It's beyond me.

But in the main, I feel like a brown bag of miscellany propped against a wall. Against a wall in company with other bags, white, red

[2] Boulevard St. Michel in Paris.

and yellow. Pour out the contents, and there is discovered a jumble of small things priceless and worthless. A first-water diamond, an empty spool, bits of broken glass, lengths of string, a key to a door long since crumbled away, a rusty knife-blade, old shoes saved for a road that never was and never will be, a nail bent under the weight of things too heavy for any nail, a dried flower or two still a little fragrant. In your hand is the brown bag. On the ground before you is the jumble it held—so much like the jumble in the bags, could they be emptied, that all might be dumped in a single heap and the bags refilled without altering the content of any greatly. A bit of colored glass more or less would not matter. Perhaps that is how the Great Stuffer of Bags filled them in the first place—who knows?

George Orwell
(1903–1950)

In the issue of Partisan Review *that carried "Reflections on Gandhi," George Orwell was identified as "formerly PR's London correspondent . . . at present living in the Hebrides where he is writing a novel." The novel was* Nineteen Eighty-Four, *Orwell's nightmare vision of life in a totalitarian world. As he was finishing his great dystopian fiction in the autumn of 1948, he wrote the essay on Gandhi, his last. Gandhi—whom his people called the Mahatma, ("great-souled") and whom Viscount Mountbatten, last viceroy of British India, hailed as "the architect of India's freedom through nonviolence"—had been assassinated earlier that year at the frail age of seventy-nine. Gandhi's autobiography, which Orwell recalls reading in an Indian newspaper during the late 1920s, was reissued by an American press, and it is this book he is turning over in his thoughts (perhaps in his hands, too) at the beginning of the essay, as though setting out to review a work and a life that now call for reassessment. The voice of this essay is not the Orwell of "Shooting an Elephant" or "A Hanging"; these are splendid literary recreations of experience with the effect of finely honed stories subject to multiple readings. In "Reflections on Gandhi," Orwell the critic tells us freely and clearly what he thinks. The opening glance at Gandhi's book leads into a critique of saintliness and humanity, pacificism and politics. It is not a question of ambivalence towards a revered leader; Orwell is not indecisively of two minds about Gandhi. This is a whole mind revealing its energetic complexity, one mind resisting the conventional, the orthodox, the reductive view of its subject, a mind capacious and supple enough to honor the political achievements of a man whose basic values it dismantles and rejects. Of Jonathan Swift, whose satires profoundly influenced his own work, Orwell remarked: "[Swift] was a great man, and yet he was partially blind. He could see only one thing at a time" ("An Imaginary Interview"). Orwell the essayist always tried to see more than one thing at a time. Totalitarianism, for him, threatens not only the political order; it is also, and most dangerously, a bondage of the intellect. The deepest Orwellian nightmare of* Nineteen Eighty-Four *is thought control. What Orwell wrote of Charles Dickens, one of his favorite authors, near the start of his literary career also describes the writer of "Reflections on Gandhi": he is "a free intelligence."*

Reflections on Gandhi

Saints should always be judged guilty until they are proved innocent, but the tests that have to be applied to them are not, of course, the same in all cases. In Gandhi's case the questions one feels inclined to ask are: to what extent was Gandhi moved by vanity—by the consciousness of himself as a humble, naked old man, sitting on a praying mat and shaking empires by sheer spiritual power—and to what extent did he compromise his own principles by entering politics, which of their nature are inseparable from coercion and fraud? To give a definite answer one would have to study Gandhi's acts and writings in immense detail, for his whole life was a sort of pilgrimage in which every act was significant. But this partial autobiography,[1] which ends in the nineteen-twenties, is strong evidence in his favor, all the more because it covers what he would have called the unregenerate part of his life and reminds one that inside the saint, or near-saint, there was a very shrewd, able person who could, if he had chosen, have been a brilliant success as a lawyer, an administrator or perhaps even a businessman.

At about the time when the autobiography first appeared I remember reading its opening chapters in the ill-printed pages of some Indian newspaper. They made a good impression on me, which Gandhi himself at that time, did not. The things that one associated with him—homespun cloth, "soul forces" and vegetarianism—were unappealing, and his medievalist program was obviously not viable in a backward, starving, over-populated country. It was also apparent that the British were making use of him, or thought they were making use of him. Strictly speaking, as a Nationalist, he was an enemy, but since in every crisis he would exert himself to prevent violence—which, from the British point of view, meant preventing any effective action whatever—he could be regarded as "our man." In private this was sometimes cynically admitted. The attitude of the Indian millionaires was similar. Gandhi called upon them to repent, and naturally they preferred him to the Socialists and Communists who, given the chance, would actually have taken their money away. How reliable such calculations are in the long run is doubtful; as Gandhi himself says, "in the end deceivers deceive only themselves"; but at any rate the gentleness with which he was nearly always handled was due partly to the feeling that he was useful. The British Conservatives only became really angry with him when, as in 1942, he was in effect turning his non-violence against a different conqueror.

[1] *The Story of My Experiments with Truth* by M. K. Gandhi, translated from the Gujerati by M. Desai, and first published in the U.S. in 1948.

But I could see even then that the British officials who spoke of him with a mixture of amusement and disapproval also genuinely liked and admired him, after a fashion. Nobody ever suggested that he was corrupt, or ambitious in any vulgar way, or that anything he did was actuated by fear or malice. In judging a man like Gandhi one seems instinctively to apply high standards, so that some of his virtues have passed almost unnoticed. For instance, it is clear even from the autobiography that his natural physical courage was quite outstanding: the manner of his death was a later illustration of this, for a public man who attached any value to his own skin would have been more adequately guarded. Again, he seems to have been quite free from that maniacal suspiciousness which, as E. M. Forster rightly says in *A Passage to India*, is the besetting Indian vice, as hypocrisy is the British vice. Although no doubt he was shrewd enough in detecting dishonesty, he seems wherever possible to have believed that other people were acting in good faith and had a better nature through which they could be approached. And though he came of a poor middle-class family, started life rather unfavorably, and was probably of unimpressive physical appearance, he was not afflicted by envy or by the feeling of inferiority. Color feeling when he first met it in its worst form in South Africa, seems rather to have astonished him. Even when he was fighting what was in effect a color war, he did not think of people in terms of race or status. The governor of a province, a cotton millionaire, a half-starved Dravidian coolie, a British private soldier were all equally human beings, to be approached in much the same way. It is noticeable that even in the worst possible circumstances, as in South Africa when he was making himself unpopular as the champion of the Indian community, he did not lack European friends.

Written in short lengths for newspaper serialization, the autobiography is not a literary masterpiece, but it is the more impressive because of the commonplaceness of much of its material. It is well to be reminded that Gandhi started out with the normal ambitions of a young Indian student and only adopted his extremist opinions by degrees and, in some cases, rather unwillingly. There was a time, it is interesting to learn, when he wore a top hat, took dancing lessons, studied French and Latin, went up the Eiffel Tower and even tried to learn the violin—all this was the idea of assimilating European civilization as thoroughly as possible. He was not one of those saints who are marked out by their phenomenal piety from childhood onwards, nor one of the other kind who forsake the world after sensational debaucheries. He makes full confession of the misdeeds of his youth, but in fact there is not much to confess. As a frontispiece to the book there is a photograph of Gandhi's possessions at the time of his death. The whole outfit could be purchased for about £5, and Gandhi's sins, at least his fleshly sins, would make the same sort of appearance if placed all in one heap. A few cigarettes, a few mouthfuls of meat, a few annas pilfered in childhood from the maidservant, two visits to a brothel (on each occasion he got away without "doing anything"), one narrowly escaped lapse with his landlady in Plymouth, one outburst of temper—that is about the whole collection. Almost from childhood onwards he had a deep earnestness, an attitude ethical rather than religious, but, until he was about thirty, no very definite sense of direction. His first entry into anything describable as public life was made by way of vegetarianism. Underneath his ordinary qualities one feels at the time the solid middleclass businessmen who were his ancestors. One feels that even after he had abandoned personal ambition he must have been a resourceful, energetic lawyer and a hard-headed political organizer, careful in keeping down expenses, an adroit handler of committees and an indefatigable chaser of subscriptions. His character was an extraordinarily mixed one, but there was almost nothing in it that you can put your finger on and call bad, and I believe that even Gandhi's worst enemies would admit that he was an interesting and unusual man who enriched the world simply by being alive. Whether he was also a lovable man, and whether his teachings can have much value for those who do not accept the religious beliefs on which they are founded, I have never felt fully certain.

Of late years it has been the fashion to talk about Gandhi as though he were not only sympathetic to the Western Left-wing movement, but were integrally part of it. Anarchists and pacifists, in particular, have claimed him for their own, noticing only that he was opposed to centralism and State violence and ignoring the other-worldly, anti-humanist tendency of his doctrines. But one should, I think, realize that Gandhi's teachings cannot be squared with the belief that Man is the measure of all things and that our job is to make life worth living on this earth, which is the only earth we have. They make sense only on the assumption that God exists and that the world of solid objects is an illusion to be escaped from. It is worth considering the disciplines which Gandhi imposed on himself and which—though he might not insist on every one of his followers observing every detail—he considered indispensable if one wanted to serve either God or humanity. First of all, no meat-eating, and if possible no animal food in any form. (Gandhi himself, for the sake of his health, had to compromise on milk, but seems to have felt this to be a backsliding.) No alcohol or tobacco, and no spices or condiments even of a vegetable kind, since food should be taken not for its own sake but solely in order to preserve one's strength. Secondly, if possible, no sexual intercourse. If sexual intercourse must happen, then it should be for the sole purpose of begetting children and presumably at long intervals. Gandhi himself, in his middle thirties, took the vow of *brahmacharya*, which means not only complete chastity but the elimination of sexual desire. This condition, it seems, is difficult to attain without a special diet and frequent fasting. One of the dangers of milk-drinking is that it is apt to arouse sexual desire. And finally—this is the cardinal point—for the seeker after goodness there must be no close friendships and no exclusive loves whatever.

Close friendships, Gandhi says, are dangerous, because "friends react on one another" and through loyalty to a friend one can be led into wrong-doing. This is unquestionably true. Moreover, if one is to love God, or to love humanity as a whole, one cannot give one's preference to any individual person. This again is true, and it marks the point at which the humanistic and the religious attitude cease to be reconcilable. To an ordinary human being, love means nothing if it does not mean loving some people more than others. The autobiography leaves it uncertain whether Gandhi behaved in an inconsiderate way to his wife and children, but at any rate it makes clear that on three occasions he was willing to let his wife or a child die rather than administer the animal food prescribed by the doctor. It is true that the threatened death never actually occurred, and also that Gandhi—with, one gathers, a good deal of moral pressure in the opposite direction—always gave the patient the choice of staying alive at the price of committing a sin: still, if the decision had been solely his own, he would have forbidden the animal food, whatever the risks might be. There must, he says, be some limit to what we will do in order to remain alive, and the limit is well on this side of chicken broth. This attitude is perhaps a noble one, but, in the sense which—I think—most people would give to the word, it is inhuman. The essence of being human is that one does not seek perfection, that one *is* sometimes willing to commit sins for the sake of loyalty, that one does not push asceticism to the point where it makes friendly intercourse impossible, and that one is prepared in the end to be defeated and broken up by life, which is the inevitable price of fastening one's love upon other human individuals. No doubt alcohol, tobacco, and so forth, are things that a saint must avoid, but sainthood is also a thing that human beings must avoid. There is an obvious retort to this, but one should be wary about making it. In this yogi-ridden age, it is too readily assumed that "non-attachment" is not only better than a full acceptance of earthly life, but that the ordinary man only rejects it because it is too difficult: in other words, that the average human being is a failed saint. It is doubtful whether this is true. Many people genuinely do not wish to be saints, and it is probable that some who achieve or aspire to sainthood have never felt much temptation to be human beings. If one could follow it to its psychological roots, one would, I believe, find that the main motive for "non-attachment" is a desire to escape from the pain of living, and above all from love, which, sexual or non-sexual, is hard work. But it is not necessary here to argue whether the otherworldly or the humanistic idea is "higher." The point is that they are incompatible. One must choose between God and Man, and all "radicals" and "progressives," from the mildest Liberal to the most extreme Anarchist, have in effect chosen Man.

However, Gandhi's pacifism can be separated to some extent from his other teachings. Its motive was religious, but he claimed also for it that it was a definite technique, a method, capable of producing desired political results. Gandhi's attitude was not that of most Western pacifists. *Satyagraha*, first evolved in South Africa, was a sort of non-violent warfare, a way of defeating the enemy without hurting him and without feeling or arousing hatred. It entailed such things as civil disobedience, strikes, lying down in front of railway trains, enduring police charges without running away and without hitting back, and the like. Gandhi objected to "passive resistance" as a translation of *Satyagraha:* in Gujarati, it seems, the word means "firmness in the truth." In his early days Gandhi served as a stretcher-bearer on the British side in the Boer War, and he was prepared to do the same again in the war of 1914–18. Even after he had completely abjured violence he was honest enough to see that in war it is usually necessary to take sides. He did not—indeed, since his whole political life centred round a struggle for national independence, he could not—take the sterile and dishonest line of pretending that in every war both sides are exactly the same and it makes no difference who wins. Nor did he, like most Western pacifists, specialize in avoiding awkward questions. In relation to the late war, one question that every pacifist had a clear obligation to answer was: "What about the Jews? Are you prepared to see them exterminated? If not, how do you propose to save them without resorting to war?" I must say that I have never heard, from any Western pacifist, an honest answer to this question, though I have heard plenty of evasions, usually of the "you're another" type. But it so happens that Gandhi was asked a somewhat similar question in 1938 and that his answer is on record in Mr. Louis Fischer's *Gandhi and Stalin*. According to Mr. Fischer, Gandhi's view was that the German Jews ought to commit collective suicide, which "would have aroused the world and the people of Germany to Hitler's violence." After the war he justified himself: the Jews had been killed anyway, and might as well have died significantly. One has the impression that this attitude staggered even so warm an admirer as Mr. Fischer, but Gandhi was merely being honest. If you are not prepared to take life, you must often be prepared for lives to be lost in some other way. When, in 1942, he urged non-violent resistance against a Japanese invasion, he was ready to admit that it might cost several million deaths.

At the same time there is reason to think that Gandhi, who after all was born in 1869, did not understand the nature of totalitarianism and saw everything in terms of his own struggle against the British government. The important point here is not so much that the British treated him forbearingly as that he was always able to command publicity. As can be seen from the phrase quoted above, he believed in "arousing the world," which is only possible if the world gets a chance to hear what you are doing. It is difficult to see how Gandhi's methods could be applied in a country where opponents of the régime disappear in the middle of the night and are never heard of again. Without a free Press and the right of assembly, it is impossible not merely to appeal to outside opinion, but to bring a mass movement into being, or even to make your intentions known to your adversary. Is there a Gandhi in Russia at this moment? And if there is, what is he accomplishing? The Russian masses could only practice civil disobedience if the same idea happened to occur to all of them simultaneously, and even then, to judge by the history of the Ukraine famine, it would make no difference. But let it be granted that non-violent resistance can be effective against one's own government, or against an occupying power: even so, how does one put it into practice internationally? Gandhi's various conflicting statements on the late war seem to show that he felt the difficulty of this. Applied to foreign politics, pacifism either stops being pacifist or becomes appeasement. Moreover the assumption, which served Gandhi so well in dealing with individuals, that all human beings are more or less approachable and will respond to a generous gesture, needs to be seriously questioned. It is not necessarily true, for example, when you are dealing with lunatics. Then the question becomes: Who is sane? Was Hitler sane? And is it not possible for one whole culture to be insane by the standards of another? And, so far as one can gauge the feelings of whole nations, is there any apparent connection between a generous deed and a friendly response? Is gratitude a factor in international politics?

These and kindred questions need discussion, and need it urgently, in the few years left to us before somebody presses the button and the rockets begin to fly. It seems doubtful whether civilization can stand another major war, and it is at least thinkable that the way out lies through non-violence. It is Gandhi's virtue that he would have been ready to give honest consideration to the kind of question that I have raised above; and, indeed, he probably did discuss most of these questions somewhere or other in his innumerable newspaper articles. One feels of him that there was much that he did not understand, but not that there was anything that he was frightened of saying or thinking. I have never been able to feel much liking for Gandhi, but I do not feel sure that as a political thinker he was wrong in the main, nor do I believe that his life was a failure. It is curious that when he was assassinated, many of his warmest admirers exclaimed sorrowfully that he had lived just long enough to see his life work in ruins, because India was engaged in a civil war which had always been foreseen as one of the by-products of the transfer of power. But it was not in trying to smooth down Hindu-Moslem rivalry that Gandhi had spent his life. His main political objective, the peaceful ending of British rule, had after all been attained. As usual the relevant facts cut across one another. On the other hand, the British did get out of India without fighting, an event which very few observers indeed would have predicted until about a year before it happened. On the other hand, this was done by a Labour government, and it is certain that a Conservative government, especially a government headed by Churchill, would have acted differently. But if, by 1945, there had grown up in Britain a large body of opinion sympathetic to Indian independence, how far was this due to Gandhi's personal influence? And if, as may happen, India and Britain finally settle down into a decent and friendly relationship, will this be partly because Gandhi, by keeping up his struggle obstinately and without hatred, disinfected the political air? That one even thinks of asking such questions indicates his stature. One may feel, as I do, a sort of aesthetic distaste for Gandhi, one may reject the claims of sainthood made on his behalf (he never made any such claim himself, by the way), one may also reject sainthood as an ideal and therefore feel that Gandhi's basic aims were anti-human and reactionary; but regarded simply as a politician, and compared with the other leading political figures of our time, how clean a smell he has managed to leave behind!

Nancy Mitford

(1904–1973)

"I don't quite know why I have felt the need to write down this well-known story, making myself cry twice. . .," writes Nancy Mitford, comic novelist of manners and biographer, at the end of "A Bad Time" (1962, The Water Beetle). *It's a compelling story, and a moving one. What makes it so is the concentration of Mitford's narrative, her careful selection of details and their cumulative power to leave one, and only one, impression of Scott's disastrous Antarctic journey in 1911–12. The result is the stuff of fiction, a memorial to an empire's myth of maleness: stiff upper lip, sporting pluck, perserverance against all odds, courage undaunted in the face of catastrophe, unquestioned faith in the humaneness of British conquest bringing civilization in its wake. Mitford's memorial gives the myth an early twentieth-century touch. Hers are the heroes of the British Empire in decline; their inevitable failure merely humanizes their moral perfection. But, curiously, the very sources she cites, hoping she "may have induced" us to read them, suggest an entirely different story, a story of blunders and lack of foresight. Amundsen's account of how his Norwegian expedition beat Scott's to the South Pole shows clearly that the terrible hardships of the British were by no means inevitable, indeed quite preventable. It is as if they made out the winner of the game to be whoever could survive the most suffering the longest—putting a good face on what could otherwise be seen as blindness to reality. Where's the truth here, if the essayist is herself writing out of a kind of fiction to save British face? Mitford's essay is a memoir of what it was that left such a "tremendous impression" on her at age seven, what still makes her cry. The truth it portrays is that of Mitford's essayistic "I," the "I" who continues to believe a myth for fifty years in spite of evidence to the contrary, the "I" who knows there's something in her material she doesn't understand: "I don't know why I have felt the need to write down this well-known story. . . ." The relationship of an essay to what we call "truth" is anything but straightforward.*

A Bad Time

Apsley Cherry-Garrard has said that "polar exploration is at once the cleanest and most isolated way of having a bad time that has yet been devised."* Nobody could deny that he and the twenty-four other members of Captain Scott's expedition to the South Pole had a bad time; in fact, all other bad times, embarked on by men of their own free will, pale before it. Theirs is the last of the great classic explorations; their equipment, though they lived in our century, curiously little different from that used by Captain Cook. Vitamin pills would probably have saved the lives of the Polar party, so would a wireless transmitter; an electric torch have mitigated the misery of the Winter Journey. How many things which we take completely as a matter of course had not yet been invented, such a little time ago! Scott's *Terra Nova* had the advantage over Cook's *Resolution* of steam as well as sail. Even this was a mixed blessing, as it involved much hated shovelling, while the coal occupied space which could have been put to better account in the little wooden barque (764 tons). Three motor-sledges lashed to the deck seemed marvellously up-to-date and were the pride and joy of Captain Scott.

The *Terra Nova* sailed from London 15th June 1910 and from New Zealand 26th November. She was fearfully overloaded; on deck, as well as the motor-sledges in their huge crates, there were 30 tons of coal in sacks, 2½ tons of petrol in drums, 33 dogs, and 19 ponies. She rode out a bad storm by a miracle. "Bowers and Campbell were standing upon the bridge and the ship rolled sluggishly over until the lee combings of the main hatch were under the sea . . . as a rule, if a ship goes that far over she goes down." It took her thirty-eight days to get to McMurdo Sound, by which time the men were in poor shape. They had slept in their clothes, lucky if they got five hours a night, and had had no proper meals. As soon as they dropped anchor they began to unload the ship. This entailed dragging its cargo over ice floes which were in constant danger of being tipped up by killer whales, a very tricky business, specially when it came to moving ponies, motor sledges and a pianola. Then they built the Hut which was henceforward to be their home. Scott, tireless himself, always drove his men hard and these things were accomplished in a fortnight. The *Terra Nova* sailed away; she was to return the following summer, when it was hoped that the Polar party would be back in time to be taken off before the freezing up of the sea forced her to leave again. If not, they would be obliged to spend a second winter on McMurdo Sound. Winter, of course, in those latitudes, happens during

* Unless otherwise stated, the quotations in this essay are from *The Worst Journey in the World*, by Cherry-Garrard. [Mitford]

our summer months and is perpetual night, as the summer is perpetual day. The stunning beauty of the scenery affected the men deeply. When the sun shone the snow was never white, but brilliant shades of pink, blue and lilac; in winter the aurora australis flamed across the sky and the summit of Mount Erebus glowed.

The Hut, unlike so much of Scott's equipment, was a total success. It was built on the shore, too near the sea, perhaps, for absolute security in the cruel winter storms, under the active volcano Mount Erebus, called after the ship in which Ross discovered these regions in 1839. It was 50 feet by 25, 9 feet high. The walls had double boarding inside and outside the frames, with layers of quilted seaweed between the boards. The roof had six layers of alternate wood, rubber and seaweed. Though 109 degrees of frost was quite usual, the men never suffered from cold indoors; in fact, with twenty-five of them living there, the cooking range at full blast and a stove at the other end, they sometimes complained of stuffiness.

Life during the first winter was very pleasant. Before turning in for good they had done several gruelling marches, laying stores in depots along the route of the Polar journey; they felt they needed and had earned a rest. Their only complaint was that there were too many lectures; Scott insisted on at least three a week and they seem to have bored the others considerably—except for Ponting's magic lantern slides of Japan. A gramophone and a pianola provided background music and there was a constant flow of witticisms which one assumes to have been unprintable until one learns that Dr. Wilson would leave the company if a coarse word were spoken. In the Hut they chiefly lived on flesh of seals, which they killed without difficulty, since these creatures are friendly and trustful by nature. "A sizzling on the fire and a smell of porridge and seal liver heralded breakfast which was at 8 A.M. in theory and a good deal later in practice." Supper was at 7. Most were in their bunks by 10 P.M., sometimes with a candle and a book; the acetylene was turned off at 10.30 to economize the fuel. Cherry-Garrard tells us that the talk at meals was never dull. Most of these men were from the Royal Navy, and sailors are often droll, entertaining fellows possessing much out-of-the-way information. (Nobody who heard them can have forgotten the performances of Commander Campbell on the B.B.C.—he was one of the greatest stars they ever had, in my view.) Heated arguments would break out on a diversity of subjects, to be settled by recourse to an encyclopedia or an atlas or sometimes a Latin dictionary. They wished they had also brought a *Who's Who*. One of their discussions, which often recurred, concerned "Why are we here? What is the force that drives us to undergo severe, sometimes ghastly hardships of our own free will?" The reply was The Interests of Science—it is important that man should know the features of the world he lives in, but this was not a complete answer. Once there was a discussion as to whether they would continue to like Polar travel if, by the aid of modern inventions, it became quite easy and comfortable. They said no, with one accord. It seems as if they really wanted to prove to themselves how much they could endure. Their rewards were a deep spiritual satisfaction and relationships between men who had become more than brothers.

Their loyalty to each other was fantastic—there was no jealousy, bickering, bullying or unkindness. Reading between the lines of their diaries and records it is impossible to guess whether anybody disliked anybody else. As for The Owner, as they called Scott, they all worshipped and blindly followed him. Cherry-Garrard, the only one who could be called an intellectual and who took a fairly objective view of the others, gives an interesting account of Scott's character: subtle, he says, full of light and shade. No sense of humour—peevish by nature, highly strung, irritable, melancholy and moody. However, such was his strength of mind that he overcame these faults, though he could not entirely conceal long periods of sadness. He was humane, so fond of animals that he refused to take dogs on long journeys, hauling the sledge himself rather than see them suffer. His idealism and intense patriotism shone through all he wrote. Of course, he had the extraordinary charm without which no man can be a leader. In his diaries he appears as an affectionate person, but shyness or the necessary isolation of a sea-captain prevented him from showing this side to the others. He was poor; he worried about provision for his family when it became obvious that he would never return to them. Indeed, he was always hampered by lack of money and never had enough to finance his voyages properly. Lady Kennet, his widow, once told me that Scott only took on Cherry-Garrard because he subscribed £2,000 to the expedition. He thought him too young (23), too delicate and too short-sighted, besides being quite inexperienced; he was the only amateur in the party. It is strange and disgraceful that Scott, who was already a world-famous explorer, should have had so little support from the Government for this prestigious voyage.

These men had an enemy, not with them in the Hut but ever present in their minds. His shadow fell across their path before they left New Zealand, when Captain Scott received a telegram dated from Madeira, with the laconic message *Am going South Amundsen*. Now, Amundsen was known to be preparing Nansen's old ship, the *Fram*, for a journey, having announced that he intended to do some further exploring in the Arctic. Only when he was actually at sea did he tell his crew that he was on his way to try and reach the South Pole. There seemed something underhand and unfair about this. Scott's men were furious; they talked of finding the Amundsen party and having it out with them, but Scott put a good face on it and pretended not to mind at all. The two leaders could hardly have been more different. Amundsen was cleverer than Scott, "an explorer of a markedly intellectual type rather Jewish than Scandinavian." There was not much humanity or idealism about him, he was a tough, brave professional. He had a sense of humour and his description of flying over the North Pole in a dirigible with General Nobile is very funny indeed. Nobile was forever in tears and Amundsen on the verge of striking him, the climax coming when, over the Pole, Nobile threw out armfuls of huge Italian flags which caught in the propeller and endangered their lives. All the same, Amundsen died going to the rescue of Nobile in 1928.

No doubt the knowledge that "the Norskies" were also on their way to the Pole was a nagging worry to Scott all those long, dark winter months, though he was very careful to hide his feelings and often remarked that Amundsen had a perfect right to go anywhere at any time. "The Pole is not a race," he would say. He (Scott) was going in the interests of science and not in order to "get there first." But he knew that everybody else would look on it as a race; he was only human, he longed to win it.

The chief of Scott's scientific staff and his greatest friend was Dr. Wilson. He was to Scott what Sir Joseph Hooker had been to Ross. (Incredible as it seems, Hooker only died that very year, 1911. Scott knew him well.) Wilson was a doctor of St. George's Hospital and a zoologist specializing in vertebrates. He had published a book on whales, penguins and seals and had prepared a report for the Royal Commission on grouse disease. While he was doing this Cherry-Garrard met him, at a shooting lodge in Scotland, and became fired with a longing to go south. Wilson was an accomplished water-colourist. Above all, he was an adorable person: "The finest character I ever met," said Scott. Now Dr. Wilson wanted to bring home the egg of an Emperor Penguin. He had studied these huge creatures when he was with Scott on his first journey to the Antarctic and thought that their embryos would be of paramount biological interest, possibly proving to be the missing link between bird and fish. The Emperors, who weigh 6½ stone, look like sad little men and were often taken by early explorers for human natives of the South Polar regions, are in a low state of evolution (and of spirits). They lay their eggs in the terrible mid-winter, because only thus can their chicks, which develop with a slowness abnormal in birds, be ready to survive the next winter. They never step on shore, even to breed; they live in rookeries on sea-ice. To incubate their eggs, they balance them on their enormous feet and press them against a patch of bare skin on the abdomen protected from the cold by a lappet of skin and feathers. Paternity is the only joy known to these wretched birds and a monstrous instinct for it is implanted in their breasts; male and female hatch out the eggs and nurse their chicks, also on their feet, indiscriminately. When a penguin has to go in the sea to catch his dinner he leaves egg or chick on the ice; there is then a mad scuffle as twenty childless birds rush to adopt it, quite often breaking or killing it in the process. They will nurse a dead chick until it falls to pieces and sit for months on an addled egg or even a stone. All this happens in darkness and about a hundred degrees of frost. I often think the R.S.P.C.A. ought to do something for the Emperor Penguins.

Dr. Wilson had reason to suppose that there was a rookery of Emperors at Cape Crozier, about sixty miles along the coast. When the ghastly winter weather had properly set in he asked for two volunteers to go with him and collect some eggs. It was one of the rules in the Hut that everybody volunteered for everything, so Wilson really chose his own companions: "Birdie" Bowers, considered by Scott to be the hardest traveller in the world, and Cherry-Garrard. The three of them left the light and warmth and good cheer of the Hut to embark upon the most appalling nightmare possible to imagine. The darkness was profound and invariable. (They steered by Jupiter.) The temperature was generally in the region of 90 degrees of frost, unless there was a blizzard, when it would rise as high as 40 degrees of frost, producing other forms of discomfort and the impossibility of moving. The human body exudes a quantity of sweat and moisture, even in the lowest temperatures, so the men's clothes were soon frozen as stiff as boards and they were condemned to remain in the bending position in which they pulled their sleigh. It was as though they were dressed in lead. The surface of the snow was so bad that they had to divide their load and bring it along by relays. They could never take off their huge gloves for fear of losing their hands by frostbite; as it was, their fingers were covered with blisters in which the liquid was always frozen, so that their hands were like bunches of marbles. The difficulty of performing the simplest action with them may be imagined; it sometimes took over an hour to light a match and as much as nine hours to pitch their tent and do the work of the camp. Everything was slow, slow. When they had a discussion it lasted a week. If Cherry-Garrard had written his book in a more uninhibited age he would no doubt have told us how they managed about what the Americans call going to the bathroom.* As it is, this interesting point remains mysterious. Dr. Wilson insisted on them spending seven hours out of the twenty-four (day and night in that total blackness were quite arbitrary) in their sleeping-bags. These were always frozen up, so that it took at least an hour to worm their way in and then they suffered the worst of

* "They [the savages] go to the bathroom in the street." (Report from a member of the Peace Corps in the Congo.) [Mitford]

all the tortures. Normally on such journeys the great comfort was sleep. Once in their warm dry sleeping-bags the men went off as if they were drugged and nothing, neither pain nor worry, could keep them awake. But now the cold was too intense for Wilson and Cherry-Garrard to close an eye. They lay shivering until they thought their backs would break, enviously listening to the regular snores of Birdie. They had got a spirit lamp—the only bearable moments they knew were when they had just swallowed a hot drink; for a little while it was like a hot-water bottle on their hearts; but the effect soon wore off. Their teeth froze and split to pieces. Their toe-nails came away. Cherry-Garrard began to long for death. It never occurred to any of them to go back. The penguin's egg assumed such importance in their minds, as they groped and plodded their four or five miles a day, that the whole future of the human race might have depended on their finding one.

At last, in the bleakest and most dreadful place imaginable, they heard the Emperors calling. To get to the rookery entailed a long, dangerous feat of mountaineering, since it was at the foot of an immense cliff. Dim twilight now glowed for an hour or two at midday, so they were able to see the birds, about a hundred of them, mournfully huddled together, trying to shuffle away from the intruders without losing the eggs from their feet and trumpeting with curious metallic voices. The men took some eggs, got lost on the cliff, were nearly killed several times by falling into crevasses and broke all the eggs but two. That night there was a hurricane and their tent blew away, carried out to sea, no doubt. Now that they faced certain death, life suddenly seemed more attractive. They lay in their sleeping-bags for two days waiting for the wind to abate and pretending to each other that they would manage somehow to get home without a tent, although they knew very well that they must perish. When it was possible to move again Bowers, by a miracle, found the tent. "We were so thankful we said nothing." They could hardly remember the journey home—it passed like a dreadful dream, and indeed they often slept while pulling their sleigh. When they arrived, moribund, at the Hut, exactly one month after setting forth, The Owner said: "Look here, you know, this is the hardest journey that has ever been done."

I once recounted this story to a hypochondriac friend, who said, horrified, "But it must have been so *bad* for them." The extraordinary thing is that it did them no harm. They were quite recovered three months later, in time for the Polar journey, from which, of course, Wilson and Bowers did not return, but which they endured longer than any except Scott himself. Cherry-Garrard did most of the Polar journey; he went through the 1914 war, in the trenches much of the time, and lived until 1959.

As for the penguins' eggs, when Cherry-Garrard got back to London the first thing he did was to take them to the Natural History Museum. Alas, nobody was very much interested in them. The Chief Custodian, when he received Cherry-Garrard after a good long delay, simply put them down on an ink stand and went on talking to a friend. Cherry-Garrard asked if he could have a receipt for the eggs? "It's not necessary. It's all right. You needn't wait," he was told.

The Winter Journey was so appalling that the journey to the Pole, which took place in daylight and in much higher temperatures seemed almost banal by comparison; but it was terribly long (over seven hundred miles each way) and often very hard. Scott left the Hut at 11 P.M. on 1st November. He soon went back, for a book; was undecided what to take, but finally chose a volume of Browning. He was accompanied by a party of about twenty men with two motor-sledges (the third had fallen into the sea while being landed), ponies and dogs. Only four men were to go to the Pole, but they were to be accompanied until the dreaded Beardmore glacier had been climbed. The men in charge of the motors turned back first, the motors having proved a failure. They delayed the party with continual breakdowns and only covered fifty miles. The dogs and their drivers went next. The ponies were shot at the foot of the glacier. The men minded this; they had become attached to the beasts, who had done their best, often in dreadful conditions. So far the journey had taken longer than it should have. The weather was bad for travelling, too warm, the snow too soft; there were constant blizzards. Now they were twelve men, without ponies or dogs, manhauling the sledges. As they laboured up the Beardmore, Scott was choosing the men who would go to the Pole with him. Of course, the disappointment of those who were sent home at this stage was acute; they had done most of the gruelling journey and were not to share in the glory. On 20th December Cherry-Garrard wrote: "This evening has been rather a shock. As I was getting my finesko on to the top of my ski Scott came up to me and said he had rather a blow for me. Of course, I knew what he was going to say, but could hardly grasp that I was going back—tomorrow night. . . . Wilson told me it was a toss-up whether Titus [Oates] or I should go on; that being so I think Titus will help him more than I can. I said all I could think of—he seemed so cut up about it, saying, 'I think somehow it is specially hard on you.' I said I hoped I had not disappointed him and he caught hold of me and said 'No, no—no,' so if that is the case all is well."

There was still one more party left to be sent back after Cherry-Garrard's. Scott said in his diary: "I dreaded this necessity of choosing, nothing could be more heartrending." He added: "We are struggling on, considering all things against odds. The weather is a constant anxiety."

The weather was against them; the winter which succeeded this disappointing summer set in early and was the worst which hardened Arctic travellers had ever experienced.

Scott had always intended to take a party of four to the Pole. He now made the fatal decision to take five. Oates was the last-minute choice; it is thought that Scott felt the Army ought to be represented. So they were: Scott aged 43, Wilson 39, Seaman Evans 37, Bowers 28, and Oates 32. The extra man was *de trop*[1] in every way. There were only four pairs of skis; the tent was too small for five, so that one man was too near the outside and always cold; worst of all, there were now five people to eat rations meant for four. It was an amazing mistake, but it showed that Scott thought he was on a good wicket. The returning parties certainly thought so; it never occurred to them that he would have much difficulty, let alone that his life might be in danger. But they were all more exhausted than they knew and the last two parties only got home by the skin of their teeth, after hair-raising experiences on the Beardmore. Scott still had 150 miles to go.

On 16 January, only a few miles from the Pole, Bowers spied something in the snow—an abandoned sledge. Then they came upon dog tracks. Man Friday's footsteps on the sand were less dramatic. They knew that the enemy had won. "The Norwegians have forestalled us," wrote Scott, "and are first at the Pole. . . . All the day dreams must go; it will be a wearisome return." And he wrote at the Pole itself: "Great God! This is an awful place!"

Amundsen had left his base on 20th October with three other men, all on skis, and sixty underfed dogs to pull his sleighs. He went over the Axel Herberg glacier, an easier climb than the Beardmore, and reached the Pole on 16th December with no more discomfort than on an ordinary Antarctic journey. His return only took thirty-eight days, by which time he had eaten most of the dogs, beginning with his own favourite. When the whole story was known there was a good deal of feeling in England over these animals. At the Royal Geographical Society's dinner to Amundsen the President, Lord Curzon, infuriated his guest by ending his speech with the words, "I think we ought to give three cheers for the dogs."

And now for the long pull home. Evans was dying, of frostbite and concussion from a fall. He never complained, just staggered along, sometimes wandering in his mind. The relief when he died was tremendous, as Scott had been tormented by feeling that perhaps he ought to abandon him, for the sake of the others. When planning the Winter Journey, Wilson had told Cherry-Garrard that he was against taking seamen on the

[1] Too much.

toughest ventures—he said they simply would not look after themselves. Indeed, Evans had concealed a wound on his hand which was the beginning of his troubles. A month later, the party was again delayed, by Oates's illness; he was in terrible pain from frostbitten feet. He bravely committed suicide, but too late to save the others. Scott wrote: "Oates' last thoughts were of his mother, but immediately before he took pride in thinking that his regiment would be pleased at the bold way in which he met his death. . . . He was a brave soul. He slept through the night, hoping not to wake; but he woke in the morning, yesterday. It was blowing a blizzard. He said 'I am just going outside and may be some time.' "

All, now, were ill. Their food was short and the petrol for their spirit lamp, left for them in the depots, had mostly evaporated. The horrible pemmican, with its low vitamin content, which was their staple diet was only bearable when made into a hot stew. Now they were eating it cold, keeping the little fuel they had to make hot cocoa. (This business of the petrol was very hard on the survivors. When on their way home, the returning parties had made use of it, carefully taking much less than they were told was their share. They always felt that Scott, who never realized that it had evaporated, must have blamed them in his heart for the shortage.) Now the weather changed. "They were in evil case but they would have been all right if the cold had not come down upon them; unexpected, unforetold and fatal. The cold in itself was not so tremendous until you realize that they had been out four months, that they had fought their way up the biggest glacier in the world, in feet of soft snow, that they had spent seven weeks under plateau conditions of rarified air, big winds and low temperatures." They struggled on and might just have succeeded in getting home if they had had ordinary good luck. But, eleven miles from the depot which would have saved them, a blizzard blew up so that they could not move. It blew for a week, at the end of which there was no more hope. On 29th March Scott wrote: "My dear Mrs. Wilson. If this reaches you, Bill and I will have gone out together. We are very near it now and I should like you to know how splendid he was at the end—everlastingly cheerful and ready to sacrifice himself for others, never a word of blame to me for leading him into this mess. He is suffering, luckily, only minor discomforts.

His eyes have a comfortable blue look of hope and his mind is peaceful with the satisfaction of his faith, in regarding himself as part of the great scheme of the Almighty. I can do no more to comfort you than to tell you that he died, as he lived, a brave, true man—the best of comrades and staunchest of friends. My whole heart goes out to you in pity. Yours R. Scott."

* * *

And to Sir James Barrie:

"We are pegging out in a very comfortless spot . . . I am not at all afraid of the end but sad to miss many a humble pleasure which I had planned for the future on our long marches. . . . We have had four days of storm in our tent and nowhere's food or fuel. We did intend to finish ourselves when things proved like this but we have decided to die naturally in the track."

On 19th March Cherry-Garrard and others in the Hut, none of them fit, began to be worried. The *Terra Nova* had duly come back, with longed-for mails and news of the outer world. They had to let her go again, taking those who were really ill. On 27th March Atkinson, the officer in charge, and a seaman went a little way to try and meet the Polar party, but it was a hopeless quest, and they were 100 miles from where Scott was already dead when they turned back. They now prepared for another winter in the Hut, the sadness of which can be imagined. Long, long after they knew all hope was gone they used to think they heard their friends coming in, or saw shadowy forms that seemed to be theirs. They mourned them and missed their company. Scott, Wilson and Bowers had been the most dynamic of them all, while "Titus" or "Farmer Hayseed" (Oates) was a dear, good-natured fellow whom everybody loved to tease. The weather was unimaginably awful. It seemed impossible that the Hut could stand up to the tempests which raged outside for weeks on end and the men quite expected that it might collapse at any time. When at last the sun reappeared they set forth to see if they could discover traces of their friends. They hardly expected any results, as they were firmly convinced that the men must have fallen down a crevasse on the Beardmore, a fate they had all escaped by inches at one time or another. Terribly soon, however, they came upon what looked like a cairn; it was, in fact, Scott's tent covered with snow.

"We have found them. To say it has been a ghastly day cannot express it. Bowers and Wilson were sleeping in their bags. Scott had thrown the flaps of his bag open at the end. His left hand was stretched over Wilson, his lifelong friend." Everything was tidy, their papers and records in perfect order. Atkinson and Cherry-Garrard read enough to find out what had happened and packed up the rest of the papers unopened. They built a cairn over the tent, which was left as they found it. Near the place where Oates disappeared they put up a cross with the inscription: "Hereabouts died a very gallant gentleman, Captain E. G. Oates of the Inniskilling Dragoons. In March 1912, returning from the Pole, he walked willingly to his death in a blizzard to try and save his comrades, beset by hardship."

In due course Cherry-Garrard and the others were taken off by the *Terra Nova*. When they arrived in New Zealand Atkinson went ashore to send cables to the dead men's wives. "The Harbour Master came out in the tug with him. 'Come down here a minute,' said Atkinson to me and 'It's made a tremendous impression. I had no idea it would make so much,' he said." Indeed it had. The present writer well remembers this impression, though only seven at the time.

Amundsen had won the race, but Scott had captured his fellow countrymen's imagination. It is one of our endearing qualities, perhaps unique, that we think no less of a man because he has failed—we even like him better for it. In any case, Amundsen complained that a year later a Norwegian boy at school in England was being taught that Captain Scott discovered the South Pole.

I don't quite know why I have felt the need to write down this well-known story, making myself cry twice, at the inscription on Oates's cross and when Atkinson said, "It has made a tremendous impression." Perhaps the bold, bald men who get, smiling, into cupboards, as if they were playing sardines, go a little way (about as far as from London to Manchester) into the air and come out of their cupboards again, a few hours later, smiling more than ever, have put me in mind of other adventurers. It is fifty years to the day, as I write this, that Scott died. Most of the wonderful books which tell of his expedition are out of print now, but they can easily be got at second hand. I should like to feel that I may have induced somebody to read them again.

Books relating to the Polar journey: *Scott's Last Expedition;* Cherry-Garrard: *The Worst Journey in the World;* Priestly: *Antarctic Adventure;* E. R. Evans: *South with Scott;* Amundsen: *My Life as an Explorer.*

Loren Eiseley
(1907–1977)

Eiseley's autobiography, out two years before his death, is called All the Strange Hours: The Excavation of a Life. *The idea of autobiography as excavation—archeology—comes from his profession as an anthropologist, a naturalist with an evolutionary and geological perspective. Over some twenty years, his essays worked at the link between natural history and personal history, the continuum of geology, biology, and psychology. In "The Winter of Man," a late essay collected in* The Star Thrower *(1978), Eiseley calls up the picture of great glacial remnants strewn on the landscape: "the dropped, transported boulders of the icefields." These "fractured mementoes of devastating cold" warn of nature's unpredictable, irrational power, even as they evoke man's own destructiveness; both the face of the earth and the human psyche are places of terror and terrorization. Both are caught in the same process of becoming and departing. There is, it has been remarked, a deep strain of melancholy in Eiseley the student of his own species. Yet, pondering a writer who deeply influenced his outlook, Eiseley writes, "We are, Emerson maintains, a 'conditional population.' If atavistic reptiles swim in the depths of man's psyche, they are not the only inhabitants of that hidden region" ("Man Against the Universe"). Essays such as "The Star Thrower," "The Last Neanderthal," "Man in the Autumn Light," and "The Brown Wasps" struggle in different ways to excavate "the depths" for whatever else may be there. But what everywhere tempers Eiseley's melancholy is the faithful exercise of vision: the dual vision of the scientist's analytical eye and the imaginative, synthesizing eye that creates the tentative joinings between natural history and individual psychic life which make our existences here, if not exactly happy, at least of some singular interest in passing. "Generation after generation the eye was among us," he wrote in connection with Thoreau's diligent efforts to grasp the human place in nature. "We were particles but we were also the recording eye that saw the sunlight." Eiseley's life, too, was "dedicated to the unexplainable eye" ("Thoreau's Vision of the Natural World").*

The Winter of Man

"We fear," remarked an Eskimo shaman responding to a religious question from the explorer Knud Rasmussen some fifty years ago. "We fear the cold and the things we do not understand. But most of all we fear the doings of the heedless ones among ourselves."

Students of the earth's climate have observed that man, in spite of the disappearance of the great continental ice fields, still lives on the steep edge of winter or early spring. The pulsations of these great ice deserts, thousands of feet thick and capable of overflowing mountains and valleys, have characterized the nature of the world since man, in his thinking and speaking phase, arose. The ice which has left the marks of its passing upon the landscape of the Northern Hemisphere has also accounted, in its long, slow advances and retreats, for movements, migrations and extinctions throughout the plant and animal kingdoms.

Though man is originally tropical in his origins, the ice has played a great role in his unwritten history. At times it has constricted his movements, affecting the genetic selection that has created him. Again, ice has established conditions in which man has had to exert all his ingenuity in order to survive. By contrast, there have been other times when the ice has withdrawn farther than today and then, like a kind of sleepy dragon, has crept forth to harry man once more. For something like a million years this strange and alternating contest has continued between man and the ice.

When the dragon withdrew again some fifteen or twenty thousand years ago, man was on the verge of literacy. He already possessed great art, as the paintings in the Lascaux cavern reveal. It was an art devoted to the unseen, to the powers that control the movement of game and the magic that drives the hunter's shaft to its target. Without such magic man felt weak and helpless against the vagaries of nature. It was his first attempt at technology, at control of nature by dominating the luck element, the principle of uncertainty in the universe.

A few millennia further on in time man had forgotten the doorway of snow through which he had emerged. He would only rediscover the traces of the Ice Age in the nineteenth century by means of the new science of geology. At first he would not believe his own history or the reality of the hidden ice dragon, even though Greenland and the polar world today lie shrouded beneath that same ice. He would not see that what the Eskimo said to Rasmussen was a belated modern enactment of an age-old drama in which we, too, had once participated. "We fear," the Eskimo sage had said in essence, "we fear the ice and cold. We fear nature which we do not understand and which provides us with food or brings famine."

Man, achieving literacy on the far Mediterranean shores in an instant of golden sunlight would take the world as it was, to be forever. He would explore the intricacies of thought and wisdom in Athens. He would dream the first dreams of science and record them upon scrolls of parchment. Twenty-five centuries later those dreams would culminate in vast agricultural projects, green revolutions, power pouring through great pipelines, or electric energy surging across continents. Voices would speak into the distances of space. Huge jet transports would hurtle through the skies. Radio telescopes would listen to cosmic whispers from beyond our galaxy. Enormous concentrations of people would gather and be fed in towering metropolises. Few would remember the Greek word *hubris*, the term for overweening pride, that pride which eventually causes some unseen balance to swing in the opposite direction.

Today the ice at the poles lies quiet. There have been times in the past when it has maintained that passivity scores of thousands of years—times longer, in fact, than the endurance of the whole of urban civilization since its first incipient beginnings no more than seven thousand years ago. The temperature gradient from the poles to the equator is still steeper than throughout much of the unglaciated periods of the past. The doorway through which man has come is just tentatively closing behind him.

So complex is the problem of the glacial rhythms that no living scientist can say with surety the ice will not return. If it does the swarming millions who now populate the planet may mostly perish in misery and darkness, inexorably pushed from their own lands to be rejected in desperation by their neighbors. Like the devouring locust swarms that gather in favorable summers, man may have some of that same light-winged ephemeral quality about him. One senses it occasionally in those places where the dropped, transported boulders of the ice fields still hint of formidable powers lurking somewhere behind the face of present nature.

These fractured mementoes of devastating cold need to be contemplated for another reason than themselves. They constitute exteriorly what may be contemplated interiorly. They contain a veiled warning, perhaps the greatest symbolic warning man has ever received from nature. The giant fragments whisper, in the words of Einstein, that "nature does not always play the same game." Nature is devious in spite of what we have learned of her. The greatest scholars have always sensed this. "She will tell you a direct lie if she can," Charles Darwin once warned a sympathetic listener. Even Darwin, however, alert as he was to vestigial traces of former evolutionary structures in our bodies, was not in a position to foresee the kind of strange mental archaeology by which Sigmund Freud would probe the depths of the human mind. Today we are aware of the latent and shadowy powers contained in the subconscious: the alternating winter and sunlight of the human soul.

Has the earth's glacial winter, for all our mastery of science, surely subsided? No, the geologist would answer. We merely stand in a transitory spot of sunshine that takes on the illusion of permanence only because the human generations are short.

Has the wintry bleakness in the troubled heart of humanity at least equally retreated?—that aspect of man referred to when the Eskimo, adorned with amulets to ward off evil, reiterated: "Most of all we fear the secret misdoings of the heedless ones among ourselves."

No, the social scientist would have to answer, the winter of man has not departed. The Eskimo standing in the snow, when questioned about his beliefs, said: "We do not believe. We only fear. We fear those things which are about us and of which we have no sure knowledge. . . ."

But surely we can counter that this old man was an ignorant remnant of the Ice Age, fearful of a nature he did not understand. Today we have science; we do not fear the Eskimo's malevolent ghosts. We do not wear amulets to ward off evil spirits. We have pierced to the far rim of the universe. We roam mentally through light-years of time.

Yes, this could be admitted, but we also fear. We fear more deeply than the old man in the snow. It comes to us, if we are honest, that perhaps nothing has changed the grip of winter in our hearts, that winter before which we cringed amidst the ice long ages ago.

For what is it that we do? We fear. We do not fear ghosts but we fear the ghost of ourselves. We have come now, in this time, to fear the water we drink, the air we breathe, the insecticides that are dusted over our giant fruits. Because of the substances we have poured into our contaminated rivers, we fear the food that comes to us from the sea. There are also those who tell us that by our own heedless acts the sea is dying.

We fear the awesome powers we have lifted out of nature and cannot return to her. We fear the weapons we have made, the hatreds we have engendered. We fear the crush of fanatic people to whom we readily sell these weapons. We fear for the value of the money in our pockets that stands symbolically for food and shelter. We fear the growing power of the state to take all these things from us. We fear to walk in our streets at evening. We have come to fear even our scientists and their gifts.

We fear, in short, as that self-sufficient Eskimo of the long night had never feared. Our minds, if not our clothes, are hung with invisible amulets: nostrums changed each year for our bodies whether it be chlorophyl toothpaste, the signs of astrology, or cold cures that do not cure: witchcraft nostrums for our society as it fractures into contending multitudes all crying for liberation without responsibility.

We fear, and never in this century will we cease to fear. We fear the end of man as that old shaman in the snow had never had cause to fear it. There is a winter still about us—the winter of man that has followed him relentlessly from the caverns and the ice. The old Eskimo spoke well. It is the winter of the heedless ones. We are in the winter. We have never left its breath.

M. F. K. Fisher

(b. 1908)

For sixty years, Mary Frances Kennedy Fisher has shared with readers what she calls "notes" made to catch powerful passing moments in her life. They're moments many can recognize in the course of living, "violent flash-like meetings" not only with people but with places, animals, things, food. "By now some of my notes sound like fabrications, invented to prove a point in an argument," she writes in the Foreword to a recent collection (Sister Age, *1983*). *"This is because it is my way of explaining. . . . When I tell of a stubbed toe or childbirth or how to serve peacocks' tongues on toast it sounds made-up, embroidered. But it is as it happened to* me.*" Fisher makes us remember that our experiences of significance are a bodily matter: if I would communicate any such experience to another person, it must be by way of a unique fit, so to speak, between my language and my own body. Her loving intimacy with food and cooking—for which she is so well known—details and documents this centrality of the body, the senses, life in the here and now. And now, in old age, she says, "I'm not hungry anymore"* (New York Times, *February 28, 1990*). *In* Sister Age, *the book that includes "Moment of Wisdom," as well as the one that preceded it,* As They Were *(1982), the range of her creativity extends far beyond the kitchen. Beyond the art of eating, another paradigm for how to live has long been taking shape in M. F. K. Fisher's "notes": the art of aging. Take her meeting as a twelve-year-old, recollected in "Moment of Wisdom," with the Bible salesman, old, fragile, alone. It "left marks to be deciphered later"* (*Foreword,* Sister Age); *yet what was mysterious then largely remains so. What the intervening years have brought is a deeper recognition of the body's wisdom and the value of recording it.*

Moment of Wisdom

Tears do come occasionally into one's eyes, and they are more often than not a good thing. At least they are salty and, no matter what invisible wound they seep from, they purge and seal the tissues. But when they roll out and down the cheeks it is a different thing, and more amazing to one unaccustomed to such an outward and visible sign of an inward cleansing.

Quick tears can sting and tease the eyeballs and their lids into suffusion and then a new clarity. The brimming and, perhaps fortunately, rarer kind, however, leaves things pale and thinned out, so that even a gross face takes on a porcelain-like quality, and—in my own case—there is a sensation of great fragility or weariness of the bones and spirit.

I have had the experience of such tears very few times. Perhaps it is a good idea to mention one or two of them, if for no other reason than to remind myself that such a pure moment may never come again.

When I was twelve years old, my family was slowly installing itself about a mile down Painter Avenue outside Whittier, California, the thriving little Quaker town where I grew up, on an orange ranch with shaggy, neglected gardens and a long row of half-wild roses along the narrow county road. Our house sat far back in the tangle, with perhaps two hundred yards of gravel driveway leading in toward it.

There was a wide screened porch across the front of the house, looking into the tangle. It was the heart of the place. We sat there long into the cool evenings of summer, talking softly. Even in winter, we were there for lunch on bright days, and in the afternoon drinking tea or beer. In one corner, there was always a good pile of wood for the hearth fire in the living room, and four wide doors led into that room. They were open most of the time, although the fire burned day and night, brightly or merely a gentle token, all the decades we lived on the Ranch.

My grandmother had her own small apartment in the house, as seemed natural and part of the way to coexist, and wandering missionaries and other men of her own cut of cloth often came down the road to see her and discuss convocations and get money and other help. They left books of earnest import and dubious literary worth, like one printed in symbols for the young or illiterate, with Jehovah an eye surrounded by shooting beams of forked fire. Grandmother's friends, of whom I remember not a single one, usually stayed for a meal. Mother was often absent from such unannounced confrontations, prey to almost ritual attacks of what were referred to as "sick headaches," but my father always carved at his seat, head of the table. Grandmother, of course, was there. Father left early, and we children went up to bed, conditioned to complete lack of interest in the murmur of respectful manly voices and our grandmother's clear-cut Victorian guidance of the churchly talk below us. That was the pattern the first months at the Ranch, before the old lady died, and I am sure we ate amply and well, and with good manners, and we accepted sober men in dusty black suits as part of being alive.

When we moved down Painter Avenue into what was then real country, I was near intoxication from the flowers growing everywhere—the scraggly roses lining the road, all viciously thorned as they reverted to wildness, and poppies and lupine in the ditches and still between the rows of orange trees (soon to disappear as their seeds got plowed too deeply into the profitable soil), and exotic bulbs springing up hit or miss in our neglected gardens. I rooted around in all of it like a virgin piglet snuffling for truffles. My mother gave me free rein to keep the house filled with my own interpretations of the word "posy." It was a fine season in life.

One day, I came inside, very dusty and hot, with a basket of roses and weeds of beauty. The house seemed mine, airy and empty, full of shade. Perhaps everyone was in Whittier, marketing. I leaned my forehead against the screening of the front porch and breathed the wonderful dry air of temporary freedom, and off from the county road and onto our long narrow driveway came a small man, smaller than I, dressed in the crumpled hot black I recognized at once as the Cloth and carrying a small valise.

I wiped at my sweaty face and went to the screen door, to be polite to another of my grandmother's visitors. I wished I had stayed out, anywhere at all, being that age and so on, and aware of rebellion's new pricks.

He was indeed tiny and frail in a way I had never noticed before in anyone. (I think this new awareness and what happened later came from the fact that I was alone in the family house and felt for the moment like a stranger made up of Grandmother and my parents and maybe God—that eye, Jehovah, but with no lightning.) He would not come in. I asked him if he would like some cool water, but he said no. His voice was thin. He asked to see Mother Holbrook, and when I told him she had died a few days before he did not seem at all bothered, and neither was I, except that he might be.

He asked if I would like to buy a Bible. I said no, we had many of them. His hands were too shaky and weak to open his satchel, but when I asked him again to come in, and started to open the door to go out to help him, he told me in such a firm way to leave him alone that I did. I did not reason about it for it seemed to be an agreement between us.

He picked up his dusty satchel, said goodbye in a very gentle voice, and walked back down the long driveway to the county road and then south, thinking God knows what hopeless thoughts. A little past our gate, he stopped to pick one of the dusty roses. I leaned my head against the screening of our porch and was astonished and mystified to feel slow fat quiet tears roll from my unblinking eyes and down my cheeks.

I could not believe it was happening. Where did they spring from, so fully formed, so unexpectedly? Where had they been waiting, all my long life as a child? What had just happened to me, to make me cry without volition, without a sound or a sob?

In a kind of justification of what I thought was a weakness, for I had been schooled to consider all tears as such, I thought, If I could have given him something of mine . . . If I were rich, I would buy him a new black suit. . . . If I had next week's allowance and had not spent this week's on three Cherry Flips . . . If I could have given him some cool water or my love . . .

But the tiny old man, dry as a ditch weed, was past all that, as I came to learn long after my first passionate protest—past or beyond.

The first of such tears as mine that dusty day, which are perhaps rightly called the tears of new wisdom, are the most startling to one's supposed equanimity. Later, they have a different taste. Perhaps they seem more bitter because they are recognizable. But they are always as unpredictable. Once, I was lying with my head back, listening to a long program of radio music from New York, with Toscanini drawing the fine blood from his gang. I was hardly conscious of the sound—with my mind, anyway—and when it ended, my two ears, which I had never thought of as cup-like, were so full of silent tears that as I sat up they drenched and darkened my whole front with little gouts of brine. I felt amazed, beyond my embarrassment in a group of near-friends, for the music I had heard was not the kind I thought I liked, and the salty water had rolled down from my half-closed eyes like October rain, with no sting to it but perhaps promising a good winter.

Such things are, I repeat to myself, fortunately rare, for they are too mysterious to accept with equanimity. I prefer not to dig too much into their comings, but it is sure that they cannot be evoked or foretold. If anger has a part in them, it is latent, indirect—not an incentive. The helpless weeping and sobbing and retching that sweeps over somebody who inadvertently hears Churchill's voice rallying Englishmen to protect their shores, or Roosevelt telling people not to be afraid of fear, or a civil-rights chieftain saying politely that there is such a thing as democracy—those violent physical reactions are proof of one's being alive and aware. But the slow, large tears that spill from the eye, flowing like unblown rain according to the laws of gravity and desolation—these are the real tears, I think. They are the ones that have been simmered, boiled, sieved, filtered past all anger and into the realm of acceptive serenity.

There is a story about a dog and an ape that came to love each other. The dog finally died, trying to keep the ape from returning to the jungle where he should have been all along and where none but another ape could follow. And one becomes the dog, the ape, no matter how clumsily the story is told. One is the hapless lover.

I am all of them. I feel again the hot dusty screening on my forehead as I watch the little man walk slowly out to the road and turn down past the ditches and stop for a moment by a scraggly rosebush. If I could only give him something, I think. If I could tell him something true.

It was a beginning for me, as the tears popped out so richly and ran down, without a sigh or cry. I could see clearly through them, with no blurring, and they did not sting. This last is perhaps the most astonishing and fearsome part, past denial of any such encounter with wisdom, or whatever it is.

Eudora Welty

(b. 1909)

Taste *is one of those rich English words that rolls body and mind into one, a single locus of knowing what pleases, what's good. My tongue distinguishes flavors in my mouth, likes some and not others. The other organs of perception know what sounds, odors, colors, textures please them; and yet another, immaterial, tongue sorts out my tastes in the symbolic realm of thought, words, texts. Eudora Welty's "A Sweet Devouring" (1957,* The Eye of the Story*) relates how one reader's taste was acquired. Born in Jackson, she lived as a child "two blocks away from the Mississippi State Capitol"; in those days, still, "the blackberry lady clanged on her bucket with a quart measure at your front door in June without fail" ("The Little Store"). There might be fresh oysters for supper, "just ladled out of the oyster barrel that the butcher got in from New Orleans," and on hot summer evenings the family would drive out for ice cream cones that you held out the window as you licked, "fast before the last bit melted" ("The Flavor of Jackson"). The world of Welty's childhood evoked in her essays is rich in tastes and "almost tangible smells—licorice recently sucked in a child's cheek, dill-pickle brine that had leaked through the paper sack in a fresh trail across the wooden floor" ("The Little Store"). Books were a part of that synaesthetic world, the pleasures of reading "like those of a Christmas cake." She swallowed books alligator-style: "snap." "There was one thing I wanted from those books," she reports of herself as a nine-year-old, "and that was for me to have ten to read at one blow"—not unlike a certain candy she fancied, whose "attraction was the number you got for a nickel" ("The Little Store"). How greed lets up and our tongues become gourmands is one of the mysteries of growing older. In Welty's case, a whole new kind of literary treat created a new appetite in books and a new satisfaction. "A Sweet Devouring" may seem to invite alligator-style reading; snap, and you have missed the artistry of this voice, its seemingly effortless modulation, phrase by phrase, of the child's experience into the adult's amused reflection on it. What Welty once said of the short story, a form of which she is a modern master, holds for her essay: "The simplest appearing work may have been brought off . . . on the sharp edge of experiment" ("Writing and Analyzing a Story").*

A Sweet Devouring

When I used to ask my mother which we were, rich or poor, she refused to tell me. I was then nine years old and of course what I was dying to hear was that we were poor. I was reading a book called *Five Little Peppers* and my heart was set on baking a cake for my mother in a stove with a hole in it. Some version of rich, crusty old Mr. King—up till that time not living on our street—was sure to come down the hill in his wheelchair and rescue me if anything went wrong. But before I could start a cake at all I had to find out if we were poor, and poor *enough;* and my mother wouldn't tell me, she said she was too busy. I couldn't wait too long; I had to go on reading and soon Polly Pepper got into more trouble, some that was a little harder on her and easier on me.

Trouble, the backbone of literature, was still to me the original property of the fairy tale, and as long as there was plenty of trouble for everybody and the rewards for it were falling in the right spots, reading was all smooth sailing. At that age a child reads with higher appetite and gratification, and with those two stars sailing close together, than ever again in his growing up. The home shelves had been providing me all along with the usual books, and I read them with love—but snap, I finished them. I read everything just alike—snap. I even came to the *Tales from Maria Edgeworth* and went right ahead, without feeling the bump—then. It *was* noticeable that when her characters suffered she punished them for it, instead of rewarding them as a reader had rather been led to hope. In her stories, the children had to make their choice between being unhappy and good about it and being unhappy and bad about it, and then she helped them to choose wrong. In *The Purple Jar*, it will be remembered, there was the little girl being taken through the shops by her mother and her downfall coming when she chooses to buy something beautiful instead of something necessary. The purple jar, when the shop sends it out, proves to have been purple only so long as it was filled with purple water, and her mother knew it all the time. They don't deliver the water. That's only the cue for stones to start coming through the hole in the victim's worn-out shoe. She bravely agrees she must keep walking on stones until such time as she is offered another choice between the beautiful and the useful. Her father tells her as far as he is concerned she can stay in the house. If I had been at all easy to disappoint, that story would have disappointed me. Of course, I did feel, what is the good of walking on rocks if they are going to let the water out of the jar too? And it seemed to me that even the illustrator fell down on the characters in that book, not alone Maria Edgeworth, for when a rich, crusty old gentleman gave Simple Susan a guinea for some kind deed she'd done him, there was a picture of the transaction and where was the guinea? I couldn't make out a feather. But I liked *reading* the book all right—except that I finished it.

My mother took me to the Public Library and introduced me: "Let her have any book she wants, except *Elsie Dinsmore*." I looked for the book I couldn't have and it was a row. That was how I learned about the Series Books. The *Five Little Peppers* belonged, so did *The Wizard of Oz*, so did *The Little Colonel*, so did *The Green Fairy Book*. There were many of everything, generations of everybody, instead of one. I wasn't coming to the end of reading, after all—I was saved.

Our library in those days was a big rotunda lined with shelves. A copy of *V. V.'s Eyes* seemed to follow you wherever you went, even after you'd read it. I didn't know what I liked, I just knew what there was a lot of. After *Randy's Spring* there came *Randy's Summer*, *Randy's Fall* and *Randy's Winter*. True, I didn't care very much myself for her spring, but it didn't occur to me that I might care for her summer, and then her summer didn't prejudice me against her fall, and I still had hopes as I moved on to her winter. I was disappointed in her whole year, as it turned out, but a thing like that didn't keep me from wanting to read every word of it. The pleasures of reading itself—who doesn't remember?—were like those of a Christmas cake, a sweet devouring. The "Randy Books" failed chiefly in being so soon over. Four seasons doesn't make a series.

All that summer I used to put on a second petticoat (our librarian wouldn't let you past the front door if she could see through you), ride my bicycle up the hill and "through the Capitol" (shortcut) to the library with my two read books in the basket (two was the limit you could take out at one time when you were a child and also as long as you lived), and tiptoe in ("Silence") and exchange them for two more in two minutes. Selection was no object. I coasted the two new books home, jumped out of my petticoat, read (I suppose I ate and bathed and answered questions put to me), then in all hope put my petticoat back on and rode those two books back to the library to get my next two.

The librarian was the lady in town who wanted to be it. She called me by my full name and said, "Does your mother know where you are? You know good and well the fixed rule of this library: *Nobody is going to come running back here with any book on the same day they took it out*. Get both those things out of here and don't come back till tomorrow. And I can practically see through you."

My great-aunt in Virginia, who understood better about needing more to read than you *could* read, sent me a book so big it had to be read on the floor—a bound volume of six or eight issues of *St. Nicholas* from a previous year. In the very first pages a serial began: *The Lucky Stone* by Abbie Farwell Brown. The illustrations were right down my alley: a heroine so poor she was ragged, a witch with an extremely pointed hat, a rich, crusty old gentleman in—better than a wheelchair—a runaway carriage; and I set to. I gobbled up installment after installment through the whole luxurious book, through the last one, and then came the words, turning me to *un*lucky stone: "To be concluded." The book had come to an end and *The Lucky Stone* wasn't finished! The witch had it! I couldn't believe this infidelity from my aunt. I still had my secret childhood feeling that if you hunted long enough in a book's pages, you could find what you were looking for, and long after I knew books better than that, I used to hunt again for the end of *The Lucky Stone*. It never occurred to me that the story had an existence anywhere else outside the pages of that single green-bound book. The last chapter was just something I would have to do without. Polly Pepper could do it. And then suddenly I tried something—I read it again, as much as I had of it. I was in love with books at least partly for what they looked like; I loved the printed page.

In my little circle books were almost never given for Christmas, they cost too much. But the year before, I'd been given a book and got a shock. It was from the same classmate who had told me there was no Santa Claus. She gave me a book, all right—*Poems by Another Little Girl*. It looked like a real book, was printed like a real book—but it was *by her*. *Homemade* poems? Illusion-dispelling was her favorite game. She was in such a hurry, she had such a pile to get rid of—her mother's electric runabout was stacked to the bud vases with copies—that she hadn't even time to say, "Merry Christmas!" With only the same raucous laugh with which she had told me, "Been filling my own stocking for years!" she shot me her book, received my Japanese pencil box with a moonlight scene on the lid and a sharpened pencil inside, jumped back into the car and was sped away by her mother. I stood right where they had left me, on the curb in my Little Nurse's uniform, and read that book, and I had no better way to prove when I got through than I had when I started that this was not a real book. But of course it wasn't. The printed page is not absolutely everything.

Then this Christmas was coming, and my grandfather in Ohio sent along in his box of presents an envelope with money it in for me to buy myself the book I wanted.

I went to Kress's. Not everybody knew Kress's sold books, but children just before Christmas know everything Kress's ever sold or will sell. My father had showed us the mirror he was giving my mother to hang above her desk, and Kress's is where my brother and I went to reproduce that by buying a mirror together to give her ourselves, and where our little brother then made us take him and he bought her one his size for fifteen cents. Kress's had also its version of the Series Books, called, exactly like another series, "The Camp Fire Girls," beginning with *The Camp Fire Girls in the Woods.*

I believe they were ten cents each and I had a dollar. But they weren't all that easy to buy, because the series stuck, and to buy some of it was like breaking into a loaf of French bread. Then after you got home, each single book was as hard to open as a box stuck in its varnish, and when it gave way it popped like a firecracker. The covers once prized apart would never close; those books once open stayed open and lay on their backs helplessly fluttering their leaves like a turned-over June bug. They were as light as a matchbox. They were printed on yellowed paper with corners that crumbled, if you pinched on them too hard, like old graham crackers, and they smelled like attic trunks, caramelized glue, their own confinement with one another and, over all, the Kress's smell—bandannas, peanuts and sandalwood from the incense counter. Even without reading them I loved them. It was hard, that year, that Christmas is a day you can't read.

What could have happened to those books?—but I can tell you about the leading character. His name was Mr. Holmes. He was not a Camp Fire Girl: he wanted to catch one. Through every book of the series he gave chase. He pursued Bessie and Zara—those were the Camp Fire Girls—and kept scooping them up in his touring car, while they just as regularly got away from him. Once Bessie escaped from the second floor of a strange inn by climbing down a gutter pipe. Once she escaped by driving away from Mr. Holmes in his own automobile, which she had learned to drive by watching him. What Mr. Holmes wanted with them—either Bessie or Zara would do—didn't give me pause; I was too young to be a Camp Fire Girl; I was just keeping up. I wasn't alarmed by Mr. Holmes—when I cared for a chill, I knew to go to Dr. Fu Manchu, who had his own series in the library. I wasn't fascinated either. There was one thing I wanted from those books, and that was for me to have ten to read at one blow.

Who in the world wrote those books? I knew all the time they were the false "Camp Fire Girls" and the ones in the library were the authorized. But book reviewers sometimes say of a book that if anyone else had written it, it might not have been this good, and I found it out as a child—their warning is justified. This was a proven case, although a case of the true not being as good as the false. In the true series the characters were either totally different or missing (Mr. Holmes was missing), and there was too much time given to teamwork. The Kress's Campers, besides getting into a more reliable kind of trouble than the Carnegie Campers, had adventures that even they themselves weren't aware of: the pages were in wrong. There were transposed pages, repeated pages, and whole sections in upside down. There was no way of telling if there was anything missing. But if you knew your way in the woods at all, you could enjoy yourself tracking it down. I read the library "Camp Fire Girls," since that's what they were there for, but though they could be read by poorer light they were not as good.

And yet, in a way, the false Campers were no better either. I wonder whether I felt some flaw at the heart of things or whether I was just tired of not having any taste; but it seemed to me when I had finished that the last nine of those books weren't as good as the first one. And the same went for all Series Books. As long as they are keeping a series going, I was afraid, nothing can really happen. The whole thing is one grand prevention. For my greed, I might have unwittingly dealt with myself in the same way Maria Edgeworth dealt with the one who put her all into the purple jar—I had received word it was just colored water.

And then I went again to the home shelves and my lucky hand reached and found Mark Twain—twenty-four volumes, not a series, and good all the way through.

Lewis Thomas

(b. 1913)

Swift's "A Modest Proposal" outlines a grisly solution to Ireland's problems. This doesn't mean what it seems to say, I think as I read; there's some unnerving split here between words and their significance, and I struggle with how to put the two back together. In the process, I have to rethink everything—what's good, what's reasonable, what's humanly possible and desirable. In "An Earnest Proposal" (The Lives of a Cell, *1974*), *Thomas is glancing back at Swift, though as with all mere glances, catching the real look in the eyes is tricky. Dr. Thomas says he's in "earnest," and the problem today is certainly deep and dire. The disease of ignorance is endangering our whole species and the planet we inhabit. In "Medical Lessons from History," he is very straightforward: "We are ignorant about how we work, where we fit in, and most of all about the enormous, imponderable system of life in which we are embedded as working parts." A physician, he looks at life from the angle of molecular biology. "All of today's DNA," he reminds us, "strung through all the cells of the earth is simply an extension and elaboration of [the] first molecule" ("The Wonderful Mistake"). But we know next to nothing of how like elements bond to form diverse things, how living assemblages are made and how they function, even where one assemblage begins and another ends. Maybe everything's one assemblage with myriad parts. Earth itself functions like a giant cell with a membrane of ozone, "far and away the grandest product of collaboration in all of nature" ("The World's Biggest Membrane"). In our state, not of nature, but of plain ignorance, we go on programming our computers to make decisions about this and that—whether we shall live or die. Who will put a stop to it? How much* do *we actually know and what kind of language can we use to talk about it, to get at what we don't know? Thomas starts things off with the language of biology; unfamiliar though it is to most of us (that's the point), it may take us down a better road, slowly. Why has Thomas, so lightly, dragged Swift into this? The doctor's earnest proposal does have its ironies when you think about it; associating himself with the greatest satirist in English must mean, at a minimum, that mechanisms for hard intellectual and moral changes are being set into motion here.*

An Earnest Proposal

There was a quarter-page advertisement in the London *Observer* for a computer service that will enmesh your name in an electronic network of fifty thousand other names, sort out your tastes, preferences, habits, and deepest desires and match them up with opposite numbers, and retrieve for you, within a matter of seconds, and for a very small fee, friends. "Already," it says, "it [the computer] has given very real happiness and lasting relationships to thousands of people, and it can do the same for you!"

Without paying a fee, or filling out a questionnaire, all of us are being linked in similar circuits, for other reasons, by credit bureaus, the census, the tax people, the local police station, or the Army. Sooner or later, if it keeps on, the various networks will begin to touch, fuse, and then, in their coalescence, they will start sorting and retrieving each other, and we will all become bits of information on an enormous grid.

I do not worry much about the computers that are wired to help me find a friend among fifty thousand. If errors are made, I can always beg off with a headache. But what of the vaster machines that will be giving instructions to cities, to nations? If they are programmed to regulate human behavior according to today's view of nature, we are surely in for for apocalypse.

The men who run the affairs of nations today are, by and large, our practical men. They have been taught that the world is an arrangement of adversary systems, that force is what counts, aggression is what drives us at the core, only the fittest can survive, and only might can make more might. Thus, it is in observance of nature's law that we have planted, like perennial tubers, the numberless nameless missiles in the soil of Russia and China and our Midwestern farmlands, with more to come, poised to fly out at a nanosecond's notice, and meticulously engineered to ignite, in the centers of all our cities, artificial suns. If we let fly enough of them at once, we can even burn out the one-celled green creatures in the sea, and thus turn off the oxygen.

Before such things are done, one hopes that the computers will contain every least bit of relevant information about the way of the world. I should think we might assume this, in fairness to all. Even the nuclear realists, busy as their minds must be with calculations of acceptable levels of megadeath, would not want to overlook anything. They should be willing to wait, for a while anyway.

I have an earnest proposal to make. I suggest that we defer further action until we have acquired a really complete set of information concerning at least one living thing. Then, at least, we shall be able to claim that we know what we are doing. The delay might take a decade; let us say a decade. We and the other nations might set it as an objective of international, collaborative science to achieve a complete understanding of a single form of life. When this is done, and the information programmed into all our computers, I for one would be willing to take my chances.

As to the subject, I propose a simple one, easily solved within ten years. It is the protozoan *Myxotricha paradoxa*, which inhabits the inner reaches of the digestive tract of Australian termites.

It is not as though we would be starting from scratch. We have a fair amount of information about this creature already—not enough to understand him, of course, but enough to inform us that he means something, perhaps a great deal. At first glance, he appears to be an ordinary, motile protozoan, remarkable chiefly for the speed and directness with which he swims from place to place, engulfing fragments of wood finely chewed by his termite host. In the termite ecosystem, an arrangement of Byzantine complexity, he stands at the epicenter. Without him, the wood, however finely chewed, would never get digested; he supplies the enzymes that break down cellulose to edible carbohydrate, leaving only the nondegradable lignin, which the termite then excretes in geometrically tidy pellets and uses as building blocks for the erection of arches and vaults in the termite nest. Without him there would be no termites, no farms of the fungi that are cultivated by termites and will grow nowhere else, and no conversion of dead trees to loam.

The flagellae that beat in synchrony to propel myxotricha with such directness turn out, on closer scrutiny with the electron microscope, not to be flagellae at all. They are outsiders, in to help with the business: fully formed, perfect spirochetes that have attached themselves at regularly spaced intervals all over the surface of the protozoan.

Then, there are oval organelles, embedded in the surface close to the point of attachment of the spirochetes, and other similar bodies drifting through the cytoplasm with the particles of still undigested wood. These, under high magnification, turn out to be bacteria, living in symbiosis with the spirochetes and the protozoan, probably contributing enzymes that break down the cellulose.

The whole animal, or ecosystem, stuck for the time being halfway along in evolution, appears to be a model for the development of cells like our own. Margulis has summarized the now considerable body of data indicating that the modern nucleated cell was made up, part by part, by the coming together of just such prokaryotic[1] animals. The blue-green algae, the original inventors of photosynthesis, entered partnership with

[1] A cell that has no nuclear membrane.

primitive bacterial cells, and became the chloroplasts of plants; their descendants remain as discrete separate animals inside plant cells, with their own DNA and RNA, replicating on their own. Other bacteria with oxidative enzymes in their membranes, makers of ATP, joined up with fermenting bacteria and became the mitochondria of the future; they have since deleted some of their genes but retain personal genomes and can only be regarded as symbionts. Spirochetes, like the ones attached to *M. paradoxa*, joined up and became the cilia of eukaryotic[2] cells. The centrioles, which hoist the microtubules on which chromosomes are strung for mitosis, are similar separate creatures; when not busy with mitosis, they become the basal bodies to which cilia are attached. And there are others, not yet clearly delineated, whose existence in the cell is indicated by the presence of cytoplasmic genes.

There is an underlying force that drives together the several creatures comprising myxotricha, and then drives the assemblage into union with the termite. If we could understand this tendency, we would catch a glimpse of the process that brought single separate cells together for the construction of metazoans, culminating in the invention of roses, dolphins, and, of course, ourselves. It might turn out that the same tendency underlies the joining of organisms into communities, communities into ecosystems, and ecosystems into the biosphere. If this is, in fact, the drift of things, the way of the world, we may come to view immune reactions, genes for the chemical marking of self, and perhaps all reflexive responses of aggression and defense as secondary developments in evolution, necessary for the regulation and modulation of symbiosis, not designed to break into the process, only to keep it from getting out of hand.

If it is in the nature of living things to pool resources, to fuse when possible, we would have a new way of accounting for the progressive enrichment and complexity of form in living things.

I take it on faith that computers, although lacking souls, are possessed of a kind of intelligence. At the end of the decade, therefore, I am willing to predict that the feeding in of all the information then available will result, after a few seconds of whirring, in something like the following message, neatly and speedily printed out: "Request more data. How are spirochetes attached? Do not fire."

[2] A cell that has a nuclear membrane.

Doris Lessing

(b. 1919)

"So you've written a good novel or a moderate novel, but what does it actually say about what you've actually experienced?" asks Doris Lessing in an interview with Florence Howe (1966). A prolific writer of novels, short stories, plays, poetry, essays and articles for well over forty years—she composed and destroyed six novels before publishing her first in 1950—Lessing has been plagued throughout with the difficulties of rendering truth, or even an idea, a glimpse, of it. How to wring or wrest truth out of experience? How to compel it to the page? In the service of that effort, her fictions make up a history of one woman's experimentation with literary possibilities. Writing first in the great European realist tradition of Tolstoy, Stendhal, Chekhov, Balzac, she moved on to The Golden Notebook, *the most famous of her novels, whose very structure mirrors the breakdown of old traditions and the consequent breakthrough into new, if undetermined, possibilities. This fracturing of modern experience occupies her in the novel series of the sixties and seventies she calls* Children of Violence*: "The idea is to write about people like myself, people my age who were born out of wars and who have lived through them, the framework of lives in conflict" (Interview with Roy Newquist, 1963). Her essay "My Father" (1963,* A Small Personal Voice) *was written during the period of her preoccupation with this "idea." It is a memoir of her father, yes, but one written out of a desire to pay off a kind of moral debt, one few even recognize, let alone discharge. The debt is incurred by our failure to be there for our parents, by the violence of using them "like recurring dreams, to be entered into when needed." Her essay attempts to rectify this situation, to be there for her father by wresting from scraps of evidence the truth of what kind of person he was. Born of this father crippled in both body and spirit by the First World War, the "I" of this painful memoir struggles to break through to a father and a man Lessing knew only "when his best years were over"; getting at truth turns into an act of love.*

My Father

We use our parents like recurring dreams, to be entered into when needed; they are always there for love or for hate; but it occurs to me that

I was not always there for my father. I've written about him before, but novels, stories, don't have to be "true." Writing this article is difficult because it has to be "true." I knew him when his best years were over.

There are photographs of him. The largest is of an officer in the 1914–18 war. A new uniform—buttoned, badged, strapped, tabbed—confines a handsome, dark young man who holds himself stiffly to confront what he certainly thought of as his duty. His eyes are steady, serious, and responsible, and show no signs of what he became later. A photograph at sixteen is of a dark, introspective youth with the same intent eyes. But it is his mouth you notice—a heavily-jutting upper lip contradicts the rest of a regular face. His moustache was to hide it: "Had to do something—a damned fleshy mouth. Always made me uncomfortable, that mouth of mine."

Earlier a baby (eyes already alert) appears in a lace waterfall that cascades from the pillowy bosom of a fat, plain woman to her feet. It is the face of a head cook. "Lord, but my mother was a practical female—almost as bad as you!" as he used to say, or throw at my mother in moments of exasperation. Beside her stands, or droops, arms dangling, his father, the source of the dark, arresting eyes, but otherwise masked by a long beard.

The birth certificate says: Born 3rd August, 1886, Walton Villa, Creffield Road, S. Mary at the Wall, R.S.D. Name, Alfred Cook. Name and surname of Father: Alfred Cook Tayler. Name and maiden name of Mother: Caroline May Batley. Rank or Profession: Bank Clerk. Colchester, Essex.

They were very poor. Clothes and boots were a problem. They "made their own amusements." Books were mostly the Bible and *The Pilgrim's Progress*. Every Saturday night they bathed in a hipbath in front of the kitchen fire. No servants. Church three times on Sundays. "Lord, when I think of those Sundays! I dreaded them all week, like a nightmare coming at you full tilt and no escape." But he rabbited with ferrets along the lanes and fields, bird-nested, stole fruit, picked nuts and mushrooms, paid visits to the blacksmith and the mill and rode a farmer's carthorse.

They ate economically, but when he got diabetes in his forties and subsisted on lean meat and lettuce leaves, he remembered suet puddings, treacle puddings, raisin and currant puddings, steak and kidney puddings, bread and butter pudding, "batter cooked in the gravy with the meat," potato cake, plum cake, butter cake, porridge with treacle, fruit tarts and pies, brawn, pig's trotters and pig's cheek and home-smoked ham and sausages. And "lashings of fresh butter and cream and eggs." He wondered if this diet had produced the diabetes, but said it was worth it.

There was an elder brother described by my father as: "Too damned clever by half. One of those quick, clever brains. Now I've always had a slow brain, but I get there in the end, damn it!"

The brothers went to a local school and the elder did well, but my father was beaten for being slow. They both became bank clerks in, I think, the Westminster Bank, and one must have found it congenial, for he became a manager, the "rich brother," who had cars and even a yacht. But my father did not like it, though he was conscientious. For instance, he changed his writing, letter by letter, because a senior criticised it. I never saw his unregenerate hand, but the one he created was elegant, spiky, careful. Did this mean he created a new personality for himself, hiding one he did not like, as he hid his "damned fleshy mouth"? I don't know.

Nor do I know when he left home to live in Luton, or why. He found family life too narrow? A safe guess—he found everything too narrow. His mother was too down-to-earth? He had to get away from his clever elder brother?

Being a young man in Luton was the best part of his life. It ended in 1914, so he had a decade of happiness. His reminiscences of it were all of pleasure, the delight of physical movement, of dancing in particular. All his girls were "a beautiful dancer, light as a feather." He played billiards and ping-pong (both for his country); he swam, boated, played cricket and football, went to picnics and horse races, sang at musical evenings. One family of a mother and two daughters treated him "like a son only better. I didn't know whether I was in love with the mother or the daughters, but oh I did love going there; we had such good times." He was engaged to one daughter, then, for a time, to the other. An engagement was broken off because she was rude to a waiter. "I could not marry a woman who allowed herself to insult someone who was defenceless." He used to say to my wryly smiling mother: "Just as well I didn't marry either of *them;* they would never have stuck it out the way you have, old girl."

Just before he died he told me he had dreamed he was standing in a kitchen on a very high mountain holding X in his arms. "Ah, yes, that's what I've missed in my life. Now don't you let yourself be cheated out of life by the old dears. They take all the colour out of everything if you let them."

But in that decade—"I'd walk 10, 15 miles to a dance two or three times a week and think nothing of it. Then I'd dance every dance and walk home again over the fields. Sometimes it was moonlight, but I liked the snow best, all crisp and fresh. I loved walking back and getting into my digs just as the sun was rising. My little dog was so happy to see me, and I'd feed her, and make myself porridge and tea, then I'd wash and shave and go off to work."

The boy who was beaten at school, who went too much to church, who carried the fear of poverty all his life, but who nevertheless was filled with the memories of country pleasures; the young bank clerk who worked such long hours for so little money but who danced, sang, played, flirted—this naturally vigorous, sensuous being was killed in 1914, 1915, 1916. I think the best of my father died in that war, that his spirit was crippled by it. The people I've met, particularly the women, who knew him young, speak of his high spirits, his energy, his enjoyment of life. Also of his kindness, his compassion and—a word that keeps recurring—his wisdom. "Even when he was just a boy he understood things that you'd think even an old man would find it easy to condemn." I do not think these people would have easily recognised the ill, irritable, abstracted, hypochondriac man I knew.

He "joined up" as an ordinary soldier out of a characteristically quirky scruple: it wasn't right to enjoy officers' privileges when the Tommies had such a bad time. But he could not stick the communal latrines, the obligatory drinking, the collective visits to brothels, the jokes about girls. So next time he was offered a commission he took it.

His childhood and young man's memories, kept fluid, were added to, grew, as living memories do. But his war memories were congealed in stories that he told again and again, with the same words and gestures, in stereotyped phrases. They were anonymous, general, as if they had come out of a communal war memoir. He met a German in no-man's-land, but both slowly lowered their rifles and smiled and walked away. The Tommies were the salt of the earth, the British fighting men the best in the world. He had never known such comradeship. A certain brutal officer was shot in a sortie by his men, but the other officers, recognising rough justice, said nothing. He had known men intimately who saw the Angels at Mons. He wished he could force all the generals on both sides into the trenches for just one day, to see what the common soldiers endured—*that* would have ended the war at once.

There was an undercurrent of memories, dreams, and emotions much deeper, more personal. This dark region in him, fate-ruled, where nothing was true but horror, was expressed inarticulately, in brief, bitter exclamations or phrases of rage, incredulity, betrayal. The men who went to fight in that war believed it when they said it was to end war. My father believed it. And he was never able to reconcile his belief in his country with his anger at the cynicism of its leaders. And the anger, the sense of betrayal, strengthened as he grew old and ill.

But in 1914 he was naïve, the German atrocities in Belgium inflamed him, and he enlisted out of idealism, although he knew he would have a hard time. He knew because a fortuneteller told him. (He could be described as uncritically superstitious or as psychically gifted.) He would be in great danger twice, yet not die—he was being protected by a famous soldier who was his ancestor. "And sure enough, later I heard from the Little Aunties that the church records showed we were descended the backstairs way from the Duke of Wellington, or was it Marlborough? Damn it, I forget. But one of them would be beside me all through the war, she said." (He was romantic, not only about this solicitous ghost, but also about being a descendant of the Huguenots, on the strength of the "e" in Tayler; and about "the wild blood" in his veins from a great uncle who, sent unjustly to prison for smuggling, came out of a ten-year sentence and earned it, very efficiently, along the coasts of Cornwall until he died.)

The luckiest thing that ever happened to my father, he said, was getting his leg shattered by shrapnel ten days before Passchendaele. His whole company was killed. He knew he was going to be wounded because of the fortuneteller, who had said he would know. "I did not understand what she meant, but both times in the trenches, first when my appendix burst and I nearly died, and then just before Passchendaele, I felt for some days as if a thick, black velvet pall was settled over me. I can't tell you what it was like. Oh, it was awful, awful, and the second time it was so bad I wrote to the old people and told them I was going to be killed."

His leg was cut off at mid-thigh, he was shell-shocked, he was very ill for many months, with a prolonged depression afterwards. "You should always remember that sometimes people are all seething underneath. You don't know what terrible things people have to fight against. You should look at a person's eyes, that's how you tell. . . . When I was like that, after I lost my leg, I went to a nice doctor man and said I was going mad, but he said, don't worry, everyone locks up things like that. You don't know—horrible, horrible awful things. I was afraid of myself, of what I used to dream. I wasn't myself at all."

In the Royal Free Hospital was my mother, Sister McVeagh. He married his nurse which, as they both said often enough (though in different tones of voice), was just as well. That was 1919. He could not face being a bank clerk in England, he said, not after the trenches. Besides, England was too narrow and conventional. Besides, the civilians did not know what the soldiers had suffered, they didn't want to know, and now it wasn't done even to remember "The Great Unmentionable." He went off to the Imperial Bank of Persia, in which country I was born.

The house was beautiful, with great stone-floored high-ceilinged rooms whose windows showed ranges of snow-streaked mountains. The gardens were full of roses, jasmine, pomegranates, walnuts. Kermanshah he spoke of with liking, but soon they went to Teheran, populous with "Embassy people," and my gregarious mother created a lively social life about which he was irritable even in recollection.

Irritableness—that note was first struck here, about Persia. He did not like, he said, "the graft and the corruption." But here it is time to try and describe something difficult—how a man's good qualities can also be his bad ones, or if not bad, a danger to him.

My father was honourable—he always knew exactly what that word meant. He had integrity. His "one does not do that sort of thing," his "no, it is *not* right," sounded throughout my childhood and were final for all of us. I am sure it was true he wanted to leave Persia because of "the corruption." But it was also because he was already unconsciously longing for something freer, because as a bank official he could not let go into the dream-logged personality that was waiting for him. And later in Rhodesia, too, what was best in him was also what prevented him from shaking away the shadows: it was always in the name of honesty or decency that he refused to take this step or that out of the slow decay of the family's fortunes.

In 1925 there was leave from Persia. That year in London there was an Empire Exhibition, and on the Southern Rhodesian stand some very fine maize cobs and a poster saying that fortunes could be made on maize at 25/-[1] a bag. So on an impulse, turning his back forever on England, washing his hands of the corruption of the East, my father collected all his capital, £800, I think, while my mother packed curtains from Liberty's, clothes from Harrods, visiting cards, a piano, Persian rugs, a governess and two small children.

Soon, there was my father in a cigar-shaped house of thatch and mud on the top of a *kopje*[2] that overlooked in all directions a great system of mountains, rivers, valleys, while overhead the sky arched from horizon to empty horizon. This was a couple of hundred miles south from the Zambesi, a hundred or so west from Mozambique, in the district of Banket, so called because certain of its reefs were of the same formation as those called *banket* on the Rand. Lomagundi—gold country, tobacco country, maize country—wild, almost empty. (The Africans had been turned off it into reserves.) Our neighbours were four, five, seven miles off. In front of the house . . . no neighbours, nothing; no farms, just wild bush with two rivers but no fences to the mountains seven miles away. And beyond these mountains and bush again to the Portuguese border, over which "our boys" used to escape when wanted by the police for pass or other offences.

[1] Twenty-five shillings.

[2] South African Dutch for "hill."

And then? There was bad luck. For instance, the price of maize dropped from 25/- to 9/- a bag. The seasons were bad, prices bad, crops failed. This was the sort of thing that made it impossible for him ever to "get off the farm," which, he agreed with my mother, was what he most wanted to do.

It was an absurd country, he said. A man could "own" a farm for years that was totally mortgaged to the Government and run from the Land Bank, meanwhile employing half-a-hundred Africans at 12/- a month and none of them knew how to do a day's work. Why, two farm labourers from Europe could do in a day what twenty of these ignorant black savages would take a week to do. (Yet he was proud that he had a name as a just employer, that he gave "a square deal.") Things got worse. A fortuneteller had told him that her heart ached when she saw the misery ahead for my father: this was the misery.

But it was my mother who suffered. After a period of neurotic illness, which was a protest against her situation, she became brave and resourceful. But she never saw that her husband was not living in a real world, that he had made a captive of her common sense. We were always about to "get off the farm." A miracle would do it—a sweepstake, a goldmine, a legacy. And then? What a question! We would go to England where life would be normal with people coming in for musical evenings and nice supper parties at the Trocadero after a show. Poor woman, for the twenty years we were on the farm, she waited for when life would begin for her and for her children, for she never understood that what was a calamity for her was for them a blessing.

Meanwhile my father sank towards his death (at 61). Everything changed in him. He had been a dandy and fastidious, now he hated to change out of shabby khaki. He had been sociable, now he was misanthropic. His body's disorders—soon diabetes and all kinds of stomach ailments—dominated him. He was brave about his wooden leg, and even went down mine shafts and climbed trees with it, but he walked clumsily and it irked him badly. He greyed fast, and slept more in the day, but would be awake half the night pondering about. . . .

It could be gold divining. For ten years he experimented on private theories to do with the attractions and repulsions of metals. His whole soul went into it but his theories were wrong or he was *unlucky*—after all, if he had found a mine he would have had to leave the farm. It could be the relation between the minerals of the earth and of the moon; his decision to make infusions of all the plants on the farm and drink them himself in the interests of science; the criminal folly of the British Government in not realising that the Germans and the Russians were conspiring as Anti-Christ to . . . the inevitability of war because no one would listen to Churchill, but it would be all right because God (by then he was a British Israelite) had destined Britain to rule the world; a prophecy said 10 million dead would surround Jerusalem—how would the corpses be cleared away?; people who wished to abolish flogging should be flogged; the natives understood nothing but a good beating; hanging must not be abolished because the Old Testament said "an eye for an eye and a tooth for a tooth. . . ."

Yet, as this side of him darkened, so that it seemed all his thoughts were of violence, illness, war, still no one dared to make an unkind comment in his presence or to gossip. Criticism of people, particularly of women, made him more and more uncomfortable till at last he burst out with: "It's all very well, but no one has the right to say that about another person."

In Africa, when the sun goes down, the stars spring up, all of them in their expected places, glittering and moving. In the rainy season, the sky flashed and thundered. In the dry season, the great dark hollow of night was lit by veld fires: the mountains burned through September and October in chains of red fire. Every night my father took out his chair to watch the sky and the mountains, smoking, silent, a thin shabby fly-away figure under the stars. "Makes you think—there are so many worlds up there, wouldn't really matter if we did blow ourselves up—plenty more where we came from."

The Second World War, so long foreseen by him, was a bad time. His son was in the Navy and in danger, and his daughter a sorrow to him. He became very ill. More and more often it was necessary to drive him into Salisbury with him in a coma, or in danger of one, on the back seat. My mother moved him into a pretty little suburban house in town near the hospitals, where he took to his bed and a couple of years later died. For the most part he was unconscious under drugs. When awake he talked obsessively (a tongue licking a nagging sore place) about "the old war." Or he remembered his youth. "I've been dreaming—Lord, to see those horses come lickety-split down the course with their necks stretched out and the sun on their coats and everyone shouting. . . . I've been dreaming how I walked along the river in the mist as the sun was rising. . . . Lord, lord, lord, what a time that was, what good times we all had then, before the old war."

James McConkey

(b. 1921)

Literature for James McConkey, teacher and writer, is not an academic subject; nor is it merely a source of pleasure. It is a way of self-knowledge and of self-creation. In 1971, he published A Journey to Sahalin, *a story of individual predicament amid the campus turmoil of the late sixties. The novel is dedicated (among others) to the great Russian writer Anton Chekhov (1860–1904) whose real-life journey from Moscow to the prison colony on Sakhalin Island in the Sea of Okhotsk inspired the title. That title, however, "had more to do with the author than with his plot," wrote McConkey years later in* To a Distant Island *(1984), where he attempted to recount, imaginatively and sympathetically, Chekhov's 6,500-mile journey to what the latter described as "a place of unbearable suffering." McConkey's searching "story of a spiritual quest" is part biography, part fictive and speculative reconstruction, part reflection on some of Chekhov's most moving post-Sakhalin stories. In these, McConkey sees Chekhov striving to articulate his conflicts of feeling and value through characters who embody antithetical parts of himself. But this meditation on another writer's life and art is also vitally autobiographical: with Chekhov's quest for freedom McConkey entwines his personal struggle, in the final years of the 1960s, to reconcile "the inner voice calling for truth with the desire for human mutuality." This had been a central theme of his novel from that period. In the still earlier essay, "In Praise of Chekhov" (1967), he imagines himself at one point as a pair of antithetical characters, Jimski and Rodneyvitch, in a Chekhovian fiction. Like Chekhov's great story "Gooseberries," which McConkey lovingly recreates in* To a Distant Island, *the essay poses fundamental questions, presumes to forge no solutions, yet "implies the possibility of a grace-bearing answer, however temporal—even evanescent—it may be." McConkey describes his teaching of literature as "my personal response to a text." So, too, these writings of nearly two decades portray an abiding personal response to a great predecessor, an artist of whom he has said, "Perhaps [Chekhov] is but a mirror of my ideal self."*

In Praise of Chekhov

Long ago—in Germany, near the end of the war—two corpsmen came into the field and lifted me into a litter. They were so careful and gentle that for their sake I gave a little groan, though I felt no pain. They strapped the litter to some metal bars above the back seat of their jeep. One of them sat beside me while the other drove. It was dark. Lying on my back, I could see nothing of the jeep. I floated slowly through the sweet air of a spring night, the head of the corpsman, with the cross outlined against the circle of white on the back of his helmet, bobbing and drifting along with me. On a hillside I saw a bonfire and heard some unfamiliar plaintive song.

"Drunk!" the corpsman said appreciatively.

"Who?" It was my voice.

"Happy! Drunk! They're supposed to stay put, them Russians from the slave camp, but whenever a freight goes east they rush at it. Some of them make it to the roofs. You should hear them laugh! We found a leg between the rails yesterday. The trains go slow through here—they never should have bivouacked them crazy homesick Russians near the tracks!"

The field hospital was a school or a church on top of a hill. Inside, the rough stone walls were whitewashed. I lay on a table looking at a pulsating overhead light; in the distance I could hear the rumble of a gasoline engine. One of the corpsmen unbuckled my boots and cut off my trousers and shirt and shorts with a pair of scissors. Snip, snip, snip: I thought it wrong to ruin clothes like that. For a moment I feel asleep. When I awoke, the corpsman was still beside me. "Would you like some water?" he asked.

"That would be nice," I said, though I wasn't thirsty. He put a moist piece of cotton in my mouth. It was like a gag, and I didn't want it; but I waited for him to be called elsewhere before hiding it under the sheet. The table was on wheels, and a Wac nurse pushed me into an adjoining room where a young doctor was waiting. I said to the doctor, "I can't move my legs."

"That's the least of our worries," he said. He looked tired, but was friendly and cheerful. The nurse was shaving my pubic hair.

"How do you know what's wrong?" I asked. "You haven't even *looked*."

He smiled. "I make it a general rule to look before I operate, whenever I can."

"But I just got here."

"That's what you think."

"Just a moment ago I was driving a jeep that flipped," I said. "I was the booby who hit the trap."

"That's what lots of my patients tell me."

The nurse had finished with the razor. I looked directly into the doctor's eyes. "I want an honest answer," I said. "Am I going to live?"

"Such a question from a healthy young man! Such an insult to my handiwork!"

"I didn't mean to insult you," I said. "I'm sorry. Will I be sterile?" I thought such a question was probably the normal response of one whose pubic hair has been shaved.

"No," he said. "You'll have a dozen children."

"I have a Luger pistol," I said. "You make this a good operation, one that won't make me sterile, and I tell you what. You can have that Luger pistol."

"It's a deal," he said. "A Luger pistol is just what I need." He placed a mask over my face. "You're higher than a kite. Breathe deeply and you'll go higher yet," and I breathed in the ether that had made me sick when I had been a child in Arkansas and the doctor had lanced both my ears. I wanted to tell him to use something else to put me to sleep, that my ears were all right now and that I didn't want to be ashamed for throwing up all over the starched sheets and pillow cases. I started to struggle; but Dr. Buckley in Little Rock was holding my arms. "Breathe deep, breathe deep," he drawled, and I was a little boy in a racing car that roared off the road into a ditch.

The Russian was trilling sweetly from the roof of the freight car. "God bless you," I said. Blood dripped from his stump. I floated past him on a cloud. I knew it a trite thing to be doing, floating on that cloud, but there it was. I vomited all over the trite cloud. "I told you so," I said reproachfully. Hitler, all in red and with horns, rose up through the cloud and came at my belly with a pitchfork. "Trite! Trite!" I screamed at him. Held down by my thick umbilical cord, I could not get away from him. I tried to yank the rubber tube out of my belly. "Don't touch that," a voice warned. Dark came and light came and another voice, a gentler Southern voice that I mistook at first for Dr. Buckley's, was praying. "Dear Jesus Christ," it prayed politely, "please in your mercy let me have a B.M." "Who is that praying?" I asked the nurse. "He was shot in the stomach," she said. The prayer went on all that day and night, but growing fainter. Another voice was screaming in German. "That sounds like a girl," I said to the nurse. "They've been using children," she said. "He's scared, but it's only his leg." The doctor roared from a distance, "If that little Nazi coward doesn't shut up, tell him I'll personally tie his hands together so tight he'll have something to cry about. God damn it, *make him shut up*." "I gave him my Luger pistol," I said, and began to weep. "Hush," the nurse said. "He's been operating for three days with hardly any rest, and the lieutenant just died." "What lieutenant?" "The one that was praying," she said. I asked, "Did the child kill the lieutenant?" "That child, or another," she said. "That's all they have left."

Because of a shortage of beds, I was evacuated by air that day to a station hospital in England. I was in a fever and drunk with morphine. The medical care was excellent and I recovered rapidly.

While I was driving to work, my car slipped just a trifle on the icy highway—it was late March, already spring, and I had not thought the rain would freeze on the asphalt—and immediately I was back on a German road and the jeep had just hit the trap and was veering into the field and rolling over. My foot trembled on the gas pedal. I make that response perhaps a dozen times a year, whenever a wheel slips on ice or gravel, and each time I am angry with myself. A person should carry away from a serious accident more than an instinctive response. But the experience had been devoid of meaning; in my role as victim I became simply what I thought was expected of me. As I knew even as I had them, my very nightmares were stereotypes. If only I could convince myself now that I had *imagined* the lieutenant's prayer, the boy's screams, the doctor's threat! Distortion of reality is at least personality. But I remain convinced of the truth of those events. Reflections of this sort I find strangely disturbing. They make me nervous, I pace about the room.

The writer who moves me most deeply is Chekhov. I like especially those tales of antithetical characters who meet by chance as they wander across immense plains, or as they travel upon the sea. In one story, a wanderer wakes in the middle of the night in a strange room in a peasant village to see a white cow in the open door. She is banging her horn against the jamb. Such images remain forever in the mind. This is the story in which the wanderer is a dispassionate creature, a man of God who is traveling across Russia begging money to rebuild his burned church. The opposing character is a near idiot, a compulsive liar and thief. While the man of God is sleeping, the thief, of course, steals the rubles intended for the church; but he returns, full of vodka, to await his victim's awakening. He returns so that he may be accused of the crime; for clearly he finds his vindication, indeed his comfort, in the resentment he arouses by his transgressions, in the ensuing quarrels and the ultimate punishment handed out by his parents, the villagers, the political authorities. But the man of God does not care; he will not fight or even argue. The matter, he tells the other, is simply between him and God. And he leaves the village with his horse-drawn cart containing an ikon and the tin money box, the thief following after, trying to draw him into anger and debate. The man of God is as impersonal and as indifferent as the natural world, as remote and as austere as the sky above them both. He remains so even after the other confesses the theft and begs forgiveness. The thief falls in terror to the ground; he weeps, he calls the man of God his kinsman, his grandfather, his uncle. Troubled, the man of God looks for a moment at the sky and feels frightened himself. "He was frightened," says Chekhov, "and he felt pity for the thief"; and so he tells the other the conventional ritual that man has established in the face of the incomprehensible Authority. If the thief will confess to the priest, if he will make a penance, if he will do this and that . . . It is noon at the end of the story; the two have reached the next town, where the thief, recovered, quarrels in the tavern with the drunken peasants and calls for the police. One can imagine the man of God moving onward into the immense afternoon landscape, a small figure growing ever smaller. Chekhov thought so little of the tale that he left it out of his collected edition. In another story, the antithetical characters are patients in a ship's infirmary on the long voyage from the Far East to their homeland. One of them is a discharged army orderly, a simple person who has been content to obey his superiors, who has no complaints and who accepts without question the most superstitious beliefs. The other is an irritable rationalist, an intellectual who rails against the injustice and tyranny to be found everywhere. Both die; their deaths are handled laconically. In the next to the last paragraph, the body of the orderly, covered in sailcloth and weighted with iron, sinks deeper and deeper as pilot fish circle about it and a shark rips the cloth; in the final paragraph the sunset above the waters is described. Chekhov imparts whatever human characteristics he can to the world of water: the pilot fish are in "ecstasy," the ocean "frowns." The clouds are given fanciful resemblances—one is an arch, one a lion, one something as domestic as a pair of shears. But all such attempts to find kinship and meaning in nature must fail, and the colors of the sunset, as they reflect upon the ocean, have a beauty—these are the last words of the story—"for which it is hard to find a name in the language of man." What does it matter, if one man accepts his condition and another protests against it? The conclusion of the story is terrible in its detachment and beauty, in its suggestion of an order far removed from human impulse and value. Whatever flaws I find in Chekhov I blame on his translators.

I have a retentive mind for wayward and useless things such as stray newspaper items, fillers among the daily reports of war and politics. One night twelve years ago, I ate dinner with my family at the Eagle's Nest restaurant on Main Street—Highway 60—in Morehead, Kentucky. I remember the taste of the chicken and hot biscuits and honey; I remember as well the display case with its Lifesavers and Beechnut gum. I remember the outline of the hill in the moonlight as we stepped outside, and I can tell anybody precisely where our car was parked. I remember all of this trivia because I had picked up a Louisville *Times* and read, while waiting by the cash register to pay my bill, the story of a Mexican who rented his town's bullfight stadium and then built a cross and had himself brutally affixed upon it. He was carried to the stadium, and his wife and children collected admission money at the gates from curious townspeople and tourists. Unfavorable publicity made the local officials cancel his contract, so his family carted him home on his cross and installed him inside. The curious still had to pay. He was, I believe, five days nailed to his cross, and came down prosperous. Reading the account, I thought, This is the end of something. I did not think of myself as a believing Christian, whatever I put down, for sake of identification, on the forms and questionnaires that all of us spend so much time filling out; and yet that news item was a personal threat—it diminished my personality in some subtle way and like an illness left me more susceptible to various kinds of contagion. I continue to hope the story false; or if it isn't, that the Mexican was desperate, that his family was starving. I hope he didn't do it for a Ford or a Chevie.

When I lived in Kentucky, I knew of a man who became so obsessed with the dual sense of the immensity of the universe and the smallness of our planet that he developed the fear that any sudden motion, even an unexpected hiccough, might send him flying into space. He walked gingerly, holding railings and touching store fronts as if he were blind, and finally was reduced to a baby's crawl. He was mad, but that is not to say his actions were beyond understanding to anybody who feels, as I think Chekhov did, that personality—whether one is a man of God, a thief, an orderly, or an intellectual—is a conscious and unconscious arrangement of attitudes and beliefs to serve as bulwark against the incomprehensible concepts of infinite time and infinite space. I consider myself a sensible person; and yet in moments of depression I can imagine the unique self to which I hold on so dearly in danger of being sucked off at any instant into the near vacuum of black space. Except, thank God, for a sense of horror, I once melted, vanished wholly away, in the swarm of a Long Island beach on an August afternoon, the quiet dispersal of my atoms accompanied less by the sound of the eternal wash of the sea than by the whisper of thousands of transistor radios each advertising the same used car. I like to look at the planets through a telescope of my own devising, because to so frame them within a magnifying lens is to make them one's own; and I highly recommend, for looking at the constellations, a plastic gadget called a Starfinder. It comes in a small cardboard box with a series of transparent discs, each showing a separate constellation and naming all the stars in it. The observer peers into the Starfinder with one eye, to see the constellation of his choice illuminated by a faint red light within the little tunnel of plastic. He holds the Starfinder upward, attempting to locate with the other eye the same constellation in the night sky. Suddenly, as if by miracle, the two eyes, which have been in danger of becoming crossed, come into focus and the observer discovers that high in the heavens the name of each star is printed beside it, and that the outlines of Bear or Hunter are traced in such a manner that the most obtuse can see the mythological figure. (Long before I knew about Orion and his hunting prowess, I was nearly killed by him. I was driving, alone, from Lexington, Kentucky, where my wife had just given birth to our second son, to our home in Morehead—a seventy-mile trip in an easterly direction—after midnight in late October. I was relaxed and happy. The three stars of Orion's belt, bright through the windshield, drew me toward them, emptied me of all feeling. I went off the shoulder of the road twice, drifted over the center line almost into the twin circles of a truck's glare, and finally pulled into the parking lot of a hilltop church to get out of the car and stare down those fierce and lovely and lonely stars.) A Starfinder costs a couple of bucks or so, a reasonable price for a device that can completely humanize the universe.

If I were Chekhov, I might have invented a character—let's call him Jimski, for my first name is James: I was named for my father's father and I have handed on the name to the third of my sons—who is, say, out for a walk in the country with a friend. Jimski tells his friend that his horse slipped and fell on the ice that morning, a trivial accident that immediately reminded him of the wound he received years before in one war or another, and of his inability to be profound on the occasion of his near-death. Jimski is in despair, conscious of the press of the universe upon him and of the shallowness of his own nature. He recounts a number of depressing incidents, each of which is intended to reinforce his view that personality is at best a precarious affair, a temporary expedient against negation. . . . Jimski wipes his nose and sighs. His friend Rodneyovitch—my middle name is Rodney, that being the name of the hero of an adventure novel my father read as a boy—is, while sympathetic, made of sterner and more practical stuff. He is, in other words, the antithetical character. "Jimski," he says, after shooting his gun aimlessly (for they are hunting quail), "what you say about the vagueness of our natures is false. Each of us has a built-in obsession, a monster within that shapes our facial expressions, that gives a special look to our noses and mouths and, yes, to the way we gesticulate and walk. We try to keep this monster hidden from the world and if possible from ourselves, even though its mark is everywhere upon us and we cannot be free of it until we die. Don't you know of moments when this secret of another's identity has been suddenly revealed to you? Listen while I tell you . . ." And Rodneyovitch, that garrulous fellow, begins his own series of sad tales, two of which—taken out of my own experiences and not yet transformed into their Russian context—can be summarized as typical examples:

Item #1. Concerning a mail orderly of an anti-tank platoon to which I was assigned for several months in World War II. He had no friends and apparently desired none. The platoon thought him a sadist. Both in training camp and abroad he would postpone as long as possible the distribution of mail. Finally he would climb upon a table or file case and cry imperiously for silence. He dispensed the letters with a flourish, as if each were a token of his personal largess. If a soldier became angry at his tyrannical slowness, he was apt to leave his perch for an hour or so, taking all the mail with him; and he was known to have withheld letters for several days from any person who displeased him. His platoon wished to murder him; he was beaten up on at least one occasion. In eastern France he appeared late one night during a snowstorm at divisional headquarters, to which I had been transferred, to pick up some packages—a task anybody else would have delayed until the following morning. We saw him suddenly fall to the ground, threshing in helpless convulsions, his little packages skittering over the snow. A medic wedged open his mouth to keep him from biting off his tongue. The mail orderly had managed to conceal until that moment the fact that he was an epileptic. Afterwards, in tears, he begged that he be permitted to remain overseas with his buddies, to whom he thought himself of use; but he was immediately shipped home. I never heard of him again.

Item #2. Concerning a former field artillery captain. In my graduate school years, I lived for a brief period with my wife and infant son in a barracks apartment in a university housing area. Every adult male resident of that area was a war veteran and a father. Some families, of course, had two or even more children; the housing area, surrounded by a stout fence with self-locking gates for the safeguarding of the infants, was little more than a gigantic playpen. A rumor developed that two voyeurs, a Mutt and a Jeff, were wandering around the area after midnight. It was said that Jeff climbed on Mutt's shoulders to peer into the high windows of the barracks; Mutt apparently was so tall that he needed no assistance. It was also also said that they were most likely to appear when a light flashed on in a bedroom late at night, for what they wished above all to see was a mother giving the milk of her breast to her child. Not much would have come of the rumors had it not been for a former field artillery captain, an older student of military bearing. He had two children. One of them, a girl of six or so, played jump rope by the hour just outside her door, but the other child, a son a year younger, was never seen. The notion of the pair of peeping Toms filled this ex-captain with a strange hatred. "Beasts," he would say of them with a snarl and a fastidious curl of the lip. "Dirty beasts." He lurked outside a friend's apartment all one night while the friend obediently clicked on and off the bedroom light. The friend's child screamed, waking the nearby families. There was quite a racket from the babies that night. Using his military experience, the undaunted ex-captain devised an elaborate communications network for capturing the pair. When any resident of the housing area saw a loiterer late at night, he was to call a certain telephone number: the person phoned was in turn to get in touch with another, and so on until the whole male populace had been alerted. Two men, designated in advance, were to conceal themselves behind the garbage cans at each of the three gates, while the other husbands were to form an advancing line that, moving from one end of the area to the other, would flush out the culprits. When this strategy produced nothing but false alarms and indignant protests from trapped but innocent prey—guests to the area, lost in the maze of corrugated huts—the ex-captain issued a daily password to all residents; and, with a few dedicated cronies, kept a vigil in the bushes at night. The loathing of the ex-captain for the Toms, the extraordinary measures he had taken (he had warned, in one of his mimeographed communiqués, that we were not to lose our heads and shoot to kill those who might turn out to be the wrong persons), kept us, even in daylight hours, from looking in confidence at anything but our own feet; no man dared to smile at a pretty girl without turning to the nearest bush and shouting, "Swallow of the north woods," or whatever the password happened to be. In short, husbands and wives began to feel guilt that they were male and female, sex itself became sinful. "Beasts! Dirty beasts!" That was all we could hear. Who were the dirty beasts? Were we? Was the ex-captain? I am sure that very few babies were conceived in the area for the month that terror reigned. Finally, of course, normality returned. A little garbage collector was jailed for indecent exposure in another barracks area. "They've caught Jeff," the ex-captain crowed. I happened to be passing his apartment when he heard the news; the wide double doors were open, and standing within I saw, for the first time, his younger child. The boy's head was tipped, his thin little arms were extended before his body like an ape's, he was drooling. I said stupidly, "Is he sick?" "We love him," the ex-captain said angrily. "The doctors were at fault, though of course they deny it. We've checked the genealogy and for generations there's been no trace, I tell you absolutely no trace; it had to be the forceps when he was born," and he slammed the doors shut and stood in front of them, erect and alert as a sentry. "They've caught the small one, the pressure's on, and by God I bet the other beast has swum the Mississippi by now!"

As I say, these are stories of the kind Rodneyovitch would tell, and you must believe me when I also say he could go on with them all afternoon, quail whizzing to safety to the right and left of his boots as he and his friend Jimski plod on. Possibly such tales should be seen as unconscious distortions of experience, each made to fit neatly into a preconceived and melancholy idea about personality. And what of consequence distinguishes Rodneyovitch's view that the monster within gives us unique identity from Jimski's that personality is but a precarious stay against negation? Rodneyovitch's argument is hardly an optimistic one. Actually we can find more that is affirmative in the medodramatic remark we can attribute to Jimski that once when happiness made him unwary the hunter in the sky nearly bagged him: for is there not the implication that he was drawn upward in communion with those strange and distant jewels that are the hunter's belt? Jimski looks outward and Rodneyovitch inward, one haunted by vacuum and the other by viscera. What else is there to say? The two walk on, their debate becoming pointless, merging into one statement as they themselves shrink into a single dot on the horizon.

It was, you will remember, a trivial slip on the ice that set me off on this particular road. It seems to have brought me to the point where I exist as a brace of bushy-faced foreigners who, if they are to become one, must be viewed as the product of a Russian writer's synthesizing mind. This is odd, and I won't wholly accept it; but I suppose that if we pursue ourselves too far, searching for a personal truth, we are apt to become fictive. I once knew an eighteenth-century scholar, a man given to a blunt kind of self-searching, who ended up the very model of Boswell's Samuel Johnson, and whose last years were severely disturbed by his uncertainty as to who he was.

I, Jimski-Rodneyovitch or whatever, am defined by my contradictions. Given at times to violent passions, I nevertheless look forward as a clear necessity to a new political entity, one that encompasses a whole world at peace. Though a religious sceptic, I find Christian imagery diffusing into my thoughts and dreams. I know from experience that newspapers distort and sentimentalize—but for years I carried in my billfold a newspaper clipping, a photograph of two dogs crossing a street. The clipping has disintegrated, but I still remember the caption:

> DOG'S BEST FRIEND—Flash, a blind greyhound, is led across a Southampton, England, street by his own "seeing eye" dog, a fox terrier named Peggy. The small dog's ability to serve as a guide for the greyhound has saved the latter from being destroyed by local authorities. Peggy, in turn, was saved from destruction several years ago by Mr. G. Corbin of Southampton. It is truly a new life for both dogs.

In short, I continue to believe, whatever the opposing evidence, in a universal brotherhood. Yet I have moved to a sparsely populated corner of a county in upstate New York, and I own nearly all the farm and woodlands surrounding my house. No poor farmer, no struggling graduate student, can build a shack or put in a trailer to disturb my view of the distant hills; and Cris, my son born in Kentucky, has already made "No Hunting" signs in his junior high print class to keep out those stout and fluorescent hunters from the city who clumsily commune with nature each deer season. Do these oppositions, as well as that related one between Jimski and Rodneyovitch, cancel each other out, leaving only the dry taste of irony as the heritage of the years since I lay in a field hospital in Germany?

Listen. When the cold spring rains ceased for a few days, my wife and I and our youngest son began to explore our new woods. Jimmy knows them so well that he will never be lost in them again. We found a grove of cedars, a stream full of rushing water from the still-melting snow, a deer trail leading down a slope into a glen that holds, in addition to a tiny field, cherry trees deformed by age—did a house once stand nearby?—and a marsh in which cattails grow. My wife cut red rags into strips so that, before the all-concealing leaves come out, we could mark the most accessible route for a path we will hack through the saplings in the long days of summer. The school bus had not yet brought our older sons home, so we left a note on the door telling them that if they wished to find us they would have to follow the strips of red cloth into the woods. We were in the glen in the center of the woods when we heard the first faint cries of Larry and Cris. We sat silently in a nest of dry weeds, listening to the nearby rush of the stream and the approaching sound of the boys as they crackled through the tangled underbrush toward us. Several burs were caught in my wife's graying hair. Our child's head barely protruded above the weeds; his eyes were round and glowing with the sense of our shared secret and with the expectancy that we would be found. For a moment I had the extraordinary sense of completion. I was a clear identity, a man of blood and soul, sitting with two of the people I loved and awaiting the other two. The glen did not become the center of the universe; from this secret navel no mystic cloak of unity moved out in waves to descend on every man and animal and tree here on earth or on the strange creatures sitting on their haunches or crawling across the vast plateaus of the dark and unknown planets circling Alpha Centauri. It was a limited victory, one that vanished as quickly as it came; but it was there, and worth the seeking. Between tasks more crucial to my survival, I can always hack a trail through my woods or re-read my Chekhov.

William Manchester

(b. 1922)

Shakespeare's soldier-hero Othello, his contentment poisoned by jealousy, bids a famous, moving farewell to all that he has known and loved: ". . . the neighing steed and the shrill trump / The spirit-stirring drum . . . / Pride, pomp, and circumstance of glorious war!" (III, iii). The magnificence of war, the glory of valor and triumph, fill much prose and poetry the world over. "As for me," writes William Manchester, a veteran of the bloody, drawn-out fight for Okinawa in the spring of 1945, "I could not reconcile that romanticized view of war that runs like a red streak through our literature . . . with the wet, green hell from which I had barely escaped." In Goodbye Darkness *(1979), his memoir of the Pacific war, and in his recent essay on "Okinawa: The Bloodiest Battle of All"* (New York Times, *1987), Manchester not only struggles to find an adequate perspective for what the essay calls "the central experience of my youth," but also to create a truthful language for conveying something as ultimate as a time in hell. The memoir portrays an American youth fervent with patriotism, when Manchester was still one of "the enchanted fighters." Until he actually experienced war, he thought that Hemingway's narratives described "the real thing"; only afterwards did he realize that they "simply replaced traditional overstatement with romantic understatement." "War," writes Manchester in* Goodbye Darkness, *"is never understated. Combat as I saw it was exorbitant, outrageous, excruciating. . . ." The sheer corporeal squalor and gore of battle must be told: how, in the rain-drenched struggle up Okinawa's Sugar Loaf Hill, men were "fighting and sleeping in one vast cesspool"; how a seven-inch Kabar knife soaks the killer "in the other man's gore." But mere squalor and gore can turn into sensationalism, and that, above all, is not part of Manchester's truth about what the war was like. His spare, fragmented narrative about the battle for Okinawa has moments of simple factual exposition ("My own regiment . . . lost more than 80 percent of the men who had landed on April 1, 1945"); eloquent moments of plain-spoken summary ("Killing by hand is hard work, and hot work"); sadly bitter retrospection ("Some of us found fighting rather different from what had been advertised"). In such a context, judgments carry a humbling conviction: "If all Americans understood the nature of battle, they might be vulnerable to the truth."*

Okinawa: The Bloodiest Battle of All

On Okinawa today, Flag Day will be observed with an extraordinary ceremony: two groups of elderly men, one Japanese, the other American, will gather for a solemn rite.

They could scarcely have less in common. Their motives are mirror images; each group honors the memory of men who tried to slay the men honored by those opposite them. But theirs is a common grief. After forty-two years the ache is still there. They are really united by death, the one great victor in modern war.

They have come to Okinawa to dedicate a lovely monument in remembrance of the Americans, Japanese and Okinawans killed there in the last and bloodiest battle of the Pacific war. More than 200,000 perished in the 82-day struggle—twice the number of Japanese lost at Hiroshima and more American blood than had been shed at Gettysburg. My own regiment—I was a sergeant in the 29th Marines—lost more than 80 percent of the men who had landed on April 1, 1945. Before the battle was over, both the Japanese and American commanding generals lay in shallow graves.

Okinawa lies 330 miles southwest of the southernmost Japanese island of Kyushu; before the war, it was Japanese soil. Had there been no atom bombs—and at that time the most powerful Americans, in Washington and at the Pentagon, doubted that the device would work—the invasion of the Nipponese homeland would have been staged from Okinawa, beginning with a landing on Kyushu to take place November 1. The six Marine divisions, storming ashore abreast, would lead the way. President Truman asked General Douglas MacArthur, whose estimates of casualties on the eve of battles had proved uncannily accurate, about Kyushu. The general predicted a million Americans would die in that first phase.

Given the assumption that nuclear weapons would contribute nothing to victory, the battle of Okinawa had to be fought. No one doubted the need to bring Japan to its knees. But some Americans came to hate the things we had to do, even when convinced that doing them was absolutely necessary; they had never understood the bestial, monstrous and vile means required to reach the objective—an unconditional Japanese surrender. As for me, I could not reconcile the romanticized view of war that runs like a red streak through our literature—and the glowing aura of selfless patriotism that had led us to put our lives at forfeit—with the wet, green hell from which I had barely escaped. Today, I understand. I was there, and was twice wounded. This is the story of what I knew and when I knew it.

To our astonishment, the Marine landing on April 1 was uncontested. The enemy had set a trap. Japanese strategy called first for kamikazes to destroy our fleet, cutting us off from supply ships; then Japanese troops would methodically annihilate the men stranded ashore using the trench-warfare tactics of World War I—cutting the Americans down as they charged heavily fortified positions. One hundred and ten thousand Japanese troops were waiting on the southern tip of the island. Intricate entrenchments, connected by tunnels, formed the enemy's defense line, which ran across the waist of Okinawa from the Pacific Ocean to the East China Sea.

By May 8, after more than five weeks of fighting, it became clear that the anchor of this line was a knoll of coral and volcanic ash, which the Marines christened Sugar Loaf Hill. My role in mastering it—the crest changed hands more than eleven times—was the central experience of my youth, and of all the military bric-a-brac that I put away after the war, I cherish most the Commendation from General Lemuel C. Shepherd, Jr., U.S.M.C., our splendid division commander, citing me for "gallantry in action and extraordinary achievement," adding, "Your courage was a constant source of inspiration . . . and your conduct throughout was in keeping with the highest tradition of the United States Naval Service."

The struggle for Sugar Loaf lasted ten days; we fought under the worst possible conditions—a driving rain that never seemed to slacken, day or night. (I remember wondering, in an idiotic moment—no man in combat is really sane—whether the battle could be called off, or at least postponed, because of bad weather.)

Newsweek called Sugar Loaf "the most critical local battle of the war." *Time* described a company of Marines—270 men—assaulting the hill. They failed; fewer than 30 returned. Fletcher Pratt, the military historian, wrote that the battle was unmatched in the Pacific war for "closeness and desperation." Casualties were almost unbelievable. In the 22d and 29th Marine regiments, two out of every three men fell. The struggle for the dominance of Sugar Loaf was probably the costliest engagement in the history of the Marine Corps. But by early evening on May 18, as night thickened over the embattled armies, the 29th Marines had taken Sugar Loaf, this time for keeps.

On Okinawa today, the ceremony will be dignified, solemn, seemly. It will also be anachronistic. If the Japanese dead of 1945 were resurrected to witness it, they would be appalled by the acceptance of defeat, the humiliation of their emperor—the very idea of burying Japanese near the barbarians from across the sea and then mourning them together. Americans, meanwhile, risen from their graves, would ponder the evolution of their own society, and might wonder, What ever happened to patriotism?

When I was a child, a bracket was screwed to the sill of a front attic window; its sole purpose was to hold the family flag. At first light, on all legal holidays—including Election Day, July 4, Memorial Day and, of course, Flag Day—I would scamper up to show it. The holidays remain, but mostly they mean long weekends.

In the late 1920s, during my childhood, the whole town of Attleboro, Massachusetts, would turn out to cheer the procession on Memorial Day. The policemen always came first, wearing their number-one uniforms and keeping perfect step. Behind them was a two-man vanguard—the mayor and, at his side, my father, hero of the 5th Marines and Belleau Wood, wearing his immaculate dress blues and looking like a poster of a Marine, with one magnificent flaw: the right sleeve of his uniform was empty. He had lost the arm in the Argonne. I now think that, as I watched him pass by, my own military future was already determined.

The main body of the parade was led by five or six survivors of the Civil War, too old to march but sitting upright in open Pierce-Arrows and Packards, wearing their blue uniforms and broad-brimmed hats. Then, in perfect step, came a contingent of men in their fifties, with their blanket rolls sloping diagonally from shoulder to hip—the Spanish-American War veterans. After these—and anticipated by a great roar from the crowd—came the doughboys of World War I, some still in their late twenties. They were acclaimed in part because theirs had been the most recent conflict, but also because they had fought in the war that—we then thought—had ended all wars.

Americans still march in Memorial Day parades, but attendance is light. One war has led to another and another and yet another, and the cruel fact is that few men, however they die, are remembered beyond the lifetimes of their closest relatives and friends. In the early 1940s, one of the forces that kept us on the line, under heavy enemy fire, was the conviction that this battle was of immense historical import, and that those of us who survived it would be forever cherished in the hearts of Americans. It was rather diminishing to return in 1945 and discover that your own parents couldn't even pronounce the names of the islands you had conquered.

But what of those who *do* remain faithful to patriotic holidays? What are they commemorating? Very rarely are they honoring what actually happened, because only a handful know, and it's not their favorite topic of conversation. In World War II, 16 million Americans entered the armed forces. Of these, fewer than a million saw action. Logistically, it took nineteen men to back up one man in combat. All who wore uniforms are called veterans, but more than 90 percent of them are as uninformed about the killing zones as those on the home front.

If all Americans understood the nature of battle, they might be vulnerable to truth. But the myths of warfare are embedded deep in our ancestral memories. By the time children have reached the age of awareness, they regard uniforms, decorations and Sousa marches as exalted, and those who argue otherwise are regarded as unpatriotic.

General MacArthur, quoting Plato, said: "Only the dead have seen the end of war." One hopes he was wrong, for war, as it had existed for over four thousand years, is now obsolete. As late as the spring of 1945, it was possible for one man, with a rifle, to make a difference, however infinitesimal, in the struggle to defeat an enemy who had attacked us and threatened our West Coast. The bomb dropped on Hiroshima made the man ludicrous, even pitiful. Soldiering has been relegated to Sartre's theater of the absurd. The image of the man as protector and defender of the home has been destroyed (and I suggest that that seed of thought eventually led women to re-examine their own role in society).

Until nuclear weapons arrived, the glorifying of militarism was the nation's hidden asset. Without it, we would almost certainly have been defeated by the Japanese, probably by 1943. In 1941 American youth was isolationist and pacifist. Then war planes from Imperial Japan destroyed our fleet at Pearl Harbor on December 7, and on December 8 recruiting stations were packed. Some of us later found fighting rather different from what had been advertised. Yet in combat these men risked their lives—and often lost them—in hope of winning medals. There is an old soldier's saying: "A man won't sell you his life, but he'll give it to you for a piece of colored ribbon."

Most of the men who hit the beaches came to scorn eloquence. They preferred the 130-year-old "Word of Cambronne." As dusk darkened the Waterloo battlefield, with the French in full retreat, the British sent word to General Pierre Cambronne, commander of the Old Guard. His position, they pointed out, was hopeless, and they suggested he capitulate. Every French textbook reports his reply as "The Old Guard dies but never surrenders." What he actually said was "*Merde.*"

If you mention this incident to members of the U.S. 101st Airborne Division, they will immediately understand. "Nuts" was not Brigadier General Anthony C. McAuliffe's answer to the Nazi demand that he hoist a white flag over Bastogne. Instead, he quoted Cambronne.

The character of combat has always been determined by the weapons available to men when their battles were fought. In the beginning they were limited to hand weapons—clubs, rocks, swords, lances. At the Battle of Camlann in 539, England's Arthur—a great warrior, not a king—led a charge that slew 930 Saxons, including their leader.

It is important to grasp the fact that those 930 men were not killed by snipers, grenades or shells. The dead were bludgeoned or stabbed to death, and we have a pretty good idea how this was done. One of the facts withheld from civilians during World War II was that Kabar fighting knives, with seven-inch blades honed to such precision that you could shave with them, were issued to Marines and that we were taught to use them. You never cut downward. You drove the point of your blade into a man's lower belly and ripped upward. In the process, you yourself became soaked in the other man's gore. After that charge at Camlann, Arthur must have been half drowned in blood.

The Battle of Agincourt, fought nearly one thousand years later, represented a slight technical advance: crossbows and long bows had appeared. All the same, Arthur would have recognized the battle. Like all engagements of the time, this one was short. Killing by hand is hard work, and hot work. It is so exhausting that even men in peak condition collapse once the issue of triumph or defeat is settled. And Henry V's spear carriers and archers were drawn from social classes that had been undernourished for as long as anyone could remember. The duration of medieval battles could have been measured in hours, even minutes.

The Battle of Waterloo, fought exactly four hundred years later, is another mater. By 1815, the Industrial Revolution had begun cranking out appliances of death, primitive by today's standards, but revolutionary for infantrymen of that time. And Napoleon had formed mass armies, pressing every available man into service. It was a long step toward total war, and its impact was immense. Infantrymen on both sides fought with single-missile weapons—muskets or rifles—and were supported by (and were the target of) artillery firing cannonballs.

The fighting at Waterloo continued for three days; for a given regiment, however, it usually lasted one full day, much longer than medieval warfare. A half century later, Gettysburg lasted three days and cost 43,497 men. Then came the marathon slaughters of 1914–1918, lasting as long as ten months (Verdun) and producing hundreds of thousands of corpses lying, as F. Scott Fitzgerald wrote afterward, "like a million bloody rugs." Winston Churchill, who had been a dashing young cavalry officer when Victoria was queen, said of the new combat: "War, which was cruel and magnificent, has become cruel and squalid."

It may be said that the history of war is one of men packed together, getting closer and closer to the ground and then deeper and deeper into it. In the densest combat of World War I, battalion frontage—the length of the line into which the 1,000-odd men were squeezed—had been 800 yards. On Okinawa, on the Japanese fortified line, it was less than 600 yards—about 18 inches per man. We were there and deadlocked for more than a week in the relentless rain. During those weeks we lost nearly 4,000 men.

And now it is time to set down what this modern battlefield was like.

All greenery had vanished; as far as one could see, heavy shellfire had denuded the scene of shrubbery. What was left resembled a cratered moonscape. But the craters were vanishing, because the rain had transformed the earth into a thin porridge—too thin even to dig foxholes. At night you lay on a poncho as a precaution against drowning during the barrages. All night, every night, shells erupted close enough to shake the mud beneath you at the rate of five or six a minute. You could hear the cries of the dying but could do nothing. Japanese infiltration was always imminent, so the order was to stay put. Any man who stood up was cut in half by machine guns manned by fellow Marines.

By day, the mud was hip deep; no vehicles could reach us. As you moved up the slope of the hill, artillery and mortar shells were bursting all around you, and, if you were fortunate enough to reach the top, you encountered the Japanese defenders, almost face to face, a few feet away. To me, they looked like badly wrapped brown paper parcels someone had soaked in a tub. Their eyes seemed glazed. So, I suppose, did ours.

Japanese bayonets were fixed; ours weren't. We used the knives, or, in my case, a .45 revolver and M1 carbine. The mud beneath our feet was deeply veined with blood. It was slippery. Blood is very slippery. So you skidded around, in deep shock, fighting as best you could until one side outnumbered the other. The outnumbered side would withdraw for reinforcements and then counterattack.

During those ten days I ate half a candy bar. I couldn't keep anything down. Everyone had dysentery, and this brings up an aspect of war even Robert Graves, Siegfried Sassoon, Edmund Blunden and Ernest Hemingway avoided. If you put more than a quarter million men in a line for three weeks, with no facilities for the disposal of human waste, you are going to confront a disgusting problem. We were fighting and sleeping in one vast cesspool. Mingled with that stench was another—the corrupt and corrupting odor of rotting human flesh.

My luck ran out on June 5, more than two weeks after we had taken Sugar Loaf Hill and killed the seven thousand Japanese soldiers defending it. I had suffered a slight gunshot wound above the right knee on June 2, and had rejoined my regiment to make an amphibious landing on Oroku Peninsula behind enemy lines. The next morning several of us were standing in a stone enclosure outside some Okinawan tombs when a six-inch rocket mortar shell landed among us.

The best man in my section was blown to pieces, and the slime of his viscera enveloped me. His body had cushioned the blow, saving my life; I still carry a piece of his shinbone in my chest. But I collapsed, and was left for dead. Hours later corpsmen found me still breathing, though blind and deaf, with my back and chest a junkpile of iron fragments—including, besides the piece of shinbone, four pieces of shrapnel too close to the heart to be removed. (They were not dangerous, a Navy surgeon assured me, but they still set off the metal detector at the Buffalo airport.)

Between June and November I underwent four major operations and was discharged as 100 percent disabled. But the young have strong recuperative powers. The blindness was caused by shock, and my vision returned. I grew new eardrums. In three years I was physically fit. The invisible wounds remain.

Most of those who were closest to me in the early 1940s had left New England campuses to join the Marines, knowing it was the most dangerous branch of the service. I remember them as bright, physically strong and inspired by an idealism and love of country they would have been too embarrassed to acknowledge. All of us despised the pompousness and pretentiousness of senior officers. It helped that, almost without exception, we admired and respected our commander in chief. But despite our enormous pride in being Marines, we saw through the scam that had lured so many of us to recruiting stations.

Once we polled a rifle company, asking each man why he had joined the Marines. A majority cited *To the Shores of Tripoli*, a marshmallow of a movie starring John Payne, Randolph Scott and Maureen O'Hara. Throughout the film the uniform of the day was dress blues; requests for liberty were always granted. The implication was that combat would be a lark, and when you returned, spangled with decorations, a Navy nurse like Maureen O'Hara would be waiting in your sack. It was peacetime again when John Wayne appeared on the silver screen as Sergeant Stryker in *Sands of Iwo Jima*, but that film underscores the point; I went to see it with another ex-Marine, and we were asked to leave the theater because we couldn't stop laughing.

After my evacuation from Okinawa, I had the enormous pleasure of seeing Wayne humiliated in person at Aiea Heights Naval Hospital in Hawaii. Only the most gravely wounded, the litter cases, were sent there. The hospital was packed, the halls lined with beds. Between Iwo Jima and Okinawa, the Marine Corps was being bled white.

Each evening, Navy corpsmen would carry litters down to the hospital theater so the men could watch a movie. One night they had a surprise for us. Before the film the curtains parted and out stepped John Wayne, wearing a cowboy outfit—ten-gallon hat, bandanna, checkered shirt, two pistols, chaps, boots and spurs. He grinned his aw-shucks grin, passed a hand over his face and said, "Hi ya, guys!" He was greeted by a stony silence. Then somebody booed. Suddenly everyone was booing.

This man was a symbol of the fake machismo we had come to hate, and we weren't going to listen to him. He tried and tried to make himself heard, but we drowned him out, and eventually he quit and left. If you liked *Sands of Iwo Jima*, I suggest you be careful. Don't tell it to the Marines.

And so we weren't macho. Yet we never doubted the justice of our cause. If we had failed—if we had lost Guadalcanal, and the Navy's pilots had lost the Battle of Midway—the Japanese would have invaded Australia and Hawaii, and California would have been in grave danger. In 1942 the possibility of an Axis victory was very real. It is possible for me to loathe war—and with reason—yet still honor the brave men, many of them boys, really, who fought with me and died beside me. I have been haunted by their loss these forty-two years, and I shall mourn them until my own death releases me. It does not seem too much to ask that they be remembered on one day each year. After all, they sacrificed their futures that you might have yours.

Yet I will not be on Okinawa for the dedication today. I would enjoy being with Marines; the ceremony will be moving, and we would be solemn, remembering our youth and the beloved friends who died there.

Few, if any, of the Japanese survivors agreed to attend the ceremony. However, Edward L. Fox, chairman of the Okinawa Memorial Shrine Committee, capped almost six years' campaigning for a monument when he heard about a former Japanese naval officer, Yoshio Yazaki—a meteorologist who had belonged to a four-thousand-man force led by Rear Admiral Minoru Ota—and persuaded him to attend.

On March 31, 1945, Yazaki-san had been recalled to Tokyo, and thus missed the battle of Okinawa. Ten week later—exactly forty-two years ago today—Admiral Ota and his men committed seppuku, killing themselves rather than face surrender. Ever since then Yazaki has been tormented by the thought that his comrades have joined their ancestors and he is here, not there.

Finding Yazaki was a great stroke of luck for Fox, for whom an Okinawa memorial had become an obsession. His own division commander tried to discourage him. The Japanese could hardly be expected to back a memorial on the site of their last great military defeat. But Yazaki made a solution possible.

If Yazaki can attend, why can't I? I played a role in the early stages of Buzz Fox's campaign and helped write the tribute to the Marines that is engraved on the monument. But when I learned that Japanese were also participating, I quietly withdrew. There are too many graves between us, too much gore, too many memories of too many atrocities.

In 1978, revisiting Guadalcanal, I encountered a Japanese businessman who had volunteered to become a kamikaze pilot in 1945 and was turned down at the last minute. Mutual friends suggested that we meet. I had expected no difficulty; neither, I think, did he. But when we confronted each other, we froze.

I trembled, suppressing the sudden, startling surge of primitive rage within. And I could see, from his expression, that this was difficult for him, too. Nations may make peace. It is harder for fighting men. On simultaneous impulse we both turned and walked away.

I set this down in neither pride nor shame. The fact is that some wounds never heal. Yazaki, unlike Fox, is dreading the ceremony. He does not expect to be shriven of his guilt. He knows he must be there but can't say why. Men are irrational, he explains, and adds that he feels very sad.

So do I, Yazaki-san, so do I.

James Baldwin

(1924–1987)

"I began to realize that I was in a country I knew nothing about, in the hands of people I did not understand at all." These words from "Equal in Paris" have a Kafkaesque ring, as does Baldwin's whole story of his eight-day entanglement in the pitiless, baffling, impersonal machinery of the French criminal-justice system. But the view of it is characteristically Baldwin's: "I began to realize . . ." opens the door to a mental world where experience is both personal and meaningful, where what hurts us and what helps us "cannot be divorced from each other" in the often anguishing movement "from one conundrum to the next." For Baldwin, experience and what one makes of it are at the heart of all that a writer has to say about himself and the world with which he must somehow come to terms—preferably as a lover but, in any case, as best he can. The artist's task is "to recreate out of the disorder of life that order which is art" ("Autobiographical Notes"). "Equal in Paris," originally published in Commentary, *became part of the artistic "order" that was Baldwin's first (and, some would say, greatest) book of essays,* Notes of a Native Son *(1955). Mostly dating from his life in Paris during the late 1940s and 1950s, these essays are concerned in one way or another with the relationship of the American, specifically the black American—ultimately Baldwin himself, as man and writer—to his personal and cultural past. What the American in Paris, black or white, has come "so blindly seeking" is his own identity—meaning, for Baldwin, "the terms on which he is related to his country, and to the world" ("A Question of Identity"). "I left America," he wrote some years after returning to it, "because I doubted my ability to survive the fury of the color problem there. . . . I wanted to find out in what way the* specialness *of my experience could be made to connect with other people instead of dividing them from me" ("The Discovery of What It Means to Be an American," 1959). The explanation offered in "Equal in Paris," an essay as sparing of explanation as it is absorbing in its narrative, is that he left his native land to escape the laughter of those "for whom the pain of living is not real." What Baldwin "realizes" by way of his Kafkaesque nightmare has to do with how deep and inescapable are the things that both connect and divide us.*

Equal in Paris

On the nineteenth of December, in 1949, when I had been living in Paris for a little over a year, I was arrested as a receiver of stolen goods and spent eight days in prison. My arrest came about through an American tourist whom I had met twice in New York, who had been given my name and address and told to look me up. I was then living on the top floor of a ludicrously grim hotel on the rue du Bac, one of those enormous dark, cold, and hideous establishments in which Paris abounds that seem to breathe forth, in their airless, humid, stone-cold halls, the weak light, scurrying chambermaids, and creaking stairs, an odor of gentility long long dead. The place was run by an ancient Frenchman dressed in an elegant black suit which was green with age, who cannot properly be described as bewildered or even as being in a state of shock, since he had really stopped breathing around 1910. There he sat at his desk in the weirdly lit, fantastically furnished lobby, day in and day out, greeting each one of his extremely impoverished and *louche*[1] lodgers with a stately inclination of the head that he had no doubt been taught in some impossibly remote time was the proper way for a *propriétaire* to greet his guests. If it had not been for his daughter, an extremely hardheaded *tricoteuse*[2]—the inclination of *her* head was chilling and abrupt, like the downbeat of an ax—the hotel would certainly have gone bankrupt long before. It was said that this old man had not gone farther than the door of his hotel for thirty years, which was not at all difficult to believe. He looked as though the daylight would have killed him.

I did not, of course, spend much of my time in this palace. The moment I began living in French hotels I understood the necessity of French cafés. This made it rather difficult to look me up, for as soon as I was out of bed I hopefully took notebook and fountain pen off to the upstairs room of the Flore, where I consumed rather a lot of coffee and, as evening approached, rather a lot of alcohol, but did not get much writing done. But one night, in one of the cafés of Saint Germain des Prés, I was discovered by this New Yorker and only because we found ourselves in Paris we immediately established the illusion that we had been fast friends back in the good old U.S.A. This illusion proved itself too thin to support an evening's drinking, but by that time it was too late. I had committed myself to getting him a room in my hotel the next day, for he was living in one of the nest of hotels near the Gare Saint Lazare, where, he said, the *propriétaire* was a thief, his wife a repressed

[1] Shady, suspicious.

[2] Literally, knitter. In this context, a real bruiser.

nymphomaniac, the chambermaids "pigs," and the rent a crime. Americans are always talking this way about the French and so it did not occur to me that he meant what he said or that he would take into his own hands the means of avenging himself on the French Republic. It did not occur to me, either, that the means which he *did* take could possibly have brought about such dire results, results which were not less dire for being also comic-opera.

It came as the last of a series of disasters which had perhaps been made inevitable by the fact that I had come to Paris originally with a little over forty dollars in my pockets, nothing in the bank, and no grasp whatever of the French language. It developed, shortly, that I had no grasp of the French character either. I considered the French an ancient, intelligent, and cultured race, which indeed they are. I did not know, however, that ancient glories imply, at least in the middle of the present century, present fatigue and, quite probably, paranoia; that there is a limit to the role of the intelligence in human affairs; and that no people come into possession of a culture without having paid a heavy price for it. This price they cannot, of course, assess, but it is revealed in their personalities and in their institutions. The very word "institutions," from my side of the ocean, where, it seemed to me, we suffered so cruelly from the lack of them, had a pleasant ring, as of safety and order and common sense; one had to come into contact with these institutions in order to understand that they were also outmoded, exasperating, completely impersonal, and very often cruel. Similarly, the personality which had seemed from a distance to be so large and free had to be dealt with before one could see that, if it was large, it was also inflexible and, for the foreigner, full of strange, high, dusty rooms which could not be inhabited. One had, in short, to come into contact with an alien culture in order to understand that a culture was not a community basket-weaving project, nor yet an act of God; was something neither desirable nor undesirable in itself, being inevitable, being nothing more or less than the recorded and visible effects on a body of people of the vicissitudes with which they had been forced to deal. And their great men are revealed as simply another of these vicissitudes, even if, quite against their will, the brief battle of their great men with them has left them richer.

When my American friend left his hotel to move to mine, he took with him, out of pique, a bedsheet belonging to the hotel and put it in his suitcase. When he arrived at my hotel I borrowed the sheet, since my own were filthy and the chambermaid showed no sign of bringing me any clean ones, and put it on my bed. The sheets belonging to *my* hotel I put out in the hall, congratulating myself on having thus forced on the attention of the Grand Hôtel du Bac the unpleasant state of its linen. Thereafter, since, as it turned out, we kept very different hours—I got up at noon, when, as I gathered by meeting him on the stairs one day, he was only just getting in—my new-found friend and I saw very little of each other.

On the evening of the nineteenth I was sitting thinking melancholy thoughts about Christmas and staring at the walls of my room. I imagine that I had sold something or that someone had sent me a Christmas present, for I remember that I had a little money. In those days in Paris, though I floated, so to speak, on a sea of acquaintances, I knew almost no one. Many people were eliminated from my orbit by virtue of the fact that they had more money than I did, which placed me, in my own eyes, in the humiliating role of a free-loader; and other people were eliminated by virtue of the fact that they enjoyed their poverty, shrilly insisting that this wretched round of hotel rooms, bad food, humiliating concierges, and unpaid bills was the Great Adventure. It couldn't, however, for me, end soon enough, this Great Adventure; there was a real question in my mind as to which would end soonest, the Great Adventure or me. This meant, however, that there were many evenings when I sat in my room, knowing that I couldn't work there, and not knowing what to do, or whom to see. On this particular evening I went down and knocked on the American's door.

There were two Frenchmen standing in the room, who immediately introduced themselves to me as policemen; which did not worry me. I had got used to policemen in Paris bobbing up at the most improbable times and places, asking to see one's *carte d'identité*. These policemen, however, showed very little interest in my papers. They were looking for something else. I could not imagine what this would be and, since I knew I certainly didn't have it, I scarcely followed the conversation they were having with my friend. I gathered that they were looking for some kind of gangster and since I wasn't a gangster and knew that gangsterism was not, insofar as he had one, my friend's style, I was sure that the two policemen would presently bow and say *Merci*, *messieurs*, and leave. For by this time, I remember very clearly, I was dying to have a drink and go to dinner.

I did not have a drink or go to dinner for many days after this, and when I did my outraged stomach promptly heaved everything up again. For now one of the policemen began to exhibit the most vivid interest in me and asked, very politely, if he might see my room. To which we mounted, making, I remember, the most civilized small talk on the way and even continuing it for some moments after we were in the room in which there was certainly nothing to be seen but the familiar poverty and disorder of that precarious group of people of whatever age, race, country, calling, or intention which Paris recognizes as *les étudiants* and sometimes, more ironically and precisely, as *les nonconformistes*. Then he moved to my bed, and in a terrible flash, not quite an instant before he lifted the bedspread, I understood what he was looking for. We looked at the sheet, on which I read, for the first time, lettered in the most brilliant scarlet I have ever seen, the name of the hotel from which it had been stolen. It was the first time the word *stolen* entered my mind. I had certainly seen the hotel monogram the day I put the sheet on the bed. It had simply meant nothing to me. In New York I had seen hotel monograms on everything from silver to soap and towels. Taking things from New York hotels was practically a custom, though, I suddenly realized, I had never known anyone to take a *sheet*. Sadly, and without a word to me, the inspector took the sheet from the bed, folded it under his arm, and we started back downstairs. I understood that I was under arrest.

And so we passed through the lobby, four of us, two of us very clearly criminal, under the eyes of the old man and his daughter, neither of whom said a word, into the streets where a light rain was falling. And I asked, in French, "But is this very serious?"

For I was thinking, it is, after all, only a sheet, not even new.

"No," said one of them. "It's not serious."

"It's nothing at all," said the other.

I took this to mean that we would receive a reprimand at the police station and be allowed to go to dinner. Later on I concluded that they were not being hypocritical or even trying to comfort us. They meant exactly what they said. It was only that they spoke another language.

In Paris everything is very slow. Also, when dealing with the bureaucracy, the man you are talking to is never the man you have to see. The man you have to see has just gone off to Belgium, or is busy with his family, or has just discovered that he is a cuckold; he will be in next Tuesday at three o'clock, or sometime in the course of the afternoon, or possibly tomorrow, or, possibly, in the next five minutes. But if he is coming in the next five minutes he will be far too busy to be able to see you today. So that I suppose I was not really astonished to learn at the commissariat that nothing could possibly be done about us before The Man arrived in the morning. But no, we could not go off and have dinner and come back in the morning. Of course he knew that we *would* come back—that was not the question. Indeed, there was no question: we would simply have to stay there for the night. We were placed in a cell which rather resembled a chicken coop. It was now about seven in the evening and I relinquished the thought of dinner and began to think of lunch.

I discouraged the chatter of my New York friend and this left me alone with my thoughts. I was beginning to be frightened and I bent all my energies, therefore, to keeping my panic under control. I began to realize that I was in a country I knew nothing about, in the hands of a people I did not understand at all. In a similar situation in New York I would have had some idea of what to do because I would have had some idea of what to expect. I am not speaking now of legality which, like most of the poor, I had never for an instant trusted, but of the temperament of the people with whom I had to deal. I had become very accomplished in New York at guessing and, therefore, to a limited extent manipulating to my advantage the reactions of the white world. But this was not New York. None of my old weapons could serve me here. I did not know what they saw when they looked at me. I knew very well what Americans saw when they looked at me and this allowed me to play endless and sinister variations on the role which they had assigned me; since I knew that it was, for them, of the utmost importance that they never be confronted with what, in their own personalities, made this role so necessary and gratifying to them, I knew that they could never call my hand or, indeed, afford to know what I was doing; so that I moved into every crucial situation with the deadly and rather desperate advantages of bitterly accumulated perception, of pride and contempt. This is an awful sword and shield to carry through the world, and the discovery that, in the game I was playing, I did myself a violence of which the world, at its most ferocious, would scarcely have been capable, was what had driven me out of New York. It was a strange feeling, in this situation, after a year in Paris, to discover that my weapons would never again serve me as they had.

It was quite clear to me that the Frenchmen in whose hands I found myself were no better or worse than their American counterparts. Certainly their uniforms frightened me quite as much, and their impersonality, and the threat, always very keenly felt by the poor, of violence, was as present in that commissariat as it had ever been for me in any police station. And I had seen, for example, what Paris policemen could do to Arab peanut vendors. The only difference here was that I did not understand these people, did not know what techniques their cruelty took, did not know enough about their personalities to see danger coming, to ward it off, did not know on what ground to meet it. That evening in the commissariat I was not a despised black man. They would simply have laughed at me if I had behaved like one. For them, I was an American. And here it was they who had the advantage, for that word, *Américain*, gave them some idea, far from inaccurate, of what to expect from me. In order to corroborate none of their ironical expectations I said nothing and did nothing—which was not the way any Frenchman, white or black, would have reacted. The question thrusting up from the bottom of my mind was not *what* I was, but *who*. And this question, since a *what* can get by with skill but a *who* demands resources, was my first real intimation of what humility must mean.

In the morning it was still raining. Between nine and ten o'clock a black Citroën took us off to the Ile de la Cité, to the great, gray Préfecture. I realize now that the questions I put to the various policemen who escorted us were always answered in such a way as to corroborate what I wished to hear. This was not out of politeness, but simply out of indifference—or, possibly, an ironical pity—since each of the policemen knew very well that nothing would speed or halt the machine in which I had become entangled. They knew I did not know this and there was certainly no point in their telling me. In one way or another I would certainly come out at the other side—for they also knew that being found with a stolen bedsheet in one's possession was not a crime punishable by the guillotine. (They had the advantage over me there, too, for there were certainly moments later on when I was not so sure.) If I did *not* come out at the other side—well, that was just too bad. So, to my question, put while we were in the Citroën—"Will it be over today?"—I received a "*Oui, bien sûr.*"[3] He was not lying. As it turned out, the *procès-verbal*[4] *was over that day. Trying to be realistic, I dismissed, in the Citroën, all thoughts of lunch and pushed my mind ahead to dinner.*

At the Préfecture we were first placed in a tiny cell, in which it was almost impossible either to sit or to lie down. After a couple of hours of this we were taken down to an office, where, for the first time, I encountered the owner of the bedsheet and where the *procès-verbal* took place. This was simply an interrogation, quite chillingly clipped and efficient (so that there was, shortly, no doubt in one's own mind that one *should* be treated as a criminal), which was recorded by a secretary. When it was over, this report was given to us to sign. One had, of course, no choice but to sign it, even though my mastery of written French was very far from certain. We were being held, according to the law in France, incommunicado, and all my angry demands to be allowed to speak to my embassy or to see a lawyer met with a stony "*Oui, oui. Plus tard.*[5] The *procès-verbal* over, we were taken back to the cell, before which, shortly, passed the owner of the bedsheet. He said he hoped we had slept well, gave a vindictive wink, and disappeared.

By this time there was only one thing clear: that we had no way of controlling the sequence of events and could not possibly guess what this sequence would be. It seemed to me, since what I regarded as the high point—the *procès-verbal*—had been passed and since the hotel-keeper was once again in possession of his sheet, that we might reasonably expect to

[3] Yes, of course.

[4] Police report, statement.

[5] Yes, yes, later.

be released from police custody in a matter of hours. We had been detained now for what would soon be twenty-four hours, during which time I had learned only that the official charge against me was *receleur*.[6] My mental shifting, between lunch and dinner, to say nothing of the physical lack of either of these delights, was beginning to make me *dizzy*. The steady chatter of my friend from New York, who was determined to keep my spirits up, made me feel murderous; I was praying that some power would release us from this freezing pile of stone before the impulse became the act. And I was beginning to wonder what was happening in that beautiful city, Paris, which lived outside these walls. I wondered how long it would take before anyone casually asked, "But where's Jimmy? He hasn't been around"—and realized, knowing the people I knew, that it would take several days.

Quite late in the afternoon we were taken from our cells; handcuffed, each to a separate officer; led through a maze of steps and corridors to the top of the building; fingerprinted; photographed. As in movies I had seen, I was placed against a wall, facing an old-fashioned camera, behind which stood one of the most completely cruel and indifferent faces I had ever seen, while someone next to me and, therefore, just outside my line of vision, read off in a voice from which all human feeling, even feeling of the most base description, had long since fled, what must be called my public characteristics—which, at that time and in that place, seemed anything but that. He might have been roaring to the hostile world secrets which I could barely, in the privacy of midnight, utter to myself. But he was only reading off my height, my features, my approximate weight, my color—that color which, in the United States, had often, odd as it may sound, been my salvation—the color of my hair, my age, my nationality. A light then flashed, the photographer and I staring at each other as though there was murder in our hearts, and then it was over. Handcuffed again, I was led downstairs to the bottom of the building, into a great enclosed shed in which had been gathered the very scrapings off the Paris streets. Old, old men, so ruined and old that life in them seemed really to prove the miracle of the quickening power of the Holy Ghost—for clearly their life was no longer their affair, it was no longer even their burden, they were simply the clay which had once been touched. And men not so old, with faces the color of lead and the consistency of oatmeal, eyes that made me think of stale *café-au-lait* spiked with arsenic, bodies which could take in food and water—any food and water—and pass it out, but which could not do anything more, except possibly, at midnight, along the riverbank where rats scurried, rape. And young men, harder and crueler than the Paris

[6] Receiver (of stolen goods).

stones, older by far than I, their chronological senior by some five to seven years. And North Africans, old and young, who seemed the only living people in this place because they yet retained the grace to be bewildered. But they were not bewildered by being in this shed: they were simply bewildered because they were no longer in North Africa. There was a great hole in the center of this shed which was the common toilet. Near it, though it was impossible to get very far from it, stood an old man with white hair, eating a piece of camembert. It was at this point, probably, that thought, for me, stopped, that physiology, if one may say so, took over. I found myself incapable of saying a word, not because I was afraid I would cry but because I was afraid I would vomit. And I did not think any longer of the city of Paris but my mind flew back to that home from which I had fled. I was sure that I would never see it anymore. And it must have seemed to me that my flight from home was the cruelest trick I had ever played on myself, since it had led me here, down to a lower point than any I could ever in my life have imagined—lower, far, than anything I had seen in that Harlem which I had so hated and so loved, the escape from which had soon become the greatest direction of my life. After we had been here an hour or so a functionary came and opened the door and called out our names. And I was sure that *this* was my release. But I was handcuffed again and led out of the Préfecture into the street—it was dark now, it was still raining—and before the steps of the Préfecture stood the great police wagon, doors facing me, wide open. The handcuffs were taken off, I entered the wagon, which was peculiarly constructed. It was divided by a narrow aisle, and on each side of the aisle was a series of narrow doors. These doors opened on a narrow cubicle, beyond which was a door which opened onto another narrow cubicle: three or four cubicles, each private, with a locking door. I was placed in one of them; I remember there was a small vent just above my head which let in a little light. The door of my cubicle was locked from the outside. I had no idea where this wagon was taking me and, as it began to move, I began to cry. I suppose I cried all the way to prison, the prison called Fresnes, which is twelve kilometers outside of Paris.

For reasons I have no way at all of understanding, prisoners whose last initial is A, B, or C are always sent to Fresnes; everybody else is sent to a prison called, rather cynically it seems to me, La Santé. I will, obviously, never be allowed to enter La Santé, but I was told by people who certainly seemed to know that it was infinitely more unbearable than Fresnes. This arouses in me, until today, a positive storm of curiosity concerning what I promptly began to think of as The Other Prison. My colleague in crime, occurring lower in the alphabet, had been sent there and I confess that the minute he was gone I missed him. I missed him because he was not French and because he was the only person in the world who knew that the story I told was true.

For, once locked in, divested of shoelaces, belt, watch, money, papers, nailfile, in a freezing cell in which both the window and the toilet were broken, with six other adventurers, the story I told of *l'affaire du drap de lit*[7] elicited only the wildest amusement or the most suspicious disbelief. Among the people who shared my cell the first three days no one, it is true, had been arrested for anything much more serious—or, at least, not serious in my eyes. I remember that there was a boy who had stolen a knitted sweater from a *monoprix*,[8] who would probably, it was agreed, receive a six-month sentence. There was an older man there who had been arrested for some kind of petty larceny. There were two North Africans, vivid, brutish, and beautiful, who alternated between gaiety and fury, not at the fact of their arrest but at the state of the cell. None poured as much emotional energy into the fact of their arrest as I did; they took it, as I would have liked to take it, as simply another unlucky happening in a very dirty world. For, though I had grown accustomed to thinking of myself as looking upon the world with a hard, penetrating eye, the truth was that they were far more realistic about the world than I, and more nearly right about it. The gap between us, which only a gesture I made could have bridged, grew steadily, during thirty-six hours, wider. I could not make any gesture simply because they frightened me. I was unable to accept my imprisonment as a fact, even as a temporary fact. I could not, even for a moment, accept my present companions as *my* companions. And they, of course, felt this and put it down, with perfect justice, to the fact that I was an American.

There was nothing to do all day long. It appeared that we would one day come to trial but no one knew when. We were awakened at seven-thirty by a rapping on what I believe is called the Judas, that small opening in the door of the cell which allows the guards to survey the prisoners. At this rapping we rose from the floor—we slept on straw pallets and each of us was covered with one thin blanket—and moved to the door of the cell. We peered through the opening into the center of the prison, which was, as I remember, three tiers high, all gray stone and gunmetal steel, precisely that prison I had seen in movies, except that, in the movies, I had not known that it was cold in prison. I had not known that when one's shoelaces and belt have been removed one is, in the strangest way, demoralized. The necessity of shuffling and the necessity of holding up one's trousers with one hand turn one into a rag doll. And the movies fail, of course, to give one any idea of what prison food is like.

[7] This business with the bedsheets.

[8] Department store for inexpensive items.

Along the corridor, at seven-thirty, came three men, each pushing before him a great garbage can, mounted on wheels. In the garbage can of the first was the bread—this was passed to one through the small opening in the door. In the can of the second was the coffee. In the can of the third was what was always called *la soupe*, a pallid paste of potatoes which had certainly been bubbling on the back of the prison stove long before that first, so momentous revolution. Naturally, it was cold by this time and, starving as I was, I could not eat it. I drank the coffee—which was not coffee—because it was hot, and spent the rest of the day, huddled in my blanket, munching on the bread. It was not the French bread one bought in bakeries. In the evening the same procession returned. At ten-thirty the lights went out. I had a recurring dream, each night, a nightmare which always involved my mother's fried chicken. At the moment I was about to eat it came the rapping at the door. Silence is really all I remember of those first three days, silence and the color gray.

I am not sure now whether it was on the third or the fourth day that I was taken to trial for the first time. The days had nothing, obviously, to distinguish them from one another. I remember that I was very much aware that Christmas Day was approaching and I wondered if I was really going to spend Christmas Day in prison. And I remember that the first trial came the day before Christmas Eve.

On the morning of the first trial I was awakened by hearing my name called. I was told, hanging in a kind of void between my mother's fried chicken and the cold prison floor, "*Vous préparez. Vous êtes extrait*"[9]—which simply terrified me, since I did not know what interpretation to put on the word "*extrait*," and since my cellmates had been amusing themselves with me by telling terrible stories about the inefficiency of French prisons, an inefficiency so extreme that it had often happened that someone who was supposed to be taken out and tried found himself on the wrong line and was guillotined instead. The best way of putting my reaction to this is to say that, though I knew they were teasing me, it was simply not possible for me to totally *dis*believe them. As far as I was concerned, once in the hands of the law in France, anything could happen. I shuffled along with the others who were *extrait* to the center of the prison, trying, rather, to linger in the office, which seemed the only warm spot in the whole world, and found myself again in that dreadful wagon, and was carried again to the Ile de la Cité, this time to the Palais de Justice. The entire day, except for ten minutes, was spent in one of the cells, first waiting to be tried, then waiting to be taken back to prison.

[9] Get ready. You're being released.

For I was *not* tried that day. By and by I was handcuffed and led through the halls, upstairs to the courtroom where I found my New York friend. We were placed together, both stage-whisperingly certain that this was the end of our ordeal. Nevertheless, while I waited for our case to be called, my eyes searched the courtroom, looking for a face I knew, hoping, anyway, that there was someone there who knew *me*, who would carry to someone outside the news that I was in trouble. But there was no one I knew there and I had had time to realize that there was probably only one man in Paris who could help me, an American patent attorney for whom I had worked as an office boy. He could have helped me because he had a quite solid position and some prestige and would have testified that, while working for him, I had handled large sums of money regularly, which made it rather unlikely that I would stoop to trafficking in bedsheets. However, he was somewhere in Paris, probably at this very moment enjoying a snack and a glass of wine and as far as the possibility of reaching him was concerned, he might as well have been on Mars. I tried to watch the proceedings and to make my mind a blank. But the proceedings were not reassuring. The boy, for example, who had stolen the sweater *did* receive a six-month sentence. It seemed to me that all the sentences meted out that day were excessive, though, again, it seemed that all the people who were sentenced that day had made, or clearly were going to make, crime their career. This seemed to be the opinion of the judge, who scarcely looked at the prisoners or listened to them; it seemed to be the opinion of the prisoners, who scarcely bothered to speak in their own behalf; it seemed to be the opinion of the lawyers, state lawyers for the most part, who were defending them. The great impulse of the courtroom seemed to be to put these people where they could not be seen—and not because they were offended at the crimes, unless, indeed, they were offended that the crimes were so petty, but because they did not wish to know that their society could be counted on to produce, probably in greater and greater numbers, a whole body of people for whom crime was the only possible career. Any society inevitably produces its criminals, but a society at once rigid and unstable can do nothing whatever to alleviate the poverty of its lowest members, cannot present to the hypothetical young man at the crucial moment that so-well-advertised right path. And the fact, perhaps, that the French are the earth's least sentimental people and must also be numbered among the most proud aggravates the plight of their lowest, youngest, and unluckiest members, for it means that the idea of rehabilitation is scarcely real to them. I confess that this attitude on their part raises in me sentiments of exasperation, admiration, and despair, revealing as it does, in both the best and the worst sense, their renowned and spectacular hard-headedness.

Finally our case was called and we rose. We gave our names. At the point that it developed that we were American the proceedings ceased, a hurried consultation took place between the judge and what I took to be several lawyers. Someone called out for an interpreter. The arresting officer had forgotten to mention our nationalities and there was, therefore, no interpreter in the court. Even if our French had been better than it was we would not have been allowed to stand trial without an interpreter. Before I clearly understood what was happening, I was handcuffed again and led out of the courtroom. The trial had been set back for the twenty-seventh of December.

I have sometimes wondered if I would *ever* have got out of prison if it had not been for the older man who had been arrested for the mysterious petty larceny. He was acquitted that day and when he returned to the cell—for he could not be released until morning—he found me sitting numbly on the floor, having just been prevented, by the sight of a man, all blood, being carried back to *his* cell on a stretcher, from seizing the bars and screaming until they let me out. The sight of the man on the stretcher proved, however, that screaming would not do much for me. The petty-larceny man went around asking if he could do anything in the world outside for those he was leaving behind. When he came to me I, at first, responded, "No, nothing"—for I suppose I had by now retreated into the attitude, the earliest I remember, that of my father, which was simply (since I had lost his God) that nothing could help me. And I suppose I will remember with gratitude until I die the fact that the man now insisted: "*Mais, êtes-vous sûr?*"[10] Then it swept over me that he was going *outside* and he instantly became my first contact since the Lord alone knew how long with the outside world. At the same time, I remember, I did not really believe that he would help me. There was no reason why he should. But I gave him the phone number of my attorney friend and my own name.

So, in the middle of the next day, Christmas Eve, I shuffled downstairs again, to meet my visitor. He looked extremely well fed and sane and clean. He told me I had nothing to worry about anymore. Only not even he could do anything to make the mill of justice grind any faster. He would, however, send me a lawyer of his acquaintance who would defend me on the 27th, and he would himself, along with several other people, appear as a character witness. He gave me a package of Lucky Strikes (which the turnkey took from me on the way upstairs) and said that, though it was doubtful that there would be any celebration in the prison, he would see to it that I got a fine Christmas dinner when I got out. And this, somehow, seemed very funny. I remember being aston-

[10] But are you sure?

ished at the discovery that I was actually laughing. I was, too, I imagine, also rather disappointed that my hair had not turned white, that my face was clearly not going to bear any marks of tragedy, disappointed at bottom, no doubt, to realize, facing him in that room, that far worse things had happened to most people and that, indeed, to paraphrase my mother, if this was the worst thing that ever happened to me I could consider myself among the luckiest people ever to be born. He injected—my visitor—into my solitary nightmare common sense, the world, and the hint of blacker things to come.

The next day, Christmas, unable to endure my cell, and feeling that, after all, the day demanded a gesture, I asked to be allowed to go to Mass, hoping to hear some music. But I found myself, for a freezing hour and a half, locked in exactly the same kind of cubicle as in the wagon which had first brought me to prison, peering through a slot placed at the level of the eye at an old Frenchman, hatted, overcoated, muffled, and gloved, preaching in this language which I did not understand, to this row of wooden boxes, the story of Jesus Christ's love for men.

The next day, the twenty-sixth, I spent learning a peculiar kind of game, played with matchsticks, with my cellmates. For, since I no longer felt that I would stay in this cell forever, I was beginning to be able to make peace with it for a time. On the twenty-seventh I went again to trial and, as had been predicted, the case against us was dismissed. The story of the *drap de lit*, finally told, caused great merriment in the courtroom, whereupon my friend decided that the French were "great." I was chilled by their merriment, even though it was meant to warm me. It could only remind me of the laughter I had often heard at home, laughter which I had sometimes deliberately elicited. This laughter is the laughter of those who consider themselves to be at a safe remove from all the wretched, for whom the pain of the living is not real. I had heard it so often in my native land that I had resolved to find a place where I would never hear it anymore. In some deep, black, stony, and liberating way, my life, in my own eyes, began during that first year in Paris, when it was borne in on me that this laughter is universal and never can be stilled.

Russell Baker

(b. 1925)

A few years ago, in a colloquium on the art of writing memoirs, the author of Growing Up *said, "Writers have to cultivate the habit early in life of listening to people other than themselves"* (Inventing the Truth, 1987). *His "Observer" column in the* New York Times, *begun in 1962, puts to regular use a confirmed habit of keeping ears—and eyes—open; "three times a week . . . grinding out a hundred thousand words a year," Baker has been compiling his wry chronicle of "the general public squalor into which the Republic is settling," the surreal goings-on of a society where nothing, it seems, can any longer outrage or shock. ("We are gathered at home to watch the end of the world on television. . . ," begins an "Observer" piece called "O Zone.") Above all, he has had fun with and made fun of the way we talk and what it says about our state of mind, everything from Washington's "Politigabble" with its evasions and its double-speak to our mass immersion, verbal and spiritual, in the myths of advertising. His language mimics and reflects back to us our degraded ideals: "man is endowed . . . with certain inalienable rights, and among these are expressways, television and the pursuit of credit." Light, witty, funny, tongue-in-cheek, humane, Baker's Observer goes through a long line of periodical essayists, straight back to Addision's Spectator. Though his irony is not of the lacerating Swiftian kind, it serves the same deeply serious ends: to expose folly and evil, to impel change. Something, though, gets in the way nowadays: "The distinction," Baker says, "between being serious and being solemn seems to be vanishing among Americans, just as surely as the distinction between "now" and "presently" and the distinction between liberty and making a mess." Mistaking solemnity for seriousness, the modern satirist's audience may no longer be attuned to satire's peculiar way of being serious: its use of ironic indirection for something more than humorous effect. In "The Flag"* (So This is Depravity, *1980), irony and humor work to expose our near-sacred national symbol as "the proud standard of the greatest men's club on earth." Baker doesn't shy away from implicating himself in the general chauvinistic hoopla; he turns his own fantasies into a butt of humor and a vehicle of satire.*

The Flag

At various times when young, I was prepared to crack skulls, kill and die for Old Glory. I never wholly agreed with the LOVE IT OR LEAVE IT bumper stickers, which held that everybody who didn't love the flag ought to be thrown out of the country, but I wouldn't have minded seeing them beaten up. In fact, I saw a man come very close to being beaten up at a baseball park one day because he didn't stand when they raised the flag in the opening ceremonies, and I joined the mob screaming for him to get to his feet like an American if he didn't want lumps all over his noodle. He stood up, all right. I was then thirteen, and a Boy Scout, and I knew you never let the flag touch the ground, or threw it out with the trash when it got dirty (you burned it), or put up with disrespect for it at the baseball park.

At eighteen, I longed to die for it. When World War II ended in 1945 before I could reach the combat zone, I moped for months about being deprived of the chance to go down in flames under the guns of a Mitsubishi Zero. There was never much doubt that I would go down in flames if given the opportunity, for my competence as a pilot was such that I could barely remember to lower the plane's landing gear before trying to set it down on a runway.

I had even visualized my death. It was splendid. Dead, I would be standing perhaps 4,000 feet up in the sky. (Everybody knew that heroes floated in those days.) Erect and dashing, surrounded by beautiful cumulus clouds, I would look just as good as ever, except for being slightly transparent. And I would smile, devil-may-care, at the camera—oh, there would be cameras there—and the American flag would unfurl behind me across 500 miles of glorious American sky, and back behind the cumulus clouds the Marine Band would be playing "The Stars and Stripes Forever," but not too fast.

Then I would look down at June Allyson and the kids, who had a gold star in the window and brave smiles shining through their tears, and I would give them a salute and one of those brave, wistful Errol Flynn grins, then turn and mount to Paradise, becoming more transparent with each step so the audience could get a great view of the flag waving over the heavenly pastures.

Okay, so it owes a lot to Louis B. Mayer in his rococo period. I couldn't help that. At eighteen, a man's imagination is too busy with sex to have much energy left for fancy embellishments of patriotic ecstasy. In the words of a popular song of the period, there was a star-spangled banner waving somewhere in The Great Beyond, and only Uncle Sam's brave heroes got to go there. I was ready to make the trip.

All this was a long time ago, and, asinine though it now may seem, I confess it here to illustrate the singularly masculine pleasures to be enjoyed in devoted service to the Stars and Stripes. Not long ago I felt a twinge of the old fire when I saw an unkempt lout on a ferryboat with a flag sewed in the crotch of his jeans. Something in me wanted to throw him overboard, but I didn't since he was a big muscular devil and the flag had already suffered so many worse indignities anyhow, having been pinned in politicians' lapels, pasted on cars to promote gasoline sales and used to sanctify the professional sports industry as the soul of patriotism even while the team owners were instructing their athletes in how to dodge the draft.

For a moment, though, I felt some of the old masculine excitement kicked up by the flag in the adrenal glands. It's a man's flag, all right. No doubt about that. Oh, it may be a scoundrel's flag, too, and a drummer's flag, and a fraud's flag, and a thief's flag. But first and foremost, it is a man's flag.

Except for decorating purposes—it looks marvelous on old New England houses—I cannot see much in it to appeal to women. Its pleasures, in fact, seem so exclusively masculine and its sanctity so unassailable by feminist iconoclasts that it may prove to be America's only enduring, uncrushable male sex symbol.

Observe that in my patriotic death fantasy, the starring role is not June Allyson's, but mine. As defender of the flag, I am able to leave a humdrum job, put June and the kids with all their humdrum problems behind me, travel the world with a great bunch of guys, do exciting things with powerful flying machines, and, fetchingly uniformed, strut exotic saloons on my nights off.

In the end, I walk off with all the glory and the big scene.

And what does June get? Poor June. She gets to sit home with the kids the rest of her life dusting my photograph and trying to pay the bills, with occasional days off to visit the grave.

No wonder the male pulse pounds with pleasure when the Stars and Stripes comes fluttering down the avenue with the band smashing out those great noises. Where was Mrs. Teddy Roosevelt when Teddy was carrying it up San Juan Hill? What was Mrs. Lincoln doing when Abe was holding it aloft for the Union? What was Martha up to while George Washington was carrying it across the Delaware? Nothing, you may be sure, that was one-tenth as absorbing as what their husbands were doing.

Consider some of the typical masculine activities associated with Old Glory: Dressing up in medals. Whipping cowards, slackers and traitors within an inch of their miserable lives. Conquering Mount Suribachi. Walking on the moon. Rescuing the wagon train. Being surrounded by the whole German Army and being asked to surrender and saying, "You can tell Schicklgruber my answer is 'Nuts.' " In brief, having a wonderful time. With the boys.

Yes, surely the American flag is the ultimate male sex symbol. Men flaunt it, wave it, punch noses for it, strut with it, fight for it, kill for it, die for it.

And women—? Well, when do you see a woman with the flag? Most commonly when she is wearing black and has just received it, neatly folded, from coffin of husband or son. Later, she may wear it to march in the Veterans Day parade, widows' division.

Male pleasures and woman's sorrow—it sounds like the old definition of sex. Yet these are the immemorial connotations of the flag, and women, having shed the whalebone girdle and stamped out the stag bar, nevertheless accept it, ostensibly at least, with the same emotional devotion that men accord it.

There are good reasons, of course, why they may be reluctant to pursue logic to its final step and say, "To hell with the flag, too." In the first place, it would almost certainly do them no good. Men hold all the political trumps in this matter. When little girls first toddle off to school, does anyone tell them the facts of life when they stand to salute the flag? Does anyone say, "You are now saluting the proud standard of the greatest men's club on earth?" You bet your chewing gum nobody tells them that. If anyone did, there would be a joint session of Congress presided over by the President of the United States to investigate the entire school system of the United States of America.

What little girls have drilled into them is that the flag stands for one nation indivisible, with liberty and justice for all. A few years ago, the men of the Congress, responding to pressure from the American Legion (all men) and parsons (mostly all men), all of whom sensed perhaps that women were not as gullible as they used to be, revised the Pledge of Allegiance with words intimating that it would be ungodly not to respect the flag. The "one nation indivisible" became one nation *under God*, indivisible," and another loophole for skeptics was sealed off. The women's movement may be brave, but it will not go far taking on national indivisibility, liberty, justice and God, all in one fight. If they tried it, a lot of us men would feel perfectly justified in raising lumps on their lovely noodles.

Philosophically speaking, the masculinity of the American flag is entirely appropriate. America, after all, is not a motherland—many places still are—but a fatherland, which is to say a vast nation-state of disparate people scattered over great distances, but held together by a belligerent, loyalty-to-the-death devotion to some highly abstract political ideas.

Since these ideas are too complex to be easily grasped, statesmen have given us the flag and told us it sums up all these noble ideas that make us a country.

Fatherland being an aggressive kind of state, the ideas it embodies must be defended, protected and propagated, often in blood. Since the flag is understood to represent these ideas, in a kind of tricolor shorthand, we emote, fight, bleed and rejoice in the name of the flag.

Before fatherland there was something that might be called motherland. It still exists here and there. In the fifties, when Washington was looking for undiscovered Asiatic terrain to save from un-American ideologies, somebody stumbled into an area called Laos, a place so remote from American consciousness that few had ever heard its name pronounced. (For the longest time, Lyndon Johnson, then Democratic leader of the Senate, referred to it as "Low Ass.") Federal inspectors sent to Laos returned with astonishing information. Most of the people living there were utterly unaware that they were living in a country. Almost none of them knew the country they were living in was called Laos. All they knew was that they lived where they had been born and where their ancestors were buried.

What Washington had discovered, of course, was an old-fashioned motherland, a society where people's loyalties ran to the place of their birth. It was a Pentagon nightmare. Here were these people, perfectly happy with their home turf and their ancestors' graves, and they had to be put into shape to die for their country, and they didn't even know they had a country to die for. They didn't even have a flag to die for. And yet, they were content!

The point is that a country is only an idea and a fairly modern one at that. Life would still be going on if nobody had ever thought of it, and would probably be a good deal more restful. No flags. Not much in the way of armies. No sharing of exciting group emotions with millions of other people ready to do or die for national honor. And so forth. Very restful, and possibly very primitive, and almost surely very nasty on occasion, although possibly not as nasty as occasions often become when countries disagree.

I hear my colleagues in masculinity protesting, "What? No country? No flag? But there would be nothing noble to defend, to fight for, to die for, in the meantime having a hell of a good time doing all those fun male things in the name of!"

Women may protest, too. I imagine some feminists may object to the suggestion that fatherland's need for prideful, warlike and aggressive citizens to keep the flag flying leaves women pretty much out of things. Those who hold that sexual roles are a simple matter of social conditioning may contend that the flag can offer the same rollicking pleasures to both sexes once baby girls are trained as thoroughly as baby boys in being prideful, warlike and aggressive.

I think there may be something in this, having seen those harridans who gather outside freshly desegregated schools to wave the American flag and terrify children. The question is whether women really want to start conditioning girl babies for this hitherto largely masculine sort of behavior, or spend their energies trying to decondition it out of the American man.

In any case, I have no quarrel with these women. Living in a fatherland, they have tough problems, and if they want to join the boys in the flag sports, it's okay with me. The only thing is, if they are going to get a chance, too, to go up to Paradise with the Marine Band playing "The Stars and Stripes Forever" back behind the cumulus clouds, I don't want to be stuck with the role of sitting home dusting their photographs the rest of my life after the big scene is ended.

Margaret Laurence

(1926–1987)

Born in the Canadian prarie town of Neepawa, Margaret Laurence spent her first twenty-three years in Manitoba province, then moved to Africa for seven years, then to England for ten, and finally back to Canada, this time to a small town "Down East" in Ontario. These biographical data were, for her, indices of her quest for the place where she belonged and that belonged to her. Of Neepawa, she writes, "My eyes were formed there." And "Everything is to be found in a town like mine. . . I did not know then that I would carry the land and town all my life within my skull, that they would form the mainspring and source of the writing I was to do" ("Where the World Began"). From her African experience came the influence of writers who "recreate their people's past in novels and plays in order to recover a sense of themselves"; from Africa, too, came the "necessary distancing," the resistance to "total identification" that she found she needed to portray character without being "too prejudiced and distorted by closeness." Her first novels and stories are about Africa; but, she writes, "I always knew that one day I would have to . . . go back to my own people, my own place of belonging" ("A Place to Stand On"). During her ten years at Elm Cottage in Buckinghamshire, England, with frequent visits to Canada, she did indeed return fictionally to her prairie hometown in her "Manawaka" novels. "It is as though in my fiction," she has observed, "I knew exactly where to go, but in my life I didn't, as yet" (Headnote, "Road from the Isles"). Long before her life caught up with her fiction, long before her "long journey back home" ended, Africa was functioning for her as a place of liberation from that very home, a first fascinating release from the life view dominating her Canadian hometown. Her earliest published essay, "The Very Best Intentions" (1964, Heart of a Stranger), *records her friendship with a Ghanaian man, a relationship formed and sustained despite cultural differences—an exploration of "those strange lands of the heart and spirit" by a "small-town prairie person" (Foreword,* Heart of a Stranger) *unwilling to settle into the parochialism of place.*

The Very Best Intentions

"Come in," Mensah said, making it sound like "Stay out."

The bungalow was small and whitewashed, overgrown with purple bougainvillaea and surrounded by pawpaw trees and giant clusters of canna lilies. The low wall around the garden gave the feeling of privacy, if not the reality. Outside, the streets buzzed and clanged with voices and bicycles, and the air was heavy with the rich cloying smell of plantains being fried in palm oil, as the trader women beside their roadside stalls blew and stirred at the red coals of their charcoal pots. This was Ghana, five years before Independence. We had come here to live because my husband, a civil engineer, was working on the new harbour at Tema, which would at last provide the capital city of Accra with an adequate port.

"Will you have tea?" Mensah enquired, waving us to chairs.

Mensah was a young barrister. We had friends in common in London, so we had decided to look him up. Now I wondered if we had not made a mistake.

"If you're busy—" I faltered, expecting and hoping that he would make the conventional response, "No, no, of course not—do stay—"

Instead he said, "Busy? Africans are never busy. Didn't you know? It is because we are such an indolent people."

As I protested, embarrassed, Mensah laughed. At the time I naively imagined that he took us to be sahib-type Europeans, and I was frantic to correct his wrong impression. Later, however—several years later—I came to see that what he really dreaded was an encounter with yet another set of white liberals who went around collecting African acquaintances as though they were rare postage stamps. And now, at this further distance, I am not at all sure that I was not doing precisely that.

Because I lived in Ghana for five years, I am often asked what Ghanaians are like. I am always tempted to reply that it depends upon which Ghanaian you mean. West Africans, in popular mythological terms, are easy-going, extroverted people who have a marvellous sense of rhythm and who can dance to *highlife* music like jazzed-up angels because it is simply born in them, something to do with the genes, perhaps. Mensah was the antithesis of this stereotyped image. He was tense as strained wire, introspective, meticulously neat, quick and even abrupt in his movements, and he would have scorned to dance *highlife* even if the salvation of his soul had depended upon it.

How our acquaintance ever survived those first few thorny years, I do not know. In the days when I first met Mensah, I still wore my militant liberalism like a heart on my sleeve. He was one of the first well-educated Africans whom I had met, and I was anxious to impress upon him not only my sympathy with African independence but also my keen appreciation of various branches of African culture—African sculpture, African literature, African traditions and proverbs. Mensah, however, as it turned out, couldn't have cared less about the African culture of the past. Strangely enough, it took me some time to realize that this represented only his own point of view and that all Africans did not necessarily think the same way. Our initial conversations were ridiculous and also (to me, anyway) painful, because whatever I happened to say always seemed to be the wrong thing.

I showed him an ebony head I had bought from a Hausa trader.

"Look—isn't this terrific? It's wonderful to see that carving is still flourishing in West Africa."

Mensah laughed disdainfully. "That? It's trash. They grind them out by the thousands. Europeans like that sort of thing, I suppose."

Both of us were exaggerating, trying to make some planned effect. I still have that carved ebony head. Now it seems neither as gorgeous as I claimed nor as awful as he said.

Mensah often employed shock treatment in talk. Once when I was extolling African drumming, telling him about a Yam Festival we had attended, and how the chief's drummer had played the *Ntumpane*, the great talking drums, Mensah clenched his hands in a sudden angry gesture.

"I am not such an admirer of these things as you are. Listen—shall I tell you something? My grandfather decorated his drums with human skulls. You see?"

He did not say any more. But I stared at him, seeing for the first time how he must look at the ancient Africa, the Africa of the talking drums and the bizarre figures cast in bronze. I could afford to be fascinated. None of it threatened me. But for Mensah, the time to move on had not only arrived, it was long overdue. What he saw in the old Africa was not the weird beauty of wood carvings or bronze vessels or the exultant pulsing of the drums. What he saw was the fear and the squalor, the superstition, the men still working the fields in this century with machetes and hoes, the children who still died by the score through lack of medical care.

As a matter of fact, I think it is highly unlikely that Mensah's grandfather ever decorated his drums with skulls, this interesting custom having died out in that part of the world many years ago. But even when I knew him better I never asked him, because it did not matter. If it wasn't actually true, it was dramatic emphasis—and it made the point all right.

But Mensah's attitude towards the totality of the past was subtle and paradoxical. On the surface, he appeared to take one clear line—the rejection of everything that had gone before.

"African history?" he would say mockingly. "Africans have no history."

At first this view distressed me, because I thought he meant it, and I would speak well-meaningly of the books on the subject which I had read, imagining him to be unacquainted with them, and insisting that Africans *had* a history, a history as long and as complex as that of any other country. Mensah would smile satirically and let me go on talking. Then he would place the tips of his fingers together as though about to make some weighty pronouncement, a mannerism of his which seemed to have been carried over from the courtroom.

"No, no," he would say, with a soft vehemence. "We are a simple people, you see. We have sprung directly from the loins of earth. History is too complicated a concept for us."

I began to comprehend, a little, his anger—which was partly a kind of self-torture. He knew as much about African history as anyone, and yet it was true that a great deal of African history was lost, perhaps lost irretrievably or perhaps awaiting partial rediscovery by archaeologists. I think Mensah reproached himself bitterly for caring that so much had been lost. I also came to see this line of his as a form of gamesmanship aimed at my white liberalism. The possession of a history, after all, is like the recognition of another person's common humanity—if it cannot be taken for granted, it means you do not really believe in it at all. Mensah never actually said this, but it was there, implicit in his sardonic laughter.

Our mistrust of one another, and perhaps of ourselves as well, must have gone deep. For a long time I did not trust Mensah enough to disagree with him, for fear of damaging what I hoped was his impression of me—which was actually only my own impression of myself: sympathetic, humanitarian, enlightened. For his part, he did not trust me enough to permit himself ever to agree with me on any issue at all. Yet the force which made us seek each other's company must have been the sense we both had of being somehow out of tune with the respective societies in which we lived. I was not only unwilling but also unable to act like a *memsahib*, even when politeness temporarily demanded it. Mensah was hypercritical of the Europeans ("these white men") who were still in positions of power, but at the same time he was unable to side entirely with any politician or statesman among his own countrymen, because he could never subdue his questioning approach toward everything. He was not much of a man for waving flags, but he was living at a time when flags were being waved mightily and anyone who did not take an enthusiastic part in this popular pastime might well feel out of step. Because he nagged away at all political parties, I told him the only solution would be for him to form his own.

"Yes," he said. "That would be a really effective political weapon, wouldn't it? A party of one."

Social occasions with Mensah were never smooth. When we invited him to our place he would invariably arrive about two hours late, and I would be trying to contain my own annoyance and to placate our Nigerian cook, who would be beside himself with rage over his ruined meal, and blowing off steam by making loud and insulting remarks about all Ghanaians. Whenever we were invited to Mensah's we would arrive on the dot, thus throwing Mensah into a frenzy of consternation over the unready dinner. To him it was exceedingly thoughtless, and even rude, for guests to arrive on time. After Mensah married, the situation eased. His wife Honour did the cooking herself because she wanted to, although this was not customary in the families of professional men. If we forgot and arrived on time, Honour would somehow contrive to hurry the dinner and our *gaffe* would not be too obvious.

Mensah's son was born about the same time as ours, and in the same hospital, so for a few months before and after the babies were born, I talked mainly to Honour when we met, since both of us were almost totally absorbed in the question of children. Honour's personality was the opposite of her husband's and this must have worked to their mutual advantage. Where Mensah was like a leopard, always pacing some invisible cage, Honour was placid and calm, very firm in her opinions but never heatedly so.

I used to envy Honour sometimes, for socially she had far more freedom than I. She never had to worry about leaving the baby in the care of someone sufficiently responsible; both grandmothers were temporarily in residence, and Honour could go out anytime she liked. I mentioned this to her, and she smiled.

"Yes, it's wonderful in some ways," she said. "But can you imagine having two women telling you what you are doing wrong with the baby? And both of them with ideas of child care which you don't accept?"

Honour was much more outspoken than Mensah when it came to family matters.

"When you put our two families together, Mensah's and mine, it adds up to a lot of people, and they all have the feeling that because Mensah is a lawyer he must be tremendously wealthy. I tell you, it is not so easy."

When at last we both emerged from our preoccupation with the babies and rejoined the general conversation, I realized that some change had gradually taken place without anyone's being aware of it. I no longer agreed, out of some need for his acceptance, with nearly everything Mensah said, and he no longer disagreed with nearly everything I said.

Perhaps we were both beginning to trust one another enough to say what we really thought. Or perhaps we had begun to exist for one another as individuals with names and families, people with specific interests and with viewpoints which were our own.

I asked Mensah once why he had decided to go into law.

"Very simple," he said. "You see, people here love litigation. With us, it is a form of entertainment. Whatever happens in this country, good times or bad, there will always be hundreds of cases being fought in court over a sack of yams that somebody's grandmother stole half a century ago. I thought—how can I lose? If I am a barrister, I am certain to make my fortune."

"And will you?"

"No," Mensah replied. "Too many of my contemporaries had the same idea."

I left Ghana just before Independence, when the entire country was in a state of frantic excitement. The bickering over the constitution had risen in the past year almost to the point of hysteria, and the province of Ashanti had threatened to secede from the union, but now the regional differences had been overcome, or at least shelved, in the interests of Independence *now*, not later.

"Free-Dom," was the chant of the big-hipped market women as they marched in the forefront of the political parades.

"Aren't you pleased?" I asked Mensah.

"I am pleased, yes, of course. But I would be even more pleased if I did not see quite such a large hotel being built by the government for visiting important personages. Well, Nkrumah is giving us circuses now. We will see if the bread comes later. At least he understands one thing that most of his faithful followers do not."

"What's that?"

"The real difficulties," Mensah said grimly, "have not yet begun."

I did not expect ever to see Mensah again after I left Ghana, but I did see him. He visited Canada one year, and we happened to be in the same city at the same time. I met him for a drink and he told me his reactions to my country.

"Canadians are so touchy. Why didn't you tell me? I never knew. I thought if you said *Americans*, that meant all North Americans. I was really in trouble here, at first."

I said that his experience was poetic justice, thinking of my own blunders in Africa, and with a grin Mensah conceded that this might be so.

He told me about Ghana. Europeans in senior posts had been replaced with Africans, which he felt was a good thing. Building had been going on rapidly. The harbour was now completed and in operation. In one sense, things were booming. But Mensah was intensely alarmed at the increasing concentration of power in the hands of one man.

"You've read about it in the newspapers, of course? Well, the reports are stupid—they speak as though Nkrumah were making himself into a European-style dictator. He's not. He's the African king-figure, the greatest of all paramount chiefs. That is the image he is trying to create. Very clever, but perhaps very dangerous also. The King—he who possesses supernatural powers. In the end, does this take us ahead—or where? Really, you know, he has accomplished a great deal in a short time. But I would feel happier if he were not so ambitious. He is called *Osagyefo* now—the Redeemer. What will bring him down, I think, is not anything within the country, but his aspirations to be the leader of pan-Africanism. That is pure fantasy."

Then Mensah laughed in the mocking way I remembered so well.

"What I really have to complain about," he said, "is that I can't listen to the radio anymore. I miss that very much."

"Why can't you listen?"

"Well, you see, every second word is *Osagyefo—Osagyefo—Osagyefo*. I am afraid that I may possibly die of boredom, so I have to turn the radio off."

Mensah's Christmas cards always bore some kind of barbed comment. That year, his card showed a picture of the triumphal Independence Arch in Accra. Opposite the words "Freedom and Justice," which appeared in large letters along the top of the arch, Mensah had penned a small question mark.

After I came to live in England, I got a postcard one day. "Am visiting England briefly. Will be in London on my way back to Ghana." And there, a few days later, was Mensah, looking a little older, but as tense and alert as always. I had invited two other friends who had attended London University with Mensah some years ago. Mensah, to my astonishment, started in once more on the "Africans have no history" line. I watched, half amused and half infuriated, while our friends pointed out gently to Mensah that there were, after all, the Benin bronzes and the ruins of Zimbabwe. The next day Mensah came over by himself.

"You really played the old tune again last night, didn't you?" I said.

He grinned. "Don't you think it's interesting to observe the reactions?"

"Oh, certainly I think so—now that I'm not being observed."

"After a while people begin to understand," Mensah said, not smiling now, "that everyone has a history, just as everyone has a skin—life isn't possible without it. But the most important thing about it is that it isn't important."

I didn't agree with him on that point, but we didn't have long to talk. It does not seem to me that we talked about anything very significant. Yet maybe it was the most significant things of which we spoke—our families, our work, where each of us thought we were going in this life and where we wanted to go. We exchanged our news quite plainly, because by this time we had known each other for a dozen years, and what happened to each of us and to our respective children was somehow important to the other. There is a point at which, without anyone having done anything to bring it about, a friend becomes an old friend. This, in the Ghanaian phrase, is something life dashes you for nothing—a present, more than you expected.

Mensah spoke scathingly of the writeups on Ghana which had appeared in the world press.

"You know what the trouble is? They see what amounts to a one-party system, and without trying to understand it or see what has formed it, they condemn it outright. It is not that I am in favour of a one-party system. It is just that I think that the western countries look at Ghana and shake their heads very sorrowfully, simply because our development obviously is not going to mirror their own. It is like saying, 'Of course I acknowledge your right to be free, as long as you always do the same as I do.' "

And yet from his point of view, the situation in Ghana was not heartening. We discussed the dismissal of a high court judge. I asked Mensah if his own position as a lawyer was not a precarious one. He nodded. The choices did not appear to be many—stay and keep one's criticism to oneself, or else go, which was not such a simple matter, either. Honour and the children had to be considered. There was the sheer practical difficulty of getting permission to leave, and there was the other thing, the inner conviction that one must stay, at least as long as possible, and find some way to speak what one felt to be true. But there was no place at the moment, it seemed, for loyal opposition. That might come later on, but what about the meantime? Mensah, standing by the window, suddenly swung around.

"To tell you the truth," he said brusquely, and with a bleakness I had never heard in his voice before, "I really do not know what to do. Perhaps I will discover."

After he had returned to Ghana, I received a Christmas card from Mensah. On the front of the card was a picture of an African woman carrying a large black cooking-pot on her head. Opposite the cooking-pot was Mensah's neatly penned comment—"Culture." I liked this very much, because it was aimed at the thing he really despises more than anything else—phoniness, whether from African supernationalists or white liberals.

I was reminded of another of Mensah's cards. It seemed to me then that if Freedom and Justice ever had any actuality, in any country, there must always, surely, be someone there who would place beside the words his own individual question mark.

Jan Morris
(b. 1926)

The artful blend of realistic detail, sociopolitical reportage, character glimpses, history, evocative memories, snatches of talk, and impressionist interpretation that distinguishes Jan Morris's travel essays creates for us an experience very like her own as she reads her favorite nineteenth-century travel writer: "One feels in his presence that the best guidebooks are far more than informational aides, more even than literature, but are manuals of sensibility" ("Through My Guidebooks"). Hers is a sensibility that searches out and vibrates to the illusions perpetrated by places, above all, cities, those collective creations of our species. Where another contemporary traveller, Shiva Naipaul (see p. 614), goes to the heart of any city by exposing the fictions promoted by and about it, Morris tracks down and sorts out what is false, what is real, what is hallucinatory, and how these merge and cross each other. For her, capturing the spirit of a place means discovering how (and how well) past, present, and future ideas of it have been realized in its look, sound, tempo, feel. All the while, she delights in the successes and ironies flowing from this play of illusion and reality—like the provincial English city of Bath, ancient but rather out of the way, making its "fantasy of greatness" true by "fostering it . . . with grace, fun, and harmony" ("A Fantasy of Greatness"). But susceptible as Morris is to the magic of places, she is not to be fooled by it. In "Fun City," we get a glimpse of this appreciative traveller's sterner, moral face: there's a difference, she implies, between illusion crafted into truth of a kind and illusion made to deceive. The latter falsifies the very idea of a place; it thrusts evil into the physicality of experience, like "the smell of Fun" clinging to her body even after she has driven away from Las Vegas into the Spring Mountains "where the snow still lay pristine." A good traveller journeying globally, on and on, with the wit to grasp the spirit of a place, Morris also knows, it seems, when and why to leave: "Fun city is no fun. . . ."

Fun City: Las Vegas, U.S.A.

It was the Piazza San Marco in Venice that first entered my mind when I strolled down from my bedroom ("A Steady Red Light Reminds You That You Have Requested A Special Service") into the casino of the MGM Grand Hotel in Las Vegas. There was no sunshine in the great room, of course, which was plunged into a timeless twilight, no sparkle of old mosaic or streaked alabaster: but what took me instantly back to Venice was the music.

On one side of the room, near the booking-office for scenic flights to the Grand Canyon, a pianist named Jerry Brown was playing *Georgia on My Mind.* On the other side, half-hidden in the gloom of the bar, Sasha Semenoff and his Romantic Strings were playing *One Enchanted Evening.* The two strains clashed somewhere in the middle, above the blackjack tables, and with their jumble of beat and style, their blend of the wistful and the ebullient, their cheerful discord and their unflagging energy, they reminded me at once of that other, older pleasure-dome far away, where the café orchestras of Quadri's and Florian's strum away in competition through the summer evenings.

And there was no denying the sense of pleasure to the MGM casino that day. The crowds that poured ceaselessly through its front doors, past the stone naiads spouting water through their nipples, fairly shone with excited anticipation. Beside Mr. Brown's piano a little crowd of southern folk, arm in arm in check shirts, was swaying sentimentally to the beat of the music, while in the bar a rather grander group in evening dress sat in a condition of frozen but distinctly flattered embarrassment as Mr. Semenoff and his Strings played *Rosemarie* very close to their ears, Mr. Semenoff smiling graciously throughout while the more winsome of his lady violinists swooped here and there to the line of the melody, throwing pretty laughs over her shoulder.

I can see her now! And beyond her, a jumbled shifting picture of the huge casino floor, the pools of its lights on the green felt of the gambling-tables, the gestulating beefy figures throwing crap, the ladderman high on his chair above the baccarat players, the ceaseless movement of the dealers' hands, the slow watchful patrol of the floor-walkers and pit-bosses, the long, long line of holiday-makers being ushered by security men, guns at their hips, towards their evening with Mr. Englebert Humperdink in the Celebrity Room (itself sealed like a lush bordello beside the cashiers' cages)—and all around, dimly glowing, the crowded ranks of the fruit machines, clanking, winking sometimes, attended by dim crouched figures holding paper cups, and now and then erupting into a shrill ringing of bells, a clatter of jackpot coins and raucous shrieks of triumph.

Even as I arrived a middle-aged lady, wearing blue slacks that sagged slightly around her buttocks, and a straw hat with uncut edges such as Huck Finn liked to sport, detached herself from these mechanisms and suddenly burst into a solitary but exuberant jitter-bug, clicking her thumbs and waving her forefinger in the half-light. The southerners around the piano whistled and clapped. Mr. Brown deftly adjusted his rhythms. "Well," I said to myself as I passed gingerly by, "this may not be so bad. It's hardly Venice after all, but it looks more fun than Gomorrah."

"Have your fun, Jan," said the Leading Citizen, "sure thing, this is a Fun Town, but what we specially do not like is these comparisons with Sodom and such. What people forget is that here in Vegas we have a thriving civic-minded community. We have 130 church buildings, Jan, in this city of ours. We have a thriving university, Jan. We are rapidly becoming the cultural center of the desert Southwest. I think I could safely say that you won't find a more lovely home environment anywhere than some of our high-grade home environments here. Mr. Wayne Newton the famous singer breeds his Arab horses in our city. Mr. Liberace is another of our distinguished residents. What I want you to remember, Jan, is this—the Spanish Trail came this way, right over this very spot, before the game of roulette ever entered the Infant Republic—that's what I always tell people like you, who come inquiring—before the game of roulette ever entered the Infant Republic of the United States!"

And it is true that around the perimeters of Las Vegas, where the ever-growing city extends raggedly into the desert, a middle-sized western railway center strives to honor family values and civilized norms. Street after street the homes of the Vegas bourgeoisie extend in wholesome conformity, and the people who hose their cars on the sidewalks, or bathe in the perpetual summer sunshine on their sprinkled lawns, have that slightly cheesy, well-meaning look indigenous to all the American West, and compounded I think of climate, religion, Swedish grandmothers and rather too much ice-cream.

Mormons actually founded Las Vegas, only its name (which means "The Meadows") being left from the overnighters of the Spanish Trail, and its original reputation was nothing if not devout. The Saints ran a mission station here, and though they were still in their polygamous phase they were certainly no Babylonians. To this day they are powerful in Las Vegas banking and commerce; the place was born again in quite another sense in 1905 when the railway town was established, and yet again in 1931 when gambling was legalized in Nevada, but still their astute rectitude seems to set the tone for Vegas suburban life.

A trace of sanctimony is inescapable among this citizenry. When a few years ago the electorate was asked whether "adult-oriented theatres and bookstores" should be allowed in the city, a three-to-one majority said no. After I left the Leading Citizen I called, at his suggestion, upon Christian Supplies, one of the best-known commercial enterprises in town. It is a very cornucopia of spiritual riches, and through it all day long Las Vegans browse for holy comics, uplifting license plates, Jesus patches or Born Again literature ("Every Tract a Proven Soulwinner"). Mrs. Shine runs the place, and I asked her which version of the Holy Bible Las Vegas Christians chiefly bought, surmising (I blush to say) that they might prefer some Inspirational Paraphrase. She answered me rather sternly. The King James Authorized version, she said, of 1611.

There is inevitably a trace of the comic to these yearnings, Las Vegas being notoriously what it is—the very face of the good lady at the airport information desk, doling out church directories, speaks to us all inescapably of humbug. But it is not all hypocrisy. Las Vegas really does contain a decent enough western town within itself, struggling if not to get out, at least to reveal or fulfill itself. There are many families here in the truest pioneer tradition, like the Cashmans who now run the Cadillac agency but whose progenitor Big Jim Cashman began by running a sandwich shop for the railroad construction workers, or the Mikulichs who now own the Vegas-Reno buses but came to the town from Yugoslavia in 1913.

You can hear good music nowadays in Vegas, if you pop up to the Artemus W. Ham Concert Hall. You can go to a straight play or a classical ballet, at the university. There is a Jewish community paper, the *Las Vegas Israelite*, which is full of Mothers of the Year and congratulations to Eli Welt on his election to the Board of Directors of the Nevada Retail Association: there is a bright young magazine called the *Las Vegan* which reports its proper share of Bubbles and Baubles fetes, lovely home environments and country club poolside barbecues.

The proprietors of the *Las Vegan*, as a matter of fact, threw a little party for me, and the people I met there were certainly not *all* humbugs. There was a novelist, and a well-known photographer, and a couple of academics, and a designer with an Australian wife, and a number of intelligent girls who said I *couldn't* write about Vegas until I had seen the Spring Mountains or the Red Rock Canyon. Agreeable infants kept burbling in and out filching canapés, and there was African folk-art on the walls.

One of my fellow guests ran an art gallery in town, and as we parted she gave me an envelope containing, she said, a little souvenir of my visit. When I opened it I found inside a photograph of a work by her father, a famous Italo-American sculptor. It showed a naked girl of total innocence sleeping side by side with an adorable little fawn, and it was called "The Dream."

"Kinky postcards, huh?" said a man looking over my shoulder.

There is always a sneer in Las Vegas. The mountains around it sneer. The desert sneers. And arrogant in the middle of its wide valley, dominating those diligent sprawling suburbs, the downtown city sneers like anything.

There is no other city center like this. Even in the early 1950s, when I first came to Las Vegas, the shape of the place was detectably Western Traditional, clustered around the railway depot and the city hall—overlaid even then indeed by the gaudy stamp of the casinos, but still recognizably a halt on the line of the Union Pacific. Today only the railroad tracks themselves delineate the past. All else is Fun City. The depot itself is actually absorbed into a casino block, so that you can step from the train direct into a gambling hall, while the downtown streets are unrecognizable as any kind of ordinary town center, the drug stores and hardware merchants, if there are any, being altogether overwhelmed in neonry and hucksterism.

Out of the old Freemont and 5th Street crossing, where Ferron's Drugs used to be, has been unleashed the blazing esplanade called the Strip, only thinly disguised as Las Vegas Boulevard South—four miles long, intermittently speckled with gigantic resort hotels, and filled in everywhere else with clubs, wedding chapels, motels with complimentary blue movies and mirror-ceilings, car rentals, Le Petit Mozart French Restaurant and Bogie's the male strip-joint (defined by its general manager recently as being "not a pornographic-type situation").

It is as though some inconceivable alien organism has fallen upon the old depot town, squatting there athwart the tracks and infecting everything with some incurable, unidentifiable but not altogether disagreeable virus. Nobody in Vegas can escape the emanations of this incubus. Even Mrs. Shine, after long wrestlings with her conscience, steels herself to pass between the gambling tables now and then to indulge herself in a buffet luncheon on the Strip. Even Pastor Harry Ward is ready sometimes to leave his Fellowship Center (Sunday School 1 P.M.) to officiate at the Chapel of the Roses round the corner, where an instant candlelight wedding with piped-in music need cost no more than 30 bucks, Amex cards accepted.

Almost nobody is immune. The Leading Citizen himself allows that gambling and whoring have always been, after all, an essential factor in the western *mores*, and Mr. Parry Thomas, the Mormon chairman of the

Valley Bank, was the very first banker to put his money behind the gaming industry. Nearly every Vegas supermarket has its own fruit machines; a stone's throw away from Christian Supplies stands the Gamblers' Bookstore, the biggest gambling bookshop on earth, where the dedicated punter may buy anything from Dr. Robert Lewis's *Taking Chances: The Psychology of Losing* to Mr. Charles Cotton's *The Compleat Gambler*, which he published in 1674, only 63 years after the Authorized Version.

This is Fun City—and as I surmised that first day, some of it *is* fun. There is the fun of gambling itself, to which I am by no means impervious. There is the somewhat blowzy fun of Showbiz, the Stars, the Hollywood Spectaculars, Sammy Davis, Jr., and all that. There is the undeniable fun of the hundreds of thousands of neon lights that emblazon the presence of Las Vegas so astonishingly upon the night. There is the fun of the ever-shifting parade of visitors—twelve million of them last year, or some 48 times the resident population.

You must be a purist indeed not to get some fun from the tomfool architecture of Las Vegas, with its monstrous classic motifs, the gigantic heroic statuary of Caesar's Palace, those breast-gushing nymphs of the MGM, and its megalomaniac suggestions of wealth, power and grandeur. The sheer loudness and brassiness of Las Vegas is entertaining, and there is a true beauty, too, to the sight of the city flashing and winking away there, a restless cauldron of lights, seen from the surrounding hills in the middle of the night—all alone in the desert, an inconceivable oasis, with the headlights streaming into town from the Los Angeles highway, and the landing lights of the jets coming and going from McCarran International.

It reaches some kind of apogee in the resort called Circus Circus, which is housed in a gigantic mock-marquee, and offers free circus acts every half-hour noon until midnight from here to eternity. This is a kind of Piranesi Big Top, a labyrinth of alcoves, ramps, roundabouts, staircases, stalls and arcades, so mysteriously constructed, so dazzling with massed battalions of fruit machines, so loud with the clanging of handles and the booming of loudspeaker voices, so rushed about by candy-floss goblins, that for myself I wander through it altogether bemused. Ever and again I seem to pass the booth where children are made up to look like clowns—at every turn I encounter that stall of grotesquely swollen teddy-bears and pink Plutos—before every fruit machine the same fat white lady goggles—at every table seems to sit the self-same dealer, in pink shirt and gypsy sleeves, bald as a coot and largely labelled "Curly"—round and round forever on revolving carousels the same solemn couples suck at their thick pink drinks beneath the transcendental lights.

When I first looked in at Circus Circus the Paulo Sisters were in the middle of their trapeze act. Their father was watching them from the side of the ring, and he told me that they were half German and half English, and had spent all their lives on the professional circuit, living in trailers. At that moment they were reaching the climax of their performance, when one sister, sustaining the other by her teeth, flips her into the Helicopter Spin and whirls her upside-down at 60 miles an hour above the ring.

It seemed to me that this must be one of life's most muddling experiences. Circus Circus is disorienting enough as it is: think how disturbing it must all look, the pink plastic dogs, the thick sweet drinks, the flashing lights, Curly and all the fat white gamblers, seen the wrong way up at a mile a minute! But the Paulo Sisters concluded their act with composure, and curtseying gracefully to the crowd, danced away offstage without a sign of vertigo. Dad collected the props together for the next time round.

The fat white woman that nobody loves is the truest familiar of Las Vegas, pulling her handle mindlessly any hour of day or night, in the roughest downtown betting parlor as in the poshest casinos of the Strip. Mention this city to travellers anywhere, and it is she they will most vividly recall—not the flashy big spenders, not the Hollywood personalities of the showrooms, not the visiting sheikhs or Japanese, certainly not the Prominent Citizen, but that tranced soul at the fruit machine, clutching her paper cup like a bowl of sacrament.

For myself it is her fatness I chiefly notice. Las Vegas is the world capital of obesity. You can buy chocolate by the yard or the bucket at the Candy Jar in town, and there are more fat people here at any one time than there are Muslims in Mecca. When each group of merry-makers enters the Circus Circus, they literally burst into view, gigantic buttocks and immeasurable thighs, paunches bulging over trouser tops, dilated white arms and bosoms like gas balloons. It is like a Hall of Mirrors, and as they lumber away into the twilight assiduously licking their ice-creams, I almost expect them to be elongated into skinny giants, or squashed into flat folk.

The Man Who Broke the Bank at Monte Carlo would not feel at home in Vegas—this is no town for a gentleman. It is the Xanadu of the second-rate. It even made me feel a bit of a snob, so coarse is the style of it, so unfastidious: according to Mr. Ralph Pearl, the chronicler of Las Vegas life, when Jacqueline Kennedy once made the mistake of coming here the check-room lady at the Dunes described her afterwards as "a broad who peed icicles"—a fitting Las Vegan epithet for disdain. I shudder to think of the dirty stories that are told in this city every night: I squirm to remember the effigies of President Carter on sale in the MGM Grand itself, with an erect cactus for his penis; I am embarrassed despite myself, for I am honestly no prude, to pick up the *Las Vegas Mirror* and find within it advertisements for Whips, Clamps and Doc Johnson's Pet Jock, "for the woman who deserves more."

It is a Xanadu of the middle-aged, too. Young America, it seems, does not generally take to gambling, and the Vegas pilgrims are likely to have learnt to throw crap in the army, or even in the Depression. The behemoth Cadillacs that are still the thing in Vegas perfectly suit their visions of fulfillment, and the aging entertainers who are super-stars of the Strip perfectly suit their tastes—Eddie Fisher, Tom Jones, Dean Martin, Liberace himself. The MGM Grand is decorated with photographs of Spencer Tracy, Clark Gable *et al.*, and its house cinema perpetually screens such nostalgic oldies as *Gone with the Wind* or *Mutiny on the Bounty:* when I squinted through my door-hole one evening I saw framed in the corridor outside an ancient pair of lovers, grey and scrawny, locked in a lascivious embrace whose very pose (she with one leg cocked behind her, he in blue suspenders) spoke to me direct from the 1940s.

They still have Happy Hours in the Las Vegas resorts. You still hear phrases like "You betcha" and "Looky here" at its bars. Gossip columns of ghastly sycophancy ornament the local papers, and Mr. Dick Maurice's nightly chat-show on local TV ("Success Speaks for Itself!") is absolutely the worst of its kind I have ever seen anywhere in the world. Every aspect of the American fraud is accentuated in Las Vegas, in rubbery victuals and false bonhomie, in meaningless greeting and programmed response. "Well, hi, howya doin'?" say the waitresses in their sincerity voices, "ready for sump'n to putya on top of the world? Howzabout our Pecan-and-Broiled-Lobster-Tail Pizza?": and when one day, just as an experiment, I rang the Secret Witness line, upon which you may give confidential evidence to the police, exactly the same voice answered me, with just the same computer brightness.

Nor is the sin of Las Vegas, the point of it all, free, frank and lusty in the western tradition. Prostitution, for instance, is legal elsewhere in Nevada, and famous bordellos like the Chicken Ranch and the Cherry Patch flourish mightily. In Las Vegas itself they are still forbidden, and so the squalid old profession is made more squalid still with pimpery and imprisonment, with patrolling plainclothes cops and 40 percent pay-offs to hotel concierges. Most of the tourists would be horrified to be seen in their Vegas circumstances, when they go home to Spring Vale or Okokie—Mrs. Hooper of the Friday coffee-meetings ogling the strippers at Bogie's, Jim from the First City Bank out on the town with the boys, picking up a tart or two like they used to over in Europe, or rolling the dice with the injunctions of his boyhood—"That's the way baby, roll it my way hon!"—as they did at Spring High long ago.

Sometimes, early in the morning, I went for a brisk walk along the Strip before the sun burst over the mountain and clamped all Vegas within its air-conditioning. This was a dispiriting experience. Just before dawn is the only moment when Vegas, just for an hour or so, abandons its pretenses. The civic make-up is distinctly worn, in that brief limbo-time; even the sincerity-smiles are dimmed. Some of the neon lights are still flashing, some are dark already, and through the open doors of the casinos you may see exhausted gamblers slumped over their coffees, or wan svelte figures in tuxedos and jewelled dresses sitting like mummies, dead already, around their ghostly baccarat.

Once or twice on these dawn forays I met joggers, incongruously sweating along the Strip, but more often, through the empty quiet, figures of the night before appeared: pale hookers on their sidewalks still, unshaven glassy revellers, taxi-loads of chorus girls going home to bed, dealers with red eyes, ash-heavy cigarettes and jackets slung over their shoulders climbing heavily into their cars. There was nothing very stimulating to this scene. It was not like the dawn hour in a really great city, when life itself seems to be changing gear around you, in the unfailing excitement of a new day. In Vegas the excitement is all contrived. Truly exciting things seldom happen here, and dawn is the time of the Vegan truth, when even the Fun flags.

On and on the fat white women wander, perfect Vegas-fodder, putting the money in, pulling the handle, and occasionally breaking away to dance alone beside the piano. And nobody, I soon discovered, was better material for Fun City than I was myself. Even at my snootiest I responded like Pavlov's dog to the conditioning of the place. Whatever I do in Las Vegas, I told myself on my first day there, I will *never* be seen clutching one of those horrible little paper cups at the fruit machines: but lo, on the very next day I caught myself before the Silverbird machines with a cup in my hand as to the manner born, clutching my complimentary Fun Book.

You have to be smarter than me to resist Dr. Pavlov in Las Vegas, for nothing is guileless here. Even the very rich, whom you may see arriving at the airport in their chartered junket flights, to be met by obsequious Cadillacs and swept away to complimentary penthouses—even the favored guests of the management, who are known in the trade as "comps," are as absolutely Vegas-fodder as the rest of us: the odds are stacked just as heavily against them, the attitude of their hosts, if rather smarmier, is just as calculating. Nothing is spontaneous in Vegas, and little is what it seems. It has all been counted beforehand, and through the one-way mirrors and hidden screens of the casinos careful eyes are watching all the time. ("Casino supervisors," darkly observes *Rouge et Noir*, the trade newsletter, "are instructed to note any significant cash action and identifying information of individuals displaying significant action.")

Las Vegas is a very clever place. It is a magnet to specialists and craftsmen of a hundred kinds, who live out there in the suburbs with Mrs. Shine and the Prominent Citizen, but who come to work each day (or each night) in the eye of the neon hurricane. They range from the electronic experts to service the fruit machines (themselves, with microprocessing, getting cleverer all the time) to the hotel landscape gardeners, the display-lighting engineers, or the professional players of Jai Alai imported specially from the Basque country for demonstration games at the MGM Grand.

It is a town, for instance, of innumerable musicians. They have come here from all over the world, they make a secure and comfortable living in the café orchestras and showbands, and off-duty they often combine for symphonic and chamber music, or play jazz for their own amusement. Take Mr. Semenoff of the Romantic Strings. He is a Latvian Jew by birth, and emerged from wartime concentration camps to study the violin in Munich. He came to Vegas twenty years ago, and now leads his delightful ensemble every evening at the MGM, when you can always find him, between performances, snatching a coffee with his violin beside him for all the world as though he were playing at the old Gellert in Budapest, say, or one of the posher cafés on the Vienna Ringstrasse.

Dancers abound here too, and designers, and animal-trainers, and choreographers, and magicians—"there's generally a magician or two in here," they told me at the Gamblers' Bookstore, looking around in vain for wizardly looking persons, "but they seem to have vanished just now." And the most dedicated specialists of all are the casino men themselves, the general staff of this motley army. They seemed to me a joyless kind of people. The ones I met seldom smoked, drank sparely, never gambled, were slow to grasp the meaning of a joke and viewed the surrounding phantasmagoria with a hard, analytical, absolutely dispassionate eye. The Vegan machine is very finely tuned, and casino men are not all the dark-joweled thugs of popular legend. Mr. Bill Friedman of the Castaways, for example, is an internationally known authority on the theory and history of gambling, and many another keen brain is at work behind these showy scenes, assessing the future in penthouse offices, observing the trends over the luncheon tables of the Las Vegas Country Club.

Most of Las Vegas's gamblers, of course, rich and poor, are pure suckers. They know they are: they are treating themselves, just for a day or two, to what the poet Coleridge defined in quite another context as "the willing suspension of disbelief." Not a trick is lost to milch them, from the fruit machines so inescapably disposed to the rock-bottom restaurant prices, genuinely cheaper than Mom can do it, that broke the resistance of Mrs. Shine (I did not myself succumb to the Circus Circus offer of a 29-cent Biscuit and Gravy Breakfast, but I did try the Four Queens $1 shrimp cocktail, of which they claim to have sold *ten million*). The look in the corporate eye of the Strip is a very cold and steady look, and its spokesmen have a habit of letting you talk your silly head off before offering any hint of a reply, a technique unnervingly reminiscent, I thought, of Lubianka.

For the Vegan cynicism at its most debased, try the wedding chapels. There are scores of them along the Strip, and with every permutation of sickly sentiment they offer immediate ecstasy to several thousand lovers every month. Everything is taken care of. Will you be requiring Honeymoon Garters, Just Married T-Shirts, Bumper Stickers, Everlasting Roses—flowers are, after all, Love's Truest Language? Will a videotape of the ceremony be needed? Witnesses can be arranged, naturally, and recorded bells can be chimed, if required, after the Reverend's matrimonial address.

I slipped into a wedding chapel one afternoon, between marriages, and tried to imagine how it would be to dedicate one's future life before the Reverend there. It was hardly a silent meditation. A rattle of air-conditioning disturbed it, and somewhere out of sight behind the artificial mahogany panelling I could hear the chapel receptionist engaged in a protracted gossip on the telephone (tantalizing gossip, too—"say, I got to see him," I heard her say, "he got married and I got to ride off with him, she was in the other car . . ."). Never mind, the Authorized Version was opened on its lectern at the Book of Proverbs, and the plastic puttis upholding the ceiling looked down at me sweetly, through their ribbons and forget-me-not posies, over the pink-bound copy of *Love Story* which each pair of them was holding.

I sat there for a moment and thought about it all, and narrowed the focus of matrimony's grand conception to this shoddy little shack of legerdemain opposite the motel check-in. I tried to hear the noble words of the great commitment spouted up there by the Reverend for his 10-buck share of the profits. I thought of love itself, the splendor of procreation, too, reduced to the thin strains of the recorded electric organ, and the Honeymoon Garter in its plastic envelope. And just for a moment—my only sententious moment, I hope, during my visit to Las Vegas—I raged within myself: to think that all this was done by choice, by people of grand heritage, born to splendor: to think that those simpering cherubs were surrogates for Michelangelo's celestial angels, or that those vibrato-melodies of Togetherness stood in the line of the mighty Bach himself!

* * *

I shook myself out of it, but anyway the fun had faded by then—and Fun, you will have noticed, is the theme word of this essay as of its subject. Fun City is no fun really, after a day or two, and when the Vegas operators speak of fun, they are using double-speak. The days when the Mafia ran Vegas were Fun Days—the Good Old Days of criminals like Bugsie Malone and Moe Sedway, the "legendary characters" of Vegas, the "old guys." In the garden of the Flamingo Hotel, now a Hilton, an inscription facetiously suggests that its roses may flourish so brightly because Bugsie buried his missing victims there: but there is nothing funny really to the hidden meanings of Las Vegas, its brutal subsoil and its often sinister compost.

Sinister? The adept manipulations of brilliant businessmen? The enterprising vulgarities of Circus Circus? The tinsel of the wedding chapels? Swinging Suzy's, which features Black, English and other Exotic Escorts? Ah, but there is to the very presence of Las Vegas, I came to feel by the end of my stay, a suggestion of true evil. This is more than a discreet city, where photography is not encouraged and anonymity is respected: it is a profoundly secret one. The myriad security men who prowl it with their guns and dogs properly represent its ruling spirit, and brooding always over it, too, is the knowledge of the nuclear explosions whose mushroom clouds rose above the Vegas horizon not so long ago, of the great Nellis Air Force base whose fighters still do their death-sweeps on its sky, of the missile-pits that lie out there in the desert waiting for Armageddon. It is a place of secrets—if I had to choose one architectural symbol to stand for Las Vegas it would not be some flashy porte-cochère or casino fantasy, but a bare enclave wall of grey concrete, such as surrounds so many of this city's lovelier home environments.

And if I had to choose an emblematic resident, it would be Howard Hughes. He lived in Las Vegas for years, immured in the ninth floor of his own Desert Inn, and at one time owned a large proportion of the Vegas resorts, besides succeeding Vera Krupp, heiress to the German munitions fortune, as proprietor of the old Wilson Ranch. Hughes's arrival on the scene is often credited with the decline of the mobsters in Las Vegas, but his legacy is not all benign. The legends of his endless conspiracies, his association with the CIA, his eerie lifestyle and his tragic destiny haunt the place with a baleful fascination, and perhaps affect its manner to this day. Coups and conspiracies in the Hughes *genre* are endemic to Las Vegas: prominent in the local news when I was there was the financier James Ray Houston, the Silver King, who was said to be minting coins for use in the rebellious island of Santo Spirito in the New Hebrides, besides running a money-laundering based upon entirely fictitious direct communication with a computer in Switzerland. I spent a day wandering around Las Vegas with one of its better-informed newspapermen, and it was instructive how often he pointed out the homes of rich recluses, from Orson Welles whom nobody seems to see to the financier who actually lives underground, with buried swimming-pool and subterranean tennis-court.

The sense of withdrawal is essential to the Vegan ambience, just as the business arrangements of this town are still shrouded in rumor and insinuation. Run through the management lists of the Las Vegas institutions—you will find them in the Chamber of Commerce's VIP List—and any criminologist will identify the unsavory names for you. There are bad men about. Sixty people were murdered in Las Vegas last year. While I was there a woman said she had been told she would be found in the desert with her legs cut off behind the knees if she refused to work as a whore. Before I arrived a citizen was killed by nineteen shots from plainclothes policemen when he stopped at a pizza bar to talk to Anthony Spilotro, better known as Tony the Ant. When they talk nostalgically about the good old days of the hit men, they are only putting to the backs of their minds the ugly truths of today—the willing suspension of disbelief come home ironically to roost! Las Vegas sometimes reminds me of the terrible little towns of inner Sicily or Sardinia, where half the population consists of murderers, kidnappers or extortionists, and the other half pretends not to notice.

The longer I stayed there, the more I was oppressed by this sense of the unthinkable, and in the end I took the advice of that girl in the party, and drove out one brilliant morning through the innocuous suburbs to the Spring Mountains, where the snow still lay pristine above the tree-line, and the air was cool and clear. The Las Vegas valley was far out of sight over the mountain ridge, but even so I could not escape the sensations of it: for through the scent of the pines and the morning wind, gradually I became conscious of another smell that I had brought along with me. It clung to me whatever I did, and it was the smell of the Strip: compounded, I think, of air-conditioning, and aerosol fresheners, and deodorants, and a trace of cigar smoke, and paper money, and chewing-gum, and something rotten or acrid which I cannot place exactly, but which I suspect to be the smell of Fun.

Franklin Russell

(b. 1926)

Ethological concerns dominate Franklin Russell's writing, especially what he has called "the great depths of behavorial mystery in the lives of animals" (The Secret Life of Animals). *A New Zealander by birth and, at the start, a farmer who later studied wilderness all over the globe, Russell has been "a professional conservationist, a planter of trees, an expert in the control of erosion." "But," he writes, "I [have] also been a professional hunter"* (The Hunting Animal). *It is the hunter's sensory alertness that he brings to his observations of natural events; the hunter's experience of them as a gripping drama of life and death that intensifies his descriptions; the hunter's psychology that positions him where he can record without flinching minute details of torn flesh, mutilated organs, and severed limbs in the killing patterns of animals, as well as convey the intimacy that arises between hunter and hunted. In "A Madness of Nature"* (New American Review, *1968*), *the hunter's eye is placed in the service of the naturalist distinguishing when, where, and under what circumstances the "colossal corporate bodies" of tiny capelin become the feast, successively, of various interested species including man, "the most voracious of all the hunters." Man comes in at the top of the chain—and, perhaps, to make the whole bloody spectacle familiar: "mass murder," Russell writes elsewhere of another such kill, "gave this scene a human aspect" ("The Cheetah"). Such natural slaughterhouses resemble nothing so much as Dionysiac frenzy, reminding us that the words* carnivore *and* carnival *have the same root. The "I" who observes this "madness" from the beach and records the hierarchy of killing remains, as ever, ignorant about the when and where of his own destruction: "warm and secure," he turns away to "take a blind step forward"—back into the behavioral mystery of his own life. Of course, it would be just too gruesome to even think of jumping in the car and dashing through traffic to the supermarket for a tin of those tasty little Norwegian capelin.*

A Madness of Nature

Beyond the northern beach, a gray swell rolls in from Greenland and runs softly along the shore. The horizon is lost in a world of gray, and gulls glide, spectral in the livid air. Watching, I am enveloped in the sullen waiting time and feel the silence, drawn out long and thin. I wait for the sea to reveal a part of itself.

A capelin is perhaps the best-hunted creature on earth. It is not more than five inches long, about the size of a young herring, and undistinguished in appearance, except that when it is freshly caught, it is the color of mercury. As the capelin dies, its silvery scales tarnish and the glitter goes out like a light, ending a small allegory about nature, a spectacle of victims, victors, and an imperative of existence. Its death illuminates a dark process of biology in which there are shadows of other, more complex lives.

The capelin are born to be eaten. They transform oceanic plankton into flesh which is then hunted greedily by almost every sea creature that swims or flies. Their only protection is fecundity. One capelin survives to adulthood from every ten thousand eggs laid, and yet a single school may stir square miles of sea.

In mid-June, the capelin gather offshore. They can be seen everywhere and at all times in history, symbols of summer and fertility, of Providence and danger. I see them along the shores of Greenland, Iceland, Norway, and near Spitsbergen. I follow them across the northern coast of Russia. Chill air, gray seas, the northern silence are the capelin's world in Alaska, in the Aleutians, around Hudson Bay, and along the northeastern shores of North America. But the capelin of the Newfoundland coast are the most visible. Here, they spawn on the beaches rather than in deep water offshore, and I have come to see their rush for eternity.

They gather a thousand feet offshore, coalescing into groups of a hundred thousand to break the water's surface with bright chuckling sounds. They gather, and grow. Soon they are in the millions, with other millions swimming up from the offshore deeps. They gather, now in the billions, so densely packed together in places that the sea shimmers silver for miles and flows, serpentine, with the swelling body of a single, composite creature.

The fish do, in fact, possess a common sense of purpose. Nothing can redirect their imperative to breed. I once swam among them and saw them parting reluctantly ahead of me, felt their bodies flicking against my hands. Looking back, I saw them closing in, filling up the space created by my passage. The passive fish tolerated me, in their anticipation of what they were about to do.

At this time of the year they are so engrossed that they barely react when a host of creatures advances to kill them. Beneath and beyond them, codfish pour up out of the deep. They overtake the capelin, eat them, plunge their sleek, dark bodies recklessly into shallow water. Some have swum so rapidly from such depths that their swim bladders are distended by the sudden drop in water pressure. The cod are gigantic by comparison with the capelin. Many weigh one hundred pounds or more, and will not be sated until they have eaten scores of capelin each. The water writhes with movement and foam where cod, headlong in pursuit, drive themselves clear out of the sea and fall back with staccato slaps.

The attack of the codfish is a brutal opening to a ritual, and a contradiction in their character. Normally, they are sedentary feeders on the sea floor. Now, however, they are possessed. Their jaws rip and tear; the water darkens with capelin blood: the shredded pieces of flesh hang suspended or rise to the surface.

Now a group of seabirds, the parrotlike puffins, clumsy in flight, turn over the capelin, their grotesque, axlike beaks probing from side to side as they watch the upper layers of the massacre. They are joined by new formations of birds until several thousand puffins are circling. They are silent, and there is no way of knowing how they were summoned from their nesting burrows on an island that is out of sight. They glide down to the water—stub-winged cargo planes—land awkwardly, taxi with fluttering wings and stamping paddle feet, then dive.

At the same time, the sea view moves with new invasions of seabirds. Each bird pumps forward with an urgency that suggests it has received the same stimulus as the cod. The gulls that breed on cliffs along a southern bay come first, gracefully light of wing, with raucous voice as they cry out their anticipation. Beneath them, flying flat, direct, silent, come murres, black-bodied, short-tailed, close relatives of the puffins. The murres land and dive without ceremony. Well offshore, as though waiting confirmation of the feast, shearwaters from Tristan da Cunha turn long, pointed wings across the troughs of waves and cackle like poultry.

The birds converge, and lose their identity in the mass thickening on the water. Small gulls—the kittiwakes, delicate in flight—screech and drop and rise and screech and drop like snowflakes on the sea. They fall among even smaller birds, lighter than they, which dangle their feet and hover at the water's surface, almost walking on water as they seek tiny pieces of shredded flesh. These are the ocean-flying petrels, the Mother Carey's chickens of mariners' legends, which rarely come within sight of land. All order is lost in the shrieking tumult of the hundreds of thousands of birds.

Underwater, the hunters meet among their prey. The puffins and murres dive below the capelin and attack, driving for the surface. The cod attack at mid-depth. The gulls smother the surface and press the capelin back among the submarine hunters. The murres and puffins fly underwater, their beating wings turning them rapidly back and forth. They meet the cod, flail wings in desperate haste, are caught, crushed, and swallowed. Now seabirds as well as capelin become the hunted. Puffin and murre tangle wings. Silver walls of capelin flicker, part, reform. Some seabirds surface abruptly, broken wings dangling. Others, with a leg or legs torn off, fly frantically, crash, skitter in shock across the water.

I see the capelin hunters spread across the sea, but also remember them in time. Each year the hunters are different because many of them depend on a fortuitous meeting with their prey. A group of small whales collides with the capelin, and in a flurry of movement they eat several tons of them. Salmon throw themselves among the capelin with the same abandon as the codfish, and in the melee become easy victims for a score of seals that kill dozens of them, then turn to the capelin and gorge themselves nearly stuporous. They rise, well beyond the tumult of the seabirds, their black heads jutting like rocks from the swell, to lie with distended bellies and doze away their feast. Capelin boil up around them for a moment but now the animals ignore them.

The capelin are hosts in a ceremony so ancient that a multitude of species have adapted to seeking a separate share of the host's bounty. The riotous collision of cod, seal, whale, and seabird obscures the smaller guests at the feast. Near the shore wait small brown fish—the cunner—one of the most voracious species. Soon they will be fighting among themselves for pieces of flesh as the capelin begin their run for the beach, or when the survivors of the spawning reel back into deep water, with the dead and dying falling to the bottom. If the water is calm and the sun bright, the cunner can be seen in two fathoms, ripping capelin corpses to pieces and scattering translucent scales like silver leaves in a wind of the sea.

Closer inshore, at the wave line, the flounder wait. They know the capelin are coming and their role is also predetermined. They cruise rapidly under the purling water in uncharacteristic excitement. They are not interested in capelin flesh. They want capelin eggs, and they will gorge as soon as spawning starts.

Now, the most voracious of all the hunters appear. Fishing vessels come up over the horizon. They brought the Portuguese of the fifteenth century, who anchored offshore, dropped their boats, and rowed ashore to take the capelin with handnets, on beaches never before walked by white men. They brought Spaniards and Dutchmen, Englishmen and Irish, from the sixteenth to the twentieth centuries. Americans, Nova Scotians, Gloucestermen, schoonermen, bankermen, longliner captains have participated in the ritual. All of them knew that fresh capelin is the finest bait when it is skillfully used, and can attract a fortune in codfish flesh, hooked on the submarine banks to the south.

But presently, these hunters are Newfoundlanders. They bring their schooners flying inshore like great brown-and-white birds, a hundred, two hundred, three hundred sail. They heel through the screaming seabirds, luff, anchor, and drop their dories with the same precision of movement of the other figures in the ritual. In an hour, three thousand men are at work from the boats. They work as the codfish work, with a frenzy that knots forearms and sends nets spilling over the sterns to encircle the capelin. They lift a thousand tons of capelin out of the sea, yet they do not measurably diminish the number of fish.

Meanwhile, landbound hunters wait for the fish to come within range of their lead-weighted handnets. Women, children, and old people crowd the beach with the able-bodied men. The old people have ancestral memories of capelin bounty. In the seventeenth and eighteenth centuries, when food was often short, only the big capelin harvest stood between them and starvation during the winter.

Many of the shore people are farmers who use the capelin for fertilizer as well as for food. Capelin corpses, spread to rot over thin northern soils, draw obedient crops of potatoes and cabbages out of the ground, and these, mixed with salted capelin flesh, become winter meals.

The children, who remember dried capelin as their candy, share the excitement of waiting. They chase one another up and down the beach and play with their own nets and fishing rods. Some are already asleep because they awoke before dawn to rouse the village, as they do every capelin morning, with the cry: "They've a-come, they've a-come!"

At the top of the beach, old women lie asleep or sit watching the seabirds squabbling and the dorymen rowing. They are Aunt Sadie and Little Nell and Bessie Blue and Mother Taunton, old ladies from several centuries. They know the capelin can save children in hard winters when the inshore cod fishery fails. They get up at two o'clock in the morning when the capelin are running, to walk miles to the nearest capelin beach. They net a barrel of fish, then roll the barrel, which weighs perhaps a hundred pounds, back home. They have finished spreading the fish on their gardens, or salting them, before the first of their grandchildren awakes.

They have clear memories of catching capelin in winter, when the sea freezes close inshore and the tide cracks the ice in places. Then millions of capelin, resting out the winter, rise in the cracks. An old woman with a good net can take tons of passive fish out of the water for as long as her strength lasts and for as far as her net reaches.

A cry rises from the beach: "Here they come!"

The ritual must be played out, according to habit. The dorymen and the seabirds, the rampaging cod and cunner cannot touch or turn the purpose of the capelin. At a moment, its genesis unknown, they start for the shore. From the top of some nearby cliffs I watch and marvel at the precision of their behavior. The capelin cease to be a great, formless mass offshore. They split into groups that the Newfoundlanders call *wads*—rippling gray lines, five to fifty feet wide—and run for the shore like advancing infantry lines. One by one, they peel away from their surviving comrades and advance, thirty to forty wads at a time.

Each wad has its discipline. The fish prepare to mate. Each male capelin seeks a female, darting from one fish to another. When he finds one, he presses against her side. Another male, perhaps two males, press against her other side. The males urge the female on toward the beach. Some are struck down by diving seabirds but others take their places. Cod dash among them and smash their sexual formations; they re-form immediately. Cunner rise and rip at them; flounder dart beneath them toward the beach.

The first wad runs into beach wavelets, and a hundred nets hit the water together; a silver avalanche of fish spills out on the beach. In each breaking wavelet the capelin maintain their formations, two or three males pressed tightly against their female until they are all flung up on the beach. There, to the whispering sound of tiny fins and tails vibrating, the female convulsively digs into the sand, which is still moving in the wake of the retreating wave. As she goes down, she extrudes up to fifty thousand eggs, and the males expel their milt.

The children shout; their bare feet fly over the spawning fish; the nets soar; sea boots grind down; the fish spill out; gulls run in the shallows under the children's feet; the flounder gorge. A codfish, two feet long, leaps out of the shallows and hits the beach. An old man scoops it up. The wads keep coming. The air is filled with birds. The dorymen shout and laugh.

The flood of eggs becomes visible. The sand glistens, then is greasy with eggs. They pile in driftlines that writhe back and forth in each wave. The female capelin wriggle into masses of eggs. The shallows are permeated with eggs. The capelin breathe eggs. Their mouths fill with eggs. Their stomachs are choked with eggs. The wads keep pouring onward, feeding the disaster on the beach.

Down come the boots and the nets, and the capelin die, mouths open and oozing eggs. The spawning is a fiasco. The tide has turned. Instead of spawning on the shore with the assurance of rising water behind them, each wad strikes ashore in retreating water. Millions are stranded but the wads keep coming.

In the background, diminished by the quantity of fish, other players gasp and pant at their nets. Barrels stack high on the beach. Horses whinny, driven hard up the bank at the back of the beach. Carts laden with barrels weave away. Carts bringing empty barrels bounce and roar down. The wads are still coming. Men use shovels to lift dead and dying fish from driftlines that are now two and three feet high. The easterly wind is freshening. The wavelets become waves. The capelin are flung up on the beach without a chance to spawn. They bounce and twist and the water flees beneath them.

It is twilight, then dark; torches now spot the beach, the offshore dories, and the schooners. The waves grow solidly and pile the capelin higher. The men shovel the heaps into pyramids, then reluctantly leave the beach. Heavy rain blots out beach and sea.

I remain to watch the blow piling up the sea. At the lowest point of the tide, it is driving waves high up on the beach, roiling the sand, digging up the partially buried eggs, and carrying them out to sea. By dawn most of the eggs are gone. The capelin have disappeared. The seabirds, the schooners, the cod, flounder, cunner, seals, whales have gone. Nothing remains except the marks of human feet, the cart tracks on the high part of the beach, the odd pyramid of dead fish. The feast is done.

The empty arena of the beach suggests a riddle. If the capelin were so perfectly adapted to spawn on a rising tide, to master the task of burying eggs in running sand between waves, to *know* when the tide was rising, why did they continue spawning after the tide turned? Was that, by the ancient rules of the ritual, intentional? If it was, then it indicated a lethal error of adaptation that did not jibe with the great numbers of capelin.

I wonder, then, if the weak died and the strong survived, but dismiss the notion after recalling the indiscriminate nature of all capelin deaths. There was no Darwinian selection for death of the stupid or the inexperienced. Men slaughtered billions, this year and last year and for three hundred years before, but the capelin never felt this pin-pricking on their colossal corporate bodies. Their spawning was a disaster for reasons well beyond the influence of men.

A nineteenth-century observer, after seeing a capelin-spawning, recorded his amazement at "the astonishing *prosperity* of these creatures, cast so wilfully away. . . ." It was in the end, and indeed throughout the entire ritual, the sheer numbers of capelin that scored the memory. The *prosperity* of the capelin preceded the disaster but then, it seemed, created it. Prosperity was not beneficial or an assurance of survival. The meaning of the ritual was slowly growning into sense. Prosperity unhinges the capelin. Prosperity, abundance, success, drive them on. They become transformed and throw themselves forward blindly. . . .

I turn from the beach, warm and secure, and take a blind step forward.

Cynthia Ozick

(b. 1928)

Cynthia Ozick has made much of her early immersion in the great European and American writers, especially her worship of Henry James whom, in "The Riddle of the Ordinary," she calls "the supreme aesthetician." Though she came to feel that she'd misunderstood what this consummate artist had to teach a young aspirant like herself, she had, by then, hungrily "assimilated the voluptuous cathedral-tones of the developed organ-master" ("The Lesson of the Master"). Whether telling about her years of devotion to "the religion of Art" or about her turn to the religion of Judaism—where she puts to use all that she gleaned from the other altar—Cynthia Ozick is as unfailingly stirring in both her fiction and nonfiction as she is untiringly ambitious. Her ambition is to reveal the Judaic eternal and to maintain her impassioned stand there as a literary artist. In "The Riddle of the Ordinary" (1975, Art & Ardor), *Ozick leads us along intricate paths of analysis and argument to see, as she sees, the "idolatry" of art for art's sake and nature for nature's sake. She compels no one to adopt her Judaic beliefs but moves us with such fine sensitivity through her intellectual landscape that we can't help but admire and appreciate it. Although she experiences writing as setting out "with empty pockets" (Foreword, Art & Ardor), it might be said with equal justice that if any writer ever embarked with pockets bulging, it's Cynthia Ozick. She who speculates so absorbingly about Virginia and Leonard Woolf ("Mrs. Virginia Woolf: A Madwoman and Her Nurse") may be said, not altogether fancifully, to be a split incarnation of them both. There is Leonard Woolf living the "soul-cracking contradictions" of being a Jew in the solidly Anglo-Saxon bastion of Bloomsbury; and there's Virginia Woolf, "hour after hour, year after year," writing. The commanding intellectuality of her prose has made Ozick something like the Virginia Woolf of our literary scene. And nothing portrays her soul-riddled situation more profoundly or with more loveliness than "A Drugstore in Winter," a memoir of early happy days spent filling her cultural pockets haphazardly, reading, reading, reading at the round glass table with her mother in the sun parlor of the Park View Pharmacy, and her father reading in Yiddish.*

The Riddle of the Ordinary

Though we all claim to be monotheists, there is one rather ordinary way in which we are all also dualists: we all divide the world into the Ordinary and the Extraordinary. This is undoubtedly the most natural division the mind is subject to—plain and fancy, simple and recondite, commonplace and awesome, usual and unusual, credible and incredible, quotidian and intrusive, natural and unnatural, regular and irregular, boring and rhapsodic, secular and sacred, profane and holy: however the distinction is characterized, there is no human being who does not, in his own everydayness, feel the difference between the Ordinary and the Extraordinary.

The Extraordinary is easy. And the more extraordinary the Extraordinary is, the easier it is: "easy" in the sense that we can almost always recognize it. There is no one who does not know when something special is happening: the high, terrifying, tragic, and ecstatic moments are unmistakable in any life. Of course the Extraordinary can sometimes be a changeling, and can make its appearance in the cradle of the Ordinary; and then it is not until long afterward that we become aware of how the visitation was not, after all, an ordinary one. But by and large the difference between special times and ordinary moments is perfectly clear, and we are never in any doubt about which are the extraordinary ones.

How do we respond to the Extraordinary? This too is easy: by paying attention to it. The Extraordinary is so powerful that it commands from us a redundancy, a repetition of itself: it seizes us so undividedly, it declares itself so dazzlingly or killingly, it is so deafening with its LOOK! SEE! NOTICE! PAY ATTENTION!, that the only answer we can give is to look, see, notice, and pay attention. The Extraordinary sets its own terms for its reception, and its terms are inescapable. The Extraordinary does not let you shrug your shoulders and walk away.

But the Ordinary is a much harder case. In the first place, by making itself so noticeable—it is around us all the time—the Ordinary has got itself in a bad fix with us: we hardly ever notice it. The Ordinary, simply by *being* so ordinary, tends to make us ignorant or neglectful; when something does not insist on being noticed, when we aren't grabbed by the collar or struck on the skull by a presence or an event, we take for granted the very things that most deserve our gratitude.

And this is the chief vein and deepest point concerning the Ordinary: that it *does* deserve our gratitude. The Ordinary lets us live out our humanity; it doesn't scare us, it doesn't excite us, it doesn't distract us—it brings us the safe return of the school bus every day, it lets us eat one meal after another, put one foot in front of the other. In short, it is equal to the earth's provisions; it grants us life, continuity, the leisure to recognize who and what we are, and who and what our fellows are, these creatures who live out their everydayness side by side with us in their own unextraordinary ways. Ordinariness can be defined as a breathing-space: the breathing-space between getting born and dying, perhaps; or else the breathing-space between rapture and rapture; or, more usually, the breathing-space between one disaster and the next. Ordinariness is sometimes the *status quo*, sometimes the slow, unseen movement of a subtle but ineluctable cycle, like a ride on the hour hand of the clock; in any case the Ordinary is above all *what is expected*.

And what is expected is not often thought of as a gift.

The second thing that ought to be said about the Ordinary is that it is sometimes extraordinarily dangerous to notice it. And this is strange, because I have just spoken of the gratitude we owe to the unnoticed foundations of our lives, and how careless we always are about this gratitude, how unthinking we are to take for granted the humdrum dailiness that is all the luxury we are ever likely to know on this planet. There are ways to try to apprehend the nature of this luxury, but they are psychological tricks, and do no good. It is pointless to contemplate, only for the sake of feeling gratitude, the bitter, vicious, crippled, drugged, diseased, deformed, despoiled, or corrupted lives that burst against their own mortality in hospitals, madhouses, prisons, all those horrendous lives chained to poverty and its variegated spawn in the long, bleak wastes on the outer margins of Ordinariness, mired in the dread of a ferocious Extraordinariness that slouches in insatiably every morning and never departs even in sleep—contemplating this, who would deny gratitude to our own Ordinariness, though it does not come easily, and has its demeaning price? Still, comparison confers relief more often than gratitude, and the gratitude that rises out of reflection on the extraordinary misfortune of others is misbegotten. —You remember how in one of the Old English poets we are told how the rejoicing hosts of heaven look down at the tortures of the damned, feeling the special pleasure of their own exemption. The consciousness of Ordinariness *is* the consciousness of exemption.

That is one way it is dangerous to take special notice of the Ordinary.

The second danger, I think, is even more terrible. But before I am ready to speak of this new, nevertheless very ancient, danger, I want to ask this question: if we are willing to see the Ordinary as a treasure and a gift, what are we to *do* about it? Or, to put it another way, what is to be gained from noticing the Ordinary? Morally and metaphysically, what are our obligations to the Ordinary? Here art and philosophy meet with a quizzical harmony unusual between contenders. "Be one of those upon whom nothing is lost," Henry James advised; and that is one answer, the answer of what would appear to be the supreme aesthetician.

For the sake of the honing of consciousness, for the sake of becoming sensitive, at every moment, *to* every moment, for the sake of making life as superlatively polished as the most sublime work of art, we ought to notice the Ordinary.

No one since the Greek sculptors and artisans has expressed this sense more powerfully than Walter Pater, that eloquent Victorian whose obsession with attaining the intensest sensations possible casts a familiar light out toward the century that followed him. Pater, like Coleridge before him and James after him, like the metaphysicians of what has come to be known as the Counterculture, was after all the highs he could accumulate in a lifetime. "We are all under sentence of death," he writes, ". . . we have an interval, and then our place knows us no more. Some spend this interval in listlessness, some in high passions, the wisest . . . in art and song. For our only chance lies in expanding that interval, in getting as many pulsations as possible into the given time. Great passions may give us this quickened sense of life. . . . Only be sure it is passion—that it does yield you this fruit of a quickened, multiplied consciousness. . . . Of this wisdom, the poetic passion, the desire for beauty, the love of art for art's sake, has most; for art comes to you professing frankly to give nothing but the highest quality to your moments as they pass, and simply for those moments' sake." And like a Zen master who seizes on the data of life only to transcend them, he announces: "Not the fruit of experience, but experience itself, is the end."

What—in this view, which once more has the allegiance of the *Zeitgeist*—what is Art? It is first noticing, and then sanctifying, the Ordinary. It is making the Ordinary into the Extraordinary. It is the impairment of the distinction between the Ordinary and the Extraordinary.

The aestheticians—the great Experiencers—can be refuted. I bring you a Hebrew melody to refute them with. It is called "The Choice"; the poet is Yeats; and since the poem is only eight lines long I would like to give over the whole of it. It begins by discriminating between essence and possession: life interpreted as *doing* beautiful things or *having* beautiful things:

The intellect of man is forced to choose
Perfection of the life, or of the work.
And if it take the second must refuse
A heavenly mansion, raging in the dark.
When all that story's finished, what's the news?
In luck or out the toil has left its mark:
That old perplexity an empty purse,
Or the day's vanity, the night's remorse.

Our choice, according to Yeats, is the choice between pursuing the life of Deed, where acts have consequences, where the fruit of experience is more gratifying than the experience itself, and pursuing the life of Art, which signifies the celebration of shape and mood. Art, he tells us, turns away from the divine preference, and finishes out a life in empty remorse; in the end the sum of the life of Art is nothing. The ironies here are multitudinous, for no one ever belonged more to the mansion of Art than Yeats himself, and it might be said that in this handful of remarkable lines Yeats condemned his own passions and his own will.

But there is a way in which the Yeats poem, though it praises Deed over Image, though it sees the human being as a creature to be judged by his acts rather than by how well he has made something—there is a way in which this poem is after all *not* a Hebrew melody. The Jewish perception of how the world is constituted also tells us that we are to go in the way of Commandment rather than symbol, goodness rather than sensation: but it will never declare that the price of Art, Beauty, Experience, Pleasure, Exaltation is a "raging in the dark" or a loss of the "heavenly mansion."

The Jewish understanding of the Ordinary is in some ways very close to Pater, and again very far from Yeats, who would punish the "perfection of the work" with an empty destiny.

With David the King we say, "All that is in the heaven and the earth is thine," meaning that it is all there for our wonder and our praise. "Be one of those upon whom nothing is lost"—James's words, but the impulse that drives them is the same as the one enjoining the observant Jew (the word "observant" is exact) to bless the moments of this world at least one hundred times a day. One hundred times: but Ordinariness is more frequent than that, Ordinariness crowds the day, we swim in the sense of our dailiness; and yet there is a blessing for every separate experience of the Ordinary.

Jewish life is crammed with such blessings—blessings that take note of every sight, sound, and smell, every rising-up and lying-down, every morsel brought to the mouth, every act of cleansing. Before he sits down to his meal, the Jew will speak the following: "Blessed are You, O Lord our God, Ruler of the Universe, whose Commandments hallow us, and who commands us to wash our hands." When he breaks his bread, he will bless God for having "brought forth bread from the earth." Each kind of food is similarly praised in turn, and every fruit in its season is praised for having renewed itself in the cycle of the seasons. And when the meal is done, a thanksgiving is said for the whole of it, and table songs are sung with exultation.

The world and its provisions, in short, are *observed*—in the two meanings of "observe." Creation is both noticed and felt to be sanctified. Everything is minutely paid attention to, and then ceremoniously praised. Here is a Talmudic saying: "Whoever makes a profane use of God's gifts—which means partaking of any worldly joy without thanking God for it—commits a theft against God." And a Talmudic dispute is recorded concerning which is the more important Scriptural utterance: loving your neighbor as yourself, or the idea that we are all the children of Adam. The sage who has the final word chooses the children-of-Adam thesis, because, he explains, our common creatureliness includes the necessity of love. But these celebrations through noticing are not self-centered and do not stop at humanity, but encompass every form of life and non-life. So there are blessings to rejoice in on smelling sweet woods or barks, fragrant plants, fruits, spices, or oils. There is a blessing on witnessing lightning, falling stars, great mountains and deserts: "Blessed are You . . . who fashioned Creation." The sound of thunder has its praise, and the sight of the sea, and a rainbow; beautiful animals are praised, and trees in their first blossoming of the year or for their beauty alone, and the new moon, and new clothing, and sexual delight. The sight of a sage brings a blessing for the creation of human wisdom, the sight of a disfigured person praises a Creator who varies the form of his creatures. From the stone to the human being, creatureliness is extolled.

This huge and unending shower of blessings on our scenes and habitations, on all the life that occupies the planet, on every plant and animal, and on every natural manifestation, serves us doubly: in the first place, what you are taught to praise you will not maim or exploit or destroy. In the second place, the categories and impulses of Art become the property of the simplest soul: because it is all the handiwork of the Creator, everything Ordinary is seen to be Extraordinary. The world, and every moment in it, is seen to be sublime, and not merely "seen to be," but brought home to the intensest part of consciousness.

Come back with me now to Pater: "The service of philosophy," he writes, "of speculative culture, toward the human spirit is to rouse, to startle it into sharp and eager observation. Every moment some form grows perfect in hand or face; some tone on the hills or the sea is choicer than the rest; some mood of passion or insight or intellectual excitement is irresistibly real and attractive to us—for that moment only." And now here at last is Pater's most celebrated phrase, so famous that it has often been burlesqued: "To burn always with this hard, gemlike flame, to maintain this ecstasy, is success in life."

But all this is astonishing. An idolator singing a Hebrew melody? I call Pater an idolator because he is one; and so is every aesthetician who sees the work of art as an end in itself. Saying "Experience itself is the end" is the very opposite of blessing the Creator as the source of all experience.

And just here is the danger I spoke of before, the danger Yeats darkly apprehended—the deepest danger our human brains are subject to. The Jew has this in common with the artist: he means nothing to be lost on him, he brings all his mind and senses to bear on noticing the Ordinary, he is equally alert to Image and Experience, nothing that passes before him is taken for granted, everything is exalted. If we are enjoined to live in the condition of noticing all things—or, to put it more extremely but more exactly, in the condition of awe—*how can we keep ourselves from sliding off from awe at God's Creation to worship of God's Creation?* And does it matter if we do?

The difference, the reason it matters, is a signal and shattering one: the difference is what keeps us from being idolators.

What is an idol? Anything that is allowed to come between ourselves and God. Anything that is *instead of* God. Anything that we call an end in itself, and yet is not God Himself.

The Mosaic vision concerning all this is uncompromisingly pure and impatient with self-deception, and this is the point on which Jews are famously stiff-necked—nothing but the Creator, no substitute and no mediator. The Creator is not contained in his own Creation; the Creator is incarnate in nothing, and is free of any image or imagining. God is not any part of Nature, or in any part of Nature; God is not any man, or in any man. When we praise Nature or man or any experience or work of man, we are worshiping the Creator, and the Creator alone.

But there is another way of thinking which is easier, and sweeter, and does not require human beings to be so tirelessly uncompromising, or to be so cautious about holding on to the distinction between delight in the world and worship of the world.

Here is a story. A Buddhist sage once rebuked a person who excoriated an idolator: "Do you think it makes any difference to God," he asked, "whether this old woman gives reverence to a block of wood? Do you think God is incapable of taking the block of wood into Himself? Do you think God will ignore anyone's desire to find Him, no matter where, and through whatever means? All worship goes up to God, who is the source of worship."

These are important words; they offer the most significant challenge to purist monotheism that has ever been stated. They tell us that the Ordinary is not merely, when contemplated with intensity, the Extraordinary, but more, much more than that—that the Ordinary is also the divine. Now there are similar comments in Jewish sources, especially in Hasidism, which dwell compassionately on the nobility of the striving for God, no matter through what means. But the striving is always toward the Creator Himself, the struggle is always toward the winnowing-out of every mediating surrogate. The Kotzker Rebbe went so far in his own striving that he even dared to interpret the command against idols as a warning not to make an idol out of a command of God. —So, in general, Jewish thought balks at taking the metaphor for the essence, at taking the block of wood as symbol or representation or mediator for God, despite the fact that the wood and its worshiper stand for everything worthy of celebration: the tree grew in its loveliness, the carver came and fashioned it into a pleasing form, the woman is alert to holiness; the tree, the carver, the woman who is alert to holiness are, all together, a loveliness and a reason to rejoice in the world. But still the wood does not mean God. It is instead of God.

It is not true, as we so often hear, that Judaism is a developmental religion, that there is a progression upward from Moses to the Prophets. The Prophets enjoined backsliders to renew themselves through the Mosaic idea, and the Mosaic idea is from then to now, and has survived unmodified: "Take heed to yourselves, that your heart be not deceived, and ye turn aside, and serve other gods, and worship them." (Deut. 11:16.) This perception has never been superseded. To seem to supersede is to trangress it.

So it is dangerous to notice and to praise the Ordinariness of the world, its inhabitants and its events. We want to do it, we rejoice to do it, above all we are commanded to do it—but there is always the easy, the sweet, the beckoning, the lenient, the *interesting* lure of the *Instead Of*: the wood of the tree instead of God, the rapture-bringing horizon instead of God, the work of art instead of God, the passion for history instead of God, philosophy and the history of philosophy instead of God, the state instead of God, the shrine instead of God, the sage instead of God, the order of the universe instead of God, the prophet instead of God.

There is no Instead Of. There is only the Creator. God is alone. That is what we mean when we utter the ultimate Idea which is the pinnacle of the Mosaic revolution in human perception: God is One.

The child of a friend of mine was taken to the Egyptian galleries of the Museum. In a glass case stood the figure of a cat resplendent in the perfection of its artfulness—long-necked, gracile, cryptic, authoritative, beautiful, spiritual, autonomous, complete in itself. "I understand," said the child, "how they wanted to bow down to this cat. I feel the same." And then she said a Hebrew word: *asur*—forbidden—the great hallowed No that tumbles down the centuries from Sinai, the No that can be said only after the world is no longer taken for granted, the No that can rise up only out of the abundant celebrations and blessings of Yes, Yes, Yes, the shower of Yeses that praise fragrant oils, and wine, and sex, and scholars, and thunder, and new clothes, and falling stars, and washing your hands before eating.

A Drugstore in Winter

This is about reading; a drugstore in winter; the gold leaf on the dome of the Boston State House; also loss, panic, and dread.

First, the gold leaf. (This part is a little like a turn-of-the-century pulp tale, though only a little. The ending is a surprise, but there is no plot.) Thirty years ago I burrowed in the Boston Public Library one whole afternoon, to find out—not out of curiosity—how the State House got its gold roof. The answer, like the answer to most Bostonian questions, was Paul Revere. So I put Paul Revere's gold dome into an "article," and took it (though I was just as scared by recklessness then as I am now) to the *Boston Globe*, on Washington Street. The Features Editor had a bare severe head, a closed parenthesis mouth, and silver Dickensian spectacles. He made me wait, standing, at the side of his desk while he read; there was no bone in me that did not rattle. Then he opened a drawer and handed me fifteen dollars. Ah, joy of Homer, joy of Milton! Grub Street bliss!

The very next Sunday, Paul Revere's gold dome saw print. Appetite for more led me to a top-floor chamber in Filene's department store: Window Dressing. But no one was in the least bit dressed—it was a dumbstruck nudist colony up there, a mob of naked frozen enigmatic manikins, tall enameled skinny ladies with bald breasts and skulls, and legs and wrists and necks that horribly unscrewed. Paul Revere's dome paled beside this gold mine! A sight—mute numb Walpurgisnacht—easily worth another fifteen dollars. I had a Master's degree (thesis topic: "Parable in the Later Novels of Henry James") and a job as an advertising copywriter (9 A.M. to 6 P.M. six days a week, forty dollars per week; if you were male and had no degree at all, sixty dollars). Filene's Sale Days—Crib Bolsters! Lulla-Buys! Jonnie-Mops! Maternity Skirts with Expanding Invisible Trick Waist! And a company show; gold watches to mark the retirement of elderly Irish salesladies; for me the chance to write song lyrics (to the tune of "On Top of Old Smoky") honoring our Store. But "Mute Numb Walpurgisnacht in Secret Downtown Chamber" never reached the *Globe*. Melancholy and meaning business, the Advertising Director forbade it. Grub Street was bad form, and I had to promise never again to sink to another article. Thus ended my life in journalism.

Next: reading, and certain drugstore winter dusks. These come together. It is an aeon before Filene's, years and years before the Later Novels of Henry James. I am scrunched on my knees at a round glass table near a plate glass door on which is inscribed, in gold leaf Paul Revere never put there, letters that must be read backward: PARK VIEW PHARMACY. There is an evening smell of late coffee from the fountain, and all the librarians are lined up in a row on the tall stools, sipping and chattering. They have just stepped in from the cold of the Traveling Library, and so have I. The Traveling Library is a big green truck that stops, once every two weeks, on the corner of Continental Avenue, just a little way in from Westchester Avenue, not far from a house that keeps a pig. Other houses fly pigeons from their roofs, other yards have chickens, and down on Mayflower there is even a goat. This is Pelham Bay, the Bronx, in the middle of the Depression, all cattails and weeds, such a lovely place and tender hour! Even though my mother takes me on the subway far, far downtown to buy my winter coat in the frenzy of Klein's on Fourteenth Street, and even though I can recognize the heavy power of a quarter, I don't know it's the Depression. On the trolley on the way to Westchester Square I see the children who live in the boxcar strangely set down in an empty lot some distance from Spy Oak (where a Revolutionary traitor was hanged—served him right for siding with redcoats); the lucky boxcar children dangle their stick-legs from their train-house maw and wave; how I envy them! I envy the orphans of the Gould Foundation, who have their own private swings and seesaws. Sometimes I imagine I am an orphan, and my father is an impostor pretending to be my father.

My father writes in his prescription book: *#59330 Dr. O'Flaherty Pow .60/ #59331 Dr. Mulligan Gtt .65/ #59332 Dr. Thron Tab .90.* Ninety cents! A terrifically expensive medicine; someone is really sick. When I deliver a prescription around the corner or down the block, I am offered a nickel tip. I always refuse, out of conscience; I am, after all, the Park View Pharmacy's own daughter, and it wouldn't be seemly. My father grinds and mixes powders, weighs them out in tiny snowy heaps on an apothecary scale, folds them into delicate translucent papers or meticulously drops them into gelatin capsules.

In the big front window of the Park View Pharmacy there is a startling display—goldfish bowls, balanced one on the other in amazing pyramids. A German lady enters, one of my father's cronies—his cronies are both women and men. My quiet father's eyes are water-color blue, he wears his small skeptical quiet smile and receives the neighborhood's life-secrets. My father is discreet and inscrutable. The German lady pokes a punchboard with a pin, pushes up a bit of rolled paper, and cries out—she has just won a goldfish bowl, with two swimming goldfish in it! Mr. Jaffe, the salesman from McKesson & Robbins, arrives, trailing two mists: winter steaminess and the animal fog of his cigar,* which melts into the coffee smell, the tarpaper smell, the eerie honeyed tangled drugstore smell. Mr. Jaffe and my mother and father are intimates by now, but because it is the 1930s, so long ago, and the old manners still survive, they address one another gravely as Mr. Jaffe, Mrs. Ozick, Mr. Ozick. My mother calls my father Mr. O, even at home, as in a Victorian novel. In the street my father tips his hat to ladies. In the winter his hat is a regular fedora; in the summer it is a straw boater with a black ribbon and a jot of blue feather.

What am I doing at this round glass table, both listening and not listening to my mother and father tell Mr. Jaffe about their struggle with "Tessie," the lion-eyed landlady who has just raised, threefold, in the middle of that Depression I have never heard of, the Park View Pharmacy's devouring rent? My mother, not yet forty, wears bandages on her ankles, covering oozing varicose veins; back and forth she strides, dashes, runs, climbing cellar stairs or ladders; she unpacks cartons, she toils behind drug counters and fountain counters. Like my father, she is on her feet until one in the morning, the Park View's closing hour. My mother and father are in trouble, and I don't know it. I am too happy. I feel the secret center of eternity, nothing will ever alter, no one will ever die. Through the window, past the lit goldfish, the gray oval sky deepens over our neighborhood wood, where all the dirt paths lead down to seagull-specked water. I am familiar with every frog-haunted monument: Pelham Bay Park is thronged with WPA art—statuary, fountains, immense rococo staircases cascading down a hillside, Bacchus-faced stelae—stone Roman glories afterward mysteriously razed by an avenging Robert Moses. One year—how distant it seems now, as if even the climate is past returning—the bay froze so hard that whole families, mine among them, crossed back and forth to City Island, strangers saluting and calling out in the ecstasy of the bright trudge over such a sudden wilderness of ice.

In the Park View Pharmacy, in the winter dusk, the heart in my body is revolving like the goldfish fleet-finned in their clear bowls. The librarians are still warming up over their coffee. They do not recognize

* Mr. Matthew Bruccoli, another Bronx drugstore child, has written to say that he remembers with certainty that Mr. Jaffe did not smoke. In my memory the cigar is somehow there, so I leave it. [Ozick]

me, though only half an hour ago I was scrabbling in the mud around the two heavy boxes from the Traveling Library—oafish crates tossed with a thump to the ground. One box contains magazines—*Boy's Life*, *The American Girl*, *Popular Mechanix*. But the other, the other! The other transforms me. It is tumbled with storybooks, with clandestine intimations and transfigurations. In school I am a luckless goosegirl, friendless and forlorn. In P.S. 71 I carry, weighty as a cloak, the ineradicable knowledge of my scandal—I am cross-eyed, dumb, an imbecile at arithmetic; in P.S. 71 I am publicly shamed in Assembly because I am caught not singing Christmas carols; in P.S. 71 I am repeatedly accused of deicide. But in the Park View Pharmacy, in the winter dusk, branches blackening in the park across the road, I am driving in rapture through the Violet Fairy Book and the Yellow Fairy Book, insubstantial chariots snatched from the box in the mud. I have never been *inside* the Traveling Library; only grownups are allowed. The boxes are for the children. No more than two books may be borrowed, so I have picked the fattest ones, to last. All the same, the Violet and the Yellow are melting away. Their pages dwindle. I sit at the round glass table, dreaming, dreaming. Mr. Jaffe is murmuring advice. He tells a joke about Wrong-Way Corrigan. The librarians are buttoning up their coats. A princess, captive of an ogre, receives a letter from her swain and hides it in her bosom. I can visualize her bosom exactly—she clutches it against her chest. It is a tall and shapely vase, with a hand-painted flower on it, like the vase on the secondhand piano at home.

I am incognito. No one knows who I truly am. The teachers in P.S. 71 don't know. Rabbi Meskin, my *cheder*[1] teacher, doesn't know. Tessie the lion-eyed landlady doesn't know. Even Hymie the fountain clerk can't know—though he understands other things better than anyone: how to tighten roller skates with a skatekey, for instance, and how to ride a horse. On Friday afternoons, when the new issue is out, Hymie and my brother fight hard over who gets to see *Life* magazine first. My brother is older than I am, and doesn't like me; he builds radios in his bedroom, he is already W2LOM, and operates his transmitter *(da-di-da-dit, da-da-di-da)* so penetratingly on Sunday mornings that Mrs. Eva Brady, across the way, complains. Mrs. Eva Brady has a subscription to *The Writer;* I fill a closet with her old copies. How to Find a Plot. Narrative and Character, the Writer's Tools. Because my brother has his ham license, I say, "I have a license too." "What kind of license?" my brother asks, falling into the trap. "Poetic license," I reply; my brother hates me, but anyhow his birthday presents are transporting: one year

[1] Hebrew school for children.

Alice in Wonderland, *Pinocchio* the next, then *Tom Sawyer*. I go after Mark Twain, and find *Joan of Arc* and my first satire, *Christian Science*. My mother surprises me with *Pollyanna*, the admiration of her Lower East Side childhood, along with *The Lady of the Lake*. Mrs. Eva Brady's daughter Jeannie has outgrown her Nancy Drews and Judy Boltons, so on rainy afternoons I cross the street and borrow them, trying not to march away with too many—the child of immigrants, I worry that the Brady's, true and virtuous Americans, will judge me greedy or careless. I wrap the Nancy Drews in paper covers to protect them. Old Mrs. Brady, Jeannie's grandmother, invites me back for more. I am so timid I can hardly speak a word, but I love her dark parlor; I love its black bookcases. Old Mrs. Brady sees me off, embracing books under an umbrella; perhaps she divines who I truly am. My brother doesn't care. My father doesn't notice. I think my mother knows. My mother reads the *Saturday Evening Post* and the *Woman's Home Companion;* sometimes the *Ladies' Home Journal*, but never *Good Housekeeping*. I read all my mother's magazines. My father reads *Drug Topics* and *Der Tog*, the Yiddish daily. In Louie Davidowitz's house (waiting our turn for the rabbi's lesson, he teaches me chess in *cheder*) there is a piece of furniture I am in awe of: a shining circular table that is also a revolving bookshelf holding a complete set of Charles Dickens. I borrow *Oliver Twist*. My cousins turn up with *Gulliver's Travels*, *Just So Stories*, *Don Quixote*, Oscar Wilde's *Fairy Tales*, uncannily different from the usual kind. Blindfolded, I reach into a Thanksgiving grabbag and pull out *Mrs. Leicester's School*, Mary Lamb's desolate stories of rejected children. Books spill out of rumor, exchange, miracle. In the Park View Pharmacy's lending library I discover, among the nurse romances, a browning, brittle miracle: *Jane Eyre*. Uncle Morris comes to visit (*his* drugstore is on the other side of the Bronx) and leaves behind, just like that, a three-volume Shakespeare. Peggy and Betty Provan, Scottish sisters around the corner, lend me their *Swiss Family Robinson*. Norma Foti, a whole year older, transmits a rumor about Louisa May Alcott; afterward I read *Little Women* a thousand times. Ten thousand! I am no longer incognito, not even to myself. I am Jo in her "vortex"; not Jo exactly, but some Jo-of-the-future. I am under an enchantment: who I truly am must be deferred, waited for and waited for. My father, silently filling capsules, is grieving over his mother in Moscow. I write letters in Yiddish to my Moscow grandmother, whom I will never know. I will never know my Russian aunts, uncles, cousins. In Moscow there is suffering, deprivation, poverty. My mother, threadbare, goes without a new winter coat so that packages can be sent to Moscow. Her fiery justice-eyes are semaphores I cannot decipher.

Someday, when I am free of P.S. 71, I will write stories; meanwhile, in winter dusk, in the Park View, in the secret bliss of the Violet Fairy Book, I both see and do not see how these grains of life will stay forever, papa and mama will live forever, Hymie will always turn my skatekey.

Hymie, after Italy, after the Battle of the Bulge, comes back from the war with a present: *From Here to Eternity*. Then he dies, young. Mama reads *Pride and Prejudice* and every single word of Willa Cather. Papa reads, in Yiddish, all of Sholem Aleichem and Peretz. He reads Malamud's *The Assistant* when I ask him to.

Papa and mama, in Staten Island, are under the ground. Some other family sits transfixed in the sun parlor where I read *Jane Eyre* and *Little Women* and, long afterward, *Middlemarch*. The Park View Pharmacy is dismantled, turned into a Hallmark card shop. It doesn't matter! I close my eyes, or else only stare, and everything is in its place again, and everyone.

A writer is dreamed and transfigured into being by spells, wishes, goldfish, silhouettes of trees, boxes of fairy tales dropped in the mud, uncles' and cousins' books, tablets and capsules and powders, papa's Moscow ache, his drugstore jacket with his special fountain pen in the pocket, his beautiful Hebrew paragraphs, his Talmudist's rationalism, his Russian-Gymnasium Latin and German, mama's furnace-heart, her masses of memoirs, her paintings of autumn walks down to the sunny water, her braveries, her reveries, her old, old school hurts.

A writer is buffeted into being by school hurts—Orwell, Forster, Mann!—but after a while other ambushes begin: sorrows, deaths, disappointments, subtle diseases, delays, guilts, the spite of the private haters of the poetry side of life, the snubs of the glamorous, the bitterness of those for whom resentment is a daily gruel, and so on and so on; and then one day you find yourself leaning here, writing at that selfsame round glass table salvaged from the Park View Pharmacy—writing this, an impossibility, a summary of how you came to be where you are now, and where, God knows, is that? Your hair is whitening, you are a well of tears, what you meant to do (beauty and justice) you have not done, papa and mama are under the earth, you live in panic and dread, the future shrinks and darkens, stories are only vapor, your inmost craving is for nothing but an old scarred pen, and what, God knows, is that?

Richard Selzer

(b. 1928)

Cicero, the great authority figure of traditional rhetoric, distinguished three kinds of style: the high, the middle, the low. There seems to be a breed of men—learned, urbane, witty, physicians either by avocation, like Robert Burton (1577–1640), or by profession, like Sir Thomas Browne (1605–82),—who, turning to the practice of prose as a way of indulging their introspective love of life's material mysteries, incline more than a little to the high style, with its involved tropes and supple syntax. Sir Thomas Browne:

> *There is no antidote against the opium of time, which temporarily considereth all things: our fathers find their graves in our short memories, and sadly tell us how we may be buried in our survivors* (Urn-Burial).

Richard Selzer, a writer-physician, loves these verbal heights but will play good-humoredly at accommodating our modern predilection for down-to-earth telegraphic simplicity. Here he is making six artful pieces out of what might be two sentences:

> *Yet what an androgynous thing a balcony is, now taking the forward thrust of power, now acting the cranny where one is tucked and snug. A place halfway to heaven, yet in touch with earth. Neither indoors nor out. In a climate of its own. Where the imagination steps off and finds wings. The balcony is just where the artist belongs ("How to Build a Balcony").*

If, like their French brother, François Rabelais, these good doctors living and dead open themselves to charges of excess, their prose styles may be said to harbor the orgasmic pleasures of language itself—shapes and sounds, significance and syntax, words, words, words, more, more. . . . Welcome relief from the reigning puritanism of the plain style is a Selzer specialty. But loftiness, even in camouflage, is by no means his only art. The hand of this teacher—of surgery and writing, at Yale—works Cicero's styles into a three-pronged instrument wielded with beautiful control and skill for explorative probes into language and feeling. "An Absence of Windows" (Confessions of a Knife, *1979), not as verbally exuberant as many of his essays, as if subdued by the shadow of the death the surgeon has just "presided over," broods on the difficulties of tempering skeptical melancholy with mystic vision in the "bloody closets" of our modern hospitals. "A Worm from*

My Notebook" (Taking the World in for Repairs, *1986) is almost a model of the plain style*—almost, *because a worm under a man's skin responding to the stroke of his finger "with slow pruritic vermiculation" makes a dizzying leap up the rhetorical ladder, demonstrating, like the essay as a whole, what can happen not only with worms but also with words.*

An Absence of Windows

Not long ago, operating rooms had windows. It was a boon and a blessing in spite of the occasional fly that managed to strain through the screens and threaten our very sterility. For the adventurous insect drawn to such a ravishing spectacle, a quick swat and, Presto! The door to the next world sprang open. But for us who battled on, there was the benediction of the sky, the applause and reproach of thunder. A Divine consultation crackled in on the lightning! And at night, in Emergency, there was the pomp, the longevity of the stars to deflate a surgeon's ego. It did no patient a disservice to have Heaven looking over his doctor's shoulder. I very much fear that, having bricked up our windows, we have lost more than the breeze; we have severed a celestial connection.

Part of my surgical training was spent in a rural hospital in eastern Connecticut. The building was situated on the slope of a modest hill. Behind it, cows grazed in a pasture. The operating theater occupied the fourth, the ultimate floor, wherefrom huge windows looked down upon the scene. To glance up from our work and see the lovely cattle about theirs, calmed the frenzy of the most temperamental of prima donnas. Intuition tells me that our patients had fewer wound infections and made speedier recoveries than those operated upon in the airless sealed boxes where now we strive. Certainly the surgeons were of a gentler stripe.

I have spent too much time in these windowless rooms. Some part of me would avoid them if I could. Still, even here, in these bloody closets, sparks fly up from the dry husks of the human body. Most go unnoticed, burn out in an instant. But now and then, they coalesce into a fire which is an inflammation of the mind of him who watches.

Not in large cities is it likely to happen, but in towns the size of ours, that an undertaker will come to preside over the funeral of a close friend; a policeman will capture a burglar only to find that the miscreant is the uncle of his brother's wife. Say that a fire breaks out. The fire truck rushes to the scene; it proves to be the very house where one of the firemen was born, and the luckless man is now called on to complete, axe and hose, the destruction of his natal place. Hardly a civic landmark, you say, but for him who gulped first air within those walls, it is a hard destiny. So it is with a hospital, which is itself a community. Its citizens—orderlies, maids, nurses, x-ray technicians, doctors, a hundred others.

A man whom I knew has died. He was the hospital mailman. It was I that presided over his death. A week ago I performed an exploratory operation upon him for acute surgical abdomen. That is the name given to an illness that is unknown, and for which there is no time to make a diagnosis with tests of the blood and urine, x-rays. I saw him writhing in pain, rolling from side to side, his knees drawn up, his breaths coming in short little draughts. The belly I lay the flat of my hand upon was hot to the touch. The slightest pressure of my fingers caused him to cry out—a great primitive howl of vowel and diphthong. This kind of pain owns no consonants. Only later, when the pain settles in, long and solid, only then does it grow a spine to sharpen the glottals and dentals a man can grip with his teeth, his throat. Fiercely then, to hide it from his wife, his children, for the pain shames him.

In the emergency room, fluid is given into the mailman's veins. Bags of blood are sent for, and poured in. Oxygen is piped into his nostrils, and a plastic tube is let down into his stomach. This, for suction. A dark tarry yield slides into a jar on the wall. In another moment, a second tube has sprouted from his penis, carrying away his urine. Such is the costume of acute surgical abdomen. In an hour, I know that nothing has helped him. At his wrist, a mouse skitters, stops, then darts away. His slaty lips insist upon still more oxygen. His blood pressure, they say, is falling. I place the earpieces of my stethoscope, this ever-asking Y, in my ears. Always, I am comforted a bit by this ungainly little hose. It is my oldest, my dearest friend. More, it is my lucky charm. I place the disc upon the tense mounding blue-tinted belly, gently, so as not to shock the viscera into commotion (those vowels!), and I listen for a long time. I hear nothing. The bowel sleeps. It plays possum in the presence of the catastrophe that engulfs it. We must go to the operating room. There must be an exploration. I tell this to the mailman. Narcotized, he nods and takes my fingers in his own, pressing. Thus has he given me all of his trust.

A woman speaks to me.

"Do your best for him, Doctor. Please."

My best? An anger rises toward her for the charge she has given. Still, I cover her hand with mine.

"Yes," I say, "my best."

An underground tunnel separates the buildings of our hospital. I accompany the stretcher that carries the mailman through that tunnel, cursing for the thousandth time the demonic architect that placed the emergency room in one building, and the operating room in the other.

Each tiny ridge in the cement floor is a rut from which rise and echo still more vowels of pain, new sounds that I have never heard before. Pain invents its own language. With this tongue, we others are not conversant. Never mind, we shall know it in our time.

We lift the mailman from the stretcher to the operating table. The anesthetist is ready with still another tube.

"Go to sleep, Pete," I say into his ear, my lips so close it is almost a kiss. "When you wake up, it will all be over, all behind you."

I should not have spoken his name aloud! No good will come of it. The syllable has peeled from me something, a skin that I need. In a minute, the chest of the mailman is studded with electrodes. From his mouth a snorkel leads to tanks of gas. Each of these tanks is painted a different color. One is bright green. That is for oxygen. They group behind the anesthetist, hissing. I have never come to this place without seeing that dreadful headless choir of gas tanks.

Now red paint tracks across the bulging flanks of the mailman. It is a harbinger of the blood to come.

"May we go ahead?" I ask the anesthetist.

"Yes," he says. And I pull the scalpel across the framed skin, skirting the navel. There are arteries and veins to be clamped, cut, tied, and cauterized, fat and fascia to divide. The details of work engage a man, hold his terror at bay. Beneath us now, the peritoneum. A slit, and we are in. Hot fluid spouts through the small opening I have made. It is gray, with flecks of black. Pancreatitis! We all speak the word at once. We have seen it many times before. It is an old enemy. I open the peritoneum its full length. My fingers swim into the purse of the belly, against the tide of the issuing fluid. The pancreas is swollen, necrotic; a dead fish that has gotten tossed in, and now lies spoiling across the upper abdomen. I withdraw my hand.

"Feel," I invite the others. They do, and murmur against the disease. But they do not say anything that I have not heard many times. Unlike the mailman, who was rendered eloquent in its presence, we others are reduced to the commonplace at the touch of such stuff.

We suction away the fluid that has escaped from the sick pancreas. It is rich in enzymes. If these enzymes remain free in the abdomen, they will digest the tissues there, the other organs. It is the pancreas alone that can contain them safely. This mailman and his pancreas—careful neighbors for fifty-two years until the night the one turned rampant and set fire to the house of the other. The digestion of tissues has already begun. Soap has formed here and there, from the compounding of the liberated calcium and the fat. It would be good to place a tube (still another tube) into the common bile duct, to siphon away the bile that is a stimulant to the pancreas. At least that. We try, but we cannot even see the approach to that duct, so swollen is the pancreas about it. and so we mop and suck and scour the floors and walls of this ruined place. Even as we do, the gutters run with new streams of the fluid. We lay in rubber drains and lead them to the outside. It is all that is left to us to do.

"Zero chromic on a Lukens," I say, and the nurse hands me the suture for closure.

I must not say too much at the operating table. There are new medical students here. I must take care what sparks I let fly toward such inflammable matter.

The mailman awakens in the recovery room. I speak his magic name once more.

"Pete." Again, "Pete," I call.

He sees me, gropes for my hand.

"What happens now?" he asks me.

"In a day or two, the pain will let up," I say. "You will get better."

"Was there any . . . ?"

"No," I say, knowing. "There was no cancer. You are clean as a whistle."

"Thank God," he whispers, and then, "Thank *you*, Doctor."

It took him a week to die in fever and pallor and pain.

It is the morning of the autopsy. It has been scheduled for eleven o'clock. Together, the students and I return from our coffee. I walk slowly. I do not want to arrive until the postmortem examination is well under way. It is twenty minutes past eleven when we enter the morgue. I pick the mailman out at once from the others. Damn! They have not even started. Anger swells in me, at being forced to face the *whole* patient again.

It isn't fair! Dismantled, he would at least be at some remove . . . a tube of flesh. But look! There is an aftertaste of life in him. In his fallen mouth a single canine tooth, perfectly embedded, gleams, a badge of better days.

The pathologist is a young resident who was once a student of mine. A tall lanky fellow with a bushy red beard. He wears the green pajamas of his trade. He pulls on rubber gloves, and turns to greet me.

"I've been waiting for you," he smiles. "Now we can start."

He steps to the table and picks up the large knife with which he will lay open the body from neck to pubis. All at once, he pauses, and, reaching with his left hand, he closes the lids of the mailman's eyes. When he removes his hand, one lid comes unstuck and slowly rises. Once more, he reaches up to press it down. This time it stays. The gesture stuns me. My heart is pounding, my head trembling. I think that the students are watching me. Perhaps my own heart has become visible, beating beneath this white laboratory coat.

The pathologist raises his knife.

"Wait," I say. "Do you always do that? Close the eyes?"

He is embarrassed. He smiles faintly. His face is beautiful, soft. "No," he says, and shakes his head. "But just then, I remembered that he brought the mail each morning . . . how his blue eyes used to twinkle."

Now he lifts the knife, and, like a vandal looting a gallery, carves open the body.

To work in windowless rooms is to live in a jungle where you cannot see the sky. Because there is no sky to see, there is no grand vision of God. Instead, there are the numberless fragmented spirits that lurk behind leaves, beneath streams. The one is no better than the other, no worse. Still, a man is entitled to the temple of his preference. Mine lies out on a prairie, wondering up at Heaven. Or in a many windowed operating room where, just outside the panes of glass, cows graze, and the stars shine down upon my carpentry.

A Worm from My Notebook

Were I a professor of the art of writing, I would coax my students to eschew all great and noble concepts—politics, women's liberation or any of the matters that affect society as a whole. There are no "great" subjects for the creative writer; there are only the singular details of a single human life. Just as there are no great subjects, there are no limits to the imagination. Send it off, I would urge my students, to wander into the side trails, the humblest burrows to seek out the exceptional and the mysterious. A doctor/writer is especially blessed in that he walks about all day in the middle of a short story. There comes that moment when he is driven to snatch up a pencil and jot it down. Only, he must take care that the pencil be in flames and that his fingers be burnt in the act. Fine writing can spring from the most surprising sources. Take parasitology, for instance. There is no more compelling drama than the life cycle of *Dracunculus medinensis*, the Guinea worm. Only to tell the story of its life and death is to peel away layers of obscurity, to shed light upon the earth and all of its creatures. That some fifty million of us are even now infested with this worm is of no literary interest whatsoever. Always, it is the affliction of one human being that captures the imagination. So it was with the passion of Jesus Christ; so it is with the infestation of single African man. Shall we write the story together? A Romance of Parasitology? Let me tell you how it goes thus far. I will give you a peek into my notebook where you will see me struggling to set words down on a blank piece of paper. At first whimsically, capriciously, even insincerely. Later, in dead earnest. You will see at precisely what moment the writer ceases to think of his character as an instrument to be manipulated and think of him as someone with whom he has fallen in love. For it is always, must always be, a matter of love.

Let us begin with a man leading his cattle to a wateringhole at the edge of the desert. We shall call him Ibrahim. Shall we locate him in Chad? No, Zaire, I think. For the beauty of the name. Such a word . . . Zaire . . . plays to the savor of the silent reader's speaking tongue. Such a word can, all by itself, sink one into a kind of reverie. Writers must think of such seemingly unimportant attributes as the sound of a written word.

Ibrahim is barefoot and wears a loose earth-colored tunic that flows to his knees. Thin, black, solitary, he walks behind his small herd of cows. Seven. Eight, if you count the calf. For counterpoise, he carries a crook taller than himself with which he poles the sand as he paces. His very stride is ceremonious. Mostly, he is solemn, silent. But at times he sings to the cows until their ears begin to move the better to catch his voice. He knows that they need song to keep going. It is clear that he loves them. Two years ago his wife died in childbirth. Her hands are what he remembers best—what they did to his body: sorted among his hair for lice which they slew between thumb and fingernail with a delicious little click, cleaned out his ears with a piece of straw, smeared him with ornamental paint, and, on the floor of their hut, crept all over him like small playful animals.

At last Ibrahim reaches the wateringhole. Only when his beasts have begun to drink, only then does he think to slake his own thirst. Wading into the pond, he bends to scoop handfuls of water to his mouth. It is a fated moment. For this is no mere water, but water inhabited by the tiny crustacean Cyclops, a microscopic crab with a large and median eye.

Unbeknownst to Ibrahim, Cyclops is harboring within its tiny body the larva of *Dracunculus medinensis*. No sooner does the little worm recognize that it has entered the intestine of a man than it casts off the Cyclops which has been for it foster parent, pantry and taxi, and it migrates into the soft tissues of the man. Shortly thereafter, somewhere inside the flesh of Ibrahim, two worms mate; immediately afterward the male dies.

Time goes by during which the worm within Ibrahim grows to a length of more than two feet and the thickness of a piece of twine. One day, while Ibrahim is squatting by his resting herd, his idle finger perceives the worm as a long undulating ridge just beneath the skin of his abdomen. Again and again he runs his finger up and down the awful ridge, feeling the creature respond with slow pruritic vermiculation. And the face of the man takes on the far-off look of someone deeply, obsessively, in love. With just that magnitude of attention does Ibrahim dote upon the worm. Look at his face! Of what can he be thinking? Of his mother? His childhood? His village? Of the forest spirits with whom he must each day, and many times each day, deal, and whom cajole? At last the spell is broken; sighing, Ibrahim takes up a small twig and, with his knife, carves a notch in one end.

At the end of a year, the intestine of the worm has shrunk away, and the uterus enlarged to occupy its entire body. It has become a tube filled with embryos. Then comes the day when an instinct, more, a diabolical urge, tells Dracunculus that the hour of its destiny has arrived; it must migrate to the foot of the man. Once having wriggled down the lateral aspect of Ibrahim's left foot midway between the malleolus and the head of the fifth metatarsal bone, the saboteur worm chews a hole from the inside out. Ibrahim feels the pain of the chewing and, peering into the hole, he sees for the first time the head of the worm advance and retreat in accordance with some occult Dracunculus rhythm. And he shudders, for it is with horror that you acknowledge the presence within your body of another creature that has a purpose and a will all its own, that eats your flesh, that you can feel. Feel moving!

Ibrahim does not know that the worm is waiting for water, that only when water covers the hole in his foot will the worm stick out its head and spew the liquid that contains the many hundreds of its get. The worm knows that it would not do to spit its precious upon the dry sand to die aborning. And so it comes to pass that once again Ibrahim has brought his cattle to the wateringhole at the edge of the desert. No sooner has he followed them into the pond than the head of the worm emerges and discharges its milky fluid from the submerged foot. Again the thirsty man stoops to slurp his palmsful of Cyclops and larvae. The cycle begins again.

But now a look of stealth and craft sidles across the otherwise impassive face of Ibrahim. His nostrils dilate, and his face, beneath the high and brilliant sun, seems to generate a kind of black sunshine of its own. Reaching into the folds of his tunic, he brings forth the little notched twig that he has fashioned those many weeks ago. Up till now, he has had the patience of the desert; now he will have the heroism of the leopard. If he has prayed to the Gods, propitiated the Spirits, we do not know it. No amulet swings at his neck. There is only the twig. Hunkering by the side of the pond, one foot in the water, Ibrahim waits. He would wait here for hours, for days, if need be. All, all has been swept aside. Even his beloved cattle are forgotten. There is in the universe only Ibrahim and his Worm. He stares down at his foot as though it were not his own, but a foreign brutish appendage that has been left lying on the desert and that had somehow been woven onto his body, attached there. At last he sees that an inch or two of the preoccupied worm is protruding from his still submerged foot. Darting, he grasps with thumb and forefinger, capturing, and, with all the grace and deftness of a surgeon ligating an artery, he ties the head of the worm in a knot around the notched end of the twig, ties it so that the worm cannot wriggle free.

Very, very slowly, a little each day and for many days, Ibrahim turns the twig which he wears at his ankle like a hideous jewel, winding the worm upon it out of a wisdom that has been passed down to him from the earliest time of mankind, through the voices of nameless ancestors, telling that the truly dangerous is not hard or stony, but soft and wet and delicate. There is no room for rashness. Ibrahim cannot be hasty. Turn the twig too quickly and the worm will break, the retained segment retracts to cause infection, gangrene, death. How dignified the man looks. Each time he squats to turn the twig, then stands up, his full height comes as a fresh surprise to the cattle who lift their horns so that the sun can gild them to celebration. In just this way, fifteen days go by. At last the whole of the worm is wrapped around the twig. It is dead. Ibrahim is healed.

Now Ibrahim turns his cattle on the long trek toward home. It is hot, hot. The world longs for a breeze, but the winds are all asleep. He feels the desert little by little envelope his solitary body. A vast sand grows even vaster. There is less and less for the cattle to eat. Each year he has had to walk them farther. See how they bob their heads with every step as if they were using them to drag along their bodies. It is true—the desert is spreading—Ibrahim thinks. At the wateringhole the men were speaking of famine. But that is far away, he says. Not here, not in the villages of Zaire. In due time, in due time, the older ones say. Ibrahim feels a vague restlessness, a longing. In three days there will be a feast in his village—the rite of circumcision when the young boys are taken into the adult life of the tribe. An animal will be slaughtered; there will be meat. Should he walk fast or slow? All at once, Ibrahim quickens his pace, calling out to the cattle to move along, hearing already the drums and the singing of the women. He has been away for three full moons. The smells of his village come out to the desert to grab him by the nose, to pull him toward home. Hurry, hurry, Ibrahim! On and on he walks and all the while the space within him where the worm had been was filling up with the music of the feast until now Ibrahim is brimful of it. And he has a moment of intoxication during which he feels the sun pounding him like a drum, and he feels his blood seeping out of the still unhealed hole in his foot to dance about his footsteps in the sand. Then, something stirs in Ibrahim, something, like a sunken branch long trapped beneath the water, bobs to the surface with considerable force. At that moment, Ibrahim decides to take a wife.

Such, such are the plots of parasitology. Ah, but now you are hooked, aren't you? I have caught you, then? You want me to go on, to write the story of Ibrahim? Well. Where should the story go from here? First to the village, I think, where Ibrahim would join the feast, find a woman with good hands and abundant breasts and make love to her. They would be married. I should like very much to describe the ritual circumcision, the ordeal of the young boys in the jungle, how they are wrapped in the skins of three animals and put in a pit for nine days from which they emerge reborn as men. I should like to render for you the passion of Ibrahim for Ntanga, his new wife, who each night lifts her throat to him for whatever he might wish to do to it; then tell of how, in time, he must once again take his little herd away from the village in search of forage. But now the terrible drought *has* come, the famine as predicted by the men at the wateringhole the year before. The desert itself is undulant, looking most like the water it craves. Ibrahim's skin and hair are soon white with the dust kicked up by the starving cows. He watches the cloud of sand rise and slowly descend. Even the desert wants to leave this place, he thinks. The knives of the sun have split one of his cows in two so that it falls apart before his eyes. Another, the sun has turned into metal. Ibrahim's fingers burst into flames as he grasps a bronze horn to ease the creature's last stumble. Still, on the scabby backs of the others, the white scavenger bird rides. Even that is almost too much for the cattle to carry. He tries singing to them, to offer them syllables of rain, a melody of cool grass, but his tongue is dry. Sand clings to the roof of his mouth. He tries to spit but he cannot. Instead he closes his lips. The last of the cattle dies within three hundred yards of the wateringhole at the edge of the desert. The faithful beast leans against something to break its fall but there is only the air into which it slumps. Ibrahim watches the dying animal collect sand in its mouth, watches death cloud the eyes in which only a short while ago he had delighted to see himself reflected. Now his own body is a knife blade across which, again and again, he draws himself, each time feeling the precise exquisite incision with undiminished pain. Ibrahim staggers on to the wateringhole—three hundred yards, yet a whole day's trek. It is a dry ditch, the bottom fissured. Sinking to his knees, he lowers his head like a cow and licks the clay. Kneeling there alone, his tongue stuck to the baked basin of the hole, Ibrahim hears a muffled clamoring as of a herd far off. A lamentation of hoofbeats and mooing swirls about him. Then all is still. The life cycle of the parasite is broken at last.

Martin Luther King, Jr.

(1929–1968)

In Why We Can't Wait, *King tells his story of the concerted effort, during April and May 1963, to "break the back of segregation" through sit-ins, boycotts, and demonstrations in Birmingham, Alabama, "the country's chief symbol of racial intolerance." The means—"direct action" undertaken by King's army of volunteers pledged to "refrain from the violence of fist, tongue, or heart"—drew its inspiration from Gandhi, whose India King had visited in 1957. When Birmingham city officials obtained a court injunction against further protests, King decided to lead a march in defiance of the order. He was arrested, cited for "civil contempt," and jailed for eight days. A prison cell is a place of enforced leisure, where things cannot be* done, *only* thought: *the "direct action" of the streets and lunch counters became the object of reflection—of calm exposition, discerning analysis, close argument, eloquent example. It became "Letter from Birmingham Jail," an urgent effort at clarification begun on the margins of a newspaper that turned into a great apologetic essay, reasoned and committed, fervent yet controlled. Through the breadth of its intellectual and moral appeals and the stirring beauties of its language, King's letter to eight local clergymen extends its reach to the reading community of all men and women of "genuine good will," everyone prepared to look beyond superficial "effects" and "grapple with underlying causes." Even as "direct action" creates the social tensions that bring individuals to re-examine their moral premises, to disentangle morality from such deceptive doubles as legality, expediency, power, and order, so King's essay in defense of what he has done both enacts as rhetoric and stimulates in its readers the second sight whereby unthinking response and unexamined judgment give way to analysis and understanding. Behind him, King makes clear, stands Socrates, the ancient Athenian "gadfly" (see Plato's* Apology). *Two years before Birmingham, James Baldwin said that "the liberation of Americans from . . . racial anguish" was becoming under King's leadership "a matter . . . of self-examination." King, he wrote, was able "to carry the battle into the individual heart and make its resolution the province of the individual will" ("The Dangerous Road Before Martin Luther King"). With his own behavior and reasoning as its focus, King's essay records just this movement from collective to individual, from public to personal.*

Letter from Birmingham Jail*

My Dear Fellow Clergymen:

While confined here in the Birmingham city jail, I came across your recent statement calling my present activities "unwise and untimely." Seldom do I pause to answer criticism of my work and ideas. If I sought to answer all the criticisms that cross my desk, my secretaries would have little time for anything other than such correspondence in the course of the day, and I would have no time for constructive work. But since I feel that you are men of genuine good will and that your criticisms are sincerely set forth, I want to try to answer your statement in what I hope will be patient and reasonable terms.

I think I should indicate why I am here in Birmingham, since you have been influenced by the view which argues against "outsiders coming in." I have the honor of serving as president of the Southern Christian Leadership Conference, an organization operating in every southern state, with headquarters in Atlanta, Georgia. We have some eighty-five affiliated organizations across the South, and one of them is the Alabama Christian Movement for Human Rights. Frequently we share staff, educational and financial resources with our affiliates. Several months ago the affiliate here in Birmingham asked us to be on call to engage in a nonviolent direct-action program if such were deemed necessary. We readily consented, and when the hour came we lived up to our promise. So I, along with several members of my staff, am here because I was invited here. I am here because I have organizational ties here.

But more basically, I am in Birmingham because injustice is here. Just as the prophets of the eighth century B.C. left their villages and carried their "thus saith the Lord" far beyond the boundaries of their home towns, and just as the Apostle Paul left his village of Tarsus and carried the gospel of Jesus Christ to the far corners of the Greco-Roman world, so am I compelled to carry the gospel of freedom beyond my own home town. Like Paul, I must constantly respond to the Macedonian call for aid.

Moreover, I am cognizant of the interrelatedness of all communities and states. I cannot sit idly by in Atlanta and not be concerned about

* This response to a published statement by eight fellow clergymen from Alabama (Bishop C. C. J. Carpenter, Bishop Joseph A. Durick, Rabbi Hilton L. Grafman, Bishop Paul Hardin, Bishop Holan B. Harmon, the Reverend George M. Murray, the Reverend Edward V. Ramage and the Reverend Earl Stallings) was composed under somewhat constricting circumstances. Begun on the margins of the newspaper in which the statement appeared while I was in jail, the letter was continued on scraps of writing paper supplied by a friendly Negro trusty, and concluded on a pad my attorneys were eventually permitted to leave me. Although the text remains in substance unaltered, I have indulged in the author's prerogative of polishing it for publication. [King]

what happens in Birmingham. Injustice anywhere is a threat to justice everywhere. We are caught in an inescapable network of mutuality, tied in a single garment of destiny. Whatever affects one directly, affects all indirectly. Never again can we afford to live with the narrow, provincial "outside agitator" idea. Anyone who lives inside the United States can never be considered an outsider anywhere within its bounds.

You deplore the demonstrations taking place in Birmingham. But your statement, I am sorry to say, fails to express a similar concern for the conditions that brought about the demonstrations. I am sure that none of you would want to rest content with the superficial kind of social analysis that deals merely with effects and does not grapple with underlying causes. It is unfortunate that demonstrations are taking place in Birmingham, but it is even more unfortunate that the city's white power structure left the Negro community with no alternative.

In any nonviolent campaign there are four basic steps: collection of the facts to determine whether injustices exist; negotiation; self-purification; and direct action. We have gone through all these steps in Birmingham. There can be no gainsaying the fact that racial injustice engulfs this community. Birmingham is probably the most thoroughly segregated city in the United States. Its ugly record of brutality is widely known. Negroes have experienced grossly unjust treatment in the courts. There have been more unsolved bombings of Negro homes and churches in Birmingham than in any other city in the nation. These are the hard, brutal facts of the case. On the basis of these conditions, Negro leaders sought to negotiate with the city fathers. But the latter consistently refused to engage in good-faith negotiation.

Then, last September, came the opportunity to talk with leaders of Birmingham's economic community. In the course of the negotiations, certain promises were made by the merchants—for example, to remove the stores' humiliating racial signs. On the basis of these promises, the Reverend Fred Shuttlesworth and the leaders of the Alabama Christian Movement for Human Rights agreed to a moratorium on all demonstrations. As the weeks and months went by, we realized that we were the victims of a broken promise. A few signs, briefly removed, returned; the others remained.

As in so many past experiences, our hopes had been blasted, and the shadow of deep disappointment settled upon us. We had no alternative except to prepare for direct action, whereby we would present our very bodies as a means of laying our case before the conscience of the local and the national community. Mindful of the difficulties involved, we decided to undertake a process of self-purification. We began a series of workshops on nonviolence, and we repeatedly asked ourselves: "Are you able to accept blows without retaliating?" "Are you able to endure the ordeal of jail?" We decided to schedule our direct-action program for the Easter season, realizing that except for Christmas, this is the main shopping period of the year. Knowing that a strong economic-withdrawal program would be the by-product of direct action, we felt that this would be the best time to bring pressure to bear on the merchants for the needed change.

Then it occurred to us that Birmingham's mayoralty election was coming up in March, and we speedily decided to postpone action until after election day. When we discovered that the Commissioner of Public Safety, Eugene "Bull" Connor, had piled up enough votes to be in the run-off, we decided again to postpone action until the day after the run-off so that the demonstrations could not be used to cloud the issues. Like many others, we waited to see Mr. Connor defeated, and to this end we endured postponement after postponement. Having aided in this community need, we felt that our direct-action program could be delayed no longer.

You may well ask: "Why direct action? Why sit-ins, marches and so forth? Isn't negotiation a better path?" You are quite right in calling for negotiation. Indeed, this is the very purpose of direct action. Nonviolent direct action seeks to create such a crisis and foster such a tension that a community which has constantly refused to negotiate is forced to confront the issue. It seeks so to dramatize the issue that it can no longer be ignored. My citing the creation of tension as part of the work of the nonviolent-resister may sound rather shocking. But I must confess that I am not afraid of the word "tension." I have earnestly opposed violent tension, but there is a type of constructive, nonviolent tension which is necessary for growth. Just as Socrates felt that it was necessary to create a tension in the mind so that individuals could rise from the bondage of myths and half-truths to the unfettered realm of creative analysis and objective appraisal, so must we see the need for nonviolent gadflies to create the kind of tension in society that will help men rise from the dark depths of prejudice and racism to the majestic heights of understanding and brotherhood.

The purpose of our direct-action program is to create a situation so crisis-packed that it will inevitably open the door to negotiation. I therefore concur with you in your call for negotiation. Too long has our beloved Southland been bogged down in a tragic effort to live in monologue rather than dialogue.

One of the basic points in your statement is that the action that I and my associates have taken in Birmingham is untimely. Some have asked: "Why didn't you give the new city administration time to act?" The only answer that I can give to this query is that the new Birmingham administration must be prodded about as much as the outgoing one, before it will act. We are sadly mistaken if we feel that the election of Albert Boutwell as mayor will bring the millennium to Birmingham. While Mr. Boutwell is a much more gentle person than Mr. Connor, they are both segregationists, dedicated to maintenance of the status quo. I have hope that Mr. Boutwell will be reasonable enough to see the futility of massive resistance to desegregation. But he will not see this without pressure from devotees of civil rights. My friends, I must say to you that we have not made a single gain in civil rights without determined legal and nonviolent pressure. Lamentably, it is an historical fact that privileged groups seldom give up their privileges voluntarily. Individuals may see the moral light and voluntarily give up their unjust posture; but, as Reinhold Niebuhr has reminded us, groups tend to be more immoral than individuals.

We know through painful experience that freedom is never voluntarily given by the oppressor; it must be demanded by the oppressed. Frankly, I have yet to engage in a direct-action campaign that was "well timed" in the view of those who have not suffered unduly from the disease of segregation. For years now I have heard the word "Wait!" It rings in the ear of every Negro with piercing familiarity. This "Wait" has almost always meant "Never." We must come to see, with one of our distinguished jurists, that "justice too long delayed is justice denied."

We have waited for more than 340 years for our constitutional and God-given rights. The nations of Asia and Africa are moving with jetlike speed toward gaining political independence, but we still creep at horse-and-buggy pace toward gaining a cup of coffee at a lunch counter. Perhaps it is easy for those who have never felt the stinging darts of segregation to say, "Wait." But when you have seen vicious mobs lynch your mothers and fathers at will and drown your sisters and brothers at whim; when you have seen hate-filled policemen curse, kick and even kill your black brothers and sisters; when you see the vast majority of your twenty million Negro brothers smothering in an airtight cage of poverty in the midst of an affluent society; when you suddenly find your tongue twisted and your speech stammering as you seek to explain to your six-year-old daughter why she can't go to the public amusement park that has just been advertised on television, and see tears welling up in her eyes when she is told that Funtown is closed to colored children, and see ominous clouds of inferiority beginning to form in her little mental sky, and see her beginning to distort her personality by developing an unconscious bitterness toward white people; when you have to concoct an answer for a five-year-old son who is asking: "Daddy, why do white people treat colored people so mean?"; when you take a cross-country drive and find it necessary to sleep night after night in the uncomfortable corners of your automobile because no motel will accept you; when you are humiliated day in and day out by nagging signs reading "white" and "colored"; when your first name becomes "nigger," your middle name becomes "boy" (however old you are) and your last name becomes "John," and your wife and mother are never given the respected title "Mrs."; when you are harried by day and haunted by night by the fact that you are a Negro, living constantly at tiptoe stance, never quite knowing what to expect next, and are plagued with inner fears and outer resentments; when you are forever fighting a degenerating sense of "nobodiness"—then you will understand why we find it difficult to wait. There comes a time when the cup of endurance runs over, and men are no longer willing to be plunged into the abyss of despair. I hope, sirs, you can understand our legitimate and unavoidable impatience.

You express a great deal of anxiety over our willingness to break laws. This is certainly a legitimate concern. Since we so diligently urge people to obey the Supreme Court's decision of 1954 outlawing segregation in the public schools, at first glance it may seem rather paradoxical for us consciously to break laws. One may well ask: "How can you advocate breaking some laws and obeying others?" The answer lies in the fact that there are two types of laws: just and unjust. I would be the first to advocate obeying just laws. One has not only a legal but a moral responsibility to obey just laws. Conversely, one has a moral responsibility to disobey unjust laws. I would agree with St. Augustine that "an unjust law is no law at all."

Now, what is the difference between the two? How does one determine whether a law is just or unjust? A just law is a man-made code that squares with the moral law or the law of God. An unjust law is a code that is out of harmony with the moral law. To put it in the terms of St. Thomas Aquinas: An unjust law is a human law that is not rooted in eternal law and natural law. Any law that uplifts human personality is just. Any law that degrades human personality is unjust. All segregation statutes are unjust because segregation distorts the soul and damages the personality. It gives the segregator a false sense of superiority and the segregated a false sense of inferiority. Segregation, to use the terminology of the Jewish philosopher Martin Buber, substitutes an "I–it" relationship for an "I–thou" relationship and ends up relegating persons to the status of things. Hence segregation is not only politically, economically and sociologically unsound, it is morally wrong and sinful. Paul Tillich has said that sin is separation. Is not segregation an existential expression of man's tragic separation, his awful estrangement, his terrible sinfulness? Thus it is that I can urge men to obey the 1954 decision of the Supreme Court, for it is morally right;

and I can urge them to disobey segregation ordinances, for they are morally wrong.

Let us consider a more concrete example of just and unjust laws. An unjust law is a code that a numerical or power majority group compels a minority group to obey but does not make binding on itself. This is *difference* made legal. By the same token, a just law is a code that a majority compels a minority to follow and that it is willing to follow itself. This is *sameness* made legal.

Let me give another explanation. A law is unjust if it is inflicted on a minority that, as a result of being denied the right to vote, had no part in enacting or devising the law. Who can say that the legislature of Alabama which set up that state's segregation laws was democratically elected? Throughout Alabama all sorts of devious methods are used to prevent Negroes from becoming registered voters, and there are some counties in which, even though Negroes constitute a majority of the population, not a single Negro is registered. Can any law enacted under such circumstances be considered democratically structured?

Sometimes a law is just on its face and unjust in its application. For instance, I have been arrested on a charge of parading without a permit. Now, there is nothing wrong in having an ordinance which requires a permit for a parade. But such an ordinance becomes unjust when it is used to maintain segregation and to deny citizens the First-Amendment privilege of peaceful assembly and protest.

I hope you are able to see the distinction I am trying to point out. In no sense do I advocate evading or defying the law, as would the rabid segregationist. That would lead to anarchy. One who breaks an unjust law must do so openly, lovingly, and with a willingness to accept the penalty. I submit that an individual who breaks a law that conscience tells him is unjust, and who willingly accepts the penalty of imprisonment in order to arouse the conscience of the community over its injustice, is in reality expressing the highest respect for law.

Of course, there is nothing new about this kind of civil disobedience. It was evidenced sublimely in the refusal of Shadrach, Meshach and Abednego to obey the laws of Nebuchadnezzar, on the ground that a higher moral law was at stake. It was practiced superbly by the early Christians, who were willing to face hungry lions and the excruciating pain of chopping blocks rather than submit to certain unjust laws of the Roman Empire. To a degree, academic freedom is a reality today because Socrates practiced civil disobedience. In our own nation, the Boston Tea Party represented a massive act of civil disobedience.

We should never forget that everything Adolf Hitler did in Germany was "legal" and everything the Hungarian freedom fighters did in Hungary was "illegal." It was "illegal" to aid and comfort a Jew in

Hitler's Germany. Even so, I am sure that, had I lived in Germany at the time, I would have aided and comforted my Jewish brothers. If today I lived in a Communist country where certain principles dear to the Christian faith are suppressed, I would openly advocate disobeying that country's antireligious laws.

I must make two honest confessions to you, my Christian and Jewish brothers. First, I must confess that over the past few years I have been gravely disappointed with the white moderate. I have almost reached the regrettable conclusion that the Negro's great stumbling block in his stride toward freedom is not the White Citizen's Counciler or the Ku Klux Klanner, but the white moderate, who is more devoted to "order" than to justice; who prefers a negative peace which is the absence of tension to a positive peace which is the presence of justice; who constantly says: "I agree with you in the goal you seek, but I cannot agree with your methods of direct action"; who paternalistically believes he can set the timetable for another man's freedom; who lives by a mythical concept of time and who constantly advises the Negro to wait for a "more convenient season." Shallow understanding from people of good will is more frustrating than absolute misunderstanding from people of ill will. Lukewarm acceptance is much more bewildering than outright rejection.

I had hoped that the white moderate would understand that law and order exist for the purpose of establishing justice and that when they fail in this purpose they become the dangerously structured dams that block the flow of social progress. I had hoped that the white moderate would understand that the present tension in the South is a necessary phase of the transition from an obnoxious negative peace, in which the Negro passively accepted his unjust plight, to a substantive and positive peace, in which all men will respect the dignity and worth of human personality. Actually, we who engage in nonviolent direct action are not the creators of tension. We merely bring to the surface the hidden tension that is already alive. We bring it out in the open, where it can be seen and dealt with. Like a boil that can never be cured so long as it is covered up but must be opened with all its ugliness to the natural medicines of air and light, injustice must be exposed, with all the tension its exposure creates, to the light of human conscience and the air of national opinion before it can be cured.

In your statement you assert that our actions, even though peaceful, must be condemned because they precipitate violence. But is this a logical assertion? Isn't this like condemning a robbed man because his possession of money precipitated the evil act of robbery? Isn't this like condemning Socrates because his unswerving commitment to truth and his philosophical inquiries precipitated the act by the misguided populace in which they made him drink hemlock? Isn't this like condemning

Jesus because his unique God-consciousness and never-ceasing devotion to God's will precipitated the evil act of crucifixion? We must come to see that, as the federal courts have consistently affirmed, it is wrong to urge an individual to cease his efforts to gain his basic constitutional rights because the quest may precipitate violence. Society must protect the robbed and punish the robber.

I had also hoped that the white moderate would reject the myth concerning time in relation to the struggle for freedom. I have just received a letter from a white brother in Texas. He writes: "All Christians know that the colored people will receive equal rights eventually, but it is possible that you are in too great a religious hurry. It has taken Christianity almost two thousand years to accomplish what it has. The teachings of Christ take time to come to earth." Such an attitude stems from a tragic misconception of time, from the strangely irrational notion that there is something in the very flow of time that will inevitably cure all ills. Actually, time itself is neutral; it can be used either destructively or constructively. More and more I feel that the people of ill will have used time much more effectively than have the people of good will. We will have to repent in this generation not merely for the hateful words and actions of the bad people but for the appalling silence of the good people. Human progress never rolls in on wheels of inevitability; it comes through the tireless efforts of men willing to be co-workers with God, and without this hard work, time itself becomes an ally of the forces of social stagnation. We must use time creatively, in the knowledge that the time is always ripe to do right. Now is the time to make real the promise of democracy and transform our pending national elegy into a creative psalm of brotherhood. Now is the time to lift our national policy from the quicksand of racial injustice to the solid rock of human dignity.

You speak of our activity in Birmingham as extreme. At first I was rather disappointed that fellow clergymen would see my nonviolent efforts as those of an extremist. I began thinking about the fact that I stand in the middle of two opposing forces in the Negro community. One is a force of complacency, made up in part of Negroes who, as a result of long years of oppression, are so drained of self-respect and a sense of "somebodiness" that they have adjusted to segregation; and in part of a few middle-class Negroes who, because of a degree of academic and economic security and because in some ways they profit by segregation, have become insensitive to the problems of the masses. The other force is one of bitterness and hatred, and it comes perilously close to advocating violence. It is expressed in the various black nationalist groups that are springing up across the nation, the largest and best-known being Elijah Muhammad's Muslim movement. Nourished by the Negro's frustration over the continued existence of racial discrimination, this movement is made up of people who have lost faith in America, who have absolutely repudiated Christianity, and who have concluded that the white man is an incorrigible "devil."

I have tried to stand between these two forces, saying that we need emulate neither the "do-nothingism" of the complacent nor the hatred and despair of the black nationalist. For there is the more excellent way of love and nonviolent protest. I am grateful to God that, through the influence of the Negro church, the way of nonviolence became an integral part of our struggle.

If this philosophy had not emerged, by now many streets of the South would, I am convinced, be flowing with blood. And I am further convinced that if our white brothers dismiss as "rabble-rousers" and "outside agitators" those of us who employ nonviolent direct action, and if they refuse to support our nonviolent efforts, millions of Negroes will, out of frustration and despair, seek solace and security in black-nationalist ideologies—a development that would inevitably lead to a frightening racial nightmare.

Oppressed people cannot remain oppressed forever. The yearning for freedom eventually manifests itself, and that is what has happened to the American Negro. Something within has reminded him of his birthright of freedom, and something without has reminded him that it can be gained. Consciously or unconsciously, he has been caught up by the *Zeitgeist*, and with his black brothers of Africa and his brown and yellow brothers of Asia, South America and the Caribbean, the United States Negro is moving with a sense of great urgency toward the promised land of racial justice. If one recognizes this vital urge that has engulfed the Negro community, one should readily understand why public demonstrations are taking place. The Negro has many pent-up resentments and latent frustrations, and he must release them. So let him march; let him make prayer pilgrimages to the city hall; let him go on freedom rides—and try to understand why he must do so. If his repressed emotions are not released in nonviolent ways, they will seek expression through violence; this is not a threat but a fact of history. So I have not said to my people: "Get rid of your discontent." Rather, I have tried to say that this normal and healthy discontent can be channeled into the creative outlet of nonviolent direct action. And now this approach is being termed extremist.

But though I was initially disappointed at being categorized as an extremist, as I continued to think about the matter I gradually gained a measure of satisfaction from the label. Was not Jesus an extremist for love: "Love your enemies, bless them that curse you, do good to them that hate you, and pray for them which despitefully use you, and persecute you." Was not Amos an extremist for justice: "Let justice roll down like waters and righteousness like an ever-flowing stream." Was not Paul an extremist for the Christian gospel: "I bear in my body the marks of the Lord Jesus." Was not Martin Luther an extremist: "Here I stand; I cannot do otherwise, so help me God." And John Bunyan: "I will stay in jail to the end of my days before I make a butchery of my conscience." And Abraham Lincoln: "This nation cannot survive half slave and half free." And Thomas Jefferson: "We hold these truths to be self-evident, that all men are created equal . . ." So the question is not whether we will be extremists, but what kind of extremists we will be. Will we be extremists for hate or for love? Will we be extremists for the preservation of injustice or for the extension of justice? In that dramatic scene on Calvary's hill three men were crucified. We must never forget that all three were crucified for the same crime—the crime of extremism. Two were extremists for immorality, and thus fell below their environment. The other, Jesus Christ, was an extremist for love, truth and goodness, and thereby rose above his environment. Perhaps the South, the nation and the world are in dire need of creative extremists.

I had hoped that the white moderate would see this need. Perhaps I was too optimistic; perhaps I expected too much. I suppose I should have realized that few members of the oppressor race can understand the deep groans and passionate yearnings of the oppressed race, and still fewer have the vision to see that injustice must be rooted out by strong, persistent and determined action. I am thankful, however, that some of our white brothers in the South have grasped the meaning of this social revolution and committed themselves to it. They are still all too few in quantity, but they are big in quality. Some—such as Ralph McGill, Lillian Smith, Harry Golden, James McBride Dabbs, Ann Braden and Sarah Patton Boyle—have written about our struggle in eloquent and prophetic terms. Others have marched with us down nameless streets of the South. They have languished in filthy, roach-infested jails, suffering the abuse and brutality of policemen who view them as "dirty nigger-lovers." Unlike so many of their moderate brothers and sisters, they have recognized the urgency of the moment and sensed the need for powerful "action" antidotes to combat the disease of segregation.

Let me take note of my other major disappointment. I have been so greatly disappointed with the white church and its leadership. Of course, there are some notable exceptions. I am not unmindful of the fact that each of you has taken some significant stands on this issue. I commend you, Reverend Stallings, for your Christian stand on this past Sunday, in welcoming Negroes to your worship service on a nonsegregated basis. I commend the Catholic leaders of this state for integrating Spring Hill College several years ago.

But despite these notable exceptions, I must honestly reiterate that I have been disappointed with the church. I do not say this as one of those negative critics who can always find something wrong with the church. I say this as a minister of the gospel, who loves the church; who was nurtured in its bosom; who has been sustained by its spiritual blessings and who will remain true to it as long as the cord of life shall lengthen.

When I was suddenly catapulted into the leadership of the bus protest in Montgomery, Alabama, a few years ago, I felt we would be supported by the white church. I felt that the white ministers, priests and rabbis of the South would be among our strongest allies. Instead, some have been outright opponents, refusing to understand the freedom movement and misrepresenting its leaders; all too many others have been more cautious than courageous and have remained silent behind the anesthetizing security of stained-glass windows.

In spite of my shattered dreams, I came to Birmingham with the hope that the white religious leadership of this community would see the justice of our cause and, with deep moral concern, would serve as the channel through which our just grievances could reach the power structure. I had hoped that each of you would understand. But again I have been disappointed.

I have heard numerous southern religious leaders admonish their worshipers to comply with a desegregation decision because it is the law, but I have longed to hear white ministers declare: "Follow this decree because integration is morally right and because the Negro is your brother." In the midst of blatant injustices inflicted upon the Negro, I have watched white churchmen stand on the sideline and mouth pious irrelevancies and sanctimonious trivialities. In the midst of a mighty struggle to rid our nation of racial and economic injustice, I have heard many ministers say: "Those are social issues, with which the gospel has no real concern." And I have watched many churches commit themselves to a completely otherworldly religion which makes a strange, un-Biblical distinction between body and soul, between the sacred and the secular.

I have traveled the length and breadth of Alabama, Mississippi and all the other southern states. On sweltering summer days and crisp autumn mornings I have looked at the South's beautiful churches with their lofty spires pointing heavenward. I have beheld the impressive outlines of her massive religious-education buildings. Over and over I have found myself asking: "What kind of people worship here? Who is their God? Where were their voices when the lips of Governor Barnett dripped with words of interposition and nullification? Where were they when Governor Wallace gave a clarion call for defiance and hatred?

Where were their voices of support when bruised and weary Negro men and women decided to rise from the dark dungeons of complacency to the bright hills of creative protest?"

Yes, these questions are still in my mind. In deep disappointment I have wept over the laxity of the church. But be assured that my tears have been tears of love. There can be no deep disappointment where there is not deep love. Yes, I love the church. How could I do otherwise? I am in the rather unique position of being the son, the grandson and the great-grandson of preachers. Yes, I see the church as the body of Christ. But, oh! How we have blemished and scarred that body through social neglect and through fear of being nonconformists.

There was a time when the church was very powerful—in the time when the early Christians rejoiced at being deemed worthy to suffer for what they believed. In those days the church was not merely a thermometer that recorded the ideas and principles of popular opinion; it was a thermostat that transformed the mores of society. Whenever the early Christians entered a town, the people in power became disturbed and immediately sought to convict the Christians for being "disturbers of the peace" and "outside agitators." But the Christians pressed on, in the conviction that they were "a colony of heaven," called to obey God rather than man. Small in number, they were big in commitment. They were too God-intoxicated to be "astronomically intimidated." By their effort and example they brought an end to such ancient evils as infanticide and gladiatorial contests.

Things are different now. So often the contemporary church is a weak, ineffectual voice with an uncertain sound. So often it is an archdefender of the status quo. Far from being disturbed by the presence of the church, the power structure of the average community is consoled by the church's silent—and often even vocal—sanction of things as they are.

But the judgment of God is upon the church as never before. If today's church does not recapture the sacrificial spirit of the early church, it will lose its authenticity, forfeit the loyalty of millions, and be dismissed as an irrelevant social club with no meaning for the twentieth century. Every day I meet young people whose disappointment with the church has turned into outright disgust.

Perhaps I have once again been too optimistic. Is organized religion too inextricably bound to the status quo to save our nation and the world? Perhaps I must turn my faith to the inner spiritual church, the church within the church, as the true *ekklesia* and the hope of the world. But again I am thankful to God that some noble souls from the ranks of organized religion have broken loose from the paralyzing chains of conformity and joined us as active partners in the struggle for freedom.

They have left their secure congregations and walked the streets of Albany, Georgia, with us. They have gone down the highways of the South on tortuous rides for freedom. Yes, they have gone to jail with us. Some have been dismissed from their churches, have lost the support of their bishops and fellow ministers. But they have acted in the faith that right defeated is stronger than evil triumphant. Their witness has been the spiritual salt that has preserved the true meaning of the gospel in these troubled times. They have carved a tunnel of hope through the dark mountain of disappointment.

I hope the church as a whole will meet the challenge of this decisive hour. But even if the church does not come to the aid of justice, I have no despair about the future. I have no fear about the outcome of our struggle in Birmingham, even if our motives are at present misunderstood. We will reach the goal of freedom in Birmingham and all over the nation, because the goal of America is freedom. Abused and scorned though we may be, our destiny is tied up with America's destiny. Before the pilgrims landed at Plymouth, we were here. Before the pen of Jefferson etched the majestic words of the Declaration of Independence across the pages of history, we were here. For more than two centuries our forebears labored in this country without wages; they made cotton king; they built the homes of their masters while suffering gross injustice and shameful humiliation—and yet out of a bottomless vitality they continued to thrive and develop. If the inexpressible cruelties of slavery could not stop us, the opposition we now face will surely fail. We will win our freedom because the sacred heritage of our nation and the eternal will of God are embodied in our echoing demands.

Before closing I feel impelled to mention one other point in your statement that has troubled me profoundly. You warmly commended the Birmingham police force for keeping "order" and "preventing violence." I doubt that you would have so warmly commended the police force if you had seen its dogs sinking their teeth into unarmed, nonviolent Negroes. I doubt that you would so quickly commend the policemen if you were to observe their ugly and inhumane treatment of Negroes here in the city jail; if you were to watch them push and curse old Negro women and young Negro girls; if you were to see them slap and kick old Negro men and young boys; if you were to observe them, as they did on two occasions, refuse to give us food because we wanted to sing our grace together. I cannot join you in your praise of the Birmingham police department.

It is true that the police have exercised a degree of discipline in handling the demonstrators. In this sense they have conducted themselves rather "nonviolently" in public. But for what purpose? To preserve the evil system of segregation. Over the past few years I have consistently preached that nonviolence demands that the means we use must be as pure as the ends we seek. I have tried to make clear that it is wrong to use immoral means to attain moral ends. But now I must affirm that it is just as wrong, or perhaps even more so, to use moral means to preserve immoral ends. Perhaps Mr. Connor and his policemen have been rather nonviolent in public, as was Chief Pritchett in Albany, Georgia, but they have used the moral means of nonviolence to maintain the immoral end of racial injustice. As T. S. Eliot has said: "The last temptation is the greatest treason: To do the right deed for the wrong reason."

I wish you had commended the Negro sit-inners and demonstrators of Birmingham for their sublime courage, their willingness to suffer and their amazing discipline in the midst of great provocation. One day the South will recognize its real heroes. They will be the James Merediths, with the noble sense of purpose that enables them to face jeering and hostile mobs, and with the agonizing loneliness that characterizes the life of the pioneer. They will be old, oppressed, battered Negro women, symbolized in a seventy-two-year-old woman in Montgomery, Alabama, who rose up with a sense of dignity and with her people decided not to ride segregated buses, and who responded with ungrammatical profundity to one who inquired about her weariness: "My feets is tired, but my soul is at rest." They will be the young high school and college students, the young ministers of the gospel and a host of their elders, courageously and nonviolently sitting in at lunch counters and willingly going to jail for conscience' sake. One day the South will know that when these disinherited children of God sat down at lunch counters, they were in reality standing up for what is best in the American dream and for the most sacred values in our Judaeo-Christian heritage, thereby bringing our nation back to those great wells of democracy which were dug deep by the founding fathers in their formulation of the Constitution and the Declaration of Independence.

Never before have I written so long a letter. I'm afraid it is much too long to take your precious time. I can assure you that it would have been much shorter if I had been writing from a comfortable desk, but what else can one do when he is alone in a narrow jail cell, other than write long letters, think long thoughts and pray long prayers?

If I have said anything in this letter that overstates the truth and indicates an unreasonable impatience, I beg you to forgive me. If I have said anything that understates the truth and indicates my having a patience that allows me to settle for anything less than brotherhood, I beg God to forgive me.

I hope this letter finds you strong in the faith. I also hope that circumstances will soon make it possible for me to meet each of you, not as an integrationist or a civil-rights leader but as a fellow clergyman and a Christian brother. Let us all hope that the dark clouds of racial prejudice will soon pass away and the deep fog of misunderstanding will be lifted from our fear-drenched communities, and in some not too distant tomorrow the radiant stars of love and brotherhood will shine over our great nation with all their scintillating beauty.

Yours for the cause of Peace and Brotherhood,
Martin Luther King, Jr.

George Steiner

(b. 1929)

Now that we know "a man can read Goethe or Rilke in the evening, that he can play Bach and Schubert, and go to his day's work at Auschwitz in the morning," what, asks George Steiner in the aftermath of the Holocaust, links the "psychological habits of high literacy and the temptations of the inhuman?" (Preface, Language and Silence: Essays on Language, Literature, and the Inhuman). *High literacy, Steiner points out, failed to prevent the fall into inhumanity; it built no effective barricade against it, no fort from which to fight it. Worse: the very language of great art can betray us, can function as the Trojan horse of the humane, and then, "better for the poet to mutilate his own tongue than to dignify the inhuman" ("Silence and the Poet"). But Steiner is "a kind of survivor" in that he continues to present the values of high literacy in his own person, his own voice, with full consciousness of their—and his—vulnerability. These values emerged historically in what he calls "Central European humanism," that confluence of Judaism and Hellenism through which Steiner the critic moves with the grace and authority natural only to one who lives there, even if only as a semipermanent guest, for Steiner acknowledges no homeland for himself as a Jew other than "six thousand years of self-awareness." Without a defined geography, non-national in its foundation, this humanistic "house of civilization" offers no protective borders. The Holocaust has permanently destroyed any illusion that a cultural home can shield its inhabitants against barbarism or that one's cultural inheritance will, in the end, prevail against the inhumane. More terrible still is the survivor's knowledge of his children's lot: theirs is an inheritance that targets them wherever, whenever, things go wrong. This has been the experience of Jews in the Diaspora. In so perilous a setting, the critic's work may seem marginal, its influence short-lived. Only "the strength and beauty" of a critic's style, Steiner says, give his writing any hope of permanence. "A Kind of Survivor" (1964) and its companion "Essays on Language, Literature, and the Inhuman" will survive, if they do, on "the strength and beauty" of this radical humanist's style. As they survive, they remind Jew and Gentile alike of a cultural abundance now more than ever to be desired, appreciated, appropriated, and enjoyed.*

A Kind of Survivor

Not literally. Due to my father's foresight (he had shown it when leaving Vienna in 1924), I came to America in January 1940, during the phony war. We left France, where I was born and brought up, in safety. So I happened not to be there when the names were called out. I did not stand in the public square with the other children, those I had grown up with. Or see my father and mother disappear when the train doors were torn open. But in another sense I am a survivor, and not intact. If I am often out of touch with my own generation, if that which haunts me and controls my habits of feeling strikes many of those I should be intimate and working with in my present world as remotely sinister and artificial, it is because the black mystery of what happened in Europe is to me indivisible from my own identity. Precisely because I was not there, because an accident of good fortune struck my name from the roll.

Often the children went alone, or held the hands of strangers. Sometimes parents saw them pass and did not dare call out their names. And they went, of course, not for anything they had done or said. But because their parents existed before them. The crime of being one's children. During the Nazi period it knew no absolution, no end. Does it now? Somewhere the determination to kill Jews, to harass them from the earth simply because they *are*, is always alive. Ordinarily, the purpose is muted, or appears in trivial spurts—the obscenity daubed on the front door, the brick through the shop window. But there are, even now, places where the murderous intent might grow heavy: in Russia, in parts of North Africa, in certain countries of Latin America. Where tomorrow? So, at moments, when I see my children in the room, or imagine that I hear them breathing in the still of the house, I grow afraid. Because I have put on their backs a burden of ancient loathing and set savagery at their heels. Because it may be that I will be able to do no more than the parents of the children gone to guard them.

That fear lies near the heart of the way in which I think of myself as a Jew. To have been a European Jew in the first half of the twentieth century was to pass sentence on one's own children, to force upon them a condition almost beyond rational understanding. And which may recur. I have to think that—it is the vital clause—so long as remembrance is real. Perhaps we Jews walk closer to our children than other men; try as they may, they cannot leap out of our shadow.

This is my self-definition. Mine, because I cannot speak for any other Jew. All of us obviously have something in common. We do tend to recognize one another wherever we meet, nearly at a glance, by some common trick of feeling, by the darkness we carry. But each of us must hammer it out for himself. That is the real meaning of the Diaspora, of the wide scattering and thinning of belief.

To the Orthodox my definition must seem desperate and shallow. Entire communities stayed close-knit to the end. There were children who did not cry out but said *Shema Yisroel*[1] and kept their eyes wide open because His kingdom lay just a step over the charnel pit; not as many as is sometimes said, but there *were*. To the strong believer the torture and massacre of six million is one chapter—one only—in the millennial dialogue between God and the people He has so terribly chosen. Though Judaism lacks a dogmatic eschatology (it leaves to the individual the imagining of transcendence), the Orthodox can meditate on the camps as a forecourt of God's house, as an almost intolerable but manifest mystery of His will. When he teaches his children the prayers and rites (my own access to these was that of history, not of present faith), when they sing at his side at the high holidays, the pious Jew looks on them not with fear, not as hostages that bear the doom of his love, but in pride and rejoicing. Through them the bread shall remain blessed and the wine sanctified. They are alive not because of a clerical oversight in a Gestapo office, but because they no less than the dead are part of God's truth. Without them history would stand empty. The Orthodox Jew defines himself (as I cannot) in the rich life of his prayer, of an inheritance both tragic and resplendent. He harvests the living echo of his own being from the voices of his community and the holiness of the word. His children are like the night turned to song.

The Orthodox Jew would not only deny me the right to speak for him, pointing to my lack of knowledge and communion; he would say, "You are not like us, you are a Jew outwardly, in name only." Exactly. But the Nazis made of the mere name necessary and sufficient cause. They did not ask whether one had ever been to synagogue, whether one's children knew any Hebrew. The anti-Semite is no theologian; but his definition is inclusive. So we would all have gone together, the Orthodox and I. And the gold teeth would have come out of our dead mouths, song or no song.

Two passages from Exodus help the mind grasp enormity. Perhaps they are mistranslations or archaic shards interpolated in the canonic text. But they help me as does poetry and metaphor, by giving imaginative logic to grim possibility. Exodus 4.24 tells how God sought to kill Moses: "And it came to pass by the way in the inn, that the Lord met him and sought to kill him." I gloss this to mean that God suffers gusts of murderous exasperation at the Jews, toward a people who have made Him a responsible party to history and to the grit of man's condition. He

[1] Hear, O Israel.

may not have wished to be involved; the people may have chosen Him, in the oasis at Kadesh, and thrust upon Him the labors of justice and right anger. It may have been the Jew who caught Him by the skirt, insisting on contract and dialogue. Perhaps before either God or living man was ready for proximity. So as in marriage, or the bond between father and child, there are moments when love is changed to something very much like itself, pure hatred.

The second text is Exodus 33.22–3. Moses is once more on Sinai, asking for a new set of Tablets (we have always been nagging Him, demanding justice and reason twice over). There follows a strange ceremony of recognition: "And it shall come to pass, while my glory passeth by, that I will put thee in a cleft of the rock, and will cover thee with my hand while I pass by: And I will take away mine hand, and thou shalt see my back parts: but my face shall not be seen." This may be the decisive clue: God can turn His back. There may be minutes or millennia—is our time His?—in which He does not see man, in which He is looking the *other way*. Why? Perhaps because through some minute, hideous error of design the universe is too large for His surveillance, because somewhere there is a millionth of an inch, it need be no more, out of His line of sight. So He must turn to look there also. When God's back parts are toward man, history is Belsen.

If the Orthodox Jew cannot allow my definition, or this use of the holy word as metaphor and paradox, neither can the Zionist and the Israeli. They do not deny the catastrophe, but they know that it bore splendid fruit. Out of the horror came the new chance. The state of Israel is undeniably a part of the legacy of German mass murder. Hope and the will to action spring from the capacity of the human mind to forget, from the instinct of necessary oblivion. The Israeli Jew cannot look back too often; his must be the dreams not of night but of day, the forward dreams. Let the dead bury the mounds of the dead. His history is not theirs; it has just begun. To someone like myself, the Israeli Jew might say: "Why aren't you here? If you fear for the lives of your children, why not send them here and let them grow up amid their own kind? Why burden them with your own perhaps literary, perhaps masochistic, remembrance of disaster? This is their future. They have a right to it. We need all the brains and sinews we can get. We're not working for ourselves alone. There isn't a Jew in the world who doesn't hold his head higher because of what we've done here, because Israel exists."

Which is obviously true. The status of the Jew everywhere has altered a little, the image he carries of himself has a new straightness of back, because Israel has shown that Jews can handle modern weapons, that they can fly jets, and turn desert into orchard. When he is pelted in Argentina or mocked in Kiev, the Jewish child knows that there is a corner of the earth where he is master, where the gun is his. If Israel were to be destroyed, no Jew would escape unscathed. The shock of failure, the need and harrying of those seeking refuge, would reach out to implicate even the most indifferent, the most anti-Zionist.

So why not go? Why not leave the various lands in which we still live, it seems to me, as more or less accepted guests? Many Russian Jews might go if they could. North African Jews are doing so even at the price of destitution. The Jews of South Africa might before too long be forced to the same resolve. So why don't I go, who am at liberty, whose children could grow up far from the spoor of the inhuman past? I don't know if there is a good answer. But there is a reason.

If the way I think of my Jewishness will appear unacceptable or self-defeating to the Orthodox and the Israeli, it will also seem remote and overdramatized to most American Jews. The idea that Jews everywhere have been maimed by the European catastrophe, that the massacre has left all who survived (even if they were nowhere near the actual scene) off balance, as does the tearing of a limb, is one which American Jews can understand in an intellectual sense. But I don't find that it has immediate personal relevance. The relationship of the American Jew to recent history is subtly and radically different from that of the European. By its very finality, the holocaust justified every previous impulse of immigration. All who had left Europe to establish the new Jewish communities in America were proved terribly right. The Jewish soldier who went to the Europe of his fathers came better armed, technologically more efficient than his murderous enemy. The few Jews he found alive were out of a hideous but spectral world, like a nightmare in a foreign tongue. In America, Jewish parents listen at night for their children; but it is to make sure the car is back in the garage, not because there is a mob out. It cannot happen in Scarsdale.

I am not sure, not completely (this is precisely where I am an outsider). Most American Jews are aware of anti-Semitism in specialized areas of life—the club, the holiday resort, the residential district, the professional guild. But in comparative terms, it tends to be mild, perhaps because America, unlike Europe or Russia, has no history of guilt toward the Jew. The size and human wealth of the American Jewish community are such, moreover, that a Jew need hardly go outside his own sphere to enjoy American life at its best and freest. The principal dynamism of American life, however, is a middle- and lower-middle-class conformity, an enforcing consensus of taste and ideal. Nearly by definition, the Jew stands in the way of uniform coherence. Economic, social, or political stress tend to make this latent disparity—the hostile recognition and reciprocal self-awareness of "difference"—more acute. Depression or a drastic increase in unemployment would isolate the status of the Jew, focusing resentment on his prosperity and on the ostentatious forms that prosperity has taken in certain aspects of Jewish life. The struggle over Negro rights, which is coming to overshadow so much of American life, has obvious bearing. Among urban Negroes anti-Semitism is often open and raw. It can be used by the Negro as a basis of temporary alliance with other underprivileged or resentful elements in the white community. Beyond these possibilities lies the larger pattern: the stiffening of consensus, the increasing concentration of American values in a standardized moralistic nationalism.

I agree that American anti-Semitism will stay mild and covert. So long as the economy expands and the racial conflict can be kept in tolerable bounds. So long as Israel is viable and can offer refuge. This is probably the root condition. The support given to Israel by the American Jewish community is both thoroughly generous and thoroughly self-interested. If a new wave of immigration occurred, if the Russian or Tunisian Jew came knocking at America's door, the status of American Jewry would be immediately affected.

These complex safeguards and conditions of acceptance can break down. America is no more immune than any other nationalistic, professedly Christian society from the contagion of anti-Semitism. In a crisis of resentment or exclusion, even the more assimilated would be driven back to our ancient legacy of fear. Though he might have forgotten it and turned Unitarian (a characteristic halfway house), Mr. Harrison's neighbors would remind him that his father was called Horowitz. To deny this is to assert that in America human character and historical forces have undergone some miraculous change—a utopian claim which the actual development of American life in the twentieth century has more than once rebuked.

Nevertheless, the sense I have of the Jew as a man who looks on his children with a dread remembrance of helplessness and an intimation of future, murderous possibility, is a very personal, isolated one. It does not relate to much that is now alive and hopeful. But it is not wholly negative either. I mean to include in it far more than the naked precedent of ruin. That which has been destroyed—the large mass of life so mocked, so hounded to oblivion that even the names are gone and the prayer for the dead can have no exact foothold—embodied a particular genius, a quality of intelligence and feeling which none of the major Jewish communities now surviving has preserved or recaptured. Because I feel that specific inheritance urgent in my own reflexes, in the work I try to do, I am a kind of survivor.

In respect of *secular* thought and achievement, the period of Jewish history which ended at Auschwitz surpassed even the brilliant age of coexistence in Islamic Spain. During roughly a century, from the emancipation of the ghettos by the French Revolution and Napoleon to the time of Hitler, the Jew took part in the moral, intellectual, and artistic noon of bourgeois Europe. The long confinement of the ghetto, the sharpening of wit and nervous insight against the whetstone of persecution, had accumulated large reserves of consciousness. Released into the light, a certain Jewish elite, and the wider middle-class circle which took pride and interest in its accomplishments, quickened and complicated the entire contour of Western thought. To every domain they brought radical imaginings; more specifically, the more gifted Jews repossessed certain crucial elements of classic European civilization in order to make them new and problematic. All this is commonplace; as is the inevitable observation that the tenor of modernity, the shapes of awareness and query by which we order our lives are, in substantial measure, the work of Marx, Freud, and Einstein.

What is far more difficult to show, though it seems to me undeniable, is the extent to which a common heritage of fairly recent emancipation, a particular bias of rational feeling—specialized in origin but broadening out to become the characteristic modern note—informs their distinct, individual genius. In all three, we discern a mastering impulse to visionary logic, to imagination in the abstract, as if the long banishment of the Eastern and European Jew from material action had given to thought a dramatic autonomy. The intimation of an energy of imagination at once sensuous and abstract, the release of the Jewish sensibility into a world dangerously new, unencumbered by reverence, is similarly at work in the subversions of Schoenberg and Kafka, and in the mathematics of Cantor. It relates Wittgenstein's *Tractatus* to that of Spinoza.

Without the contribution made by the Jews between 1830 and 1930, Western culture would be obviously different and diminished. At the same time, of course, it was his collision with established European values, with classic modes of art and argument, which compelled the emancipated Jew to define his range and identity. In this collision, in the attempt to achieve poise in an essentially borrowed milieu, the converted Jew or half-Jew, the Jew whose relation to his own past grew covert or antagonistic—Heine, Bergson, Hofmannsthal, Proust—played a particularly subtle and creative role.

Those who helped define and shared in this *Central European humanism* (each of the three terms carrying its full charge of implication and meaning) showed characteristic traits, characteristic habits of taste and recognition. They had a quick way with languages. Heine is the first, perhaps the only great poet whom it is difficult to locate in any single linguistic sensibility. The habits of reference of this European Jewish generation often point to the Greek and Latin classics; but these were seen through the special focus of Winckelmann, Lessing, and Goethe. An almost axiomatic sense of Goethe's transcendent stature, of the incredible ripeness and humanity of his art, colors the entire European-Jewish enlightenment, and continues to mark its few survivors (Goethe's fragment *On Nature* converted Freud from an early interest in law to the study of the biological sciences). The Central European Jewish bourgeoisie was frequently intimate with the plays of Shakespeare and assumed, rightly, that the performance of Shakespearean drama in Vienna, Munich, or Berlin, often acted and staged by Jews, more than matched what could be found in England. It read Balzac and Stendhal (one recalls Léon Blum's pioneer study of Beyle), Tolstoy, Ibsen, and Zola. But it often read them in a special, almost heightened context. The Jews who welcomed Scandinavian drama and the Russian novel tended to see in the new realism and iconoclasm of literature a part of the general liberation of spirit. Zola was not only the explorer of erotic and economic realities, as were Freud, Weininger, or Marx: he was the champion of Dreyfus.

The relationship of Jewish consciousness to Wagner was passionate, though uneasy. We see late instances of this duality in the musicology of Adorno and the fiction of Werfel. It recognized in Wagner the radicalism and histrionic tactics of a great outsider. It caught in Wagner's anti-Semitism a queer, intimate note, and gave occasional heed to the stubborn myth that Wagner was himself of Jewish descent. Being new to the plastic arts, hence beautifully free and empiric in its responses, Jewish taste, in the guise of dealer, patron, and critic, backed Impressionism and the blaze of the modern. Through Reinhardt and Piscator it renovated the theater; through Gustav Mahler the relations between serious music and society. In its golden period, from 1870 to 1914, then again in the 1920's, the Jewish leaven gave to Prague and Berlin, to Vienna and Paris a specific vitality of feeling and expression, an atmosphere both quintessentially European and "off-center." The nuance of spirit is delicately mocked and made memorable in the unquiet hedonism, in the erudite urbanity of Proust's Swann.

Almost nothing of it survives. This is what makes my own, almost involuntary, identification with it so shadowy a condition. European Jewry and its intelligentsia were caught between two waves of murder, Nazism and Stalinism. The implication of the European and Russian Jew in Marxism had natural causes. As has often been said, the dream of a secular millennium—which is still alive in Georg Lukács and the master historian of hope, Ernst Bloch—relates the social utopia of Communism to the messianic tradition. For both Jew and Communist, history is a scenario of gradual humanization, an immensely difficult attempt by man to become man. In both modes of feeling there is an obsession with the prophetic authority of moral or historical law, with the right reading of canonic revelations. But from Eduard Bernstein to Trotsky, from

Isaac Babel to Pasternak, the involvement of the Jewish personality in Communism and the Russian revolution follows an ironic pattern. Nearly invariably it ends in dissent or heresy—in that heresy which claims to be orthodox because it is seeking to restore the betrayed meaning of Marx (the Polish Marxist Adam Schaff would be a contemporary instance of this "Talmudic revisionism"). As Stalinism turned to nationalism and technocracy—the new Russia of the managerial middle class has its precise origins in the Stalinist period—the revolutionary intelligentsia went to the wall. The Jewish Marxist, the Trotskyite, the socialist fellow-traveler were trapped in the ruins of utopia. The Jew who had joined Communism in order to fight the Nazis, the Jewish Communist who had broken with the party after the purge trials, fell into the net of the Hitler-Stalin pact.

In one of the vilest episodes in modern history, the militia and police of European appeasement and European totalitarianism collaborated in handing over Jews. The French delivered to the Gestapo those who had fled from Spain and Germany. Himmler and the G.P.U. exchanged anti-Stalinist and anti-Nazi Jews for further torture and elimination. One thinks of Walter Benjamin—one of the most brilliant representatives of radical humanism—committing suicide lest the French or Spanish border-guards hand him over to the invading S.S.; of Buber-Neumann whose widow was nearly hounded to death by Stalinist cadres *inside* a Nazi concentration camp; of a score of others trapped between the Nazi and the Stalinist hunter (the memoirs of Victor Serge close with the roll of their several and hideous deaths). Which bestial bargain and exchange at the frontier made eloquent the decision to hound the Jew out of European history. But also the peculiar dignity of his torment. Perhaps we can define ourselves thus: *the Jews are a people whom totalitarian barbarism must choose for its hatred.*

A certain number escaped. It is easily demonstrable that much important work in American scholarship in the period from 1934 to circa 1955, in the arts, in the exact and social sciences, is the afterlife of the Central European renascence and embodied the talent of the refugee. But the particular cast of the American Jewish intelligence on native ground, which I first met at the University of Chicago in the late 1940's, and which now plays so obviously powerful a role in American intellectual and artistic life, is something very different. There is little of Karl Kraus's notion of style and human literacy in, say, *Partisan Review.* Kraus is very nearly a touchstone. Ask a man if he has heard of him or read his *Literature and Lies.* If so, he is probably one of the survivors.

In Kraus, as in Kafka and Hermann Broch, there is a mortal premonition and finality. Broch, who seems to me the major European novelist after Joyce and Mann, is a defining figure. His *Death of Virgil*, his philosophic essays, are an epilogue to humanism. They focus on the deed which should dominate our rational lives so far as we still conduct them, which should persistently bewilder our sense of self—the turn of civilization to mass murder. Like certain parables of Kafka and the epistemology of the early Wittgenstein, the art of Broch goes near the edge of necessary silence. It asks whether speech, whether the shapes of moral judgment and imagination which the Judaic-Hellenic tradition founds on the authority of the Word, are viable in the face of the inhuman. Is the poet's verse not an insult to the naked cry? Broch died in America in a strange, vital solitude, giving voice to a civilization, to an inheritance of humane striving, already done to death.

The humanism of the European Jew lies in literal ash. In the accent of survivors—Hannah Arendt, Ernst Bloch, T. W. Adorno, Erich Kahler, Lévi-Strauss—whose interests and commitments are, of course, diverse, you will hear a common note as of desolation. Yet it is these voices which seem to me contemporary, whose work and context of reference are indispensable to an understanding of the philosophic, political, aesthetic roots of the inhuman; of the paradox that modern barbarism sprang, in some intimate, perhaps necessary way, from the very core and locale of humanistic civilization. If this is so, why do we try to teach, to write, to contend for literacy? Which question, and I know of none more urgent, or the idiom in which it is put, probably puts the asker thirty years out of date—on either side of the present.

As do certain other questions, increasingly muted and out of focus. Yet which cannot go unasked if we are to argue the values and possibilities of our culture. I mean the general complicity, in the massacre. There were superb exceptions (in Denmark, Norway, Bulgaria), but the tale is sordid and much of it remains an ugly riddle. At a time when nine thousand Jews were being exterminated *each day*, neither the R.A.F. nor the U.S. Air Force bombed the ovens or sought to blow open the camps (as Mosquitoes, flying low, had broken wide a prison in France to liberate agents of the *maquis*[2]). Though the Jewish and Polish underground made desperate pleas, though the German bureaucracy made little secret of the fact that the "final solution" depended on rail transport, the lines to Belsen and Auschwitz were not bombed. Why? The question has been asked of Churchill and Tedder. Has there been an adequate answer? When the *Wehrmacht* and *Waffen-S.S.*[3] poured into Russia, Soviet intelligence quickly noted the mass killing of the Jews. Stalin forbade any public announcement of the fact. Here again, the reasons are obscure. He may not have wanted a rekindling of separate

[2] French resistance to German occupation forces.

[3] Branches of the German armed forces.

Jewish consciousness; he may have feared implicit reference to his own anti-Semitic policies. Whatever the cause, many Jews who could have fled eastward stayed behind unknowing. Later on, in the Ukraine, local gangs helped the Germans round up those who cowered in cellars and woods.

I wonder what would have happened if Hitler had played the game after Munich, if he had simply said, "I will make no move outside the Reich so long as I am allowed a free hand inside my borders." Dachau, Buchenwald, and Theresienstadt would have operated in the middle of twentieth-century European civilization until the last Jew in reach had been made soap. There would have been brave words on Trafalgar Square and in Carnegie Hall, to audiences diminishing and bored. Society might, on occasion, have boycotted German wines. But no foreign power would have taken action. Tourists would have crowded the *Autobahn* and spas of the Reich, passing near but not too near the death-camps as we now pass Portuguese jails or Greek prison-islands. There would have been numerous pundits and journalists to assure us that rumors were exaggerated, that Dachau had pleasant walks. And the Red Cross would have sent Christmas parcels.

Below his breath, the Jew asks of his gentile neighbor: "If you had known, would you have cried in the face of God and man that this hideousness must stop? Would you have made some attempt to get my children out? Or planned a skiing party to Garmisch?" The Jew is a living reproach.

Men are accomplices to that which leaves them indifferent. It is this fact which must, I think, make the Jew wary inside Western culture, which must lead him to re-examine ideals and historical traditions that, certainly in Europe, had enlisted the best of his hopes and genius. The house of civilization proved no shelter.

But then, I have never been sure about houses. Perforce, the Jew has often been wanderer and guest. He can buy an old manse and plant a garden. An anxious pastoralism is a distinctive part of the attempt of many American middle-class and intellectual Jews to assimilate to the Anglo-Saxon background. But I wonder whether it's quite the same. The dolls in the attic were not ours; the ghosts have a rented air. Characteristically, Marx, Freud, Einstein end their lives far from their native ground, in exile or refuge. The Jew has his anchorage not in place but in time, in his highly developed sense of history as personal context. Six thousand years of self-awareness are a homeland.

I find that the edge of strangeness and temporary habitation carries over into language, though here again my experience is obviously different from that of the native-born American Jew. European Jews learned languages quickly; often they had to as they wandered. But a final "at homeness" may elude us, that unconscious, immemorial intimacy which a man has with his native idiom as he does with the rock, earth, and ash of his acre. Hence the particular strategies of the two greatest European Jewish writers. Heine's German, as Adorno has pointed out, is a brilliantly personal, European idiom on which his fluent knowledge of French exercised a constant pressure. Kafka wrote German as if it were all bone, as if none of the enveloping texture of colloquialism, of historical and regional overtone, had been allowed him. He used each word as if he had borrowed it at high interest. Many great actors are or have been Jews. Language passes *through* them, and they shape it almost too well, like a treasure acquired, not inalienable. This may be pertinent also to the Jewish excellence in music, physics, and mathematics, whose languages are international and codes of pure denotation.

The European Jew did not want to remain a guest. He strove, as he has done in America, to take root. He gave strenuous, even macabre proof of his loyalty. In 1933–4, Jewish veterans of the First World War assured Herr Hitler of their patriotism, of their devotion to the German ideal. Shortly thereafter, even the limbless and the decorated were hauled to the camps. In 1940, when Vichy stripped French Jews of their rights, veterans of Verdun, holders of the *Médaille militaire*, men whose families had lived in France since the early nineteenth century, found themselves harried and stateless. In the Soviet Union a Jew is so designated on his identity card. Is it foolish or hysterical to suppose that, labor as he may, the Jew in a gentile nation-state sits near the door? Where, inevitably, he arouses distrust.

From Dreyfus to Oppenheimer, every burst of nationalism, of patriotic hysteria, has focused suspicion on the Jew. Such statistics probably have no real meaning, but it may well be that the proportion of Jews actually implicated in ideological or scientific disloyalty has been high. Perhaps because they have been vulnerable to blackmail and clandestine menace, because they are natural middle-men with an ancient ease in the export and import of ideas. But more essentially, I imagine, because they are pariahs whose sense of nationality has been made critical and unsteady. To a man who may tomorrow be in desperate flight across his own border, whose graveyard may be ploughed up and strewn with garbage, the nation-state is an ambiguous haven. Citizenship becomes not an inalienable right, a sacrament of *Blut und Boden*,[4] but a contract which he must re-negotiate, warily, with each host.

The rootlessness of the Jew, the "cosmopolitanism" denounced by Hitler, by Stalin, by Mosley, by every right-wing hooligan, is historically an enforced condition. The Jew finds no comfort in "squatting on

[4] Blood and earth.

the window sill" (T. S. Eliot's courteous phrase). He would rather have been *echt Deutsch*[5] or *Français de vieille souche*[6] or Minuteman born than "Chicago Semite Viennese." At most times he has been given no choice. But though uncomfortable in the extreme, this condition is, if we accept it, not without a larger meaning.

Nationalism is the venom of our age. It has brought Europe to the edge of ruin. It drives the new states of Asia and Africa like crazed lemmings. By proclaiming himself a Ghanaean, a Nicaraguan, a Maltese, a man spares himself vexation. He need not ravel out what he is, where his humanity lies. He becomes one of an armed, coherent pack. Every mob impulse in modern politics, every totalitarian design, feeds on nationalism, on the drug of hatred which makes human beings bare their teeth across a wall, across ten yards of waste ground. Even if it be against his harried will, his weariness, the Jew—or some Jews, at least—may have an exemplary role. To show that whereas trees have roots, men have legs and are each other's guests. If the potential of civilization is not to be destroyed, we shall have to develop more complex, more provisional loyalties. There are, as Socrates taught, necessary treasons to make the city freer and more open to man. Even a Great Society is a bounded, transient thing compared to the free play of the mind and the anarchic discipline of its dreams.

When a Jew opposes the parochial ferocity into which nationalism so easily (inevitably) degenerates, he is paying an old debt. By one of the cruel, deep ironies of history, the concept of a chosen people, of a nation exalted above others by particular destiny, was born in Israel. In the vocabulary of Nazism there were elements of a vengeful parody on the Judaic claim. The theological motif of a people elected at Sinai is echoed in the pretense of the master race and its chiliastic dominion. Thus there was in the obsessed relation of Nazi to Jew a minute but fearful grain of logic.

But if the poison is, in ancient part, Jewish, so perhaps is the antidote, the radical humanism which sees man on the road to becoming man. This is where Marx is most profoundly a Jew—while at the same time arguing the dissolution of Jewish identity. He believed that class and economic status knew no frontiers, that misery had a common citizenship. He postulated that the revolutionary process would abolish national distinctions and antagonisms as industrial technology had all but eroded regional autonomy. The entire socialist utopia and dialectic of history is based on an international premise.

Marx was wrong; here, as in other respects, he thought too romantically, too well of men. Nationalism has been a major cause and bene-

[5] A genuine German.

[6] A Frenchman of old stock.

ficiary of two world wars. The workers of the world did not unite; they tore at each other's throats. Even beggars wrap themselves in flags. It was Russian patriotism, the outrage of national consciousness, not the vision of socialism and class solidarity, which enabled the Soviet Union to survive in 1941. In Eastern Europe, state socialism has left national rivalries fierce and archaic. A thousand miles of empty Siberian steppe may come to matter more to Russia and China than the entire fabric of Communist fraternity.

But though Marx was wrong, though the ideal of a non-national society seems mockingly remote, there is in the last analysis no other alternative to self-destruction. The earth grows too crowded, too harassed by the shadow of famine, to waste soil on barbed wire. Where he can survive as guest, where he can re-examine the relations between conscience and commitment, making his exercise of national loyalty scrupulous but also skeptical and humane, the Jew can act as a valuable irritant. The chauvinist will snarl at his heels. But it is in the nature of a chase that those who are hunted are in advance of the pack.

That is why I have not, until now, been able to accept the notion of going to live in Israel. The State of Israel is, in one sense, a sad miracle. Herzl's Zionist program bore the obvious marks of the rising nationalism of the late nineteenth century. Sprung of inhumanity and the imminence of massacre, Israel has had to make itself a closed fist. No one is more tense with national feeling than an Israeli. He must be if his strip of home is to survive the wolfpack at its doors. Chauvinism is almost the requisite condition of life. But although the strength of Israel reaches deep into the awareness of every Jew, though the survival of the Jewish people may depend on it, the nation-state bristling with arms is a bitter relic, an absurdity in the century of crowded men. And it is alien to some of the most radical, most humane elements in the Jewish spirit.

So a few may want to stay in the cold, outside the sanctuary of nationalism—even though it is, at last, their own. A man need not be buried in Israel. Highgate or Golders Green or the wind will do.

If my children should happen to read this one day, and if luck has held, it may seem as remote to them as it will to a good many of my contemporaries. If things go awry, it may help remind them that somewhere stupidity and barbarism have already chosen them for a target. This is their inheritance. More ancient, more inalienable than any patent of nobility.

Chinua Achebe

(b. 1930)

But for the easy informality with which it brings together so wide an intellectual range of reference, "Language and the Destiny of Man" (1972, Morning Yet on Creation Day) *might come across as erudite. But this is erudition in a radically different service. As a boy in his hometown of Ogidi in eastern Nigeria, before it* was *Nigeria, Chinua Achebe had no notion of becoming a writer, because, he writes, "I did not know of the existence of such creatures until fairly late." From his mother and older sister, he heard traditional, orally transmitted stories of the Igbo people. No one claimed authorship of these stories; no one owned them. They had for him "the immemorial quality of sky and forests and rivers" ("Named for Victoria, Queen of England"). Then, at age eight, he learned English and was introduced, in due course, to the European world of authored texts—of the individual writer creating stories and poems that are marked with his own name. Since the late 1950s, Achebe has been producing (among poems, lectures, stories, and essays) a stunning group of novels in English about the cultural and individual costs of colonialism and its aftermath:* Things Fall Apart, No Longer at Ease, Arrow of God, Man of the People. *All the while, he has been creating another sort of text by way of his life and example: the modern African artist. "Let no one be fooled by the fact that we write in English," he says of himself and fellow artists working in the colonizer's medium, "for we intend to do unheard of things with it" ("Colonialist Criticism"). Deeply committed to his art and as deeply absorbed in the task of cultural transformation, Achebe links his own work as a writer with the practice of traditional African storytellers "who lived and moved and had their being in society, and created their works for the good of that society" ("Africa and Her Writers"). Through the imaginative experience of literature, oral or written, the artist works like a teacher leading others to explore who they are and what kind of world they want to create. Our "perilous destiny" as human beings is this freedom to shape our existence, and the vital medium of that shaping is language—how we use it or abuse it. In "Language and the Destiny of Man" (1972,* Morning Yet on Creation Day), *Chinua Achebe joins his own literate cosmopolitan voice to the traditional voices of mythic narratives, repeating in a new way their old wisdom about words and truth, and about the importance of not letting them become severed.*

Language and the Destiny of Man

In his long evolutionary history man has scored few greater successes than his creation of human society. For it was on that primeval achievement that he has built those special qualities of mind and of behavior which, in his own view at least, separate him from lower forms of life. If we sometimes tend to overlook this fact, it is only because we have lived so long under the protective ambiance of society that we have come to take its benefits for granted. Which, in a way, might be called the ultimate tribute; rather like the unspoken worship and thanksgiving which a man renders with every breath he draws. If it were different, we would not be men but angels, incapable of boredom.

Unquestionably, language was crucial to the creation of society. There is no way in which human society could exist without speech. By society we do not, of course, mean the mechanical and mindless association of the beehive or the anthill which employs certain rudimentary forms of communication to achieve an unvarying, instinctual purpose, but a community where man "doomed to be free"—to use Joyce Cary's remarkable phrase—is yet able to challenge that peculiar and perilous destiny with an even chance of wresting from it a purposeful, creative existence.

Speech too, like society itself, seems so natural that we rarely give much thought to it or contemplate man's circumstance before its invention. But we know that language is not inherent in man—the capacity for language, yes; but not language. Therefore there must have been a time in the very distant past when our ancestors did not have it. Let us imagine a very simple incident in those days. A man strays into a rock shelter without knowing that another is there finishing a meal in the dark interior. The first hint our newcomer gets of this fact is a loose rock hurled at his head. In a different kind of situation, which we shall call (with all kinds of guilty reservations) *human*, that confrontation might have been resolved less destructively by the simple question: *What do you want?* or even an angry: *Get out of here!*

Nobody is, of course, going to be so naïve as to claim for language the power to dispose of all, or even most, violence. After all man is not less violent than other animals, but more—apparently the only one which consistently visits violence on its own kind. Yet in spite of this (or perhaps because of it) one does have a feeling that without language we should have long been extinct.

Many people, following the fascinating progress of Dr. L. S. B. Leakey's famous excavations in the Olduvai Gorge in eastern Africa in the 1950s, were shocked by his claim that the so-called "pre-Zinjanthropus" child, the discovery of whose remains stirred many hearts and was one of the high lights of modern paleontology, was probably murdered, aged about twelve. Another excavator, Professor Raymond Dart, working farther south, has collected much similar evidence of homicide in the caves of Transvaal.[1] But we should not have been surprised or shocked unless we had overlooked the psychological probability of the murder outside the Garden of Eden.

Let us take a second and quite different kind of example. Let us imagine an infant crying. Its mother assumes that it is hungry and offers it food; but it refuses to eat and goes on crying. Is it wet? Does it have pain? If so, where? Has an ant crawled into its dress and bitten it? Does it want to sleep? etc., etc. Thus the mother, especially if she lacks experience (as more and more mothers tend to do), will grope from one impulse to another, from one possibility to its opposite until she stumbles on the right one. Meanwhile the child suffers distress, and she, mental anguish. In other words, because of a child's inadequate vocabulary, even its simplest needs cannot be quickly known and satisfied. From which rather silly example we can see, I hope, the value of language in facilitating the affairs and transactions of society by enabling its members to pass on their message quickly and exactly.

In small close-knit societies, such as we often call primitive, the importance of language is seen in pristine clarity. For instance, in the creation myth of the Hebrews, God made the world by word of mouth; and in the Christian myth, as recorded in St. John's Gospel, the Word became God himself.

African societies in the past held similar notions about language and the potency of words. Writing about Igbo society in Nigeria, Igwe and Green had this to say:

> a speaker who could use language effectively and had a good command of idioms and proverbs was respected by his fellows and was often a leader in the community.[2]

From another part of Africa a Kenyan, Mugo Gatheru, in his autobiographical book gives even stronger testimony from his people:

> among the Kikuyu those who speak well have always been honoured, and the very word *chief* means *good talker*.[3]

There is a remarkable creation myth among the Wapangwa people of Tanzania which begins thus:

[1] Sonia Cole, *The Prehistory of East Africa*. London: Wedenfeld & Nicolson. [All footnotes in the essay are Achebe's.]

[2] G. E. Igwe & M. M. Green, *Igbo Language Course*. London: Oxford University Press.

[3] Mugo Gatheru, *A Child of Two Worlds*. London: Heinemann Educational Books, p. 40.

> The sky was large, white, and very clear. It was empty; there were no stars and no moon; only a tree stood in the air and there was wind. This tree fed on the atmosphere and ants lived on it. Wind, tree, ants, and atmosphere were controlled by the power of the Word, but the Word was not something that could be seen. It was a force that enabled one thing to create another.[4]

But although contemporary societies in Africa and elsewhere have moved away from beliefs and attitudes which had invested language with such ritual qualities, we can still find remains of the old dignity in certain places and circumstances. In his famous autobiography, Camara Laye records the survival of such an attitude in the Guinea of his boyhood: the strong impression that the traditional village could make on the visitor from the town.

> In everything, I noticed a kind of dignity which was often lacking in town life. . . . And if their minds seemed to work slower in the country, that was because they always spoke only after due reflection, and because speech itself was a most serious matter.[5]

And finally, from a totally different environment, these lines of a traditional Eskimo poem, "Magic Words," from Jerome Rothenberg's excellent anthology, *Shaking the Pumpkin:*

> That was the time when words were like magic
> The human mind had mysterious powers.
> A word spoken by chance
> might have strange consequences.
> It would suddenly come alive
> and what people wanted to happen could happen—
> all you had to do was say it.[6]

In small and self-sufficient societies such as gave birth to these myths, the integrity of language is safeguarded by the fact that what goes on in the community can easily be ascertained, understood, and evaluated by all. The line between truth and falsehood thus tends to be sharp, and when a man addresses his fellows, they know already what kind of person he is, whether (as Igbo people would put it) he is one with whose words something can be done; or else who, if he tells you to stand, you know you must immediately flee!

[4] Ulli Beier, ed., *The Origin of Life and Death.* London: Heinemann.

[5] Camara Laye, *The African Child.* London and Glasgow: Fontana, p. 53.

[6] Jerome Rothenberg, ed., *Shaking the Pumpkin.* New York: Doubleday.

But as society becomes larger and more complex, we find that we can no longer be in command of all the facts but are obliged to take a good deal of what we hear on trust. We delegate to others the power to take certain decisions on our behalf, and they may not always be people we know or can vouch for. I shall return shortly to a consideration of this phenomenon. But first I shall consider a different, though related, problem—the pressure to which language is subjected by the mere fact that it can never change fast enough to deal with every new factor in the ever-increasing complexity of the life of the community, to say nothing of the private perceptions and idiosyncracies of particular speakers. T. S. Eliot comes readily to mind with those memorable lines in which he suggests to us the constant struggle, frustration, and anguish which this situation imposes on a poet:

> . . . Trying to learn to use words, and every attempt
> Is a wholly new start and a different kind of failure
> Because one has only learnt to get the better of words
> For the thing one no longer has to say, or the way in which
> One is no longer disposed to say it. . . .

Of course one might wonder whether this problem was a real one for ordinary people like ourselves or a peculiar species of self-flagellation by a high-strung devotee seeking through torment to become worthy of his deity. For, as in these well-known lines, Eliot's celebration of his ideal can sometimes assume accents of holy intoxication:

> And every phrase
> And sentence that is right (where every word is at home,
> Taking its place to support the others
> The word neither diffident nor ostentatious,
> An easy commerce of the old and the new,
> The common word exact without vulgarity,
> The formal word precise but not pedantic,
> The complete consort dancing together)
> Every phrase and every sentence is an end and a beginning,
> Every poem an epitaph.

This curious mix of high purpose and carnival jollity may leave us a little puzzled, but there is no doubt whatever about Eliot's concern and solicitude for the integrity of words. And let us not imagine, even the most prosaic among us, that this concern and the stringent practice Eliot advocates are appropriate only to poets. For we all stand to lose when language is debased, just as every one of us is affected when the nation's currency is devalued; not just the Secretary of the Treasury, or controllers of our banks.

Talking about secretaries of the Treasury and devaluation, there was an amusing quotation by Professor Douglas Bush in an essay entitled "Polluting Our Languages" in the Spring 1972 issue of *The American Scholar*. The Secretary of the Treasury, John Connally, had said: "In the early sixties we were strong; we were virulent." Clearly that was only a slip, albeit of a kind that might interest Freudians. But it might not be entirely unfair to see a tendency to devaluation inherent in certain occupations!

We must now turn from considering the necessary struggle with language arising, as it were, from its very nature and the nature of the society it serves to the more ominous threat to its integrity brought about neither by its innate inadequacy nor yet by the incompetence and carelessness of its ordinary users, but rather engineered deliberately by those who will manipulate words for their own ends. It has long been known that language, like any other human invention, can be abused, can be turned from its original purpose into something useless or even deadly. George Orwell, who was very much concerned in his writings with this modern menace, reminds us that language can be used not only for expressing thought but for concealing thought or even preventing thought.[7] I guess we are all too familiar with this—from the mild assault of the sales pitch which exhorts you: "Be progressive! Use ABC toothpaste!" or invites you to a *saving spree* in a department store; through the mystifications of learned people jealously guarding the precincts of their secret societies with such shibboleths as: "Bilateral mastectomy was performed" instead of "Both breasts were removed";[8] to the politician who employs government prose to keep you in the dark about affairs on which your life or the lives of your children may depend, or the official statistician who assures you that crime rates "are increasing at a decreasing rate of increase." I shall not waste your time about this well-known fact of modern life. But let me round off this aspect of the matter by quoting a little of the comment made by W. H. Auden in an interview published by the New York *Times* (October 19, 1971):

> As a poet—not as a citizen—there is only one political duty, and that is to defend one's language from corruption. And that is particularly serious now. It's being so quickly corrupted. When it is corrupted, people lose faith in what they hear, and this leads to violence.

And leads also full circle to the cave-man situation with which we began. And the heart of my purpose is to suggest that our remote an-

[7] George Orwell, "Politics and the English Language," in *Essays*. New York: Doubleday.
[8] Dr. F. Nwako, "Disorders in Medical Education," in *Nsukkascope*, 1972.

cestors who made and preserved language for us, who, you might say, crossed the first threshold from bestiality to humanness, left us also adequate warning, wrapped in symbols, against its misuse.

Every people has a body of myths or sacred tales received from its antiquity. They are supernatural stories which man created to explain the problems and mysteries of life and death—his attempt to make sense of the bewildering complexity of existence. There is a proud, nomadic people, the Fulani, who inhabit the northern savannahs of Western Africa from Cameroun and Nigeria westward to Mali and Senegal. They are very much attached to their cattle, whose milk is their staff of life. Here is a Fulani myth of creation from Mali:

At the beginning there was a huge drop of milk.
Then Doondari came and he created the stone.
Then the stone created iron;
And iron created fire;
And fire created water;
And water created air.

Then Doondari descended the second time.
And he took the five elements,
And he shaped them into man.
But man was proud.
Then Doondari created blindness and blindness defeated man.
But when blindness became too proud,
Doondari created sleep, and sleep defeated blindness;
But when sleep became too proud,
Doondari created worry, and worry defeated sleep;
But when worry became too proud,
Doondari created death, and death defeated worry.

But when death became too proud,
Doondari descended for the third time,
And he came as Gueno, the eternal one
And Gueno defeated death.[9]

You notice, don't you, how in the second section of that poem, after the creation of man, we have that phrase *became too proud* coming back again and again like the recurrence of a dominant beat in rhythmic music? Clearly the makers of that myth intended us not to miss it. So it was at the very heart of their purpose. MAN IS DESTROYED BY PRIDE. It is said over and over again; it is shouted like a message across vast distances until the man at the other end of the savannah has defi-

[9] Ulli Beier, op. cit.

nitely got it, despite the noise of rushing winds. Or if you prefer a modern metaphor, it is like making a long-distance call when the line is faulty or in bad weather. You shout your message and repeat it again and again just to make sure.

Claude Lévi-Strauss, the French structural anthropologist, has indeed sought to explain the repetitive factor in myth in this way, relating it to general information theory. Our forefathers and ancestors are seen in the role of *senders* of the message, and we, the novices of society, as *receivers*.[10] The ancestors are sending us signals from the long history and experience of by-gone days about the meaning of life, the qualities we should cultivate, and the values that are important. Because they are so far away and because we are surrounded by the tumult and distractions of daily life, they have to shout and repeat themselves not only in phrase after phrase but also in myth after myth, varying the form slightly now and again until the central message goes home.

If this interpretation is right, then the Fulani myth of creation delivers not only a particular message on the danger of pride but also exemplifies beautifully the general intention and purpose of myths. Let us now look at another short myth from the Igbo people in Nigeria which bears more directly on the question of language:

> When death first entered the world, men sent a messenger to Chuku, asking him whether the dead could not be restored to life and sent back to their old homes. They chose the dog as their messenger.
>
> The dog, however, did not go straight to Chuku, and dallied on the way. The toad had overheard the message, and as he wished to punish mankind, he overtook the dog and reached Chuku first. He said he had been sent by men to say that after death they had no desire at all to return to the world. Chuku declared that he would respect their wishes, and when the dog arrived with the true message he refused to alter his decision.
>
> Thus although a human being may be born again, he cannot return with the same body and the same personality.[11]

It has been pointed out that there are more than seven hundred different versions of this myth all over Africa. Thus the element of repetition, which we have seen in the form of a phrase recurring in time within one myth, takes on the formidable power of spatial dispersion across a continent. Clearly the ancestral senders regard this particular signal as of

[10] Edmund Leach, *Lévi-Strauss*. London: Fontana/Collins.

[11] Ulli Beier, op. cit.

desperate importance, hence its ubiquity and the profuse variations of its theme. Sometimes the messenger is the dog; sometimes, the chameleon or the lizard or some other animal. In some versions the message is garbled through the incompetence of the messenger, or through his calculated malice against men. In others man in his impatience sends a second messenger to God who in anger withdraws the gift of immortality. But whatever variations in the detail, the dominant theme remains: Men send a messenger to their Creator with a plea for immortality and He is disposed to grant their request. But something goes wrong with the message at the last moment. And this bounty which mankind has all but held in its grasp, this monumental gift that would have made man more like the gods, is snatched from him forever. And he knows that there is a way to hell even from the gates of heaven!

This, to my mind, is the great myth about language and the destiny of man. Its lesson should be clear to all. It is as though the ancestors, who made language and knew from what bestiality its use rescued them, are saying to us: Beware of interfering with its purpose! For when language is seriously interfered with, when it is disjoined from truth, be it from mere incompetence or worse, from malice, horrors can descend again on mankind.

Carol Bly

(b. 1930)

Whether by deliberation or "unconsciously," as she herself might put it, Carol Bly assumes in her collection of essays, Letters from the Country, *Emerson's idea of "a correspondence between the human soul and everything that exists in the world"* (Journal, *September 8, 1833*). *A quotation from the poet Robert Bly heads her fine essay "Great Snows": "How strange to think of giving up all ambition! / Suddenly I see with such clear eyes / The white flake of snow / That has just fallen in the horse's mane." In the spirit of the poem, the essayist concludes that the two things which "make nature lovely to people"—even its great snowstorms—are "enforced, extended leisure in a natural place" and "planning our lives instead of just following along." She imagines mundane life situations, like the moment someone decides to turn down an ecologically damaging job, or refuses to pad an expense account after all. In such moments—and surely all of us have had such experiences—"ice and snow and bare trunks look better, less happenstance, less pointless"; with rare clarity, you suddenly see the beauty of snow in the horse's mane. The exercise of our moral nature puts us back into right relation with the world and brings a compensation that comes no other way. Bly's subject in* Letters from the Country *is the people of rural Minnesota—their "psychic reality." Determined to expose all that goes wrong between them and the world, she tackles particulars of government, business, schooling, family, church, small towns, grant-giving—anything that helps or hinders that relationship through which the individual receives his or her natural reward. And that reward is a happiness emerging from the unity of moral behavior and aesthetic insight. "Getting Tired" (1973) reads like a description of how to be happy, of one woman seeing clearly the world around her. Nor is this a sentimentalized or romanticized happiness, but one in which the hard realities, tiredness and death, ride the open tractor with her. We tend, she suggests, to look for compensation in the wrong places. Bly's very American voice strives for a language, unpretentious but forcefully wrought, to articulate what she considers the only satisfying human heritage.*

Getting Tired

The men have left a gigantic 6600 combine a few yards from our grove, at the edge of the stubble. For days it was working around the farm; we heard it on the east, later on the west, and finally we could see it grinding back and forth over the windrows on the south. But now it has been simply squatting at the field's edge, huge, tremendously still, very professional, slightly dangerous.

We all have the correct feelings about this new combine: this isn't the good old farming where man and soil are dusted together all day; this isn't farming a poor man can afford, either, and therefore it further threatens his hold on the American "family farm" operation. We have been sneering at this machine for days, as its transistor radio, amplified well over the engine roar, has been grinding up our silence, spreading a kind of shrill ghetto evening all over the farm.

But now it is parked, and after a while I walk over to it and climb up its neat little John-Deere-green ladder on the left. Entering the big cab up there is like coming up into a large ship's bridge on visitors' day—heady stuff to see the inside workings of a huge operation like the Queen Elizabeth II. On the other hand I feel left out, being only a dumbfounded passenger. The combine cab has huge windows flaring wider at the top; they lean forward over the ground, and the driver sits so high behind the glass in its rubber moldings it is like a movie-set spaceship. He has obviously come to dominate the field, whether he farms it or not.

The value of the 66 is that it can do anything, and to change it from a combine into a cornpicker takes one man about half an hour, whereas most machine conversions on farms take several men a half day. It frees its owner from a lot of monkeying.

Monkeying, in city life, is what little boys do to clocks so they never run again. In farming it has two quite different meanings. The first is small side projects. You monkey with poultry, unless you're a major egg handler. Or you monkey with ducks or geese. If you have a very small milk herd, and finally decide that prices plus state regulations don't make your few Holsteins worthwhile, you "quit monkeying with them." There is a hidden dignity in this word: it precludes mention of money. It lets the wife of a very marginal farmer have a conversation with a woman who may be helping her husband run fifteen hundred acres. "How you coming with those geese?" "Oh, we've been real disgusted. We're thinking of quitting monkeying with them." It saves her having to say, "We lost our shirts on those darn geese."

The other meaning of monkeying is wrestling with and maintaining machinery, such as changing heads from combining to cornpicking. Farmers who cornpick the old way, in which the corn isn't shelled automatically during picking in the field but must be elevated to the top of a pile by belt and then shelled, put up with some monkeying.

Still, cornpicking and plowing is a marvelous time of the year on farms; one of the best autumns I've had recently had a few days of fieldwork in it. We were outside all day, from six in the morning to eight at night—coming in only for noon dinner. We ate our lunches on a messy truck flatbed. (For city people who don't know it: *lunch* isn't a noon meal; it is what you eat out of a black lunch pail at 9 A.M. and 3 P.M. If you offer a farmer a cup of coffee at 3:30 P.M. he or she is likely to say, "No thanks, I've already had lunch.") There were four of us hired to help—a couple to plow, Celia (a skilled farmhand who worked steady for our boss), and me. Lunch was always two sandwiches of white commercial bread with luncheon meat, and one very generous piece of cake-mix cake carefully wrapped in Saran Wrap. (I never found anyone around here self-conscious about using Saran Wrap when the Dow Chemical Company was also making napalm.)

It was very pleasant on the flatbed, squinting out over the yellow picked cornstalks—each time we stopped for lunch, a larger part of the field had been plowed black. We fell into the easy psychic habit of farmworkers: admiration of the boss. "Ja, I see he's buying one of those big 4010s," someone would say. We always perked up at inside information like that. Or "Ja," as the woman hired steady told us, "he's going to plow the home fields first this time, instead of the other way round." We temporary help were impressed by that, too. Then, with real flair, she brushed a crumb of luncheon meat off her jeans, the way you would make sure to flick a gnat off spotless tennis whites. It is the true feminine touch to brush a crumb off pants that are encrusted with Minnesota Profile A heavy loam, many swipes of SAE 40 oil, and grain dust.

All those days, we never tired of exchanging information on how *he* was making out, what *he* was buying, whom *he* was going to let drive the new tractor, and so on. There is always something to talk about with the other hands, because farming is genuinely absorbing. It has the best quality of work: nothing else seems real. And everyone doing it, even the cheapest helpers like me, can see the layout of the whole—from spring work, to cultivating, to small grain harvest, to cornpicking, to fall plowing.

The second day I was promoted from elevating corncobs at the corn pile to actual plowing. Hour after hour I sat up there on the old Alice, as she was called (an Allis-Chalmers WC that looked rusted from the

Flood). You have to sit twisted part way around, checking that the plowshares are scouring clean, turning over and dropping the dead crop and soil, not clogging. For the first two hours I was very political. I thought about what would be good for American farming—stronger marketing organizations, or maybe a law like the Norwegian Odal law, preventing the breaking up of small farms or selling them to business interests. Then the sun got high, and each time I reached the headlands area at the field's end I dumped off something else, now my cap, next my jacket, finally my sweater.

Since the headlands are the last to be plowed, they serve as a field road until the very end. There are usually things parked there—a pickup or a corn trailer—and things dumped—my warmer clothing, our afternoon lunch pails, a broken furrow wheel someone picked up.

By noon I'd dropped all political interest, and was thinking only: how unlike this all is to Keats's picture of autumn, a "season of mists and mellow fruitfulness." This gigantic expanse of horizon, with everywhere the easy growl of tractors, was simply teeming with extrovert energy. It wouldn't calm down for another week, when whoever was lowest on the totem pole would be sent out to check a field for dropped parts or to drive away the last machines left around.

The worst hours for all common labor are the hours after noon dinner. Nothing is inspiring then. That is when people wonder how they ever got stuck in the line of work they've chosen for life. Or they wonder where the cool Indian smoke of secrets and messages began to vanish from their marriage. Instead of plugging along like a cheerful beast working for me, the Allis now smelled particularly gassy. To stay awake I froze my eyes onto an indented circle in the hood around the gas cap. Someone had apparently knocked the screw cap fitting down into the hood, so there was a moat around it. In this moat some overflow gas leapt in tiny waves. Sometimes the gas cap was a castle, this was the moat; sometimes it was a nuclear-fission plant, this was the horrible hot-water waste. Sometimes it was just the gas cap on the old Alice with the spilt gas bouncing on the hot metal.

Row after row. I was stupefied. But then around 2:30 the shadows appeared again, and the light, which had been dazing and white, grew fragile. The whole prairie began to gather itself for the cool evening. All of a sudden it was wonderful to be plowing again, and when I came to the field end, the filthy jackets and the busted furrow wheel were just benign mistakes: that is, if it chose to, the jacket could be a church robe, and the old wheel could be something with some pride to it, like a helm. And I felt the same about myself: instead of being someone with a half interest in literature and a half interest in farming doing a half-decent job plowing, I could have been someone desperately needed in Washington or Zurich. I drank my three o'clock coffee joyously, and traded the other plowman a Super-Valu cake-mix lemon cake slice for a Holsum baloney sandwich because it had garlic in it.

By seven at night we had been plowing with headlights for an hour. I tried to make up games to keep going, on my second wind, on my third wind, but labor is labor after the whole day of it; the mind refuses to think of ancestors. It refuses to pretend the stalks marching up to the right wheel in the spooky light are men-at-arms, or to imagine a new generation coming along. It doesn't care. Now the Republicans could have announced a local meeting in which they would propose a new farm program whereby every farmer owning less than five hundred acres must take half price for his crop, and every farmer owning more than a thousand acres shall receive triple price for his crop, and I was so tired I wouldn't have shown up to protest.

A million hours later we sit around in a daze at the dining-room table, and nobody says anything. In low, courteous mutters we ask for the macaroni hotdish down this way, please. Then we get up in ones and twos and go home. Now the farm help are all so tired we *are* a little like the various things left out on the headlands—some tools, a jacket, someone's thermos top—used up for that day. Thoughts won't even stick to us anymore.

Such tiredness must be part of farmers' wanting huge machinery like the Deere 6600. That tiredness that feels so good to the occasional laborer and the athlete is disturbing to a man destined to it eight months of every year. But there is a more hidden psychology in the issue of enclosed combines versus open tractors. It is this: one gets too many impressions on the open tractor. A thousand impressions enter as you work up and down the rows: nature's beauty or nature's stubbornness, politics, exhaustion, but mainly the feeling that all this repetition—last year's cornpicking, this year's cornpicking, next year's cornpicking—is taking up your lifetime. The mere repetition reveals your eventual death.

When you sit inside a modern combine, on the other hand, you are so isolated from field, sky, all the real world, that the brain is dulled. You are not sensitized to your own mortality. You aren't sensitive to anything at all.

This must be a common choice of our mechanical era: to hide from life inside our machinery. If we can hide from life in there, some idiotic part of the psyche reasons, we can hide from death in there as well.

Donald Barthelme

(1931–1989)

Barthelme's "Not-Knowing" illustrates, in a delightful way, the fact that no kind of discourse, no device fictional or nonfictional, no turn of mind, is excluded from the essayist's repertoire; any of it may be worked into the structure of an essay. It isn't a matter of destroying generic boundaries, breaking down this literary wall or that. Nothing so violent; this essay slides so lightly from story to commentary, to story, to theory, to analysis, to story, to report, to ethics, that we can hardly fail to see in its "activity of mind" a demonstration of how to move freely without boundaries. What creates boundaries is observance; don't observe them and they don't exist—except as a background of possibilities not being observed. "This is fun for everyone" (said, in the essay, in reference to a critic who has managed to reduce one of the author's stories to a footnote). Barthelme's novels and stories began appearing in the early 1960s about the time theory was summoning up a phenomenon called "postmodernism," of which his writing was shortly seen as a signal instance. Writing, he says here, is "a process of not-knowing" (yet language purports to convey knowledge); but there's another kind of not-knowing, namely ignorance of what postmodern writers are up to, especially on the part of critics. You might miss it in the fun of reading, but this is a didactic essay that teaches by showing what one postmodern writer does and how he does it. He dramatizes the trouble we're always in: that language is deaf and dumb to itself; it can't hear its own duplicities or say what it's doing in the moment of doing it, and so it has to be caught off guard, lured by the writer into revealing little things about itself. Above all, language has to be constantly monitored and fiddled with, disciplined not to support any myths or rituals, old or new, of power. Because: it's just by means of these rituals of power that language enters into the complicity whereby culture represents itself as reality and so compels our deepest allegiances, exacts a piety of violence from us in defense of this "reality." (Witness the ideological languages of nationalism, and all the other -isms.) The postmodern writer subverts this complicity by draining language of its power to function as the sine qua non *of cultural violence. Left with this gentling of language and its artful, peaceful pleasures excluding no one, we're led to ask: if art's so good, why ain't it life? Now that's the right question—about yet another boundary we might not always wish to observe. The writer's problem: how to render "the as-yet unspeakable, the as-yet unspoken."*

Not-Knowing

Let us suppose that someone is writing a story. From the world of conventional signs he takes an azalea bush, plants it in a pleasant park. He takes a gold pocket watch from the world of conventional signs and places it under the azalea bush. He takes from the same rich source a handsome thief and a chastity belt, places the thief in the chastity belt and lays him tenderly under the azalea, not neglecting to wind the gold pocket watch so that its ticking will, at length, awaken the now-sleeping thief. From the Sarah Lawrence campus he borrows a pair of seniors. Jacqueline and Jemima, and sets them to walking in the vicinity of the azalea bush and the handsome, chaste thief. Jacqueline and Jemima have just failed the Graduate Record Examination and are cursing God in colorful Sarah Lawrence language. What happens next?

Of course, I don't know.

It's appropriate to pause and say that the writer is one who, embarking upon a task, does not know what to do. I cannot tell you, at this moment, whether Jacqueline and Jemima will succeed or fail in their effort to jimmy the chastity belt's lock, or whether the thief, whose name is Zeno and who has stolen the answer sheets for the next set of Graduate Record Examinations, will pocket the pocket watch or turn it over to the nearest park employee. The fate of the azalea bush, whether it will bloom or strangle in a killing frost, is unknown to me.

A very conscientious writer might purchase an azalea at the Downtown Nursery and a gold watch at Tiffany's, hire a handsome thief fresh from Riker's Island, obtain the loan of a chastity belt from the Metropolitan, inveigle Jacqueline and Jemima in from Bronxville, and arrange them all under glass for study, writing up the results in honest, even fastidious prose. But in so doing he places himself in the realm of journalism or sociology. The not-knowing is crucial to art, is what permits art to be made. Without the scanning process engendered by not-knowing, without the possibility of having the mind move in unanticipated directions, there would be no invention.

This is not to say that I don't know anything about Jacqueline or Jemima, but what I do know comes into being at the instant it's inscribed. Jacqueline, for example, loathes her mother, whereas Jemima dotes on hers—I discover this by writing the sentence that announces it. Zeno was fathered by a—what? Polar bear? Roller skate? Shower of gold? I opt for the shower of gold, for Zeno is a hero (although he's just become one by virtue of his golden parent). Inside the pocket watch there is engraved a legend. Can I make it out? I think so: *Drink me*, it says. No no, can't use it, that's Lewis Carroll's. But could Zeno be a watch swallower rather than a thief? No again, Zeno'd choke on it, and so would the reader. There are rules.

Writing is a process of dealing with not-knowing, a forcing of what and how. We have all heard novelists testify to the fact that, beginning a new book, they are utterly baffled as to how to proceed, what should be written and how it might be written, even though they've done a dozen. At best there's a slender intuition, not much greater than an itch. The anxiety attached to this situation is not inconsiderable. "Nothing to paint and nothing to paint with," as Beckett says of Bram van Velde. The not-knowing is not simple, because it's hedged about with prohibitions, roads that may not be taken. The more serious the artist, the more problems he takes into account and the more considerations limit his possible initiatives—a point to which I shall return.

What kind of fellow is Zeno? How do I know until he's opened his mouth?

"*Gently, ladies, gently,*" says Zeno, as Jacqueline and Jemima bash away at the belt with a spade borrowed from a friendly park employee. And to the park employee: "Somebody seems to have lost thishere watch."

Let us change the scene.

Alphonse, the park employee from the preceding episode, he who lent the spade, is alone in his dismal room on West Street (I could position him as well in a four-story townhouse on East Seventy-second, but you'd object, and rightly so, verisimilitude forbids it, nothing's calculated quicker than a salary). Alphonse, like so many toilers in the great city, is not as simple as he seems. Like those waiters who are really actors and those cab drivers who are really composers of electronic music, Alphonse is sunlighting as a Parks Department employee although he is, in reality, a literary critic. We find him writing a letter to his friend Gaston, also a literary critic although masquerading pro tem as a guard at the Whitney Museum. Alphonse poises paws over his Smith-Corona and writes:

> Dear Gaston,
> Yes, you are absolutely right—Postmodernism is dead. A stunning blow, but not entirely surprising. I am spreading the news as rapidly as possible, so that all of our friends who are in the Postmodernist "bag" can get out of it before their cars are repossessed and the insurance companies tear up their policies. Sad to see Postmodernism go (and so quickly!). I was fond of it. As fond, almost, as I was of its grave and noble predecessor, Modernism. But we cannot dwell in the done-for. The death of a movement is

a natural part of life, as was understood so well by the partisans of Naturalism, which is dead.

I remember exactly where I was when I realized that Postmodernism had bought it. I was in my study with a cup of tequila and William Y's new book, *One-Half*. Y's work is, we agree, good—*very* good. But who can make the leap to greatness while dragging after him the burnt-out boxcars of a dead aesthetic? Perhaps we can find new employment for him. On the roads, for example. When the insight overtook me, I started to my feet, knocking over the tequila, and said aloud (although there was no one to hear), "What? Postmodernism, too?" So many, so many. I put Y's book away on a high shelf and turned to the contemplation of the death of Plainsong, A.D. 958.

By the way: Structuralism's tottering. I heard it from Gerald, who is at Johns Hopkins and thus in the thick of things. You don't have to tell everybody. Frequently, idle talk is enough to give a movement that last little "push" that topples it into its grave. I'm convinced that's what happened to the New Criticism. I'm persuaded that it was Gerald, whispering in the corridors.

On the bright side, one thing that is dead that I don't feel too bad about is Existentialism, which I never thought was anything more than Phenomenology's bathwater anyway. It had a good run, but how peeving it was to hear all those artists going around talking about "the existential moment" and similar claptrap. Luckily, they have stopped doing that now. Similarly, the Nouveau Roman's passing did not disturb me overmuch. "Made dreariness into a religion," you said, quite correctly. I know this was one of your pared-to-the-bone movements and all that, but I didn't even like what they left out. A neat omission usually raises the hairs on the back of my neck. Not here. Robbe-Grillet's only true success, for my money, was with *Jealousy*, which I'm told he wrote in a fit of.

Well, where are we? Surrealism gone, got a little sweet toward the end, you could watch the wine of life turning into Gatorade. Sticky. Altar Poems—those constructed in the shape of an altar for the greater honor and glory of God—have not been seen much lately: missing and presumed dead. The Anti-Novel is dead; I read it in the *Times*. The Anti-Hero and the Anti-Heroine had a thing going which resulted in three Anti-Children, all of them now at M.I.T. The Novel of the Soil is dead, as are Expressionism, Impressionism, Futurism, Imagism, Vorticism, Regionalism, Realism, the Kitchen Sink School of Drama, the Theatre of the Absurd, the Theatre of Cruelty, Black Humor, and Gongorism. You know all this; I'm just totting up. To be a Pre-Raphaelite in the present era is to be somewhat out of touch. And, of course, Concrete Poetry—sank like a stone.

So we have a difficulty. What shall we call the New Thing, which I haven't encountered yet but which is bound to be out there somewhere? Post-Postmodernism sounds, to me, a little lumpy. I've been toying with the Revolution of the Word, II, or the New Revolution of the Word, but I'm afraid the Jolas estate may hold a copyright. It should have the word *new* in it somewhere. The New Newness? Or maybe the Post-New? It's a problem. I await your comments and suggestions. If we're going to slap a saddle on this rough beast, we've got to get moving.

Yours,
Alphonse

If I am slightly more sanguine than Alphonse about Post-modernism, however dubious about the term itself and not altogether clear as to who is supposed to be on the bus and who is not, it's because I locate it in relation to a series of problems, and feel that the problems are durable ones. Problems are a comfort. Wittgenstein said, of philosophers, that some of them suffer from "loss of problems," a development in which everything seems quite simple to them and what they write becomes "immeasurably shallow and trivial." The same can be said of writers. Before I mention some of the specific difficulties I have in mind, I'd like to at least glance at some of the criticisms that have been leveled at the alleged Postmodernists—let's say John Barth, William Gass, John Hawkes, Robert Coover, William Gaddis, Thomas Pynchon, and myself in this country, Calvino in Italy, Peter Handke and Thomas Bernhard in Germany, although other names could be invoked. The criticisms run roughly as follows: that this kind of writing has turned its back on the world, is in some sense not about the world but about its own processes, that it is masturbatory, certainly chilly, that is excludes readers by design, speaks only to the already tenured, or that it does not speak at all, but instead, like Frost's Secret, sits in the center of a ring and Knows.

I would ardently contest each of these propositions, but it's rather easy to see what gives rise to them. The problems that seem to me to define the writer's task at this moment (to the extent that he has chosen them as his problems) are not of a kind that make for ease of communication, for work that rushes toward the reader with outflung arms—rather, they're the reverse. Let me cite three such difficulties that I take to be important, all having to do with language. First, there is art's own project, since Mallarmé, of restoring freshness to a much-handled language, essentially an effort toward finding a language in which making art is possible at all. This remains a ground theme, as potent, problematically, today as it was a century ago. Secondly, there is the political and social contamination of language by its use in manipulation of various kinds over time and the effort to find what might be called a "clean" language, problems associated with the Roland Barthes of *Writing Degree Zero* but also discussed by Lukács and others. Finally, there is the pressure on language from contemporary culture in the broadest sense—I mean our devouring commercial culture—which results in a double impoverishment: theft of complexity from the reader, theft of the reader from the writer.

These are by no means the only thorny matters with which the writer has to deal, nor (allowing for the very great differences among the practitioners under discussion) does every writer called Postmodern respond to them in the same way and to the same degree, nor is it the case that other writers of quite different tendencies are innocent of these concerns. If I call these matters "thorny," it's because any adequate attempt to deal with them automatically creates barriers to the ready assimilation of the work. Art is not difficult because it wishes to be difficult, but because it wishes to be art. However much the writer might long to be, in his work, simple, honest, and straightforward, these virtues are no longer available to him. He discovers that in being simple, honest, and straightforward, nothing much happens: he speaks the speakable, whereas what we are looking for is the as-yet unspeakable, the as-yet unspoken.

With Mallarmé the effort toward mimesis, the representation of the external world, becomes a much more complex thing than it had been previously. Mallarmé shakes words loose from their attachments and bestows new meanings upon them, meanings which point not toward the external world but toward the Absolute, acts of poetic intuition. This is a fateful step; not for nothing does Barthes call him the Hamlet of literature. It produces, for one thing, a poetry of unprecedented difficulty. You will find no Mallarmé in Bartlett's *Familiar Quotations*. Even so ardent an admirer as Charles Mauron speaks of the sense of alienation enforced by his work. Mauron writes: "All who remember the day when first they looked into the *Poems* or the *Divagations* will testify to that curious feeling of *exclusion* which put them, in the face of a text written with *their* words (and moreover, as they could somehow feel, magnificently written), suddenly outside their own language, deprived of their rights in a common speech, and, as it were, rejected by their oldest friends." Mallarmé's work is also, and perhaps most importantly, a step toward establishing a new ontological status for the poem, as an object in the world rather than a representation of the world. But the ground seized is dangerous ground. After Mallarmé the struggle to renew language becomes a given for the writer, his exemplary quest an imperative.

Mallarmé's work, "this whisper that is so close to silence," as Marcel Raymond calls it, is at once a liberation and a loss to silence of a great deal of territory.

The silencing of an existing rhetoric (in Harold Rosenberg's phrase) is also what is at issue in Barthes's deliberations in *Writing Degree Zero* and after—in this case a variety of rhetorics seen as actively pernicious rather than passively inhibiting. The question is, what is the complicity of language in the massive crimes of Fascism, Stalinism, or (by implication) our own policies in Vietnam? In the control of societies by the powerful and their busy functionaries? If these abominations are all in some sense facilitated by, made possible by, language, to what degree is that language ruinously contaminated (considerations also raised by George Steiner in his well-known essay "The Hollow Miracle" and, much earlier, by George Orwell)? I am sketching here, inadequately, a fairly complex argument; I am not particularly taken with Barthes's tentative solutions but the problems command the greatest respect. Again, we have language deeply suspicious of its own behavior; although this suspicion is not different in kind from Hemingway's noticing, early in the century, that words like *honor*, *glory*, and *country* were perjured, bought, the skepticism is far deeper now, and informed as well by the investigations of linguistic philosophers, structuralists, semioticians. Even conjunctions must be inspected carefully. "I read each word with the feeling appropriate to it," says Wittgenstein. "The word 'but' for example with the but-feeling. . . ." He is not wrong. Isn't the but-feeling, as he calls it, already sending us headlong down a greased slide before we've had the time to contemplate the proposition it's abutting? Quickly now, quickly—when you hear the phrase "our vital interests" do you stop to wonder whether you were invited to the den, Zen, Klan, or coven meeting at which these were defined? Did you speak?

In turning to the action of contemporary culture on language, and thus on the writer, the first thing to be noticed is a loss of reference. If I want a world of reference to which all possible readers in this country can respond, there is only one universe of discourse available, that in which the Love Boat sails on seas of passion like a Flying Dutchman of passion and the dedicated men in white of *General Hospital* pursue, with evenhanded diligence, triple bypasses and the nursing staff. This limits things somewhat. The earlier newspaper culture, which once dealt in a certain amount of nuance and zestful, highly literate hurly-burly, has deteriorated shockingly. The newspaper I worked for as a raw youth, thirty years ago, is today a pallid imitation of its former self. Where once we could put spurious quotes in the paper and attribute them to Ambrose Bierce and be fairly sure that enough readers would get the joke to make the joke worthwhile, from the point of view of both reader and writer, no such common ground now exists. The situation is not peculiar to this country. Steiner remarks of the best current journalism in Germany that, read against an average number of the *Frankfurter Zeitung* of pre-Hitler days, it's difficult at times to believe that both are written in German. At the other end of the scale much of the most exquisite description of the world, discourse about the world, is now being carried on in mathematical languages obscure to most people—certainly to me—and the contributions the sciences once made to our common language in the form of coinages, new words and concepts, are now available only to specialists. When one adds the ferocious appropriation of high culture by commercial culture—it takes, by my estimate, about forty-five minutes for any given novelty in art to travel from the Mary Boone Gallery on West Broadway to the display windows of Henri Bendel on Fifty-seventh Street—one begins to appreciate the seductions of silence.

Problems in part define the kind of work the writer chooses to do, and are not to be avoided but embraced. A writer, says Karl Kraus, is a man who can make a riddle out of an answer.

Let me begin again.

Jacqueline and Jemima are instructing Zeno, who has returned the purloined GRE documents and is thus restored to dull respectability, in Postmodernism. Postmodernism, they tell him, has turned its back on the world, is not about the world but about its own processes, is masturbatory, certainly chilly, excludes readers by design, speaks only to the already tenured, or does not speak at all, but instead—

Zeno, to demonstrate that he too knows a thing or two, quotes the critic Perry Meisel on semiotics. "Semiotics," he says, "is in a position to claim that no phenomenon has ontological status outside its place in the particular information system from which it draws its meaning"—he takes a large gulp of his Gibson—"and therefore, all language is finally groundless." I am eavesdropping and I am much reassured. This insight is one I can use. Gaston, the critic who is a guard at the Whitney Museum, is in love with an IRS agent named Madelaine, the very IRS agent, in fact, who is auditing my return for the year 1982. "Madelaine," I say kindly to her over lunch, "semiotics is in a position to claim that no phenomenon has any ontological status outside its place in the particular information system from which it draws its meaning, and therefore, all language is finally groundless, including that of those funny little notices you've been sending me." "Yes," says Madelaine kindly, pulling from her pocket a large gold pocket watch that Alphonse has sold Gaston for twenty dollars, her lovely violet eyes atwitter, "but some information systems are more enforceable than others." Alas, she's right.

If the writer is taken to be the work's way of getting itself written, a sort of lightning rod for an accumulation of atmospheric disturbances, a St. Sebastian absorbing in his tattered breast the arrows of the Zeitgeist, this changes not very much the traditional view of the artist. But it does license a very great deal of critical imperialism.

This is fun for everyone. A couple of years ago I received a letter from a critic requesting permission to reprint a story of mine as an addendum to the piece he had written about it. He attached the copy of my story he proposed to reproduce, and I was amazed to find that my poor story had sprouted a set of tiny numbers—one to eighty-eight, as I recall—an army of tiny numbers marching over the surface of my poor distracted text. Resisting the temptation to tell him that all the tiny numbers were in the wrong places, I gave him permission to do what he wished, but I did notice that by a species of literary judo the status of my text had been reduced to that of footnote.

There is, in this kind of criticism, an element of aggression that gives one pause. Deconstruction is an enterprise that announces its intentions with startling candor. Any work of art depends upon a complex series of interdependences. If I wrench the rubber tire from the belly of Rauschenberg's famous goat to determine, in the interest of a finer understanding of same, whether the tire is a B. F. Goodrich or a Uniroyal, the work collapses, more or less behind my back. I say this not because I find this kind of study valueless but because the mystery worthy of study, for me, is not the signification of parts but how they come together, the tire wrestled over the goat's hind legs. Calvin Tomkins tells us in *The Bride and the Bachelors* that Rauschenberg himself says that the tire seemed "something as unavoidable as the goat." To see both goat and tire as "unavoidable" choices, in the context of art-making, is to illuminate just how strange the combinatorial process can be. Nor was the choice a hasty one; Tomkins tells us that the goat had been in the studio for three years and had appeared in two previous versions (the final version is titled "Monogram") before it met the tire.

Modern-day critics speak of "recuperating" a text, suggesting an accelerated and possibly strenuous nursing back to health of a basically sickly text, very likely one that did not even know itself to be ill. I would argue that in the competing methodologies of contemporary criticism, many of them quite rich in implications, a sort of tyranny of great expectations obtains, a rage for final explanations, a refusal to allow a work that mystery which is essential to it. I hope I am not myself engaging in mystification if I say, not that the attempt should not be made, but that the mystery exists. I see no immediate way out of the paradox—tear a mystery to tatters and you have tatters, not mystery—I merely note it and pass on.

We can, however, wonder for a moment why the goat girdled with its tire is somehow a magical object, rather than, say, only a dumb idea. Harold Rosenberg speaks of the contemporary artwork as "anxious," as wondering: Am I a masterpiece or simply a pile of junk? (If I take many of my examples here from the art world rather than the world of literature it is because the issues are more quickly seen in terms of the first: "goat" and "tire" are standing in for pages of prose, pounds of poetry.) What precisely is it in the coming together of goat and tire that is magical? It's not the surprise of seeing the goat attired, although that's part of it. One might say, for example, that the tire *contests* the goat, *contradicts* the goat, as a mode of being, even that the tire *reproaches* the goat, in some sense. On the simplest punning level, the goat is *tired*. Or that the unfortunate tire has *been caught* by the goat, which has been fishing in the Hudson—goats eat anything, as everyone knows—or that the goat is being *consumed by* the tire; it's outside, after all, mechanization takes command. Or that the goateed goat is protesting the fatigue of its friend, the tire, by wearing it as a sort of STRIKE button. Or that two contrasting models of infinity are being presented, tires and goats both being infinitely reproducible, the first depending on the good fortunes of the B. F. Goodrich company and the second upon the copulatory enthusiasm of goats—parallel production lines suddenly met. And so on. What is magical about the object is that it at once invites and resists interpretation. Its artistic worth is measurable by the degree to which it remains, after interpretation, vital—no interpretation or cardiopulmonary push-pull can exhaust or empty it.

In what sense is the work "about" the world, the world that Jacqueline and Jemima have earnestly assured Zeno the work has turned its scarlet rump to? It is to this vexing question that we shall turn next.

Let us discuss the condition of my desk. It is messy, mildly messy. The messiness is both physical (coffee cups, cigarette ash) and spiritual (unpaid bills, unwritten novels). The emotional life of the man who sits at the desk is also messy—I am in love with a set of twins, Hilda and Heidi, and in a fit of enthusiasm I have joined the Bolivian army. The apartment in which the desk is located seems to have been sublet from Moonbeam McSwine. In the streets outside the apartment melting snow has revealed a choice assortment of decaying et cetera. Furthermore, the social organization of the country is untidy, the world situation in disarray. How do I render all this messiness, and if I succeed, what have I done?

In a common-sense way we agree that I attempt to find verbal equivalents for whatever it is I wish to render. The unpaid bills are easy enough. I need merely quote one: FINAL DISCONNECT NOTICE.

Hilda and Heidi are somewhat more difficult. I can say that they are beautiful—why not?—and you will more or less agree, although the bald statement has hardly stirred your senses. I can described them—Hilda has the map of Bolivia tattooed on her right cheek and Heidi habitually wears, on her left hand, a set of brass knuckles wrought of solid silver—and they move a step closer. Best of all, perhaps, I can permit them to speak, for they speak much as we do.

> "On Valentine's Day," says Hilda, "he sent me oysters, a dozen and a half."
>
> "He sent me oysters too," said Heidi, "two dozen."
>
> "Mine were long-stemmed oysters," says Hilda, "on a bed of the most wonderful spinach."
>
> "Oh yes, spinach," says Heidi, "he sent me spinach too, miles and miles of spinach, wrote every bit of it himself."

To render "messy" adequately, to the point that you are enabled to feel it—it should, ideally, frighten your shoes—I would have to be more graphic than the decorum of the occasion allows. What should be emphasized is that one proceeds by way of particulars. If I know how a set of brass knuckles feels on Heidi's left hand it's because I bought one once, in a pawn-shop, not to smash up someone's face but to exhibit on a pedestal in a museum show devoted to cultural artifacts of ambivalent status. The world enters the work as it enters our ordinary lives, not as world-view or system but in sharp particularity: a tax notice from Madelaine, a snowball containing a résumé from Gaston.

The words with which I attempt to render "messy," like any other words, are not inert, rather they are furiously busy. We do not mistake the words *the taste of chocolate* for the taste of chocolate itself, but neither do we miss the tease in *taste*, the shock in *chocolate*. Words have halos, patinas, overhangs, echoes. The word *halo*, for instance, may invoke St. Hilarius, of whom we've seen too little lately. The word *patina* brings back the fine pewtery shine on the saint's halo. The word *overhang* reminds us that we have, hanging over us, a dinner date with St. Hilarius, that crashing bore. The word *echo* restores us to Echo herself, poised like the White Rock girl on the overhang of a patina of a halo—infirm ground, we don't want the poor spirit to pitch into the pond where Narcissus blooms eternally, they'll bump foreheads, or maybe other parts closer to the feet, a scandal. There's chocolate smeared all over Hilarius' halo—messy, messy. . . .

The combinatorial agility of words, the exponential generation of meaning once they're allowed to go to bed together, allows the writer to surprise himself, makes art possible, reveals how much of Being we haven't yet encountered. It could be argued that computers can do this sort of thing for us, with critic-computers monitoring their output. When computers learn how to make jokes, artists will be in serious trouble. But artists will respond in such a way as to make art impossible for the computer. They will redefine art to take into account (that is, to exclude) technology—photography's impact upon painting and painting's brilliant response being a clear and comparatively recent example.

The prior history of words is one of the aspects of language the world uses to smuggle itself into the work. If words can be contaminated by the world, they can also carry with them into the work trace elements of world which can be used in a positive sense. We must allow ourselves the advantages of our disadvantages.

A late bulletin: Hilda and Heidi have had a baby, with which they're thoroughly displeased, it's got no credit cards and can't speak French, they'll send it back. . . . Messy.

Style is not much a matter of choice. One does not sit down to write and think: Is this poem going to be a Queen Anne poem, a Biedermeier poem, a Vienna Secession poem, or a Chinese Chippendale poem? Rather it is both a response to constraint and a seizing of opportunity. Very often a constraint is an opportunity. It would seem impossible to write *Don Quixote* once again, yet Borges has done so with great style, improving on the original (as he is not slow to tell us) while remaining faithful to it, faithful as a tick on a dog's belly. I don't mean that whim does not intrude. Why do I avoid, as much as possible, using the semicolon? Let me be plain: the semicolon is ugly, ugly as a tick on a dog's belly. I pinch them out of my prose. The great German writer Arno Schmidt, punctuation-drunk, averages eleven to a page.

Style is of course *how*. And the degree to which *how* has become *what*—since, say, Flaubert—is a question that men of conscience wax wroth about, and should. If I say of my friend that on this issue his marbles are a little flat on one side, this does not mean that I do not love my friend. He, on the other hand, considers that I am ridden by strange imperatives, and that the little piece I gave to the world last week, while nice enough in its own way, would have been vastly better had not my deplorable aesthetics caused me to score it for banjulele, cross between a banjo and a uke. Bless Babel.

Let us suppose that I am the toughest banjulele player in town and that I have contracted to play "Melancholy Baby" for six hours before an audience that will include the four next-toughest banjulele players in town. We imagine the smoky basement club, the hustling waiters (themselves students of the jazz banjulele), Jacqueline, Jemima, Zeno, Alphonse, Gaston, Madelaine, Hilda, and Heidi forming a congenial group at the bar. There is one thing of which you may be sure: I am not going to play "Melancholy Baby" as written. Rather I will play something that is parallel, in some sense, to "Melancholy Baby," based upon the chords of "Melancholy Baby," made out of "Melancholy Baby," *having to do with* "Melancholy Baby"—commentary, exegesis, elaboration, contradiction. The interest of my construction, if any, is to be located in the space between the new entity I have constructed and the "real" "Melancholy Baby," which remains in the mind as the horizon which bounds my efforts.

This is, I think, the relation of art to world. I suggest that art is always a mediation upon external reality rather than a representation of external reality or a jackleg attempt to "be" external reality. If I perform even reasonably well, no one will accuse me of not providing a true, verifiable, note-for-note reproduction of "Melancholy Baby"—it will be recognized that this was not what I was after. Twenty years ago I was much more convinced of the autonomy of the literary object than I am now, and even wrote a rather persuasive defense of the proposition that I have just rejected: that the object is itself world. Beguiled by the rhetoric of the time—the sculptor Phillip Pavia was publishing a quite good magazine called *It Is*, and this was typical—I felt that the high ground had been claimed and wanted to place my scuffed cowboy boots right there. The proposition's still attractive. What's the right answer? Bless Babel.

A couple of years ago I visited Willem de Kooning's studio in East Hampton, and when the big doors are opened one can't help seeing—it's a shock—the relation between the rushing green world outside and the paintings. Precisely how de Kooning manages to distill nature into art is a mystery, but the explosive relation is there, I've seen it. Once when I was in Elaine de Kooning's studio on Broadway, at a time when the metal sculptor Herbert Ferber occupied the studio immediately above, there came through the floor a most horrible crashing and banging. "What in the world is that?" I asked, and Elaine said, "Oh, that's Herbert thinking."

Art is a true account of the activity of mind. Because consciousness, in Husserl's formulation, is always consciousness *of* something, art thinks ever of the world, cannot not think of the world, could not turn its back on the world even if it wished to. This does not mean that it's going to be honest as a mailman; it's more likely to appear as a drag queen. The problems I mentioned earlier, as well as others not taken up, enforce complexity. "We do not spend much time in front of a canvas whose intentions are plain," writes Cioran, "music of a specific character, unquestionable contours, exhausts our patience, the over-explicit poem seems . . . incomprehensible." Flannery O'Connor, an artist of the first rank, famously disliked anything that looked funny on the page, and her distaste has widely been taken as a tough-minded put-down of puerile experimentalism. But did she also dislike anything that looked funny on the wall? If so, a severe deprivation. Art cannot remain in one place. A certain amount of movement, up, down, across, even a gallop toward the past, is a necessary precondition.

Style enables us to speak, to imagine again. Beckett speaks of "the long sonata of the dead"—where on earth did the word *sonata* come from, imposing as it does an orderly, even exalted design upon the most disorderly, distressing phenomenon known to us? The fact is not challenged, but understood, momentarily, in a new way. It's our good fortune to be able to imagine alternative realities, other possibilities. We can quarrel with the world, constructively (no one alive has quarreled with the world more extensively or splendidly than Beckett). "Belief in progress," says Baudelaire, "is a doctrine of idlers and Belgians." Perhaps. But if I have anything unorthodox to offer here, it's that I think art's project is fundamentally meliorative. The aim of meditating about the world is finally to change the world. It is this meliorative aspect of literature that provides its ethical dimension. We are all Upton Sinclairs, even that Hamlet, Stéphane Mallarmé.

Caroline Blackwood

(b. 1931)

Joseph Hall, Thomas Overbury, John Earle—these were the immensely popular seventeenth-century English writers of "characters," those typical and pointed human portraits that exercised so lively an influence on the early development of the essay. The prolific Jean de la Bruyère translated the Greek father of them all, Theophrastus, into French and supplemented the latter's thirty portraits of vices and virtues with 390 caractères *of his own, then added more and more with each new edition until there were 1,130 at his death. Widely read on both sides of the Channel, la Bruyère's satiric pictures, with their range and penetration, established the character as an essayistic vehicle for social criticism. Caroline Blackwood's "Portrait of a Beatnik" (1964) falls squarely into this old and productive tradition. Like la Bruyère, she observes actual people in their surroundings at a particular time in history—in this case, the early 1960s California community of self-styled revolutionaries bodying forth the "Beat" character. A Beatnik theoretician informs her, "You might really describe us in fact as a community of individuals seeking only for The Beatific Vision, The Experience of Holiness, The Orgiastic Fulfillment, in Self." Like her observer's eye, Blackwood's ear filters most tellingly; an acute and shrewdly selective transmission device, it gives back literally what it takes in but with the persistent ironic modulations created by placement and context. Not altogether irrelevant to the relentless wit of this essayist, novelist, and writer of short stories may be the fact that she was born and raised in County Down, Northern Ireland. Then, too, there may be more here than a freak phenomenon of American social life at mid-century. Through the voice of the Beatnik theoretician, no literate American can fail to hear echoes of another: "the great Idea of great and perfect individuals," "myself, typical before all," "endless as it was beginningless," "to know the universe itself as a road," "afoot with my vision," "Bathing myself . . . my songs in Sex," "the true New World . . . I merely thee ejaculate . . . ." Walt Whitman, of course, declaring in the nineteenth century: "I project the history of the future."* (Leaves of Grass)

Portrait of the Beatnik

Almost every day in some newspaper or magazine, the American Housewife makes her new complaint. A Beatnik philosopher has told her that she lives in "the Age of the White Rhinoceros," and another has told her that it is "the Age of Fried Shoes." "Where," she asked, "is all this Beatnik Movement leading us?" Her question is gratuitous. There has never been a Movement, merely a mirage, merely a masquerade.

The Beatnik is simply a bourgeois fantasy that has become incarnated and incarcerated, in a coffee-house and a "pad"; he is merely the Bohemian in every American business-man that has got out. He is a luxury product, the revolutionary who offers no threat, the nonconformist whose nonconformity is commercial. He shocks and scandalises without creating anxiety; he is the rebel not without cause, but the rebel without repercussion.

Supposedly revolutionary, the "Beatnik Movement" is unique in that it enjoys the recognition, the support, and succour of the very society whose dictates is pretends to flout. It has all the trappings of the subversive, the meeting in the darkened cellar, the conspiratorial whisper behind the candle in the chianti bottle, the nihilistic mutter, without the mildest element of subversion. No one in the future, when filling in an official form, will ever be made to swear that they have never been a Beatnik.

The American working man in unconcerned with the Beat Generation and its quest for "the primitive Beginnings." The Beatnik scandalises and interests only the middle-class public from which he springs. As opposed to the Bum (who might well be said to be more truly Beat) he is quite popular. He presents no obvious social incitement or question. He is "cool" and polite. Whereas the Bum rolls in the streets of downtown Los Angeles, drunk and cursing, the Beatnik sits peacefully in his coffee-house, nonconforming over capuccino, a safely-licenced anarchist. Everyone knows where to find him: he is always in his Beatnik Joint or in his "pad." Everyone knows who he is because of his beard, and *Life* Magazine can photograph him whenever it wishes.

Unlike the delinquent (with whom he is often confused), the Beatnik only ever troubles the Police over the technical issue of whether or not, if he reads his own poem to Jazz in a coffee-house, it constitutes "entertainment" and therefore invokes the need for an entertainment licence.

The Beatnik in his bold rebellion against American Bourgeois Values, is about as dangerous as the three revolutionaries in Orwell's *1984*. Like them, he has been put by the State safely in front of a chess-set in the Chestnut Tree Café, and there he is allowed to sit being revolutionary.

The Beat Generation has declared that it will take no part in the "middle-class rat race"; it has protested "a sacred dedication to poverty"; it has denounced all Western civilisation as "square shuck" (phoney).

A popular misconception is that the term "Beatnik" signifies one who is *beat* in the sense of "down beat," or "licked"—whereas to the Beat Generation it signifies "the beatific one."

The ego-ideal of the Beatnik is the "cool hipster"—the man who sits detached with his own flask in his own hip pocket, the man who is "way out," the man who doesn't "wig" (care), the man who finds beatitude in noncommitment.

The "square" is often not "hip" to the fact that despite similarities of dress, the Beatnik is by no means his existentialist predecessor. An obscure Beat philosopher finally clarified this point when he said, "The existentialist cat dug like that the positive answer of nothingness, in the face of nothingness, is positivism—we dig that the positive answer of nothingness, to nothingness, is nothingness—Man, isn't that farther out?"

The Beatnik rejects articulateness, speech involving a conversational commitment constituting lack of "coolness." Paradoxically, therefore, the Beat Generation can only speak in order to say that it will not speak, and Jack Kerouac and Alan Ginsberg who are generally known as the Beat spokesmen, are by very definition, as well as by their success and achievements, nonhipsters.

Ideally, a truly "cool cat" should be *completely* self-contained and therefore *completely* silent. The average Beatnik compromises, however, by speaking in language cut to the maximum. His talk, an abbreviated version of already abbreviated Jazz talk, amounts to complete code. A "T.O.," for example, is a much-used Beat word for a rich society woman who questions prostitutes, with half-thrilled envy, about the physical mechanics of their trade. An amateur hipster might be trapped into thinking that a "T.O." was an initiate, for it derives from "To be turned out," meaning initiated, deriving from "To be turned on," referring to "On pot," which stems in turn from "on the pod" of marijuana. The expression is now, however, *only* used to describe not the initiate but the would-be but too-afraid initiate. It is often claimed by the Beatniks that many women living in Park Avenue pent-houses, and many wives of successful movie stars living in Beverly Hills mansions, are secret "T.O.'s" in regard to Beat.

No professor of semantics could be more severe about misuse of vernacular than the hipster. The charlatan can be spotted instantly, and denounced as a "square." He often, for example, makes incorrect use of the term "to ball" which (in the forties) meant to make love. Now, however, the expression "I balled the cat" could only mean to the truly

Beat, that you were grateful to someone, so grateful in fact that you would only have *liked* to have balled them in the old-fashioned sense.

Beatific talk is the very soul of brevity, if not wit. It is deliberately functional, for the hipster rejects euphemism. He "sets a scene" when he tells, "wigs" when he's worried, "gigs" when he works, "bugs" when he's annoyed, "wails" when he functions, "floats" when he's drunk, "grazes" when he's content, "bends" when he's tired, "scenes" when he arrives, "splits" when he goes.

The Beatnik, in his rejection of the popular American concept that Success equates with Manhood, stresses a non-virility often mistaken for homosexuality. He is essentially a-sexual. Once again the ideal of the "cool" precluding the personal commitment demanded by sexual activity. He has, however, no particular objection to sexual intercourse as long as it is conducted quickly, clinically, and above all wordlessly. The Beat "cat" approaches the Beat "chick" with the ritualistic "Pad me"—his "pad" being his home where he keeps his foam rubber mattress. The "chick" can either reply "Dig" (a sign of cool acquiescence), or otherwise she can merely snap "Drop!" (a much-used abbreviation of "Drop dead"). In reverse, the "chick's" approach to the male is equally formalised; she must say "I'm frigid," to which he can either reply "I'll make you wail" (function) or, otherwise, "Don't bug."

Despite his rejection of marriage as middle-class "shuck" (phoney), the Beatnik's Wedding is an important event in any Beat community. He marries in the Ocean, only at midnight. He and his Beat Bride-to-be stand naked in the waves while the rites are performed by a Beatific friend who reads a self-composed hymeneal ritual poem, which is then followed by a lunar incantation. The Bridegroom then silently hands the "chick" a ring of flowers which she must throw into the waves in order to symbolise that her hipster is giving himself to "The real mama, the Ocean, the mama of the whole race of Man," while she is herself uniting with "The Old Man of the Sea."

Non-Beatnik grandmothers and aunts are invited to attend these services, and often leave in tears before the wedding breakfast, which naturally takes place in a "pad" and is as formal as the Sea Wedding. The newly-weds sit in a semi-circle composed of silently contemplative friends, "light up on muggles" (smoke marijuana), and continue their search for "the inner luminous experience."

Beat philosophy is misty, mystical, and eclectic. Claiming to embrace Zen, the Beatnik philosopher paradoxically rejects discipline; he therefore replaces the Zen Ideal of a total commitment to the moment by a Beat ideal of a striving towards a state of totally noncommitted contemplation. As a result he often merely arrives at a condition very similar to the one in which the American Housewife watches her television.

He prefers Jung to Freud, the concept of the collective, as opposed to the personal, subconscious being "*cooler*" in the sense that it predisposes less commitment to self. Other influences on his thought have been St. Francis of Assisi, Nietzsche, Ouspenski, and St. John of the Cross. He admires Joyce for his obscurity.

Within the confines that he has set himself, the Beatnik adheres to his conventions of nonconventionality with the enthusiasm of the Rotarian Club member for his rules. Every hipster wears the strict uniform of classical Bohemianism. He is heavily bearded. He has an open sandal, a chunky raw-wool sweater, and a little leather cap with a button on it. All his clothes *must* be bought second-hand. A similar Beat regulation is that his "pad" or mattress must be acquired *only* from the Salvation Army. Beds are considered "square" so it must therefore be put straight on the floor of his "pad" which is also his home, and ideally should be a battered shack. He must also hand-paint his floorboards with enigmatic and abstract ("*way-out*") designs, for one of his slogans is "*In the meaningless lies the meaning.*"

The true Beatnik should never "hustle" (do any paid work). He must sleep all day and only emerge by night. In the corner of every Beat "pad" there must necessarily be a gigantic stack of unwashed dishes.

As a deliberate reaction against the Hollywood emphasis on the breast and the flashing lipsticked smile, the appearance of his female Beatnik is characterised by a studied and aggressive a-sexuality. Pale-lipped and unsmiling she sits in a high-necked shapeless tunic made of woven wool. Her legs must always be crossed and heavily encased in black woolly stockings. Her cheeks are whitened with thick, white make-up base, her hair hangs dank and darkly jagged. She is to be seen nightly alone, staring over an unplayed chess-game with a mystic and heavily mascara'd eye.

In order to ensure the correct attire of visitors, many a Beatnik coffee-house has an adjoining dress shop: a Beatnik boutique. There, on sale, are elaborately-designed thirty-dollar Beat Generation tunics made of raw Mexican wool, sackcloth shirts, primitive leather water-pouches, the Beat jewellery made of iron.

I spoke with an ex-Beatnik turned Beat dress designer. She sat in her workshop and sewed the thong on a raw-hide sandal. She spoke of her Beat past with the apologetic nostalgia sometimes found in retired members of the Communist Party. "Jesus, I dug Beatific—Man, the swinginest (it's the best)—I like dug splittin' (I felt obliged to leave it)—I dug giggin' for bread to wail (I was obliged to work for the money to go on functioning). . . ."

Her friend, another renegade Beatnik, who was sitting in the corner painting papier-maché model figurines of Beatniks (later to be sold in a boutique) was less enthusiastic about the Movement. "Beatific's a bug," she said.

The Beat coffee-houses are characterised by their extreme gloom, and by their cathedral silences. They attract not only the hipster but also the wandering psychotic who gets mistaken for Beat because he is "way out." They also shelter two unfortunate by-products of Beat. First, the Bogus Beatnik: the Hollywood agent and the successful car-salesman, who, having worked by day go corruptly Beat by night. Secondly, the hypocritical hipster, who, unaware of the deeper philosophical significance of the Movement, has taken out "Beat" as he might take out an insurance policy, merely to protect himself against any future censor from a success-worshipping society. Failure is impossible to anyone who is Beat, for they have rejected aspiration.

The entertainment at the Beat coffee-house consists of "Prose and Poetry readings" and folk-singing, the latter being part of the quest for the "primitive beginnings." No alcohol is served, for the Beatnik rejects "lushing" (drinking) as part of bourgeois "shuck."

Short, silent, home-made Beat movies are also shown. As there would appear to be only a limited number of these films, the more popular and "farther out" ones are shown up to four or five times on the same night. An old man looms upon the screen, huge and fearful. The camera remains lengthily upon the vast cigar which he holds between his teeth. An adolescent appears, white-faced and knuckle-clenching, his eyes roll, his face contorts. The Jazz background music mounts to a crescendo. The boy "splits a gut" (laughs), he lifts his hand, and with a sudden frenzied violence, strikes the cigar from the old man's mouth. The camera follows the cigar which rolls in the dust. The old man shivers. He rocks, holding his head in agony. He staggers to a lavatory. He vomits. The camera remains upon the lavatory pan until it slowly dissolves into a vagina. The audience slowly turn their heads to see if everyone else is "hip." A voice always says, "Dig that crazy sequence!"

Between the runnings of films, Beatific poem-reading takes place to the accompaniment of Bongo drums.

The take-off
                                on one
                                    and
a half
                              push up
not all
                                at once
                              just cool
hip.

The unsuspecting tourist suffering from the "square" illusion that it is possible to drop in at a coffee-house for only a few minutes, then becomes "hip" to his error. Once "Beat readings" are in progress only someone with the courage or the insensitivity that would enable him to leave the front pew of an Anglican church while the parson is delivering his Easter sermon, can even conceive of making an exit under the condemnatory scrutiny of the Beatific congregation's culturally pious eye.

The tourist often finds towards dawn (for there is an important Beat tenet: "*Night sleep is for Squares*") that after a whole evening on capuccino and "Modigliani's" (described on Beat menus as "Murals of ham and gherkin on rye"), he is slowly becoming "cooler and cooler," and "further and further out."

The "entertainment" often ends with a famous Beat musician, Lord Buckley, giving a nasal rendering of the story of Jesus of Nazareth walking on the waters. *And der Naz said*, "*Walk cool*, *Baby*, *walk cool*. . . ."

Ever since the publication of *On the Road*, which focused upon the Beatnik a furore of public interest and attention, Jack Kerouac's right to the title of "Father of the Beat Generation" has been jealously contested. Kenneth Rexroth, an elderly and obscure San Franciscan poet, made the first violent attempt to secure the title for himself when he protested angrily to the Press that he had been living all his life "the kind of life that Kerouac just writes about."

Another far more powerful figure then emerged in the form of a lesser-known (and therefore "cooler") poet named Lawrence Lipton. A man approaching sixty, he denounced Kerouac for being in his thirties, and therefore unfitted to represent the Beat Generation who were essentially a product of the 1950's. He was appointed "Grand Lama" in Venice West, a slum area of Los Angeles, where there are many suitably Beat and dilapidated shacks, and he is now hoping to establish it as the new Beat World Capital.

I spoke with the "Grand Lama," he reclined on his "pad" Pasha-like and smoked a cigar. "Our pad," he said, "has the same symbolical importance to us, as did the couch of the Bohemians of the thirties. Beat, you will understand, my dear young woman, is far more than a religion. Beat, my dear young lady, is a way of Life."

He closed his eyes.

"Here, down in Venice West," he continued, "we have a new kind of Beat, the real Beat, the Beat Generation of the future. I have called them by their true title, 'The Holy Barbarians,' and the report that I have just finished making about them will be called by that very name. I have already received extensive enquiries about it, not only from the Book-of-the-Month Club, but also from several television programmes, the

M.-G.-M. Studios, and many anthropologists from U.C.L.A. I tell you all this, you will understand, merely so that you will really grasp how big this whole thing is. Already my poems are being scribbled on the lavatory walls of New York, already our Movement is spreading to Japan, Italy, France, Germany, and Great Britain. The Holy Barbarians, you will see, my dear young woman, will very soon be world-wide interest!"

We had a long silence.

"I," he continued, speaking with a slow and portentous solemnity, "am the Mentor of the Holy Barbarians. They call me 'The Shaman of the Tribe.' I interpret their way of life to the public. I have probably made more tape-recordings of Beatnik conversations than any other living man." He languidly waved his hand at a mountainous stack of tape spools lying on his floor. "There," he said, "you have one hundred hours' worth of authentic Beat conversations, private philosophic conversations, you understand, taking place in simple pads, amongst young and simple people, but ones who are asking, more profoundly, more honestly than any previous generation, who they are, and where they are going. . . ."

Once again he closed his eyes. "We, the Holy Barbarians, finding nothing in the West, have turned towards the East. We reject your Audens and your Spenders and all their affiliations. Our poets' Search goes inwards for The Luminous Experience. We reject and scorn your Angry Young Men with their social preoccupations. We seek much further for the non-political Answer." "The Lama" suddenly looked at me with a suspicious, visionary eye. "That does not in the least mean to say," he added quickly, "that we do not utterly reject the Russian way of life. We in fact even have an expression amongst our hipsters, *'There's no Square like a red Square.'* "

Once again we had a silence. "We, the Holy Barbarians, have totally rejected racial barriers," he went on. "We call a negro a *nigger* and a *spade*, for he knows we say the words with Love. You might really describe us in fact as a Community of individuals seeking only for The Beatific Vision, The Experience of Holiness, The Orgiastic Fulfilment, in Self. Our hipsters would say that we seek only *to flip our wings.*

"I'm afraid," he said, suddenly smiling with scornful patronage, "that that will have very little meaning to you.

"We," he continued, making heavy use of the Papal *we*, "might well be compared to the Early Christians. We are the Outlaws from the Social Lie. We are the Persecuted People, the Apocalyptic People, the Nocturnal People. The people of the night," he added, for fear I had not understood.

As I was leaving, "The Lama" stood in the doorway of his shack. "We have many, many Artists down here in Venice West," he said, "all of them living in dedicated poverty. Some of them are among the most creative talents in America. I should very much like you to have a look at them. I will telephone you as soon as I have arranged to have you shown round their pads." Suddenly I became cool, visionary. I saw that "The Lama" had already, mystically, ruthlessly, appointed my future Duties. He had ordained how my life from then on was to be spent. Like a Florence Nightingale, or a conscientious Inspector of an Insane Asylum, making daily rounds of condemned Artists in padded cells.

John McPhee
(b. 1931)

The work of John McPhee, a New Yorker *staff writer for twenty-five years, gives the deceptive—which is to say artful—impression of being impersonal. Rather than directly voicing what he feels and thinks about his material, McPhee characteristically devises narrative structures that regulate how we read and respond to what he writes. In "The Search for Marvin Gardens" (1972,* Pieces of the Frame), *he reports on Atlantic City's anarchic decay after more than a century of capitalistic enterprise. Using Monopoly—the board game Americans have been cutting their entrepreneurial teeth on for two generations—like a map for looking at the real Atlantic City, he makes his apparently one-dimensional language sustain a multiple reference for the game-in-progress. Streets running away from the beach have names like Pennsylvania, Indiana, North Carolina, Vermont; hearing them recited reminds us that "the quick kill" is in full play throughout these United States. Parallel to the beach, streets named after the seven seas suggest that the stakes are world-wide. (Sorry global results are prefigured in this seaside gambling resort where "Mediterranean and Baltic are the principal avenues of the ghetto.") More often than not, McPhee appears as a minor character in his own narratives. But here, the "I" is fictionalized as the absurd major player who narrates his own absorption in the capitalistic game, whose only goal is to win, and only hope, possession of Marvin Gardens. The person who wrote the essay, the "I" who gives himself a fictional role in it, can only be got at as the one pulling the strings, structuring the narrative. Far more than Addison, McPhee might have fashioned his essayistic self after the motto for* Spectator *No. 562: "Be present as if absent." He cultivates unobtrusiveness, seldom allowing any idiosyncrasies into his writing. Yet nobody can anticipate what McPhee will choose to write about next, or how he will handle his material; in short, his choice of subject tends to be so personal as to be idiosyncratic, and what he does with it reveals his artistry as that of a director, always off stage but alertly controlling the smallest details. His brief portrait of Marvin Gardens, "the ultimate outwash of Monopoly," ends the story of the quick kill with an ironic, never explicit, but crystal-clear personal view of the game.*

The Search for Marvin Gardens

Go. I roll the dice—a six and a two. Through the air I move my token, the flatiron, to Vermont Avenue, where dog packs range.

The dogs are moving (some are limping) through ruins, rubble, fire damage, open garbage. Doorways are gone. Lath is visible in the crumbling walls of the buildings. The street sparkles with shattered glass. I have never seen, anywhere, so many broken windows. A sign—"Slow, Children at Play"—has been bent backward by an automobile. At the lighthouse, the dogs turn up Pacific and disappear. George Meade, Army engineer, built the lighthouse—brick upon brick, six hundred thousand bricks, to reach up high enough to throw a beam twenty miles over the sea. Meade, seven years later, saved the Union at Gettysburg.

I buy Vermont Avenue for $100. My opponent is a tall, shadowy figure, across from me, but I know him well, and I know his game like a favorite tune. If he can, he will always go for the quick kill. And when it is foolish to go for the quick kill he will be foolish. On the whole, though, he is a master assessor of percentages. It is a mistake to underestimate him. His eleven carries his top hat to St. Charles Place, which he buys for $140.

The sidewalks of St. Charles Place have been cracked to shards by through-growing weeds. There are no buildings. Mansions, hotels once stood here. A few street lamps now drop cones of light on broken glass and vacant space behind a chain-link fence that some great machine has in places bent to the ground. Five plane trees—in full summer leaf, flecking the light—are all that live on St. Charles Place.

Block upon block, gradually, we are cancelling each other out—in the blues, the lavenders, the oranges, the greens. My opponent follows a plan of his own devising. I use the Hornblower & Weeks opening and the Zuricher defense. The first game draws tight, will soon finish. In 1971, a group of people in Racine, Wisconsin, played for seven hundred and sixty-eight hours. A game begun a month later in Danville, California, lasted eight hundred and twenty hours. These are official records, and they stun us. We have been playing for eight minutes. It amazes us that Monopoly is thought of as a long game. It is possible to play to a complete, absolute, and final conclusion in less than fifteen minutes, all within the rules as written. My opponent and I have done so thousands of times. No wonder we are sitting across from each other now in this best-of-seven series for the international singles championship of the world.

On Illinois Avenue, three men lean out from second-story windows. A girl is coming down the street. She wears dungarees and a bright-red shirt, has ample breasts and a Hadendoan Afro, a black halo, two feet in diameter. Ice rattles in the glasses in the hands of the men.

"Hey, sister!"

"Come on up!"

She looks up, looks from one to another to the other, looks them flat in the eye.

"What for?" she says, and she walks on.

I buy Illinois for $240. It solidifies my chances, for I already own Kentucky and Indiana. My opponent pales. If he had landed first on Illinois, the game would have been over then and there, for he has houses built on Boardwalk and Park Place, we share the railroads equally, and we have cancelled each other everywhere else. We never trade.

In 1852, R. B. Osborne, an immigrant Englishman, civil engineer, surveyed the route of a railroad line that would run from Camden to Absecon Island, in New Jersey, traversing the state from the Delaware River to the barrier beaches of the sea. He then sketched in the plan of a "bathing village" that would surround the eastern terminus of the line. His pen flew glibly, framing and naming spacious avenues parallel to the shore—Mediterranean, Baltic, Oriental, Ventnor—and narrower transsecting avenues: North Carolina, Pennsylvania, Vermont, Connecticut, States, Virginia, Tennessee, New York, Kentucky, Indiana, Illinois. The place as a whole had no name, so when he had completed the plan Osborne wrote in large letters over the ocean, "Atlantic City." No one ever challenged the name, or the names of Osborne's streets. Monopoly was invented in the early nineteen-thirties by Charles B. Darrow, but Darrow was only transliterating what Osborne had created. The railroads, crucial to any player, were the making of Atlantic City. After the rails were down, houses and hotels burgeoned from Mediterranean and Baltic to New York and Kentucky. Properties—building lots—sold for as little as six dollars apiece and as much as a thousand dollars. The original investors in the railroads and the real estate called themselves the Camden & Atlantic Land Company. Reverently, I repeat their names: Dwight Bell, William Coffin, John DaCosta, Daniel Deal, William Fleming, Andrew Hay, Joseph Porter,

Jonathan Pitney, Samuel Richards—founders, fathers, forerunners, archetypical masters of the quick kill.

My opponent and I are now in a deep situation of classical Monopoly. The torsion is almost perfect—Boardwalk and Park Place versus the brilliant reds. His cash position is weak, though, and if I escape him now he may fade. I land on Luxury Tax, contiguous to but in sanctuary from his power. I have four houses on Indiana. He lands there. He concedes.

Indiana Avenue was the address of the Brighton Hotel, gone now. The Brighton was exclusive—a word that no longer has retail value in the city. If you arrived by automobile and tried to register at the Brighton, you were sent away. Brighton-class people came in private railroad cars. Brighton-class people had other private railroad cars for their horses—dawn rides on the firm sand at water's edge, skirts flying. Colonel Anthony J. Drexel Biddle—the sort of name that would constrict throats in Philadelphia—lived, much of the year, in the Brighton.

Colonel Sanders' fried chicken is on Kentucky Avenue. So is Clifton's Club Harlem, with the Sepia Revue and the Sepia Follies, featuring the Honey Bees, the Fashions, and the Lords.

My opponent and I, many years ago, played 2,428 games of Monopoly in a single season. He was then a recent graduate of the Harvard Law School, and he was working for a downtown firm, looking up law. Two people we knew—one from Chase Manhattan, the other from Morgan, Stanley—tried to get into the game, but after a few rounds we found that they were not in the conversation and we sent them home. Monopoly should always be *mano a mano*[1] anyway. My opponent won 1,199 games, and so did I. Thirty were ties. He was called into the Army, and we stopped just there. Now, in Game 2 of the series, I go immediately to jail, and again to jail while my opponent seines property. He is dumbfoundingly lucky. He wins in twelve minutes.

Visiting hours are daily, eleven to two; Sunday, eleven to one; evenings, six to nine. "NO MINORS, NO FOOD, Immediate Family Only Allowed in Jail." All this above a blue steel door in a blue cement wall in the windowless interior of the basement of the city hall. The desk sergeant sits opposite the door to the jail. In a cigar box in front of him are pills in every color, a banquet of fruit salad an inch and a half deep—leapers, co-pilots, footballs, truck drivers, peanuts, blue angels, yellow jackets,

[1] Hand in hand, *i.e.*, one on one.

redbirds, rainbows. Near the desk are two soldiers, waiting to go through the blue door. They are about eighteen years old. One of them is trying hard to light a cigarette. His wrists are in steel cuffs. A military policeman waits, too. He is a year or so older than the soldiers, taller, studious in appearance, gentle, fat. On a bench against a wall sits a good-looking girl in slacks. The blue door rattles, swings heavily open. A turnkey stands in the doorway. "Don't you guys kill yourselves back there now," says the sergeant to the soldiers.

"One kid, he overdosed himself about ten and a half hours ago," says the M.P.

The M.P., the soldiers, the turnkey, and the girl on the bench are white. The sergeant is black. "If you take off the handcuffs, take off the belts," says the sergeant to the M.P. "I don't want them hanging themselves back there." The door shuts and its tumblers move. When it opens again, five minutes later, a young white man in sandals and dungarees and a blue polo shirt emerges. His hair is in a ponytail. He has no beard. He grins at the good-looking girl. She rises, joins him. The sergeant hands him a manila envelope. From it he removes his belt and a small notebook. He borrows a pencil, makes an entry in the notebook. He is out of jail, free. What did he do? He offended Atlantic City in some way. He spent a night in the jail. In the nineteen-thirties, men visiting Atlantic City went to jail, directly to jail, did not pass Go, for appearing in topless bathing suits on the beach. A city statute requiring all men to wear full-length bathing suits was not seriously challenged until 1937, and the first year in which a man could legally go bare-chested on the beach was 1940.

Game 3. After seventeen minutes, I am ready to begin construction on overpriced and sluggish Pacific, North Carolina, and Pennsylvania. Nothing else being open, opponent concedes.

The physical profile of streets perpendicular to the shore is something like a playground slide. It begins in the high skyline of Boardwalk hotels, plummets into warrens of "side-avenue" motels, crosses Pacific, slopes through church missions, convalescent homes, burlesque houses, rooming houses, and liquor stores, crosses Atlantic, and runs level through the bombed-out ghetto as far—Baltic, Mediterranean—as the eye can see. North Carolina Avenue, for example, is flanked at its beach end by the Chalfonte and the Haddon Hall (908 rooms, air-conditioned), where, according to one biographer, John Philip Sousa (1854–1932) first played when he was twenty-two, insisting, even then, that everyone call him by his entire name. Behind these big hotels, motels—Barbizon, Catalina—crouch. Between Pacific and Atlantic is an occasional house from 1910—

wooden porch, wooden mullions, old yellow paint—and two churches, a package store, a strip show, a dealer in fruits and vegetables. Then, beyond Atlantic Avenue, North Carolina moves on into the vast ghetto, the bulk of the city, and it looks like Metz in 1919, Cologne in 1944. Nothing has actually exploded. It is not bomb damage. It is deep and complex decay. Roofs are off. Bricks are scattered in the street. People sit on porches, six deep, at nine on a Monday morning. When they go off to wait in unemployment lines, they wait sometimes two hours. Between Mediterranean and Baltic runs a chain-link fence, enclosing rubble. A patrol car sits idling by the curb. In the back seat is a German shepherd. A sign on the fence says, "Beware of Bad Dogs."

Mediterranean and Baltic are the principal avenues of the ghetto. Dogs are everywhere. A pack of seven passes me. Block after block, there are three-story brick row houses. Whole segments of them are abandoned, a thousand broken windows. Some parts are intact, occupied. A mattress lies in the street, soaking in a pool of water. Wet stuffing is coming out of the mattress. A postman is having a rye and a beer in the Plantation Bar at nine-fifteen in the morning. I ask him idly if he knows where Marvin Gardens is. He does not. "HOOKED AND NEED HELP? CONTACT N.A.R.C.O." "REVIVAL NOW GOING ON, CONDUCTED BY REVEREND H. HENDERSON OF TEXAS." These are signboards on Mediterranean and Baltic. The second one is upside down and leans against a boarded-up window of the Faith Temple Church of God in Christ. There is an old peeling poster on a warehouse wall showing a figure in an electric chair. "The Black Panther Manifesto" is the title of the poster, and its message is, or was, that "the fascists have already decided in advance to murder Chairman Bobby Seale in the electric chair." I pass an old woman who carries a bucket. She wears blue sneakers, worn through. Her feet spill out. She wears red socks, rolled at the knees. A white handkerchief, spread over her head, is knotted at the corners. Does she know where Marvin Gardens is? "I sure don't know," she says, setting down the bucket. "I sure don't know. I've heard of it somewhere, but I just can't say where." I walk on, through a block of shattered glass. The glass crunches underfoot like coarse sand. I remember when I first came here—a long train ride from Trenton, long ago, games of poker in the train—to play basketball against Atlantic City. We were half black, they were all black. We scored forty points, they scored eighty, or something like it. What I remember most is that they had glass backboards—glittering, pendent, expensive glass backboards, a rarity then in high schools, even in colleges, the only ones we played on all year.

I turn on Pennsylvania, and start back toward the sea. The windows of the Hotel Astoria, on Pennsylvania near Baltic, are boarded up. A sheet of unpainted plywood is the door, and in it is a triangular peephole that now frames an eye. The plywood door opens. A man answers my question. Rooms there are six, seven, and ten dollars a week. I thank him for the information and move on, emerging from the ghetto at the Catholic Daughters of America Women's Guest House, between Atlantic and Pacific. Between Pacific and the Boardwalk are the blinking vacancy signs of the Aristocrat and Colton Manor motels. Pennsylvania terminates at the Sheraton-Seaside—thirty-two dollars a day, ocean corner. I take a walk on the Boardwalk and into the Holiday Inn (twenty-three stories). A guest is registering. "You reserved for Wednesday, and this is Monday," the clerk tells him. "But that's all right. We have *plenty* of rooms." The clerk is very young, female, and has soft brown hair that hangs below her waist. Her superior kicks her.

He is a middle-aged man with red spiderwebs in his face. He is jacketed and tied. He takes her aside. "Don't say 'plenty,' " he says. "Say 'You are fortunate, sir. We have rooms available.' "

The face of the young woman turns sour. "We have all the rooms you need," she says to the customer, and, to her superior, "How's that?"

Game 4. My opponent's luck has become abrasive. He has Boardwalk and Park Place, and has sealed the board.

Darrow was a plumber. He was, specifically, a radiator repairman who lived in Germantown, Pennsylvania. His first Monopoly board was a sheet of linoleum. On it he placed houses and hotels that he had carved from blocks of wood. The game he thus invented was brilliantly conceived, for it was an uncannily exact reflection of the business milieu at large. In its depth, range, and subtlety, in its luck-skill ratio, in its sense of infrastructure and socio-economic parameters, in its philosophical characteristics, it reached to the profundity of the financial community. It was as scientific as the stock market. It suggested the manner and means through which an underdeveloped world had been developed. It was chess at Wall Street level. "Advance token to the nearest Railroad and pay owner twice the rental to which he is otherwise entitled. If Railroad is unowned, you may buy it from the Bank. Get out of Jail, free. Advance token to nearest Utility. If unowned, you may buy it from Bank. If owned, throw dice and pay owner a total ten times the amount thrown. You are assessed for street repairs: $40 per house, $115 per hotel. Pay poor tax of $15. Go to Jail. Go directly to Jail. Do not pass Go. Do not collect $200."

The turnkey opens the blue door. The turnkey is known to the inmates as Sidney K. Above his desk are ten closed-circuit-TV screens—assorted viewpoints of the jail. There are three cellblocks—men, women, juvenile boys. Six days is the average stay. Showers twice a week. The steel doors and the equipment that operates them were made in San Antonio. The prisoners sleep on bunks of butcher block. There are no mattresses. There are three prisoners to a cell. In winter, it is cold in here. Prisoners burn newspapers to keep warm. Cell corners are black with smudge. The jail is three years old. The men's block echoes with chatter. The man in the cell nearest Sidney K. is pacing. His shirt is covered with broad stains of blood. The block for juvenile boys is, by contrast, utterly silent—empty corridor, empty cells. There is only one prisoner. He is small and black and appears to be thirteen. He says he is sixteen and that he has been alone in here for three days.

"Why are you here? What did you do?"

"I hit a jitney driver."

The series stands at three all. We have split the fifth and sixth games. We are scrambling for property. Around the board we fairly fly. We move so fast because we do our own banking and search our own deeds. My opponent grows tense.

Ventnor Avenue, a street of delicatessens and doctors' offices, is leafy with plane trees and hydrangeas, the city flower. Water Works is on the mainland. The water comes over in submarine pipes. Electric Company gets power from across the state, on the Delaware River, in Deepwater. States Avenue, now a wasteland like St. Charles, once had gardens running down the middle of the street, a horse-drawn trolley, private homes. States Avenue was as exclusive as the Brighton. Only an apartment house, a small motel, and the All Wars Memorial Building—monadnocks spaced widely apart—stand along States Avenue now. Pawnshops, convalescent homes, and the Paradise Soul Saving Station are on Virginia Avenue. The soul-saving station is pink, orange, and yellow. In the windows flanking the door of the Virginia Money Loan Office are Nikons, Polaroids, Yashicas, Sony TVs, Underwood typewriters, Singer sewing machines, and pictures of Christ. On the far side of town, beside a single track and locked up most of the time, is the new railroad station, a small hut made of glazed firebrick, all that is left of the lines that built the city. An authentic phrenologist works on New York Avenue close to Frank's Extra Dry Bar and a church where the sermon today is "Death in the Pot." The church is of pink brick, has blue and amber windows and two red doors. St. James Place, narrow and twisting, is lined with boarding houses that have wooden porches on each of three stories, suggesting a New Orleans made of salt-bleached pine. In a vacant lot on Tennessee is a white Ford station wagon stripped to the chassis. The windows are smashed. A plastic Clorox bottle sits on the driver's seat. The wind has pressed newspaper against the chain-link fence around the lot. Atlantic Avenue, the city's principal thoroughfare, could be seventeen American Main Streets placed end to end—discount vitamins and Vienna Corset shops, movie theatres, shoe stores, and funeral homes. The Boardwalk is made of yellow pine and Douglas fir, soaked in pentachlorophenol. Downbeach, it reaches far beyond the city. Signs everywhere—on windows, lampposts, trash baskets—proclaim "Bienvenue Canadiens!"[2] The salt air is full of Canadian French. In the Claridge Hotel, on Park Place, I ask a clerk if she knows where Marvin Gardens is. She says, "Is it a floral shop?" I ask a cab-driver, parked outside. He says, "Never heard of it." Park Place is one block long, Pacific to Boardwalk. On the roof of the Claridge is the Solarium, the highest point in town—panoramic view of the ocean, the bay, the salt-water ghetto. I look down at the rooftops of the side-avenue motels and into swimming pools. There are hundreds of people around the rooftop pools, sunbathing, reading—many more people than are on the beach. Walls, windows, and a block of sky are all that is visible from these pools—no sand, no sea. The pools are craters, and with the people around them they are countersunk into the motels.

The seventh, and final, game is ten minutes old and I have hotels on Oriental, Vermont, and Connecticut. I have Tennessee and St. James. I have North Carolina and Pacific. I have Boardwalk, Atlantic, Ventnor, Illinois, Indiana. My fingers are forming a "V." I have mortgaged most of these properties in order to pay for others, and I have mortgaged the other to pay for the hotels. I have seven dollars. I will pay off the mortgages and build my reserves with income from the three hotels. My cash position may be low, but I feel like a rocket in an underground silo. Meanwhile, if I could just go to jail for a time I could pause there, wait there, until my opponent, in his inescapable rounds, pays the rates of my hotels. Jail, at times, is the strategic place to be. I roll boxcars from the Reading and move the flatiron to Community Chest. "Go to Jail. Go directly to Jail."

The prisoners, of course, have no pens and no pencils. They take paper napkins, roll them tight as crayons, char the ends with matches, and write on the walls. The things they write are not entirely idiomatic; for example, "In God We Trust." All is in carbon. Time is required in the writing. "Only humanity could know of such pain." "God So Loved the World." "There is no greater pain than life itself." In the women's block now, there are six blacks, giggling, and a white asleep in red shoes. She

[2] Welcome, Canadians!

is drunk. The others are pushers, prostitutes, an auto thief, a burglar caught with pistol in purse. A sixteen-year-old accused of murder was in here last week. These words are written on the wall of a now empty cell: "Laying here I see two bunks about six inches thick, not counting the one I'm laying on, which is hard as brick. No cushion for my back. No pillow for my head. Just a couple scratchy blankets which is best to use it's said. I wake up in the morning so shivery and cold, waiting and waiting till I am told the food is coming. It's on its way. It's not worth waiting for, but I eat it anyway. I know one thing when they set me free I'm gonna be good if it kills me."

How many years must a game be played to produce an Anthony J. Drexel Biddle and chestnut geldings on the beach? About half a century was the original answer, from the first railroad to Biddle at his peak. Biddle, at his peak, hit an Atlantic City streetcar conductor with his fist, laid him out with one punch. This increased Biddle's legend. He did not go to jail. While John Philip Sousa led his band along the Boardwalk playing "The Stars and Stripes Forever" and Jack Dempsey ran up and down in training for his fight with Gene Tunney, the city crossed the high curve of its parabola. Al Capone held conventions here—upstairs with his sleeves rolled, apportioning among his lieutenant governors the states of the Eastern seaboard. The natural history of an American resort proceeds from Indians to French Canadians via Biddles and Capones. French Canadians, whatever they may be at home, are Visigoths here. *Bienvenue Visigoths!*

My opponent plods along incredibly well. He has got his fourth railroad, and patiently, unbelievably, he has picked up my potential winners until he has blocked me everywhere but Marvin Gardens. He has avoided, in the fifty-dollar zoning, my increasingly petty hotels. His cash flow swells. His railroads are costing me two hundred dollars a minute. He is building hotels on States, Virginia, and St. Charles. He has temporarily reversed the current. With the yellow monopolies and my blue monopolies, I could probably defeat his lavenders and his railroads. I have Atlantic and Ventnor. I need Marvin Gardens. My only hope is Marvin Gardens.

There is a plaque at Boardwalk and Park Place, and on it in relief is the leonine profile of a man who looks like an officer in a metropolitan bank—"Charles B. Darrow, 1889–1967, inventor of the game of Monopoly." "Darrow," I address him, aloud. "Where is Marvin Gardens?" There is, of course, no answer. Bronze, impassive, Darrow looks south down the Boardwalk. "Mr. Darrow, please, where is Marvin Gardens?" Nothing. Not a sign. He just looks south down the Boardwalk.

My opponent accepts the trophy with his natural ease, and I make, from notes, remarks that are even less graceful than his.

Marvin Gardens is the one color-block Monopoly property that is not in Atlantic City. It is a suburb within a suburb, secluded. It is a planned compound of seventy-two handsome houses set on curvilinear private streets under yews and cedars, poplars and willows. The compound was built around 1920, in Margate, New Jersey, and consists of solid buildings of stucco, brick, and wood, with slate roofs, tile roofs, multimullioned porches, Giraldic towers, and Spanish grilles. Marvin Gardens, the ultimate outwash of Monopoly, is a citadel and sanctuary of the middle class. "We're heavily patrolled by police here. We don't take no chances. Me? I'm living here nine years. I paid seventeen thousand dollars and I've been offered thirty. Number one, I don't want to move. Number two, I don't need the money. I have four bedrooms, two and a half baths, front den, back den. No basement. The Atlantic is down there. Six feet down and you float. A lot of people have a hard time finding this place. People that lived in Atlantic City all their life don't know how to find it. They don't know where the hell they're going. They just know it's south, down the Boardwalk."

Edward Hoagland

(b. 1932)

A long, beautiful essay of Hoagland's called "Home Is Two Places" opens in a brooding mood: "Things are worse than many of us are admitting." By the last paragraph, nine or ten thousand words later, he has come around to "Perhaps I might as well have begun this essay by saying that things are better than we think." It's all the ground he has covered meanwhile, of time and geography, of speculation and feeling, that makes this reversal the farthest thing imaginable from a coy whimsy to end an essay with. There's the "now" of 1970, with its "uncertainties and abysses" of middle age, when a city person may discover the need for more than one home to "set to work in"; and the "then" of Hoagland's childhood in woods and fields, of "sensing other wavelengths in the world besides the human gabble," along with the more distant "then" of his parents and their beginnings. There's the "here" of northern Vermont and the "there" of Greenwich Village, Hoagland's two homes: "one foot in the seventies and one foot in an earlier decade—the foot that doesn't mind going to sleep and maybe missing something." Now, then; here, there; this way, that: a Hoagland essay stays on the move inventing itself across such transitions, limber as a pair of well-grown, well-used legs that make their way with equal ease and sapience through a metropolis or up a mountain. "City Walking" (1975, Heart's Desire*) attains the same agility of form, miraculously, for it does it in a tenth of the space. In about a thousand words, Hoagland moves from the "now" of New York City to the "then" of life as a young writer in the fifties, to the fictive past of Huck Finn's America; from "here" by the Hudson, to "there" by the Mississippi; from the sheer exhilaration of city walking—"brutality is strength"—to the cramped wariness induced by urban predators. Whether in living or writing, staying limber is of the essence, the premier mark of sanity and beauty. "A personal essay," writes Hoagland, "is like the human voice talking, its order the mind's natural flow" ("What I Think, What I Am"; see p. 690). For this prolific and widely admired essayist, the essay draws its lovely suppleness of form from the suppleness of the human self knowing how to "live intelligently," a suppleness that is the "chameleon strength" of all life in its evolutionary unfolding: "days well-lived . . . energy, zappy sex, sunshine shored up, inventiveness, competitiveness, and the whole fun of busy brain cells." ("Thoughts on Returning to the City After Five Months on a Mountain Where the Wolves Howled").*

City Walking

There is a time of life somewhere between the sullen fugues of adolescence and the retrenchments of middle age when human nature becomes so absolutely absorbing one wants to be in the city constantly, even at the height of the summer. Nature can't seem to hold a candle to it. One gobbles the blocks, and if the weather is sweaty, so much the better; it brings everybody else out too. To the enthusiast's eye, what might later look to be human avarice is simply energy, brutality is strength, ambition is not wearisome or repellent or even alarming. In my own case, aiming to be a writer, I knew that every mile I walked, the better writer I'd be; and I went to Twentieth Street and the Hudson River to smell the yeasty redolence of the Nabisco factory, and to West Twelfth Street to sniff the police stables. In the meat-market district nearby, if a tyro complained that his back ached, the saying was "Don't bleed on me!"

Down close to the Battery the banana boats used to unload (now they are processed in Albany). Banana boats were the very definition of seagoing grubbiness, but bejeweled snakes could be discovered aboard which had arrived from the tropics as stowaways. On Bleecker Street you could get a dozen clams on the half shell for fifty cents if you ate them outdoors; and on Avenue A, piroshki, kielbasa, and suchlike. Kids still swam from piers west of the theater district in the Hudson and under Brooklyn Bridge, and I was on the lookout among them for Huckleberry Finn. He was there, all right, diving in, then scrambling up a piling, spitting water because he hadn't quite learned how to swim. In the evening I saw him again on Delancey Street, caught by the ear by a storekeeper for pilfering.

Oh yes, oh yes! one says, revisiting these old walking neighborhoods. Yorkville, Inwood, Columbus Avenue. Our New York sky is not muscular with cloud formations as is San Francisco's, or as green-smelling as London's, and rounding a corner here, one doesn't stop stock-still to gaze at the buildings as in Venice. The bartenders like to boast that in this city we have "the best and worst," yet intelligent conversation, for example, is mostly ad-libbed and comes in fits and starts, anywhere or nowhere; one cannot trot out of an evening and go looking for it. We have our famous New York energy instead, as well as its reverse, which is the keening misery, the special New York craziness, as if every thirteenth person standing on the street is wearing a gauzy hospital smock and paper shower slippers.

Edmund G. Love wrote a good city walker's book some years ago called *Subways Are for Sleeping*. Indeed they were, but now if the transit police didn't prevent old bums from snoozing the night away while rumbling back and forth from Brooklyn to the Bronx, somebody would set them on fire. Up the street hunting parties are abroad, whom the walker must take cognizance of; it's not enough to have your historical guidebook and go maundering about to the Old Merchant's House on East Forth Street. A pair of bravos will ask you for a light and want a light; another pair, when your hands are in your pockets, will slug you. If you're lucky they will slug you; the old bar fighters complain about how risky fighting has become. You must have a considerable feel for these things, an extra sense, eyes in the back of your head: or call it a walker's *emotional range*. You must know when a pistol pointed at you playfully by a ten-year-old is a cap pistol and when it's not; whether someone coming toward you with a broken bottle is really going for you or not. We have grown to be students of police work—watching a bank robber scram as the squad cars converge, watching a burglar tackled, watching four hoodlums unmercifully beating a cop until four patrol cars scream to a halt and eight policemen club down the hoods.

Nevertheless, if you ask people who have some choice in the matter why they live in a particular neighborhood, one answer they will give is that they "like to walk." Walking is a universal form of exercise, not age-oriented or bound to any national heritage, and costs and implies nothing except maybe a tolerant heart. Like other sports, it calls for a good eye as well as cheerful legs—those chunky gluteus muscles that are the butt of mankind's oldest jokes—because the rhythm of walking is in the sights and one's response as much as simply in how one steps. In America at the moment it may seem like something of a reader's or an individualist's sport, because we are becoming suburban, and the suburbs have not yet adjusted to the avocation of walking. But they will.

And yet times do change. Only this spring I was in a river town on the Mississippi, loafing on a dock the barges tie to, on the lookout for Huckleberry Finn once again. He was there, all right, with a barefoot, redheaded, towheaded gang. They had sandy freckles and wore torn pants; Miss Watson still cut their hair. They were carrying a pailful of red-eared turtles and green frogs from the borrow pit behind the levee, and were boasting about the garfish they had noosed with a piece of piano wire. They began daring each other, and what the dare turned out to be—the best they could think of—was which of them had nerve enough to reach down and taste the Mississippi!

Now, muggers are herd creatures like the rest of us; they too have a "rush hour." So if a walker is indeed an individualist there is nowhere he can't go at dawn and not many places he can't go at noon. But just as it demeans life to live alongside a great river you can no longer swim in or drink from, to be crowded into the safer areas and hours takes much of the gloss off walking—one sport you shouldn't have to reserve a time and a court for.

Joan Didion

(b. 1934)

No one is more conscious than Joan Didion of the kind of ignorance that moves the essayist in the act of writing: the ignorance of the "I" that's doing the writing. The essayistic "I." The "I" being written into being—Joan Didion "arranging words on paper," playing grammar "by ear" like a piano, but with a precision so peculiarly her own that one would have to be tone deaf to miss the player in the music, the messenger in the message: the "I" being constructed through "the infinite power" of grammar. "I write entirely to find out what I'm thinking, what I'm looking at, what I see and what it means. What I want and what I fear" ("Why I Write," 1976). Acts of writing, for Didion, are radically creative, for what they create is this self coming to know itself. Her early essay, "On Morality" (1965, Slouching Toward Bethlehem) *exemplifies this creative movement from ignorance to knowledge. Can there be any surprise in the fact that it turns out to be anything but an abstract knowledge of right and wrong, do's and don'ts? Given the assignment to think about "morality," Didion writes what comes to mind, and what comes to mind is happenings—past and present—in Death Valley, where she herself happens to be writing "in a room at the Enterprise Motel and Trailer Park" with the mercury at 119°, not far from where the Jayhawkers, a splinter group of goldseekers on a short cut to California in the rush of 1849, died in the breakdown of social cohesion. There are, she decides, loyalties to groups of which we're members, those primitive loyalties that work to ensure survival; apart from that, what passes for "moral imperatives" is merely something we deeply need or want. Her autobiographical essay "On Going Home" (1967) depicts with characteristic economy the time and place that established her own primitive morality: her loyalties to family and home. "We are what we learned as children"; but the realities of life with her daughter now, in Los Angeles, demand something other than perpetuating old family bonds. "I give her a xylophone and a sundress from Madeira, and promise to tell her a funny story": what she has to give her child comes not out of any "morality," Didion might say, but out of "pragmatic necessity." And out of the pragmatic necessity of "saying I" ("Why I Write") come these essays offering their brilliant synchrony of realistically reported detail and personal response.*

On Morality

As it happens I am in Death Valley, in a room at the Enterprise Motel and Trailer Park, and it is July, and it is hot. In fact it is 119°. I cannot seem to make the air conditioner work, but there is a small refrigerator, and I can wrap ice cubes in a towel and hold them against the small of by back. With the help of the ice cubes I have been trying to think, because *The American Scholar* asked me to, in some abstract way about "morality," a word I distrust more every day, but my mind veers inflexibly toward the particular.

Here are some particulars. At midnight last night, on the road in from Las Vegas to Death Valley Junction, a car hit a shoulder and turned over. The driver, very young and apparently drunk, was killed instantly. His girl was found alive but bleeding internally, deep in shock. I talked this afternoon to the nurse who had driven the girl to the nearest doctor, 185 miles across the floor of the Valley and three ranges of lethal mountain road. The nurse explained that her husband, a talc miner, had stayed on the highway with the boy's body until the coroner could get over the mountains from Bishop, at dawn today. "You can't just leave a body on the highway," she said. "It's immoral."

It was one instance in which I did not distrust the word, because she meant something quite specific. She meant that if a body is left alone for even a few minutes on the desert, the coyotes close in and eat the flesh. Whether or not a corpse is torn apart by coyotes may seem only a sentimental consideration, but of course it is more: one of the promises we make to one another is that we will try to retrieve our casualties, try not to abandon our dead to the coyotes. If we have been taught to keep our promises—if, in the simplest terms, our upbringing is good enough—we stay with the body, or have bad dreams.

I am talking, of course, about the kind of social code that is sometimes called, usually pejoratively, "wagon-train morality." In fact that is precisely what it is. For better or worse, we are what we learned as children: my own childhood was illuminated by graphic litanies of the grief awaiting those who failed in their loyalties to each other. The Donner-Reed Party, starving in the Sierra snows, all the ephemera of civilization gone save that one vestigial taboo, the provision that no one should eat his own blood kin. The Jayhawkers, who quarreled and separated not far from where I am tonight. Some of them died in the Funerals and some of them died down near Badwater and most of the rest of them died in the Panamints. A woman who got through gave the Valley its name. Some might say that the Jayhawkers were killed by the desert summer, and the Donner Party by the mountain winter, by circumstances beyond control; we were taught instead that they had somewhere abdicated their responsibilities, somehow breached their primary loyalties, or they would not have found themselves helpless in the mountain winter or the desert summer, would not have given way to acrimony, would not have deserted one another, would not have *failed*. In brief, we heard such stories as cautionary tales, and they still suggest the only kind of "morality" that seems to me to have any but the most potentially mendacious meaning.

You are quite possibly impatient with me by now; I am talking, you want to say, about a "morality" so primitive that it scarcely deserves the name, a code that has as its point only survival, not the attainment of the ideal good. Exactly. Particularly out here tonight, in this country so ominous and terrible that to live in it is to live with antimatter, it is difficult to believe that "the good" is a knowable quantity. Let me tell you what it is like out here tonight. Stories travel at night on the desert. Someone gets in his pickup and drives a couple of hundred miles for a beer, and he carries news of what is happening, back wherever he came from. Then he drives another hundred miles for another beer, and passes along stories from the last place as well as from the one before; it is a network kept alive by people whose instincts tell them that if they do not keep moving at night on the desert they will lose all reason. Here is a story that is going around the desert tonight: over across the Nevada line, sheriff's deputies are diving in some underground pools, trying to retrieve a couple of bodies known to be in the hole. The widow of one of the drowned boys is over there; she is eighteen, and pregnant, and is said not to leave the hole. The divers go down and come up, and she just stands there and stares into the water. They have been diving for ten days but have found no bottom to the caves, no bodies and no trace of them, only the black 90° water going down and down and down, and a single translucent fish, not classified. The story tonight is that one of the divers has been hauled up incoherent, out of his head, shouting—until they got him out of there so that the widow could not hear—about water that got hotter instead of cooler as he went down, about light flickering through the water, about magma, about underground nuclear testing.

That is the tone stories take out here, and there are quite a few of them tonight. And it is more than the stories alone. Across the road at the Faith Community Church a couple of dozen old people, come here to live in trailers and die in the sun, are holding a prayer sing. I cannot hear them and do not want to. What I can hear are occasional coyotes and a constant chorus of "Baby the Rain Must Fall" from the jukebox in the Snake Room next door, and if I were also to hear those dying voices, those Midwestern voices drawn to this lunar country for some unimaginable atavistic rites, *rock of ages cleft for me*, I think I would lose my own reason. Every now and then I imagine I hear a rattlesnake, but my husband says that it is a faucet, a paper rustling, the wind. Then he stands by a window, and plays a flashlight over the dry wash outside.

What does it mean? It means nothing manageable. There is some sinister hysteria in the air out here tonight, some hint of the monstrous perversion to which any human idea can come. "I followed my own conscience." "I did what I thought was right." How many madmen have said it and meant it? How many murderers? Klaus Fuchs said it, and the men who committed the Mountain Meadows Massacre said it, and Alfred Rosenberg said it. And, as we are rotely and rather presumptuously reminded by those who would say it now, Jesus said it. Maybe we have all said it, and maybe we have been wrong. Except on that most primitive level—our loyalties to those we love—what could be more arrogant than to claim the primacy of personal conscience? ("Tell me," a rabbi asked Daniel Bell when he said, as a child, that he did not believe in God. "Do you think God cares?") At least some of the time, the world appears to me as a painting by Hieronymous Bosch; were I to follow my conscience then, it would lead me out onto the desert with Marion Faye, out to where he stood in *The Deer Park* looking east to Los Alamos and praying, as if for rain, that it would happen: ". . . *let it come and clear the rot and the stench and the stink, let it come for all of everywhere, just so it comes and the world stands clear in the white dead dawn.*"

Of course you will say that I do not have the right, even if I had the power, to inflict that unreasonable conscience upon you; nor do I want you to inflict your conscience, however reasonable, however enlightened, upon me. ("We must be aware of the dangers which lie in our most generous wishes," Lionel Trilling once wrote. "Some paradox of our nature leads us, when once we have made our fellow men the objects of our enlightened interest, to go on to make them the objects of our pity, then of our wisdom, ultimately of our coercion.") That the ethic of conscience is intrinsically insidious seems scarcely a revelatory point, but it is one raised with increasing infrequency; even those who do raise it tend to *segue* with troubling readiness into the quite contradictory position that the ethic of conscience is dangerous when it is "wrong," and admirable when it is "right."

You see I want to be quite obstinate about insisting that we have no way of knowing—beyond that fundamental loyalty to the social code—what is "right" and what is "wrong," what is "good" and what "evil." I dwell so upon this because the most disturbing aspect of "morality" seems to me to be the frequency with which the word now appears; in the press, on television, in the most perfunctory kinds of conversation.

Questions of straightforward power (or survival) politics, questions of quite indifferent public policy, question of almost anything: they are all assigned these factitious moral burdens. There is something facile going on, some self-indulgence at work. Of course we would all like to "believe" in something, like to assuage our private guilts in public causes, like to lose our tiresome selves; like, perhaps, to transform the white flag of defeat at home into the brave white banner of battle away from home. And of course it is all right to do that; that is how, immemorially, things have gotten done. But I think it is all right only so long as we do not delude ourselves about what we are doing, and why. It is all right only so long as we remember that all the *ad hoc* committees, all the picket lines, all the brave signatures in *The New York Times*, all the tools of agitprop straight across the spectrum, do not confer upon anyone any *ipso facto* virtue. It is all right only so long as we recognize that the end may or may not be expedient, may or may not be a good idea, but in any case has nothing to do with "morality." Because when we start deceiving ourselves into thinking not that we want something or need something, not that it is a pragmatic necessity for us to have it, but that it is a *moral imperative* that we have it, then is when we join the fashionable madmen, and then is when the thin whine of hysteria is heard in the land, and then is when we are in bad trouble. And I suspect we are already there.

On Going Home

I am home for my daughter's first birthday. By "home" I do not mean the house in Los Angeles where my husband and I and the baby live, but the place where my family is, in the Central Valley of California. It is a vital although troublesome distinction. My husband likes my family but is uneasy in their house, because once there I fall into their ways, which are difficult, oblique, deliberately inarticulate, not my husband's ways. We live in dusty houses ("D-U-S-T," he once wrote with his finger on surfaces all over the house, but no one noticed it) filled with mementos quite without value to him (what could the Canton dessert plates mean to him? how could he have known about the assay scales, why should he care if he did know?), and we appear to talk exclusively about people we know who have been committed to mental hospitals, about people we know who have been booked on drunk-driving charges, and about property, particularly about property, land, price per acre and C-2 zoning and assessments and freeway access. My brother does not understand my husband's inability to perceive the advantage in the rather common real-estate transaction known as "sale-leaseback," and my husband in turn does not understand why so many of the people he hears about in my father's house have recently been committed to mental hospitals or booked on drunk-driving charges. Nor does he understand that when we talk about sale-leasebacks and right-of-way condemnations we are talking in code about the things we like best, the yellow fields and the cottonwoods and the rivers rising and falling and the mountain roads closing when the heavy snow comes in. We miss each other's points, have another drink and regard the fire. My brother refers to my husband, in his presence, as "Joan's husband." Marriage is the classic betrayal.

Or perhaps it is not anymore. Sometimes I think that those of us who are now in our thirties were born into the last generation to carry the burden of "home," to find in family life the source of all tension and drama. I had by all objective accounts a "normal" and a "happy" family situation, and yet I was almost thirty years old before I could talk to my family on the telephone without crying after I had hung up. We did not fight. Nothing was wrong. And yet some nameless anxiety colored the emotional charges between me and the place that I came from. The question of whether or not you could go home again was a very real part of the sentimental and largely literary baggage with which we left home in the fifties; I suspect that is irrelevant to the children born of the fragmentation after World War II. A few weeks ago in a San Francisco bar I saw a pretty young girl on crystal take off her clothes and dance for the cash prize in an "amateur-topless" contest. There was no particular sense of moment about this, none of the effect of romantic degradation, of "dark journey," for which my generation strived so assiduously. What sense could that girl possibly make of, say *Long Day's Journey into Night*? Who is beside the point?

That I am trapped in this particular irrelevancy is never more apparent to me than when I am home. Paralyzed by the neurotic lassitude engendered by meeting one's past at every turn, around every corner, inside every cupboard, I go aimlessly from room to room. I decide to meet it head-on and clean out a drawer, and I spread the contents on the bed. A bathing suit I wore the summer I was seventeen. A letter of rejection from *The Nation*, an aerial photograph of the site for a shopping center my father did not build in 1954. Three teacups hand-painted with cabbage roses and signed "E.M.," my grandmother's initials. There is no final solution for letters of rejection from *The Nation* and teacups hand-painted in 1900. Nor is there any answer to snapshots of one's grandfather as a young man on skis, surveying around Donner Pass in the year 1910. I smooth out the snapshot and look into his face, and do and do not see my own. I close the drawer, and have another cup of coffee with my mother. We get along very well, veterans of a guerrilla war we never understood.

Days pass. I see no one. I come to dread my husband's evening call, not only because he is full of news of what by now seems to me our remote life in Los Angeles, people he has seen, letters which require attention, but because he asks what I have been doing, suggests uneasily that I get out, drive to San Francisco or Berkeley. Instead I drive across the river to a family graveyard. It has been vandalized since my last visit and the monuments are broken, overturned in the dry grass. Because I once saw a rattlesnake in the grass I stay in the car and listen to a country-and-Western station. Later I drive with my father to a ranch he has in the foothills. The man who runs his cattle on it asks us to the roundup, a week from Sunday, and although I know that I will be in Los Angeles I say, in the oblique way my family talks, that I will come. Once home I mention the broken monuments in the graveyard. My mother shrugs.

I go to visit my great-aunts. A few of them think now that I am my cousin, or their daughter who died young. We recall an anecdote about a relative last seen in 1948, and they ask if I still like living in New York City. I have lived in Los Angeles for three years, but I say that I do. The baby is offered a horehound drop, and I am slipped a dollar bill "to buy a treat." Questions trail off, answers are abandoned, the baby plays with the dust motes in a shaft of afternoon sun.

It is time for the baby's birthday party: a white cake, strawberry-marshmallow ice cream, a bottle of champagne saved from another party. In the evening, after she has gone to sleep, I kneel beside the crib and touch her face, where it pressed against the slats, with mine. She is an open and trusting child, unprepared for and unaccustomed to the ambushes of family life, and perhaps it is just as well that I can offer her little of that life. I would like to give her more. I would like to promise her that she will grow up with a sense of her cousins and of rivers and of her great-grandmother's teacups, would like to pledge her a picnic on a river with fried chicken and her hair uncombed, would like to give her *home* for her birthday, but we live differently now and I can promise her nothing like that. I give her a xylophone and a sundress from Madeira, and promise to tell her a funny story.

N. Scott Momaday

(b. 1934)

Among the Kiowa people, according to N. Scott Momaday, himself half Kiowa, names are not arbitrary, mere conventional signs; names give substance to all things. As the Priest of the Sun tells it in House Made of Dawn, *John the Evangelist spoke truly when he said, "In the beginning was the Word"; but when he kept talking, he padded the truth with verbiage, "fat." In verbiage—words for the sake of artifice, words for the sake of words—the name is desacrilized and the world profaned. The Sun Priest again: "the white man's regard for language—for the Word itself—as an instrument of creation has diminished nearly to the point of no return. It may be that he will perish by the Word." For the Kiowa, no overall divinity rules what happens within nature or beyond it; there is only the sacred Word, the spirit of things existing in their names. Thus the Kiowa literary artist is a creator of the sacred, and as a Kiowa artist Momaday strives to eliminate word-fat. In his first year of life, this poet, painter, novelist, essayist, received the name Tsoaitalee, or Rock-tree-boy, after Devil's Tower, the huge shaft of volcanic rock that rises above a Wyoming river. A place not of conflict but of creative power, as if "the motion of the world was begun" here, Devil's Tower is the source of myths, legends, history, and poetry keeping "the idea" of the Kiowa people alive. Momaday has chosen not to write about what he calls "the mean and ordinary agonies of human history," how the Kiowa culture was destroyed along with the buffalo herds; his subject is the sacred time of his people, their "time of great adventure and nobility and fulfillment." In* The Way to Rainy Mountain, *he recreates "the journey" by which the Kiowas "conceived a good idea of themselves" and by which that idea endures. The essay of the same title (originally published in* The Reporter, *1967, then used to introduce the book) records a visit to his grandmother's grave and opens into the sacred time of Aho, born when "the Kiowa were living the last great moment of their history." She was, for her grandson, the last member of the Sun Dance culture, the last of them with a "holy regard that now is all but gone out of mankind." The essay's plain but lyrical style, if read from the Kiowa viewpoint, is a reclamation of words for their natural—their sacred—function.*

The Way to Rainy Mountain

A single knoll rises out of the plain in Oklahoma, north and west of the Wichita Range. For my people, the Kiowas, it is an old landmark, and they gave it the name Rainy Mountain. The hardest weather in the world is there. Winter brings blizzards, hot tornadic winds arise in the spring, and in summer the prairie is an anvil's edge. The grass turns brittle and brown, and it cracks beneath your feet. There are green belts along the rivers and creeks, linear groves of hickory and pecan, willow and witch hazel. At a distance in July or August the steaming foliage seems almost to writhe in fire. Great green-and-yellow grasshoppers are everywhere in the tall grass, popping up like corn to sting the flesh, and tortoises crawl about on the red earth, going nowhere in the plenty of time. Loneliness is an aspect of the land. All things in the plain are isolate; there is no confusion of objects in the eye, but *one* hill or *one* tree or *one* man. To look upon that landscape in the early morning, with the sun at your back, is to lose the sense of proportion. Your imagination comes to life, and this, you think, is where Creation was begun.

I returned to Rainy Mountain in July. My grandmother had died in the spring, and I wanted to be at her grave. She had lived to be very old and at last infirm. Her only living daughter was with her when she died, and I was told that in death her face was that of a child.

I like to think of her as a child. When she was born, the Kiowas were living that last great moment of their history. For more than a hundred years they had controlled the open range from the Smoky Hill River to the Red, from the headwaters of the Canadian to the fork of the Arkansas and Cimarron. In alliance with the Comanches, they had ruled the whole of the southern Plains. War was their sacred business, and they were among the finest horsemen the world has ever known. But warfare for the Kiowas was preeminently a matter of disposition rather than of survival, and they never understood the grim, unrelenting advance of the U.S. Cavalry. When at last, divided and ill-provisioned, they were driven onto the Staked Plains in the cold rains of autumn, they fell into panic. In Palo Duro Canyon they abandoned their crucial stores to pillage and had nothing then but their lives. In order to save themselves, they surrendered to the soldiers at Fort Sill and were imprisoned in the old stone corral that now stands as a military museum. My grandmother was spared the humiliation of those high gray walls by eight or ten years, but she must have known from birth the affliction of defeat, the dark brooding of old warriors.

Her name was Aho, and she belonged to the last culture to evolve in North America. Her forebears came down from the high country in western Montana nearly three centuries ago. They were a mountain people, a mysterious tribe of hunters whose language has never been positively classified in any major group. In the late seventeenth century they began a long migration to the south and east. It was a long journey toward the dawn, and it led to a golden age. Along the way the Kiowas were befriended by the Crows, who gave them the culture and religion of the Plains. They acquired horses, and their ancient nomadic spirit was suddenly free of the ground. They acquired Tai-me, the sacred Sun Dance doll, from that moment the object and symbol of their worship, and so shared in the divinity of the sun. Not least, they acquired the sense of destiny, therefore courage and pride. When they entered upon the southern Plains, they had been transformed. No longer were they slaves to the simple necessity of survival; they were a lordly and dangerous society of fighters and thieves, hunters and priests of the sun. According to their origin myth, they entered the world through a hollow log. From one point of view, their migration was the fruit of an old prophecy, for indeed they emerged from a sunless world.

Although my grandmother lived out her long life in the shadow of Rainy Mountain, the immense landscape of the continental interior lay like memory in her blood. She could tell of the Crows, whom she had never seen, and of the Black Hills, where she had never been. I wanted to see in reality what she had seen more perfectly in the mind's eye, and traveled fifteen hundred miles to begin my pilgrimage.

Yellowstone, it seemed to me, was the top of the world, a region of deep lakes and dark timber, canyons and waterfalls. But, beautiful as it is, one might have the sense of confinement there. The skyline in all directions is close at hand, the high wall of the woods and deep cleavages of shade. There is a perfect freedom in the mountains, but it belongs to the eagle and the elk, the badger and the bear. The Kiowas reckoned their stature by the distance they could see, and they were bent and blind in the wilderness.

Descending eastward, the highland meadows are a stairway to the plain. In July the inland slope of the Rockies is luxuriant with flax and buckwheat, stonecrop and larkspur. The earth unfolds and the limit of the land recedes. Clusters of trees and animals grazing far in the distance cause the vision to reach away and wonder to build upon the mind. The sun follows a longer course in the day, and the sky is immense beyond all comparison. The great billowing clouds that sail upon it are shadows that move upon the grain like water, dividing light. Farther down, in the land of the Crows and Blackfeet, the plain is yellow. Sweet clover takes hold of the hills and bends upon itself to cover and seal the soil. There the Kiowas paused on their way; they had come to the place where they must change their lives. The sun is at home on the plains. Precisely there does it have the certain character of a god. When the Kiowas came to the land of the Crows, they could see the dark lees of the hill at dawn across the Bighorn River, the profusion of light on the grain shelves, the oldest deity ranging after the solstices. Not yet would they veer southward to the caldron of the land that lay below; they must wean their blood from the northern winter and hold the mountains a while longer in their view. They bore Tai-me in procession to the east.

A dark mist lay over the Black Hills, and the land was like iron. At the top of a ridge I caught sight of Devil's Tower upthrust against the gray sky as if in the birth of time the core of the earth had broken through its crust and the motion of the world was begun. There are things in nature that engender an awful quiet in the heart of man; Devil's Tower is one of them. Two centuries ago, because they could not do otherwise, the Kiowas made a legend at the base of the rock. My grandmother said:

> Eight children were there at play, seven sisters and their brother. Suddenly the boy was struck dumb; he trembled and began to run upon his hands and feet. His fingers became claws, and his body was covered with fur. Directly there was a bear where the boy had been. The sisters were terrified; they ran, and the bear after them. They came to the stump of a great tree, and the tree spoke to them. It bade them climb upon it and as they did so, it began to rise into the air. The bear came to kill them, but they were just beyond its reach. It reared against the tree and scored the bark all around with its claws. The seven sisters were borne into the sky, and they became the stars of the Big Dipper.

From that moment, and so long as the legend lives, the Kiowas have kinsmen in the night sky. Whatever they were in the mountains, they could be no more. However tenuous their well-being, however much they had suffered and would suffer again, they had found a way out of the wilderness.

My grandmother had a reverence for the sun, a holy regard that now is all but gone out of mankind. There was a wariness in her and an ancient awe. She was a Christian in her later years, but she had come a long way about, and she never forgot her birthright. As a child she had been to the Sun Dances; she had taken part in those annual rites, and by them she had learned the restoration of her people in the presence of Tai-me. She was about seven when the last Kiowa Sun Dance was held in 1887 on the Washita River above Rainy Mountain Creek. The buffalo were gone. In order to consummate the ancient sacrifice—to impale the head of the buffalo bull upon the medicine tree—a delegation of old men journeyed into

Texas, there to beg and barter for an animal from the Goodnight herd. She was ten when the Kiowas came together for the last time as a living Sun Dance culture. They could find no buffalo; they had to hang an old hide from the sacred tree. Before the dance could begin, a company of soldiers rode out from Fort Sill under orders to disperse the tribe. Forbidden without cause the essential act of their faith, having seen the wild herds slaughtered and left to rot upon the ground, the Kiowas backed away forever from the medicine tree. That was July 20, 1890, at the great bend of the Washita. My grandmother was there. Without bitterness, and for as long as she lived, she bore a vision of deicide.

Now that I can have her only in memory, I see my grandmother in the several postures that were peculiar to her: standing at the wood stove on a winter morning and turning meat in a great iron skillet; sitting at the south window, bent above her beadwork, and afterwards, when her vision had failed, looking down for a long time into the fold of her hands; going out upon a cane, very slowly as she did when the weight of age came upon her; praying. I remember her most often at prayer. She made long, rambling prayers out of suffering and hope, having seen many things. I was never sure that I had the right to hear, so exclusive were they of all mere custom and company. The last time I saw her she prayed standing by the side of her bed at night, naked to the waist, the light of a kerosene lamp moving upon her dark skin. Her long, black hair, always drawn and braided in the day, lay upon her shoulders and against her breasts like a shawl. I do not speak Kiowa, and I never understood her prayers, but there was something inherently sad in the sound, some merest hesitation upon the syllables of sorrow. She began in a high and descending pitch, exhausting her breath to silence; then again and again—and always the same intensity of effort, of something that is, and is not, like urgency in the human voice. Transported so in the dancing light among the shadows of her room, she seemed beyond the reach of time. But that was illusion; I think I knew then that I should not see her again.

Houses are like sentinels in the plain, old keepers of the weather watch. There, in a very little while, wood takes on the appearance of great age. All colors wear soon away in the wind and rain, and then the wood is burned gray and the grain appears and the nails turn red with rust. The windowpanes are black and opaque; you imagine there is nothing within, and indeed there are many ghosts, bones given up to the land. They stand here and there against the sky, and you approach them for a longer time than you expect. They belong in the distance; it is their domain.

Once there was a lot of sound in my grandmother's house, a lot of coming and going, feasting and talk. The summers there were full of excitement and reunion. The Kiowas are a summer people; they abide the cold and keep to themselves; but when the season turns and the land becomes warm and vital, they cannot hold still; an old love of going returns upon them. The aged visitors who came to my grandmother's house when I was a child were made of lean and leather, and they bore themselves upright. They wore great black hats and bright ample shirts that shook in the wind. They rubbed fat upon their hair and wound their braids with strips of colored cloth. Some of them painted their faces and carried the scars of old and cherished enmities. They were an old council of warlords, come to remind and be reminded of who they were. Their wives and daughters served them well. The women might indulge themselves; gossip was at once the mark and compensation of their servitude. They made loud and elaborate talk among themselves, full of jest and gesture, fright and false alarm. They went abroad in fringed and flowered shawls, bright beadwork and German silver. They were at home in the kitchen, and they prepared meals that were banquets.

There were frequent prayer meetings, and great nocturnal feasts. When I was a child, I played with my cousins outside, where the lamplight fell upon the ground and the singing of the old people rose up around us and carried away into the darkness. There were a lot of good things to eat, a lot of laughter and surprise. And afterwards, when the quiet returned, I lay down with my grandmother and could hear the frogs away by the river and feel the motion of the air.

Now there is a funeral silence in the rooms, the endless wake of some final word. The walls have closed in upon my grandmother's house. When I returned to it in mourning, I saw for the first time in my life how small it was. It was late at night, and there was a white moon, nearly full. I sat for a long time on the stone steps by the kitchen door. From there I could see out across the land; I could see the long row of trees by the creek, the low light upon the rolling plains, and the stars of the Big Dipper. Once I looked at the moon and caught sight of a strange thing. A cricket had perched upon the handrail, only a few inches away from me. My line of vision was such that the creature filled the moon like a fossil. It had gone there, I thought, to live and die, for there of all places, was its small definition made whole and eternal. A warm wind rose up and purled like the longing within me.

The next morning I awoke at dawn and went out on the dirt road to Rainy Mountain. It was already hot, and the grasshoppers began to fill the air. Still, it was early in the morning, and the birds sang out of the shadows. The long yellow grass on the mountain shone in the bright light, and a scissortail hied above the land. There, where it ought to be, at the end of a long and legendary way, was my grandmother's grave. Here and there on the dark stones were ancestral names. Looking back once, I saw the mountain and came away.

Richard Rhodes

(b. 1937)

What are we trying to save when we agree to "preserve the wilderness"? Take the Everglades: some 13,000 square miles extending east, west, and south from Lake Okeechobee down to the shallow-water keys of Florida Bay; that major portion of South Florida "still officially a wilderness"—in the words of Richard Rhodes, "the rag left over when the wilderness wears away." His journey there was one of many he made in the 1970s, "looking for America," hoping "to approach the riddle of who we are and why we came here and what we intend to do." As his models in this investigation, he claimed "not the new journalists or the old, but Emerson and Whitman and Thoreau." And of the essay, his chosen form, he says, "It is a spiral rather than a circle, by definition unfinished . . . an old and honorable form, invented at a time when men believed an individual sensibility, an individual intelligence, could be a useful and sometimes revealing measure of the world" (Foreword, Looking for America, 1979). *Yet Rhodes's "individual sensibility" as an essayist, his voicing of personal conscience in the tradition of the New England transcendentalists, is, nonetheless, sustained by a time-honored journalistic combination of reliable reporting and crusading in the public interest. Expository narrative, lucid analysis, lush descriptive passages—all are skillfully interwoven to create a moving argument for saving what is left of the Everglades ecosystem. Key West as the haunt of Audubon and Hemingway leads artfully into a potent stream of images characteristic of Rhodes the novelist: "Why the wilderness is insane. It destroys with pluralities. It skins off our flesh and shows us branching vessels and twitching meat and bubbling fluids and bones round and sturdy as tree trunks." Then the closing "spiral," the return to Naples (his temporary base) where his look at the Everglades moves him to an urgently personal moral stance: "We should preserve the wilderness because we need to know . . . that we are not finally compelled by our raging and whimpering always and forever to destroy." In 1974, the 2,400 square miles of Big Cypress Swamp—threatened, at the time of writing (1971) by plans for development—became Big Cypress National Preserve and thereby escaped drainage; the struggle to save the Everglades from the ecological consequences of its water-control systems continues.*

The Death of the Everglades

The old man saw the lizard slip from under a bush in front of the drugstore where he had gone to test his blood pressure and saw it sprawl on the flagstone path beside the sidewalk and hunched toward it propping himself with his cane. He raised the cane over his head baring his teeth and jammed the cane down and pinned the lizard to the flagstone tearing its belly out and it twisted over, its four infant hands clutching the air and its mouth opening and closing and the man jerked the cane up and jammed it down and jammed it up and down until he had mashed the lizard into the stone. The black tip of his cane smeared now, the old man looked uneasily around and breathing hard set the cane to the walk staining the white stone red and lurched away, teeming Florida jerking across his narrowed eyes.

He didn't understand.
That the lizard was harmless?
Yes.
But he did understand. It wasn't harmless.
A lizard?
It was a fuse running back into the swamp. He put it out.
One of many fuses then.
We put them out whenever we can. They mean us no good.
They mean us no harm.
They mean us no harm. They mean us nothing at all.

The Everglades, the wilderness Everglades that was once the wonder of the world, is not dying. It is already dead. The shell is left, the shell of a wilderness, and should be saved. We save shells. They are symmetrical and can be understood. The silent things that live inside them are not symmetrical and cannot be understood. They must be taken for what they are or destroyed. They do not care if they are taken or not. They live and die in silence. The old man raged. The lizard never said a word.

I am not cynical. I am not wedded to death, though at one time I thought I might be. I do not know Florida as well as the men and women who live there who would save it from itself, but I know land, and know when it is failing. South Florida will be a garden or it will be a desert. It will never again be a wilderness. It is not a wilderness now. It is the rag left over when the wilderness wears away.

Amerigo Vespucci named this western continent with a name better than his own. In a letter to Lorenzo de Medici he called it a New World. It tore men's eyes open. They could not believe what they saw. On their maps they shrank it into comprehension. Leonardo da Vinci, the most visionary of Renaissance men, drew the New World as a string of islands. Jacques le Moyne, the first artist to visit North America, drew Florida smaller than Cuba and located the Great Lakes in Tennessee.

Men came to the New World to plunder. Later they came to live. They could choose to move through the wilderness and make it their own or they could choose to push it back before them, destroying it as they went. Having money and courage but lacking the genius that might transform them into a new kind of people, they chose to push the wilderness back. They chose to remain European, with European notions of land ownership and European beliefs in man's authority over the natural world. That is why, though we think of ourselves today as American, we do not think of ourselves as an American race. We are separate from one another. We are Italian or Polish or Black or Wasp. The only people in America who feel they belong to the land, and so to each other, are the people we call Indian. They are the people who made the wilderness their own.

You can easily locate the places that pass for wilderness in the United States. The United States Geological Survey has not yet found time to record them on its most intimate series of topographical maps, the 7½-minute series, scaled one inch to two thousand feet. Barrens of western Nebraska, Wyoming, Utah, Nevada, have not yet been mapped for the 7½-minute series. The Everglades from Lake Okeechobee to Cape Sable has not yet been mapped for the series, though a jetport almost rose on the edge of the Big Cypress Swamp, though most of the Everglades has been leveed and ditched for water storage, though canals have been cut for new towns near the Big Cypress' Fakahatchee Strand, though acres of Nike missiles point toward Cuba from the center of the national park. The Everglades is still officially a wilderness, but it has already been pushed back. It teemed once with life. It teems no more.

"How shall I express myself," the traveler William Bartram wrote from upper Florida in the eighteenth century, "to avoid raising suspicions of my veracity? Should I say the river (in this place) from shore to shore, and perhaps near half a mile above and below me, appeared to be one solid bank of fish, of various kinds, pushing through this narrow pass of the St. Juan's into the little lake, on their return down the river, and that the alligators were in such incredible numbers, and so close together from shore to shore, that it would have been easy to have walked across on their heads, had the animals been harmless?" Bartram saw alligators twenty feet long, with bodies, he said, big as horses'. The longest recorded in the twentieth century was thirteen feet.

Birds, countless millions of birds, came to Florida once from all the reaches of the world, so thick in the sky that they darkened the sun, so thick in the shallow rookeries that their droppings turned the brown water white for miles. At the height of Florida's trade in egret plumes, eighty years ago, one Jacksonville merchant in one shipment sent 130,000 egret skins to New York. The birds come now in shrunken numbers, fewer than fifty thousand of them a year, and many do not stay. Some species will never be seen again. They are extinct, and to understand the dead finality of that word you must imagine what you would feel if you were the last human being alive anywhere in the world.

The first pictures of wilderness America to reach Europe were Jacques le Moyne's drawings of savage Florida. For a time, Florida *was* the New World to European eyes. William Bartram's *Travels* fired the imaginations of the English Romantic poets, of William and Dorothy Wordsworth and of Samuel Taylor Coleridge. Coleridge read Bartram and dreamed of building a utopia in Florida. Young men in groups of twelve would sail there and work only half a day and discuss philosophy in the long afternoons. Coleridge never left the English Lake District, but Bartram's Florida worked its way into his opium dream and came out *Kubla Khan:*

> Where Alph, the sacred river, ran
> Through caverns measureless to man
> Down to a sunless sea.

Alph was a Florida spring. But the caverns proved treacherous. They were caverns of time, and we moved through them as if the only lives that concerned us were our own.

We took the land and made it ours. "After we had strooken sayle and cast anker athwart the River," wrote an early French explorer of Florida, "I determined to goe on shore to discover the same." Religion strengthened him. He was only a little lower than the angels. He was lord of the earth. The men who planned the Everglades jetport felt the same. "We will do our best," one of them wrote, "to meet our responsibilities and the responsibilities of all men to exercise dominion over the land, sea, and air above us as the higher order of man intends." You can hear the Great Chain of Being rattling in there, the old medieval hierarchy of stone and plant and animal and man and angel and God. The preservationists who fought the jetport down heard only greed, but the old belief in the sovereignty of man impelled men to discover America and justified our existence here for three hundred years. Those who hold that belief today cannot understand why others do not. They smell subversion.

"How," asks a broadside circulating these days in South Florida, "can anyone legally stop a useless land from becoming a community of churches, schools, hospitals, universities, playground parks, golf courses, and beautiful homes where thousands of precious children will be born and raised to be useful citizens?" That the swamps and floodplains are not useless, that they collect and store and purify all the water South Florida will ever have, that the worst thing that could happen to the region would be the addition of more thousands of precious children to its present load, are not assertions easy to prove.

"Before this century is done," Peter Matthiessen writes in the Sierra Club book *The Everglades*, "there will be an evolution in our values and the values of human society, not because man has become more civilized but because, on a blighted earth, he will have no choice. This evolution—actually a revolution whose violence will depend on the violence with which it is met—must aim at an order of things that treats man and his habitat with respect." Nowhere in America is the conflict more directly engaged than in South Florida. If its primeval wilderness is gone, its ecosystem is not yet irrevocably damaged. Birds still sing and trees still grow. There is something left to save, a water supply and a way of life. New and terrifying problems have not yet displaced the old. Miami is not yet New York, nor Okeechobee Lake Erie. But how much time remains for South Florida is a question on which few people agree.

The Everglades was once a vast and grassy river. It began in the flood-and-hurricane spill of Lake Okeechobee and flowed south and southwest a hundred miles to merge with the ocean above Cape Sable, on the southwestern tip of Florida. Sawgrass and water and peat muck, a river fifty, seventy miles wide, bound on the east by a limestone ridge and on the west by a broad and shadowed cypress swamp, it looked like a marsh, but the water flowed sluggishly down. One foot of falloff in ten months. An inch and a little more a month. From new moon to new moon in the summer the land might receive thirty inches of rain and fill up like a tipped bowl. Alligators spread out then to feed, and deer and the panthers that harvested them found refuge on hammocks, tree islands shaped like longboats that interrupted the monotony of sawgrass. In the late summer and early autumn, hurricanes thrashed the sawgrass and tore the tops off the royal palms. The hurricanes dropped the last of the rains the land would see until summer came again. The water crept down the land or evaporated away in the sun or transpired away through the pores of green plants and trees. Disappearing, it concentrated the life that swarmed within it, mosquito fish and killifish and crayfish and the larger predators that lived on them, and the birds came to feed in the broth and reproduce. The water level dropped lower and lower and alligators dug out holes, tearing the grass and the peat away with their tails, making room not only for themselves but also for a seed crop of fish and turtles and frogs that would grow to populate the land when the next rains came. The first thunderstorms of late winter brought fire that burned away the old cover of sawgrass. On the higher land, the fire destroyed brush and the shoots of hardwoods but left behind the corky, fire-resistant pines.

When the water that flooded over Okeechobee reached the mangrove estuaries that lined the coasts, it mixed with seawater, stirred by the tides. The brackish solution that resulted from the mixing was a thousand times more fertile than the sea itself, haven for adolescent pink shrimp whose shells gave the roseate spoonbill its color, haven for young fish that men would later hook for sport and net for food. Crowds of crocodiles swarmed in the deltas of mangrove rivers, the only place in North America they were ever found. The mangrove forest itself was one of the largest in the world, trees that reclaimed the land from the sea, trees denser on their islands and peninsulas than any rain forest.

Aboriginal Indians lived on the mangrove coast and hunted the Everglades, men who came down from the continental wilderness and exchanged their buckskins for breechclouts of woven palm engorged in back with the tails of raccoons, women who bared their brown breasts and hung their bellies with Spanish moss like tropical growths of pubic hair. They piled up mounds of feasted shells that later whole farms would occupy, roared out to slaughter the fat manatee, dug coontie root and learned to wash it free of its alkaloid and pound it into white flour, harvested the land and the ocean and threw the waste over their shoulders and moved on. In other mounds, they piled up their dead without ceremony until a dream of death came down the peninsula from the interior of America and then they saw through to the other side and began to leave tokens in the graves of those of their blood who would pass over. The idea of death brought an idea of life and they flowered out in decoration, scratched patterns on their pots, carved wooden deer heads with knives made from the teeth of sharks, pushed smoothed knucklebones through their earlobes, took scalps and arms and legs from their enemies. And these, the Calusa and Tequesta, greeted the Spanish when they arrived. Greeted the Spanish with poisoned arrows and night hatchetings, but within a hundred years all of them were gone, killed by new diseases or shipped off to slavery in Cuban sugar fields.

The Everglades was not fit to live on, not fit to farm. White men left it alone while they tackled the northern wilderness. They pushed all the way to Oregon before they began to look seriously at the young peninsula that reached farther south than any other land in the United States. In the late nineteenth century sporadic efforts at drainage began. A muck dike went up along the lower rim of Lake Okeechobee to stop the spill of water and farmers moved in with cattle and sugar cane. Where the Everglades peat was exposed to the sun it began to oxidize, crumbling from fertile muck into gray silica-brightened ash that fed nothing. It is still oxidizing today, and will be gone, the work of five thousand years, in a few decades more. America's winter vegetable garden, Florida people call it.

The Okeechobee dike held the lake water back, but it was no match for hurricanes. One hit the lake in 1926 and drove the shallow water through the dike and killed three hundred people determined enough to try to make their living on a floodplain. A worse hurricane hit in 1928, and this time rescue workers stacked the bodies up like cordwood and burned them because there was no place to bury them in the flooded ground. Two thousand people died. Herbert Hoover came to Florida to survey the destruction. The new levee he caused to be built stands today. It began the federal-state program to control the lake and the Everglades below, although most of the canal work wasn't started until the late 1940s, at about the same time that President Truman announced the creation of a new national park at the lower end of the state.

Today only the part of the Everglades that lies within the national park—6 per cent of its original area—escapes direct control, and even that 6 per cent depends during the dry season on water draining into it from spillways on the Tamiami Trail and from a canal on the eastern edge of the park. The Everglades south of Okeechobee for a distance of twenty-five miles is farmland. Three water-conservation areas now lie where most of the Everglades ran before. They are surrounded by canals and levees. The Central and Southern Florida Flood Control District, the FCD, using stations constructed by the Army Corps of Engineers, pumps water into the water-conservation areas for storage in dry times and pumps water out of them to the ocean in times of potential flood. They are maintained as wilderness areas, and as many people visit them for hunting and fishing and airboating annually as visit the national park. But they are only historically Everglades, because the water flows through them now only at the behest of man. Nor are they particularly effective for storage. One scientist estimates that all the rain water they catch is evaporated or transpired away before it can be used. They are essentially shallow lagoons. It was in these areas that the worst of last winter's fires burned. It was in one of these areas, in 1966, when flood followed five years of drought, that the stress of high water killed thousands of deer. People blamed the Corps of Engineers. The Corps of Engineers correctly pointed out that the water-conservation area where the deer were killed had not been designed for wildlife preservation but for water control.

The park suffered during the same drought. Lacking the rainfall that supplies it with 80 per cent of its water, it needed the flow south from Okeechobee, but the spillways on the Tamiami Trail were closed.

The Engineers explained that they had not planned the water-conservation system to feed the park.

Hurricanes in the 1920s, fires in 1945, flood in 1947, severe drought in the early 1960s, flood in 1966, more fires in 1970 and 1971—South Florida and the Everglades have had their woes. But cycles of flood and drought have always worked their changes on the South Florida landscape. The difference today is that men are there, men who are working their changes too.

The jetport controversy has been resolved. Forty thousand flights a month still use the single training strip north of the Tamiami Trail above Everglades National Park, but the training strip will be moved and the jetport built elsewhere in Florida, on a site where the natural order has already given way completely to the man-made. It is worth remembering that the preservationists' victory was only a relative victory. The jetport has not been canceled. It will only be moved, to a place where it will cause less damage because the damage has already been done. That is what rankles the landowners of southwestern Florida. They have held their land for years, paid taxes on cypress swamp and wet prairie and everglades, waited their turn while the Gold Coast yielded up its wealth. The jetport would have sustained a major city. A government far away, an Interior Secretary from Alaska, a President from California, denied them their dream. Gave it away to other landowners. Encouraged by wilderness activists and hordes of newsmen, just such people as Spiro Agnew warned against.

The dream of city building, the dream of land bought at one hundred dollars an acre and sold for twenty golden thousand, has not faded. The jetport released energies in South Florida that will not easily be discharged. Twenty-five years ago the same landowners watched a new national park devour huge areas of Dade and Monroe counties. They say bitterly today what they must have thought bitterly then, that the Park is *already larger than the state of Delaware*. They mean, *how much land does a park need?* And not a notably scenic park at that, a water park, a biological park, a park for alligators and birds and gumbo-limbo trees. Then the jetport, a second chance. Lost because it would damage the park. Then, in 1970, the possibility that a leg of Interstate 75 might be cut from Naples to Miami to replace the Tamiami Trail. A panel of scientists and engineers recommended that no road at all be built. Florida's Secretary of Transportation compromised on Alligator Alley, which runs from Naples straight to Fort Lauderdale and avoids most of the Big Cypress. But even the new highway won't do landowners much good, because it will probably have few access roads.

Having successfully expelled the Everglades Jetport, preservationists are fighting today to save the Big Cypress Swamp from development. Only from the Big Cypress does water still drift freely into the park. The preservationists would like the federal government to buy half a million acres north of the park to protect its western water supply, a water supply that amounts to 15 per cent of the park's total water resources but 40 per cent of its dry-season flow. Burdened with deficits, the Nixon administration would prefer to preserve the land without buying it by converting the Tamiami Trail into a scenic parkway and federally zoning the swamp around it for recreation only.

The landowners, the big ones, are fighting back, and fighting the harder because they know this fight may be their last chance. Much of the Big Cypress was originally intended to be included in the park. It is still raw today, but development is beginning. New towns are going up on its western edge. A Miami real estate firm is selling land within the park itself for "waterfront estates," land still privately owned because Congress has not yet provided funds to buy it. Oil companies would like to drill in the Big Cypress, laying down access roads that would further alter its sheet-water flow and encourage development. Speculators are dredging out canals. If the Everglades Jetport was yesterday's South Florida controversy, the Big Cypress is today's.

You can walk in the Big Cypress if you don't mind getting wet. Roberts Lake Strand is surrounded by Loop Road 94, in the heart of the land the preservationists hope Congress will buy. It is one of the smaller strands in the Big Cypress and one still unmarred except for the scars of old logging and the deprivations of boy scouts in search of cypress knees. The strand begins at roadside, a screen of brush and cypress trees. If you do not know the swamp you do not enter it easily, no more easily than you would parachute for the first time from a plane. Panthers. Water moccasins. Alligators. The water creeps over your shoes. Firm bottom, sometimes bare limestone pitted with solution holes dissolved out over the centuries by plant acids, more often a tangle of leaves. Cool water, brown but entirely clear. Small plants like green stars grow on the bottom. You can drink the water. It tastes of plant decay, but no more so than most Florida water. The cypress trees close overhead and sunlight breaks fitfully through. Lichens grow on the tree trunks, gray-green, bright green, even pink, and moss soft as velvet, wet home for things too small to see. On the cypress branches sit air plants like isolated pineapples, their pointed leaves cupped to catch rain. Some of the air plants catch enough water to support life, natural aquariums with a crawfish and a tadpole or two up there in the trees. The nooks and crannies of life, a tadpole in an air plant on a cypress in the swamp. You realize you will not be attacked by predators and you relax, enjoying the cool water in the summer heat. You slog back into the swamp and farther back, heading toward a pond, passing a few cut stumps, then big trees never cut, trees that have grown in silence since before Columbus' first voyage, trees towering like the columns of cathedrals up to the sun. And rooted in the water, in the slow southward flow.

The pond is in a clearing, one of the water holes around which the cypresses grow. It is still choked with grass from the winter drought. The grass will die, flooded out by summer rain and thrashed down by alligators. You wade to your waist in the water now, taking caution in the dense grass. Ahead of you, out of sight, frogs bleat and jump. The distance is exact, an exact defensive boundary. Cross the boundary and you throw a switch and the frogs bleat and jump. The grass is indifferent. It has grown and seeded. It has done its job. It hangs in bunches on your legs. From time to time you reach under the water and push the grass behind you. You are making an alligator trail. You are an alligator pushing through lime grass in the Florida sun. You reach the edge of the pond and climb over a floating log and re-enter the cypress shade. You could walk into eternity in a cypress swamp. It has no corners. It is not abstract and knows no titles or plats. It flows and changes in patterns we only dimly begin to understand. The South Florida ecosystem has been studied seriously for less than thirty years.

If you find bogeymen in a cypress swamp, then you put them here. It is only itself, green in tooth and claw. It is what we left behind, territorial frogs and silent trees. You could live here if you took the trouble to learn how. An alligator might get you. There are worse deaths. Death means nothing and less than nothing here. Death leads back to life as surely as a circle turns in upon itself. If you died, the moss would still hang from the trees and the air plants still sit like comic birds nursing along a tadpole or two. The resurrection ferns, come summer and summer rain, would still resurrect. The gods who designed the swamp had a sense of humor. They put air plants on the trees and gray-green pads of periphyton in the water and they canceled death. The periphyton is spongy and slippery. You can mold it like clay. It feeds small things that feed larger things that eventually feed alligators, and the alligators belch and bed down in cypress ponds. Gar hover like broken branches. Leaves float by. A spider shakes its web strung on struts that reach high up into the trees. Cypress knees bend above the water. They might be shaggy ladies offering an accommodation. "How could anyone want to tear this beautiful place down?" asks my guide, a friend of the earth. How could they not, with its old mysteries scratching at their souls? It denies them their sovereignties. It reminds them that life, all life, their own life too, is a swarm of molecules thrown up momentarily in fantastic shapes and washed down and thrown up again, like waves breaking forever against a shore. Cowering behind antique metaphysics, believing life a constitutional right and death an obscenity, most of us find such reminders hard to cherish.

As love does when it decays, the debate over the future of the Big Cypress Swamp is rapidly resolving into a power struggle. Those who believe some wild land should be preserved in America, for itself and as a hedge against the unknown effects of massive ecological change, are fighting to preserve the Big Cypress. Those who believe the land is infinitely bountiful and was put here for human use are fighting to develop the Big Cypress. Wedged between the two positions is the tender science of ecology, and it is no more capable of taking a clear stand than a child is capable of deciding between parents in a divorce.

Joe Browder, Washington secretary to the Friends of the Earth and the one man more responsible than any other for bringing the Everglades Jetport to national attention and national censure, believes that Big Cypress development would be a catastrophe. "Failure to protect that portion of the Big Cypress that supplies water to Everglades National Park," he has written, "would, in addition to destroying the existing natural values in much of the Everglades, decrease water supply and increase water demand in southwest Florida to such a degree that additional pressures would be placed on the other major Everglades watershed, the sawgrass glades managed by the [Flood Control District]. The extra water demand would diminish the supply available for urban, industrial, and agricultural users in southeast Florida, and would further stimulate the conflict between all other users and Everglades National Park."

Landowners in Collier County, the county in southwestern Florida that includes most of the Big Cypress, completely disagree. They believe the water is plentiful, the swamp useless and dangerous, development desirable, and water into the park merely a matter of aiming a few canals its way. Their plans, they have said publicly, "could make this park into a living garden for wild life and plant life the year around." It is that already, but never mind.

The facts, so far as they are known, fall somewhere between.

The Big Cypress is presently an unusual and largely undamaged South Florida swamp, most of it privately owned. All of its water comes from rain. The rain that falls on the Big Cypress recharges the freshwater aquifer that supplies water for human use on the southwestern coast of Florida. It is the only natural water supply available to the coast. When the aquifer is full, water left standing on the ground drifts slowly down into the coastal portion of Everglades National Park, maintaining the life there under natural conditions.

If the Big Cypress were drained, its ecology would be altered from that of a swamp to that of dry land. Most of the life that thrives there now would die away. So would the coastal estuary. The park would take its water from canals, and the canals would certainly change and might permanently disrupt the ecology of the land within the park itself. The park's chief biologist, William Robertson, thinks the effect of development "highly unpredictable" but probably damaging.

The water-resources division of the United States Geological Survey, in a report prepared for Interior Secretary Walter Hickel before he departed Washington, implied that controlled development of the Big Cypress would cause some damage to the park but would not seriously impair the Gulf Coast's water supply. "No estimate is available," the report said, "of the total water-supply potential of [the western Big Cypress]. The present total water use in those areas is insignificant compared with the quantity evaporated, transpired, and discharged through the canal systems."

Draining the Big Cypress, then, would deliver up an enormous tract of land for human use. It would destroy the Big Cypress itself. It would turn the park into a giant zoo, an ecosystem that would look natural to casual visitors but would in fact be artificially maintained through canals. Pesticides used for mosquito control in the new towns north of the park would take their toll on the park, but the effects would be long-term. Any adverse effects on the Gulf Coast water supply would also be long-term.

The question of the Big Cypress becomes a long-term question, though it must be answered now, before development proceeds any further: what kind of future do the people of South Florida envision for themselves? And that question is part of a larger dilemma: what kind of future do all of us in America envision for ourselves? Assuming that we have a choice, do we want to live entirely in cities under artificial conditions or do we want a little of the natural world around us?

The larger dilemma begins to answer itself not in the speeches of our leaders but in the actions of individual citizens moving forward along parallel lines. We laid out the land long ago, in square sections that looked logical on a map but had nothing to do with the natural divisions of the land itself and little to do with the interests of the people who lived on it. Nowhere did the fine Enlightenment minds that devised our Constitution fail us more completely. Over the grid of sections, they fitted a Balkanized grid of political institutions, of townships and counties and states. Each had its particular sovereignties. Each developed its particular structures of power, some informal, some legally constituted. The old boundaries worked when the nation was poor in people and overrich in resources. They worked when those who differed from the established authorities had at least the possibility of moving on.

They are strained almost to breaking today, and the points of stress locate problems the entire nation is scrambling to solve. Our cities need money because their legal boundaries no longer define the metropolitan areas in which we live, areas that may well cut across city, town, village, county, and even state lines, areas chopped up into small authorities that drain away tax money to duplicate services the city has traditionally supplied. Citizens in nearly every state struggle with state legislatures still gerrymandering to give dominance to rural interests. Pollution control continues by law to be the responsibility of state and local governments, while pollution blows across state and county lines. The shape of our political institutions no longer matches the shape of our purposes and our need.

Consider Florida. The Everglades, which is all one watershed from Okeechobee to Cape Sable, is divided into three counties, a state-federal water conservation district and a national park, each with its own priorities of water and development.

The Big Cypress Swamp is being developed by men who have no legal or political responsibility to consider the ultimate effects of that development. The area of the Big Cypress that preservationists would like the federal government to buy is situated in Monroe County. Most of the large developers live in Collier County or in Miami. The Monroe County seat is in Key West, two hundred miles away across the Florida Bay.

Lake Okeechobee supplies water for Miami and most of Florida's Gold Coast. The water that feeds Okeechobee and is beginning to pollute it with pesticides and fertilizers rushes down the channelized Kissimmee River from farms and towns to the north, farms and towns that draw their own water supply from sources other than the big lake.

The list could be longer, and it could be duplicated anywhere in America. It demonstrates a failure of responsibility on the part of institutions that no longer fit our needs but are unwilling to rearrange the authority they have held so many years. But we have never been a people to let institutions stand in our way. When they have not worked, we have either abolished them or left them to die of neglect while we moved on to others that could do the job we wanted done. That is why a few activist men and women could work through the courts, the press, the television networks and the lobbies of Congress to convince a President that he should personally cancel one county-sponsored jetport. That is why Congress, not the state of Florida or the governments of Collier and Monroe counties, will probably find some way to buy or otherwise control the Big Cypress Swamp. But that is also why the battle to save the wild lands, in South Florida and elsewhere, has been so difficult for those who believe land deserves its day in court as surely as people do: because the idea is new and the institutions that will make it work are still being shaped.

The battle may be won, if there is time. No one knows how much time is left. However abstractly we divided the land, and however much we may want today to redivide it into shapes more consistent with its natural patterns, it has never been attendant to our laws. It changes with the certainty of the old laws of chemistry and physics. We can misuse it, if that is what we are doing, for an unknown length of time before it fails any longer to serve our needs, but when that time is up it fails suddenly and totally and without much hope of recovery. Poisonous algal blooms have already appeared at the northern end of Lake Okeechobee. Miami imposed water rationing last winter. "The Everglades," says Arthur Marshall, an ecologist at the University of Miami who has studied South Florida for eighteen years, "has all the symptoms of environmental stress and approaching catastrophic decline."

Perhaps it has. The men who believe the Lord gave us land to build on aren't worried. "Look at the Dutch," one of them, Ben Shepard, a commissioner of the Dade County Port Authority, said recently. "They completely destroyed the ecology of their land and yet it's supporting human life satisfactorily. The Dutch are some of the best-adjusted, prosperous, happiest people today." It probably does him no justice to recite John Maynard Keynes's jape at such men. "Practical men," Keynes said, "who believe themselves to be quite exempt from any intellectual influences, are usually the slaves of some defunct economist." Because Florida, having everything else, also has its own little Netherlands: Key West.

Key West. A waterless island of fossilized coral surrounded by the sea. If the continent were water and the water land, Key West is where all the sweetness and bitterness, all the honey and sour acids of our complicated American lives would drain. The southernmost point in the United States. Land's end. Old glory and present decay. Haven for disgruntled Cubans paddling the ninety miles from Havana in rafts of canvas and old inner tubes. Tourist trap meringued with Key Lime pie. Swabbies' town clipped to a drab naval base where black submarines cruise the harbor like sharks. Where developers reclaim land from the sea, the dying mangroves stinking of sulfur. Where an aquarium displays ocean fish in narrow tanks, white fungus blinding their eyes. Hemingway's home and Audubon's shrine.

Some of Key West's water comes from the Everglades. When the Navy decided to settle permanently on the island, it ran a pipeline down the Overseas Highway to supply it with water. Before the pipeline came in, the natives collected rainwater in cisterns behind their houses or bought it from commercial cisterns that dotted the island like small-town Mexican jails. With its population growing today in response to the tourist trade, Key West has gone to desalinization. Westinghouse built it a nuclear-powered desalinization plant, the largest of its kind in the United States. If we run out of water we can always distill the sea. With water, the motels in Key West may fill their swimming pools for tourists who come to see the turtle stockyards or to bend an elbow in Hemingway's favorite bar hung with parachute canopies and open to the street. And no one can complain of ecological damage, because there isn't much you can do to a dry Florida key once you've kicked out the dwarf Key deer. There ought to be no wilderness here at all except the wilderness of the sea, but even here the wilderness intrudes like a hypodermic injecting blood into a dying man.

Hemingway's house hangs back on a side street, a wide, gracious house surrounded on four sides with gardens and tropical trees, a huge banyan, shading palms, a royal poinciana with all its fired flowers burning. Cats prowl the corridors and sleep under the trees. Here the man lived for twenty years, tightening down the screws on his inner life even as his public life thickened with poisonous fame, writing less and less well. Describing love with the naïveté of a schoolgirl. Hunting Nazi submarines in the Caribbean. Converting heroism into mere bravado by dividing it from its vital source, the idea of death, his best and only theme, the theme he avoided more and more. Avoided until it killed him.

He was a hunter and a fisherman. He tried to come to grips with the land and the sea and at his occasional best he succeeded as well as anyone ever has, but to hunt and to fish is only to use the natural world, and to recover that world in all its intimacy you must be used by it, must give yourself up to it as nakedly as any Indian. He could not. He walked the narrow catwalk to his study over the garage and sharpened his pencils and fought to find feelings he progressively lost because he could not bear the crowd of fantasies that came with them. "There is no timber," an Irish playwright once wrote, "that has not strong roots among the clay and the worms." You must be buried alive like a seed or a larva to grow up into the sun, and to write about that growth you must willingly bury yourself alive over and over again. Paralyzed by private grief, Hemingway wielded his shovel clumsily over his own grave. Below his study, so they say in Key West, in a rusted steel safe, Hemingway's last wife found the manuscripts he had locked away there from prying eyes. She would publish them after his death to add a few thousand years more to his trial in purgatory. He bent to the wilderness and it devoured him.

Audubon owned no house in Key West, but he stayed in one that is more than a match for Hemingway's. It is a shrine today, decked out with expensive antiques that command more attention than they deserve. The house belonged to a Key West salvager named Geiger, a plump, bespectacled old scholar and hypocrite who made his living hauling in the lucrative stores of ships wrecked on the coral reef east of the island. Key West was a wealthy town when Miami was still an Indian village, and the islanders weren't above rearranging reef markers to keep it that way. Captain Geiger salvaged with the best of them and got rich on the proceeds.

Down one day came Audubon to work up the Florida birds. The captain housed him, Audubon a rare bird himself. Once, in New Orleans, broke, months from home and marriage bed, he accepted a beautiful courtesan's commission to paint her portrait. He hauled his palette to her backstreet house and found her naked before him on the couch. She lay naked for ten long afternoons while he stared and cartooned and oiled. It was the most difficult commission he ever accepted, he told a friend later.

He brought the same compaction of frustrated lust to his birds. They perch life-size on the pages of the enormous elephant folios displayed today in Captain Geiger's house. Audubon's eye raped them alive, tore them free from the clay and the worms. They rend their prey or fix the water at their feet with high metabolic intensity or poise to leap from the paper and claw out your heart. He saw the wilderness through them, made them transparent as any lantern slide. Their hollow, whistling bones and their racing wings beat from the interstices of the creamy paper against which they were thrown. Making them, building them up with remembered motions of the eye and the hand that first described them alive in the Everglades, he lived with the fear that trickled sweat down his back and pushed through to the swarming mystery beyond. The Aztec priests who never cut their hair and never knew a woman molded seeds and fresh human blood and black dirt into idols in black rooms off the main halls of their temples, and Audubon, sweating in an upstairs parlor at raffish Captain Geiger's house in Key West, molded seed and blood and black dirt into birds and discovered the essential Florida, the Florida that not even the most ardent preservationist dares speak of, the Florida that sent William Bartram into paroxyms of hysterical bliss and Samuel Coleridge into opium dreams. Why, the wilderness is insane. It destroys us with pluralities. It skins off our flesh and shows us branching vessels and twitching meat and bubbling fluids and bones round and sturdy as tree trunks. The alligator in its drying pond chews up its young, the wild boar breeds moaning with its mother, the panther licks its wet member, the mantis eats the male it has coupled with, the strangler fig chokes to death its guardian tree, the shrimp feasts on rot and the buzzard on decay and the proud eagle on carrion, and we see into ourselves and are horrified to live in such a world, a world that so mirrors our own depths, that delights in acts we have thought depraved, have worked from the beginning of our consciousness to fence in and legislate away. We wear pants and write laws and turn over the earth and only at the climax of our feverish couplings do we dimly sense how far we have removed ourselves from the moment-by-moment ecstasies of any animal's ordinary day. And that is one reason to keep what is left of wilderness in this civilized land, not to fish and hunt but to see the complexities that lay dormant within us, the possibilities we have not yet understood, because Shakespeare and the old Indian tales and the myths of Greece and Rome together do not begin to reveal as many metamorphoses as one walk through a cypress swamp or one descent into a coral reef. Audubon knew, and pushed through his fear to the other side and came back bird-maddened and showed us what he saw, the Florida that pulses inside. And for his trouble he is enshrined today on a barren Florida key fed by foul water recovered from the ocean. That is Key West, a little Netherlands. We can convert the whole continent over if we choose. Look at the Dutch.

When we came to Florida, my wife and two children and I, we took a house on the white beach at Naples, and we returned to it now by air from Key West like birds returning to an old and favored nest. At Naples the land meets the sea casually. Nothing there of rugged coast or coral reef. You must swim out seven miles to find a depth of thirty feet. No undertow will claim you, or any shark. Deceptive shallows, as Florida with its imperceptible seaweed tilt is deceptive, a beach itself dropping slowly into the water, a ramp on which the smallest creature may generation by generation crawl out onto the land. We came from the sea, by degrees teaching our flesh to wrap the sea inside it. It courses through us every day of our lives, reddened now with hungry iron. We never returned. The fish left the sea and returned, most of them. Their blood, like ours, is less salty than sea water, because while they lived in the estuaries or in fresh water the sea increased its load of salt leached from the land. The shark, with his bitter blood, never left the sea. He is old and well adapted. Older still are the airless bacteria that lie at the bottom of the lakes we have poisoned and the most terrible of disease organisms we suffer, botulism and tetanus and gangrene. The airless bacteria evolved before the fresh wind blew across the face of the world, evolved in vapors of methane and a saltless world of water. And learned to encyst themselves against the deadly oxygen that gives us life. Learned to wait their turn in a world gone wild with life. They wait now and will always be waiting, until sun and fresh air sting them no more.

Florida summer oppresses. Sweat collects. Clothes do not dry. You move in an invisible cloud of steam smelling sea metals and the dust of palm trees. Sun on the white beach reverses colors in your eyes. At low tide in the early evening, beachcombers pull piles of Naples starfish from the wet sand and lay them out on towels to dry, to die. My son flushes an ivory crab from its hole. It stands high on jointed legs, its eyes like black pearls glued to its carapace, and it turns in little jumps to face the boy as he moves. It is a head without a trunk jumping on jointed legs. It skitters sideways and collects itself and runs away to dig another hole and wait in the shadow inside and the boy is awed to silence.

Near sunset, the pier down the beach that reaches out a thousand feet into the Gulf fills up with fishermen. Young people with long hair, elderly couples in pale blue shorts and yachting caps. A hunchback whose shrunken legs dangle over the rim of his wheelchair. A fat woman with curlers in her cropped gray hair smoking a pipe, her enormous breasts hanging loose beneath a dirty tee shirt. Fish flop on the pier and lie still, one silver eye fixed on the moon. Schools, universities of bream flash among the pilings, bream enough to repopulate the ocean if it were ever in need, bream that sound the water like an orchestra of harps as they jump and dodge the predators that chase them. A black ray, one of its wings chopped off for bait, stains the pier. The tension of the fishermen smells like boiling lead. They have come out to catch fish in the low tide. Men cast their lines and reel them up. Boys drop lines between the floor boards and lie on their bellies peering into the darkness below. A woman baits the four prongs of a hook as big as a man's fist. Back on the land, a mosquito-control truck pumps mists of Dibrom through the streets and Naples disappears like Brigadoon. Brown pelicans, birds as comic and serene as Polynesian girls, birds that look like benevolent pterodactyls, circle the water beside the pier and casually fold their wings and dive and bring up fish no fisherman can touch. And fly a little way off and settle on the water and flip the fish in the air and swallow them.

The sun thickens to a giant red ball. It touches the water and flattens out at its base. The lead tension holds, vibrating like a dulled gong. At the moment of the sun's setting, everyone on the pier stops fishing and looks up to watch, pulled alert by an old compulsion. The water and the sky turn pink. The red ball grows, careless of the energy that gives everything in the world its single life. It drops into the ocean, feeding the water. Something breaks inside. The sea has eaten the sun. A few at a time, the fishermen reel up and walk away. The Dibrom settles on trees and houses and Naples returns to life minus mosquitoes. Out of sight in the swamp, in the sawgrass, living mosquitoes sniff the air, the males searching nectar, the females seeking blood.

Florida night. The thunderstorms of late afternoon have blown away. The sun has set and the fishermen are gone. The moon is down. On the porch of our house I am drinking bourbon and talking to a friend of the earth. It is our last night in Florida and we are ready to return home because Florida has come to seem some enormous conspiracy of contentious men and pregnant silence and I need distance to sort it out. The friend of the earth believes the wild lands will be saved because they must be if he is to find any peace in the world. Bitter at the confusion of my own life, I believe they will be turned and plowed and paved so that homes can be built where children will grow up guarded from the stews of birth and the stink of death, out of sight of the real life of the world. He is optimistic and his optimism makes no sense. We have everywhere destroyed the wilderness, raging and whimpering as we went. Yet he believes we will put aside our old autocracies and become natural democrats.

My wife remembers then a time, as a child, when she found a shell on the Naples beach and took it to her Victorian grandmother, who told her to throw it into a pot of boiling water to clean it out. A child, she did, and something alive shot out of the shell and flailed its legs in agony up to the roiling surface of the water and died, died as terribly as anything can ever die. She understood later what it was, a hermit crab. She would never again clean out a shell. The friend of the earth remembers a time when he was lost in the mountains of New Mexico and feared that he would die. He walked out in three days without food, marveling that he felt, after the first day, no hunger, only the compulsion to put one foot in front of the other lest he lie down and give up. He is camping in the same mountains as I write.

We are a wild species, Darwin said long ago. We were never scientifically bred. We are a various and colorful pack of mongrels, and the wilderness made us what we are: it is the place from which we came, and the place, clay and worms, where we shall go. For most of the life of man we could not live with that knowledge. Rather than live with it we pushed the wilderness away from us as a child pushes away the mother who would smother him with complexity. We go into the wilderness today, what is left of it, to find out who we are, but that is not the reason we should preserve it. We should preserve it because we need to know now, and our children and our children's children will need even more to know later, that we are not finally compelled by our raging and whimpering always and forever to destroy, that we are not entirely wedded to death. We need to leave a little food on our plates to prove that we are not impoverished. We need magnanimity, more today than we have ever needed it before.

At midnight we wade into the Gulf, my wife and the friend of the earth and I, into one small shore of the sea. The sky is clear and filled with stars, constellations we can see, formations we have never named, galaxies and suns too far from us for any except spiritual vision. They glow over the swamp, over the Everglades, over the great ramp of land that rises out of the water to cause men contention they have not yet decided how to still. Shall there be homes on the land? Oil pumped out of it? Water drawn up to wash away sweat and the spendings of the night? Shall old lizards crawl through muck there, green moss riding on their backs? And birds nest, and the used shells of their eggs drop down through the branches to float on the brown water? The things that live there, in the grass and in the swamp, will not know nor care what we do. They will go on as they have gone or they will not go at all. They do not choose. They only live. And the sharks circle forever, waiting for their prey.

The sea water glows around our bodies as we move: night plankton: they come alive with the light in the moving water we make, dots, sparkles, flashes, flares. We stare under water at a flood of stars glowing around the tips of our fingers, lighting our kicking feet and our stroking arms. They were here all along in the bright day and we did not know. We swirl them into light and they decorate us, imitating the stars above, microscopic things glowing in the water like the giant stars reduced by incomprehensible distances to points of white in the black sky. The stars in the sky and night plankton making stars in the water wherever we go: layers, and layers under layers down into the very center of things, and layers there too small to see, and layers below those layers until the head swims and still more layers then. We are no more divided from the world than the water itself is divided. When we damage the world we damage ourselves. If we destroy it we destroy ourselves. A piece at a time, we think, a part at a time, but the world has no pieces and does not come apart. Wherever we put our hands, points of energy trail off from us like the tails of comets. The tree that falls without sound falls within our hearing.

Margaret Atwood

(b. 1939)

Widely read and admired for her novels, poems, and short stories, this Canadian writer also exhibits a fine command of a more unusual genre: the prose poem. To this genre (whose invention is ascribed to the French poet Charles Baudelaire) Atwood assigns "Happy Endings," collected in her book Murder in the Dark: Short Fictions and Prose Poems *(1983). Look at this sentence—printed here with line breaks—from story B:*

This other John will emerge
like a butterfly from a cocoon,
like a Jack from a box,
like a pit from a prune,
if the first John is only squeezed enough.

The internal triad of parallel phrases, the run of similes, the rhythmic forward momentum, the half-comic foray into rhyme (cocoon/prune), the wry balance of the outer clauses—all suggest the concerted verbal economy of poetry honing form to feeling and sense. Atwood's three-line epigraph introduces not only the ideas but the rhythms developed and varied in each successive story, the initial "John and Mary meet" finding its inexorable echo in the thrice-repeated "John and Mary die." Colloquial language (an important convention of prose poetry) amounts, in Atwood's ironic treatment, to no more than the repetition of clichés. A terrible everyday language talking about individuals shorn of all differences yields only a terrible skeleton story: the human life story. Yet "Happy Endings," like Eliot's very different "Tradition and the Individual Talent," is a writer's meditation on her métier; like Selzer's "A Worm from My Notebook," it is a writing lesson—and a reading lesson, about what we should demand from fiction in the way of truthfulness, and from the storyteller, whom Atwood elsewhere calls a "truthteller" ("An End to Audience?" Second Words). *Even as Ehrlich's dazzlingly metaphoric essay "The Smooth Skull of Winter," may be read as a prose poem, so "Happy Endings," with its unmistakable personal voice, may, without violence to its highly self-conscious artistry, be read as an essay. Or perhaps a quasi-essay, a piece of prose on the frontiers of story and poem. Was Addison's "The Royal Exchange" not composed as what we would today call a "column"? Was Franklin's "The Ephemera" not, in its immediate context, a letter? Is Fielding's "An Essay on Nothing" not a treatise, albeit in a spirit of mockery? Yet all are equally and legitimately essays. By intention, Atwood writes a prose poem about fiction's plots, and about humans as victims of one and only one ending: you and I die. By variations on this theme, her prose poem relentlessly assays our inescapable victimage but ends by turning our attention elsewhere, to the "How and Why"—the nitty-gritty of truthful story-telling and of human survival.*

Happy Endings

John and Mary meet. What happens next? If you want a happy ending, try A.

A

John and Mary fall in love and get married. They both have worthwhile and remunerative jobs which they find stimulating and challenging. They buy a charming house. Real estate values go up. Eventually, when they can afford live-in help, they have two children, to whom they are devoted. The children turn out well. John and Mary have a stimulating and challenging sex life and worthwhile friends. They go on fun vacations together. They retire. They both have hobbies which they find stimulating and challenging. Eventually they die. This is the end of the story.

B

Mary falls in love with John but John doesn't fall in love with Mary. He merely uses her body for selfish pleasure and ego gratification of a tepid kind. He comes to her apartment twice a week and she cooks him dinner, you'll notice that he doesn't even consider her worth the price of a dinner out, and after he's eaten the dinner he fucks her and after that he falls asleep, while she does the dishes so he won't think she's untidy, having all those dirty dishes lying around, and puts on fresh lipstick so she'll look good when he wakes up, but when he wakes up he doesn't even notice, he puts on his socks and his shorts and his pants and his shirt and his tie and his shoes, the reverse order from the one in which he took them off. He doesn't take off Mary's clothes, she takes them off herself, she acts as if she's dying for it every time, not because she likes sex exactly, she doesn't but she wants John to think she does because if they do it often enough surely he'll get used to her, he'll come to depend on her and they will get married, but John goes out the door with hardly so much as a good-night and three days later he turns up at six o'clock and they do the whole thing over again.

Mary gets run down. Crying is bad for your face, everyone knows that and so does Mary but she can't stop. People at work notice. Her friends tell her John is a rat, a pig, a dog, he isn't good enough for her, but she can't believe it. Inside John, she thinks, is another John, who is much nicer. This other John will emerge like a butterfly from a cocoon, a Jack from a box, a pit from a prune, if the first John is only squeezed enough.

One evening John complains about the food. He has never complained about the food before. Mary is hurt.

Her friends tell her they've seen him in a restaurant with another woman, whose name is Madge. It's not even Madge that finally gets to Mary: it's the restaurant. John has never taken Mary to a restaurant. Mary collects all the sleeping pills and aspirins she can find, and takes them and half a bottle of sherry. You can see what kind of a woman she is by the fact that it's not even whiskey. She leaves a note for John. She hopes he'll discover her and get her to the hospital in time and repent and then they can get married, but this fails to happen and she dies.

John marries Madge and everything continues as in A.

C

John, who is an older man, falls in love with Mary, and Mary, who is only twenty-two, feels sorry for him because he's worried about his hair falling out. She sleeps with him even though she's not in love with him. She met him at work. She's in love with someone called James, who is twenty-two also and not yet ready to settle down.

John on the contrary settled down long ago: this is what is bothering him. John has a steady respectable job and is getting ahead in his field, but Mary isn't impressed by him, she's impressed by James, who has a motorcycle, being free. Freedom isn't the same for girls, so in the meantime Mary spends Thursday evenings with John. Thursdays are the only days John can get away.

John is married to a woman called Madge and they have two children, a charming house which they bought just before the real estate values went up, and hobbies which they find stimulating and challenging, when they have the time. John tells Mary how important she is to him, but of course he can't leave his wife because a commitment is a commitment. He goes on about this more than is necessary and Mary finds it boring, but older men can keep it up longer so on the whole she has a fairly good time.

One day James breezes in on his motorcycle with some top-grade California hybrid and James and Mary get higher than you'd believe possible and they climb into bed. Everything becomes very underwater, but along comes John, who has a key to Mary's apartment. He finds them stoned and entwined. He's hardly in any position to be jealous, considering Madge, but nevertheless he's overcome with despair. Finally he's middle-aged, in two years he'll be bald as an egg and he can't stand it. He purchases a handgun, saying he needs it for target practice—this is the thin part of the plot, but it can be dealt with later—and shoots the two of them and himself.

Madge, after a suitable period of mourning, marries an understanding man called Fred and everything continues as in A, but under different names.

D

Fred and Madge have no problems. They get along exceptionally well and are good at working out any little difficulties that may arise. But their charming house is by the seashore and one day a giant tidal wave approaches. Real estate values go down. The rest of the story is about what caused the tidal wave and how they escape from it. They do, though thousands drown. Some of the story is about how the thousands drown, but Fred and Madge are virtuous and lucky. Finally on high ground they clasp each other, wet and dripping and grateful, and continue as in A.

E

Yes, but Fred has a bad heart. The rest of the story is about how kind and understanding they both are until Fred dies. Then Madge devotes herself to charity work until the end of A. If you like, it can be "Madge," "cancer," "guilty and confused," and "birdwatching."

F

If you think this is all too bourgeois, make John a revolutionary and Mary a counterespionage agent and see how far that gets you. You'll still end up with A, though in between you may get a lustful brawling saga of passionate involvement, a chronicle of our times, sort of.

* * *

You'll have to face it, the endings are the same however you slice it. Don't be deluded by any other endings, they're all fake, either deliberately fake, with malicious intent to deceive, or just motivated by excessive optimism if not by downright sentimentality.

The only authentic ending is the one provided here:

John and Mary die. John and Mary die. John and Mary die.

So much for endings. Beginnings are always more fun. True connoisseurs, however, are known to favor the stretch in between, since it's the hardest to do anything with.

That's about all that can be said for plots, which anyway are just one thing after another, a what and a what and a what.

Now try How and Why.

Stephen Jay Gould

(b. 1941)

Kingdom: Animals; Phylum: Chordate; Subphylum: Vertebrata; Class: Mammalia; Order: Primates; Family: Hominidae; Genus: Homo; Species: Homo sapiens. *If such categories are the sum total of taxonomy, what could it possibly have to tell a nonspecialist? Stephen Jay Gould has shown (in four collections of his monthly essays compiled from* Natural History *magazine) that taxonomic practice, like reading and writing, is never a mechanical procedure, never a matter of simple pigeonholing. It does not assume the existence of "correct and unchanging categories." Taxonomy is "method" in the etymological sense: "going after" the changes produced in a population by natural selection. Natural selection is the mechanism of evolution, evolution provides the raw material of natural history, and natural history is the story of these material variations in time, our account of what evolution has wrought. It stands to reason that if you want a straight version of this story, it should come from a natural historian like Gould, one, that is, who practices taxonomy in all things and whose preferred method is "letting generalities cascade out of particulars." As an essayist he has been fortunate in his attraction to evolutionary theory, for no other theme, he says, "so beautifully encompasses both the particulars that fascinate and the generalities that instruct" (Prologue,* The Flamingo's Smile, 1985). *Gould's essays certainly "fascinate," even as they "instruct" by making something of the taxonomic experience generally available. Without a trained eye, that experience is easy to miss, for it turns up where we least expect it: in our own midst, for example. We may no longer condemn Kinsey's report on the human female's sexual behavior with the McCarthyite righteousness of 1954, yet most of us still read it with scarcely more understanding than if we had only censorship on our minds. You can't understand what you don't know how to read. In the playfully titled "Of Wasps and WASPs"* (The Flamingo's Smile), *Gould confronts taxonomic illiteracy by introducing Kinsey the philosopher of taxonomy who transferred his research techniques from insects to humans; in this way, Gould brings the language of natural history—its terminology of variations constituting continua—into the center of our social and moral concerns. Like any good teacher, he fascinates by the sheer knowledge and love of his subject.*

Of Wasps and WASPs

"He is hurling the insult of the century against our mothers, wives, daughters and sisters, under the pretext of making a great contribution to scientific research." Thus did Louis B. Heller, congressman from New York, label the Kinsey report on *Sexual Behavior in the Human Female* (1953) in a letter to the postmaster general, urging that the book be banned from the mails. Dr. Henry Van Dusen, president of the Union Theological Seminary, doubted Kinsey's facts but proclaimed that if true nonetheless, "they reveal a prevailing degradation in American morality approximating the worst decadence of the Roman empire." "The most disturbing thing," Van Dusen continued in castigating Kinsey's report, "is the absence of a spontaneous, ethical revulsion from the premises of the study."

Yet the premises seemed uncomplicated enough. Kinsey had sought, through extensive interviews with more than 5,000 women, to compile a statistical record of what people do do, rather than what law and custom say they should do. He passed no judgment and merely reported his findings; he did, however, discover a frequency of premarital and extramarital sexual relations that, to say the least, disturbed the chivalric code of many naïve, hypocritical, or smugly satisfied people—particularly older men in power.

Alfred C. Kinsey suffered the misfortune of publishing his report in 1953 at the height of McCarthyite hysteria in America (his earlier 1948 report on *Sexual Behavior in the Human Male* had caused a stir but had not inspired such calumny, perhaps because society has always accepted a wider range of behavior among males and because the early political climate of post-war years had been much more liberal). Many labeled Kinsey's report on female sexuality as an exercise in communism or, if not directly subversive, sufficiently weakening of American moral fiber to allow easy communist access to our troubled shores. A special House Committee, established to investigate the use of funds by tax-exempt foundations and led by noted cold warrior B. Carroll Reece, dragged the Rockefeller Foundation onto its carpet. The foundation capitulated to these and other pressures, and Kinsey's main source of support ended abruptly in 1954. The Reece Committee issued its majority report in December 1954, accusing some foundations of using tax-exempt monies for studies "directly supporting subversion." The Kinsey reports were explicitly cited as unworthy of the aid they had received. Kinsey never did find an alternate source of support; he died two years later, overworked, angry, and distressed that so many years of further data might never see publication (renewed funding arrived later, but not in time for Kinsey's personal vindication).

Kinsey was no lifelong crusader for sexual enlightenment. He drifted into sex research almost by accident (though not without prior interest). He had been trained as an entomologist and was, at the time of his shift in careers, one of America's foremost taxonomists of wasps (six-legged, not two-legged). Soon after his switch, he began a Phi Beta Kappa lecture at Indiana University with these words:

> With individual variation as a biologic phenomenon I have been concerned during some twenty years of field exploration and laboratory research. In the intensive and extensive measurement of tens of thousands of small insects which you have probably never seen, and about which you certainly cannot care, I have made some attempt to secure the specific data and the quantity of data on which scientific scholarship must be based. During the past two years, as a result of a convergence of circumstances, I have found myself confronted with material on variation in certain types of human behavior.

Most people, when they learn about Kinsey's earlier career, tend to regard the discovery with quaint amusement. How odd that a man who later shook America should have spent most of his professional career on the taxonomy of tiny insects. Surely there can be no relationship between two such disparate careers. As one wag wrote in a graffito on the title page to Harvard's only copy of Kinsey's greatest monograph on wasps: "Why don't you write about something more interesting, Al?"

I wish to argue, however, that Kinsey's wasps and WASPs were intimately related by his common intellectual approach to both. And since wasps preceded WASPs, Kinsey's career as a taxonomist had a direct and profound impact upon his sex research. In fact, Kinsey pursued his sex research by following a particular "taxonomic way of thought," a valid style of science that does not match most stereotypes of the enterprise. The special character of Kinsey's work—the aspects that brought him such fame and trouble—flowed directly from the taxonomic approach he had learned and perfected as an entomologist.

Aside from the specific conclusions that so shocked America—basically the high frequency of things that nice people supposedly didn't do, from homosexuality to premarital and extramarital sex among women to the high frequency of sexual contact with animals among men who had grown up on farms—Kinsey stirred the world with his different procedural approach to sex research. He worked with three basic premises, all flowing directly from his taxonomic perspective. First, he would base his conclusions upon samples far larger than any previous researcher had gathered. No more extrapolations to all of humanity from a small and homogeneous population of college students. Second, his sample would be heterogeneous—old and young, farm and city, poor and rich, illiterate and college educated. As wasps varied from tree to tree, classes, sexes, and generations might differ widely in their sexual behavior. Third, he would pass no judgments but merely describe what people did.

Kinsey received his Ph.D. in entomology from Harvard and then accepted a post as assistant professor of zoology at the University of Indiana, where he remained all his life. He spent the first twenty years of his career in a study, conducted with unprecedented detail, of the taxonomy, evolution, and biogeography of gall-forming wasps in the genus *Cynips*. These small wasps lay their eggs within the tissues of plants (usually the leaves or stems of oaks). When the larvae hatch, they induce the plant to form a gall about them, thus securing both protection and a source of food. The larvae mature within their galls, eventually emerging as winged insects to begin the process anew. Kinsey presented his work on *Cynips* in a number of shorter papers and two large monographs, *The Gall Wasp Genus* Cynips: *A Study in the Origin of Species* (1930) and *The Origin of Higher Categories in* Cynips (1936).

In 1938, in response to student petition, the university established a noncredit course on marriage (a euphemism, I suppose, for some sex education). Kinsey, who had planned to spend the rest of his life studying wasps, was asked to serve as chairman of the committee to regulate this course and to give three lectures on the biology of sex. Kinsey was conscientious and empirically oriented to a fault. He went to the library to find the required information about human sexual response—and he couldn't. So he decided that he would have to compile it himself. He began by interviewing students but soon realized that he was not getting representative information about American heterogeneity. He began to travel on weekends, gathering information in nearby towns at his own expense. He developed an extensive format for interviews and wrote the responses in code to assure anonymity (Kinsey's intuitive skill as an interviewer became legendary). He recorded enormous variation in sexual behavior among people of different economic status, extending his researches to Gary, Chicago, Saint Louis, and to Indiana prisons. As his work became more public, criticism mounted, but the university remained firm in its support of Kinsey's right to know.

Eventually, with the university's backing, he established the Institute for Sex Research and secured Rockefeller Foundation money for his burgeoning interviews and their publication. His work culminated in two great volumes, *Sexual Behavior in the Human Male* and *Sexual Behavior in the Human Female*, each based on more than 5,000 interviews with white Americans of diversified backgrounds. (True to his convictions about the fundamental character of variability, Kinsey knew that he did not have enough data to reach conclusions about black Americans or to extrapolate to other nations and cultures.) Long before these volumes appeared, Kinsey had, with great reluctance and sadness but with creeping inevitability, abandoned the wasp studies that had brought him so much pleasure and had set his standards of scientific work.

Although Kinsey confined his major works on wasps to a single family, the Cynipidae, his aims were as broad as natural history itself. He thought deeply about the practice and meaning of classification and hoped to reformulate the principles of taxonomy. He wrote in 1927:

> From our work on Cynipidae, in connection with a study of the published work in other fields of taxonomy, I propose to attempt a formulation of the philosophy of taxonomy, its usefulness as a means of portraying and explaining species as they exist in nature, and its importance in the coordination and elucidation of biologic data.

Kinsey felt that he could achieve these larger goals by performing a specific study with such unprecedented factual detail that larger principles would emerge from the volume of information itself. Kinsey was a workaholic before the word was invented. On a traveling fellowship in 1919–1920, he logged 18,000 miles (2,500 on foot) in southern and western regions of the United States and collected some 300,000 specimens of gall wasps. His two trips to rural Mexico and Central America in the 1930s were monuments to his insatiable industry. Still, he was never satisfied. In his 1936 monograph, he lamented that for each of his 165 species, he had collected, on average, "only" 214 insects and 755 galls. For 51 of these species (variable groups in regions of uniform topography), he stated that he would not be satisfied until he had gathered a grand total of 1,530,000 insects and 3 to 4 million galls!

More than mere collection mania underlay Kinsey's expressed desires and actual efforts. A modern statistician might well argue that Kinsey had an inadequate appreciation of sampling theory; you really don't need to get every one. Still, Kinsey pursued his copious collecting because he operated and centered his biological beliefs upon one cardinal principle: the primacy and irreducibility of variation.

Ironically, much of taxonomic practice had not fully assimilated this fundamental change brought to biology by evolutionary theory. Many taxonomists still viewed the work as a series of pigeonholes, each housing a species. Species, in this view, should be defined by their "essences"—fundamental features separating them from all others. Variation was regarded as a nuisance at best—a kind of accidental splaying out around the essential form, and serving only to create confusion in the correct assignment of pigeonholes. Most classical taxonomists treated variation as a necessary evil and often established species after studying only a few specimens.

Taxonomists like Kinsey, who understood the full implications of evolutionary theory, developed a radically different attitude to variation. Islands of form exist, to be sure: cats do not flow together in a sea of continuity, but rather come to us as lions, tigers, lynxes, tabbies, and so forth. Still, although species may be discrete, they have no immutable essence. Variation is the raw material of evolutionary change. It represents the fundamental reality of nature, not an accident about a created norm. Variation is primary; essences are illusory. Species must be defined as ranges of irreducible variation.

This antiessentialist way of thinking has profound consequences for our basic view of reality. Ever since Plato cast shadows on the cave wall, essentialism has dominated Western thought, encouraging us to neglect continua and to divide reality into a set of correct and unchanging categories. Essentialism establishes criteria for judgment and worth: individual objects that lie close to their essence are good; those that depart are bad, if not unreal.

Antiessentialist thinking forces us to view the world differently. We must accept shadings and continua as fundamental. We lose criteria for judgment by comparison to some ideal: short people, retarded people, people of other beliefs, colors, and religions are people of full status. The taxonomic essentialist scoops up a handful of fossil snails in a single species, tries to abstract an essence, and rates his snails by their match to this average. The antiessentialist sees something entirely different in his hand—a range of irreducible variation defining the species, some variants more frequent than others, but all perfectly good snails. Ernst Mayr, our leading taxonomic theorist, has written elegantly and at length on the difference between essentialism and variation as an ultimate reality ("population thinking" in his terminology—see his recent book, *The Growth of Biological Thought*).

Kinsey, who understood the implications of evolutionary theory so well, was a radical antiessentialist in taxonomy. His belief in the primacy of variation spurred an almost frantic effort to collect ever more specimens. His belief in continua forced him to explore virtually every square foot of suitable territory for *Cynips* in North America—for whenever he found large gaps, he strongly suspected (usually correctly) that intermediate forms would be found in some geographically contiguous area.

In the end, Kinsey's antiessentialism became almost too radical. He was so convinced that species would grade into other species that he began to name truly intermediate geographical variants *within* a single species as separate entities, and established a bloated taxonomy of full names for transient and minor local variants. (Kinsey decided that species arose by the spread through local populations of discrete mutations with small effects. Thus, whenever he found a local population differing from others by mutations of the sort produced in laboratory stocks, he established a new species. But local populations within a species often establish small mutations without losing their central tie to the rest of the species—the ability to interbreed.)

More important for American social history, Kinsey transported bodily to his sex research the radical antiessentialism of his entomological studies. Kinsey's twenty years with *Cynips* may not be judged as a wasteful diversion compared with the later source of his fame. Rather, Kinsey's wasp work established both the methodology and principles of reasoning that made him a pioneer in sex research.

I am not merely making learned inferences about continuities that the master of antiessentialism didn't recognize. Kinsey knew perfectly well what he was doing. He regretted not a moment spent on wasps, both because he loved them too, and because their study had set his intellectual sights. In the first chapter of his first treatise on *Sexual Behavior in the Human Male*, Kinsey included a remarkable section on "the taxonomic approach," with two subheadings—"in biology," followed by the explicit transfer, "in applied and social sciences." Kinsey wrote:

> The techniques of this research have been taxonomic, in the sense in which modern biologists employ the term. It was born out of the senior author's long-time experience with a problem in insect taxonomy. The transfer from insect to human material is not illogical, for it has been a transfer of a method that may be applied to the study of any variable population.

Extensive sampling was the hallmark of Kinsey's work. Most earlier studies of human sexual behavior had either confined their reporting to unusual cases (Krafft-Ebing's *Psychopathia Sexualis*, for example) or had generalized from small and homogeneous samples. If Kinsey had hoped for millions of wasps and their galls, he would at least interview many thousands of humans. He knew that he needed such large numbers because his antiessentialist perspective proclaimed two truths about variation for wasps and people alike—apparently homogeneous populations in one place (all college students at Indiana or all murderers at Alcatraz) would exhibit an enormous range of irreducible variation, and discrete local populations in different places (older middle-class women in Illinois or poor young men in New York) would differ greatly in average sexual behaviors. (Biologists refer to these two types of variation as within-population and between-population.) Kinsey decided that he would have to sample many differing groups and large numbers within each group. He wrote in the first paragraph of his treatise on males:

> It is a fact-finding survey in which an attempt is made to discover what people do sexually, and what factors account for differences in sexual behavior among individuals, and among various segments as of the population.

In his section on "the taxonomic approach in biology" he explained why his experience with wasps had set his methods for humans:

> Modern taxonomy is the product of an increasing awareness among biologists of the uniqueness of individuals, and of the wide range of variation which may occur in any population of individuals. The taxonomist is, therefore, primarily concerned with the measurement of variation in series of individuals which stand as representatives of the species in which he is interested.

Kinsey's belief in the primacy of variation and diversity became a crusade. His 1939 Phi Beta Kappa lecture, "Individuals," focused on the "unlimited nonidentity" among organisms in any population and castigated both biological and social scientists for drawing general conclusions from small and relatively homogeneous samples. For example:

> A mouse in a maze, today, is taken as a sample of all individuals, of all species of mice under all sorts of conditions, yesterday, today, and tomorrow. A half dozen dogs, pedigrees unknown and breeds unnamed, are reported on as "dogs"—meaning all kinds of dogs—if, indeed, the conclusions are not explicitly or at least implicitly applied to you, to your cousins, and to all other kinds and descriptions of humans. . . . A noted American colloid chemist startles the country with the announcement of a new cure for drug addicts; and it is not until other laboratories report failure to obtain similar results that we learn that the original experiments were based on a half dozen individuals.

As a second important transfer from his entomologically based antiessentialism, Kinsey repeatedly emphasized the impossibility of pigeonholing human sexual response by allocating people into rigidly defined categories. As his wasps formed chains of continuity from one species to the next, human sexual response could be fluid, changing, and devoid of sharp boundaries. Of male homosexuality, he wrote:

> Males do not represent two discrete populations, heterosexual and homosexual. The world is not to be divided into sheep and

> goats. Not all things are black nor all things white. It is fundamental of taxonomy that nature rarely deals with discrete categories. Only the human mind invents categories and tries to force facts into separate pigeon-holes. The living world is a continuum in each and every one of its aspects. The sooner we learn this concerning human sexual behavior the sooner we shall reach a sound understanding of the realities of sex.

The third transfer—the one that ultimately brought Kinsey so much trouble—raised the contentious issue of judgment. If variation is primary, copious, and irreducible, and if species have no essences, then what "natural" criterion can we discover for judgment? An odd variant is as much a member of its species as an average individual. Even if average individuals are more common than peculiar organisms, who can identify one or the other as "better"—for species have no "right" form defined by an immutable essence. Kinsey wrote in "Individuals," again making explicit reference to wasps:

> Prescriptions are merely public confessions of prescriptionists. . . . What is right for one individual may be wrong for the next; and what is sin and abomination to one may be a worthwhile part of the next individual's life. The range of individual variation, in any particular case, is usually much greater than is generally understood. Some of the structural characters in my insects vary as much as twelve hundred percent. This means that populations from a single locality may contain individuals with wings 15 units in length, and other individuals with wings 175 units in length. In some of the morphologic and physiologic characters which are basic to the human behavior which I am studying, the variation is a good twelve thousand percent. And yet social forms and moral codes are prescribed as though all individuals were identical; and we pass judgments, make awards, and heap penalties without regard to the diverse difficulties involved when such different people face uniform demands.

Kinsey often claimed in his two great reports that he had merely recorded the facts of sexual behavior without either passing or even implying judgment. On the prefatory page to his report on males, he wrote:

> For some time now there has been an increasing awareness among many people of the desirability of obtaining data about sex which would represent an accumulation of scientific fact completely divorced from questions of moral value and social custom.

His critics countered by arguing that an absence of judgment in the context of such extensive recording is, itself, a form of judgment. I think I would have to agree. I see no possibility for a completely "value-free" social science. Kinsey may have disclaimed in the reports themselves, but the statement just quoted from his 1939 essay makes no bones about his conviction that nonjudgmental attitudes are morally preferable—and his basic belief in the primacy of variation has evident implications itself. Can one despise what nature provides as fundamental? (One can, of course, but few people will favor an ethic that rejects life and the world as we inevitably find them.)

What, in any case, is the alternative? Should we not compile the factual data of human sexual behavior? Or should people who undertake such a study sprinkle each finding with an irrelevant assessment of its moral worth from their personal point of view? That would be hubris indeed. Ultimately, however, I must confess that my approval of Kinsey, and my strong attraction to him, arises from our shared values. I too am a taxonomist.

At the beginning of *The Grapes of Wrath*, as Tom Joad heads home after a prison term, he meets Casy, his old preacher. Casy explains that he no longer holds revivals because he could not reconcile his own sexual behavior (often inspired by the fervor of the revival meeting itself) with the content of his preaching:

> I says, "Maybe it ain't a sin. Maybe it's just the way folks is." . . . Well, I was layin' under a tree when I figured that out, and I went to sleep. And it come night, an' it was dark when I come to. They was a coyote squawkin' near by. Before I knowed it, I was sayin' out loud . . . "There ain't no sin and there ain't no virtue. There's just stuff people do. . . . And some of the things folks do is nice, and some ain't nice, but that's as far as any man got a right to say."

Paul Theroux

(b. 1941)

"In the experience I have of myself I find enough to make me wise, if I were a good scholar," wrote Montaigne at fifty-six ("Of Experience"). Paul Theroux at twenty-six—sitting "in a cool dark room in the middle of Africa" far away from his draft board—demonstrates the alliance between writing an essay and making the first, rough, tentative moves toward becoming a "good scholar": someone who knows how to read aright the book of his own experience. Such scholarship of the self brings the wisdom "to play the man well and properly," Montaigne said, "to enjoy our being rightfully." In 1967, when "Cowardice" was written, the sociopolitical controversy surrounding the Vietnam War was at full pitch. Theroux's story of resistance to any association with the military had an immediacy not easily realized nowadays when war and conscription—or so we imagine—become ever more hypothetical. Theroux's picture of himself as a draft dodger is provocative; his suggestion that fear "may prove the truest motive" for nonviolence goes against the grain, and deliberately so: no winning autobiographical details here, on the part of this brash anti-hero; no conciliatory gestures to the reader, pacifist or warmonger. Theroux highlights details of his experience like pieces of a shocking text that compels notice, that can't simply be shelved. There is a truth in it that will not go away: fear is bodily. Of an encounter with armed border guards in Malawi, he reports, "When the guns were pointed at me my body started to shake, my legs felt as if they had gone suddenly boneless." We live in the flesh, however much we may "force ourselves on dogma"—or, as Didion might say, embrace "moral imperatives" (see "On Morality"). Here again is Montaigne: "What is the use of these lofty points of philosophy on which no human being can settle, and these rules that exceed our use and our strength?" ("Of Vanity"). Is there, perhaps, some as yet unstudied moral art lodged in the beauty and legitimacy of the flesh with all its weakness? As recently as 1984, in the long, elliptically narrated title essay of his collection Sunrise with Seamonsters, *it is still a matter, for Theroux, of testing the "use and strength" of his own body, older now, in a continuing study of how "to play the man well and properly," "to live appropriately."*

Cowardice

In the old days, young boys with nothing to do used to stand around drugstores talking excitedly of picking up girls. They now have other choices—they can pick up guns or protest signs. I tend to take the druggist's view: have an ice cream and forget the choices. I intend to give in neither to the army nor to the peace movement.

I am now certain of my reason for thinking this: I am a coward.

It has not always been this way. I used to think I was a person of high principles. The crooked thing about high principles is that they can live in thin air. I am fairly sure mine did. For the past five years my reaction to anything military was based on borrowed shock.

I still believe that war is degrading, that it gets us no place, and that one must not hurt anyone else. The pacifists say this and the government calls them cowards. The pacifists protest that they are not cowards. I feel no kinship with the government. I have some sympathy for the folk who call themselves pacifists because I believe many of them to be as cowardly as I am. But I see no reason to be defensive about it. Certainly they should not have to put up with all that humiliation on the sidewalk. As cowards they should be entitled to a little peace. They should not have to waste their time and risk arrest scrawling slogans on the subway or walking for hours carrying heavy signs. Guns may be heavier, but why carry either one?

A soldier shuffled nervously in front of me while I stood in line at the East Side Airlines Terminal in New York two years ago. He turned abruptly and told me that he was going to Oakland, California. I told him I was going to London and then to Uganda. Harmless talk—the kind that travelers make with ease. He surprised me by breaking convention and continuing what should have been an ended conversation. After Oakland he would be going to Vietnam. I clucked at his misfortune and as we both thought presumably of death he said, "Somebody's got to go."

But not me, I thought. I got my ticket confirmed and a week later I was in Africa, far from the draft board, even farther from Vietnam. Five years ago I would have hectored the soldier with some soul-swelling arguments. I was a pacifist and a very noisy one at that.

When I was told that I must join the ROTC at the University of Massachusetts in 1960 I refused. Then I tried to think why I had refused. I had no friends who were pacifists but I did not need a manual to tell me that I hated violence. I dreaded the thought of marching or taking guns apart; I quietly resolved never to go into the army, the ROTC, or anything that was vaguely military. The thought of wearing a uniform appalled me and the thought of being barked at frightened me. I wanted to write a book and be left alone. In two hours I was a pacifist, a month later I was the only healthy non-Quaker at the University exempt from ROTC. A few years later I was arrested by the campus police for leading a demonstration (that was in 1962 when demonstrations were rare and actually bothered people). I bunched together with a dozen more pacifists, organized some more protests, and, the year I graduated, ROTC was put on a voluntary basis by a faculty committee. Although the committee was composed of friends of mine it was not really a put-up job. ROTC was just not consistent with high principles.

Before I was excused from ROTC I had to meet an ad hoc committee: the colonels of the army and the air force ROTC, the chaplain, and the provost. The army colonel, a man with a passion for writing patriotic letters to the student newspaper, listened to my woolly tirade against the military (quotations from Jesus, Norman Mailer, Tolstoy, and Eugene V. Debs). He rose, his medals jangled at me, and he thundered: "What do you know about war!"

It couldn't have been plainer, but for a pacifist it is an easy question to answer. "Nothing, but . . ." And then the atrocity stories, a smattering of religion, and a few abstract nouns. I could have appealed to the governor if they had not let me out of ROTC. The governor was coming up for reelection and would not have wanted to appear a jingo by making me take ROTC or a communist by excusing me. The committee quietly released me from my obligation.

If I had told them I was a coward they would not have wasted a minute with me. I would have been given regulation shoes and told to keep them clean; I would have been expected to know all the parts of an M-1 carbine; I would have had to stab sandbags with a bayonet every Tuesday after entomology class. So I did not tell them I was a coward, although that would have been the most honest thing to do. The colonel, a man experienced in these matters, insinuated that I was one, but good taste prevented his speaking the word.

The ROTC has never done much more than bruise a man. Its contribution has been to teach college boys marching. Ironically, the people who object to ROTC end up marching many more miles than the sophomores on the parade ground. Peace movements are successful usually because they are so militaristic in organization and attitude. The language of the peace groups is always military-sounding: fighting, campaign, movement, ranks, marches—even freedom awards, for valor. There is keen envy among the groups: which college has the most picketers, the bloodiest and most agonizing signs, which men have the handsome beards. Tempers are short among demonstrators; they have ridden a long way to be grim. The protester from the Amherst area gets off near the White House and begins grousing: "Jesus, we just got here and they expect us to start picketing!"

I was persuaded by a friend to picket in Times Square against nuclear testing one cold night in 1962. We had to report to a cigar-smoking gentleman who gave each of us a sign and instructions: "Walk clockwise, single file around the army recruiter booth. Remember, don't talk, don't stop walking, and if you want to leave just raise your hand and I'll get someone to carry your sign. Let's practice walking without the sign first, then we'll start. Okay, everyone line up here . . ."

The little man did not carry a sign. He was the sergeant, we were the privates. He marched beside us and used his big cigar as a swagger stick. Every so often he would tell someone to pipe down or walk straight. We got off to a rough start, but soon got the hang of it, convincing me that, if nothing else, we responded well to discipline and would all have made pretty good soldiers.

Many pacifists I have known are scared out of their wits that they will be drafted. Is this fright caused by seeing moral laws broken and all Gandhi's hunger strikes made worthless by a man's head—or let's say, a pacifist's head—being blown apart? Is the fright a fear of death or a fear of failed principles? Is the refusal to join in the slaughter inspired by feelings of cowardice or moral conviction? I am thinking of pacifists who have been taught their fear after being beaten up, threatened by armed boys, and seeing brutality up close.

I lived in a crowded suburb of a large city in the United States and I had to pass through an alley—the lights at the opposite end: salvation—to get a bus when I went to the movies. The last time I passed through that alley five figures came toward me. I knew they wanted to beat me up. I stood still and hoped they would pass by, although what I imagined—being surrounded, having the youngest one push me down in the snow and punch me while I curled up and groaned, hearing them laugh and then running away, until my throat ached—actually happened, and the next ten minutes were a blur of cruelty. I was frightened but I would not let anger take the place of my fright.

This is really what a coward is, I believe: a person who is afraid of nearly everything and most of all afraid of anger. His own anger is a special danger to him. He accepts his solitary hardship and pays the price of withdrawing. He knows that each attempt to deal with violence may require summoning all the inhuman bravado he can contain. The bravery is a cover. Its weight intimidates the flesh beneath it. Since bravery implies a willingness to risk death, the fear to be brave becomes the fear to die. I am unable to understand what could make me risk death: neither patriotism, a desire to preserve anything, nor a hatred of anyone could rouse me to fight.

I have always wondered how people do things which require risk, whether there is not a gap in their consciousness, a suspension of judgment while the dangerous act is performed. I have never felt this release, even momentarily, from the consequences of risk. Remembered incidents intrude: street fights I could not bear to watch, threats I walked away from, vicious glares that made me sick, and some time ago being in a bar in Washington, D.C., where a woman on a stool kept calling the dishwasher a nigger. She leaned on the bar and slobbered: "You a nigger, ain't you? You know you are; you nothin' but a nigger. You ain't no Creole like you say. You a nigger . . ." And the Negro behind the bar whistled and looked at no one. I wanted to shout at the woman. But with a fear that quickly became nausea I left.

Leaving is a cure for nothing, though if one goes to the right spot one may have time to reflect usefully on why one left. Four years ago I joined the Peace Corps, was sent to Malawi, in Central Africa, and taught school. Unlike most people in their early twenties, I had personal servants, a big house, and good public relations. My relatives said I was really sacrificing and doing good work (there is a school of thought that assumes if one is in Africa one is, *ipso facto*, doing good work). I was happy in my job. I was not overworked. And I had joined the Peace Corps for what I now see were selfish reasons: I had thought of responsibilities I did not want—marriage seemed too permanent, graduate school too hard, and the army too brutal. The Peace Corps is a sort of Howard Johnson's on the main drag into maturity. Usually life is pleasant, sometimes difficult, occasionally violent. A good time to find out whether or not you are a coward.

Violence in Malawi became common. The resignation of several high-ranking politicians and the firing of a few others threw the country into a nightmare of suspicion late in 1964. Many people suspected of collaborating with the ex-cabinet members were choked or hacked to death. One day I was walking home along the dirt road that led to my house. I saw smoke. Up ahead I saw three Youth Leaguers dashing into the bush. I knew they had just burned something, but I was not sure what it was. I was sure that it was serious and became worried. Just over the hill was a truck in flames. The cab of the truck was crackling and I could make out stiff black shapes in the holes of the flames. I detoured around the burning truck and went home. At home I had a drink, locked the door, and went to bed.

About a week later I was on a train and going North to the lake shore. At each stop, boys, Youth Leaguers anywhere from ten to forty years old, got on the train and demanded to see the party cards of the African travelers. If a person did not have a card he was beaten. An old man next to me was dragged out of his seat, thrown to the floor, and kicked. Just before they dragged him out of the seat he looked at me (we had been talking about how terrible it was this thing was happening and I said that it made me very angry) and his hand reached out for my sleeve. I moved—a timid reflex—against the window and he missed my sleeve. They quickly got him onto the floor. His screams were terrific and he wept as they kicked him. No one in the car moved. Several minutes later, another and another were thrown to the floor and beaten. Outside the train a man was being chased and punched as he ran through a gauntlet of people. His hands were pushed against his face for protection. He reeled across the platform and bumped into a fence. I saw him huddled against the fence—the boys hitting him with sticks—as the train pulled away. I could not tell if he was screaming. I had closed the window. By the time the train had gone about a hundred miles, the car was almost empty; most of the occupants had been dragged out and beaten. I stepped out at my station and walked to a taxi. It was hard to suppress an intense feeling of relief. The cards that the men were being asked to produce were sold by the Youth Leaguers for two shillings. Many refused to buy them because they did not believe in the present regime and would not compromise their principles.

In August of 1965 I drove a car through the Northern region of Malawi. I passed through fourteen roadblocks and reached the border-post at about ten in the evening. The gate—the customs' barrier—was closed. I saw some men standing near it. My headlights were still on and the windows of the car were rolled up. The men appeared to be saying something but I could not hear them. Only after a few moments did I realize that my headlights were shining into their eyes. I shut off the engine and rolled down the window. As soon as the window was open a crack I heard the loud shouting of the men. They stood where they were and ordered me out of the car. They raised their rifles to my face. When the guns were pointed at me my body started to shake, my legs felt as if they had gone suddenly boneless. I was numb. I knew I was about to be shot. I was waiting to be murdered. *If they're going to shoot me let them do it quickly!* flashed through my mind. The feeling of standing there on that border—a border that had been raided four times, resulting in the deaths of many more people than even the large number reported in the press—in the darkness, the bullets crashing into my shirt, bursting through my back with a fist-sized lump of flesh and clotted blood, my body dropping into the sand by the light of a fizzing lantern, the men standing over me and firing into my inert body, my head broken open . . . It was unbearable. And my papers were in order, my passport was in my hand high above my head. But the guns! The shouting! I was so afraid that I think I could have been moved to action—I felt capable of killing them, or attempting it. Yet this would have been absurd because I had done nothing wrong. The guns remained pointed into my face. The feeling persisted: I wanted to shoot them or be shot. I wanted something to happen, something violent that would settle the whole affair.

They told me I must walk toward them. This I did, all the while trying to prevent myself from lunging at them in an attempt to incite them to shoot me and get it over with. But they did not shoot me. They swore at me and took me into the police station. I pleaded with them to let me through the barrier (I felt that as long as I remained on their side of the border I was guilty of something). I convinced them and that night drove until two in the morning along the narrow bush track into Tanzania.

When my Peace Corps stretch was over I decided to stay in Africa. I realized that there was violence in Africa, but I started to understand it. I had reached two conclusions: one, the violence was either tribal or political—I had no tribe and was not involved in politics and so the violence was not directed against me; two, life in Africa is simple, provincial, dull generally but with stirrings here and there, evidence of growth that I might help with. Day-to-day life in Africa is much like day-to-day life in New Hampshire: people strolling in the sunshine or standing around the local bar spitting on the sidewalk; there is gossip about love affairs and car-buying, there is time for talking or reading or writing. Sometimes there is trouble at the castle and the gun-shots echo down through the huts. Trouble happens around powerful people, politicians and chiefs. I live among neither.

On my way to work, gliding through the green in my car, I think: *you can be drafted today*. I am twenty-five; I have bad eyes, but am otherwise physically fit. I have no wife. My job as a teacher here in Uganda may exempt me from the draft, but there is no guarantee of that. My draft board knows where I am. President Johnson has said that he will again increase the number of troops in Vietnam. The war is a jumble of figures: the number of troops and planes, the number of bombings and raids, the number of dead or wounded. The numbers appear every day in the Uganda papers as cold as football scores. I add flesh and blood to them and I am afraid.

As a coward I can expect nothing except an even stronger insistence that I go and fight. *Fight whom?* A paradox emerges; the coward recognizes no enemies. Because he wants always to think that he will not be harmed (although he is plagued by the thought that he will be), there is no evil in his world. He wills evil out of his world. Evil is something that provokes feelings of cowardice in him; this feeling is unwelcome, he wants to forget it. In order to forget it he must not risk hating it. Indeed, the coward hates nothing just as he loves nothing. These emotions are a gamble for him; he merely tolerates them in others and tries to squash or escape them in himself. He will condemn no one when he is free from threat.

The word coward is loaded with awful connotations. It does not ordinarily lend itself to inclusion in logical discourse because it quickly inspires two assumptions. The first is that cowardice does not indicate how we really feel; the second is that we have principles which are in no way related to, and always more powerful than, our feelings, our flesh. The first assumption implies that the feeling of cowardice is somehow fraudulent; a coward is discounted as authentic because of the word's associations: it is allied to "tail" (Latin: *cauda*), one of its synonyms is "fainthearted" or, more plainly, "womanish." To accept this definition is to reach the conclusion that the coward's head will clear, that he will cease to become weak if he thinks a bit. The second assumption is that one's principles will overcome one's feelings. I would suggest, if my flesh is any indicator, that this is not the case.

Talking a mixture of rubbish and rhetoric to get out of ROTC, picketing the Military Ball, sympathizing with those Californians who were dragged down cement stairs by the police, their spines bumping over the edges, seeing some logic in Wolfgang Borchert's simple advice to pacifists ("Sag, 'NEIN'!"[1])—these are ego-inspired feelings; the ego fights for air, rejects absorption, anonymity, and death. Since we have perhaps far less dogma cluttering our lives than any other people in history, these ego-inspired feelings which can move us to acts of protest may prove essentially good, the principle of non-violence made out of a deep feeling of cowardice may prove the truest. It is bound to have its opposite motives: Cardinal Spellman's blessing of the war in Vietnam was one of these acts of the ego and certainly not the result of any biblical dogma he had been taught.

All of this goes against existing laws. It is illegal to be afraid to go into the army. If I tell the draft board to count me out because I am afraid, they will answer, "That's impossible . . ." But this not impossible, it is only illegal, I will say; I saw a man die, I saw a man kicked to death, I held the crumbling blue body of a drowned man in my hands . . . This is feeling; I will be asked for principles, not feelings. Fear is selfish and so no amount of fear, even if it stems from observed violence, is acceptable grounds for exemption.

Yet ours is not a military-minded nation; this is clear to everyone. The president of a Chicago draft board was quoted as saying a few months ago: "I've been threatened half-a-dozen times. Guys say they're gonna kill me if they see me on the street . . ." Is it the thought that war

[1] "Say NO!"

is degrading and immoral that makes this half-dozen take the trouble to threaten the life of their draft board president? Or is it something else? We know we are terrible soldiers, that we are not bold; we have placed our trust in the hardware of war. ("Thank God for the atom bomb," my brother's sergeant said when he saw the platoon marching higgledy-piggledy across the parade ground.)

I say "we"—I mean "I." If I allow myself to be drafted into the army I will be committing suicide. The army is to a coward what a desert is to an agoraphobe, an elaborate torment from which the only escape serves to torment him further. The coward marches with death; the agoraphobe stalks the rolling dunes in search of an enclosure.

I sit here in a cool dark room in the middle of Africa thousands of miles from the people in the city hall who want to draft me. I sit down in the middle of it all and try to decide why I do not want to go. And that is all anyone can do, try to be honest about what he feels, what he's seen or thinks he's seen. He can offer this disturbing vision to those who are not sure why they are unwilling. Folksongs and slogans and great heroes are no good for us now, and neither is the half-truth that is in every poem or every melodious sentence that hides barbaric notions.

When I think of people trying to convince themselves that high principles result from merely hugging answers I think of the reverse of the old fairy story: a princess in her hunger kisses a handsome prince and turns him into a toad. The answers will not come by forcing ourselves upon dogma. The issue is that we should admit once and for all that we are frightened. We will not have told ourselves a lie and, after this truth which is a simple one, maybe even ugly, we can begin to ask new questions.

Phyllis Rose

(b. 1942)

Essaying as an exploration in words on some subject begins, precisely insofar as it is *an exploration, with the explorer's ignorance of where she is, where she is moving and where she will end up. In this sense, every essayist is cutting through a personal wilderness; how she does it maps, so to speak, the itinerary of her desire. Phyllis Rose, author of two earlier biographies, recently published a controversial third,* Jazz Cleopatra, *about Josephine Baker, the extraordinary African-American who sang and danced her way from poverty in St. Louis to the mythical heart of Parisian intellectual life. It reads like an extended essay pondering, among other things, Rose's own unlikely identification with Baker: " . . . in our phantasies . . . we cross . . . she wanted to be remembered for her ideas . . . I am on stage in fox and feathers with an audience madly applauding." It seems no accident that Rose wrote "Tools of Torture: An Essay on Beauty and Pain"* (The Atlantic, *1986) while engaged in her work on Baker; the great music hall star embodies for Rose "the spirit of Paris." And that—the spirit of Paris—is what this essayist is after. The ideal of glamor staged in the Parisian music hall may now be outdated, but its aesthetic still thrives: "Spending time and money on* soins esthétiques *[beauty treatments] is appropriate and necessary," she insists, "not self-indulgent." Appropriate, in that "loving attention to the body" recognizes and respects "you" as a unique embodiment of human culture. And necessary, Rose implies, to protect this "you" from the abuse of any culture that, rather than satisfying "you" forces "you" to satisfy it. The "radical hedonism" of which Paris is "civilization's reminder" equalizes us in the common pleasures of body care and the common need for protection from pain. It is therefore, says Rose, "a moral touchstone standing for the frivolity that keeps priorities straight." Every instance of torture—like every hungry person in our path or on our TV screen—witnesses to a lack of radical love: the love that cares for the body first. It is, after all, a profound frivolity Phyllis Rose explores with so little rhetorical fuss and entirely without the coercion to suffer that one might expect on such high and serious subjects as beauty and pain.*

Tools of Torture: An Essay on Beauty and Pain

In a gallery off the rue Dauphine, near the *parfumerie* where I get my massage, I happened upon an exhibit of medieval torture instruments. It made me think that pain must be as great a challenge to the human imagination as pleasure. Otherwise there's no accounting for the number of torture instruments. One would be quite enough. The simple pincer, let's say, which rips out flesh. Or the head crusher, which breaks first your tooth sockets, then your skull. But in addition I saw tongs, thumbscrews, a rack, a ladder, ropes and pulleys, a grill, a garrote, a Spanish horse, a Judas cradle, an iron maiden, a cage, a gag, a strappado, a stretching table, a saw, a wheel, a twisting stork, an inquisitor's chair, a breast breaker, and a scourge. You don't need complicated machinery to cause incredible pain. If you want to saw your victim down the middle, for example, all you need is a slightly bigger than usual saw. If you hold the victim upside down so the blood stays in his head, hold his legs apart, and start sawing at the groin, you can get as far as the navel before he loses consciousness.

Even in the Middle Ages, before electricity, there were many things you could do to torment a person. You could tie him up in an iron belt that held the arms and legs up to the chest and left no point of rest, so that all his muscles went into spasm within minutes and he was driven mad within hours. This was the twisting stork, a benign-looking object. You could stretch him out backward over a thin piece of wood so that his whole body weight rested on his spine, which pressed against the sharp wood. Then you could stop up his nostrils and force water into his stomach through his mouth. Then, if you wanted to finish him off, you and your helper could jump on his stomach, causing internal hemorrhage. This torture was called the rack. If you wanted to burn someone to death without hearing him scream, you could use a tongue lock, a metal rod between the jaw and collarbone that prevented him from opening his mouth. You could put a person in a chair with spikes on the seat and arms, tie him down against the spikes, and beat him, so that every time he flinched from the beating he drove his own flesh deeper onto the spikes. This was the inquisitor's chair. If you wanted to make it worse, you could heat the spikes. You could suspend a person over a pointed wooden pyramid and whenever he started to fall asleep, you could drop him onto the point. If you were Ippolito Marsili, the inventor of this torture, known as the Judas cradle, you could tell yourself you had invented something humane, a torture that worked without burning flesh or breaking bones. For the torture here was supposed to be sleep deprivation.

The secret of torture, like the secret of French cuisine, is that nothing is unthinkable. The human body is like a foodstuff, to be grilled, pounded, filleted. Every opening exists to be stuffed, all flesh to be carved off the bone. You take an ordinary wheel, a heavy wooden wheel with spokes. You lay the victim on the ground with blocks of wood at strategic points under his shoulders, legs, and arms. You use the wheel to break every bone in his body. Next you tie his body onto the wheel. With all its bones broken, it will be pliable. However, the victim will not be dead. If you want to kill him, you hoist the wheel aloft on the end of a pole and leave him to starve. Who would have thought to do this with a man and a wheel? But, then, who would have thought to take the disgusting snail, force it to render its ooze, stuff it in its own shell with garlic butter, bake it, and eat it?

Not long ago I had a facial—only in part because I thought I needed one. It was research into the nature and function of pleasure. In a dark booth at the back of the beauty salon the aesthetician put me on a table and applied a series of ointments to my face, some cool, some warmed. After a while she put something into my hand, cold and metallic. "Don't be afraid, madame," she said. "It is an electrode. It will not hurt you. The other end is attached to two metal cylinders, which I roll over your face. They break down the electricity barrier on your skin and allow the moisturizers to penetrate deeply." I didn't believe this hocus-pocus. I didn't believe in the electricity barrier or in the ability of these rollers to break it down. But it all felt very good. The cold metal on my face was a pleasant change from the soft warmth of the aesthetician's fingers. Still, since Algeria it's hard to hear the word *electrode* without fear. So when she left me for a few minutes with a moist, refreshing cheesecloth over my face, I thought, What if the goal of her expertise had been pain, not moisture? What if the electrodes had been electrodes in the Algerian sense? What if the cheesecloth mask were dipped in acid?

In Paris, where the body is so pampered, torture seems particularly sinister, not because it's hard to understand but because—as the dark side of sensuality—it seems so easy. Beauty care is among the glories of Paris. *Soins esthétiques* include makeup, facials, massages (both relaxing and reducing), depilations (partial and complete), manicures, pedicures, and tanning, in addition to the usual run of *soins* for the hair: cutting, brushing, setting, waving, styling, blowing, coloring, and streaking. In Paris the state of your skin, hair, and nerves is taken seriously, and there is little of the puritanical thinking that tries to persuade us that beauty comes from within. Nor do the French think, as Americans do, that beauty should be offhand and low-maintenance. Spending time and money on *soins esthétiques* is appropriate and necessary, not self-indulgent. Should that loving attention to the body turn malevolent, you have torture. You have the procedure—the aesthetic, as it were—of torture, the explanation for the rich diversity of torture instruments, but you do not have the cause.

Historically torture has been a tool of legal systems, used to get information needed for a trial or, more directly, to determine guilt or innocence. In the Middle Ages confession was considered the best of all proofs, and torture was the way to produce a confession. In other words, torture didn't come into existence to give vent to human sadism. It is not always private and perverse but sometimes social and institutional, vetted by the government and, of course, the Church. (There have been few bigger fans of torture than Christianity and Islam.) Righteousness, as much as viciousness, produces torture. There aren't squads of sadists beating down the doors to the torture chambers begging for jobs. Rather, as a recent book on torture by Edward Peters says, the institution of torture creates sadists; the weight of a culture, Peters suggests, is necessary to recruit torturers. You have to convince people that they are working for a great goal in order to get them to overcome their repugnance to the task of causing physical pain to another person. Usually the great goal is the preservation of society, and the victim is presented to the torturer as being in some way out to destroy it.

From another point of view, what's horrifying is how easily you can persuade someone that he is working for the common good. Perhaps the most appalling psychological experiment of modern times, by Stanley Milgram, showed that ordinary, decent people in New Haven, Connecticut, could be brought to the point of inflicting (as they thought) severe electric shocks on other people in obedience to an authority and in pursuit of a goal, the advancement of knowledge, of which they approved. Milgram used—some would say abused—the prestige of science and the university to make his point, but his point is chilling nonetheless. We can cluck over torture, but the evidence at least suggests that with intelligent handling most of us could be brought to do it ourselves.

In the Middle Ages, Milgram's experiment would have had no point. It would have shocked no one that people were capable of cruelty in the interest of something they believed in. That was as it should be. Only recently in the history of human thought has the avoidance of cruelty moved in the forefront of ethics. "Putting cruelty first," as Judith Shklar says in *Ordinary Vices*, is comparatively new. The belief that the "pursuit of happiness" is one of man's inalienable rights, the idea that "cruel and unusual punishment" is an evil in itself, the Benthamite notion that behavior should be guided by what will produce the greatest happiness for the greatest number—all these principles are only two centuries old. They were born with the eighteenth-century democratic revolutions. And in two hundred years they have not been universally accepted. Wherever people believe strongly in some cause, they will justify torture—not just the Nazis, but the French in Algeria.

Many people who wouldn't hurt a fly have annexed to fashion the imagery of torture—the thongs and spikes and metal studs—hence reducing it to the frivolous and transitory. Because torture has been in the mainstream and not on the margins of history, nothing could be healthier. For torture to be merely kinky would be a big advance. Exhibitions like the one I saw in Paris, which presented itself as educational, may be guilty of pandering to the tastes they deplore. Solemnity may be the wrong tone. If taking one's goals too seriously is the danger, the best discouragement of torture may be a radical hedonism that denies that any goal is worth the means, that refuses to allow the nobly abstract to seduce us from the sweetness of the concrete. Give people a good croissant and a good cup of coffee in the morning. Give them an occasional facial and a plate of escargots. Marie Antoinette picked a bad moment to say "Let them eat cake," but I've often thought she was on the right track.

All of which brings me back to Paris, for Paris exists in the imagination of much of the world as the capital of pleasure—of fun, food, art, folly, seduction, gallantry, and beauty. Paris is civilization's reminder to itself that nothing leads you less wrong than your awareness of your own pleasure and a genial desire to spread it around. In that sense the myth of Paris constitutes a moral touchstone, standing for the selfish frivolity that helps keep priorities straight.

Alice Walker
(b. 1944)

When "Looking for Zora" first appeared in Ms. *magazine (March 1975), Alice Walker had published poetry, a novel, and a book of stories about black women. One of these, "The Revenge of Hanna Kemhoff"—she calls it "my story about voodoo"—had led her, just when she was asking "Where are the* black *collectors of folklore?", to Zora Neale Hurston (see p. 292). "What I discovered," says Walker, was "a model," one who "had provided, as if she knew someday I would come along wandering in the wilderness, a nearly complete record of her life" ("Saving the Life That Is Your Own"). The vital thing about that "life" for Alice Walker—young, black, female, setting out in the perilous profession of letters—was Hurston the black woman as artist, a Southerner like herself, and "made of some of the universe's most naturally free stuff" (Dedication,* I Love Myself When I Am Laughing: A Zora Neale Hurston Reader*). Sharing Hurston's folklore collection,* Mules and Men, *with her own relatives in rural Georgia, Walker observed how the book "gave them back all the stories they had forgotten and of which they had grown ashamed"; she recorded their "joy over who [Hurston] was showing them to be: descendants of an inventive, joyous, courageous, and outrageous people" ("A Cautionary Tale and a Partisan View"). So, when, in the summer of 1973, Alive Walker went "looking for Zora" in an unkempt Florida cemetery, Hurston the writer was very much alive in the future author of* The Color Purple; *alive, too, was Walker's indignation at the neglect that had befallen this "Genius of the South"—her books out of print, her last years spent in obscure poverty, and, before that, "the misleading, deliberately belittling, inaccurate, and generally irresponsible attacks on her work and life by almost everyone" ("A Cautionary Tale"). The snatches of commentary that alternate in the essay with Walker's own economical and, at moments, tensely funny account evoke some of this critical context while emphasizing the more recent, restorative assessments of Hurston's biographer, Robert Hemenway. To go "looking for Zora" was, for Alice Walker, a small personal act of restitution towards the greatest and most beloved of those artistic "mothers" she writes about so feelingly in the title essay of* In Search of Our Mothers' Gardens. *It was, too, a larger symbolic act: "A people do not throw their geniuses away. And if they are thrown away, it is our duty as artists and as witnesses for the future to collect them again for the sake of our children, and, if necessary, bone by bone" ("A Cautionary Tale").*

Looking for Zora

On January 16, 1959, Zora Neale Hurston, suffering from the effects of a stroke and writing painfully in longhand, composed a letter to the "editorial department" of Harper & Brothers inquiring if they would be interested in seeing "the book I am laboring upon at present—a life of Herod the Great." One year and twelve days later, Zora Neale Hurston died without funds to provide for her burial, a resident of the St. Lucie County, Florida, Welfare Home. She lies today in an unmarked grave in a segregated cemetery in Fort Pierce, Florida, a resting place generally symbolic of the black writer's fate in America.

Zora Neale Hurston is one of the most significant unread authors in America, the author of two minor classics and four other major books.

—Robert Hemenway,
"Zora Hurston and the Eatonville Anthropology,"
in *The Harlem Renaissance Remembered*

On August 15, 1973, I wake up just as the plane is lowering over Sanford, Florida, which means I am also looking down on Eatonville, Zora Neale Hurston's birthplace. I recognize it from Zora's description in *Mules and Men:* "the city of five lakes, three croquet courts, three hundred brown skins, three hundred good swimmers, plenty guavas, two schools, and no jailhouse." Of course I cannot see the guavas, but the five lakes are still there, and it is the lakes I count as the plane prepares to land in Orlando.

From the air, Florida looks completely flat, and as we near the ground this impression does not change. This is the first time I have seen the interior of the state, which Zora wrote about so well, but there are the acres of orange groves, the sand, mangrove trees, and scrub pine that I know from her books. Getting off the plane I walk through the humid air of midday into the tacky but air-conditioned airport. I search for Charlotte Hunt, my companion on the Zora Hurston expedition. She lives in Winter Park, Florida, very near Eatonville, and is writing her graduate dissertation on Zora. I see her waving—a large, pleasant-faced white woman in dark glasses. We have written to each other for several weeks, swapping our latest finds (mostly hers) on Zora, and trying to make sense out of the mass of information obtained (often erroneous or simply confusing) from Zora herself—through her stories and autobiography—and from people who wrote about her.

Eatonville has lived for such a long time in my imagination that I can hardly believe it will be found existing in its own right. But after twenty minutes on the expressway, Charlotte turns off and I see a small settlement of houses and stores set with no particular pattern in the sandy soil off the road. We stop in front of a neat gray building that has two fascinating signs: EATONVILLE POST OFFICE and EATONVILLE CITY HALL.

Inside the Eatonville City Hall half of the building, a slender, dark-brown-skin woman sits looking through letters on a desk. When she hears we are searching for anyone who might have known Zora Neale Hurston, she leans back in thought. Because I don't wish to inspire foot-dragging in people who might know something about Zora they're not sure they should tell, I have decided on a simple, but I feel profoundly *useful*, lie.

"I am Miss Hurston's niece," I prompt the young woman, who brings her head down with a smile.

"I think Mrs. Moseley is about the only one still living who might remember her," she says.

"Do you mean *Mathilda* Moseley, the woman who tells those 'woman-is-smarter-than-man' lies in Zora's book?"

"Yes," says the young woman. "Mrs. Moseley is real old now, of course. But this time of day, she should be at home."

I stand at the counter looking down on her, the first Eatonville resident I have spoken to. Because of Zora's books, I feel I know something about her; at least I know what the town she grew up in was like years before she was born.

"Tell me something," I say. "Do the schools teach Zora's books here?"

"No," she says, "they don't. I don't think most people know anything about Zora Neale Hurston, or know about any of the great things she did. She was a fine lady. I've read all of her books myself, but I don't think many other folks in Eatonville have."

"Many of the church people around here, as I understand it," says Charlotte in a murmured aside, "thought Zora was pretty loose. I don't think they appreciated her writing about them."

"Well," I say to the young woman, "thank you for your help." She clarifies her directions to Mrs. Moseley's house and smiles as Charlotte and I turn to go.

> The letter to Harper's does not expose a publisher's rejection of an unknown masterpiece, but it does reveal how the bright promise of the Harlem Renaissance deteriorated for many of the writers who shared in its exuberance. It also indicates the personal tragedy of Zora Neale Hurston: Barnard graduate, author of four novels, two books of folklore, one volume of autobiography, the most important collector of Afro-American

folklore in America, reduced by poverty and circumstance to seek a publisher by unsolicited mail.

—Robert Hemenway

Zora Hurston was born in 1901, 1902, or 1903—depending on how old she felt herself to be at the time someone asked.

—Librarian, Beinecke Library, Yale University

The Moseley house is small and white and snug, its tiny yard nearly swallowed up by oleanders and hibiscus bushes. Charlotte and I knock on the door. I call out. But there is no answer. This strikes us as peculiar. We have had time to figure out an age for Mrs. Moseley—not dates or a number, just old. I am thinking of a quivery, bedridden invalid when we hear the car. We look behind us to see an old black-and-white Buick—paint peeling and grillwork rusty—pulling into the drive. A neat old lady in a purple dress and with white hair is straining at the wheel. She is frowning because Charlotte's car is in the way.

Mrs. Moseley looks at us suspiciously. "Yes, I knew Zora Neale," she says, unsmilingly and with a rather cold stare at Charlotte (who, I imagine, feels very *white* at that moment), "but that was a long time ago, and I don't want to talk about it."

"Yes, ma'am," I murmur, bringing all my sympathy to bear on the situation.

"Not only that," Mrs. Moseley continues, "I've been sick. Been in the hospital for an operation. Ruptured artery. The doctors didn't believe I was going to live, but you see me alive, don't you?"

"Looking well, too," I comment.

Mrs. Moseley is out of her car. A thin, sprightly woman with nice gold-studded false teeth, uppers and lowers. I like her because she stands there *straight* beside her car, with a hand on her hip and her straw pocketbook on her arm. She wears white T-strap shoes with heels that show off her well-shaped legs.

"I'm eighty-two years old, you know," she says. "And I just can't remember things the way I used to. Anyhow, Zora Neale left here to go to school and she never really came back to live. She'd come here for material for her books, but that was all. She spent most of her time down in South Florida."

"You know, Mrs. Moseley, I saw your name in one of Zora's books."

"You did?" She looks at me with only slightly more interest. "I read some of her books a long time ago, but then people got to borrowing and borrowing and they borrowed them all away."

"I could send you a copy of everything that's been reprinted," I offer. "Would you like me to do that?"

"No," says Mrs. Moseley promptly. "I don't read much any more. Besides, all of that was *so* long ago. . . ."

Charlotte and I settle back against the car in the sun. Mrs. Moseley tells us at length and with exact recall every step in her recent operation, ending with: "What those doctors didn't know—when they were expecting me to die (and they didn't even think I'd live long enough for them to have to take out my stitches!)—is that Jesus is the best doctor, and if *He* says for you to get well, that's all that counts."

With this philosophy, Charlotte and I murmur quick assent: being Southerners and church bred, we have heard that belief before. But what we learn from Mrs. Moseley is that she does not remember much beyond the year 1938. She shows us a picture of her father and mother and says that her father was Joe Clarke's brother. Joe Clarke, as every Zora Hurston reader knows, was the first mayor of Eatonville; his fictional counterpart is Jody Starks of *Their Eyes Were Watching God.* We also got directions to where Joe Clarke's store *was*—where Club Eaton is now. Club Eaton, a long orange-beige nightspot we had seen on the main road, is apparently famous for the good times in it regularly had by all. It is, perhaps, the modern equivalent of the store porch, where all the men of Zora's childhood came to tell "lies," that is, black folk tales, that were "made and used on the spot," to take a line from Zora. As for Zora's exact birthplace, Mrs. Moseley has no idea.

After I have commented on the healthy growth of her hibiscus bushes, she becomes more talkative. She mentions how much she *loved* to dance, when she was a young woman, and talks about how good her husband was. When he was alive, she says, she was completely happy because he allowed her to be completely free. "I was so free I had to pinch myself sometimes to tell if I was a married woman."

Relaxed now, she tells us about going to school with Zora. "Zora and I went to the same school. It's called Hungerford High now. It *was* only to the eighth grade. But our teachers were so good that by the time you left you knew college subjects. When I went to Morris Brown in Atlanta, the teachers there were just teaching me the same things I had already learned right in Eatonville. I wrote Mama and told her I was going to come home and help her with her babies. I wasn't learning anything new."

"Tell me something, Mrs. Moseley," I ask. "Why do you suppose Zora was against integration? I read somewhere that she was against school desegregation because she felt it was an insult to black teachers."

"Oh, one of them [white people] came around asking me about integration. One day I was doing my shopping. I heard 'em over there talking about it in the store, about the schools. And I got on out of the way because I knew if they asked me, they wouldn't like what I was going to tell 'em. But they came up and asked me anyhow. 'What do you think about this integration?' one of them said. I acted like I thought I had heard wrong. 'You're asking *me* what *I* think about integration?' I said. 'Well, as you can see, I'm just an old colored woman'—I was seventy-five or seventy-six then—'and this is the first time anybody ever asked me about integration. And nobody asked my grandmother what she thought, either, but her daddy was one of you all.' " Mrs. Moseley seems satisfied with this memory of her rejoinder. She looks at Charlotte. "I have the blood of three races in my veins," she says belligerently, "white, black, and Indian, and nobody asked me *anything* before."

"Do you think living in Eatonville made integration less appealing to you?"

"Well, I can tell you this: I have lived in Eatonville all my life, and I've been in the governing of this town. I've been everything but mayor and I've been *assistant* mayor. Eatonville was and is an all-black town. We have our own police department, post office, and town hall. Our own school and good teachers. Do I need integration?

"They took over Goldsboro, because the black people who lived there never incorporated, like we did. And now I don't even know if any black folks live there. They built big houses up there around the lakes. But we didn't let that happen in Eatonville, and we don't sell land to just anybody. And you see, we're still here."

When we leave, Mrs. Moseley is standing by her car, waving. I think of the letter Roy Wilkins wrote to a black newspaper blasting Zora Neale for her lack of enthusiasm about the integration of schools. I wonder if he knew the experience of Eatonville she was coming from. Not many black people in America have come from a self-contained, all-black community where loyalty and unity are taken for granted. A place where black pride is nothing new.

There is, however, one thing Mrs. Moseley said that bothered me.

"Tell me, Mrs. Moseley," I had asked, "why is it that thirteen years after Zora's death, no marker has been put on her grave?"

And Mrs. Moseley answered: "The reason she doesn't have a stone is because she wasn't buried here. She was buried down in South Florida somewhere. I don't think anybody really knew where she was."

> Only to reach a wider audience, need she ever write books—because she is a perfect book of entertainment in herself. In her youth she was always getting scholarships and things from wealthy white people, some of whom simply paid her just to sit around and represent the Negro race for them, she did it in such a racy fashion. She was full of sidesplitting anecdotes, humorous tales, and tragicomic stories, remembered out of her

> life in the South as a daughter of a traveling minister of God. She could make you laugh one minute and cry the next. To many of her white friends, no doubt, she was a perfect "darkie," in the nice meaning they give the term—that is, a naïve, childlike, sweet, humorous, and highly colored Negro.
>
> But Miss Hurston was clever, too—a student who didn't let college give her a broad "a" and who had great scorn for all pretensions, academic or otherwise. That is why she was such a fine folklore collector, able to go among the people and never act as if she had been to school at all. Almost nobody else could stop the average Harlemite on Lenox Avenue and measure his head with a strange-looking, anthropological device and not get bawled out for the attempt, except Zora, who used to stop anyone whose head looked interesting, and measure it.
>
> —Langston Hughes, *The Big Sea*

> What does it matter what white folks must have thought about her?
>
> —Student, black women writers class, Wellesley College

Mrs. Sarah Peek Patterson is a handsome, red-haired woman in her late forties, wearing orange slacks and gold earrings. She is the director of Lee-Peek Mortuary in Fort Pierce, the establishment that handled Zora's burial. Unlike most black funeral homes in Southern towns that sit like palaces among the general poverty, Lee-Peek has a run-down, *small* look. Perhaps this is because it is painted purple and white, as are its Cadillac chariots. These colors do not age well. The rooms are cluttered and grimy, and the bathroom is a tiny, stale-smelling prison, with a bottle of black hair dye (apparently used to touch up the hair of the corpses) dripping into the face bowl. Two pine burial boxes are resting in the bathtub.

Mrs. Patterson herself is pleasant and helpful.

"As I told you over the phone, Mrs. Patterson," I begin, shaking her hand and looking into her penny-brown eyes, "I am Zora Neale Hurston's niece, and I would like to have a marker put on her grave. You said, when I called you last week, that you could tell me where the grave is."

By this time I am, of course, completely into being Zora's niece, and the lie comes with perfect naturalness to my lips. Besides, as far as I'm concerned, she *is* my aunt—and that of all black people as well.

"She was buried in 1960," exclaims Mrs. Patterson. "That was when my father was running this funeral home. He's sick now or I'd let you talk to him. But I know where she's buried. She's in the old cemetery, the Garden of the Heavenly Rest, on Seventeenth Street. Just when you go in the gate there's a circle, and she's buried right in the middle of it. Hers is the only grave in that circle—because people don't bury in that cemetery anymore."

She turns to a stocky, black-skinned woman in her thirties, wearing a green polo shirt and white jeans cut off at the knee. "This lady will show you where it is," she says.

"I can't tell you how much I appreciate this," I say to Mrs. Patterson, as I rise to go. "And could you tell me something else? You see, I never met my aunt. When she died, I was still a junior in high school. But could you tell me what she died of, and what kind of funeral she had?"

"I don't know exactly what she died of," Mrs. Patterson says. "I know she didn't have any money. Folks took up a collection to bury her. . . . I believe she died of malnutrition."

"*Malnutrition?*"

Outside, in the blistering sun, I lean my head against Charlotte's even more blistering car top. The sting of the hot metal only intensifies my anger. "*Malnutrition,*" I manage to mutter. "Hell, our condition hasn't changed *any* since Phillis Wheatley's time. *She* died of malnutrition!"

"Really?" says Charlotte. "I didn't know that."

> One cannot overemphasize the extent of her commitment. It was so great that her marriage in the spring of 1927 to Herbert Sheen was short-lived. Although divorce did not come officially until 1931, the two separated amicably after only a few months, Hurston to continue her collecting, Sheen to attend Medical School. Hurston never married again.
>
> —Robert Hemenway

"What is your name?" I ask the woman who has climbed into the back seat.

"Rosalee," she says. She has a rough, pleasant voice, as if she is a singer who also smokes a lot. She is homely, and has an air of ready indifference.

"Another woman came by here wanting to see the grave," she says, lighting up a cigarette. "She was a little short, dumpty white lady from one of these Florida schools. Orlando or Daytona. But let me tell you something before we gets started. All I know is where the cemetery is. I don't know one thing about that grave. You better go back in and ask her to draw you a map."

A few moments later, with Mrs. Patterson's diagram of where the grave is, we head for the cemetery.

We drive past blocks of small, pastel-colored houses and turn right onto Seventeenth Street. At the very end, we reach a tall curving gate, with the words "Garden of the Heavenly Rest" fading into the stone. I expected, from Mrs. Patterson's small drawing, to find a small circle—which would have placed Zora's grave five or ten paces from the road. But the "circle" is over an acre large and looks more like an abandoned field. Tall weeds choke the dirt road and scrape against the sides of the car. It doesn't help either that I step out into an active ant hill.

"I don't know about y'all," I say, "but I don't even believe this." I am used to the haphazard cemetery-keeping that is traditional in most Southern black communities, but this neglect is staggering. As far as I can see there is nothing but bushes and weeds, some as tall as my waist. One grave is near the road, and Charlotte elects to investigate it. It is fairly clean, and belongs to someone who died in 1963.

Rosalee and I plunge into the weeds; I pull my long dress up to my hips. The weeds scratch my knees, and the insects have a feast. Looking back, I see Charlotte standing resolutely near the road.

"Aren't you coming?" I call.

"No," she calls back. "I'm from these parts and I know what's out there." She means snakes.

"Shit," I say, my whole life and the people I love flashing melodramatically before my eyes. Rosalee is a few yards to my right.

"How're you going to find anything out here?" she asks. And I stand still a few seconds, looking at the weeds. Some of them are quite pretty, with tiny yellow flowers. They are thick and healthy, but dead weeds under them have formed a thick gray carpet on the ground. A snake could be lying six inches from my big toe and I wouldn't see it. We move slowly, very slowly, our eyes alert, our legs trembly. It is hard to tell where the center of the circle is since the circle is not really round, but more like half of something round. There are things crackling and hissing in the grass. Sandspurs are sticking to the inside of my skirt. Sand and ants cover my feet. I look toward the road and notice that there are, indeed, *two* large curving stones, making an entrance and exit to the cemetery. I take my bearings from them and try to navigate to exact center. But the center of anything can be very large, and a grave is not a pinpoint. Finding the grave seems positively hopeless. There is only one thing to do:

"Zora!" I yell, as loud as I can (causing Rosalee to jump). "Are you out here?"

"If she is, I sho hope she don't answer you. If she do, I'm gone."

"Zora!" I call again. "I'm here. Are you?"

"If she is," grumbles Rosalee, "I hope she'll keep it to herself."

"Zora!" Then I start fussing with her. "I hope you don't think I'm going to stand out here all day, with these snakes watching me and these ants having a field day. In fact, I'm going to call you just one or two more times." On a clump of dried grass, near a small bushy tree, my eye falls on one of the largest bugs I have ever seen. It is on its back, and is as large as three of my fingers. I walk toward it, and yell "Zo-ra!" and my foot sinks into a hole. I look down. I am standing in a sunken rectangle that is about six feet long and about three or four feet wide. I look up to see where the two gates are.

"Well," I say, "this is the center, or approximately anyhow. It's also the only sunken spot we've found. Doesn't this look like a grave to you?"

"For the sake of not going no farther through these bushes," Rosalee growls, "yes, it do."

"Wait a minute," I say, "I have to look around some more to be sure this is the only spot that resembles a grave. But you don't have to come."

Rosalee smiles—a grin, really—beautiful and tough.

"Naw," she says, "I feels sorry for you. If one of these snakes got ahold of you out here by yourself I'd feel *real* bad." She laughs. "I done come this far, I'll go on with you."

"Thank you, Rosalee," I say. "Zora thanks you too."

"Just as long as she don't try to tell me in person," she says, and together we walk down the field.

> The gusto and flavor of Zora Neal[e] Hurston's storytelling, for example, long before the yarns were published in "Mules and Men" and other books, became a local legend which might . . . have spread further under different conditions. A tiny shift in the center of gravity could have made them best-sellers.
>
> —Arna Bontemps, *Personals*

> Bitter over the rejection of her folklore's value, especially in the black community, frustrated by what she felt was her failure to convert the Afro-American world view into the forms of prose fiction, Hurston finally gave up.
>
> —Robert Hemenway

When Charlotte and I drive up to the Merritt Monument Company, I immediately see the headstone I want.

"How much is this one?" I ask the young woman in charge, pointing to a tall black stone. It looks as majestic as Zora herself must have been when she was learning voodoo from those root doctors down in New Orleans.

"Oh, *that* one," she says, "that's our finest. That's Ebony Mist."

"Well, how much is it?"

"I don't know. But wait," she says, looking around in relief, "here comes somebody who'll know."

A small sunburned man with squinty green eyes comes up. He must be the engraver, I think, because his eyes are contracted into slits, as if he has been keeping stone dust out of them for years.

"That's Ebony Mist," he says. "That's our best."

"How much is it?" I ask, beginning to realize I probably *can't* afford it.

He gives me a price that would feed a dozen Sahelian drought victims for three years. I realize I must honor the dead, but between the dead great and the living starving, there is no choice.

"I have a lot of letters to be engraved," I say, standing by the plain gray marker I have chosen. It is pale and ordinary, not at all like Zora, and makes me momentarily angry that I am not rich.

We go into his office and I hand him a sheet of paper that has:

ZORA NEALE HURSTON
"A GENIUS OF THE SOUTH"
NOVELIST FOLKLORIST
ANTHROPOLOGIST
1901 1960

"A genius of the South" is from one of Jean Toomer's poems.

"Where is this grave?" the monument man asks. "If it's in a new cemetery, the stone has to be flat."

"Well, it's not a new cemetery and Zora—my aunt—doesn't need anything flat, because with the weeds out there, you'd never be able to see it. You'll have to go out there with me."

He grunts.

"And take a long pole and 'sound' the spot," I add. "Because there's no way of telling it's a grave, except that it's sunken."

"Well," he says, after taking my money and writing up a receipt, in the full awareness that he's the only monument dealer for miles, "you take this flag" (he hands me a four-foot-long pole with a red-metal marker on top) "and take it out to the cemetery and put it where you think the grave is. It'll take us about three weeks to get a stone out there."

I wonder if he knows he is sending me to another confrontation with the snakes. He probably does. Charlotte has told me she will cut my leg and suck out the blood if I am bit.

"At least send me a photograph when it's done, won't you?"

He says he will.

Hurston's return to her folklore-collecting in December of 1927 was made possible by Mrs. R. Osgood Mason, an elderly white patron of the arts, who at various times also helped Langston Hughes, Alain Locke, Richmond Barthe, and Miguel Covarrubias. Hurston apparently came to her attention through the intercession of Locke, who frequently served as a kind of liaison between the young black talent and Mrs. Mason. The entire relationship between this woman and the Harlem Renaissance deserves extended study, for it represents much of the ambiguity involved in white patronage of black artists. All her artists were instructed to call her "Godmother"; there was a decided emphasis on the "primitive" aspects of black culture, apparently a holdover from Mrs. Mason's interest in the Plains Indians. In Hurston's case there were special restrictions imposed by her patron: although she was to be paid a handsome salary for her folklore collecting, she was to limit her correspondence and publish nothing of her research without prior approval.

—Robert Hemenway

You have to read the chapters Zora *left out* of her autobiography.

—Student, Special Collections Room, Beinecke Library, Yale University

Dr. Benton, a friend of Zora's and practicing M.D. in Fort Pierce, is one of those old, good-looking men whom I always have trouble not liking. (It no longer bothers me that I may be constantly searching for father figures; by this time, I have found several and dearly enjoyed knowing them all.) He is shrewd, with steady brown eyes under hair that is almost white. He is probably in his seventies, but doesn't look it. He carries himself with dignity, and has cause to be proud of the new clinic where he now practices medicine. His nurse looks at us with suspicion, but Dr. Benton's eyes have the penetration of a scalpel cutting through skin. I guess right away that if he knows anything at all about Zora Hurston, he will not believe I am her niece. "Eatonville?" Dr. Benton says, leaning forward in his chair, looking first at me, then at Charlotte. "Yes, I know Eatonville; I grew up not far from there. I knew the whole bunch of Zora's family." (He looks at the shape of my cheekbones, the size of my eyes, and the nappiness of my hair.) "I knew her daddy. The old man. He was a hard-working, Christian man. Did the best he could for his family. He was the mayor of Eatonville for a while, you know.

"My father was the mayor of Goldsboro. You probably never heard of it. It never incorporated like Eatonville did, and has just about disappeared. But Eatonville is still all black."

He pauses and looks at me. "And you're Zora's niece," he says wonderingly.

"Well," I say with shy dignity, yet with some tinge, I hope, of a nineteenth-century blush, "I'm illegitimate. That's why I never knew Aunt Zora."

I love him for the way he comes to my rescue. "You're *not* illegitimate!" he cries, his eyes resting on me fondly. "All of us are God's children! Don't you even *think* such a thing!"

And I hate myself for lying to him. Still, I ask myself, would I have gotten this far toward getting the headstone and finding out about Zora Hurston's last days without telling my lie? Actually, I probably would have. But I don't like taking chances that could get me stranded in central Florida.

"Zora didn't get along with her family. I don't know why. Did you read her autobiography, *Dust Tracks on a Road?*"

"Yes, I did," I say. "It pained me to see Zora pretending to be naïve and grateful about the old white 'Godmother' who helped finance her research, but I loved the part where she ran off from home after falling out with her brother's wife."

Dr. Benton nods. "When she got sick, I tried to get her to go back to her family, but she refused. There wasn't any real hatred; they just never had gotten along and Zora wouldn't go to them. She didn't want to go to the county home, either, but she had to, because she couldn't do a thing for herself."

"I was surprised to learn she died of malnutrition."

Dr. Benton seems startled. "Zora *didn't* die of malnutrition," he says indignantly. "Where did you get that story from? She had a stroke and she died in the welfare home." He seems peculiarly upset, distressed, but sits back reflectively in his chair. "She was an incredible woman," he muses. "Sometimes when I closed my office, I'd go by her house and just talk to her for an hour or two. She was a well-read, well-traveled woman and always had her own ideas about what was going on. . . ."

"I never knew her, you know. Only some of Carl Van Vechten's photographs and some newspaper photographs . . . What did she look like?"

"When I knew her, in the fifties, she was a big woman, *erect*. Not quite as light as I am (Dr. Benton is dark beige), and about five foot, seven inches, and she weighed about two hundred pounds. Probably more. She . . ."

"What! Zora was *fat!* She wasn't, in Van Vechten's pictures!"

"Zora loved to eat," Dr. Benton says complacently. "She could sit down with a mound of ice cream and just eat and talk till it was all gone."

While Dr. Benton is talking, I recall that the Van Vechten pictures were taken when Zora was still a young woman. In them she appears tall, tan, and healthy. In later newspaper photographs—when she was in her forties—I remembered that she seemed heavier and several shades lighter. I reasoned that the earlier photographs were taken while she was busy collecting folklore materials in the hot Florida sun.

"She had high blood pressure. Her health wasn't good. . . . She used to live in one of my houses—on School Court Street. It's a block house. . . . I don't recall the number. But my wife and I used to invite her over to the house for dinner. *She always ate well,*" he says emphatically.

"That's comforting to know," I say, wondering where Zora ate when she wasn't with the Bentons.

"Sometimes she would run out of groceries—after she got sick—and she'd call me. 'Come over here and see 'bout me,' she'd say. And I'd take her shopping and buy her groceries.

"She was always studying. Her mind—before the stroke—just worked all the time. She was always going somewhere, too. She once went to Honduras to study something. And when she died, she was working on that book about Herod the Great. She was so intelligent! And really had perfect expressions. Her English was beautiful." (I suspect this is a clever way to let me know Zora herself didn't speak in the "black English" her characters used.)

"I used to read all of her books," Dr. Benton continues, "but it was a long time ago. I remember one about . . . it was called, I think, 'The Children of God' [*Their Eyes Were Watching God*], and I remember Janie and Teapot [Teacake] and the mad dog riding on the cow in that hurricane and bit old Teapot on the cheek. . . ."

I am delighted that he remembers even this much of the story, even if the names are wrong, but seeing his affection for Zora I feel I must ask him about her burial. "Did she *really* have a pauper's funeral?"

"She *didn't* have a pauper's funeral!" he says with great heat. "Everybody around here *loved* Zora."

"We just came back from ordering a headstone," I say quietly, because he *is* an old man and the color is coming and going on his face, "but to tell the truth, I can't be positive what I found is the grave. All I know is the spot I found was the only grave-size hole in the area."

"I remember it wasn't near the road," says Dr. Benton, more calmly. "Some other lady came by here and we went out looking for the grave and I took a long iron stick and poked all over that part of the cemetery but we didn't find anything. She took some pictures of the general area. Do the weeds still come up to your knees?"

"And beyond," I murmur. This time there isn't any doubt. Dr. Benton feels ashamed.

As he walks us to our car, he continues to talk about Zora. "She couldn't really write much near the end. She had the stroke and it left her weak; her mind was affected. She couldn't think about anything for long.

"She came here from Daytona, I think. She owned a houseboat over there. When she came here, she sold it. She lived on that money, then she worked as a maid—for an article on maids she was writing—and she worked for the *Chronicle* writing the horoscope column.

"I think black people here in Florida got mad at her because she was for some politician they were against. She said this politician *built* schools for blacks while the one they wanted just talked about it. And although Zora wasn't egotistical, what she thought, she thought; and generally what she thought, she said."

When we leave Dr. Benton's office, I realize I have missed my plane back home to Jackson, Mississippi. That being so, Charlotte and I decide to find the house Zora lived in before she was taken to the county welfare home to die. From among her many notes, Charlotte locates a letter of Zora's she has copied that carries the address: 1734 School Court Street. We ask several people for directions. Finally, two old gentlemen in a dusty gray Plymouth offer to lead us there. School Court Street is not paved, and the road is full of mud puddles. It is dismal and squalid, redeemed only by the brightness of the late afternoon sun. Now I can understand what a "block" house is. It is a house shaped like a block, for one thing, surrounded by others just like it. Some houses are blue and some are green or yellow. Zora's is light green. They are tiny—about fifty by fifty feet, squatty with flat roofs. The house Zora lived in looks worse than the others, but that is its only distinction. It also has three ragged and dirty children sitting on the steps.

"Is this where y'all live?" I ask, aiming my camera.

"No, ma'am," they say in unison, looking at me earnestly. "We live over yonder. This Miss So-and-So's house; but she in the horspital."

We chatter inconsequentially while I take more pictures. A car drives up with a young black couple in it. They scowl fiercely at Charlotte and don't look at me with friendliness, either. They get out and stand in their doorway across the street. I go up to them to explain. "Did you know Zora Hurston used to live right across from you?" I ask.

"Who?" They stare at me blankly, then become curiously attentive, as if they think I made the name up. They are both Afroed and he is somberly dashikied.

I suddenly feel frail and exhausted. "It's too long a story," I say, "but tell me something: is there anybody on this street who's lived here for more than thirteen years?"

"That old man down there," the young man says, pointing. Sure enough, there is a man sitting on his steps three houses down. He has graying hair and is very neat, but there is a weakness about him. He reminds me of Mrs. Turner's husband in *Their Eyes Were Watching God*. He's rather "vanishing"-looking, as if his features have been sanded down. In the old days, before black was beautiful, he was probably considered attractive, because he had wavy hair and light-brown skin; but now, well, light skin has ceased to be its own reward.

After the preliminaries, there is only one thing I want to know: "Tell me something," I begin, looking down at Zora's house. "Did Zora like flowers?"

He looks at me queerly. "As a matter of fact," he says, looking regretfully at the bare, rough yard that surrounds her former house, "she was crazy about them. And she was a great gardener. She loved azaleas, and that running and blooming vine (morning-glories), and she really loved that night-smelling flower (gardenia). She kept a vegetable garden year-round, too. She raised collards and tomatoes and things like that.

"Everyone in this community thought well of Miss Hurston. When she died, people all up and down this street took up a collection for her burial. We put her away nice."

"Why didn't somebody put up a headstone?"

"Well, you know, one was never requested. Her and her family didn't get along. They didn't even come to the funeral."

"And did she live down there by herself?"

"Yes, until they took her away. She lived with—just her and her companion, Sport."

My ears perk up. "Who?"

"Sport, you know, her dog. He was her only companion. He was a big brown-and-white dog."

When I walk back to the car, Charlotte is talking to the young couple on their porch. They are relaxed and smiling.

"I told them about the famous lady who used to live across the street from them," says Charlotte as we drive off. "Of course they had no idea Zora ever lived, let alone that she lived across the street. I think I'll send some of her books to them."

"That's real kind of you," I say.

> I am not tragically colored. There is no great sorrow dammed up in my soul, nor lurking behind my eyes. I do not mind at all. I do not belong to the sobbing school of Negrohood who hold that nature somehow has given them a lowdown dirty deal and whose feelings are all hurt about it. . . . No, I do not weep at the world—I am too busy sharpening my oyster knife.
>
> —Zora Neale Hurston, "How It Feels to Be Colored Me," *World Tomorrow*, 1928

There are times—and finding Zora Hurston's grave was one of them—when normal responses of grief, horror, and so on do not make sense because they bear no real relation to the depth of the emotion one feels. It was impossible for me to cry when I saw the field full of weeds where Zora is. Partly this is because I have come to know Zora through her books and she was not a teary sort of person herself; but partly, too, it is because there is a point at which even grief feels absurd. And at this point, laughter gushes up to retrieve sanity.

It is only later, when the pain is not so direct a threat to one's own existence, that what was learned in that moment of comical lunacy is understood. Such moments rob us of both youth and vanity. But perhaps they are also times when greater disciplines are born.

Annie Dillard

(b. 1945)

At sixteen, Annie Dillard was reading Emerson's Essays *and writing a paper on his concept of the soul. Emerson "excited me enormously," she writes, because he "was a thinker, full-time, as Pasteur and Salk were full-time biologists"; he required "each native to cobble up an original relation with the universe"* (An American Childhood). *Dillard has been cobbling up hers with so attentive and fine an eye to both the universe and her craft one wants a more fastidious image to describe what she's doing, working at it like a diligent naturalist on the one hand, like a disciplined poet on the other. "We are here to witness," she states in the title essay of her remarkable book,* Teaching a Stone to Talk *(1982). Finding herself alive and conscious amid "the whole inhuman array" of the world, this "native" sets out "to keep an eye on things." No better place than the Galápagos Islands, which are "just plain there . . . almost wholly uncluttered by human culture or history," yet wonderfully rich in wildlife, including the tortoises and finches that so occupied Darwin. Dillard's long, finely structured essay, "Life on the Rocks," witnesses to a moment in evolutionary time: "Well—here we all are," sea lions, birds, algae, iguanas, and the human creature on the lookout. To witness is to see and to say what has been seen—no simple task, since consciousness is always transforming what passes through the senses into objects of reflection and playthings of imagination. Like any expert, Dillard "plays the edges" of her form* (The Writing Life); *evocation and speculation verge on lyric: "I sing of the Galápagos Islands. . . ." More insistently than most, Dillard's essays will not be still on the page; they are made for listening, for sounding, even if only in the silence of the mind's ear. "The white beach was a havoc of lava boulders black as clinkers, sleek as spray, and lambent as brass in the sinking sun." This is a bit of what she would call "fancy" writing* (Living By Fiction), *rhythmic, thick with images, with assonances and clashes. But even a piece of "plain" writing like "The animals are tame" can make a sounding sequence when varied and carried across paragraphs like a refrain. Dillard's work invites us to read all essays as heard discourse, to slow our eyes to the sound of the voice talking, the sensuous pace of shapely, artful speech.*

Life on the Rocks: The Galápagos

I

First there was nothing, and although you know with your reason that nothing is nothing, it is easier to visualize it as a limitless slosh of sea—say, the Pacific. Then energy contracted into matter, and although you know that even an invisible gas is matter, it is easier to visualize it as a massive squeeze of volcanic lava spattered inchoate from the secret pit of the ocean and hardening mute and intractable on nothing's lapping shore—like a series of islands, an archipelago. Like: the Galápagos. Then a softer strain of matter began to twitch. It was a kind of shaped water; it flowed, hardening here and there at its tips. There were blue-green algae; there were tortoises.

The ice rolled up, the ice rolled back, and I knelt on a plain of lava boulders in the islands called Galápagos, stroking a giant tortoise's neck. The tortoise closed its eyes and stretched its neck to its greatest height and vulnerability. I rubbed that neck, and when I pulled away my hand, my palm was green with a slick of single-celled algae. I stared at the algae, and at the tortoise, the way you stare at any life on a lava flow, and thought: Well—here we all are.

Being here is being here on the rocks. These Galapagonian rocks, one of them seventy-five miles long, have dried under the equatorial sun between five and six hundred miles west of the South American continent; they lie at the latitude of the Republic of Ecuador, to which they belong.

There is a way a small island rises from the ocean affronting all reason. It is a chunk of chaos pounded into visibility *ex nihilo:*[1] here rough, here smooth, shaped just so by a matrix of physical necessities too weird to contemplate, here instead of there, here instead of not at all. It is a fantastic utterance, as though I were to open my mouth and emit a French horn, or a vase, or a knob of tellurium. It smacks of folly, of first causes.

I think of the island called Daphnecita, little Daphne, on which I never set foot. It's in half of my few photographs, though, because it obsessed me: a dome of gray lava like a pitted loaf, the size of the Plaza Hotel, glazed with guano and crawling with red-orange crabs. Sometimes I attributed to this island's cliff face a surly, infantile consciousness, as though it were sulking in the silent moment after it had just shouted, to the sea and the sky, "I didn't ask to be born." Or sometimes

[1] Out of nothing.

it aged to a raging adolescent, a kid who's just learned that the game is fixed, demanding, "What did you have me for, if you're just going to push me around?" Daphnecita: again, a wise old island, mute, leading the life of pure creaturehood open to any antelope or saint. After you've blown the ocean sky-high, what's there to say? What if we the people had the sense or grace to live as cooled islands in an archipelago live, with dignity, passion, and no comment?

It is worth flying to Guayaquil, Ecuador, and then to Baltra in the Galápagos just to see the rocks. But these rocks are animal gardens. They are home to a Hieronymus Bosch assortment of windblown, stowaway, castaway, flotsam, and shipwrecked creatures. Most exist nowhere else on earth. These reptiles and insects, small mammals and birds, evolved unmolested on the various islands on which they were cast into unique species adapted to the boulder-wrecked shores, the cactus deserts of the lowlands, or the elevated jungles of the large islands' interiors. You come for the animals. You come to see the curious shapes soft proteins can take, to impress yourself with their reality, and to greet them.

You walk among clattering four-foot marine iguanas heaped on the shore lava, and on each other, like slag. You swim with penguins; you watch flightless cormorants dance beside you, ignoring you, waving the black nubs of their useless wings. Here are nesting blue-footed boobies, real birds with real feathers, whose legs and feet are nevertheless patently fake, manufactured by Mattel. The tortoises are big as stoves. The enormous land iguanas at your feet change color in the sunlight, from gold to blotchy red as you watch.

There is always some creature going about its beautiful business. I missed the boat back to my ship, and was left behind momentarily on uninhabited South Plaza island, because I was watching the Audubon's shearwaters. These dark pelagic birds flick along pleated seas in stitching flocks, flailing their wings rapidly—because if they don't, they'll stall. A shearwater must fly fast, or not at all. Consequently it has evolved two nice behaviors which serve to bring it into its nest alive. The nest is a shearwater-sized hole in the lava cliff. The shearwater circles over the water, ranging out from the nest a quarter of a mile, and veers gradually toward the cliff, making passes at its nest. If the flight angle is precisely right, the bird will fold its wings at the hole's entrance and stall directly onto its floor. The angle is perhaps seldom right, however; one shearwater I watched made a dozen suicidal-looking passes before it vanished into a chink. The other behavior is spectacular. It involves choosing the nest hole in a site below a prominent rock with a downward-angled face. The shearwater comes careering in at full tilt, claps its wings, stalls itself into the rock, and the rock, acting as a backboard, banks it home.

The animals are tame. They have not been persecuted, and show no fear of man. You pass among them as though you were wind, spindrift, sunlight, leaves. The songbirds are tame. On Hood Island I sat beside a nesting waved albatross while a mockingbird scratched in my hair, another mockingbird jabbed at my fingernail, and a third mockingbird made an exquisite progression of pokes at my bare feet up the long series of eyelets in my basketball shoes. The marine iguanas are tame. One settler, Carl Angermeyer, built his house on the site of a marine iguana colony. The gray iguanas, instead of moving out, moved up on the roof, which is corrugated steel. Twice daily on the patio, Angermeyer feeds them a mixture of boiled rice and tuna fish from a plastic basin. Their names are all, unaccountably, Annie. Angermeyer beats on the basin with a long-handled spoon, calling, "Here AnnieAnnieAnnieAnnie"—and the spiny reptiles, fifty or sixty strong, click along the steel roof, finger their way down the lava boulder and mortar walls, and swarm around his bare legs to elbow into the basin and be elbowed out again smeared with a mash of boiled rice on their bellies and on their protuberant, black, plated lips.

The wild hawk is tame. The Galápagos hawk is related to North America's Swainson's hawk; I have read that if you take pains, you can walk up and pat it. I never tried. We people don't walk up and pat each other; enough is enough. The animals' critical distance and mine tend to coincide, so we could enjoy an easy sociability without threat of violence or unwonted intimacy. The hawk, which is not notably sociable, nevertheless endures even a blundering approach, and is apparently as content to perch on a scrub tree at your shoulder as anyplace else.

In the Galápagos, even the flies are tame. Although most of the land is Ecuadorian national park, and as such rigidly protected, I confess I gave the evolutionary ball an offsides shove by dispatching every fly that bit me, marveling the while at its pristine ignorance, its blithe failure to register a flight trigger at the sweep of my descending hand—an insouciance that was almost, but not quite, disarming. After you kill a fly, you pick it up and feed it to a lava lizard, a bright-throated four-inch lizard that scavenges everywhere in the arid lowlands. And you walk on, passing among the innocent mobs on every rock hillside; or you sit, and they come to you.

We are strangers and sojourners, soft dots on the rocks. You have walked along the strand and seen where birds have landed, walked, and flown;

their tracks begin in sand, and go, and suddenly end. Our tracks do that: but we go down. And stay down. While we're here, during the seasons our tents are pitched in the light, we pass among each other crying "greetings" in a thousand tongues, and "welcome," and "good-bye." Inhabitants of uncrowded colonies tend to offer the stranger famously warm hospitality—and such are the Galápagos sea lions. Theirs is the greeting the first creatures must have given Adam—a hero's welcome, a universal and undeserved huzzah. Go, and be greeted by sea lions.

I was sitting with ship's naturalist Soames Summerhays on a sand beach under cliffs on uninhabited Hood Island. The white beach was a havoc of lava boulders black as clinkers, sleek with spray, and lambent as brass in the sinking sun. To our left a dozen sea lions were body-surfing in the long green combers that rose, translucent, half a mile offshore. When the combers broke, the shoreline boulders rolled. I could feel the roar in the rough rock on which I sat; I could hear the grate inside each long backsweeping sea, the rumble of a rolled million rocks muffled in splashes and the seethe before the next wave's heave.

To our right, a sea lion slipped from the ocean. It was a young bull; in another few years he would be dangerous, bellowing at intruders and biting off great dirty chunks of the ones he caught. Now this young bull, which weighed maybe 120 pounds, sprawled silhouetted in the late light, slick as a drop of quicksilver, his glistening whiskers radii of gold like any crown. He hauled his packed bulk toward us up on the long beach; he flung himself with an enormous surge of fur-clad muscle onto the boulder where I sat. "Soames," I said—very quietly, "he's here because *we're* here, isn't he?" The naturalist nodded. I felt water drip on my elbow behind me, then the fragile scrape of whiskers, and finally the wet warmth and weight of a muzzle, as the creature settled to sleep on my arm. I was catching on to sea lions.

Walk into the water. Instantly sea lions surround you, even if none has been in sight. To say that they come to play with you is not especially anthropomorphic. Animals play. The bull sea lions are off patrolling their territorial shores; these are the cows and young, which range freely. A five-foot sea lion peers intently into your face, then urges her muzzle gently against your underwater mask and searches your eyes without blinking. Next she rolls upside down and slides along the length of your floating body, rolls again, and casts a long glance back at your eyes. You are, I believe, supposed to follow, and think up something clever in return. You can play games with sea lions in the water using shells or bits of leaf, if you are willing. You can spin on your vertical axis and a sea lion will swim circles around you, keeping her face always six inches from yours, as though she were tethered. You can make a game of touching their back flippers, say, and the sea lions will understand at once; somersaulting conveniently before your clumsy hands, they will give you an excellent field of back flippers.

And when you leave the water, they follow. They don't want you to go. They porpoise to the shore, popping their heads up when they lose you and casting about, then speeding to your side and emitting a choked series of vocal notes. If you won't relent, they disappear, barking; but if you sit on the beach with so much as a foot in the water, two or three will station with you, floating on their backs and saying, Urr.

Few people come to the Galápagos. Buccaneers used to anchor in the bays to avoid pursuit, to rest, and to lighter on fresh water. The world's whaling ships stopped here as well, to glut their holds with fresh meat in the form of giant tortoises. The whalers used to let the tortoises bang around on deck for a few days to empty their guts; then they stacked them below on their backs to live—if you call that living—without food or water for a year. When they wanted fresh meat, they killed one.

Early inhabitants of the islands were a desiccated assortment of grouches, cranks, and ships' deserters. These hardies shot, poisoned, and enslaved each other off, leaving behind a fecund gang of feral goats, cats, dogs, and pigs whose descendants skulk in the sloping jungles and take their tortoise hatchlings neat. Now scientists at the Charles Darwin Research Station, on the island of Santa Cruz, rear the tortoise hatchlings for several years until their shells are tough enough to resist the crunch; then they release them in the wilds of their respective islands. Today, some few thousand people live on three of the islands; settlers from Ecuador, Norway, Germany, and France make a livestock or pineapple living from the rich volcanic soils. The settlers themselves seem to embody a high degree of courteous and conscious humanity, perhaps because of their relative isolation.

On the island of Santa Cruz, eleven fellow passengers and I climb in an open truck up the Galápagos' longest road; we shift to horses, burros, and mules, and visit the lonely farm of Alf Kastdalen. He came to the islands as a child with his immigrant parents from Norway. Now a broad, blond man in his late forties with children of his own, he lives in an isolated house of finished timbers imported from the mainland, on four hundred acres he claimed from the jungle by hand. He raises cattle. He walks us round part of his farm, smiling expansively and meeting our chatter with a willing, open gaze and kind words. The pasture looks like any pasture—but the rocks under the grass are round lava ankle-breakers, the copses are a tangle of thorny bamboo and bromeliads, and the bordering trees dripping in epiphytes are breadfruit, papaya, avocado, and orange.

Kastdalen's isolated house is heaped with books in three languages. He knows animal husbandry; he also knows botany and zoology. He feeds us soup, chicken worth chewing for, green *naranjilla*[2] juice, noodles, pork in big chunks, marinated mixed vegetables, rice, and bowl after bowl of bright mixed fruits.

And his isolated Norwegian mother sees us off; our beasts are ready. We will ride down the mud forest track to the truck at the Ecuadorian settlement, down the long road to the boat, and across the bay to the ship. I lean down to catch her words. She is gazing at me with enormous warmth. "Your hair," she says softly. I am blond. *Adiós.*

II

Charles Darwin came to the Galápagos in 1835, on the *Beagle;* he was twenty-six. He threw the marine iguanas as far as he could into the water; he rode the tortoises and sampled their meat. He noticed that the tortoises' carapaces varied wildly from island to island; so also did the forms of various mockingbirds. He made collections. Nine years later he wrote in a letter, "I am almost convinced (quite contrary to the opinion I started with) that species are not (it is like confessing a murder) immutable." In 1859 he published *On the Origin of Species*, and in 1871 *The Descent of Man.* It is fashionable now to disparage Darwin's originality; not even the surliest of his detractors, however, faults his painstaking methods or denies his impact.

Darwinism today is more properly called neo-Darwinism. It is organic evolutionary theory informed by the spate of new data from modern genetics, molecular biology, paleobiology—from the new wave of the biologic revolution which spread after Darwin's announcement like a tsunami. The data are not all in. Crucial first appearances of major invertebrate groups are missing from the fossil record—but these early forms, sometimes modified larvae, tended to be fragile either by virtue of their actual malleability or by virtue of their scarcity and rapid variation into "hardened," successful forms. Lack of proof in this direction doesn't worry scientists. What neo-Darwinism seriously lacks, however, is a description of the actual mechanism of mutation in the chromosomal nucleotides.

In the larger sense, neo-Darwinism also lacks, for many, sheer plausibility. The triplet splendors of random mutation, natural selection, and Mendelian inheritance are neither energies nor gods; the words merely describe a gibbering tumult of materials. Many things are unexplained,

[2] Little orange.

many discrepancies unaccounted for. Appending a very modified neo-Lamarckism to Darwinism would solve many problems—and create new ones. Neo-Lamarckism holds, without any proof, that certain useful acquired characteristics may be inherited. Read C. H. Waddington, *The Strategy of the Genes*, and Arthur Koestler, *The Ghost in the Machine*. The Lamarckism/Darwinism issue is not only complex, hinging perhaps on whether DNA can be copied from RNA, but also politically hot. The upshot of it all is that while a form of Lamarckism holds sway in Russia, neo-Darwinism is supreme in the West, and its basic assumptions, though variously modified, are not overthrown.

So much for scientists. The rest of us didn't hear Darwin as a signal to dive down into the wet nucleus of a cell and surface with handfuls of strange new objects. We were still worried about the book with the unfortunate word in the title: *The Descent of Man*. It was dismaying to imagine great-grandma and great-grandpa effecting a literal, nimble descent from some liana-covered tree to terra firma, scratching themselves, and demanding bananas.

Fundamentalist Christians, of course, still reject Darwinism because it conflicts with the creation account in Genesis. Fundamentalist Christians have a very bad press. Ill feeling surfaces when, from time to time in small towns, they object again to the public schools' teaching evolutionary theory. Tragically, these people feel they have to make a choice between the Bible and modern science. They live and work in the same world as we, and know the derision they face from people whose areas of ignorance are perhaps different, who dismantled their mangers when they moved to town and threw out the baby with the straw.

Even less appealing in their response to the new evolutionary picture were, and are, the social Darwinists. Social Darwinists seized Herbert Spencer's phrase, "the survival of the fittest," applied it to capitalism, and used it to sanction ruthless and corrupt business practices. A social Darwinist is unlikely to identify himself with the term; social Darwinism is, as the saying goes, not a religion but a way of life. A modern social Darwinist wrote the slogan "If you're so smart, why ain't you rich?" The notion still obtains, I believe, wherever people seek power: that the race is to the swift, that everybody is *in* the race, with varying and merited degrees of success or failure, and that reward is its own virtue.

Philosophy reacted to Darwin with unaccustomed good cheer. William Paley's fixed and harmonious universe was gone, and with it its meticulous watchmaker god. Nobody mourned. Instead philosophy shrugged and turned its attention from first and final causes to analysis of certain values here in time. "Faith in progress," the man-in-the-street philosophy, collapsed in two world wars. Philosophers were more guarded; pragmatically, they held a very refined "faith in process"—which, it would seem, could hardly lose. Christian thinkers, too, outside of Fundamentalism, examined with fresh eyes the world's burgeoning change. Some Protestants, taking their cue from Whitehead, posited a dynamic god who lives alongside the universe, himself charged and changed by the process of becoming. Catholic Pierre Teilhard de Chardin, a paleontologist, examined the evolution of species itself, and discovered in that flow a surge toward complexity and consciousness, a free ascent capped with man and propelled from within and attracted from without by god, the holy freedom and awareness that is creation's beginning and end. And so forth. Like flatworms, like languages, ideas evolve. And they evolve, as Arthur Koestler suggests, not from hardened final forms, but from the softest plasmic germs in a cell's heart, in the nub of a word's root, in the supple flux of an open mind.

Darwin gave us time. Before Darwin (and Huxley, Wallace, et al.) there was in the nineteenth century what must have been a fairly nauseating period: people knew about fossils of extinct species, but did not yet know about organic evolution. They thought the fossils were litter from a series of past creations. At any rate, for many, this creation, the world as we know it, had begun in 4004 B.C., a date set by Irish Archbishop James Ussher in the seventeenth century. We were all crouched in a small room against the comforting back wall, awaiting the millennium which had been gathering impetus since Adam and Eve. Up there was a universe, and down here would be a small strip of man come and gone, created, taught, redeemed, and gathered up in a bright twinkling, like a sprinkling of confetti torn from colored papers, tossed from windows, and swept from the streets by morning.

The Darwinian revolution knocked out the back wall, revealing eerie lighted landscapes as far back as we can see. Almost at once, Albert Einstein and astronomers with reflector telescopes and radio telescopes knocked out the other walls and the ceiling, leaving us sunlit, exposed, and drifting—leaving us puckers, albeit evolving puckers, on the inbound curve of space-time.

III

It all began in the Galápagos, with these finches. The finches in the Galápagos are called Darwin's finches; they are everywhere in the islands, sparrowlike, and almost identical but for their differing beaks. At first Darwin scarcely noticed their importance. But by 1839, when he revised his *Journal* of the *Beagle* voyage, he added a key sentence about the finches' beaks: "Seeing this gradation and diversity of structure in one small, intimately related group of birds, one might really fancy that from an original paucity of birds in this archipelago, one species had been taken and modified for different ends." And so it was.

The finches come when called. I don't know why it works, but it does. Scientists in the Galápagos have passed down the call: you say pssssssh psssssh psssssh psssssh psssssh until you run out of breath; then you say it again until the island runs out of birds. You stand on a flat of sand by a shallow lagoon rimmed in mangrove thickets and call the birds right out of the sky. It works anywhere, from island to island.

Once, on the island of James, I was standing propped against a leafless *palo santo* tree on a semiarid inland slope, when the naturalist called the birds.

From other leafless *palo santo* trees flew the yellow warblers, speckling the air with bright bounced sun. Gray mockingbirds came running. And from the green prickly pear cactus, from the thorny acacias, sere grasses, bracken and manzanilla, from the loose black lava, the bare dust, the fern-hung mouths of caverns or the tops of sunlit logs—came the finches. They fell in from every direction like colored bits in a turning kaleidoscope. They circled and homed to a vortex, like a whirlwind of chips, like draining water. The tree on which I leaned was the vortex. A dry series of puffs hit my cheeks. Then a rough pulse from the tree's thin trunk met my palm and rang up my arm—and another, and another. The tree trunk agitated against my hand like a captured cricket: I looked up. The lighting birds were rocking the tree. It was an appearing act: before there were barren branches; now there were birds like leaves.

Darwin's finches are not brightly colored; they are black, gray, brown, or faintly olive. Their names are even duller: the large ground finch, the medium ground finch, the small ground finch; the large insectivorous tree finch; the vegetarian tree finch; the cactus ground finch, and so forth. But the beaks are interesting, and the beaks' origins even more so.

Some finches wield chunky parrot beaks modified for cracking seeds. Some have slender warbler beaks, short for nabbing insects, long for probing plants. One sports the long chisel beak of a woodpecker; it bores wood for insect grubs and often uses a twig or cactus spine as a pickle fork when the grub won't dislodge. They have all evolved, fanwise, from one bird.

The finches evolved in isolation. So did everything else on earth. With the finches, you can see how it happened. The Galápagos islands are near enough to the mainland that some strays could hazard there;

they are far enough away that those strays could evolve in isolation from parent species. And the separate islands are near enough to each other for further dispersal, further isolation, and the eventual reassembling of distinct species. (In other words, finches blew to the Galápagos, blew to various islands, evolved into differing species, and blew back together again.) The tree finches and the ground finches, the woodpecker finch and the warbler finch, veered into being on isolated rocks. The witless green sea shaped those beaks as surely as it shaped the beaches. Now on the finches in the *palo santo* tree you see adaptive radiation's results, a fluorescent splay of horn. It is as though an archipelago were an arpeggio, a rapid series of distinct but related notes. If the Galápagos had been one unified island, there would be one dull note, one super-dull finch.

IV

Now let me carry matters to an imaginary, and impossible, extreme. If the earth were one unified island, a smooth ball, we would all be one species, a tremulous muck. The fact is that when you get down to this business of species formation, you eventually hit some form of reproductive isolation. Cells tend to fuse. Cells tend to engulf each other; primitive creatures tend to move in on each other and on us, to colonize, aggregate, blur. (Within species, individuals have evolved immune reactions, which help preserve individual integrity; you might reject my liver—or someday my brain.) As much of the world's energy seems to be devoted to keeping us apart as was directed to bringing us here in the first place. All sorts of different creatures can mate and produce fertile offspring; two species of snapdragon, for instance, or mallard and pintail ducks. But they don't. They live apart, so they don't mate. When you scratch the varying behaviors and conditions behind reproductive isolation, you find, ultimately, geographical isolation. Once the isolation has occurred, of course, forms harden out, enforcing reproductive isolation, so that snapdragons will never mate with pintail ducks.

Geography is the key, the crucial accident of birth. A piece of protein could be a snail, a sea lion, or a systems analyst, but it had to start somewhere. This is not science; it is merely metaphor. And the landscape in which the protein "starts" shapes its end as surely as bowls shape water.

We have all, as it were, blown back together like the finches, and it's hard to imagine the isolation from parent species in which we evolved. The frail beginnings of great phyla are lost in the crushed histories of cells. Now we see the embellishments of random chromosomal mutations selected by natural selection and preserved in geographically isolate gene pools as *faits accomplis*, as the differentiated fringe of brittle knobs that is life as we know it. The process is still going on, but there is no turning back; it happened, in the cells. Geographical determination is not the cow-caught-in-a-crevice business I make it seem. I'm dealing in imagery, working toward a picture.

Geography is life's limiting factor. Speciation—life itself—is ultimately a matter of warm and cool currents, rich and bare soils, deserts and forests, fresh and salt waters, deltas and jungles and plains. Species arise in isolation. A plaster cast is as intricate as its mold; life is a gloss on geography. And if you dig your fists into the earth and crumble geography, you strike geology. Climate is the wind of the mineral earth's rondure, tilt, and orbit modified by local geological conditions. The Pacific Ocean, the Negev Desert, and the rain forest in Brazil are local geological conditions. So are the slow carp pools and splashing trout riffles of any backyard creek. It is all, God help us, a matter of rocks.

The rocks shape life like hands around swelling dough. In Virginia, the salamanders vary from mountain ridge to mountain ridge; so do the fiddle tunes the old men play. All this is because it is hard to move from mountain to mountain. These are not merely anomalous details. This is what life is all about: salamanders, fiddle tunes, you and me and things, the split and burr of it all, the fizz into particulars. No mountains and one salamander, one fiddle tune, would be a lesser world. No continents, no fiddlers. No possum, no sop, no taters. The earth, without form, is void.

The mountains are time's machines; in effect, they roll out protoplasm like printers' rollers pressing out news. But life is already part of the landscape, a limiting factor in space; life too shapes life. Geology's rocks and climate have already become Brazil's rain forest, yielding shocking bright birds. To say that all life is an interconnected membrane, a weft of linkages like chain mail, is truism. But in this case, too, the Galápagos islands afford a clear picture.

On Santa Cruz island, for instance, the saddleback carapaces of tortoises enable them to stretch high and reach the succulent pads of prickly pear cactus. But the prickly pear cactus on that island, and on other tortoise islands, has evolved a treelike habit; those lower pads get harder to come by. Without limiting factors, the two populations could stretch right into the stratosphere.

Ça va. It goes on everywhere, tit for tat, action and reaction, triggers and inhibitors ascending in a spiral like spatting butterflies. Within life, we are pushing each other around. How many animal forms have evolved just so because there are, for instance, trees? We pass the nitrogen around, and vital gases; we feed and nest, plucking this and that and planting seeds. The protoplasm responds, nudged and nudging, bearing the news.

And the rocks themselves shall be moved. The rocks themselves are not pure necessity, given, like vast, complex molds around which the rest of us swirl. They heave to their own necessities, to stirrings and prickings from within and without.

The mountains are no more fixed than the stars. Granite, for example, contains much oxygen and is relatively light. It "floats." When granite forms under the earth's crust, great chunks of it bob up, I read somewhere, like dumplings. The continents themselves are beautiful pea-green boats. The Galápagos archipelago as a whole is surfing toward Ecuador; South America is sliding toward the Galápagos; North America, too, is sailing westward. We're on floating islands, shaky ground.

So the rocks shape life, and then life shapes life, and the rocks are moving. The completed picture needs one more element: life shapes the rocks.

Life is more than a live green scum on a dead pool, a shimmering scurf like slime mold on rock. Look at the planet. Everywhere freedom twines its way around necessity, inventing new strings of occasions, lassoing time and putting it through its varied and spirited paces. Everywhere live things lash at the rocks. Softness is vulnerable, but it has a will; tube worms bore and coral atolls rise. Lichens in delicate lobes are chewing the granite mountains; forests in serried ranks trammel the hills. Man has more freedom than other live things; anti-entropically, he batters a bigger dent in the given, damming the rivers, planting the plains, drawing in his mind's eye dotted lines between the stars.

The old ark's a moverin'. Each live thing wags its home waters, rumples the turf, rearranges the air. The rocks press out protoplasm; the protoplasm pummels the rocks. It could be that this is the one world, and that world a bright snarl.

Like boys on dolphins, the continents ride their crustal plates. New lands shoulder up from the waves, and old lands buckle under. The very landscapes heave; change burgeons into change. Gray granite bobs up, red clay compresses; yellow sandstone tilts, surging in forests, incised by streams. The mountains tremble, the ice rasps back and forth, and the protoplasm furls in shock waves, up the rock valleys and down, ramifying possibilities, riddling the mountains. Life and the rocks, like spirit and matter, are a fringed matrix, lapped and lapping, clasping and held. It is like hand washing hand. It is like hand washing hand and the whole tumult hurled. The planet spins, rapt inside its intricate mists. The galaxy is a flung thing, loose in the night, and our solar system is one of many dotted campfires ringed with tossed rocks. What shall we sing?

What shall we sing, while the fire burns down? We can sing only specifics, time's rambling tune, the places we have seen, the faces we have known. I will sing you the Galápagos islands, the sea lions soft on the rocks. It's all still happening there, in real light, the cool currents upwelling, the finches falling on the wind, the shearwaters looping the waves. I could go back, or I could go on; or I could sit down, like Kubla Khan:

> Weave a circle round him thrice,
> And close your eyes with holy dread,
> For he on honey-dew hath fed,
> And drunk the milk of Paradise.

Shiva Naipaul
(1945–1985)

*Remembering the end of his student days at Oxford, Shiva Naipaul concludes, "For me, there were no tribal hopes or structures upon which to lean. I had no vision of myself; I would have to start afresh; to discover, unaided, my human possibility" ("From The Dragon's Mouth"). Born into an Indian family of Brahman caste transplanted to Trinidad, Shiva Naipaul, like his famous older brother, V. S. Naipaul, became a world traveller and a master of both fiction and nonfiction. "I write out of necessity," he explains, "to understand the world in which I live" ("My Brother and I"). The world in which he lives—*lived, *for Shiva Naipaul died suddenly and young, of a heart attack at forty, at the peak of his severely disciplined powers as an artist—is a postcolonial world, where the colonized are set adrift without cultural moorings and the colonizers' cultural heirs stay like uncomprehending zombies in the graveyards of their inheritance. The world's human places maintain themselves largely by fantasy. No matter if it is an African island paradise ("Fall from Innocence"), or a postindustrial English urban jungle ("On Cannibal Farm"), or a vast, teeming Asian city like Bombay where people come "to hustle," every place "perched on the edge of the abyss, frenziedly hammers together a makeshift existence" ("An Unfinished Journey"). "Bombay gives everyone a chance to live," according to "City by the Sea" (*Beyond the Dragon's Mouth, 1985). *But irony builds on irony in this simple statement of fact, much as in Naipaul's original title for the essay: "Taking Shelter in Bombay"* (Geo, *1981). Unlike other Indian cities, which "effectively destroy the free play of personality," Bombay may "offer liberation," may give even its seventy million rats a chance at living; but the place gives little enough "shelter" and, besides "liberation," offers its infamous "cages": "Bombay deceives at every level." Naipaul moves through it all as one of "the detribalized" ("My Brother and I"), recording and reporting, at every level, the "variety, color, comforts, culture" of these deceptions. For a "man compounded of ruins," as he described himself in his last essay ("An Unfinished Journey"), a man with no apparent ideological agenda, the question is "how to become properly real." The key would seem to be "properly"; and the "properly real" of this culturally disinherited and immensely hard-working writer seems to lie in the trail of his writing, which, like travel, is for Naipaul not a process of self-definition but a way of laying to rest any culturally shaped egoistic remainders: "a form of gradual self-extinction."*

The City by the Sea

The middle-class lady frowned.

"Bombay?" she said. "There's nothing specially interesting about Bombay. It's just another big cosmopolitan city, like any other. Only more people. That's all."

Below us, on a floodlit tennis court, an international tennis tournament was in progress. Pretty Indian girls in T-shirts and fashionably patched jeans dotted the wooden terraces erected for the occasion. The warm night was scented with a smell of dust. Lit-up skyscrapers loomed like mountain ranges. The match ended, the victorious Indian player shaking hands with his American opponent. Without warning, the spell was broken.

Out of nowhere, as if born of the musty night itself, a small army of sweepers invaded the court, meagre, stick-limbed men wielding short, soft brooms. Crouched on their haunches, their gaze anchored to the ground, they began brushing the playing surface. The middle-class lady did not look at this dwarfish, less-than-human crew. They were not supposed to be looked at: they were excluded from her vision of the cosmopolitan city. The sweepers, their job done, vanished as silently and as suddenly as they had come. Another match began; we left. Outside, established on the pavement, was a colony of five or six squatter huts. Within the low, dark interiors, fires burned. A smell of excrement tainted the smoky air. Ragged children crawled in the dust. Nearby, a group of dhoti-clad men lounged under a banyan tree. A beggar whined and was ignored. All about us the seething city hummed. The lady, lifting the border of her sari, looked at nothing.

I was seeing the city with the uncharitable eyes of the freshly arrived visitor. My responses on that first evening were raw, touched with a mild hysteria. Bombay, it is said, offers no "foreplay." It makes no concessions. Like New York, it plunges you straight in. I had arrived only hours before, in a dawn white with unseasonal rain. Even at that early hour a sea of urgent brown faces was to be seen pressed up against the glass doors of the terminal building. What were they waiting for? What did they want? There had been a moment of recoil; a dread of venturing out into the nightmare at which they hinted.

It was a long ride through the grey, humid morning to the city centre, through mile after mile of endlessly repeated suburban squalor—always, it seemed, the same squatter colonies (they spring up like mould on every available space), the same moss-blackened, uncared-for apartment blocks draped with washing, the same gaudy film posters adorned with fleshy, pink-faced women, the same rows of cramped shops, the same overwhelming sense of too many people spilling from crowded pavement into crowded street. At the traffic lights the beggars descended, thrusting their hands through the window, whining a litany of want, pointing now at their mouths, now at their bellies, now at the dirt-encrusted baby invariably attached to their hips. My driver was garrulous. Was it true that in London a man would be paid by the Government even if he did no work? A friend had told him that. If that was so, London must be a truly wonderful place. In Bombay, if a man did no work, he starved. "Bombay no good, sahib. No good at all." He fell silent for a while.

Then: "I have nice girl cousin, sahib."

"I'm glad to hear that."

"College girl. Educated. Very modern."

I waited.

"Eight hundred rupees one whole night, sahib. Modern girl."

"Would you really sell your girl cousin to me?"

He laughed; and began to tell me of men who sold their wives, their daughters, their sisters. "When life is hard, sahib, a man will do anything."

On that first day, then, it seemed a city of terror, of despair. But I was wrong—or, at any rate, only partly right. It takes time to read Bombay. It takes time to understand that those moss-blackened apartment blocks are not slums, that they very probably are the homes of middle-class people and that the outer neglect is deceptive. It takes time to understand that those squatter huts occupying the pavement outside the stadium may contain transistor radios and gas cookers, that the men who live in them may have regular clerkly jobs and be earning three or four hundred rupees a month—a decent wage by Indian standards. It takes time to penetrate the veil of apparently hopeless dereliction and to see that the city still works reasonably well: buses run; trains run; electricity lights the roads and skyscrapers; water (more or less) flows; telephones (more or less) work. Bombay lives.

So it happens that, after an interval, the nightmare begins to fade and another idea of Bombay becomes possible. This is the vision of the city as it can be seen from Marine Drive, that lovely stretch of road, curving round a bay washed by the waters of the Arabian Sea, bordered to the north by the residential towers of Malabar Hill, home of businessmen and film-stars, and, to the south, by the towers of Nariman Point, reclaimed from the sea within the last ten years. To enhance the vision, go to the Taj Mahal Hotel. Sit in its marbled, air-conditioned lobby, which looks east, toward the Gateway of India, the harbour and the Indian mainland. Middle-class Bombay uses this lobby as a kind of grand piazza—a piazza locked away behind glass and protected from unseemly invasion by stern-faced Sikhs. Watch the carefully dressed families who come to parade, to examine the rich displays of jewellery and textiles, to read the advertisements for holidays in Goa. Or go, in the late afternoon, to the Gymkhana Club. Sit out on its long veranda with views of the towers, domes and spires of Victorian Bombay. Watch the young men playing rugger and the white-clad tennis players strolling to and from the courts. Or go, at lunch time, to the restaurant attached to the Jehangir Art Gallery and observe the young journalists, secretaries and advertising executives who gather there. Gradually, the visitor begins to sense the liveliness, the glamour, of the city; he begins to appreciate—if not wholly to accept—some of the claims that are made for it.

That glamour, at its most extreme, slides into the dreams and fantasies spawned by the film world. Bombay, the centre of the prolific Indian film industry, churns out about eighty films a year. Nearly all are bad—so bad that they indicate a collective derangement of the intelligence. But this does not matter because, ultimately, it is not the films that count (in most of these films the actors simply play up their popular "images") but the stars themselves. Magazines like *Stardust*, *Filmfare* and *Super* (to name only those published in English) are entirely devoted to chronicling their doings. The stars exist to embody all the lusts and longings of a deprived urban population. Film after bad film recycles elemental dreams of riches, of fair women, of virility, of humble virtue conquering arrogant vice.

The wealth accumulated by the more successful actors and actresses verges on the fabulous: some are paid a million or more rupees per film and a few are so versatile that they will have five or six films on hand at any one time. Their houses are palatial. At their parties, Scotch whisky, selling in India from thirty pounds a bottle, is rumoured to flow like water. They drive about in air-conditioned Cadillacs and Mercedes Benzes—though one actor of left-wing persuasion contents himself with a red, chauffeur-driven Volkswagen.

Now and then they descend from their celestial mansions and display themselves to their devotees. One such manifestation occurred while I was there. Its heavily publicised purpose was to collect money for the victims of the cyclone which had struck the state of Andhra a week or two before. Dressed in specially made white suits, the stars toured the streets of the city on the backs of lorries. How much money was actually collected remains obscure. More memorable was the assault on two gossip columnists by one of the white-clad actors: he had been outraged by something they had written about him. It was *that* which made the headlines in the newspapers next day. The victims of the cyclone were forgotten.

The stars are the tutelary deities of Bombay—in a curious way the photographs that appear in the film magazines do echo the gaudy representations of the Hindu pantheon sold on every street corner. They are the guardians of the city's glamour and its promise. In a town where millions are compelled to eke out choked, near-impossible lives, they allow the imagination room to expand. They speak directly to the destitute. At all hours of the day Bombay's cinema houses are surrounded by gawking crowds of young men staring up at the glittering posters. Within, for a few rupees, they will be offered cloud-capped dreams. Bombay's cinemas are the opium dens of the masses.

Bombay, you will be told time and again, is like no other city in India. Indeed, its enthusiasts will point out, it is India's only "real" city. Delhi is dismissed as too Punjabi-dominated, too obsessed by political intrigue and the niceties of the bureaucratic pecking order. Calcutta, despite its surviving pockets of English-influenced gentility, remains, at bottom, a Bengali preserve. Madras is of the orthodox Hindu South. Bombay, on the other hand, belongs to no one and everyone. Hindu, Muslim, Parsi, British—all have played a part in the creation of the city.

In the Indian sense of home, of what is quaintly referred to as a "native place," Bombay is home to very few of its seven million people—with the possible exception of the Parsis who began migrating from Gujerat to the comforts of British rule in the seventeenth century. "If a man tells you Bombay is his home," I was told, "that means he is without roots." This lack of ancestral attachment adds yet another dimension to the glamour of the city. It undermines the constraints traditionally imposed by the varied and stifling communalisms—of family, caste, religion, region—which drive such deep and damaging fissures through all layers of Indian society and effectively destroy the free play of personality.

Bombay offers liberation. The individual can flower. He can, if he so wishes, cultivate his eccentricities. "Here," the journalist said, "I can wear cheap rubber slippers to the office. I can dress how I like. Nobody cares. Nobody gives a damn. I couldn't do that in Allahabad." A small victory, but, for him, one worth celebrating and savouring. In Bombay you can lead your own life. You can be anonymous. You can go up to your flat on the twentieth floor and lock yourself away. In Bombay, you can have a lover; you can have a mistress.

But, if the visitor has to be on guard against over-reacting to the outer dereliction of the city, he has also to guard against overemphasising its modernity. Bombay is still of India. Its universality can be exaggerated. Everyone may belong to Bombay. But everyone—Parsi, Gujerati, Bohra, Goan, Maratha, Tamil, Sindhi—belongs in his own way. The city is a loose federation of communalisms, each of which tends to look after itself, each of which tends to mind its own business. The Parsis, running their own hospitals, schools and residential enclaves, are, perhaps, the most extreme example of communal self-sufficiency; but all the other communities, to a greater or lesser degree, follow the pattern.

Much of the life of the city is invisible. It runs underground, rarely surfacing, conducted through the parallel but non-communicating channels of the varied communalisms. Parsi politics (for example) touches only Parsis and is, in fact, known to few outsiders. It is entirely self-contained. One of the first things that strikes one about the city—and Bombay, it should be noted, crawls with journalists—is the absence of any overall community of news and intellectual exchange. "Bombay," as such, is an administrative abstraction. A strike of thousands of government workers passes almost unnoticed: no one discusses the issues involved. Who, you ask, are those people marching down the street waving banners? What are they protesting about? Nobody is certain. Every event is isolated, as significant or insignificant as any other, appearing out of the blue and disappearing into the blue. Nothing joins up to make a coherent picture. In countries where journalism is a developed art, the newspapers tell a continuing story. The stranger finds himself, as it were, plunged into the middle of a long-running serial. After a while, however, he begins to pick up the strands of the plot. He becomes familiar with the issues and the main characters of the drama. This does not happen in Bombay. The city is permanently out of focus.

Universalism exists only in the upper reaches of Bombay society. It is in this tiny area that one finds the "cosmopolitanism" referred to by the middle-class lady. This cosmopolitanism looks to the West for inspiration and sustenance; but it too must be treated with caution and not over-rated. The concern, for instance, with pollution and the environment is little more than a modish affectation, a direct, unadapted import. Bombay matrons will weep over the victims of thalidomide but lose interest when the talk turns to the one hundred thousand waifs at large in the city. A favourable review of an Indian film in a foreign newspaper will be presented as an immutable, eternal judgment, the final guarantee of its worth. The actress whose chief claim to fame in her own and the city's eyes is that she once played a part in an American film tells you how much she adores London, how, really, it is her true spiritual home. As it happens, she is not all that successful by the standards of the Indian cinema. This, her friends say admiringly, is because she is far too "westernised," far too "sophisticated" (in the American film she bared her breasts) for simple Indian audiences. As we talk, three white-haired poodles play about her feet—dogs, especially large, protein-consuming dogs, are very fashionable in Bombay just now.

"Where do you take them for walks?" I ask. The animals do not look well. They must suffer from the heat and the physical constrictions of life in a Bombay high-rise flat.

She looks shocked. "*I* don't take them for walks," she replies. "That's *her* job." She points at a ragged maid-servant hovering in the background.

Thus dog-ownership is separated from its implications. It is carried on in a void. Her dog-keeping is purely imitative, a gesture of homage to London and its spacious parks.

A group of architecture students is on strike. Surrounded by slogans, they sprawl under a geodesic dome. They are on strike because, at the end of their course, they will be awarded diplomas, not degrees. To justify their case, they tell the story of the professor of architecture who had a daughter of marriageable age. Two of the professor's students fell in love with the girl. One was reading for a diploma, the other for a degree. The degree student got the girl. I could get nothing more out of them. Architecture was irrelevant. They had no ideas, no plans. The geodesic dome implied nothing; it led nowhere. It was a misleading symbol of modernity.

Bombay is littered with misleading symbols of modernity. You soon learn not to be surprised at the girl who, looking as if she has stepped straight out of the pages of *Vogue* and doing what she calls an "international" job, can speak quite calmly of the arranged marriage (correct caste guaranteed) that may be lying ahead of her. You learn not to be surprised that an Australian cabaret star, making the simplest of sexual jokes, can reduce a "sophisticated" night-club audience to howls of laughter.

Bombay deceives at every level.

Over the last three years, on a hill-top in the suburb of Worli, a public garden has come into being. Previously, the hill was covered with the shacks of a shanty colony. Now there are terraced banks of flowers, well-tended lawns, an illuminated waterfall. The garden is not yet complete. In time there will be a lotus pool and a pavilion. In a city so choked for space, the creation of this garden is a small miracle. But it is worth a visit for another reason: it affords a visual summary of Bombay. To the west is the sea and the city of faery towers—the city of dreams. To the east are tightly-packed colonies of hutments. Beyond rise the chimneys of the textile mills, hazing the air with smoke—the city of labour and struggle. The Mill Area is another world. There are few connections between it and the middle-class town. Two hundred thousand people work in Bombay's textile industry—the mills are the largest employers of labour. Within them a stark industrial life is carried on. In vast sheds, swirling with cotton dust and humid as greenhouses (the humidity is deliberate—the cotton threads would break in a dry atmosphere), bare-backed men day and night tend ranks of clattering machinery. One in every six of these men will eventually develop tuberculosis; most call it a day after five or six years. Clustered round the mills are the densely-populated tenements known as *chawls*—one of the distinctive features of the architecture of old Bombay—where the mill-hands live. Twenty or more men (the vast majority of the mill-hands are migrant workers who have left their families behind in the village) may share a cell in these chawls, sleeping in shifts. But the money is reasonably good (the average wage is around five hundred rupees a month) and the competition for jobs is fierce: when life is hard, men will do anything.

It was the mills which, in the latter half of the nineteenth century, brought industrial boom and the beginnings of population explosion to Bombay. Until then, the town had grown slowly, outstripped in importance by Calcutta and Madras. The Portuguese had been the first European overlords of the area. They, however, did not do a great deal with it—a fort or two remains, not much else. In 1660 the island (or, rather, the series of tiny islands out of which Bombay is compounded) passed into the possession of the English king Charles II as part of the dowry brought by his Portuguese bride Catherine of Braganza. Eight years later, in return for an annual rent of ten pounds, he leased it to the merchants of the East India Company. At that time the Company—still struggling to establish a secure foothold in India—had its main trading station further to the north, at Surat in Gujerat. There they were vulnerable not only to the exactions of the corrupt officials of the Mughal Empire but to the depredations of the Mughals' enemies—the Hindu Marathas. Sea-girthed Bombay offered escape from both these plagues.

The Company, unlike its Portuguese predecessors, was free of sectarian passion. Profitable, unharassed trade—that was its sole concern. By the end of the seventeenth century, Bombay had already acquired the features by which it can still be recognised. "The people that live here," wrote one of the Company's surgeons, "are a mixture of most of the neighbouring countries, most of them fugitives and vagabonds, no account being here taken of them; others perhaps invited here by the liberty granted them in their several religions, which here are solemnised with variety of fopperies . . ." Across the sub-continent, in Calcutta and Madras, the British Raj soon hardened into the inflexible rituals and habits of imperial rule. That did not happen to quite the same extent in Bombay where the barriers to social contact between rulers and ruled were not as insurmountable as they were elsewhere. The influence of the westernised Parsis must have helped—in the 1830s Sir Jamsetjee Jeejeebhoy was entertaining Englishmen at his famous parties. So must have the pride of the Marathas, heirs to a powerful martial tradition—they would sit down as a matter of course in the presence of Englishmen. Such behaviour would have been unthinkable in Calcutta. But most important may have been the fact that everyone who lived in the city that offered refuge to all but was home to none was, to a certain degree, an adventurer. Everyone was on the make. Men came to Bombay to earn a living, to hustle. And that is why, after three hundred years, they still keep coming.

The migrants come, it has been estimated, at the rate of three hundred families a day. They come from everywhere, from Tamil Nadu (formerly Madras State), from Andhra Pradesh, from Kerala, from Mysore, from Assam in the distant north-east, from the hinterland of Maharashtra—of which Bombay happens to be the state capital. All India makes its claims on the cosmopolitan city. Six years ago the population of Bombay was six million; today it is seven and a half million; in 1990, at present rates of growth, it will have reached ten million; and by the year 2000 it will be fifteen or sixteen million. The migrants pour into an area that is just under 350 square kilometres in extent.

The statistics numb—as they always do in India. Every night one and a half million people sleep out on the city's streets and pavements. The number who live permanently on the pavements is put—conservatively in my opinion—at one hundred thousand. Because Bombay is built on a series of narrow islands (they call it a linear city), the suburbs stretch northwards to the point of absurdity. It is possible to spend four or more hours a day in travelling to and from one's place of work. At rush hours the lemming-like crowds stampeding in and out of the Victoria Terminus are a frightening spectacle. Suburban trains carry nearly twice the number of passengers for which they are designed. As a result, three or four people are killed or seriously maimed every day, accidents which the newspapers do not even bother to report. The water supply is hopelessly inadequate. Improvements are being undertaken with the help of the World Bank but, by the time those have been completed, demand would once again have outstripped supply. Raw sewage washes into the sea. Nearly a third of the population is without sanitary facilities. Not surprisingly, millions are afflicted with energy-sapping gastric complaints.

Towards dusk the rats—there are supposed to be seventy million rats in Bombay, ten for every human being—and the cockroaches make their appearance, swarming about the Gateway of India and the broad promenade that borders the Worli Seaface. In the early evening, every yellow-lit window in every multi-storey block thrown wide open to the stagnant air rich with the smell of smoke and food, every transistor radio turned to full volume, every car horn blaring, every voice raised to a shout, the human immensity rages with something approaching frenzy. Bombay, while it remains awake, knows no stillness, no solitude. Only late at night does an exhausted peace descend as the yellow squares of light blink out, the cars disappear from the roads and the blanketed bodies ranged along the pavements assume all the abandoned attitudes of deep repose. Then, on the Worli Seaface, you can hear the wash of the waves on the rocks. For a few hours the city belongs to its seventy million rats and its as yet uncounted cockroaches; for a few hours man is held at bay.

Bombay looks for rescue—but without any great conviction—to its projected "twin city" (New Bombay) which, it is hoped, will arise one day on the mainland. The plans are both grandiose (they include the construction of six-mile-long bridges linking the island with the mainland) and detailed (even the optimum distance between bus-stops has been calculated). But the little that exists of the new city—a down-at-heel shopping precinct, a block or two of flats, a cluster of capital-intensive factories—still has about it the forlorn air of make-believe. There is certainly no correspondence between what exists and the fantasies of the planners—"Entering the harbour one would see the city on both sides, on the one side extending over the island, and on the other rising above its shores into the hills beyond. In the harbour and across the bridges one would see a constant and busy movement . . . Citizens from all over the island . . . would cross to the Eastern waterfront where would be located large, magnificent plazas . . ." It is a dream that no one really believes in. The State government, in a burst of enthusiasm, did promise to move to the new city but so far has shown no signs of actually being prepared to do so. In any case, India, under its new Janata rulers, is in the grip of a Gandhian resurgence which seeks salvation in village regeneration. Metropolitan grandeur is out of step with the humble mood of the times. While New Bombay languishes for lack of interest and money, Old Bombay continues to draw to itself the redundant humanity of unregenerated village India.

The stress shows. It is there in the middle-class obsession with housing: despite the spate of high-rise building in the last ten years, flats—and even single rooms—are not easy to come by. "Would you believe that I am forced to share one room with three other people?" the young, smartly-dressed executive asked. "I would like to get married. But how can I? Where can I take my wife? It's intolerable. It's no way to live." He could not stay any length of time in that room. To keep himself sane he walked. "I just walk and walk and walk when I have nothing better to do." The psychoanalyst adds his portion to the tale, telling of the fears of impotency that can arise from overcrowding and the lack of privacy it entails. In the squatter colonies drugs and cheap country liquor bring easy release at the weekends. That is the time for wife-beating and child-beating. In his dark, airless cell, the post office peon squats nervelessly. It is a public holiday, the Muslim festival of

Muharram. He has no plans to make use of the day. His eyes are glazed with apathy; he can hardly summon up the energy to speak. Outside, on the crumbling landing, inches away from the spot where his wife crouches preparing his midday meal, the leaking drainage pige has deposited a pool of fetid water. He will do nothing about that. He will do nothing about anything. He will not even complain. Occasionally, though, explosions do occur. Some years ago, the mobs of the Shiv Sena (the Army of Shiva), the vehicle of a revived Maratha nationalism which takes as its cult figure Sivaji, the seventeenth century Maratha warrior-hero, rampaged through the streets of the city beating up South Indian migrants and smashing their shops and restaurants. The surprising thing is that such outbreaks do not occur more often.

The migrants, despite everything, keep coming. A visit to a typical area out of which Bombay sucks people helps to explain why. Ratnagiri lies (by road) some two hundred miles south of Bombay. The land, sea-edged, traversed by rivers and hills, is full of beauty. But it is a cruel beauty. A largely landless peasantry lives off a diet of rice, coconut and—when they can get it—dried fish. Malnutrition has led to an incapacity for sustained labour, mental and physical. Prawns are caught in the sea off Ratnagiri, but these, deep-frozen and put into pretty boxes, are all exported to the United States and Japan. The trade is controlled by a handful of Bombay entrepreneurs. Ratnagiri benefits only in the form of the semi-sweated labour employed in the packaging factories. No other industrial development worth the name has taken place in the entire district. Men must depend on what the land can give; and the land by itself can give very little. Those who can, leave.

In one village I visited virtually the only people left were those too old and too young to go anywhere. At the entrance to the village I came upon a scene that could have come straight out of one of Hollywood's Biblical epics. Perhaps a dozen men, emaciated, all but naked, sun-blackened torsoes glistening with sweat, were at work in the red depths of a neatly-terraced laterite pit, quarrying the rock, shaping the blocks which are the basic building material of the district. On that diet of rice and coconut, on that burning, cloudless morning, their labour must have seemed like a punishment inflicted by a malevolent god. At best, a man could hack nine blocks a day out of the rock. For that, he would earn about six rupees—just enough, perhaps, to feed him, to give him the energy he needed to hack another nine blocks the next day.

Uncultivated plots surrounded the huts. The topsoil was so thin that, in many places, the rock floor was exposed. To make this land produce anything, mud has to be brought in every year. Only one crop a year was possible because of the village's total dependence on the rains. If the monsoon played truant for a week or so that crop would be ruined. Everyone was locked into a deathly dance with the rains; the relationship between a man and his food was direct and brutal. I entered a lightless hut. Children rose out of the darkness, surrounding me. My host—legs and arms as thin as sticks—had four brothers. They were all away in Bombay working on construction sites. Without their remittances, the children would starve. It was as simple as that. The land did not produce enough, could not produce enough, to feed even those who were left behind; and, in Ratnagiri, there was nothing but the land. They counted as rich the man who had enough to eat all the year round. In every hut I went into, the story was the same: sons in Bombay, husbands in Bombay, brothers and sisters in Bombay. Without Bombay they would die.

In Bombay, it seems, there is always work, always some way of earning a few rupees, of keeping body and soul together. Consider this family living on the pavement, seeking shelter under a lean-to built up from scraps of polythene, sacking, cardboard and wood. Three years ago they migrated from a village near Poona, walking all the way. Husband and wife and children scour the streets and refuse dumps of the city collecting rags, paper, discarded cigarette packets—anything that can be recycled. Their gleanings bring in seven or eight rupees a day. On that they can just about manage. In their home district such a thing would not have been possible. Bombay allows them to survive. The family next door also comes from a village near Poona. They roam the railway tracks collecting charcoal. That too brings in seven or eight rupees a day. Bombay gives everyone a chance to live.

Sometimes it gives more than that: it is a place where miracles of a sort may happen. A year ago this shoe-shine boy, who now wanders about the Gateway of India in search of customers, left his family in Calcutta and came to Bombay. He cannot be much more than thirteen years old. Usually he makes anything from five to twenty rupees a day. Today, he tells me, he has earned nothing. However, he was not too worried. Some weeks before he had had an amazing stroke of good fortune. One of his customers, a Frenchman, had, rather strangely, taken him along as a "guide" on a six-week tour of the country. They had been to Madras, Bangalore, Agra . . . they had gone everywhere, flying from place to place. The Frenchman had paid him fifty rupees a day. He had been able to save, he said, about two thousand rupees. A friend of his (as youthful and solitary as he was and also in the shoe-shine trade) confirmed the story.

"He very bright fellow," he said, nodding admiringly. He too, as it turned out, had his expectations. These were centred on a Dutchman who had promised to take him to Holland.

"He will go as houseboy," said the waif from Calcutta.

"No, no. Not houseboy," the other insisted. "I go as *tourist.* I go to see the place as tourist."

Bombay gives everyone a chance. A walk along any stretch of pavement will reveal a hundred minute specialisations of function, a hundred strategies for survival. You can hawk anything; water, nuts, cheap pens, toys, peacock feathers, religious bric-à-brac, plastic flowers, aphrodisiacs, quack medicines, lottery tickets, hard-luck stories—"Ladies and Gentlemen," says the handwritten appeal thrust into my hand by the teary-eyed, demurely dressed young girl, "we are unfortunate people, we have been driven from our land by poverty. We ask donations from charitable and human people . . ."; you can grind lenses, repair broken locks, stitch leather, sell cage-birds, charm snakes, read palms, interpret dreams, clean out the ears of passers-by; you can parade your dancing monkey, display your acrobatic skills, pick pockets. The will to live is capable of infinite articulation. When life is hard, a man will do anything.

The variety, the colour, of Bombay street life disguise its terrors. There are those who will deny that there are any terrors. The architect points to the photograph pinned on his office wall. It shows a man and a woman sitting down to their evening meal in a drainage pipe. "Isn't it wonderful!" he exclaims. "Look at them. Such formal poses. It's like a Mughal miniature painting!" You begin to protest. No!—he says. No! They may be poor. But what is wrong with poverty? Had I seen Detroit? Glasgow? Frankfurt? The people in these places were no happier than that couple who lived in a drainage pipe. Affluence breeds ugliness; it is degrading. In that drainage pipe a new "life-style" was being created. The photograph demonstrated the grandeur, the tenacity, of the human spirit.

Blessed are the hot, overcrowded cities of the Poor.

Mr. Narayan shuffled into the hotel. He stood there, in the marbled lobby, staring uneasily about him, a small, very dark man dressed in white shirt and white trousers. About him milled the gorgeous, nocturnal pageant of middle-class Bombay.

"Is it," he said, "as cool as this in London?"

"Often it's cooler. Quite a bit cooler."

"Then," he said, "they are right. London must be a paradise. All my friends say it's a kind of paradise over there. Is that true?"

"I think your friends exaggerate."

"But to be so cool . . . where I live it is never cool. But you will soon see for yourself. You will see how the poor people of Bombay live."

It was why he had come: to take me to his room, to show me how the poor people of Bombay lived. We went out into the warm night in search of a bus—he had responded with something like alarm to my suggestion that we take a taxi. Mr. Narayan (he came from Andhra) was a typesetter. For several months now he had been unemployed and was living off the savings he had managed to accumulate. "I have applied for how many jobs, sir, I cannot tell you. Typesetters are not greatly in demand at the moment."

Our double-decker bus moved like a Juggernaut through crowded, noisy streets. Mr. Narayan's fingers drummed nervously on the knees of his spotless white trousers. It was men like him—small men with small skills, for whom the life of the street represented not opportunity but the betrayal of possibility—it was men such as he who suffered most in Bombay. He took a sheaf of assorted documents out of his pocket and handed it to me—passport, health certificates, typesetting diploma, a letter from his previous employer stating that he had been a good and faithful worker. Mr. Narayan's life was contained in those papers and he never separated himself from them. "Now," he said, "I am concentrating all my efforts on going to the Gulf."

The Gulf was, of course, the Persian Gulf. It is the new El Dorado for those with any kind of expertise; and India is a bottomless reservoir of the middle- to low-range skills required by the oil-rich desert sheikdoms. Engineers, plumbers, waiters, motor-mechanics—they all want to go to the Gulf for a few years and make a small fortune. Every week the Kuwaiti consul in Bombay issues nearly one hundred work permits. The Arab, as ubiquitous a figure in Bombay as he is in London, has come to rival the film star in popular mythology.

But Mr. Narayan was afraid. The human traffic to the Gulf was controlled by a network of agents. It was these agents who located the going jobs, who fixed you up, and many were unscrupulous. The agent was asking Mr. Narayan four thousand rupees for his services and he had no idea what to do. He knew of several men who had been swindled out of their life-savings. "I will go mad if that happened to me, sir. I know it." Fearful of committing his money, yet knowing of no other way to get to the Gulf, he lived in an agony of indecision. Meanwhile, day by day, his savings dwindled.

We got off the bus. The street was thick with people. Music poured from brightly-lit foodshops.

"This," Mr. Narayan announced solemnly, "is red-light area."

There were women everywhere, roaming the pavements, standing on corners, looking down from the balconies and windows of upper floors. Soon we were among Bombay's notorious "cages." In cell after iron-barred cell stood or squatted groups of prostitutes, the younger and more nubile dressed in short skirts, the older in grimy, if colourful, saris.

In every nook and cranny overworked, ugly flesh was up for sale. Painted faces leered, pouted, simpered—or merely stared vacantly. A man could obtain animal relief in one of these pestilential dens for as little as three or four rupees.

A high proportion of the girls came from the South, from Mysore, where, apparently, there was still a lingering tradition of temple prostitution. Daughters were sacrificed by their families to the deva—the god. Many of these *devadasis* (slaves of the god), their lives effectively ruined, drifted to Bombay in due course, to a life of unvarnished prostitution. Others had been kidnapped or simply sold off by desperate fathers and husbands. Yet others had been lured into the trade by pimps who had promised to turn them into actresses: these men haunted the railway stations of Bombay, on the look-out for country girls coming to the city for the first time. For these, the dreams inspired by Bombay could melt swiftly into nightmare. A fortunate few might buy themselves freedom after five or six years; some might even find husbands. But the majority worked until they dropped dead, killed off by disease.

The cages fell away behind us. We turned down a lane teeming with children. "I will show you an aunt of mine," Mr. Narayan said. He led the way into an airless room, about ten foot square, on the ground floor of a tenement. A greying, wrinkled woman sat cross-legged on the floor. In front of her was a basin filled with loose tobacco and a bundle of tobacco leaves. Pictures of Hindu gods and goddesses lined the wall above her head. Cooking utensils were stacked neatly in a corner. The only item of furniture was a chest of drawers. Seven people lived in that room—the woman, her daughter, her son-in-law and her four grandchildren. The woman was making *bidis*, the hand-rolled cigarettes that are sold for next to nothing. She was able to roll one thousand bidis in twelve hours and worked seven days a week. In an average month she would earn about two hundred and fifty rupees. She had been rolling bidis for forty years. It was all she had ever done.

"Like a machine," Mr. Narayan whispered. "Like a machine."

The woman looked up at us and smiled. I watched the busy, expert fingers. They seemed to have a life of their own. Perhaps they were the only part of her that really lived. Age, Mr. Narayan explained, was beginning to catch up with his aunt. In the room next door was a younger woman who could roll fifteen hundred bidis in eight hours. His aunt, to compensate, had begun to train her twelve-year-old granddaughter in the art—the girl had been taken out of school; her fingers were too valuable an asset to be wasted. Already the child could roll five hundred in a day. A vicious karma had closed in about her. I looked at the girl who, covered from head to toe by a blanket, lay fast sleep, stretched out like a corpse against the far wall of the cell.

Mr. Narayan's room—it was in the same building—lay up a shaky, ladder-like flight of stairs. It was as tiny and airless as the one we had been into on the ground floor. But here there were definite signs of refinement—the name-plate on the door, the green-painted walls, the ceiling fan, the glass-fronted cabinet in which was stored the family's brassware, the rows of books on a wooden shelf and, most surprising of all, the small tank full of brightly-coloured tropical fish. Mr. Narayan's three children—two girls and a boy—lay asleep on the floor. A metal folding chair, obviously a highly prized possession, was presented with a flourish. I sat down and looked at the tropical fish.

"It is for *him* I got it," Mr. Narayan said, following my gaze. He pointed at his sleeping son. "I thought it would be educative for him to have such a thing to look at."

The boy was about seven years old. Mr. Narayan centred all his remaining ambitions on him.

"It is really for his sake that I wish to go to the Gulf," he said. "No way else can I get the money for him to pursue his studies. If he has no education what will become of him? It makes me afraid to think of that."

"What would you like your son to be when he grows up?"

"Maybe doctor. Maybe engineer. I am not sure. The choice will be his."

The boy stirred restlessly, half-opening his eyes. Mr. Narayan, reaching forward, caressed him. The boy slept again. He was being educated at a special "convent" school which cost his father thirty-five rupees a month—a not insubstantial sum. Mr. Narayan took down a leather schoolbag from the bookshelf and showed me an exercise book filled with drawings and Biblical maxims. I read and admired.

"One day my son will be a great man," he said.

I wanted to believe him.

The outdoor sleepers had already taken up their positions for the night when Mr. Narayan escorted me down the rickety stairs to the street. Bodies lined both sides of the roadway. In the cages the girls leaned sleepily against the bars, staring vacantly.

On Chowpatty beach the smell of excrement mingled with the smell of the sea. The pressure lamps of the foodstalls shone with flaring, painful brilliance. From afar came the cacophonous clatter of a temple. To the south curved Marine Drive. The faery towers of the dream city blazed with light. Indistinct figures squatted or walked along the water's edge. Nearby, a group of men and women sat in a circle, drumming and singing. Masseurs rose out of the darkness, soliciting custom. A statue of the elephant-headed god, Ganesh, grotesquely painted and ornamented, had been carved out of the sand. Offerings of money and flowers were strewn around the base. Strange city! It confounded hope and despair. One could never be sure where the one ended and the other began, so blurred was the boundary between realism and fantasy. "Citizens from all over the island . . . would cross to the Eastern waterfront where would be located large, magnificent plazas . . . one day my son will be a great man . . ." I listened to the drumming and singing.

Bombay lives because it denies its terrors.

Scott Russell Sanders

(b. 1945)

> *The working class and the employing class have nothing in common. There can be no peace so long as hunger and want are found among millions of working people and the few, who make up the employing class, have all the good things of life. (Preamble to the Constitution of the Industrial Workers of the World, or I.W.W.—nickname: Wobblies)*

In "Doing Time in the Thirteenth Chair" (The Paradise of Bombs, *1987*), *Scott Sanders, hoping to be excused from jury duty, describes, tongue in cheek, how he wishes the court to perceive him: "unreliable," "confessed fabulist," "marginal Quaker," "Wobbly socialist." Interested in both science and the arts, Cambridge-educated, claiming the "dirt-road soul" of a country boy* ("Coming from the Country") *as stubbornly as Huck Finn, author of folktales, essays, literary criticism, realistic and science fiction for adults and juveniles, this man who delights with his many faces and who believes the essay is for speaking "without disguise" may perhaps be glimpsed in his singular wholeness under the persona of a Wobbly. The IWW, or Wobblies, lost their organizational force within the U.S. labor movement by the 1920s; they remain in legendary memory as a kind of final surge of the old West: virile, singing, high-spirited workers pouring forth from Wobbly halls to take possession of a socioeconomic frontier freed from debilitating, exploitative capitalists lodged in the industrial East. The Wobblies spoke for the poorest, the dispossessed; they still do. As the thirteenth juror, Sanders suspends judgment on Bennie's guilt; his voice speaks for a Bennie that he himself might have become but for the grace of circumstance. The two who "stare across the courtroom at one another as into a funhouse mirror"—Bennie and Sanders—are, for the observer with a Wobbly conscience, distorted images of each other produced by class struggle. "I find myself brooding in essay after essay on the origins of violence," says Sanders (Introduction,* The Paradise of Bombs). *And Bennie's life is lived in a world of violence from which there is no apparent escape, down to the most pernicious violence of all: dispossessing a person of his time. Sanders narrates the fate of Bennie with all the historical self-awareness and pathos of workers' poetry, but the essay's grip on us is that of a lean, beautifully wrought short story.*

Doing Time in the Thirteenth Chair

The courtroom is filled with the ticking of a clock and the smell of mold. Listening to the minutes click away, I imagine bombs or mechanical hearts sealed behind the limestone walls. Forty of us have been yanked out of our usual orbits and called to appear for jury duty in this ominous room, beneath the stained-glass dome of the county courthouse. We sit in rows like strangers in a theater, coats rumpled in our laps, crossing and uncrossing our legs, waiting for the show to start.

I feel sulky and rebellious, the way I used to feel when a grade-school teacher made me stay inside during recess. This was supposed to have been the first day of my Christmas vacation, and the plain, uncitizenly fact is that I don't want to be here. I want to be home hammering together some bookshelves for my wife. I want to be out tromping the shores of Lake Monroe with my eye cocked skyward for bald eagles and sharp-shinned hawks.

But the computer-printed letter said to report today for jury duty, and so here I sit. The judge beams down at us from his bench. Tortoise-shell glasses, twenty-dollar haircut, square boyish face: although probably in his early forties, he could pass for a student-body president. He reminds me of an owlish television know-it-all named Mr. Wizard who used to conduct scientific experiments (Magnetism! Litmus tests! Sulphur dioxide!) on a kids' show in the 1950s. Like Mr. Wizard, he lectures us in slow, pedantic speech: trial by one's peers, tradition stretching back centuries to England, defendant innocent until proven guilty beyond a reasonable doubt, and so abundantly on. I spy around for the clock. It must be overhead, I figure, up in the cupola above the dome, raining its ticktocks down on us.

When the lecture is finished, the judge orders us to rise, lift our hands, and swear to uphold the truth. There is a cracking of winter-stiff knees as we stand and again as we sit down. Then he introduces the principal actors: the sleek young prosecutor, who peacocks around like a politician on the hustings; the married pair of brooding, elegantly dressed defense lawyers; and the defendant. I don't want to look at this man who is charged with crimes against the "peace and dignity" of the State of Indiana. I don't want anything to do with his troubles. But I grab an image anyway, of a squat, slit-eyed man about my age, mid-thirties, stringy black hair parted in the middle and dangling like curtains across his face, sparse black beard. The chin whiskers and squinted-up eyes make him look faintly Chinese, and faintly grimacing.

Next the judge reads a list of twelve names, none of them mine, and twelve sworn citizens shuffle into the jury box. The lawyers have at them, darting questions. How do you feel about drugs? Would you say the defendant there looks guilty because he has a beard? Are you related to any police officers? Are you pregnant? When these twelve have finished answering, the attorneys scribble names on sheets of paper which they hand to the judge, and eight of the first bunch are sent packing. The judge reads eight more names, the jury box fills up with fresh bodies, the questioning resumes. Six of these get the heave-ho. And so the lawyers cull through the potential jurors, testing and chucking them like two men picking over apples in the supermarket. At length they agree on a dozen, and still my name has not been called. Hooray, I think. I can build those bookshelves after all, can watch those hawks.

Before setting the rest of us free, however, the judge consults his list. "I am calling alternate juror number one," he says, and then he pronounces my name.

Groans echo down my inmost corridors. For the first time I notice a thirteenth chair beside the jury box, and that is where the judge orders me to go.

"Yours is the most frustrating job," the judge advises me soothingly. "Unless someone else falls ill or gets called away, you will have to listen to all the proceedings without taking part in the jury's final deliberations or decisions."

I feel as though I have been invited to watch the first four acts of a five-act play. Never mind, I console myself: the lawyers will throw me out. I'm the only one in the courtroom besides the defendant who sports a beard or long hair. A backpack decorated with NO NUKES and PEACE NOW and SAVE THE WHALES buttons leans against my boots. How can they expect me, a fiction writer, to confine myself to facts? I am unreliable, a confessed fabulist, a marginal Quaker and Wobbly socialist, a man so out of phase with my community that I am thrown into fits of rage by the local newspaper. The lawyers will take a good look at me and race one another to the bench for the privilege of having the judge boot me out.

But neither Mr. Defense nor Mr. Prosecution quite brings himself to focus on my shady features. Each asks me a perfunctory question, the way vacationers will press a casual thumb against the spare tire before hopping into the car for a trip. If there's air in the tire, you don't bother about blemishes. And that is all I am, a spare juror stashed away in the trunk of the court, in case one of the twelve originals gives out during the trial.

Ticktock. The judge assures us that we should be finished in five days, just in time for Christmas. The real jurors exchange forlorn glances. Here I sit, number thirteen, and nobody looks my way. Knowing I am stuck here for the duration, I perk up, blink my eyes. Like the bear going over the mountain, I might as well see what I can see.

* * *

What I see is a parade of mangled souls. Some of them sit on the witness stand and reveal their wounds; some of them remain offstage, summoned up only by the words of those who testify. The case has to do with the alleged sale, earlier this year, of hashish and cocaine to a confidential informer. First the prosecutor stands at a podium in front of the jury and tells us how it all happened, detail by criminal detail, and promises to prove every fact to our utter satisfaction. Next, one of the defense attorneys has a fling at us. It is the husband of the Mr.-and-Mrs. team, a melancholy-looking man with bald pate and mutton-chop sideburns, deep creases in the chocolate skin of his forehead. Leaning on the podium, he vows that he will raise a flock of doubts in our minds—grave doubts, reasonable doubts—particularly regarding the seedy character of the confidential informer. They both speak well, without hemming and hawing, without stumbling over syntactic cliffs, better than senators at a press conference. Thus, like rival suitors, they begin to woo the jury.

At mid-morning, before hearing from the first witness, we take a recess. (It sounds more and more like school.) Thirteen of us with peel-away JUROR tags stuck to our shirts and sweaters retreat to the jury room. We drink coffee and make polite chat. Since the only thing we have in common is this trial, and since the judge has just forbidden us to talk about that, we grind our gears trying to get a conversation started. I find out what everybody does in the way of work: a bar waitress, a TV repairman (losing customers while he sits here), a department store security guard, a dentist's assistant, an accountant, a nursing home nurse, a cleaning woman, a caterer, a mason, a boisterous old lady retired from rearing children (and married, she tells us, to a school-crossing guard), a meek college student with the demeanor of a groundhog, a teacher. Three of them right now are unemployed. Six men, six women, with ages ranging from twenty-one to somewhere above seventy. Chaucer could gather this bunch together for a literary pilgrimage, and he would not have a bad sampling of smalltown America.

Presently the bailiff looks in to see what we're up to. She is a jowly woman, fiftyish, with short hair the color and texture of buffed aluminum. She wears silvery half-glasses of the sort favored by librarians; in the courtroom she peers at us above the frames with a librarian's skeptical glance, as if to make sure we are awake. To each of us she now gives a small yellow pad and a ballpoint pen. We are to write our names on the back, take notes on them during the trial, and surrender them to her whenever we leave the courtroom. (School again.) Without saying so directly, she lets us know that we are her flock and she is our shepherd. Anything we need, any yen we get for traveling, we should let her know.

I ask her whether I can go downstairs for a breath of air, and the bailiff answers "sure." On the stairway I pass a teenage boy who is listlessly polishing with a rag the wrought-iron filigree that supports the banister. Old men sheltering from December slouch on benches just inside the ground-floor entrance of the courthouse. Their faces have been caved in by disappointment and the loss of teeth. Two-dollar cotton work gloves, the cheapest winter hand-covers, stick out of their back pockets. They are veterans of this place; so when they see me coming with the blue JUROR label pasted on my chest, they look away. Don't tamper with jurors, especially under the very nose of the law. I want to tell them I'm not a real juror, only a spare, number thirteen. I want to pry old stories out of them, gossip about hunting and dogs, about their favorite pickup trucks, their worst jobs. I want to ask them when and how it all started to go wrong for them. Did they hear a snap when the seams of their life began to come apart? But they will not be fooled into looking at me, not these wily old men with the crumpled faces. They believe the label on my chest and stare down at their unlaced shoes.

I stick my head out the door and swallow some air. The lighted thermometer on the bank reads twenty-eight degrees. Schmaltzy Christmas organ music rebounds from the brick-and-limestone shopfronts of the town square. The Salvation Army bell rings and rings. Delivery trucks hustling through yellow lights blare their horns at jaywalkers.

The bailiff must finally come fetch me, and I feel like a wayward sheep. On my way back upstairs, I notice the boy dusting the same square foot of iron filigree, and realize that he is doing this as a penance. Some judge ordered him to clean the metalwork. I'd like to ask the kid what mischief he's done, but the bailiff, looking very dour, is at my heels.

In the hallway she lines us up in our proper order, me last. Everybody stands up when we enter the courtroom, and then, as if we have rehearsed these routines, we all sit down at once. Now come the facts.

The facts are a mess. They are full of gaps, chuckholes, switchbacks, and dead ends—just like life.

At the outset we are shown three small plastic bags. Inside the first is a wad of aluminum foil about the size of an earlobe; the second contains two white pills; the third holds a pair of stamp-sized, squarish pockets of folded brown paper. A chemist from the state police lab testifies that he examined these items and found cocaine inside the brown packets, hashish inside the wad of aluminum foil. As for the white pills, they are counterfeits of a popular barbiturate, one favored by politicians and movie stars. They're depressants—downers—but they contain no "controlled substances."

There follows half a day's worth of testimony about how the bags were sealed, who locked them in the narcotics safe at the Bloomington police station, which officer drove them up to the lab in Indianapolis and which drove them back again, who carried them in his coat pocket and who carried them in his briefcase. Even the judge grows bored during this tedious business. He yawns, tips back in his chair, sips coffee from a mug, folds and unfolds with deft thumbs a square of paper about the size of the cocaine packets. The wheels of justice grind slowly. We hear from police officers in uniform, their handcuffs clanking, and from mustachioed officers in civvies, revolvers bulging under their suitcoats. From across the courtroom, the bailiff glares at us above her librarian's glasses, alert to catch us napping. She must be an expert at judging the degrees of tedium.

"Do you have to go back and be in the jail again tomorrow?" my little boy asks me at supper.

"Not jail," I correct him. "*Jury*. I'm in the jury."

"With real police?"

"Yes."

"And guns?"

"Yes, real guns."

On the second day there is much shifting of limbs in the jury box when the confidential informer, whom the police call I90, takes the stand. Curly-haired, thirty-three years old, bear-built and muscular like a middle-range wrestler, slow of eye, calm under the crossfire of questions, I90 works—when he works—as a drywall finisher. (In other words, he gets plasterboard ready for painting. It's a dusty, blinding job; you go home powdered white as a ghost, and you taste the joint-filler all night.) Like roughly one-quarter of the construction workers in the country, right now he's unemployed.

The story he tells is essentially this: Just under a year ago, two cops showed up at his house. They'd been tipped off that he had a mess of stolen goods in his basement, stuff he'd swiped from over in a neighboring county. "Now look here," the cops said to him, "you help us out with some cases we've got going, and we'll see what we can do to help you when this here burglary business comes to court." "Like how?" he said. "Like tell us what you know about hot property, and maybe finger a drug dealer or so." He said yes to that, with the two cops sitting at his kitchen table, and—zap!—he was transformed into I90. (Hearing of this miraculous conversion, I am reminded of Saul on the road to Damascus, the devil's agent suddenly seeing the light and joining the angels.) In this new guise he gave information that led to several arrests and some prison terms, including one for his cousin and two or three for other buddies.

In this particular case, his story goes on, he asked a good friend of his where a guy could buy some, you know, drugs. The friend's brother led him to Bennie's trailer, where Bennie offered to sell I90 about any kind of drug a man's heart could desire. "All I want's some hash," I90 told him, "but I got to go get some money off my old lady first." "Then go get it," said Bennie.

Where I90 went was to the police station. There they fixed him up to make a "controlled buy": searched him, searched his car; strapped a radio transmitter around his waist; took his money and gave him twenty police dollars to make the deal. Back I90 drove to Bennie's place, and on his tail in an unmarked police car drove Officer B., listening over the radio to every burp and glitch sent out by I90's secret transmitter. On the way, I90 picked up a six-pack of Budweiser. ("If you walk into a suspect's house drinking a can of beer," Officer B. later tell us, "usually nobody'll guess you're working for the police.") Inside the trailer, the woman Bennie lives with was now fixing supper, and her three young daughters were playing cards on the linoleum floor. I90 bought a gram of blond Lebanese hashish from Bennie for six dollars. Then I90 said that his old lady was on him bad to get her some downers, and Bennie obliged by selling him a couple of 714's (the white pills favored by movie stars and politicians) at seven dollars for the pair. They shot the bull awhile, Bennie bragging about how big a dealer he used to be (ten pounds of hash and five hundred hits of acid a week), I90 jawing along like an old customer. After about twenty minutes in the trailer, I90 drove to a secluded spot near the L & N railroad depot, and there he handed over the hash and pills to Officer B., who milked the details out of him.

Four days later, I90 went through the same routine, this time buying two packs of cocaine—two "dimes" worth—from Bennie for twenty dollars. Inside the trailer were half a dozen or so of Bennie's friends, drinking whiskey and smoking pot and watching TV and playing backgammon and generally getting the most out of a Friday night. Again Officer B. tailed I90, listened to the secret radio transmission, and took it all down in a debriefing afterwards behind the Colonial Bakery.

The lawyers burn up a full day leading I90 through this story, dropping questions like breadcrumbs to lure him on, Mr. Prosecutor trying to guide him out of the labyrinth of memory and Mr. Defense trying to get him lost. I90 refuses to get lost. He tells and retells his story without stumbling, intent as a wrestler on a dangerous hold.

On the radio news I hear that U.S. ships have intercepted freighters bound out from Beirut carrying tons and tons of Lebanese hashish, the very same prize strain of hash that I90 claims he bought from Bennie.

Not wanting to irk the Lebanese government, the radio says, our ships let the freighters through. Tons and tons sailing across the Mediterranean—into how many one-gram slugs could that cargo be divided?

Out of jail the defense lawyers subpoena one of I90's brothers, who is awaiting his own trial on felony charges. He has a rabbity look about him, face pinched with fear, ready to bolt for the nearest exit. His canary yellow T-shirt is emblazoned with a scarlet silhouette of the Golden Gate Bridge. The shirt and the fear make looking at him painful. He is one of seven brothers and four sisters. Hearing that total of eleven children—the same number as in my father's family—I wonder if the parents were ever booked for burglary or other gestures of despair.

This skittish gent tells us that he always buys his drugs from his brother, good old I90. And good old I90, he tells us further, has a special fondness for snorting cocaine. Glowing there on the witness stand in his yellow shirt, dear brother gives the lie to one after another of I90's claims. But just when I'm about ready, hearing all of this fraternal gossip, to consign I90 to the level of hell reserved by Dante for liars, the prosecutor takes over the questioning. He soon draws out a confession that there has been a bitter feud recently between the two brothers. "And haven't you been found on three occasions to be mentally incompetent to stand trial?" the prosecutor demands.

"Yessir," mutters the brother.

"And haven't you spent most of the past year in and out of mental institutions?"

"Yessir."

This second admission is so faint, like a wheeze, that I must lean forward to hear it, even though I am less than two yards away. While the prosecutor lets this damning confession sink into the jury, the rabbity brother just sits there, as if exposed on a rock while the hawks dive, his eyes pinched closed.

By day three of the trial, we jurors are no longer strangers to one another. Awaiting our entry into court, we exhibit wallet photos of our children, of nieces and nephews. We moan in chorus about our Christmas shopping lists. The caterer tells about serving 3,000 people at a basketball banquet. The boisterous old lady, to whom we have all taken a liking, explains how the long hairs on her white cats used to get on her husband's black suit pants until she put the cats out in the garage with heating pads in their boxes.

"Where do you leave your car?" the accountant asks.

"On the street," explains the lady. "I don't want to crowd those cats. They're particular as all get-out."

People compare their bowling scores, their insurance rates, their diets. The mason, who now weighs about 300 pounds, recounts how he once lost 129 pounds in nine months. His blood pressure got so bad he had to give up dieting, and inside of a year he'd gained all his weight back and then some. The nurse, who wrestles the bloated or shriveled bodies of elderly paupers at the city's old folks' home, complains about her leg joints, and we all sympathize. The security guard entertains us with sagas about shoplifters. We compare notes on car wrecks, on where to get a transmission overhauled, on the outgoing college football coach and the incoming city mayor. We talk, in fact, about everything under the sun except the trial.

In the hall, where we line up for our reentry into the courtroom, a sullen boy sits at a table scrawling on a legal pad. Line after line he copies the same sentence: "I never will steal anything ever again." More penance. He's balancing on the first rung of a ladder that leads up—or down—to the electric chair. Somewhere in the middle of the ladder is a good long prison sentence, and that, I calculate, is what is at stake in our little drug-dealing case.

On the third day of testimony, we learn that I90 has been hidden away overnight by police. After he stepped down from the witness stand yesterday, Bennie's mate, Rebecca, greeted the informant outside in the lobby and threatened to pull a bread knife out of her purse and carve him into mincemeat. I look with new interest at the stolid, bulky, black-haired woman who has been sitting since the beginning of the trial right behind the defendant. From time to time she has leaned forward, touched Bennie on the shoulder, and bent close to whisper something in his good ear. She reminds me of the Amish farm wives of my Ohio childhood—stern, unpainted, built stoutly for heavy chores, her face a fortress against outsiders.

When Rebecca takes the stand, just half a dozen feet from where I sit in chair thirteen, I sense a tigerish fierceness beneath her numb surface. She plods along behind the prosecutor's questions until he asks her, rhetorically, whether she would like to see Bennie X put in jail; then she lashes out. God no, she doesn't want him locked away. Didn't he take her in when she had two kids already and a third in the oven, and her first husband run off, and the cupboards empty? And haven't they been living together just as good as married for eight years, except while he was in jail, and don't her three little girls call him Daddy? And hasn't he been working on the city garbage trucks, getting up at four in the morning, coming home smelling like other people's trash, and hasn't she been bagging groceries at the supermarket, her hands slashed with paper cuts, and her mother looking after the girls, all so they can keep off the welfare? Damn right she doesn't want him going to any prison.

What's more, Rebecca declares, Bennie don't deserve prison because he's clean. Ever since he got out of the slammer a year ago, he's quit dealing. He's done his time and he's mended his ways and he's gone straight. What about the sale of cocaine? the prosecutor wants to know. It never happened, Rebecca vows. She was there in the trailer the whole blessed night, and she never saw Bennie sell nobody nothing, least of all cocaine, which he never used because it's too expensive—it'll run you seventy-five dollars a day—and which he never sold even when he was dealing. The prosecutor needles her: How can she remember that particular night so confidently? She can remember, she flares at him, because early that evening she got a call saying her sister's ten-year-old crippled boy was fixing to die, and all the family was going to the children's hospital in Indianapolis to watch him pass away. That was a night she'll never forget as long as she lives.

When I was a boy, my friends and I believed that if you killed a snake, the mate would hunt you out in your very bed and strangle or gnaw or smother you. We held a similar belief regarding bears, wolves, and mountain lions, although we were much less likely to run into any of those particular beasts. I have gone years without remembering that bit of child's lore, until today, when Rebecca's tigerish turn on the witness stand revives it. I can well imagine her stashing a bread knife in her purse. And if she loses her man for years and stony years, and has to rear those three girls alone, the cupboards empty again, she might well jerk that knife out of her purse one night and use it on something other than bread.

During recess, we thirteen sit in the jury room and pointedly avoid talking about the bread knife. The mason tells how a neighbor kid's Ford Pinto skidded across his lawn and onto his front porch, blocking the door and nosing against the picture window. "I took the wheels off and chained the bumper to my maple tree until his daddy paid for fixing my porch."

Everyone, it seems, has been assaulted by a car or truck. Our vehicular yarns wind closer and closer about the courthouse. Finally, two of the women jurors—the cigarillo-smoking caterer and the elderly cat lady—laugh nervously. The two of them were standing just inside the plate-glass door of the courthouse last night, the caterer says, when along came a pickup truck, out poked an arm from the window, up flew a smoking beer can, and then BAM! the can exploded. "We jumped a yard in the air!" cries the old woman. "We thought it was some of Bennie's mean-looking friends," the caterer admits. Everybody laughs at the tableau of speeding truck, smoking can, exploding cherry bomb, leaping jurors. Then we choke into sudden silence, as if someone has grabbed each of us by the throat.

Four of Bennie's friends—looking not so much mean as broken, like shell-shocked refugees—testify on his behalf during the afternoon of day three. Two of them are out-of-work men in their twenties, with greasy hair to their shoulders, fatigue jackets, and clodhopper boots: their outfits and world-weary expressions are borrowed from record jackets. They are younger versions of the old men with caved-in faces who crouch on benches downstairs, sheltering from December. The other two witnesses are young women with reputations to keep up, neater than the scruffy men; gold crosses dangle over their sweaters, and gum cracks between crooked teeth. All four speak in muttered monosyllables and orphaned phrases, as if they are breaking a long vow of silence and must fetch bits and pieces of language from the archives of memory. They were all at Bennie's place on the night of the alleged cocaine sale, and they swear in unison that no such sale took place.

Officer B., the puppetmaster who pulled the strings on I90, swears just as adamantly that both the sales, of cocaine and of hash, *did* take place, for he listened to the proceedings over the radio in his unmarked blue Buick. He is a sleepy-eyed man in his mid-thirties, about the age of the informant and the defendant, a law-upholding alter ego for those skewed souls.

Double-chinned, padded with the considerable paunch that seems to be issued along with the police badge, Officer B. answers Mr. Prosecutor and Mr. Defense in a flat, walkie-talkie drawl, consulting a sheaf of notes in his lap, never contradicting himself. Yes, he neglected to tape the opening few minutes of the first buy, the minutes when the exchange of hashish and money actually took place. Why? "I had a suspicion my batteries were weak, and I wanted to hold off." And, yes, he did erase the tape of the debriefing that followed buy number one. Why? "It's policy to reuse the old cassettes. Saves the taxpayers' money." And, yes, the tape of the second buy is raw, indecipherable noise, because a blaring TV in the background drowns out all human voices. (Listening to the tape, we can understand nothing in the scrawking except an ad for the American Express Card.) The tapes, in other words, don't prove a thing. What it all boils down to is the word of the law and of the unsavory informer versus the word of the many-times-convicted defendant, his mate, and his friends.

Toward the end of Officer B.'s testimony, there is a resounding clunk, like a muffled explosion, at the base of the witness stand. We all jump—witness, judge, jury, onlookers—and only relax when the prosecutor squats down and discovers that a pair of handcuffs has fallen out of Officer B.'s belt. Just a little reminder of the law's muscle. All of us were envisioning bombs. When Officer B. steps down, the tail of his sportcoat is hitched up over the butt of his gun.

The arrest: A squad car pulls up to the front of the trailer, and out the trailer's back door jumps Bennie, barefooted, wearing T-shirt and cut-off jeans. He dashes away between tarpaper shacks, through dog yards, over a stubbled field (his bare feet bleeding), through a patch of woods to a railroad cut. Behind him puffs a skinny cop (who recounts this scene in court), shouting, "Halt! Police!" But Bennie never slows down until he reaches that railroad cut, where he stumbles, falls, rolls down to the tracks like the sorriest hobo. The officer draws his gun. Bennie lifts his hands for the familiar steel cuffs. The two of them trudge back to the squad car, where Officer B. reads the arrest warrant and Bennie blisters everybody with curses.

The judge later instructs us that flight from arrest may be regarded as evidence, not of guilt but of *consciousness* of guilt. Oh ho! A fine distinction! Guilt for what! Selling drugs? Playing hooky? Original sin? Losing his job at Coca-Cola? I think of those bleeding feet, the sad chase. I remember a drunken uncle who stumbled down a railroad cut, fell asleep between the tracks, and died of fear when a train passed over.

On day four of the trial, Bennie himself takes the stand. He is shorter than I thought, and fatter—too many months of starchy jail food and no exercise. With exceedingly long thumbnails he scratches his jaw. When asked a question, he rolls his eyes, stares at the ceiling, then answers in a gravelly country voice, the voice of a late-night disk jockey. At first he is gruffly polite, brief in his replies, but soon he gets cranked up and rants in a grating monologue about his painful history.

He graduated from high school in 1968, worked eight months at RCA and Coca-Cola, had a good start, had a sweetheart, then the Army got him, made him a cook, shipped him to Vietnam. After a few weeks in the kitchen, he was transferred to the infantry because the fodder-machine was short of foot soldiers. "Hey, listen, man, I ain't nothing but a cook," he told them. "I ain't been trained for combat." And they said, "Don't you worry; you'll get on-the-job training. Learn or die." The artillery ruined his hearing. (Throughout the trial he has held a hand cupped behind one ear, and has followed the proceedings like a grandfather.) Some of his buddies got shot up. He learned to kill people. "We didn't even know what we was there for." To relieve his constant terror, he started doing drugs: marijuana, opium, just about anything that would ease a man's mind. Came home from Vietnam in 1971 a wreck, got treated like dirt, like a babykiller, like a murdering scumbag, and found no jobs. His sweetheart married an insurance salesman.

Within a year after his return he was convicted of shoplifting and burglary. He was framed on the second charge by a friend, but couldn't use his only alibi because he had spent the day of the robbery in bed with a sixteen-year-old girl, whose father would have put him away for statutory rape. As it was, he paid out two years in the pen, where he sank deeper into drugs than ever before. "If you got anything to buy or trade with, you can score more stuff in the state prisons than on the streets of Indianapolis." After prison, he still couldn't find work, couldn't get any help for his drug-thing from the Veterans' Administration, moved in with Rebecca and her three girls, eventually started selling marijuana and LSD. "Every time I went to somebody for drugs, I got ripped off. That's how I got into dealing. If you're a user, you're always looking for a better deal."

In 1979 he was busted for selling hash, in 1980 for possessing acid, betrayed in both cases by the man from whom he had bought his stock. "He's a snitch, just a filthy snitch. You can't trust nobody." Back to prison for a year, back out again in December 1981. No jobs, no jobs, no damn jobs; then part-time on the city garbage truck, up at four in the morning, minus five degrees and the wind blowing and the streets so cold his gloves stuck to the trash cans. Then March came, and this I90 guy showed up, wanted to buy some drugs, and "I told him I wasn't dealing anymore. I done my time and gone straight. I told him he didn't have enough money to pay me for no thirty years in the can." (The prosecutor bristles, the judge leans meaningfully forward: we jurors are not supposed to have any notion of the sentence that might follow a conviction on this drug charge.)

In his disk-jockey voice, Bennie denies ever selling anything to this I90 snitch. (He keeps using the word "snitch": I think of tattle-tales, not this adult betrayal.) It was I90, he swears, who tried to sell *him* the hash. Now the pills, why, those he had lying around for a friend who never picked them up, and so he just gave them to I90. "They was give to me, and so I couldn't charge him nothing. They wasn't for me anyway. Downers I do not use. To me, life is a downer. Just to cope with every day, that is way down low enough for me." And as for the cocaine, he never laid eyes on it until the man produced that little plastic bag in court. "I don't use coke. It's too expensive. That's for the bigwigs and the upstanding citizens, as got the money."

Sure, he admits, he ran when the police showed up at his trailer. "I'm flat scared of cops. I don't like talking to them about anything. Since I got back from Vietnam, every time they cross my path they put bracelets on me." (He holds up his wrists. They are bare now, but earlier this morning, when I saw a deputy escorting him into the courthouse, they were handcuffed.) He refuses to concede that he is a drug addict, but agrees he has a terrible habit, "a gift from my country in exchange for me going overseas and killing a bunch of strangers."

After the arrest, forced to go cold turkey on his dope, he begged the jail doctor—"He's no kind of doctor, just one of them that fixes babies"—to zonk him out on something. And so, until the trial, he has spent eight months drowsing under Valium and Thorazine. "You can look down your nose at me for that if you want, but last month another vet hung himself two cells down from me." (The other guy was a scoutmaster, awaiting trial for sexually molesting one of his boys. He had a record of severe depression dating from the war, and used his belt for the suicide.)

"The problem with my life," says Bennie, "is Vietnam." For a while after coming home, he slept with a knife under his pillow. Once, wakened suddenly, thinking he was still in Vietnam, he nearly killed his best friend. During the week of our trial, another Vietnam vet up in Indianapolis shot his wife in the head, imagining she was a gook. Neighbors got to him before he could pull out her teeth, as he used to pull out the teeth of the enemies he bagged over in Vietnam.

When I look at Bennie, I see a double image. He was drafted during the same month in which I, studying in England, gave Uncle Sam the slip. I hated that war, and feared it, for exactly the reasons he describes—because it was foul slaughter, shameful, sinful, pointless butchery. While he was over there killing and dodging, sinking into the quicksand of drugs, losing his hearing, storing up a lifetime's worth of nightmares, I was snug in England, filling my head with words. We both came home to America in the same year, I to job and family, he to nothing. Ten years after that homecoming, we stare across the courtroom at one another as into a fun-house mirror.

As the twelve jurors file past me into the room where they will decide on Bennie's guilt or innocence, three of them pat my arm in a comradely way. They withdraw beyond a brass-barred gate; I sit down to wait on a deacon's bench in the hallway outside the courtroom. I feel stymied, as if I have rocketed to the moon only to be left riding the ship round and round in idle orbit while my fellow astronauts descend to the moon's surface. At the same time I feel profoundly relieved, because, after the four days of testimony, I still cannot decide whether Bennie truly sold those drugs, or whether I90, to cut down on his own prison time, set up this ill-starred Bennie for yet another fall. Time, time—it always comes down to time: in jail, job, and jury box we are spending and hoarding our only wealth, the currency of days.

Even through the closed doors of the courtroom, I still hear the ticking of the clock. The sound reminds me of listening to my daughter's pulse through a stethoscope when she was still riding, curled up like a stowaway, in my wife's womb. Ask not for whom this heart ticks, whispered my unborn daughter through the stethoscope: it ticks for thee. So does the courtroom clock. It grabs me by the ear and makes me fret about time—about how little there is of it, about how we are forever bumming it from one another as if it were cups of sugar or pints of blood ("You got a minute?" "Sorry, have to run, not a second to spare"). Seize the day, we shout, to cheer ourselves; but the day has seized us and flings us forward pell-mell toward the end of all days.

Now and again there is a burst of laughter from the jury room, but it is always squelched in a hurry. They are tense, and laugh to relieve the tension, and then feel ashamed of their giddiness. Lawyers traipse past me—the men smoking, striking poses, their faces like lollipops atop their ties; the women teetering on high heels. The bailiff walks into our judge's office carrying a bread knife. To slice her lunch? As evidence against Rebecca? A moment later she emerges bearing a piece of cake and licking her fingers. Christmas parties are breaking out all over the courthouse.

Rebecca herself paces back and forth at the far end of my hallway, her steps as regular as the clock's tick, killing time. Her bearded and cross-wearing friends sidle up to comfort her, but she shrugs them away. Once she paces down my way, glances at the barred door of the jury room, hears muffled shouts. This she must take for good news, because she throws me a rueful smile before turning back.

Evidently the other twelve are as muddled by the blurred and contradictory "facts" of the case as I am, for they spend from noon until five reaching their decision. They ask for lunch. They ask for a dictionary. They listen again to the tapes. Sullen teenagers, following in the footsteps of Bennie and I90, slouch into the misdemeanor office across the hall from me; by and by they slouch back out again, looking unrepentant. At length the 300-pound mason lumbers up to the gate of the jury room and calls the bailiff. "We're ready as we're going to be." He looks bone-weary, unhappy, and dignified. Raising his eyebrows at me, he shrugs. Comrades in uncertainty.

The cast reassembles in the courtroom, the judge asks the jury for its decision, and the mason stands up to pronounce Bennie guilty. I stare at my boots. Finally I glance up, not at Bennie or Rebecca or the lawyers, but at my fellow jurors. They look distraught, wrung-out and despairing, as if they have just crawled out of a mine after an explosion and have left some of their buddies behind. Before quitting the jury room, they composed and signed a letter to the judge pleading with him to get some help—drug help, mind help, any help—for Bennie.

The ticking of the clock sounds louder in my ears than the judge's closing recital. But I do, with astonishment, hear him say that we must all come back tomorrow for one last piece of business. He is sorry, he knows we are worn out, but the law has prevented him from warning us ahead of time that we might have to decide on one more question of guilt.

The legal question posed for us on the morning of day five is simple: Has Bennie been convicted, prior to this case, of two or more unrelated felonies? If so, then he is defined by Indiana state law as a "habitual offender," and we must declare him to be such. We are shown affidavits for those earlier convictions—burglary, sale of marijuana, possession of LSD—and so the answer to the legal question is clear.

But the moral and psychological questions are tangled, and they occupy the jury for nearly five more hours on this last day of the trial. Is it fair to sentence a person again, after he has already served time for his earlier offenses? How does the prosecutor decide when to apply the habitual offender statute, and does its use in this case have anything to do with the political ambitions of the sleek young attorney? Did Bennie really steal that $150 stereo, for which he was convicted a decade ago, or did he really spend the day in bed with his sixteen-year-old girlfriend? Did Vietnam poison his mind and blight his life?

Two sheriff's deputies guard the jury today; another guards me in my own little cell. The bailiff would not let me stay out on the deacon's bench in the hall, and so, while a plainclothes detective occupies my old seat, I sit in a room lined with file cabinets and stare out like a prisoner through the glass door. "I have concluded," wrote Pascal, "that the whole misfortune of men comes from a single thing, and that is their inability to remain at rest in a room." I agree with him; nothing but that cruising deputy would keep me here.

This time, when the verdict is announced, Rebecca has her daughters with her, three little girls frightened into unchildlike stillness by the courtroom. Their lank hair and washed-out eyes remind me of my childhood playmates, the children of dead-end, used-up West Virginia coalminers who'd moved to Ohio in search of work. The mother and daughter are surrounded by half a dozen rough customers, guys my age with hair down over their shoulders and rings in their ears, with flannel shirts, unfocused eyes. Doubtless they are the reason so many holstered deputies and upholstered detectives are patrolling the courthouse, and the reason I was locked safely away in a cell while the jury deliberated.

When the mason stands to pronounce another verdict of guilty, I glimpse what I do not want to glimpse: Bennie flinging his head back, Rebecca snapping hers forward into her palms, the girls wailing.

* * *

The judge accompanies all thirteen of us into the jury room, where he keeps us for an hour while the deputies clear the rough customers from the courthouse. We are not to be alarmed, he reassures us; he is simply being cautious, since so much was at stake for the defendant. "How much?" the mason asks. "Up to twenty-four years for the drug convictions, plus a mandatory thirty years for the habitual offender charges," the judge replies. The cleaning woman, the nurse, and the TV repairman begin crying. I swallow carefully. For whatever it's worth, the judge declares comfortingly, he agrees with our decisions. If we knew as much about this Bennie as he knows, we would not be troubled. And that is just the splinter in the brain, the fact that we know so little—about Bennie, about Vietnam, about drugs, about ourselves—and yet we must grope along in our ignorance, pronouncing people guilty or innocent, squeezing out of one another that precious fluid, time.

And so I do my five days in the thirteenth chair. Bennie may do as many as fifty-four years in prison, buying his drugs from meaner dealers, dreaming of land mines and of his adopted girls, checking the date on his watch, wondering at what precise moment the hinges of his future slammed shut.

Gretel Ehrlich

(b. 1946)

In 1976, while she was in Wyoming to film a documentary on sheepherders for PBS, Gretel Ehrlich's lover died of cancer in New York, a loss that severed her from her old life and brought, amid the dislocation of grief, "an odd kind of fullness." This fullness is, in one word, Wyoming: where she "was able to take up residence on earth with no alibis, no self-promoting schemes"; where she has worked at herding, calving, branding, and writing poetry, fiction, essays; a place, she says, where we are invited "constantly to be what we are." In her essays about Wyoming, The Solace of Open Spaces *(1985), her energetic and finely developed poetic sensibility is focussed on detailing "what is already there" in a landscape unobstructed by cultural "fillers." A landscape of desolation where winter lasts six months, of "great arid valleys," "hundred-mile views"—a place on anything but a human scale, or so it would seem. "Space," writes Ehrlich, "has a spiritual equivalent and can heal what is divided and burdensome in us" ("The Solace of Open Spaces"). It is this affinity between herself and the land, the correspondence between "what is already there" and human consciousness of it, that she has set out to express. Thus her writing tends towards a rich poetics of simile and metaphor: "We are often like rivers: careless and forceful, timid and dangerous, lucid and muddied, eddying, gleaming, still" ("On Water"). "The Smooth Skull of Winter," with its densely imagined landscape, reads like a poem worked into the prose of an essay. Here, correspondence appears to work initially in the other direction: it's nature who, like an artist—a novelist, a poet—writes out a wintry text, a "scroll" unfolding the yearly dying in the whiteness of snow. As the essay goes on, the qualities of nature's wintering and of human participation in that wintering become so intricately joined we scarcely know whether the closing image speaks of nature's sentience or our own—or whether the distinction matters. As Ehrlich puts it: "The truest art I would strive for in any work would be to give the page the same qualities as earth: weather would land on it harshly; light would elucidate the most difficult truths; wind would sweep away obtuse padding" (Preface,* The Solace of Open Spaces*).*

The Smooth Skull of Winter

Winter looks like a fictional place, an elaborate simplicity, a Nabokovian invention of rarefied detail. Winds howl all night and day, pushing litters of storm fronts from the Beartooth to the Big Horn Mountains. When it lets up, the mountains disappear. The hayfield that runs east from my house ends in a curl of clouds that have fallen like sails luffing from sky to ground. Snow returns across the field to me, and the cows, dusted with white, look like snowcapped continents drifting.

The poet Seamus Heaney said that landscape is sacramental, to be read as text. Earth is instinct: perfect, irrational, semiotic. If I read winter right, it is a scroll—the white growing wider and wider like the sweep of an arm—and from it we gain a peripheral vision, a capacity for what Nabokov calls "those asides of spirit, those footnotes in the volume of life by which we know life and find it to be good."

Not unlike emotional transitions—the loss of a friend or the beginning of new work—the passage of seasons is often so belabored and quixotic as to deserve separate names so the year might be divided eight ways instead of four.

This fall ducks flew across the sky in great "V"s as if that one letter were defecting from the alphabet, and when the songbirds climbed to the memorized pathways that route them to winter quarters, they lifted off in a confusion, like paper scraps blown from my writing room.

A Wyoming winter laminates the earth with white, then hardens the lacquer work with wind. Storms come announced by what old-timers call "mare's tails"—long wisps that lash out from a snow cloud's body. Jack Davis, a packer who used to trail his mules all the way from Wyoming to southern Arizona when the first snows came, said, "The first snowball that hits you is God's fault; the second one is yours."

Every three days or so white pastures glide overhead and drop themselves like skeins of hair to earth. The Chinese call snow that has drifted "white jade mountains," but winter looks oceanic to me. Snow swells, drops back, and hits the hulls of our lives with a course-bending sound. Tides of white are overtaken by tides of blue, and the logs in the woodstove, like sister ships, tick toward oblivion.

On the winter solstice it is thirty-four degrees below zero and there is very little in the way of daylight. The deep ache of this audacious Arctic air is also the ache in our lives made physical. Patches of frostbite show up on our noses, toes, and ears. Skin blisters as if cold were a kind of radiation to which we've been exposed. It strips what is ornamental in us. Part of the ache we feel is also a softness growing. Our connections with neighbors—whether strong or tenuous, as lovers or friends—

become too urgent to disregard. We rub the frozen toes of a stranger whose pickup has veered off the road; we open water gaps with a tamping bar and an ax; we splice a friend's frozen water pipe; we take mittens and blankets to the men who herd sheep. Twenty or thirty below makes the breath we exchange visible: all of mine for all of yours. It is the tacit way we express the intimacy no one talks about.

One of our recent winters is sure to make the history books because of not the depth of snow but, rather, the depth of cold. For a month the mercury never rose above zero and at night it was fifty below. Cows and sheep froze in place and an oil field worker who tried taking a shortcut home was found next spring two hundred yards from his back door. To say you were snowed in didn't express the problem. You were either "froze in," "froze up," or "froze out," depending on where your pickup or legs stopped working. The day I helped tend sheep camp we drove through a five-mile tunnel of snow. The herder had marked his location for us by deliberately cutting his finger and writing a big "X" on the ice with his blood.

When it's fifty below, the mercury bottoms out and jiggles there as if laughing at those of us still above ground. Once I caught myself on tiptoes, peering down into the thermometer as if there were an extension inside inscribed with higher and higher declarations of physical misery: ninety below to the power of ten and so on.

Winter sets up curious oppositions in us. Where a wall of snow can seem threatening, it also protects our staggering psyches. All this cold has an anesthetizing effect: the pulse lowers and blankets of snow induce sleep. Though the rancher's workload is lightened in winter because of the short days, the work that does need to be done requires an exhausting patience. And while earth's sudden frigidity can seem to dispossess us, the teamwork on cold nights during calving, for instance, creates a profound camaraderie—one that's laced with dark humor, an effervescent lunacy, and unexpected fits of anger and tears. To offset Wyoming's Arctic seascape, a nightly flush of Northern Lights dances above the Big Horns, irradiating winter's pallor and reminding us that even though at this time of year we veer toward our various nests and seclusions, nature expresses itself as a bright fuse, irrepressible and orgasmic.

Winter is smooth-skulled, and all our skids on black ice are cerebral. When we begin to feel cabin-feverish, the brain pistons thump against bone and mind irrupts—literally invading itself—unable to get fresh air. With the songbirds gone only scavengers are left: magpies, crows, eagles. As they pick on road-killed deer we humans are apt to practice the small cruelties on each other.

We suffer from snow blindness, selecting what we see and feel while our pain whites itself out. But where there is suffocation and self-imposed ignorance, there is also refreshment—snow on flushed cheeks and a pristine kind of thinking. All winter we skate the small ponds—places that in summer are water holes for cattle and sheep—and here a reflection of mind appears, sharp, vigilant, precise. Thoughts, bright as frostfall, skate through our brains. In winter, consciousness looks like an etching.

David Quammen

(b. 1948)

Quammen confesses to "a lifelong and deep-seated revulsion towards spiders." He knows the feeling is widespread. Yet here, almost in the same breath, is how he describes Latrodectus mactans: *"Dangerous but not malicious, exotic-seeming but in truth rather common, ruthless . . . tender . . . death-dealing and life-seeking, fierce and vulnerable, gorgeous or hideous depending upon how we happen to see it, the black widow spider* is *nature" ("A Mouse Is Miracle Enough,"* The Flight of the Iguana, *1988). An enthralled spectator at what he calls the "pageant of nature," Quammen has for some years been writing a column for* Outside *magazine called "Natural Acts." Nature, he says, may seem "like a freak show," but isn't; what may look to any of us like quirks and monstrosities are "the natural and true-born practitioners of life on this planet."* Latrodectus mactans *included. We humans are, of course, part of this planetary life, and our attitudes—revulsions, affinities, principles—are part of us, part of this pageantry of the natural. These attitudes of ours (and his) intrigue Quammen every bit as much as any other apparently freakish "natural acts," iguanas flying or Australian earthworms growing ten feet long. The Whitmanesque side of him wants to give all of nature a "great epic hug," to embrace, as did "our crazy wild poet," every leaf of grass, pismire, and tree toad. But Quammen is no twentieth-century mystic—see his critique of Teilhard de Chardin in "Thinking About Earthworms"* (The Flight of the Iguana). *Nature's most absorbing mystery is infinite diversity, endless particularity. And that goes for us and our attitudes, and what may be happening inside our individual and collective heads at any given time. It's as if that other "self-righteous crank," Thoreau of Walden Pond, were making an irresistibly didactic appearance in the middle of Quammen's essay: "Break stride. Wander off mentally. Pick a subject so perversely obscure that it can't help but have neglected significance." Who knows what evil lurks in this great, good "pageant of nature"? David Quammen seems pretty sure it's "homogenization of mind," people collectively making what Darwin called "an approach to intelligence," when—by nature—we're equipped, unlike earthworms, to go all the way, one at a time.*

Thinking About Earthworms

An Unpopular Meditation on Darwin's Silent Choir

Somewhere between the ages of thirty and forty each of us comes to the shocking realization that a lifetime is not infinite. The world is big and rich, options are many, but time is limited. Once that dire truth has revealed itself, everything afterward becomes a matter of highly consequential choices. Every hour of cello practice is an hour that might have been spent rereading Dostoyevski, but wasn't; every day of honest work is a day of lost skiing, and vice versa; every inclusion is also an exclusion, every embracement is also a casting aside, every *do* is also a *didn't*. Then presto: Time is up, and each *didn't* goes down on the scroll as a *never did*. Yikes, why is he punishing us with this platitudinous drivel? you may ask. It's because I've just spent the entire first week of my thirty-ninth year thinking about earthworms.

Now I ask you to give the subject ten minutes. That figure includes a small margin, I hope, for divagations concerning television, the Super Bowl, the philosophy of Teilhard de Chardin, the late space shuttle *Challenger*, and other closely related matters, not least of which is the far-ranging curiosity of Charles Darwin.

Darwin spent forty-four years of his life, off and on, thinking about earthworms. This fact isn't something they bother to tell you in freshman biology. Even Darwin himself seems to have harbored some ambivalence over the investment of time and attention. In an addendum to his autobiography, written not long before he died, he confided: "This is a subject of but small importance; and I know not whether it will interest any readers, but it has interested me." The interest had begun back in 1837, when he was just home from his voyage on the *Beagle*, and it endured until very near the end of his life. He performed worm-related experiments that stretched across decades. Finally in 1881 he wrote a book about earthworms, a book in which the words "evolution" and "natural selection" are not (unless I blinked and missed them) even mentioned. That book is titled *The Formation of Vegetable Mould, Through the Action of Worms, With Observations of Their Habits*. By "vegetable mould" he meant what today would be called humus, or simply topsoil. It was his last published work.

Darwin seems to have found something congenial about these animals. "As I was led to keep in my study during many months worms in pots filled with earth," he wrote, "I became interested in them, and wished to learn how far they acted consciously, and how much mental power they displayed." Among his typically methodical observations of wormish habits was the following: "Worms do not possess any sense of hearing. They took not the least notice of the shrill notes from a metal whistle, which was repeatedly sounded near them; nor did they of the deepest and loudest tones of a bassoon. They were indifferent to shouts, if care was taken that the breath did not strike them. When placed on a table close to the keys of a piano, which was played as loudly as possible, they remained perfectly quiet." It's an image to be inscribed on all human memory, I think, as an antidote to pomposity and aloofness: Charles Darwin, alone in his study with a tin whistle and a bassoon and a piano, trying to get a rise out of worms. Under the category "Mental Qualities," he stated, as though regretfully: "There is little to be said on this head. We have seen that worms are timid." Later in the book, though, he described some experiments—designed to distinguish instinct, in their leaf-gathering behavior, from judgment—that inclined him to credit them with "a near approach to intelligence."

But what mainly concerned Darwin was the collective and cumulative impact of worms in the wild. On this count, he made large claims for them. He knew they were numerous, powerful, and busy. A German scientist had recently come up with the figure 53,767 as the average earthworm population on each acre of the land he was studying, and to Darwin this sounded about right for his own turf too. Every one of those 53,767 worms, he realized, spent much of its time swallowing. It swallowed dead plant material for its sustenance, and it swallowed almost anything else in its path (including tiny rock particles) as it burrowed. The rock particles were smashed even finer in the worm's gizzard, mixed with the plant material and the digestive juices in its gut, and passed out behind in the form of "castings." The castings contained enough natural glue to give them a nice crumb structure, characteristic of good soil, and were also biochemically ideal for nurturing vegetation. Collectively, over years and decades and centuries, this process transformed dead leaves and fractured rock into the famous and all-important "vegetable mould." But that wasn't all.

At least some of those species of earthworm had the habit of depositing their castings above ground. A worm would back tail-first out of its burrow and unload a neat castellated pile around the entrance. As a result, Darwin recognized, soil from a foot or more underground was steadily being carried up to the surface. In many parts of England, he figured, the worm population swallowed and brought up ten tons of earth each year on each acre of land. Earthworms therefore were not only creating the planet's thin layer of fertile soil; they were also constantly turning it inside out. They were burying old Roman ruins. They were causing the monoliths of Stonehenge to subside and topple. On sloping land, where rainwater and wind would sweep their castings away and down into valleys, they were making a huge contribution to erosion. No wonder Darwin concluded: "Worms have played a more important part in the history of the world than most persons would at first suppose."

His worm book sold well in the early editions. By one account, in fact, it was a greater commercial success for him than *The Origin of Species*. Nowadays the book is generally ignored by everyone except soil scientists—who themselves nod to it devoutly but don't seem to take its contents too seriously. Sometimes these scientists mention that Darwin rather overstated the role of worms while he underestimated such other soil organisms as bacteria, fungi, protozoa, and subterranean insects. *The Formation of Vegetable Mould, Through the Action of Worms* is nevertheless a readable volume, mild and affable and modest in tone, containing a few curious facts and some telling glimpses of the author's fastidious methodology. But the most interesting thing about the book, in my view, is simply that this particular man took the trouble to write it. At the time, evolution by natural selection was the hottest idea in science; yet Charles Darwin spent his last year of work thinking about earthworms.

And thank goodness he did. That sort of stubborn mental contrariety is as precious to our planet as worm castings. It is equally essential that some people *do* think about earthworms, at least sometimes, as it is that *not everyone does*. It is essential not for the worms' sake but for our own.

More and more in recent years, we are all thinking about the same things at the same time. Electromagnetic radiation is chiefly responsible; microwaves, macrowaves, dashing and dancing electrons unite us instantly and constantly with the waves of each other's brain. We can't step out into the yard without being bonked by a signal that has come caroming off some satellite, and when we step back inside, there's Dan Rather, ready with the day's subject for thought. One day we think about an explosion in the sky above Cape Canaveral. Another day we think about a gutshot pope. On a designated Sunday in January we gather in clusters to focus our thoughts upon the Super Bowl. Occasionally we ponder a matter of somewhat less consequence, like the early returns from the New Hampshire primary or the question of who shot J. R. Ewing. Late in the evening we think about what Ted Koppel thinks it's important we think about. Over large parts of the planet we think quite intently about the World Cup soccer final. My point is not that some of these subjects are trivial while others are undeniably and terrifyingly significant; my point is that we think about them together in great national (sometimes global) waves of wrinkling brows, and on cue. God himself has never summoned so much precisely synchronized, prayerful attention as Mary Lou Retton got for doing back flips. And maybe God is envious. Of course now He too has His own cable network.

The Jesuit philosopher and paleontologist Pierre Teilhard de Chardin gave a label to this phenomenon. He called it the *noosphere*, and he considered it just wonderful. In Teilhard's view, the noosphere (*noös* being Greek for mind, and the rest by analogy with lithosphere, biosphere, atmosphere) was the ultimate product of organic evolution, the culmination of all nature's progress toward man and perfection—a layer of pure homogenized mind enwrapping the Earth, hovering there above us as "the sphere of reflexion, of conscious invention, of the conscious unity of souls." It was prescient of him, I think, to have shaped this idea back at a time when even radio was an inestimable new toy. But in my heartfelt opinion, his enthusiasm was misguided. Too much "conscious unity of souls" is unhealthy, probably even pernicious. It yields polarized thought, in the same sense that a polarized filter yields polarized light: nice neat alignments of attention and interest (which is different from, but a step toward, unanimity of opinion), with everyone smugly in agreement that such-and-such matters are worth contemplation, and that the rest by implication are not. Such unity is a form of overall mental impoverishment. For just one particular instance, it tends to neglect earthworms.

You will have sensed by now that I am a self-righteous crank on this subject. I believe that unanimity is always a bad thing. The prospect of all five billion of us human beings getting our alpha waves into perfect sync appalls me. My own minuscule contribution to the quixotic battle—the battle against homogenization of mind, the battle to preserve a cacophonous disunity of souls, the hopeless fingers-in-ears campaign of abstention from the noosphere—lies chiefly in not owning a television.

Pitiful, I know. It sounds like the most facile sort of pseudointellectual snobbery, I know. It is backward and petulant, and I am missing lots of terrific nature documentaries on the high-minded channels, I know. It's grim work, but somebody's got to do it. Anyway, I am not at all opposed to television. I am merely opposed to the notion that *everybody* should be dutifully, simultaneously plugged in. Maybe someday, for some unforeseeable reason, society will have need of a person who has never seen, say, a video replay of the space shuttle explosion. If so, I'll be ready. It's a personal sacrifice that I've been quite willing to make.

On the other hand, so as not to sound too tediously righteous, I want to confess that I did watch the Super Bowl this year, on a friend's set, thereby merging for three hours my somnolent brain with those millions of somnolent others. It was a sublime waste of time, and I'm glad I did it. Next year I won't.

You yourself can join in the good fight without even unplugging your television. Just take a day or an hour each month to think carefully about something that nobody else deems worthy of contemplation. Break stride. Wander off mentally. Pick a subject so perversely obscure that it can't help but have neglected significance. If everyone else is thinking about the sad and highly visible deaths of seven astronauts, think about the Scottsboro Boys. If everyone else is thinking about the Super Bowl, think about a quiet little story called "The Loneliness of the Long-Distance Runner." If everyone else is busy despising Ferdinand Marcos, devote a few minutes of loathing to Fulgencio Batista. Or think about earthworms.

Think about the Australian species, *Megascolides australis*, that grows ten feet long and as big around as a bratwurst. Think about *Lumbricus terrestris*, familiar to soil scientists as the common European earthworm and to generations of American boyhood as the night crawler, nowadays gathered at night by professional pickers on Canadian golf courses and imported into the U.S. for a total value of $13 million per year. Think about how hard it is to tell front from rear, especially so since they can back up. Think about the curious reproductive arrangement of earthworm species generally, hermaphroditic but not self-fertilizing, so that each one during the act of mating provides sperm for its partner's eggs while receiving back the partner's sperm for its own eggs; now imagine having a full sister whose mother was your father. Think about the fact that these animals can regenerate a lost head. Think about the formation of vegetable mould, and the relentless swallowing, digesting, burrowing, and casting off of waste by which earthworms topple and bury the monuments of defunct civilizations while freshening the soil for new growth. Think about how sometimes it's the little things that turn the world inside out.

Kenneth A. McClane

(b. 1951)

People turn to essay writing for all kinds of reasons, from wanting to change the world to hoping to improve the state of their pocketbooks. Kenneth McClane, who describes himself as "a poet by training and yearning" (his poems fill more than six books), came to the craft of prose by way of grief over his brother Paul's death from alcoholism at age twenty-nine, grief and the guilt peculiar to those who, improbably, survive where others—as gifted, as deserving—perish. McClane's first essay, "A Death in the Family" (1985), "is a brother's testimony" voiced amid resonances of James Baldwin's great novella of love and estrangement between two brothers, one a teacher, the other a musician and junkie, Sonny's Blues. *Baldwin's portrayal of the "hidden menace" of growing up in Harlem speaks to the imperilled condition of all life, love, and human possibility, to the truth that no one is ever safe: "Safe, hell!" cries one character, "Ain't no place safe for kids, for nobody." McClane's essays (collected in* Walls, *1990) work from the premise that living honestly means accepting "menace"—from without and within—as the fundamental reality of all individual effort. Writing, for this poet, essayist, and devoted teacher, is the cultivation of an essential "attitude": that "placing one's thoughts before another," however perilous it may be, "signifies . . . a celebration of interdependence" ("Baxter's Program"). In "Walls: A Journey to Auburn," this "attitude" takes McClane from his university to a maximum-security prison. Full of trepidation, not least of all about his own fitness for the task, he goes to testify to the possibility of communication, to "our willingness to become interconnected" across the physical and social walls that both protect and threaten our public safety, and across those equally adamant private walls of hurt that "seem forever rising." While "so much of life remains the inevitable, unremarkable, unalterable chain of despair" ("The School"), the writer is at work forging different chains, different linkages between himself and others. The brotherhood—and, McClane would urge, sisterhood—of reader and writer, artist and audience, forms in the knowledge that each of us is a "vast spiritual conundrum, capable of love and destruction" ("Baxter's Program"). Destruction, hence perpetual "menace"; love—hence the "mercy" that, even if it cannot save another, draws us near.*

Walls: A Journey to Auburn

PAUL
The willows are gold again
and now the season seems past thinking
seems past remembrances, seems past
the long lean taking of your breath:

I remember you Paul, always, how you strutted
among the city—Lord of the manor: how you
fought with the drivers, how you never
let one person call you *nigger*. I remember how

you struggled with Dad—loving him in the stridency
of your ill-covered conquest: you wanted to love him
and he you: Yours is the story too often repeated:
the city boy driven to alcohol, death:

But the willow once green is golden:
and I remember you part in desire, part in fact:
You would have hated the lie I make of you; you
would have hated the fact:

Still the willow turns green to golden and still
you visit me in mid-morning, telling me of this awful
place, of the omnipresent *them*, who would not let you live
and I listen:

You who were too proud to equivocate: you who loved as freely
and deeply, as messily, as the world could imagine:
Paul, I miss you. I miss your hear-bearing, stern confidence,
your anger which made ghettos of all of us:

No one struggled more; no one asked more; no one
took the risk of presence more sacredly: in your loss
I understood not only the shores of grief,
but how its walls seem forever rising.

—Kenneth A. McClane

At first glance, Auburn Correctional Facility calls to mind a feudal castle or a stone and brick edifice worthy of Humphrey Bogart or Edward G. Robinson. One readily envisions prisoners dragging their balls and chains, the late night prison break, or the lights slowly flickering, presaging the imminent electrocution. This is the stuff of movies, of prison lore. Yet for most of us, these images, dispatched out of Hollywood, are all we shall ever know about the real life in our nation's prisons. Most of us will certainly not be sentenced there; few of us will choose one as a place to visit.

Yet in every stereotype, there is also a residuum of truth: people employ generalizations to celebrate a certain verity about the world; and no myth would have any currency if it did not, to some unassailable extent, identify something in actual experience. Certainly these cinematic incarnations are not the prison's reality, but they contain a grain of truth, nonetheless. Undeniably, though we may not know what a prison is, our imaginings, however incompletely, convey that the prison is a *hellish* place. Indeed, nothing in our arsenal of national fictions suggests that the prison is other than horrific. In this case, it is not a matter of correctness but degree. The prisons—at least the prisons I have encountered—are infinitely more hellish than our Hollywood dream makers relate. Inmates in these places are not planning breakouts or prison riots; they are not planning anything. To dream of escape is to believe that one has something worthy of salvaging; to believe, that is, in the proposition of a self-orchestrated future. The prisons I have visited are spirit killers: the inmates—no matter how smart, capable, or engaging—have little sense of their own inextinguishable worth, their own human possibility. And this is not by accident.

Auburn Prison is certainly not the worst reformatory in this country, nor is it the best. Like most, it probably sits in the thick middle range: no inmate would ask to be sentenced there; certainly some might wish to be transferred out; a few of the hard-nosed might even like it, its attraction resting in its utter banality. Neither good (that is, experimental) nor bad (and the word here has almost no meaning, since Auburn, at least to my eyes—and no doubt to those of its inmates—is bad enough), Auburn just is.

At bottom, to cast out is not to cast off, and the long trek to Auburn Prison—through the mill town and over the proverbial railroad tracks—is our reminder that the great prison is a great industry: people earn their livings there; whole towns, including Auburn, are built on the day-to-day catering to our national pariah. And like anything which both haunts and fascinates us, we come to the prison's gates armed with rocks and wonder.

Inescapably, and with great trepidation, we know that the inhabitants of our man-made Siberias are our brethren: indeed, it is this weighty realization, this sense that the murderer we so ruthlessly banish may not eternally quiet the potential murderer within, which so frightens us. For it takes but a few precious seconds for the mind's knife to become the hand's weapon. And all of us, at some terrible time, have walked that narrow footpath between the imagined and the horrific.

At Auburn, the first thing one confronts is its massive guard tower, with its rifle-shouldering, no-nonsense officer. By the time you have noticed him, he has noticed you. For a minute or so, he looks down at you, looks around you and, always unsmiling, moves back to his elevation and privacy. What is so astonishing is that *you* feel condemned. You sense in that coldly dismissive gaze, in the backdrop of the great prison, that Gandhi was right: *to think of evil is to act evilly.* And you feel—and this is essential to the prison's apparatus—that the common denominator of your humanity has been discovered: that you are a writer, or a college professor, or a dutiful husband is of little significance. Here, as the guard corroborates, there is no room for romanticism: he's seen your kind before.

One enters Auburn Prison through two gigantic brass doors, each heavily tooled with elaborate metalwork, at the center of which, like an uneasy coupling, sits the famous symbol of Justice, with its blindfolded woman supporting her two deliberately balanced weights. The rest of the portraiture is oddly cherubic, even sexual, as it seems the neoclassical invariably is. It is a celebration of everything, or a reminder of how everything—be it lust or justice—fights in this great amphitheater of a world. I wonder how I might understand this, should I be a prisoner passing on my way to serve a life sentence. He, certainly, knows that life is a great chaos—though this, I hazard, was not the artist's intention. It is, however, a possible interpretation; and it certainly was mine.

The prison's receiving room is reminiscent of an airport security check area, with much the same ingenious technology. At Auburn, there are two guards who inspect both your clothing and carriables. Since I had come to read from my poetry, I had a canvas bag filled with books, and never have my works been so finely perused. Each page was rigorously examined; the bag was checked and rechecked.

After all of us had passed through the metal detector, the guard stamped our right hands with an invisible substance. Then we were counted. Indeed, at the next twelve checkpoints, we were counted and counted again. At each checkpoint there is a "lock in": a holding area where one must remain until a guard electronically dislodges the massive gates. The twelve of us, eleven teachers from Elmira Community College's Inmate Higher Education Program and myself, journeyed from checkpoint to checkpoint like wary salmon. The group was a strange conglomeration. All, with the exception of myself, were white; two of the twelve were women. Six had taught at Auburn for the last two years, and four had worked at the prison for more than a decade. One of the teachers, who wore a jaunty red hat, was the frailest young man I had ever seen: I wondered how he had negotiated his twenty-five years, not to mention the prison's exactings. Yet no one was particularly large or muscular. Sporting his Special Forces army jacket, one man nearly looked the part. But most were aging college and high school teachers, stomachs a notch wider, dreams a bit more remote, than all would like.

Finally we reached "the Yard," and began the long walk through the corridor by cell block D. I say long walk, but it was only a thousand yards. All of a sudden, as if a wall of sound, the prisoners began chanting "Baby, you're beautiful" to the two women with us. Loosened through the stone and Plexiglas, the sound recalled that haunting, terrifying Malabar Caves sojourn in Forster's *A Passage to India*, where human inadequacy and racism are shown as helpmeets. I kept thinking, *This is not sound; it is an indictment*. And then I realized, undeniably, shamefully, as if for the first time, what it must *cost* to be a woman: to have your body become, day in and day out, the receptacle for so much need, so much ill-digested, inchoate, dangerously poised lust.

I watched as the two women bore it, the college-aged one as strong as a serf in a Breton painting. Quickly her thin face closed down; she walked with a studied, disciplined bearing. Then someone, everyone yelling: *I'll kill you white motherfuckers*. The sound booming and pounding, as if the prison were a giant tuning fork.

Auburn Prison, built in 1816, is one of the oldest maximum security institutions in the United States. A pioneer in penology, Auburn was constructed with individual cells for each inmate, although the original design for these cells, the so-called "Auburn System," was pernicious to say the least. During the early part of the nineteenth century, Auburn became the focus for a unique penal "experiment," in which the most incorrigible inmates were sentenced to absolute, uninterrupted solitary confinement. Permitted neither to leave their cells nor to read or work, the one hundred "selected" inmates were forced to stand for eight hours a day in total silence. Moreover, in the disturbingly convoluted thinking of the time, this practice was considered "a humane gesture," since it was assumed that an eternity of forced motionlessness might lead to muscle atrophy. No one, of course, questioned whether solitary confinement was in itself inhumane. No, in the rigidly Calvinistic teaching of the day, a prisoner's lot was to be cruel. One burned in hell for one's sins; and prison, most certainly, was this earth's hell.

As might be surmised, in the first year of this heinous experiment, of the hundred prisoners involved, nearly half went mad, while the others succumbed to tuberculosis and pneumonia. Yet, as is so often the case with prisons, the public was of two minds: on the one hand, it wanted its "custodial houses" to keep the dangerous miscreants away from the community and expected the prison to salve the commonwealth of a serious problem; on the other, it was only willing to permit the prison such "corrective leeway" as might preserve the community's conscience. Clearly, although the public had wanted these Auburn convicts to be severely punished, it did not wish to see them die in plaguelike numbers, at least not within *its* institution. And so, after its first barbarous year, the experiment was ended.

Yet ideas die slowly, and the Auburn penologists—zealots that they were—still believed that solitary confinement was the only way to discipline the abject criminal. Indeed, just two years after their first ill-fated attempt, they began a new, yet no less severe, improvisation on the same theme. Realizing that absolute, forced human isolation encouraged death and psychosis, the Auburn authorities proposed a modified system where inmates would work in a closely monitored common area, while always returning to their individual cells to sleep. Although the prisoners might come in contact with one another at work and at meals, at no time would they be permitted to talk, exchange letters, or communicate. In 1822, this rigid denial of human intercourse—which is still the rubric in many of the world's penal systems—found its most eloquent spokesperson in Auburn's Warden Gersham Powers:

> The demands of nature must indeed be complied with; their [the prisoners'] bodies must be fed and clothed . . . but they ought to be deprived of every enjoyment arising from social or kindred feelings and affections; of all knowledge of each other, the world, and their connections with it. Force them to reflection, and let self-tormenting guilt harrow up the tortures of accusing conscience, keener than scorpion stings; until the intensity of their sufferings subdues their stubborn spirits, and humbles them to a realizing sense of the enormity of their crimes and their obligation to reform.

Thankfully, the Auburn Prison of 1822 is not the institution that one confronts today. In 1986, as a case in point, even the term "prison" is anachronistic: Auburn is a "correctional facility." Yet even though Warden Powers is long buried, his philosophy, I surmise, still informs these halls. For Auburn, like any architecturally planned, functional structure, was constructed to facilitate a certain notion of reality. When these long tiers of individual cells were created—small, dark, and cramped—certain expectations were being fulfilled; certain others, suggested. Hopefully, the prisoner in 1986 will not die from long hours of standing in his cell, as fifty of his brethren once did; but he still will find his room terribly constrictive; he still will notice how the walls of his cell jut out into the corridor, a further hindrance to "unwanted talk"; and he still will discover—and this he will relish, albeit silently—that this is *his* cell: however cramped, squalid, and dark.

This, of course, is no insignificant development. However small his quarters, the inmate possesses something which is *his:* he can hang something on the wall (provided he has something to hang) and can, as much as is humanly possible, leave his mark on his space. For a time, he does not have to worry about someone else's belongings, feelings, or privacy—at least while *they* are in *their* cells. And if you are a prisoner, this is essential and important rest. Certainly, one may murder oneself in one's own cell; but amongst the prison community, there are literally hundreds of people who might potentially murder you, and all for some supposed slight, and one not even necessarily directed at them but at their friend, lover, or even, God knows, at someone who is just a resident of their cell block. In one's cell—for a few precious hours then—one can safely "watch one's back." Of course, there might be a fire and one might perish; but there might be a nuclear disaster in New York, and all New York might evaporate in the conflagration. A prisoner, like most New Yorkers, is willing to live with that possibility. But he does not relish placing his life in harm's way, amongst people who know all too much about harm. And thus his cell is, in this darkest of places, "heaven sent."

Yet none of this enlightened humanitarianism—that social architects might applaud and Anton Chekhov, weary of Sahalin, might, understandably, envy—has much effect on the visitor. He is far too much a victim of his own life, and the perilous nature of it. If he has not valued his freedom before coming to Auburn, if he has not thought about who he is (and therefore what he must protect), he does so now. For whatever else a prison does, it demands that one confront it. If you are a prisoner, it might take you a dozen years to realize that the life you *hope* to create requires, above all else, that it be lived *within* these walls, for these *walls do not go away*. Here, of all the world's places, there is everything to accept.

For those of us who are *visiting*—and this, indeed, is the greatest privilege—our status is in our faces, our movements, our bowels. We know, and we cling to this as we might to our children, that *we shall walk out of here, tonight, at a certain time.*

And it is just this privilege which both the prisoners and, to a lesser degree, the guards wish to cost us dear. When we walked through the corridors, the catcalls, the *Baby, you look beautiful,* and *I'll kill you white motherfuckers,* were an expression of lust, anger, and bitterness; but they were also an expression of our enviable ability to put off that which the inmates could not elude. In our quick, stuttering movements, in our downturned faces, in our trying to look courageous, we possessed a vulnerability—and how powerfully, in a different way, we sensed it—that they could ill afford. Indeed, it was this flabby indulgence, this possibility for openly embracing fear (swimming in it, as one might a fur coat), for which they despised us. Fear would set them to the barbells late at night; fear would turn them taciturn; fear would cause them to stuff the fork into another's ribs before he jabbed it into theirs; fear was *not* that mad dash between buildings, that shrinking, scared, trying-to-look-not-so movement which so claimed us.

I had been invited to Auburn Correctional Facility to read and talk about my poetry for an incredible two-and-a-half-hour class. I remember how my stomach tightened when I first learned that I had to perform for that length of time. By nature I am a one-hour person. Indeed, whenever I attend a lecture that swells on beyond that point, I find myself imaginatively melding with the audience, thinking how I must meet someone in three minutes, catch the late bus, or do the laundry. But more accurately, I clung to the question of time because it was the easiest thing on which to cling. Although it would be difficult to fill one hundred and fifty minutes, my great confrontation was not with the clock, but with those time would place before me.

The forty inmates who made up my class were participants in Elmira Community College's Inmate Higher Education Program. Most of the students were black and in their early twenties; one man had gray hair. Conspicuously, the three white prisoners clustered together, in much the same way blacks often huddle together in the outer world. At Cornell, where I teach, this behavior is often looked upon as unfriendly at best and racist at worst. Few whites would concede that blacks, like themselves, are merely desirous of fraternizing with people with whom they share a common interest and experience. Whites, because this is America, have never had to justify their actions; they sit with and entertain whomever they wish. Yet when blacks exercise the same human prerogative, it is considered an act of dismissal, subterfuge, or war.

At Auburn I couldn't help but wonder what those white inmates felt with the tables turned. Was their isolation that of the lonely island, or the citadel beyond assault? Clearly they were in the minority in the prison population, but they were also white; and I sensed, even in this last outcrop of civilization, that their color still had some sting. And even if it didn't call the heavens down, it did testify that they were, in prison parlance, some "bad muthafuckas." For the few whites who found themselves sent up to Auburn had been convicted of repeated, unusually brutal offenses. Indeed, the viciousness of the whites' crimes seemed in inverse proportion to their numbers. As one of the black inmates described them, and not without a touch of envy, "If evil walked, them cats be Jesse Owens."

At Auburn one thing was immediately apparent: the inmates were delighted that I had come. In the first instance, I was someone they didn't know who took them away from the tedium of the ordinary; but, more importantly, I was the first black teacher they had encountered in twelve months. Once I read two poems, the questions began: Where had I been raised? What was my background? How had I managed to evade prison? I breathlessly explained that I had grown up in Harlem, with two good parents "who rode my ass" but offered little else.

This, of course, was an oversimplification, if not a direct lie. I had been raised in Harlem, but in the most unusual of circumstances. My father was a physician, my mother was a brilliant artist and writer, and I had attended one of the finest—and personally most ruinous—independent schools in the city. I lived in Harlem, which is to say that I saw much, but I certainly hadn't lived the lives these inmates had: indeed, I had spent my entire life keeping myself at a safe remove from anything which might bring me to Harlem's reality. Yes, I had done a little of this and a bit of that, but I was always at the sidelines. I knew where the deep water was—everyone knew that. But I remained a shore bird.

My brother, however, paid for my escape. A talented drummer who had the same IQ as I did (something my mother was wont to remind me of), he lived in those streets, and it, and the difficult contradictions he faced, broke him. My brother Paul would ultimately drink himself to death at twenty-nine. He was tough, independent, and full of bitterness. He was, as I read that evening, "hungry for the end of the world."

The inmates particularly liked my "brother" poems: they too had brothers they missed and loved, brothers whose ultimate lives might be even more menaced than their own. This I found oddly comforting: in our desire to transcend the horror of crime, we hasten to view the criminal as someone without any notion of family or community. Certainly, this is our clumsy way of insulating ourselves from *their* human truth: for it is far too frightening to imagine ourselves as potential criminals, and far more convenient, and comforting, to see the criminal as truly subhuman. Indeed, had they been born with twelve heads or twenty spikes, we might finally, irrevocably, divorce ourselves from them. But as they come with two arms, two legs, a pumping heart, and a wondrous mind, their profanation suggests our own ratty flesh; their banishment, our own ever possible exile.

In truth, the lies we fabricate to distance ourselves from others invariably rise to haunt us. We may lie *to* ourselves, but others are under no obligation to lie *for* us. Whatever these inmates were—and all of them were sentenced to Auburn for corporal crimes—they would not permit me to view them merely as maniacs, psychopaths, or what have you. They were people, cussed and joy-filled: people capable of tenderness and murder: people like me and yet unlike me, because I haven't yet, thank goodness, killed anyone.

I learned a great deal in those two hours and thirty minutes; much more, I trust, than those inmates learned from me. At one point, one of the students asked me to describe how it felt to enter the prison. I shall never forget how dangerous that question seemed to me, dangerous because it gave voice to all my inner disquiet. Quickly I found myself looking about the room, noticing that there were no guards within immediate reach. To this day I don't know what made me sense my immediate vulnerability: certainly it had to do with the poignancy of the question, for in some profound way, the inmate was asking me to unburden myself, to tell him how I had found a means to live with fear; yet just as centrally—and this was as palpable as air—he wanted to know if I thought he was a beast, if I had cast him beyond the shores of humanity (and if I had, he might make my suspicions *real*); but most fundamentally, most crucially, I realized that he, Lord knows how, had given language to my own questioning, my own inadequate "sew-work." I hadn't made peace with the prison, with him, or with myself. And he knew it.

After some time—it seemed like hours, it was merely seconds—I told him the truth. I stated that the prison was the most frightening, scary place I had ever seen. He was quiet for a moment, and then he smiled. He agreed with me. *Agreed with me. Yes*, this place was as hellish as he imagined. In my own terror, I had thought that he had been holding me to my life; in truth, I had been holding him to his. He, like all of us, needed to affirm that his own powers of discrimination were accurate, that his experience might be mirrored by others. Although Auburn was brutal and spirit-crushing, it had not yet destroyed his ability to perceive and differentiate shades of horror; it had not yet destroyed him. To this, at least, I could bear witness.

There were two questions which were asked again and again of me. Inmate after inmate wanted to know if I thought I would continue to write and to teach. At first, I was not at all surprised at this question: it is a common one, asked eternally of writers. Yet on this particular occasion, whenever I attempted to answer the question, the audience would neither hear nor accept my response. Again and again I would state that Yes, I thought I would continue to teach, and again and again I would be presented with the same question. It was maddening.

Finally I realized what was happening. To these inmates, my tacit belief in the probability of an *assured* future, my notion that I could reasonably expect to find myself in a *certain* circumstance, at a *certain* time, was as mind-boggling as if I had just sprouted wings. For them, there had never been *one* veritable day of certainty: when they were in the streets, they had to live on mother wit; now, in prison, every minute brought new perils. Indeed, if there was one inexpugnable axiom for them, it was the present tense, the resounding *I am*. Of nothing else could they be certain.

Ultimately, their questions were, if you will, *pre*-questions: they were the first, tentative vocalizations of wonder. The inmates wanted me to repeat myself, because they could not understand the specifics of my answer until they understood the astonishing grammar from which it sprang. Miraculously, although we shared the ability to make sounds, we had yet to forge a common language. And it was just this which made us tongue-tied at revelation: having so much to say, and no means, no suitable lexicon for conveying it, we were exiles in a country more hideous, terrible, and unreachable than any Kafka had ever imagined.

If Auburn cut the prisoners off from the world, it, more horribly, sealed them into their *futureless* selves. Usually, thankfully, human beings—because of imagination, spirit, and plain cantankerousness—evolve the means to transcend most anything, even the grim ghetto of self. Yet at Auburn, and I trust at most prisons, this could not be tolerated (*jails, we must remember, are to keep people in*). As any jailer knows, the walls of the present are always dismantled in the future; but if there is *no* future, if there is no ability to set aside and reconstitute, to interdict and reposition, then the present becomes the almighty, and the walls become unconquerable. Although I did not interview the jailors, I did see the jailed. For most of them, the walls without had become the walls within; and such walls never, no matter what Joshua does, *come a-tumbling down.*

After I had finished reading, one student, who had heretofore been silent, spoke up, reminding me that although "we prisoners might seem like nice guys, we're here because we killed people," the last statement clearly intended to elicit a reaction from me, the naïve college professor. Now, after two long hours, I found myself getting angry: I wondered why he so wanted to frighten me, especially since it seemed that my easy fright was all he desired. But then I realized that he might be attempting something far more humanly essential and generous. As I had told him of my brother, had offered that intimate bond of personal experience and blood, so too would he share his only sacred gift—his experience—with me. Difficult and tentative as his motions were (and confession, by nature, is always stony), this man wanted to speak to me as man to man, witness to witness.

What first I had taken as a vitriolic assault was merely this man's life: he had offered it up, in the ready language at his disposal. I might not like the life he had, or the brutal language by which he expressed it, but I certainly should permit him his truth. It might sting; I might refuse to listen; but this is the privilege of the listener. The teller, sadly, can only recount his tale: he can lie, but that, in itself, is just another corner of revelation.

At bottom, this man was trying to claim his humanity as he tested mine. If I had my naïveté to lose, he had something far more essential to win, his personhood; and he would struggle for that at all costs. Indeed, it was the lopsidedness of this battle, the vast inequality of our two involvements, which so charged the moment. I, since I had not yet truly become pariah, had the privilege of arguing over the nature of my privilege (or even tossing it away if I so desired); while he, on the other hand, had no choice but to plead for his essential humanity. He, certainly, would not choose to walk into this prison—not with what he knew. Indeed, if there was light at the end of the proverbial tunnel for him, he had not only to create the light but the instrument by which it might be seen. And since our predicaments were far from being reciprocal, the wolves loomed at every corner.

And yet remembering my childhood joy when I "acted the nigger" on the New York City bus, negotiating that delicious netherworld that only the marginalized are allowed, I understood what that inmate felt. When those "high-class" whites saw me, the chocolate-faced boy, they knew that I was the flesh and blood repository of their assumptions—the authentic ghetto type; and I, even though I attended the crème-de-la-crème private school in the city, gave them a show worthy of their concern. Although I didn't have any real power, I could certainly fool those people. I'd talk jive, look evil, and "badmouth" the toughest looking white boy I could find. And then, laughing all the way, I'd romp over to the Collegiate School, the place where ninety percent of *their* children failed to gain entrance.

Yet notwithstanding my minor triumph, I bitterly decried the subterra in which it was purchased. Certainly one can, in extreme cases, extricate some pleasure out of hell; but hell is nonetheless hell; it is certainly never heaven. And thus the inmate, though he needed me to facilitate his journey to self-announcement, could excuse neither the brashness of my declaration—I was asking him to justify himself—nor the insubstantiality of my presence. Whatever else I was, to him and the rest of the prison population, my credentials were dubious at best. A Cornell professorship might mean something in the outer world; but here, it was as valuable as an expired driver's license, or an old football ticket. Power, we must remember, is negotiable only where it has validity: in the prison, had I been physically strong or good at cards, I might expect a measure of admiration, respect, and fellowship; but *sans* these talents, my degrees and professional standing, understandably, met with little interest. Indeed, the value system which had so honored me had exiled them. For those who had been ritually cast out, certainly, it would be an inhumanly bitter pill to swallow to be expected to salute the son as they suffered under his father. Blake to the contrary, the cut worm does *not* forgive the plow.

Ultimately the human voice is a very wondrous thing: it can show, at rare moments, everything which propels it. That these men had once been murderers meant that they could also be something else; at least, that was what the new wavering in this young man's voice suggested. I watched him slowly negotiate the incline of possibility, his voice swelling into a trill of astonishment, at first slow, gravelly, and then steady. Certainly this wasn't a wave of spontaneous announcement: he had seen far too much for that. More, it was the hard, pruned, strained depth-taking of someone who sensed, albeit bitterly, that the world might return nothing. But still he, with no reason that I could fathom, kept speaking, his own narrative building, gathering. Suddenly, words suggested words, listening suggested listeners, confession suggested healing; and he said, both to himself and to me, "Man, you ain't bad." And that was enough.

At ten o'clock the bell rang, and the prisoners began to file back to their cells. Of the forty I spoke with, twenty or so came up to me, shook my hand, and asked if I might come back. None of these congratulations came from the three white prisoners, something which I can only presume to understand. My poems are not overly racial: I didn't read a large number of racial poems. Possibly I had neglected them; possibly they did not like my reading. I just do not know.

The journey out of the prison seemed more efficacious. When we entered the yard this time, it was filled with inmates pumping iron, smoking, and chatting. Again we were escorted by four guards. Now the towers, with their no-nonsense sentries, were well lighted, although the lights were not dancing over the grounds as in the movies. For the first time I looked at the one-hundred-year-old granite. These walls had been made to last: hell, as Gersham Powers had so wanted, would remain interminable.

Near the first checkpoint, I saw one of the inmates who had been at my seminar. He smiled—a long, good smile—a smile that seemed almost hungry, a smile much like my brother's. I wished him well.

Then we began the elaborate countings until we reached the last checkpoint, where they asked us to put our right hands under an ultraviolet light. The light illuminated the invisible stamp that had been placed on our wrists when we first entered the prison. It seemed such a fitting way to leave this place: the once invisible stamp, now glowing luminously green, as yet again another mystery.

Resources for Readers and Writers

Montaigne and the Essay

This lively old Gascon has woven all his bodily infirmities into his works and, after having spoken of the faults or virtues of any other man, immediately publishes to the world how it stands with himself in that particular. Had he kept his own counsel, he might have passed for a much better man, though perhaps he would not have been so diverting an author.

—Joseph Addison, *Spectator* No. 562 (July 2, 1714)

All the writers on common life since him have done nothing but echo him. You cannot open him without detecting a *Spectator* or starting a *Rambler*; besides that, his own character pervades the whole and binds it sweetly together.

—Charles Lamb, "Books With One Idea In Them," *The Examiner* (July 18, 1813)

A single odd volume of Cotton's translation of the *Essays* remained to me from my father's library, when a boy. It lay long neglected, until, after many years, when I was newly escaped from college, I read the book, and procured the remaining volumes. I remember the delight and wonder in which I lived with it. It seemed to me as if I had myself written the book, in some former life, so sincerely it spoke to my thought and experience.

—Ralph Waldo Emerson, "Montaigne: Or, The Skeptic," *Representative Men* (1850)

After all, in the whole of literature, how many people have succeeded in drawing themselves with a pen? . . . As the centuries go by, there is always a crowd before that picture, gazing into its depths, seeing their own faces reflected in it, seeing more the longer they look, never being able to say quite what it is that they see.

—Virginia Woolf, "Montaigne," *The Common Reader* (1925)

. . . what makes Montaigne a very great figure is that he succeeded, God knows how—for Montaigne very likely did not know that he had done it—it is not the sort of thing that men

can observe about themselves, for it is essentially bigger than the individual's consciousness—he succeeded in giving expression to the skepticism in *every* human being.
—T. S. Eliot, "The 'Pensées' of Pascal," *Essays Ancient and Modern* (1936)

Free association artistically controlled—this is the paradoxical secret of Montaigne's best essays. One damned thing after another—but in a sequence that in some almost miraculous way develops a central theme and relates it to the rest of human experience.
—Aldous Huxley, Preface, *Collected Essays* (1959)

It became my habit to turn the top corner of any page on which something so remarkable was written that I knew I would want to find it again. I have a poor memory and need to do this sort of thing. Now, eight years or so later, more than half the corners are turned, so that the book looks twice as thick sitting on the table, and I have discovered a new interest in Montaigne: what is there on all those unturned pages that I have read but forgotten, still there to be discovered?
—Lewis Thomas, "Why Montaigne Is Not A Bore," *The Medusa and the Snail* (1979)

. . . having decided that "the most barbarous of our maladies is to despise our being," he did succeed *via* the *Essays* in learning to accept himself, by making friends with his mind.
—Philip Lopate, "The Essay Lives—in Disguise," *New York Times Book Review* (November 18, 1984)

What is it about the *Essais* of Michel de Montaigne—the first two volumes published in 1580, the third in 1588—that keeps practitioners of the genre turning back, folding down corners, and paying tribute to "this lively old Gascon" by adding to his one hundred and seven essays more and more of their own? Why the "crowd before that picture"? Montaigne set out to "portray" himself in his writing—for the sake of friends and neighbors, he said, who might "take pleasure in associating and conversing with me again in this image" (II, 18).[1] Posthumous fame as such seemed to hold little attraction for him: "I shall no longer have any grip by which to seize reputation, nor by which it can touch me or reach me." Without the man, a name is nothing: "What can it mark when I am no

[1] All references are to *The Complete Essays of Montaigne*, translated by Donald M. Frame (1957). Parenthetical numbers refer to book and essay in this volume.

longer here?" (II, 16). His essays kept him busy writing and rewriting for two decades, but with no literary pretensions. He refers to them as "these things of mine . . . monstrous bodies, pieced together of diverse members, having no order, sequence or proportion" (I, 28); "this bundle . . . of disparate pieces"; "all this fricassee that I am scribbling here . . ." (III, 13).

Monstrous bodies, bundles, fricassees. Why should they have compelled so much attention, emulation, love, right down to our own day? Where is the essayist in English with that kind of stature and durability? Bacon and Addison, whose influence on the essay, its moral concerns and its penchant for informality, has been immeasurable, elicit their share of praise, even (especially in Addison's case) of imitators. Bacon, wrote Thomas Macaulay, knew how to talk "in language which everybody understands, about things in which everybody is interested." And of Addison he said (with the matchless confidence that was his mark as a critic): "As an observer of life, manners, of all the shades of human character, he stands in the first class." Yet the names of Bacon and Addison don't run all through the tradition as does Montaigne's, like a rich lode, that, however deeply mined, is never exhausted but holds incalculably more gold than four hundred years of essay writing in French, English, and other modern languages can carry away. And you don't even have to dig very deep. See Lewis Thomas, who knows his Montaigne as lovingly as Montaigne knew his own favorite old authors: the goods in the *Essais*, says Thomas, lie strewn about on practically every page, for the picking.

Montaigne's appeal, finally, must be as various and as private as any one reader's memories, tastes, interests, aspirations. Who knows why the young Emerson, home from Harvard, took down that "long neglected" first volume when he did? As with all books, all ideas, it's a matter of readiness: you "discover" a writer or a book when you're prepared for what is there to be had. But that verity of literary influence only presses the question harder: what *is* it one turns back to in the *Essais* of Montaigne?

Whom does one meet there? A man in middle age and, given the state of medicine in the later sixteenth century, one nearer to old age than might be supposed (a fact of which Montaigne was acutely aware). A comfortable man who liked being comfortable, heir to a wealthy merchant's estate in the countryside east of Bordeaux; married (but so unobtrusively you'd hardly know it from his writings) and well cared for by his staff of servants; getting on with daily living in an equable manner while bloody religious wars raged all around. A man with an unremarkable career behind him as a magistrate and, by his own testimony, a remarkable friendship with a colleague, Étienne de la Boétie, who died in 1563 at age thirty-two, when Montaigne himself was just thirty. It was a friendship he valued above all things in his life and for which his essays are perhaps a kind of surrogate. "My essential pattern is suited to communication and revelation," he wrote many years after his friend's death; "I am all in the open and in full view, born for company and friendship" (III, 3)—even, towards the end of his life, friendship with a remarkable woman, the brilliant young Marie de Gournay who became his literary executor. At thirty-eight ("while still entire") Montaigne retired from his job as magistrate in the Bordeaux Parliament and solemnized the decision by inscribing a short account of it on his library wall. Thinking that retirement would bring leisure, he came up against a common dilemma: what to do with my leisure? how to pass the time? His mind, seeking stoic unperturbedness, thinking "to entertain itself in full idleness and stay and settle itself," instead gave birth to "chimeras and fantastic monsters." In order "to contemplate their ineptitude and strangeness at [his] pleasure," he began "to put them in writing" (I, 8). He was a humanist, in the historical sense: one who knows and loves the learning of the ancients (in his case, Plutarch and Seneca, above all). And in the more diffuse sense: one who takes as the focus of his interest and study "man," by which he meant the human character, mainly as he found it expressed in himself. He was also a skeptic, a student of the newly rediscovered late Classical philosopher, Sextus Empiricus. His library's most famous inscription was: "Que sais-je?" What do I know? "There is virtually nothing that I know I know, or that I dare give my word I can do," he writes in "Of Presumption," one of the longer essays of Book II. "I am as doubtful of myself as of anything else. . . ." And so it is of himself that he writes, himself that he studies and probes and tests, giving to his writing the name *essai*: "If my mind could gain a firm foothold, I would not make essays, I would make decisions; but it is always in apprenticeship and on trial" (III, 2).

By 1580, at age forty-seven, Montaigne had written two books of essays; he had also developed a long-dreaded, excruciating kidney disease but managed a trip to Italy, nonetheless, and two terms as mayor of Bordeaux in the early eighties. His third book of generally much longer, richer, more complicated and more difficult essays appeared in 1588, alongside revisions of Books I and II. In failing health, he wrote his last revisions down the margins of the 1588 edition. Death, which he had rehearsed often and amiably in his essays, came at age fifty-nine—still young, we would say; "old age," in Montaigne's eyes (III, 13).

"If the world complains that I speak too much of myself, I complain that it does not even think of itself," he remarked in one of his late essays (III, 3). He'd already dismissed the notion, earlier on, that he was wasting his time "by taking stock of [himself] so continually, so carefully" in writing:

> For those who go over themselves only in their minds or occasionally in speech do not penetrate to essentials in their examination as does a man who makes that his study, his work, and his trade, who binds himself to keep an enduring account, with all his faith, with all his strength (II, 18).

The writing way of thinking about oneself becomes a way of life, an occupation and a way of being true to oneself—a kind of morality. It is true that the *Essais* brim with observations and insights. The best of them, moreover, are marvels of suppleness that turn and meander and gather meaning almost as life itself does, one passage at a time; one can't help feeling, with Charles Lamb, that, after Montaigne, "there is nothing new under the sun." Everywhere, too, there's the sense of identification with this Frenchman of the sixteenth century: of seeing yourself figured, like the young Emerson, in that all too human portrait drawn with a pen, locating there the permutations of your own disorderliness, the peripheries of your own doubt and that of "every human being," as Eliot said. Not least important, Montaigne shows us not only how but where to write essays: in a place of privacy, a condition of solitariness. We must retire, somehow create for ourselves "a back shop all our own," as he calls it, "in which to establish our real liberty and our principal retreat and solitude" (I, 39). All these things go a long way towards explaining why this old "bundle" of Montaigne's has kept its freshness for so long, why these essays bear more weight in the aggregate, radiate more significance, disseminate more than we can, strictly speaking, account for textually.

But easy to miss, perhaps because it's so prominent (or simply because we have a perverse habit of not taking authors at their word) is this: Montaigne reminds all of us who are alive, as he once was, that living is what we least know how to do and what we most need to learn for our own good.

> We are great fools. "He has spent his life in idleness," we say. "I have done nothing today." What, have you not lived? That is not only the fundamental but the most illustrious of your occupations. "If I had been placed in a position to manage great affairs, I would have shown what I could do." Have you been able to think out and manage your own life? You have done the greatest task of all. . . . To compose our character is our duty, not to compose books, and to win, not battles and provinces,

> but order and tranquillity in our conduct. Our great and glorious masterpiece is to live appropriately (III, 13).

A book is written, bound, published, lasts for centuries; but, no, says Montaigne, that is not itself the "great and glorious masterpiece." A book is only a kind of remnant, what is left over afterwards when the real composition—the work of knowing how to live—is finished. Still, these leavings do matter, for they are the chosen marks of living: here's how *I* do it. The doing, the writing itself, is both a path *to* knowing and a path *of* knowing; as I write, I am "forming my life" (II, 37), which is "the greatest task of all."

We inquire after the "art" of the essay; Montaigne long ago made the essay into a medium for the art of living. It's easy to bristle, to object: look at how much privilege of wealth, class, sex went into practicing the gentleman's art. Yet, can any of us, however circumstanced, however tried and pressed, afford *not* to practice it, however we can? In a time when we write "for" a course, or "for" publication, or "for" money, "this lively old Gascon" lingers in his book—"a book," he said, "consubstantial with its author" (II, 18)—to show us what it is like to write for one's living in a more primary sense. "I am not building here a statue to erect at the town crossroads . . . ," he said of his *Essais.* Whatever the work was to him, to us it has become a monument after all, a monument to a certain vital relationship between living and writing. Can it be this that keeps us "gazing" through the centuries?

Michel de Montaigne

(1533–1592)

Of Practice

(Translated by Donald Frame)

Reasoning and education, though we are willing to put our trust in them, can hardly be powerful enough to lead us to action, unless besides we exercise and form our soul by experience to the way we want it to go; otherwise, when it comes to the time for action, it will undoubtedly find itself at a loss. That is why, among the philosophers, those who have wanted to attain some greater excellence have not been content to await the rigors of Fortune in shelter and repose, for fear she might surprise them inexperienced and new to the combat; rather they have gone forth to meet her and have flung themselves deliberately into the test of difficulties. Some of them have abandoned riches to exercise themselves in a voluntary poverty; others have sought labor and a painful austerity of life to toughen themselves against toil and trouble; others have deprived themselves of the most precious parts of the body, such as sight and the organs of generation, for fear that their services, too pleasant and easy, might relax and soften the firmness of their soul.

But for dying, which is the greatest task we have to perform, practice cannot help us. A man can, by habit and experience, fortify himself against pain, shame, indigence, and such other accidents; but as for death, we can try it only once: we are all apprentices when we come to it.

In ancient times there were men who husbanded their time so excellently that they tried to taste and savor it even at the point of death, and strained their minds to see what this passage was; but they have not come back to tell us news of it:

> No man awakes
> Whom once the icy end of living overtakes.
> Lucretius

Canius Julius, a Roman nobleman of singular virtue and firmness, after being condemned to death by that scoundrel Caligula, gave this among many prodigious proofs of his resoluteness. As he was on the point of being executed, a philosopher friend of his asked him: "Well,

Canius, how stands your soul at this moment? What is it doing? What are your thoughts?" "I was thinking," he replied, "about holding myself ready and with all my powers intent to see whether in that instant of death, so short and brief, I shall be able to perceive any dislodgment of the soul, and whether it will have any feeling of its departure; so that, if I learn anything about it, I may return later, if I can, to give the information to my friends." This man philosophizes not only unto death, but even in death itself. What assurance it was, and what proud courage, to want his death to serve as a lesson to him, and to have leisure to think about other things in such a great business!

> Such sway he had over his dying soul.
> Lucan

It seems to me, however, that there is a certain way of familiarizing ourselves with death and trying it out to some extent. We can have an experience of it that is, if not entire and perfect, at least not useless, and that makes us more fortified and assured. If we cannot reach it, we can approach it, we can reconnoiter it; and if we do not penetrate as far as its fort, at least we shall see and become acquainted with the approaches to it.

It is not without reason that we are taught to study even our sleep for the resemblance it has with death. How easily we pass from waking to sleeping! With how little sense of loss we lose consciousness of the light and of ourselves! Perhaps the faculty of sleep, which deprives us of all action and all feeling, might seem useless and contrary to nature, were it not that thereby Nature teaches us that she has made us for dying and living alike, and from the start of life presents to us the eternal state that she reserves for us after we die, to accustom us to it and take away our fear of it.

But those who by some violent accident have fallen into a faint and lost all sensation, those, in my opinion, have been very close to seeing death's true and natural face. For as for the instant and point of passing away, it is not to be feared that it carries with it any travail or pain, since we can have no feeling without leisure. Our sufferings need time, which in death is so short and precipitate that it must necessarily be imperceptible. It is the approaches that we have to fear; and these may fall within our experience.

Many things seem to us greater in imagination than in reality. I have spent a good part of my life in perfect and entire health; I mean not merely entire, but even blithe and ebullient. This state, full of verdure and cheer, made me find the thought of illnesses so horrible that when

I came to experience them I found their pains mild and easy compared with my fears.

Here is what I experience every day: if I am warmly sheltered in a nice room during a stormy and tempestuous night, I am appalled and distressed for those who are then in the open country; if I am myself outside, I do not even wish to be anywhere else.

The mere idea of being always shut up in a room seemed to me unbearable. Suddenly I had to get used to being there a week, or a month, full of agitation, alteration, and weakness. And I have found that in time of health I used to pity the sick much more than I now think I deserve to be pitied when I am sick myself; and that the power of my apprehension made its object appear almost half again as fearful as it was in its truth and essence. I hope that the same thing will happen to me with death, and that it is not worth the trouble I take, the many preparations that I make, and all the many aids that I invoke and assemble to sustain the shock of it. But at all events, we can never be well enough prepared.

During our third civil war, or the second (I do not quite remember which), I went riding one day about a league from my house, which is situated at the very hub of all the turmoil of the civil wars of France. Thinking myself perfectly safe, and so near my home that I needed no better equipage, I took a very easy but not very strong horse. On my return, when a sudden occasion came up for me to use this horse for a service to which it was not accustomed, one of my men, big and strong, riding a powerful work horse who had a desperately hard mouth and was moreover fresh and vigorous—this man, in order to show his daring and get ahead of his companions, spurred his horse at full speed up the path behind me, came down like a colossus on the little man and little horse, and hit us like a thunderbolt with all his strength and weight, sending us both head over heels. So that there lay the horse bowled over and stunned, and I ten or twelve paces beyond, dead, stretched on my back, my face all bruised and skinned, my sword, which I had had in my hand, more than ten paces away, my belt in pieces, having no more motion or feeling than a log. It is the only swoon that I have experienced to this day.

Those who were with me, after having tried all the means they could to bring me round, thinking me dead, took me in their arms and were carrying me with great difficulty to my house, which was about half a French league from there. On the way, and after I had been taken for dead for more than two full hours, I began to move and breathe; for so great an abundance of blood had fallen into my stomach that nature had to revive its forces to discharge it. They set me up on my feet, where I threw up a whole bucketful of clots of pure blood, and several times on the way I had to do the same thing. In so doing I began to recover a little life, but it was bit by bit and over so long a stretch of time that my first feelings were much closer to death than to life:

> Because the shaken soul, uncertain yet
> Of its return, is still not firmly set.
>
> Tasso

This recollection, which is strongly implanted on my soul, showing me the face and idea of death so true to nature, reconciles me to it somewhat.

When I began to see anything, it was with a vision so blurred, weak, and dead, that I still could distinguish nothing but the light,

> As one 'twixt wakefulness and doze,
> Whose eyes now open, now again they close.
>
> Tasso

As for the functions of the soul, they were reviving with the same progress as those of the body. I saw myself all bloody, for my doublet was stained all over with the blood I had thrown up. The first thought that came to me was that I had gotten a harquebus shot in the head; indeed several were being fired around us at the time of the accident. It seemed to me that my life was hanging only by the tip of my lips; I closed my eyes in order, it seemed to me, to help push it out, and took pleasure in growing languid and letting myself go. It was an idea that was only floating on the surface of my soul, as delicate and feeble as all the rest, but in truth not only free from distress but mingled with that sweet feeling that people have who let themselves slide into sleep.

I believe that this is the same state in which people find themselves whom we see fainting with weakness in the agony of death; and I maintain that we pity them without cause, supposing that they are agitated by grievous pains or have their soul oppressed by painful thoughts. This has always been my view, against the opinion of many, and even of Étienne de La Boétie, concerning those whom we see thus prostrate and comatose as their end approaches, or overwhelmed by the length of the disease, or by a stroke of apoplexy, or by epilepsy—

> This do we often see:
> A man, struck, as by lightning, by some malady,
> Falls down all foaming at the mouth, shivers and rants;
> He moans under the torture, writhes his muscles, pants,
> And in fitful tossing exhausts his weary limbs
>
> Lucretius

—or wounded in the head: When we hear them groan and from time to time utter poignant sighs, or see them make certain movements of the body, we seem to see signs that they still have some consciousness left; but I have always thought, I say, that their soul and body were buried in sleep.

> He lives, and is unconscious of his life.
>
> Ovid

And I could not believe that with so great a paralysis of the limbs, and so great a failing of the senses, the soul could maintain any force within by which to be conscious of itself; and so I believed that they had no reflections to torment them, nothing able to make them judge and feel the misery of their condition, and that consequently they were not much to be pitied.

I can imagine no state so horrible and unbearable for me as to have my soul alive and afflicted, without means to express itself. I should say the same of those who are sent to execution with their tongue cut out, were it not that in this sort of death the most silent seems to be the most becoming, if it goes with a firm, grave countenance; and the same of those miserable prisoners who fall into the hands of the villainous murdering soldiers of these days, who torture them with every kind of cruel treatment to force them to pay some excessive and impossible ransom, keeping them meanwhile in a condition and in a place where they have no means whatever of expressing or signifying their thoughts and their misery.

The poets have portrayed some gods as favorable to the deliverance of those who thus drag out a lingering death:

> I bear to Pluto, by decree,
> This lock of hair, and from your body set you free.
>
> Virgil

Nonetheless, the short and incoherent words and replies that are extorted from them by dint of shouting about their ears and storming at them, or the movements that seem to have some connection with what is asked them, are not evidence that they are alive, at least fully alive. So it happens to us in the early stages of sleep, before it has seized us completely, to sense as in a dream what is happening around us, and to follow voices with a blurred and uncertain hearing which seems to touch on only the edges of the soul; and following the last words spoken to us, we make answers that are more random than sensible.

Now I have no doubt, now that I have tried this out by experience, that I judged this matter rightly all along. For from the first, while wholly unconscious, I was laboring to rip open my doublet with my nails (for I was not in armor); and yet I know that I felt nothing in my imagination that hurt me; for there are many movements of ours that do not come from our will:

> And half-dead fingers writhe and seize the sword again.
> Virgil

Thus those who are falling throw out their arms in front of them, by a natural impulse which makes our limbs lend each other their services and have stirrings apart from our reason:

> They say that chariots bearing scythes will cut so fast
> That severed limbs are writhing on the ground below
> Before the victim's soul and strength can ever know
> Or even feel the pain, so swift has been the hurt.
> Lucretius

My stomach was oppressed with the clotted blood; my hands flew to it of their own accord, as they often do where we itch, against the intention of our will.

There are many animals, and even men, whose muscles we can see contract and move after they are dead. Every man knows by experience that there are parts that often move, stand up, and lie down, without his leave. Now these passions which touch only the rind of us cannot be called ours. To make them ours, the whole man must be involved; and the pains which the foot or the hand feel while we are asleep are not ours.

As I approached my house, where the alarm of my fall had already come, and the members of my family had met me with the outcries customary in such cases, not only did I make some sort of answer to what was asked me, but also (they say) I thought of ordering them to give a horse to my wife, whom I saw stumbling and having trouble on the road, which is steep and rugged. It would seem that this consideration must have proceeded from a wide-awake soul; yet the fact is that I was not there at all. These were idle thoughts, in the clouds, set in motion by the sensations of the eyes and ears; they did not come from within me. I did not know, for all that, where I was coming from or where I was going, nor could I weigh and consider what I was asked. These are slight effects which the senses produce of themselves, as if by habit; what the soul contributed was in a dream, touched very lightly, and merely licked and sprinkled, as it were, by the soft impression of the senses.

Meanwhile my condition was, in truth, very pleasant and peaceful; I felt no affliction either for others or for myself; it was a languor and an extreme weakness, without any pain. I saw my house without recognizing it. When they had put me to bed, I felt infinite sweetness in this repose, for I had been villainously yanked about by those poor fellows, who had taken the pains to carry me in their arms over a long and very bad road, and had tired themselves out two or three times in relays. They offered me many remedies, of which I accepted none, holding it for certain that I was mortally wounded in the head. It would, in truth, have been a very happy death; for the weakness of my understanding kept me from having any judgment of it, and that of my body from having any feeling of it. I was letting myself slip away so gently, so gradually and easily, that I hardly ever did anything with less of a feeling of effort.

When I came back to life and regained my powers,

When my senses at last regained their strength,
Ovid

which was two or three hours later, I felt myself all of a sudden caught up again in the pains, my limbs being all battered and bruised by my fall; and I felt so bad two or three nights after that I thought I was going to die all over again, but by a more painful death; and I still feel the effect of the shock of that collision.

I do not want to forget this, that the last thing I was able to recover was the memory of this accident; I had people repeat to me several times where I was going, where I was coming from, at what time it had happened to me, before I could take it in. As for the manner of my fall, they concealed it from me and made up other versions for the sake of the man who had been the cause of it. But a long time after, and the next day, when my memory came to open up and picture to me the state I had been in at the instant I had perceived that horse bearing down on me (for I had seen him at my heels and thought I was a dead man, but that thought had been so sudden that I had no time to be afraid), it seemed to me that a flash of lightning was striking my soul with a violent shock, and that I was coming back from the other world.

This account of so trivial an event would be rather pointless, were it not for the instruction that I have derived from it for myself; for in truth, in order to get used to the idea of death, I find there is nothing like coming close to it. Now as Pliny says, each man is a good education to himself, provided he has the capacity to spy on himself from close up. What I write here is not my teaching, but my study; it is not a lesson for others, but for me.

And yet it should not be held against me if I publish what I write. What is useful to me may also by accident be useful to another. Moreover, I am not spoiling anything, I am using only what is mine. And if I play the fool, it is at my expense and without harm to anyone. For it is a folly that will die with me, and will have no consequences. We have heard of only two or three ancients who opened up this road, and even of them we cannot say whether their manner in the least resembled mine, since we know only their names. No one since has followed their lead. It is a thorny undertaking, and more so than it seems, to follow a movement so wandering as that of our mind, to penetrate the opaque depths of its innermost folds, to pick out and immobilize the innumerable flutterings that agitate it. And it is new and extraordinary amusement, which withdraws us from the ordinary occupations of the world, yes, even from those most recommended.

It is many years now that I have had only myself as object of my thoughts, that I have been examining and studying only myself; and if I study anything else, it is in order promptly to apply it to myself, or rather within myself. And it does not seem to me that I am making a mistake if—as is done in the other sciences, which are incomparably less useful—I impart what I have learned in this one, though I am hardly satisfied with the progress I have made in it. There is no description equal in difficulty, or certainly in usefulness, to the description of oneself. Even so one must spruce up, even so one must present oneself in an orderly arrangement, if one would go out in public. Now, I am constantly adorning myself, for I am constantly describing myself.

Custom has made speaking of oneself a vice, and obstinately forbids it out of hatred for the boasting that seems always to accompany it. Instead of blowing the child's nose, as we should, this amounts to pulling it off.

> Flight from a fault will lead us into crime.
>
> Horace

I find more harm than good in this remedy. But even if it were true that it is presumptuous, no matter what the circumstances, to talk to the public about oneself, I still must not, according to my general plan, refrain from an action that openly displays this morbid quality, since it is in me; nor may I conceal this fault, which I not only practice but profess. However, to say what I think about it, custom is wrong to condemn wine because many get drunk on it. We can misuse only things which are good. And I believe that the rule against speaking of oneself applies only to the vulgar form of this failing. Such rules are bridles for calves, with which neither the saints, whom we hear speaking so boldly about themselves, nor the philosophers, nor the theologians curb themselves. Nor do I, though I am none of these. If they do not write about themselves expressly, at least when the occasion leads them to it they do not hesitate to put themselves prominently on display. What does Socrates treat of more fully than himself? To what does he lead his disciples' conversation more often than to talk about themselves, not about the lesson of their book, but about the essence and movement of their soul? We speak our thoughts religiously to God, and to our confessor, as our neighbors do to the whole people. But, someone will answer, we speak only our self-accusations. Then we speak everything: for our very virtue is faulty and fit for repentance.

My trade and my art is living. He who forbids me to speak about it according to my sense, experience, and practice, let him order the architect to speak of buildings not according to himself but according to his neighbor; according to another man's knowledge, not according to his own. If it is vainglory for a man himself to publish his own merits, why doesn't Cicero proclaim the eloquence of Hortensius, Hortensius that of Cicero?

Perhaps they mean that I should testify about myself by works and deeds, not by bare words. What I chiefly portray is my cogitations, a shapeless subject that does not lend itself to expression in actions. It is all I can do to couch my thoughts in this airy medium of words. Some of the wisest and most devout men have lived avoiding all noticeable actions. My actions would tell more about fortune than about me. They bear witness to their own part, not to mine, unless it be by conjecture and without certainty: they are samples which display only details. I expose myself entire: my portrait is a cadaver on which the veins, the muscles, and the tendons appear at a glance, each part in its place. One part of what I am was produced by a cough, another by a pallor or a palpitation of the heart—in any case dubiously. It is not my deeds that I write down; it is myself, it is my essence.

I hold that a man should be cautious in making an estimate of himself, and equally conscientious in testifying about himself—whether he rates himself high or low makes no difference. If I seemed to myself good and wise or nearly so, I would shout it out at the top of my voice. To say less of yourself than is true is stupidity, not modesty. To pay yourself less than you are worth is cowardice and pusillanimity, according to Aristotle. No virtue is helped by falsehood, and truth is never subject to error. To say more of yourself than is true is not always presumption; it too is often stupidity. To be immoderately pleased with what you are, to fall therefore into an undiscerning self-love, is in my opinion the substance of this vice. The supreme remedy to cure it is to do just the opposite of what those people prescribe who, by prohibiting talking about oneself, even more strongly prohibit thinking about oneself. The pride lies in the thought; the tongue can have only a very slight share in it.

It seems to them that to be occupied with oneself means to be pleased with oneself, that to frequent and associate with oneself means to cherish oneself too much. That may be. But this excess arises only in those who touch themselves no more than superficially; who observe themselves only after taking care of their business; who call it daydreaming and idleness to be concerned with oneself, and making castles in Spain to furnish and build oneself; who think themselves something alien and foreign to themselves.

If anyone gets intoxicated with his knowledge when he looks beneath him, let him turn his eyes upward toward past ages, and he will lower his horns, finding there so many thousands of minds that trample him underfoot. If he gets into some flattering presumption about his valor, let him remember the lives of the two Scipios, so many armies, so many nations, all of whom leave him so far behind them. No particular quality will make a man proud who balances it against the many weaknesses and imperfections that are also in him, and, in the end, against the nullity of man's estate.

Because Socrates alone had seriously digested the precept of his god—to know himself—and because by that study he had come to despise himself, he alone was deemed worthy of the name *wise*. Whoever knows himself thus, let him boldly make himself known by his own mouth.

Essayists On Their Art

No subject, as this book indicates, is off limits to the essayist. Whatever can pass through experience by way of the senses, the reason, the imagination, passes through the essay. When Montaigne said, "I meddle rashly with every sort of subject . . ." (I, 56), he spoke for the many writers who would, in their different ways, follow his lead. "Everything I see or hear is an essay in bud," wrote Alexander Smith, the nineteenth-century author of a once widely noted, now practically forgotten piece called "On the Writing of Essays." All experience flowers in the essay, pushes towards elaboration and definition—form.

Part of what passes through experience is, of course, the essay itself: essayists stay busy at their work and read other people's. And so, like other genres—but more explicitly, because the essay's impetus is, in the long run, an impetus to explain—our genre has a tendency to become fascinated by its own processes: to become self-absorbed, reflexive. To talk about what it means to *be* an essay. The form likes to keep track of itself; by ruminating, whether at length or in the occasional digression, on why and how they do what they do, essayists keep an eye on their practice. Maybe they have to, the form being so elusive, so open to reinvention at each new writing; maybe pondering the essay is a way of making it stand still, at least for the nonce, of limning its mobile features and thereby recalling the essayist to a sense of what can and can't be done. Formal openness has its traps. The pull may be irresistible to follow more firmly charted directions, to fall in with what may present themselves as more sharply delineated conventions than the essay upholds. Explanation and argument may stir up so many things in the mind and on the page that the discourse starts arraying itself, as if defensively, under "thesis statements," in neatly mustered paragraphs led by "topic sentences," and marches on towards "conclusions" like any respectable academic "paper"; storytelling may take off on the writer's inventive energies and soar into outright fiction—making it all (or mostly) up; beauties of imagery or sentence shape may grow so compelling in and of themselves the prose turns more poetic than the essayistic motive calls for. What one contemporary practitioner, Joseph Epstein, describes as "that shapeless, bottomless, lovely receptacle, the essay" ("Piece Work:

Writing the Essay") is always in danger of being made to shape up, mold itself to demands other than its own.

All this writing about the essay, then, appears to serve a paradoxical function: on one hand, to pin down, to stabilize and get a good look at what is so marvellously and fearfully mobile; on the other, to preserve just this mobility, this elasticity, of the form and to keep reminding anyone who attempts it how self-defeating all defections to treatise and article, fiction, or poetry are bound to be. In a house with as many entrances and exits as the essay, it becomes imperative, if you're going to take up residence, to hold in mind where they all are and where they lead.

However one accounts for it, the literary self-absorption of the essay has been, from the beginning, one of its special delights. Essayistic musings on the essay have not only kept the genre in communication with itself but have been its best and most enticing advertisement over the years. What follows is a collage of such writings, necessarily selective but diverse, from the ruminations of various essayists on their art. Being a collage it brings everything and everybody down to the same level, so to speak, irrespective of age or renown, where they have no choice but to inhabit a common space and engage in a dialogue of sorts. Somebody has to go to the trouble to get a conversation going, so it seems only fair to grant the first voice the longest hearing. Another reason to hear Edward Hoagland (see p. 518) out is simply that "What I Think, What I Am" must be the best short essay in English on what an essay is. Needless to say, it *shows* even as it *tells*.

What I Think, What I Am

Our loneliness makes us avoid column readers these days. The personalities in the San Francisco *Chronicle*, Chicago *Daily News*, New York *Post* constitute our neighbors now, some of them local characters but also the opinionated national stars. And movie reviewers thrive on our yearning for somebody emotional who is willing to pay attention to us and return week after week, year after year, through all the to-and-fro of other friends, to flatter us by pouring out his/her heart. They are essayists of a type, as Elizabeth Hardwick is, James Baldwin was.

We sometimes hear that essays are an old-fashioned form, that so-and-so is the "last essayist," but the facts of the marketplace argue quite otherwise. Essays of nearly any kind are so much easier than short stories for a writer to sell, so many more see print, it's strange that though two fine anthologies remain that publish the year's best stories, no comparable collection exists for essays.[1] Such changes in the reading public's taste aren't always to the good, needless to say. The art of telling stories predated even cave painting, surely; and if we ever find ourselves living in caves again, it (with painting and drumming) will be the only art left, after movies, novels, photography, essays, biography, and all the rest have gone down the drain—the art to build from.

One has the sense with the short story as a form that while everything may have been done, nothing has been overdone; it has a permanence. Essays, if a comparison is to be made, although they go back four hundred years to Montaigne, seem a mercurial, newfangled, sometimes hokey affair that has lent itself to many of the excesses of the age, from spurious autobiography to spurious hallucination, as well as to the shabby careerism of traditional journalism. It's a greased pig. Essays are associated with the way young writers fashion a name—on plain, crowded newsprint in hybrid vehicles like the *Village Voice*, *Rolling Stone*, the *New York Review of Books*, instead of the thick paper stock and thin readership of *Partisan Review*.

Essays, however, hang somewhere on a line between two sturdy poles: this is what I think, and this is what I am. Autobiographies which aren't novels are generally extended essays, indeed. A personal essay is like the human voice talking, its order the mind's natural flow, instead of a systematized outline of ideas. Though more wayward or informal than an article or treatise, somewhere it contains a point which is its real center, even if the point couldn't be uttered in fewer words than the essayist has used. Essays don't usually boil down to a summary, as articles do, and the style of the writer has a "nap" to it, a combination of personality and originality and energetic loose ends that stand up like the nap on a piece of wool and can't be brushed flat. Essays belong to the animal kingdom, with a surface that generates sparks, like a coat of fur, compared with the flat, conventional cotton of the magazine article writer, who works in the vegetable kingdom, instead. But essays, on the other hand, may have fewer "levels" than fiction, because we are not supposed to argue much about their meaning. In the old distinction between teaching and storytelling, the essayist, however cleverly he camouflages his intentions, is a bit of a teacher or reformer, and an essay is intended to convey the same point to each of us.

This emphasis upon mind speaking to mind is what makes essays less universal in their appeal than stories. They are addressed to an educated, perhaps a middle-class, reader, with certain presuppositions,

[1] Since 1985, Ticknor & Fields has been publishing *The Best American Essays* annually, under the general editorship of Robert Atwan.

a frame of reference, even a commitment to civility that is shared—not the grand and golden empathy inherent in every man or woman that a storyteller has a chance to tap.

Nevertheless, the artful "I" of an essay can be as chameleon as any narrator in fiction; and essays do tell a story quite as often as a short story stakes a claim to a particular viewpoint. Mark Twain's piece called "Corn-pone Opinions," for example, which is about public opinion, begins with a vignette as vivid as any in *Huckleberry Finn*. Twain says that when he was a boy of fifteen, he used to hang out a back window and listen to the sermons preached by a neighbor's slave standing on top of a woodpile: "He imitated the pulpit style of the several clergymen of the village, and did it well and with fine passion and energy. To me he was a wonder. I believed he was the greatest orator in the United States and would some day be heard from. But it did not happen; in the distribution of rewards he was overlooked. . . . He interrupted his preaching now and then to saw a stick of wood, but the sawing was a pretense—he did it with his mouth, exactly imitating the sound the bucksaw makes in shrieking its way through the wood. But it served its purpose, it kept his master from coming out to see how the work was getting along."

A novel would go on and tell us what happened next in the life of the slave—and we miss that. But the extraordinary flexibility of essays is what has enabled them to ride out rough weather and hybridize into forms that suit the times. And just as one of the first things a fiction writer learns is that he needn't actually be writing fiction to write a short story—that he can tell his own history or anybody else's as exactly as he remembers it and it will be "fiction" if it remains primarily a story—an essayist soon discovers that he doesn't have to tell the whole truth and nothing but the truth; he can shape or shave his memories, as long as the purpose is served of elucidating a truthful point. A personal essay frequently is not autobiographical at all, but what it does keep in common with autobiography is that, through its tone and tumbling progression, it conveys the quality of the author's mind. Nothing gets in the way. Because essays are directly concerned with the mind and the mind's idiosyncrasy, the very freedom the mind possesses is bestowed on this branch of literature that does honor to it, and the fascination of the mind is the fascination of the essay.

From *The Tugman's Passage* (1976)

Aside from the breathtaking skill with which Hoagland crafts this "tumbling progression" of an essay (breathtaking because it feels so simply spontaneous), there's the wealth of issues he touches on, however lightly and passingly, concerning the essay's art. In his casual manner, in fact, he lays out just about the whole range of questions entertained by essayists through the ages: questions of motive, of praxis, of generic bounds, of form, of voice, of truth, of style, of value.

The writers quoted in the following pages treat these topics in very different ways, partly for historical reasons, partly because of differences in temperament. This one may take for granted what that one has barely even thought of; assumptions vary, both about the human condition and that of the essay. Not everybody means the same thing by key words like "knowledge," "intimacy," "plain," "familiar," "methodical," "free"— and, of course, "essay." One writer's concern may be specific to his or her own practice; another's may extend to the whole field. Yet each voice carries conviction; each has the authority of a single writer's experience as a working essayist. They know whereof they speak. And, of course, each writer's perspective indicates (and, to some extent, seeks to justify) the kind of essay that particular writer values and, therefore, tends to write.

Although the arrangement of this material is deliberately tentative— to be dismantled and reassembled at will—it isn't arbitrary: it does, *as* an arrangement, make a certain kind of sense. It tries to stimulate certain lines of inquiry and suggests certain insights. That goes for the whole collage as well as for the sequences within each of its sections. Yet, the excerpts are also to be played with. Move them around into new sequences—the first one in the section last, the third one second, and so on, as fancy and curiosity dictate. Every move will alter the configuration, suggest new affinities or qualifications, expose interesting tangents, complicate or subvert what only moments ago seemed definitive. Any rearrangement will modulate the conversation in progress, alter its dynamic and shift its implications.

Essays in the Academy

Given what essayists are trying to do, is there a place for such work in the typical college setting, with its compartmentalized intellectual life? Are essays "composition," or "literature," or something else again?

> The essay is a pair of baggy pants into which nearly anyone and anything can fit. In the college catalogue of this term's offerings, it does not fall under "creative writing"; it is not, strictly speaking, even imaginative, though there has never been a want of imagination among its best practitioners. In range of interest, it is multivarious: there are literary essays, philosophical essays,

and historical essays; there are formal essays and familiar essays. The essay is in large part defined by the general temperament of the essayist. He is without pedantry; he is not, as they say in university English departments, "in the profession."

—Joseph Epstein, "Piece Work: Writing the Essay," *Plausible Prejudices* (1985)

An essayist deals with personal experiences, opinions, tastes, notions, and prejudices. For him, a fact is at best a peg to hang something on.

—Joseph Wood Krutch, "We Need More Than More Facts," *If You Don't Mind My Saying So* (1964)

I set forth notions that are human and my own, simply as human notions considered in themselves. . . .

—Michel de Montaigne, "Of Prayers" (I, 56), *The Complete Essays of Montaigne*, trans. Donald Frame (1957)

In days of more single purpose than these, young men and maidens, in the first flush of summer, set up a maypole on the green; but before they joined hands and danced round about it they had done honour to what it stood for by draping it with swags of flowers and green-stuff, hanging it with streamers of divers colours, and sticking it with as many gilt hearts as there were hearts among them of votive inclination. So they transfigured the thing signified, and turned a shaven tree-trunk from a very crude emblem into a thing of happy fantasy. That will serve me for a figure of how the poet deals with his little idea, or great one; and in his more sober mood it is open to the essayist so to deal with his, supposing he have one. He must hang his pole, or concept, not with rhyme but with wise or witty talk. He must turn it about and about, not to set the ornaments jingling, or little bells ringing; rather that you may see its shapeliness enhanced, its proportions emphasized, and in all the shifting lights and shadows of its ornamentation discern it still for the notion that it is.

—Maurice Hewlett, "The Maypole and the Column," *Extemporary Essays* (1922)

Essays are usually taught all wrong: instead of being celebrated for their delights as literature, they are harnessed to rhetoric and composition, in a two-birds-with-one-stone approach designed to sharpen the students' skills at argumentative persuasion.

—Philip Lopate, "The Essay Lives—in Disguise," *New York Times Book Review* (November 18, 1984)

Amplification and Form

How does an essay grow and take shape? How does one amplify—elaborate, develop, sustain—a topic? What kind of freedom does the essay offer—freedom from what, to do what? What control can/should an essayist exercise, and at what points in the process of amplification, and to what end? Is the achieved form of an essay merely the path of amplification itself?

> I had not written anything for fun since medical school and a couple of years thereafter, except for occasional light verse and once in a while a serious but not very clear or very good poem. Good bad verse was what I was pretty good at. The only other writing I'd done was scientific papers, around two hundred of them, composed in the relentlessly flat style required for absolute unambiguity in every word, hideous language as I read it today. The chance to break free of that kind of prose, and to try the essay form, raised my spirits, but at the same time worried me. I tried outlining some ideas for essays, making lists of items I'd like to cover in each piece, organizing my thoughts in orderly sequences, and wrote several dreadful essays which I could not bring myself to reread, and decided to give up being orderly. I changed the method to no method at all, picked out some suitable times late at night, usually on the weekend two days after I'd already passed the deadline, and wrote without outline or planning in advance, as fast as I could. This worked better, or at least was more fun, and I was able to get started.
> —Lewis Thomas, "Essays and Gaia," *The Youngest Science* (1983)

> Among my daily papers which I bestow on the public, there are some which are written with regularity and method and others that run out into the wildness of those compositions which go by the name of *essays*. As for the first, I have the whole scheme of the discourse in my mind, before I set pen to paper. In the other kind of writing, it is sufficient that I have several thoughts on the subject, without troubling myself to range them in such order that they may seem to grow out of one another and be disposed under the proper heads. Seneca and Montaigne are patterns for writing in this last kind, as Tully [Cicero] excels in the other. When I read an author of genius who writes without method, I fancy myself in a wood that abounds with a great many noble objects rising among one another in the greatest confusion and disorder. When I read a

methodical discourse, I am in a regular plantation and can place myself in several centers, so as to take a view of all the lines and walks that are struck from them. You may ramble in the one a whole day altogether and every moment discover something or other that is new to you, but when you have done you will have but a confused imperfect notion of the place; in the other, your eye commands the whole prospect and gives you such an idea of it as is not easily worn out of the memory.
—Joseph Addison, *Spectator* No. 476 (Friday, September 4, 1712)

To write just treatises requireth leisure in the writer and leisure in the reader . . . which is the cause that hath made me choose to write certain brief notes, set down rather significantly than curiously,[1] which I have called *essays*. . . . But my hope is they may be as grains of salt that will rather give you an appetite than offend you with satiety.
—Francis Bacon, Dedicatory Epistle, *Essays* (1610–12)

I know of no other written form so extemporaneous as the essay. It is a spiral rather than a circle, by definition unfinished.
—Richard Rhodes, Foreword, *Looking for America* (1979)

I hold neither Plutarch's nor none of those ancient short manner of writing, nor Montaigne's, nor such of this latter time to be rightly termed *essays*; for though they be short, yet they are strong and able to endure the sharpest trial. But mine are essays, who am but newly bound apprentice to the inquisition of knowledge and use these papers as a painter's boy a board, that is trying to bring his hand and his fancy acquainted. It is a manner of writing well befitting undigested motions, or a head not knowing his strength, like a circumspect runner trying for a start, or providence that tastes before it buys.
—William Cornwallis, "Of Essays and Books," *Essays* (1601)

All the same, essays seem a deviation, a diversion: the region of the trivial, no matter how momentous the subject. We can speculate why. Essays summarize. They do not invent. In undertaking the writing of an essay. . . . I know beforehand what I think. I see the end, it is all the while uncompromisingly, inflexibly, in sight, and my task is to traverse the space between. The risks are small. The way is predictable. It is a

[1] Suggestively or expressively, rather than carefully and elaborately.

journey of obligation within borders, not an adventure. . . . Essays know too much.

Except sometimes. Knowledge is not made out of knowledge. Knowing swims up from invention and imagination—from ardor—and sometimes even an essay can invent, burn, guess, try out, dig up, hurtle forward, succumb to that flood of sign and nuance that adds up to intuition, disclosure, discovery. The only nonfiction worth writing—at least for me—lacks the summarizing gift, is heir to nothing, and sets out with empty pockets from scratch. Sensibility (or intellect, or susceptibility) is most provoked when most deprived of scaffolding; then it has to knot sheets for the climb.

—Cynthia Ozick, Foreword, *Art & Ardor* (1983)

My conceptions and my judgment move only by groping, staggering, stumbling, and blundering, and when I have gone ahead as far as I can, still I am not at all satisfied: I can still see country beyond, but with a dim and clouded vision, so that I cannot clearly distinguish it.

—Montaigne, "Of the Education of Children," (I, 26)

Montaigne's generous development of the essay form, taking it to its outer limits right away, was . . . daunting. Afterward came an inevitable specialization, which included the very un-Montaignean split between formal and informal essays. It is difficult even now to draw a firm distinction between the two, because elements of one often turn up in the other, and because most of the great essayists were adept at both modes.

—Lopate, "The Essay Lives—in Disguise"

For me the writing of a personal essay is like finding my way through a forest without being quite sure what game I am chasing, what landmark I am seeking. I sniff down one path until some heady smell tugs me in a new direction, and then off I go, dodging and circling, lured on by the calls of unfamiliar birds, puzzled by the tracks of strange beasts, leaping from stone to stone across rivers, barking up one tree after another. The pleasure in writing an essay—and when the writing is any good in reading it—comes from this dodging and leaping, this movement of the mind.

It must not be idle movement, however, if the essay is to hold up; it must yield a pattern, draw a map of experience, be driven by deep concerns. The surface of a river is alive with lights and reflections, the breaking of foam over rocks, but

> underneath that dazzle it is going somewhere. We should expect as much from an essay: the shimmer and play of mind on the surface and in the depths a strong current.
>
> —Scott Russell Sanders, Introduction, *The Paradise of Bombs* (1987)

> When you write, you lay out a line of words. The line of words is a miner's pick, a woodcarver's gouge, a surgeon's probe. You wield it, and it digs a path you follow. Soon you find yourself in new territory. . . . You make the path boldly and follow it fearfully. You go where the path leads. . . . The writing has changed, in your hands, and in a twinkling, from an expression of your notions to an epistemological tool. The new place interests you because it is not clear. You attend. In your humility, you lay down the words carefully, watching all the angles. Now the earlier writing looks soft and careless. Process is nothing; erase your tracks. The path is not the work.
>
> —Annie Dillard, *The Writing Life* (1989)

Motive

Why write essays, why read them? What motives impel any particular essayist, any given essay? Can a reader tell from the rhetoric of a given essay what motive(s) drive(s) it?

> . . . the art of writing has for backbone some fierce attachment to an idea. It is on the back of an idea, something believed in with conviction or seen with precision and thus compelling words to its shape, that the diverse company which included Lamb and Bacon, Mr. Beerbohm and Hudson, and Vernon Lee and Mr. Conrad, and Leslie Stephen and Butler and Walter Pater reaches the farther shore.
>
> —Virginia Woolf, "The Modern Essay," *The Common Reader* (1925)

> The essayist is someone with a strong urge to write and no other place to exercise his urge but the essay. He wishes to leave the stamp of his personality on the page—and, with great good luck, who knows, on the age.
>
> —Epstein, "Piece Work: Writing the Essay"

> . . . when I consider how much I have seen, read and heard, I begin to blame my own taciturnity; and since I have neither

time nor inclination to communicate the fullness of my heart in speech, I am resolved to do it in writing and to print myself out, if possible, before I die. . . . I shall publish a sheet-full of thoughts every morning, for the benefit of my contemporaries, and if I can any way contribute to the diversion or improvement of the country in which I live, I shall leave it, when I am summoned out of it, with the secret satisfaction of thinking that I have not lived in vain.

—Joseph Addison, *Spectator* No. 1 (Thursday, March 1, 1711)

Putting aside the need to earn a living, I think there are four great motives for writing, at any rate for writing prose. They exist in different degrees in every writer, and in any one writer the proportions will vary from time to time, according to the atmosphere in which he is living. They are:

(1) Sheer egoism. Desire to seem clever, to be talked about, to be remembered after death, to get your own back on grownups who snubbed you in childhood, etc., etc. It is humbug to pretend that this is not a motive, and a strong one. . . .

(2) Esthetic enthusiasm. Perception of beauty in the external world, or, on the other hand, in words and their right arrangement. Pleasure in the impact of one sound on another, in the firmness of good prose or the rhythms of a good story. Desire to share an experience which one feels is valuable and ought not to be missed. . . .

(3) Historical impulse. Desire to see things as they are, to find out true facts and store them up for the use of posterity.

(4) Political purpose—using the world "political" in the widest possible sense. Desire to push the world in a certain direction, to alter other people's idea of the kind of society that they should strive for.

—George Orwell, "Why I Write," *Such, Such Were the Joys* (1953)

What many of the best essayists have had . . . was a quick access to their own blood reactions, so that the merest flash of a prejudice or taste-discrimination might be dragged into the open and defended.

—Lopate, "The Essay Lives—in Disguise"

On the subject of letter writing, I want to say this: that it is a kind of work in which my friends think I have some ability.

> And I would have preferred to adopt this form to publish my sallies, if I had had someone to talk to.
>
> —Montaigne, "A Consideration upon Cicero," (I, 40)

> In many ways writing is the act of saying *I*, of imposing oneself upon other people, of saying *listen to me*, *see it my way*, *change your mind*. It's an aggressive, even hostile act. You can disguise its aggressiveness all you want with veils of subordinate clauses and qualifiers and tentative subjunctives, with ellipses and evasions—with the whole manner of intimating rather than claiming, of alluding rather than stating—but there's no getting around the fact that setting words on paper is the tactic of a secret bully, an invasion, an imposition of the writer's sensibility on the reader's most private space.
>
> —Joan Didion, "Why I Write," *New York Times Book Review* (1976)

Voice

What does it mean to call an essayist's voice "intimate"? Is being "personal" congruent with being "intimate"? Can/Should an essayist be able to manage a range of voices? What range of voices does the genre as a whole accommodate? How does voice relate to motive, and to modes of amplification within the essay?

> The most delightful parts of Montaigne's essays are those where he breaks from the consideration of some abstract quality to explore the pecularities of his body or his soul. It is the same with Hazlitt, or with Thackeray. . . . None of these men has the least fear of giving himself away, and, perhaps, in a short piece that is the only thing of value that one can give away. . . . When we consider that this gift of intimacy is the most difficult of all to make, and that to convey anything so personal needs the impersonality of the highest art, we need not wonder that it is not often offered us between the politics and the reviews.
>
> —Virginia Woolf, "A Book of Essays," *The Essays of Virginia Woolf*, Vol. II, ed. Andrew McNeillie (1987)

> We commonly do not remember that it is, after all, always the first person that is speaking.
>
> —Henry David Thoreau, *Walden: or, Life in the Woods* (1854)

> A certain modesty of intention resides in the essay. It is a modesty inherent in the French verb that gives the form its

name—*essayer*: to try, to attempt, to taste, to try on, to assay. However many words the essayist may avail himself of, he instinctively knows, or ought to know, that the last word cannot be his. If it is the last word an author wants, let him go write books.

—Epstein, "Piece Work: Writing the Essay"

Though the early essayists' habit of quotation may seem excessive to modern taste, it was this display of learning that linked them to their educated reading public and ultimately gave them the authority to speak so personally about themselves.

—Lopate, "The Essay Lives—in Disguise"

Essays belong to a literary species whose extreme variability can be studied most effectively within a three-poled frame of reference. There is the pole of the personal and the autobiographical; there is the pole of the objective, the factual, the concrete-particular; and there is the pole of the abstract-universal. Most essayists are at home and at their best in the neighborhood of only one of the essay's three poles, or at the most only in the neighborhood of two of them. There are the predominantly personal essayists, who write fragments of reflective autobiography and who look at the world through the keyhole of anecdote and description. There are the predominantly objective essayists who do not speak directly of themselves, but turn their attention outward to some literary or scientific or political theme. Their arts consist of setting forth, passing judgment upon, and drawing general conclusions from, the relevant data. In the third group we find those essayists who do their work in the world of high abstractions, who never condescend to be personal and who hardly deign to take notice of the particular facts from which their generalizations were originally drawn. . . .

The most richly satisfying essays are those which make the best not of one, not of two, but of all the three worlds in which it is possible for the essay to exist.

—Aldous Huxley, Preface, *Collected Essays* (1959)

The essay is a haven for the private idiosyncratic voice in an era of anonymous babble. Like the blandburgers served in their millions along highways, most language served up in public these days is textureless tasteless mush. On television, over the phone, in the newspaper, wherever human beings bandy words, we encounter more and more abstractions, more empty formulas. Think of the pablum ladled out by politicians. Think of the fluffy white bread of advertising. Think, lord help us, of committee reports. By contrast the essay remains stubbornly concrete and particular: it confronts you with an oil-smeared toilet seat at the Sunoco station, a red vinyl purse shaped like a valentine heart, a bowlegged dentist hunting deer with an elephant gun. As Orwell forcefully argued, and as dictators seem to agree, such a bypassing of abstractions, such an insistence on the concrete, is a politically subversive act. Clinging to this door, that child, this grief, following the zigzag motions of an inquisitive mind, the essay renews language and clears trash from the springs of thought. A century and a half ago Emerson called on a new generation of writers to cast off the hand-me-down rhetoric of the day, to "pierce this rotten diction and fasten words again to visible things." The essayist aspires to do just that.

—Scott Russell Sanders, "The Singular First Person," *Sewanee Review* (Fall 1988)

The essay, as a literary form, resembles the lyric, in so far as it is moulded by some central mood—whimsical, serious, or satirical. Give the mood, and the essay, from the first sentence to the last, grows around it as the cocoon grows around the silkworm.

—Alexander Smith, "On the Writing of Essays," *Dreamthorp* (1863)

Never to be yourself and yet always—that is the problem.

—Woolf, "The Modern Essay"

There are as many kinds of essays as there are human attitudes or poses, as many essay flavors as there are Howard Johnson ice creams. The essayist arises in the morning and, if he has work to do, selects his garb from an unusually extensive wardrobe: he can pull on any sort of shirt, be any sort of person, according to his mood or his subject matter—philosopher, scold, jester, raconteur, confidant, pundit, devil's advocate, enthusiast.

—E. B. White, Foreword, *Essays of E. B. White* (1977)

Truth

Is an essay an instrument of truth—a means of getting at some truth, of telling the truth? What does it mean to be truthful, to tell the truth in an essay? Has an essay failed if it fails to deliver up the truth about some subject? Where's the line between shaping experience and making it up, between essay and fiction? Can a reader know the difference? Can a reader detect fakery? What's the connection between self-knowledge and being truthful in an essay? Can an essayist's voice deceive?

> I put forward formless and unresolved notions, as do those who publish doubtful questions to debate in the schools, not to establish the truth but to seek it.
>
> —Montaigne, "Of Prayers," (I, 56)

> The essay offers the chance to wrestle with one's own intellectual confusion and to set down one's ideas in a manner both more straightforward and more exposed than in fiction. . . .
>
> —Lopate, "The Essay Lives—in Disguise"

> There is one thing the essayist cannot do, though—he cannot indulge himself in deceit or in concealment, for he will be found out in no time.
>
> —White, Foreword, *Essays of E. B. White*

> Sir Francis Bacon observes that a well-written book compared with its rivals and antagonists is like Moses' serpent that immediately swallow'd up and devoured those of the Egyptians. I shall not be so vain as to think that where the *Spectator* appears the other public prints will vanish, but shall leave it to my reader's consideration whether it is not much better to be let into the knowledge of oneself than to hear what passes in Muscovy or Poland, and to amuse ourselves with such writings as tend to the wearing out of ignorance, passion, and prejudices, than such as naturally conduce to inflame hatreds and make enmities irreconcilable.
>
> —Joseph Addison, *Spectator* No. 10 (Monday, March 12, 1711)

> . . . the essayist's habit of not only giving you his thoughts, but telling you how he came by them, is interesting, because it shows you by what alchemy the ruder world becomes transmuted into the finer. We like to know the lineage of ideas just as we like to know the lineage of great earls and swift racehorses. We like to know that the discovery of the law of gravitation was born of the fall of an apple in an English garden on a summer afternoon. Essays written after this fashion are racy of the soil in which they grow, as you taste the lava in the vines grown on the slopes of Etna, they say.
>
> —Smith, "On the Writing of Essays"

And although [my essays] handle those things wherein both men's lives and their pens are most conversant, yet . . . I have endeavoured to make them not vulgar, but of a nature whereof a man shall find much in experience, little in books, so as they are neither repetitions nor fancies.

—Bacon, Dedicatory Epistle, *Essays*

Most of the fictions of the past twenty years have led away from candor—toward irony, satire, artsy jokes, close-lipped coyness, anything but serious, direct statement of what the author thinks and feels. If you hide behind enough screens, no one will ever hold you to an opinion or demand from you a coherent vision or take you for a charlatan. The essay appeals to me because it is not hedged round by these literary inhibitions. You may speak without disguise of what moves and worries and excites you. If the words you put down are foolish, then at least everyone knows who the fool is.

—Sanders, Introduction, *The Paradise of Bombs*

The essay can do everything a poem can do, and everything a short story can do—everything but fake it. The elements in any nonfiction should be true not only artistically—the connections must hold at base and must be veracious, for that is the convention and the covenant between the nonfiction writer and his reader. Veracity isn't much of a drawback to the writer; there's a lot of truth out there to work with. And veracity isn't much of a drawback to the reader. The real world arguably exerts a greater fascination on people than any fictional one; many people, at least, spend their whole lives there, apparently by choice. The essayist does what we do with our lives; the essayist thinks about actual things. He can make sense of them analytically or artistically. In either case he renders the real world coherent and meaningful, even if only bits of it, and even if that coherence and meaning reside only inside small texts.

—Annie Dillard, Introduction, *The Best American Essays* (1988)

In all the questioning about what makes a writer, and especially perhaps the personal essayist, I have seen little reference to this fact; namely, that the brain has become a kind of unseen artist's loft. There are pictures that hang askew, pictures with outlines barely chalked in, pictures torn, pictures the artist has striven unsuccessfully to erase, pictures that only emerge and glow in a certain light. They have all been teleported, stolen, as it were, out of time. They represent no longer the sequential flow of ordinary memory. They can be pulled about on easels, examined within the mind itself. The act is not one of total recall like that of the professional mnemonist. Rather it is the use of things extracted from their context in such a way that they have become the unique possession of a single life. The writer sees back to these transports alone, bare, perhaps few in number, but endowed with a symbolic life. He cannot obliterate them. He can only drag them about, magnify or reduce them as his artistic sense dictates, or juxtapose them in order to enhance a pattern. One thing he cannot do. He cannot destroy what will not be destroyed; he cannot determine in advance what will enter his mind.

—Loren Eiseley, *All the Strange Hours* (1975)

I am here only at revealing myself, who will perhaps be different tomorrow, if I learn something new which changes me.

—Montaigne, "Of the Education of Children," (I, 26)

Any essayist, setting out in a frail apparatus of noticings and jottings, is a brave person. Maybe this is why there are so few good ones at work today. . . . Stand-up musings are tricky, because the closer they come to the bone, the more they are imperiled by silliness, sentimentality, or egotism. . . .

—Diane Johnson, "The Traveling Self: Edward Hoagland," *Terrorists and Novelists* (1982)

To tell the truth about oneself, to discover oneself near at hand, is not easy.

—Virginia Woolf, "Montaigne," *The Common Reader*

Style

Does the language matter? Should essays strive to sound colloquial? Is a plain style necessarily colloquial? Is a colloquial style necessarily plain? Does figurative language have a place in essays? Is syntactical complexity a good thing? What is a "beautiful" style? Should an essay be stylistically homogeneous? What relations does style have to voice, to amplification, to truth?

A novel has a story, a poem rhyme; but what art can the essayist use in these short lengths of prose to sting us wide awake and fix us in a trance which is not sleep but rather an intensification of life—a basking, with every faculty alert, in the sun of pleasure? He must know—that is the first essential—how to write.

—Woolf, "The Modern Essay"

. . . he has failed because he has tried to write beautifully. The danger of trying to write beautifully in English lies in the ease with which it is possible to do something very like it. There are the old cadences humming in one's head, the old phrases covering nothing so decently that it seems to be something after all. Preoccupied with the effort to be smooth, rotund, demure, and irreproachable, sentimentality slips past unnoticed, and platitudes spread themselves abroad with an air of impeccable virtue.

—Virginia Woolf, "Imitative Essays," *The Essays of Virginia Woolf*, Vol. II

It is not easy to write a familiar style. Many people mistake a familiar for a vulgar style, and suppose that to write without affectation is to write at random. On the contrary, there is nothing that requires more precision, and, if I may so say, purity of expression, than the style I am speaking of. It utterly rejects not only all unmeaning pomp, but all low, cant phrases, and loose, unconnected slipshod allusions. It is not to take the first word that offers, but the best word in common use; it is not to throw words together in any combinations we please, but to follow and avail ourselves of the true idiom of the language. To write a genuine familiar or truly English style, is to write as anyone would speak in common conversation who had a thorough command and choice of words, or who could discourse with ease, force, and perspicuity, setting aside all pedantic and oratorical flourishes.

—William Hazlitt, "On Familiar Style," *Selected Essays*, ed. Geoffrey Keynes (1948)

I cannot go along with those who say, "The art of conversation has died," because I have no idea what such a statement means. . . . What has departed is conversationally-flavored writing, which implies a speaking relationship between writer and reader.

—Lopate, "The Essay Lives—in Disguise"

Fine writing is still with us. Density, even lushness, and elegance, forceful rhythms, dramatically fused imagery, and a degree of metaphorical splendor—these qualities still obtain and are the hallmark of fine writing.

—Annie Dillard, "Fine Writing, Cranks, and the New Morality: Prose Styles," *Living by Fiction* (1982)

The temptation to decorate is great where the theme may be slight.

—Woolf, "The Modern Essay"

Plain writing is by no means easy writing. The *mot juste* is an intellectual achievement.

—Dillard, "Fine Writing, Cranks, and the New Morality: Prose Styles"

The essay may deal in metaphor better than the poem can, in some ways, because prose may expand what the lyric poem must compress. Instead of confining a metaphor to half a line, the essayist can devote to it a narrative, descriptive, or reflective couple of pages, and bring forth vividly its meanings. Prose welcomes all sorts of figurative language, of course, as well as alliteration, and even rhyme. The range of rhythms in prose is larger and grander than that of poetry. And it can handle discoursive idea, and plain fact, as well as character and story.

—Dillard, Introduction, *The Best American Essays* (1988)

Style is an increment in writing. . . . Every writer, by the way he uses the language, reveals something of his spirit, his habits, his capacities, his bias. This is inevitable, as well as enjoyable. All writing is communication; creative writing is communication through revelation—it is the Self escaping into the open. No writer long remains incognito.

—E. B. White, "An Approach to Style," *The Elements of Style* (1959)

Praxis

Under what conditions is an essayist likely to do his or her best work? How much leisure does one need, and for what? Should an essayist make notes, keep a journal? What kinds of things are worth noting? What use are deadlines? What is a regimen? Are inspiration and habit mutually exclusive factors in writing essays?

Essays lie all over the land, stored up like the unused wheat of a decade ago in the silos of old magazines and modest collec-

tions. In the midst of this clumsy abundance, there are rare lovers of the form, the great lovers being some few who practice it as the romance this dedication can be.
—Elizabeth Hardwick, Introduction, *A Susan Sontag Reader* (1982)

This bundle of so many disparate pieces is being composed in this manner: I set my hand to it only when pressed by too unnerving an idleness, and nowhere but at home.
—Montaigne, "Of the Resemblance of Children to Fathers" (II, 37)

A writer who has his sights trained on the Nobel Prize or other earthly triumphs had best write a novel, or a poem, or a play, and leave the essayist to ramble about, content with living a free life and enjoying the satisfactions of a somewhat undisciplined existence.

—White, Foreword, *Essays of E. B. White*

As it is the fashion for modern tourists to travel pencil in hand and bring home their portfolios filled with sketches, I am disposed to get up a few for the entertainment of my friends. When, however, I look over the hints and memorandums I have taken down for the purpose, my heart almost fails me at finding how my idle humor has led me aside from the great objects studied by every regular traveller who would make a book. I fear I shall give equal disappointment with an unlucky landscape-painter, who had travelled on the continent, but, following the bent of his vagrant inclination, had sketched in nooks, and corners, and by-places. His sketch-book was accordingly crowded with cottages, and landscapes, and obscure ruins; but he had neglected to paint St. Peter's or the Coliseum, the cascade of Terni, or the bay of Naples, and had not a single glacier or volcano in his whole collection.
—Washington Irving, "The Author's Account of Himself," *The Sketchbook* (1819–20)

The present writing is only to admonish the world that they shall not find me an idle but a very busy Spectator.
—Richard Steele, *Spectator* No. 4 (Monday, March 5, 1711)

How it felt to me: that is getting closer to the truth about a notebook. I sometimes delude myself about why I keep a notebook, imagine that some thrifty virtue derives from preserving everything observed. See enough and write it down, I tell myself, and then some morning when the world seems drained of wonder, some day when I am only going through the motions of doing what I am supposed to do, which is write—on that bankrupt morning I will simply open my notebook and there it will be. . . .

—Joan Didion, "On Keeping a Notebook," *Slouching Towards Bethlehem* (1966)

He that condemns himself to compose on a stated day will often bring to his task an attention dissipated, a memory embarrassed, an imagination overwhelmed, a mind distracted with anxieties, a body languishing with disease: he will labour on a barren topic, 'till it is too late to change it, or in the ardour of invention, diffuse his thoughts into wild exuberance which the pressing hour of publication cannot suffer judgment to examine or reduce.

—Samuel Johnson, *Rambler* No. 208 (Saturday, March 14, 1752)

After a while it became a kind of habit, and I continued writing with fair regularity for something over four years. . . . Having caught the habit, I kept on writing short essays, some for the *New England Journal*, some unpublished, and four years later there were enough for a second book. . . .

—Lewis Thomas, "Essays and Gaia"

Value

What are essays for? *Who* are they for? Can essays—reading them and writing them—make life better?

In this era of pre-packaged thought the essay is the closest thing we have, on paper, to a record of the individual mind at work and play. It is an amateur's raid in a world of specialists. Feeling overwhelmed by data, random information, the flotsam and jetsam of mass culture, we relish the spectacle of a single consciousness making sense of a part of the chaos.

—Sanders, "The Singular First Person"

It was said of Socrates that he brought philosophy down from heaven to inhabit among men, and I shall be ambitious to have it said of me that I have brought philosophy out of closets and libraries, schools and colleges, to dwell in clubs and assemblies, at tea tables, and in coffee houses.

—Joseph Addison, *Spectator* No. 10

'Tis with great pleasure I observe that men of letters in this age have lost, in great measure, that shyness and bashfulness of temper which kept them at a distance from mankind, and, at the same time, that men of the world are proud of borrowing from books their most agreeable topics of conversation. 'Tis to be hop'd that this league betwixt the learned and conversible worlds which is so happily begun will be still farther improv'd to their mutual advantage; and to that end I know nothing more advantageous than such essays as these with which I endeavour to entertain the public. In this view, I cannot but consider myself as a kind of resident ambassador from the dominions of learning to those of conversation, and shall think it my constant duty to promote a good correspondence betwixt these two states which have so great a dependence on each other. I shall give intelligence to the learned of whatever passes in company, and shall endeavour to import into company whatever commodities I find in my native country proper to their use and entertainment.

—David Hume, "On Essay Writing," *Essays Moral and Political* (1742)

It [the essay] has been too much an indulgence of gentlemen, and so has lost repute, but it is an old and honorable form, invented at a time when men believed an individual sensibility, an individual intelligence, could be a useful and sometimes revealing measure of the world.

—Rhodes, Foreword, *Looking for America*

I am not building here a statue to erect at the town crossroads, or in a church or a public square. . . . This is for a nook in a library, and to amuse a neighbor, a relative, a friend, who may take pleasure in associating and conversing with me again in this image.

—Montaigne, "Of Giving the Lie" (II, 18)

The essay is a vulnerable form. Rooted in middle-class civility, it presupposes not only that the essayist himself be demonstrably sane, but that his readers also operate upon a set of widely held assumptions. Fiction can be hallucinatory if it wishes, and journalism impassive, and so each continues through thick and thin, but essays presuppose a certain standard of education in the reader, a world ruled by some sort of order—where government is constitutional, or at least monarchical, perhaps where sex hasn't wandered too far from its home base and religion isn't so smothering that nobody knows where babies come from—where people seek not fragmentation but a common bond.

—Edward Hoagland, "That Gorgeous Great Novelist," *Red Wolves & Black Bears* (1976)

It is a form with distinguished predecessors and a rich tradition, and within its generous boundaries one can do almost anything one wishes: report anecdotes, tell jokes, make literary criticisms, polemicize, bring in odd scraps of scholarship, recount human idiosyncrasy in its full bountifulness, let the imagination roam free.

—Epstein, "Piece Work: Writing the Essay"

The principle which controls it is simply that it should give pleasure; the desire which impels us when we take it from the shelf is simply to receive pleasure. Everything in an essay must be subdued to that end. It should lay us under a spell with its first word, and we should only wake, refreshed, with its last. In the interval we may pass through the most various experiences of amusement, surprise, interest, indignation; we may soar to the heights of fancy with Lamb or plunge to the depths of wisdom with Bacon, but we must be roused. The essay must lap us about and draw its curtain across the world.

—Woolf, "The Modern Essay"

Talking About Style

In *The Writing Life* (1989) Annie Dillard tells this story:

> A well-known writer got collared by a university student who asked, "Do you think I could be a writer?"
>
> "Well," the writer said, "I don't know. . . .Do you like sentences?"

Sentences are what we spend all our time getting in and out of when we write. You can't get away from them any more than a dancer from her own body. Writing is thought moving in sentences, from one to the next, one sentence at a time. An essay is a stream of sentences if one thinks of discourse as a process—being written or read—or an aggregate of sentences if one considers it as a crafted object, a finished text. Style has to do with the way each sentence works, what shape it makes as it moves, and with the cumulative effect of such shapes in the run of language, the discourse.

A reader tends to experience this cumulative effect not as *style* (unless one is actually looking *at* sentence structures) but as *voice:* as a speaking presence. Someone intimate, or detached, or ironic, or sarcastic, or nostalgic, or ruminative, or playful, or learned, or didactic, or modest, or provocative, or coolly analytical, or subtly or forcefully persuasive, and so on. There are as many voices as there are essays to contain them. But voice, in writing, is a sort of metaphor, as is the closely related term *tone*, the attitude towards subject and audience that a reader infers from a text. The words on the page don't literally speak; literally, there's no one there. (Strictly, there are no words as such there, no sentences; there are only marks on paper which we activate into significance by the decoding processes we call "reading.") What happens to us as we read is very *like* hearing a living, thinking, feeling person speak; in a genre such as the essay that experience is, by design, inescapable and part of the fun. To be absorbed by an essay means to forget that you're decoding marks on paper and to experience what you're doing as engaging in a particular kind of relationship with someone over something.

Voice is the essayistic self constructed *as* and *by means of* style. The words you choose (*diction*) and how you order and relate them in sentences (*syntax*) create your style. Style, as E. B. White suggests, is inevitable: your writing will have a style no matter what; the only question, always, is whether the style has been crafted, shaped—chosen in accord with an essayistic motive—or whether it has simply happened, inadvertent as the smudge of a bad ribbon, beyond the writer's intelligent grasp. To recognize that writing is, as White says, "the Self escaping into the open," may be a chilling thought, enough to put anybody off writing permanently; or it may become the impetus to learning how the resources of language, its range of diction and its plasticity of syntax, serve the writer's art of communication. Style is the realm of choice, of freedom, in langauge; it is the realm of invention, of self-definition—even, in the final analysis, of truth. A style may betray the truth, even against the writer's will, or it may help to tell the truth by its capacity to meld with experience and with the writer's sense of self.

But what is there to talk about, when we talk about style? Can we say any more than: a pleasing style, an ugly style, a dull style, a pompous style, a labored style, an awkward style, a careless style, a graceful style? *Need* we say more than that?

We can talk about how sentences work, take note of style *descriptively* rather than in purely *evaluative* ways, to praise or condemn. The utility of stylistic description is at least threefold. In a community of writers and readers (such as a college class), it offers a rudimentary common language to account for what people think is going on in a text—not as they contemplate it at a distance, but as they actually engage it, word for word. In the effort of any one writer to learn from accomplished others, knowledge of style serves as a tool for analyzing models one may wish to imitate so as to try out one's own verbal skills for mastering one's own stylistic range. And, in one's own craft as an essayist, awareness of diction and syntax becomes indispensable the more one cares about shaping and polishing the work-in-progress, rewriting and editing until the thing "sounds right," until it says what one wants it to say in the way necessary to say it. It may not be essential to know how to describe a sentence in order to write it; but it *is* essential to know something of what it is possible to do with words in sentences, to cultivate an intelligent ear for sentence shapes, in order to appropriate the resources of language for one's own motives and sensibilities as a writer.

Diction: The Words Chosen

In considering the diction of an essay, or a passage in an essay, one might pose questions such as:

1. Which of the semantically most weighted words (the verbs, nouns, adjectives, adverbs) are *general* and *abstract*, which are *specific* and *concrete?* Are there, for instance, words that create images—evoke sensory experience?

2. At what *levels of usage* (sometimes called *registers*) do the significant words operate? Specifically, does the diction tend to be *colloquial*, or does it draw upon *learned* or *technical* vocabulary (*i.e.*, belonging to some field like molecular biology, literary criticism, computer programming, etc.)?

3. Do any of the words work non-literally, to create metaphors, similes, and other *figures of speech?*

No essay—if it *is* an essay, rather than a treatise or an article—can survive a wholly abstract diction, or a consistently learned, or a technical one; not even the most poetic of essays can sustain a purely figurative diction, nor, on the other hand, will even the most colloquial discourse be utterly devoid of metaphoric play. What is most telling, therefore, about an essay's diction, is not the bare count of abstract and concrete, colloquial and learned, literal and figurative, but the essayist's movement between and among these poles; such verbal shifts create the semantic range of a given style and the modulations we hear as the essayist's voice.

Consider these passages:

> There was a delicious sensation of mingled security and awe with which I looked down, from my giddy height, on the monsters of the deep at their uncouth gambols. Shoals of porpoises tumbling about the bow of the ship; the grampus slowly heaving his huge form above the surface; or the ravenous shark, darting, like a spectre, through the blue waters. (Irving, "The Voyage").

> A political emergency brings out the corn-pone opinion in fine force in its two chief varieties—the pocketbook variety, which has its origin in self-interest, and the bigger variety, the sentimental variety—the one which can't bear to be outside the pale; can't bear to be in disfavor; can't endure the averted face and the cold shoulder; wants to stand well with his friends, wants to be smiled upon, wants to be welcome, wants to hear the precious words, "*He's* on the right track!" Uttered, perhaps by an ass, but still an ass of high degree, an ass whose approval is gold and diamonds to a smaller ass, and confers glory and honor and happiness, and membership in the herd. (Twain, "Corn-pone Opinions").

Note how Irving's first sentence announces in *general* terms—"the monsters of the deep at their uncouth gambols"—what the more *specific* and *concrete* images go on to depict in the next sentence (actually a fragment): "porpoises tumbling . . . the grampus slowly heaving . . . the ravenous shark, darting. . . ." In the Twain passage, shifts of diction are more complex: the *abstract* "corn-pone opinion" of the opening clause is first specified under two kinds (the "pocketbook variety" and the "sentimental variety"), then turns *concrete*, acquiring the solidity and particularity of a feeling, thinking, sensing individual, with full personification of the original "corn-pone opinion" in the verb phrase "wants to stand well with his friends"; near the close, the concrete "gold and diamonds" gives way to the abstract "glory and honor and happiness," with a slight reversal towards the concrete pole yet again at "membership in the herd."

In the next three examples, mobility of diction sustains the stylistic ease and accessibility we expect from essays, while drawing on *learned* and/or *technical* words appropriate to the topic each writer attempts:

> In the course of evolution man is supposed to have sacrificed the greater part of his olfactory center to his cortex, his sense of smell to his intelligence (Huxley, "Hyperion to a Satyr").

> The antiessentialist sees something entirely different in his hand—a range of irreducible variation defining the species, some variations more frequent than others, but all perfectly good snails (Gould, "Of Wasps and WASPs").

> The flagellae that beat in synchrony to propel myxotricha with such directness turn out, on closer scrutiny with the electron microscope, not to be flagellae at all. They are outsiders, in to help with the business: fully formed, perfect spirochetes that have attached themselves at regularly spaced intervals all over the surface of the protozoan (Thomas, "An Earnest Proposal").

Huxley, in a move characteristic of his elegantly wrought essays, balances a learned, semi-scientific phrase ("his olfactory center to his cortex") with a precise and colloquial one ("his sense of smell to his intelligence"). Gould's reflections on taxonomy take him from the learned "antiessentialist" and the technical "variation" and "species" to the solidly colloquial (and more concrete) "but perfectly good snails." And Thomas, the student of molecular biology who loves the perenially colloquial Montaigne, makes an art of weaving technical language ("flagellae," "myxotricha," "electron microscope," "spirochetes") through the common threads of everyday speech ("beat," "turn out," "in to help with the business," etc.)—or perhaps the weave works the other way around; in a Thomas essay, it's often impossible to say which layer of diction is the warp and which the woof.

The following eight passages all exhibit, in a variety of ways, the play of *literal* and *figurative* language.

An extended *metaphor* amplifies an initial analogy formulated in literal terms:

> Thoreau's assault on the Concord society of the mid-nineteenth century has the quality of a modern Western: he rides into the subject at top speed, shooting in all directions. Many of his shots ricochet and nick him on the rebound, and throughout the melee there is a horrendous cloud of inconsistencies and contradictions, and when the shooting dies down and the air clears, one is impressed chiefly by the courage of the rider and by how splendid it was that somebody should have ridden in there and raised all that ruckus (White, "A Slight Sound at Evening").

A series of literal images climaxes in a metaphoric one—likening the busy, naked feet of London's hustling street-children to soft rain falling on the pavement—that places the whole descriptive sequence in a complex moral perspective, yet so subtly, and with such compression, one has to work at it a bit:

> But one of the worst sights I know in London, is to be found in the children who prowl about this place; who sleep in the baskets, fight for the offal, dart at any object they think they can lay their thieving hands on, dive under the carts and barrows, dodge the constables, and are perpetually making a blunt pattering on the pavement of the Piazza with the rain of their naked feet (Dickens, "Night Walks").

This next one looks innocently literal; but Welty's "snap" evokes the swift efficiency of predation, of an alligator, perhaps, ingesting its prey whole:

> The home shelves had been providing me all along with the usual books, and I read them with love—but snap, I finished them. I read everything just alike—snap (Welty, "A Sweet Devouring").

John Earle's seventeenth-century prose, too, wears an unassuming literal face which only a close look reveals to be densely figurative:

> It is a heap of stones and men, with a vast confusion of languages, and were the steeple not sanctified, nothing liker Babel. The noise in it is like that of bees, a strange humming or buzz,

> mixed of walking, tongues and feet. It is a kind of still roar or whisper (Earle, "Paul's Walk").

The bee *simile* snags our attention first, leads to the *metonymic* "tongue" (for "talking") and "foot" (for "walking," "movement"), followed by an *oxymoron*, "still roar," instantly transliterated to plain "whisper." Back at the beginning, the pairing of "stones" and "men" under "heap" is an instance of *zeugma*.

In this passage, by contrast, the figure of speech stands out—wildly— in the unexpected comic *simile* of semicolons and ticks:

> Why do I avoid, as much as possible, using the semicolon? Let me be plain: the semicolon is ugly, ugly as a tick on a dog's belly. I pinch them out of my prose (Barthelme, "Not-Knowing").

Here, too, a prominent *metaphor* following the first, literally worded sentence intensifies the image of drought-striken land by a kind of cruel double-exposure—a desert looking like a great wavy lake:

> But now the terrible drought *has* come, the famine as predicted by the men at the wateringhole the year before. The desert itself is undulant, looking most like the water it craves (Selzer, "A Worm from My Notebook").

In these two very different passages, the literal finish undercuts and modulates the elaborate metaphor at the start, effecting shifts in both mood (*i.e.*, feeling) and tone (attitude to material):

> In this flat swamp of convalescence, left by the ebb of sickness, yet far enough from *terra firma* of established health, your note, dear editor, reached me, requesting—an article (Lamb, "The Convalescent").

> These dark pelagic birds flick along pleated seas in stitching flocks, flailing their wings rapidly—because if they don't, they'll stall (Dillard, "Life on the Rocks").

Interesting things happen in the next three passages, in each of which the essayist wrests a lucid and vital metaphor out of what are already figurative clichés, stylistic dead matter, language so worn only the magic of real artistry can revive it with fresh meaning and renewed impact:

> No, I do not weep at the world—I am too busy sharpening my oyster knife (Hurston, "How It Feels to be Colored Me").

> They can do nothing for us if we herd ourselves under their authority and lie down like sheep in the shade of a hedge (Woolf, "How Should One Read a Book?")

> And so I do my five days in the thirteenth chair. Bennie may do as many as fifty-four years in prison, buying his drugs from meaner dealers, dreaming of land mines and of his adopted girls, checking the date on his watch, wondering at what precise moment the hinges of his future slammed shut (Sanders, "Doing Time in the Thirteenth Chair").

Hurston's zestful "sharpening my oyster knife" springs from the metaphoric cliché "the world is my oyster"; Woolf gives a thought-provoking turn to the hackneyed association of passivity with sheep by pairing the concrete verb "herd" with the surprising, abstract "authority"; Sanders, somewhat like Dickens, walks through a series of hard-hitting literal images to a figure (*synecdoche*) that startlingly substitutes the vital *part*—"hinges"—for the more conventional, even clichéd *whole*—doors: the literal prison door that will close behind Bennie, and the figurative door to his future.

Finally, here is a set of quotations where movements along the *literal-figurative* axis cross other paths: between *abstract* and *concrete*, *general* and *specific*, even traces of *learned* and *technical*. In this lovely quotation from Hazlitt, initial abstraction, cast in almost learned terms ("synthetical method" and "analytical") is succeeded by the more concrete diction of two low-key metaphors: storing and anatomizing experience. Then comes a series of picturesquely concrete and specific images expressed in an extended simile:

> I am for the synthetical method on a journey, in preference to the analytical. I am content to lay in a stock of ideas then, and to examine and anatomize them afterwards. I want to see my vague notions float like the down of the thistle before the breeze, and not to have them entangled in the briars and thorns of controversy (Hazlitt, "On Going a Journey").

Bacon and Momaday make similar shifts from abstract to concrete, by way of simile and metaphor:

> They [studies] perfect nature, and are perfected by experience; for natural abilities are like natural plants, that need pruning by study: and studies themselves, do give forth directions too much at large, except they be bounded in by experience (Bacon, "Of Studies").

> The sun follows a longer course in the day, and the sky is immense beyond comparison. The great billowing clouds that sail upon it are shadows that move upon the grain like water, dividing light (Momaday, "The Way to Rainy Mountain").

Naipaul produces a powerful rhetorical climax by moving oppositely, not from literal and abstract to figurative and concrete, but from descriptive language that is both literal and concrete to the high abstraction of "human immensity" personified by the expressive verb "rages":

> In the early evening, every yellow-lit window in every multistory block thrown wide open to the stagnant air rich with the smell of smoke and food, every transistor radio turned to full volume, every car horn blaring, every voice raised to a shout, the human immensity rages with something approaching frenzy (Naipaul, "City by the Sea").

Dillard is a writer who plays with words every which way, almost as if intent upon missing no possible path or trail of movement. Here she jumps sideways from the concreteness and specificity of metaphor in the first sentence to the concreteness and specificity of literal language in the second:

> The rocks shape life like hands around swelling dough. In Virginia the salamanders vary from mountain ridge to mountain ridge; so do the fiddle tunes the old men play (Dillard, "Life on the Rocks").

And in this, the first, more general metaphor (mountains as "time's machines") generates a second, more specific metaphor (mountains as "printers' rollers"):

> The mountains are time's machines; in effect, they roll out protoplasm like printers' rollers pressing out news (Dillard, "Life on the Rocks").

Syntax: Words in their Order and Relation

Sentences exist so to speak in motion. Sentences, in other words, make *discourse*, a word whose etymology goes back to the Latin *currere:* to run. And so, to study the syntax of a given style, to understand how it arranges words into sentences, one must look both at what goes on within a given sentence and at what is happening between and among consecutive sentences. The stylistic effects of syntax make themselves felt in the run of the prose; as E. B. White said, "Style is an increment in writing." To pull out a sentence or two, or even several, as is done in what follows here, is like arresting a mere phrase in a longer and larger melody. It is, of course, the melody one is after—the "increment" that is the style of the discourse, the essay, as a whole. Understanding the stylistic habits of an essay means putting your specimen sentence, or sequence, back into its context, its paragraph at the very least; and it means sounding out the essay as a whole for its characteristic patterns, the variety and range of syntax at work.

What patterns? What shall we look for? Here's a list, by no means complete, but it makes a useful start that can take one quite a long way:

1. What is the *order* of basic elements in the sentence—subject, verb, complement (if there is one)? Is it *regular* or *inverted?*

2. Is the meaning of sentences concentrated mainly in their *verbs* or in their *nouns* (and attendant modifiers)?

3. What is the *architecture* of the sentence like? Does meaning build *periodically* or *cumulatively*, by suspension or by accretion?

4. How are *connections* made? How do words, phrases, clauses, sentences link up grammatically and/or rhetorically?

Order

English sentences tend to move from subject to verb to complement, in that order: S-V-C. "The sea is deep and dark." If you invert that and write "Deep and dark is the sea" (C-V-S), something a little unusual is felt to be happening, a change in mood perhaps, and in tone, even in genre: the inverted sentence feels not only more somber and more formal, but more poetic. Something similar happens in the common shift of an adverbial complement (*e.g.*, a prepositional phrase) from the end of the sentence to the front, which entails a verb-subject reversal: not the *regular* "A pale moon hangs in the sky" (S-V-C), but the *inverted* "In the sky hangs a pale moon" (C-V-S). Here is D. H. Lawrence making just this reversal, with a long phrasal complement in the sentence opening, then the verb "lies," then the subject, "silver potentiality," creating a C-V-S-order:

> Under the surge of ruin, unmitigated winter, lies the silver potentiality of all blossom ("Whistling of Birds").

Again:

> In the bottoms of impenetrable blackthorn, each evening and morning now, out flickers a whistling of birds.

And again:

> In his song is heard the first brokenness and uncertainty of the transition.

Inversion turns out to be a marked feature of this poetically evocative essay about—in fact—transition, from winter to spring, death to life, silence to sound, suffering to song. It is as if the syntax itself, by reversing expected progressions, wanted to astonish us with the very idea of movement and progression: the marvelous, unthinkable changes in the world that the essay celebrates.

The slightly archaic air of such inversions suggests, too, that contemporary English may be losing some of its tolerance for this kind of syntactic play; yet an inversion like the following feels thoroughly colloquial and current:

> To the world's business he is dead (Lamb, "The Convalescent").

This inverted sentence interrupts a series of short paragraphs dominated by perfectly regular S-V-C syntax, rendered even more insistent by a repeated "He + predicate" structure (a figure known in traditional rhetoric as *anaphora*—see also p. 735):

> He has put on the strong armour of sickness . . . He lies pitying himself . . . He is forever plotting . . . He makes the most of himself . . . He compassionates himself all over . . . He is his own sympathiser . . . He cares for few spectators . . . He likes it . . .

The short inverted sentence, "To the world's business he is dead," reverses the enumerative momentum of the anaphoric S-V-C series and opens the way for change. It is like a neat, strong hinge on which the style can turn to new subject matter and new structural patterns.

Inverted syntax serves both to summarize the cumulative sense of a passage and to intimate some uncertainty about it, in this excerpt from Woolf's "The Death of the Moth":

> He [the moth at her window] flew vigorously to one corner of his compartment, and, after waiting there a second, flew across to the other. What remained for him but to fly to a third corner and then to a fourth? That was all he could do, in spite of the size of the downs, the width of the sky, the far-off smoke of houses, and the romantic voice, now and then, of a steamer out at sea. *What he could do he did.* Watching . . .

The questioner at once answers her own question and makes as if to sound it out afresh: "What," the relative pronoun of the inverted answering sentence (in italics), echoes the earlier interrogative "What," an effect that's amplified by the initial sound group of the next sentence, "Watching . . ." It is an apt local stylist effect in an essay concerned with the mystery of individual lives—a moth's, a writer's—and their potency in the great scheme of life and death: "What he *could* do . . ." What?

Verb or Noun

On the face of it, the choice of what will predominate in a sentence, its verbs or its nouns, seems like a matter of diction. *Verb* and *noun* are not lexical notions but syntactical ones bearing on the structures of sentences: *noun* refers to words in the sentence which designate agency or condition, words (like "Cynthia," or "pesticides," or "loneliness") capable of serving as the subjects of clauses; *verb* refers to words designating action or being, words (like "says," "destroy" or "is") capable of predicating things about subjects. It is of course in the nature of sentences that they require both subjects and predicates, both nouns and verbs, in order to work *as* grammatical sentences. In most styles, nouns and verbs—the chief carriers of meaning within sentences—do equal work in tandem with each other; but certain styles, or certain phases of a given style, tend to foreground either their nouns or their verbs. In a *nominal* (*i.e.*, noun-centered) style, the verbs—grammatically indispensable though they are—pale into the background by being kept at a minimum, with relatively colorless, weak, or general meanings; the message of the sentence clusters into its nouns and noun phrases (subject phrases, complement phrases, prepositional phrases), gliding over the verbs as if they were so much filler, glue. A dominantly *verbal* style, on the other hand, exploits the concreteness and specificity of verbs to create a vigorous and/or evocative prose that dispenses with all but structurally essential nouns; action and movement tend to subdue, even overwhelm, agency and condition.

Here is a passage from Franklin Russell's "A Madness of Nature," an essay whose subject pushes its style towards the *verbal* pole:

> The attack of the codfish is a brutal opening to a ritual, and a contradiction in their character. Normally, they are sedentary feeders on the sea floor. Now, however, they are possessed. Their jaws rip and tear; the water darkens with capelin blood: the shredded pieces of flesh hang suspended or rise to the surface.

The first two sentences are nominal, filling their verb slots with the inactive words "is" and "are." After "Now, however, they are possessed," the syntax turns energetically verbal in picturing the "possessed" frenzy—the "madness"—of the attack: "rip," "tear," "darkens"; participles—"shredded," "suspended"—specify and intensify the verbs "hang" and "rise." Here, a few paragraphs later, is the hunting and feeding frenzy in full force (verbs and verb-based forms italicized):

> The cod *attack* in mid-depth. The gulls *smother* the surface and *press* the capelin back among the submarine hunters. The murres and puffins *fly* underwater, their *beating* wings *turning* them rapidly back and forth. They *meet* the cod, *flail* wings in desperate haste, *are caught*, *crushed*, and *swallowed*. Now seabirds as well as capelin *become* the *hunted*. Puffin and murre *tangle* wings. Silver walls of capelin *flicker*, *part*, *reform*. Some seabirds *surface* abruptly, *broken* wings *dangling*. Others with a leg or legs *torn* off, *fly* frantically, *crash*, *skitter* in shock across the water.

Verbs and their participial forms (with -ed or -ing) graphically render the underwater killing melee, thickening into twos and threes around nouns: in this bloody havoc, identity ceases to matter along with agency; there is only killing and being killed.

Contrast this with a noun-dominated passage from Gould's expository-argumentative essay, "Of Wasps and WASPs" with its analytic focus on the concept "taxonomy" (itself, of course, a noun):

> Still, although species may be discrete, they have no immutable essence. Variation is the raw material of evolutionary change. It represents the fundamental reality of nature, not an accident about a created norm. Variation is primary; essences are illusory. Species must be defined as ranges of irreducible variation.

The working verbs, here, are primarily forms of the verb "to be": "may be," "is," "are," "must be"; add to those the bland verbs "have," "represents," and the passive "must be defined." The meaning of this passage, in its fine exactitude, is concentrated not in its verbs but in its nouns and their related adjectives: "species . . . discrete," "immutable essence," "variation," "raw material," "evolutionary change," etc. Gould's essay is by no means persistently nominal. The accessibility of his writing owes much to skillful, exact use of concrete verbs where appropriate. But his is a style that shifts easily and comfortably in and out of a lucid nominal syntax—a rare thing to bring off effectively in an informal discourse like an essay, which tends to prefer the concreteness and specificity that verbs are so good at delivering.

In parts of Russell's essay, verbal dominance is so strong that even nominal concepts, *e.g.*, "the hunted," and absolute phrases like "broken wings dangling" bear the verbal imprint. Annie Dillard takes the possibility of verbal dominance to an interesting extreme by making words commonly used as verbs do the work of nouns (called, by linguists, "conversion," or "functional shift") in this passage from "Life on the Rocks":

> I could feel *the roar* in the rough rock on which I sat; I could hear *the grate* inside each long backsweeping sea, *the rumble* of a rolled million rocks muffled *in splashes* and *the seethe* before the next wave's *heave*.

The effect of these conversions (note also the verb-based adjectives "backsweeping" and "rolled") is extraordinary: it is as if the world of *things* perceived by her senses were self-activating, both being and doing, agency and action in one. Is this, then, a *verbal* syntax, or—since so many verbs are acting like nouns—is it an ultimately *nominal* one?

Architecture: Periodic and Cumulative Sentences

One of the most resonant and riveting arguments in King's "Letter from Birmingham Jail" begins: "We have waited for more than 340 years for our constitutional and God-given rights." It's easy, King points out, "for those who have never felt the stinging dart of segregation to say 'Wait.' " Then comes this famous passage—a *single* sentence:

> But when you have seen vicious mobs lynch your mothers and fathers at will and drown your sisters and brothers at whim; when you have seen hate-filled policemen curse, kick and even kill your black brothers and sisters; when you see the vast majority of your twenty million Negro brothers smothering in an airtight cage of poverty in the midst of an affluent society; when you suddenly find your tongue twisted and your speech stammering as you seek to explain to your six-year-old daughter why she can't go to the public amusement park that has just been advertised on television, and see tears welling up in her eyes when she is told that Funtown is closed to colored children, and see ominous clouds of inferiority beginning to form in her little mental sky, and see her beginning to distort her personality by developing an unconscious bitterness toward white people; when you have to concoct an answer for a five-year-old son who is asking, "Daddy, why do white people treat colored people so mean?"; when you take a cross-country drive

> and find it necessary to sleep night after night in the uncomfortable corners of your automobile because no motel will accept you; when you are humiliated day in and day out by nagging signs reading "white" and "colored"; when your first name becomes "nigger," your middle name becomes "boy" (however old you are) and your last name becomes "John," and your wife and mother are never given the respected title "Mrs"; when you are harried by day and haunted by night by the fact that you are a Negro, living constantly at tiptoe stance, never quite knowing what to expect next, and are plagued with inner fears and outer resentments; when you are forever fighting a degenerating sense of "nobodiness"—then you will understand why we find it difficult to wait.

And here, utterly different in subject, feeling, purpose, and impact, is another very long sentence (also a *single* sentence from the standpoint of grammar—the exclamation mark near the beginning is purely expressive):

> I can see her now! And beyond her, a jumbled shifting picture of the huge casino floor, the pools of its lights on the green felt of the gambling-tables, the gesticulating beefy figures throwing crap, the ladderman high on his chair above the baccarat players, the ceaseless movement of the dealers' hands, the slow watchful patrol of the floorwalkers and pitbosses, the long, long line of holiday-makers being ushered by security men, guns at their hips, towards their evening with Mr. Englebert Humperdink in the Celebrity Room (itself sealed like a lush bordello) beside the cashiers' cage—and all around, dimly glowing, the crowded ranks of the fruit machines, clanking, winking, sometimes attended by dim crouched figures holding paper cups, and now and then erupting into a shrill ringing of bells, a clatter of jackpot coins and raucous shrieks of triumph (Morris, "Fun City").

Long, amassed sentences like these don't simply happen; they are fashioned—built up element by element. How, in each case, is this done?

The King sentence, if you read it aloud, will take your breath away—literally. Trying to get through it all in a single breath won't work; take a new breath at each of those long, internally complicated "when . . ." clauses, and you find yourself unable to pump it all back out because of the powerful sense of being in mid-stream, *not yet finished*—not finished, in fact, 'till you get to "*then* you will understand . . ." That, of course, is the main clause one waits for throughout those ten consecutive subordinate clauses leading up to it. It's only with the main clause that the sense is complete and the sentence ends. This kind of *suspension* of meaning across the unfolding syntax creates a sentence design known as *periodic*. Its forms in English go back to classical Ciceronian rhetoric; it is, in fact, the very kind of syntax that many of the early essayists, including Montaigne, Bacon, and Cornwallis, rebelled against, forsaking its elaborate engineering, its high formality, for what they felt to be less artfully manipulated, less ornate, looser sentence patterns. But periodic syntax has remained very much alive these four hundred years, as this splendidly oratorical instance from King demonstrates. Its sustained suspension, the long-delayed completing clause, has the effect of evoking in the very pace and patterning of language the realities of experience King is attempting to portray: how very long the wait for racial justice has been, how slow is the passage of 340 years.

Now back to the Morris sentence: her woman (one of the "lady violinists" from the preceding paragraph of the essay) and "beyond her, a jumbled shifting picture of the huge casino floor." With the word "floor" ends a perfectly satisfactory sentence—short (and cut in two by that exclamation mark) but grammatically complete: "I" = subject; "can see" = verb; "her. . . . And . . . a jumbled shifting picture" = direct object complement. All that follows ("the pools of its lights . . . the gesticulating beefy figures . . . the ladderman . . . ," *etc.*, *etc.*) is pure elaboration; this long string reopens the sentence by building detail upon detail to amplify its complement. Rather than delaying completion of the syntax and building details into that delay as does King's periodic sentence, this one achieves grammatical completeness at the start, then lets details accumulate afterwards (theoretically *ad infinitum*), after the basic sentence has already closed. This kind of sentence is known as *cumulative*, also called *running*, or *loose*. It tends to create the illusion—only an illusion—of utter spontaneity, as though the mind were spinning itself out naturally, portraying itself in the very process of thinking. The art of this kind of sentence lies in getting the gist of your idea exactly right at the beginning, laying out in brief, at the start, what is going to accumulate once the sentence is allowed to "run," and, then, working out the "run" itself, the controlled accretion and linking of syntactically compatible elements. Morris is a master of this kind of elongated loose sentence, deploying it again and again in her essay—most memorably, perhaps, at the very end.

The scope of a sentence may be smaller and show the design just as clearly, as in this pair of sentences from E. B. White's "A Slight Sound at Evening," the first of them *periodic*, the second *cumulative:*

> If Thoreau had merely left us an account of man's life in the woods or if he had simply retreated to the woods and there recorded his complaints about society, or even if he had contrived to include both records in one essay, *Walden* would probably not have lived a hundred years.

> At any rate, I'd like to stroll about the countryside in Thoreau's company for a day, observing the modern scene, inspecting today's snowstorm, pointing out the sights, and offering belated apologies for my sins.

In the periodic sentence, subordinate clauses build toward the delayed main clause "*Walden* would . . ."; in the *cumulative* or *loose* sentence, a string of participial phrases ("observing . . . , inspecting . . . , pointing out . . . , and offering . . .") known as *free modifiers* (because, although separated, they look syntactically back to the earlier subject "I") spin out the details of White's grammatically complete opening clause ". . . I'd like to stroll. . . ." The amble of the cumulative details suggests something of the strolling pace itself.

To appreciate how irregular alternation of periodic and running syntax can help create the fluid stylistic texture of a colloquial, contemporary essay made out of relatively short sentences, read through this sequence chosen from Scott Sanders's "Doing Time in the Thirteenth Chair":

> We sit in rows like strangers in a theatre, coats rumpled in our laps, crossing and uncrossing our legs, better than senators at a press conference.

> Curly-haired, thirty-three years old, bear-built and muscular like a middle-range wrestler, slow of eye, calm under the cross-fire of questions, I90 works—when he works—as a drywall finisher.

> They shot the bull a while, Bennie bragging about how big a dealer he used to be (ten pounds of hash and five hundred hits of acid a week), I90 jawing along like an old customer.

> She reminds me of the Amish farm wives of my Ohio childhood—stern, unpainted, built stoutly for heavy chores, her face a fortress against outsiders.

> And hasn't he been working on the city garbage trucks, getting up at four in the morning, coming home smelling like other people's trash, and hasn't she been bagging groceries at the supermarket, her hands slashed with paper cuts, and

> her mother looking after the girls, all so they can keep off the welfare?
>
> And if she loses her man for years and stony years, and has to rear those three girls alone, the cupboards empty again, she might well jerk that knife out of her purse one night and use it on something other than bread.

In respect to design, these sentences are (in order): *running*, *periodic*, *running*, *running*, *running* (compound sentence), *periodic*.

The possibilities of periodic and cumulative sentence designs are so manifold that a general discussion like this one barely makes a scratch. For instance: though postponing the main clause to the end of a sentence is the most common modern device of a periodic architecture, suspension may be created in other ways. The main *verb* of a sentence and/or its *complement* may be delayed, as in the following:

> *A pretty severe fit of indisposition* which, under the name of a nervous fever, has made a prisoner of me for some weeks past, and is but slowly leaving me, *has reduced me to an incapacity of reflecting upon any topic foreign to itself* (Lamb, "The Convalescent").
>
> And *Shelley*, whom I knew in the most superficial way, who remained essentially a stranger to me to the very end, *led me*, without in the least ever knowing what he had done, *into one of the most important and lasting experiences of my life* (Porter, "St. Augustine and the Bullfight").

Suspension is achieved in the first instance by embedding a long relative clause ("which . . . me") between the subject phrase and its verb + complement (both italicized). The periodic sentence from Porter creates a kind of staggered delay by embedding material first between subject and verb, then between verb and complementary phrase (all italicized).

In one of the nicest, most fluid sentence designs, an initial move toward periodicity may be loosened, a suspended structure may start to run and accumulate new material—and perhaps even reverse itself again:

> When I am in a serious humour, I very often walk by myself in Westminster Abbey; where the gloominess of the place, and the use to which it is applied, with the solemnity of the building, and the condition of the people who lie in it, are apt to fill my mind with a kind of melancholy, or rather thoughtfulness, that is not disagreeable (Addison, *Spectator* No. 26).

The initial subordinate clause ("When . . . humour") with main clause following ("I . . . Abbey") takes a periodic direction; but then, grammatically complete, the sentence takes off anew, in another subordinate clause ("where . . ."), which turns out to have a compound subject ("gloominess" and "use") followed by a compound prepositional phrase ("with . . .")—by this time, we're in the middle of another suspension, for, here, at last, comes the verb belonging to "gloominess" and "use": "are apt to fill . . ." At the last moment, the interposed "or rather thoughtfulness" loosens the suspension once more. The overall effect of this suspend-run, suspend-run pattern is so much like the to-and-fro of spoken language, one feels that the sentence simply "flows," like the unpremeditated talk of a superbly disciplined conversationalist—the very style, in fact, for which Addison is admired.

A last thought, on how the design of a significantly positioned sentence can affect the reader's response to a whole essay. Like several others in this book, Sanders's and Morris's essays just cited close with beautiful cumulative sentences. Because such sentences could, in theory, run on and on, accumulating more and more detail of a suitable syntactic kind, any essay ending in this manner leaves its reader with a sense of incomplete closure, of the final sentence stopped on the page while the discourse remains open, unconcluded. For different versions of this effect in context, see the endings of *e.g.*: Belloc's "The Mowing of a Field," Welty's "A Sweet Devouring," Porter's "St. Augustine and the Bullfight," Ozick's "The Riddle of the Ordinary," Selzer's "An Absence of Windows."

Making Connections

Here are two brief quotations from W. E. B. Du Bois's "On Being Black," an essay of subtle stylistic artistry:

> I arise at seven. The milkman has neglected me. He pays little attention to colored districts. My white neighbor glares elaborately.

> You are apt to have the company of a sheriff and a couple of meek or sullen black prisoners on part of your way, and dirty colored section hands will pour in toward night and drive you to the smallest corner.

The two passages not only look different on the page, they have a very different momentum when read; they engage the mind in distinct ways. The first passage is made up of four very short, grammatically simple sentences set end to end; the spaces between them are indeterminate, as are the logical relationships that underlie the sequence. The unexpressed link between the first and second sentence is surely temporal: "When (or "whenever") I arise at seven (I discover that) the milkman has neglected me." The third sentence appears to make an inference from the second—or is it the other way around? And what is the link between the neighbor's glare and the milkman's neglect? Is the former the result of the latter, or is it, in some intricate sociopolitical way, the cause of the latter? It is only by attending to the essay as a whole that the reader can begin to construe and interpret these unexpressed relationships; the power of this prose lies in recording with such apparent simplicity what is by no means simple—what is, for this essayist, the central riddle of his social existence. Now for the second passage: it is, most obviously, a single sentence compounded of two clauses (" You . . . your ways" + "dirty . . . corner") each of which, in turn, contains two smaller compounded elements; these compounds, at both the clausal and the phrasal level, are created by the conjunction "and." One moves through this sentence with great ease—no spaces, no pauses (except for the brief syntactical one at the medial comma). The idea is to say what it's like to travel in a Jim Crow car, and the sentence gets through it all in one smooth sweep. One may be as hard put to distinguish logical relationships among the parts as in the first passage, but this sentence doesn't invite that kind of scrutiny; it averts it by a unity of effect, of things adding up and falling into place with a terrible coherence.

The first passage suppresses connections by omitting *conjunctions;* this is known as *asyndeton* (from the Greek, "not bound together"). The second passage emphasizes connections by repeating the *coordinating conjunction* "and"; this is *polysyndeton* ("many/much" + "bound together"). Other coordinating conjunctions that can create similar effects are: so, or, nor, for, but, yet. In a general sense, polysyndetic writing is a mode of artful coherence, asyndetic writing a mode of artful incoherence. To understand how each might be working in a given essay, one needs, of course, to consider the whole discourse—its subject, voice, form, purpose, stylistic shifts and range.

For a somewhat fuller illustration of connected and disconnected styles, consider the following pairs of examples, each of which juxtaposes a predominantly *asyndetic* (*a*) and a *polysyndetic* (*b*) passage by the same writer:

a. The world is a place of business. What an infinite bustle! I am awakened almost every night by the panting locomotive. It interrupts my dreams. There is no sabbath. It would be glorious to see mankind at leisure for once. It is nothing but work, work, work (Thoreau, "Life without Principle").

b. The day went by, and at evening I passed the yard of another neighbor, who keeps many servants, and spends much money foolishly, while he adds nothing to the common stock, and there I saw the stone of the morning lying beside a whimsical structure intended to adorn his Lord Timothy Dexter's premises, and the dignity forthwith departed from the teamster's labor, in my eyes (Thoreau, "Life without Principle").

a. Your hair is whitening, you are a well of tears, what you meant to do (beauty and justice) you have not done, papa and mama are under the earth, you live in panic and dread, the future shrinks and darkens, stories are only vapor, your inmost craving is for nothing but an old scarred pen, and what, God knows, is that? (Ozick, "A Drugstore in Winter").

b. The sound of thunder has its praise, and the sight of the sea, and a rainbow; beautiful animals are praised, and trees in their first blossoming of the year or for their beauty alone, and the new moon, and new clothing, and sexual delight (Ozick, "The Riddle of the Ordinary").

a. If you do not know the swamp you do not enter it easily, no more easily than you would parachute for the first time from a plane. Panthers. Water moccasins. Alligators. The water creeps over your shoes. Firm bottom, sometimes bare limestone pitted with solution holes dissolved out over the centuries by plant acids, more often a tangle of leaves. Cool water, brown but entirely clear. Small plants like green stars grow on the bottom. You can drink the water (Rhodes, "The Death of the Everglades").

b. He raised the cane over his head baring his teeth and jammed the cane down and pinned the lizard to the flagstone tearing its belly out and it twisted over, its four infant hands clutching the air and its mouth opening and closing and the man jerked the cane up and jammed it down and jammed it up and down until he had smashed the lizard into the stone (Rhodes, "The Death of the Everglades").

Note that the absence of connection (asyndeton) between simple, short sentences in a row may be marked either by periods (Thoreau, [a]) or by commas (Ozick, [a]). In the asyndetic excerpt from Rhodes (a), pieces of sentences (words, phrases) are set side by side in the same way as full clauses, without connection of any kind.

A characteristic feature of polysyndeton—connection by coordinating conjunctions—is the levelling of the sentence's structural hierarchies.

In the polysyndetic example from Rhodes (b) the conjunction "and" joins full clauses (subject + predicate units) as well as single words and phrases *within* those clauses. The mere fact of connection takes over as the ranking of sentence elements collapses; the longer it gets, the more the sentence seems merely to be running on and on. In Rhodes's lizard story, this device is beautifully calculated to mesmerize and stun.

But coordinating conjunctions are not the only means of grammatical connection; there are the *subordinating conjunctions* (if, when, although, because, while, as, so that, etc.) and the *relative pronouns* (that, which, who, whom, by which, etc). These grammatical links clarify hierarchical patterns in complex sentences to show exactly how elements are ranked in relation to each other. Where this means of connection predominates, the result is *hypotaxis* (from Greek, "to arrange under"). On the face of it, a *hypotactic* style may demand more from its reader than a style formed out of short, disconnected elements or pieces loosely joined by "and," "or," and the like. Try these two excerpts from Baldwin's "Equal in Paris," the first one a single complex sentence, the second a shorter sentence followed by a very long one:

> As in movies I have seen, I was placed against the wall, facing an old-fashioned camera, *behind which* stood one of the most completely cruel and indifferent faces I have ever seen, *while* someone next to me and, therefore, just outside my line of vision, read off in a voice *from which* all human feeling, even feeling of the most base description, had long since fled, *what* must be called my public characteristics—*which*, at that time and in that place, seemed anything but that.

> I knew very well *what* Americans saw *when* they looked at me and this allowed me to play endless and sinister variations on the role *which* they had assigned me; *since* I knew *that* it was, for them, of the utmost importance *that* they never be confronted with *what*, in their own personalities, made this role so necessary and gratifying to them, I knew *that* they could never call my hand or, indeed, afford to know *what* I was doing; *so that* I moved into every crucial situation with the deadly and rather desperate advantages of bitterly accumulated perception, of pride and contempt.

Both passages bristle with relative pronouns and subordinating conjunctions (in italics). It is these logical links that enable Baldwin to render so precise a dramatic situation in the first instance, so exact and finely analyzed an interior reality in the second passage. Hypotaxis, because it builds logical relationships among sentence elements rather than merely linking them serially, is able to articulate ideas with great conciseness and clarity—but only if the reader pays the closest attention. It's in that sense that hypotactic styles are demanding: your wits must be fully engaged in the syntax; it will not let you daydream between clauses or encourage you to glide along a smooth path of "ands." But a good stretch of hypotaxis leaves very little unsaid: there are no spaces to get lost in, no gaps to construe, no loose joints to wonder about.

One of the early masters of modern English prose style, John Donne, demands much from his reader and gives much in return. Here is a magnificent, predominantly hypotactic sentence from his Meditation No. 4, which opens, almost innocently, in a simple polysyndetic string (all conjunctions and relative pronouns in italics):

> God hath taken man's creature, death, into his hand, *and* mended it; *and whereas* it hath in itself a fearful form *and* aspect, *so that* man is afraid of his own creature, God presents it to him, in a familiar, in an assiduous, in an agreeable, *and* acceptable form, in sleep, *that so when* he awakes from sleep, *and* says to himself, shall I be no otherwise *when* I am dead, *than* I was even now, *when* I was asleep, he may be ashamed of his waking dreams, *and* of his melancholic fancying out a horrid *and* an affrightful figure of that death *which* is so like sleep.

In a hypotactic prose, as these examples show, the syntax presses towards maximal fullness and specificity of articulation by linking clauses grammatically with apt conjunctions. In its structure and effects, this style is the antithesis of the short, disconnected, incoherent sentence stream discussed at the beginning of this section: "I arise at seven. The milkman has neglected me." And so on. In opposition to *hypotaxis* ("to arrange under"), this kind of asyndetic style is known as *parataxis* ("to arrange side by side"). One way, of course, to make explicit the connections suppressed by parataxis would be to transform such sentences grammatically into a long hypotactic one; another way—a very important and interesting one in the life of English prose style—is to retain the grammatical asyndeton and to suggest connection and relationship by *rhetorical* means. That means, almost infinitely variable and rich, is *parallelism:* giving similar form to elements having similar function or status. Any syntactic entity can participate in a parallel series: a sentence, a dependent clause, a subject phrase, a verb phrase, a complement phrase, a phrasal modifier, a single word.

Here, from Bacon's "Of Studies," is a series of three short *paratactic* sentences bound by parallelism:

> To spend too much time in studies is sloth; to use them too much for ornament is affectation; to make judgment wholly by their rules is the humour of a scholar.

Bacon's analysis of how studies may be misused—and by implication, how they may be rightly used—is clear and coherent despite the lack of grammatical connections. The form of the first two sentences is identical at all levels of structure; the third member of the series lengthens two of its parts: the phrasal modifier "wholly by their rules" and the complement "the humour of a scholar." Such variation within parallel structures is common, perhaps to avoid the stiffness of perfect symmetry. As with other stylistic devices, the unexpected keeps the design vital. Two additional examples from later essayists show similar tripartite parallelism with parataxis, and the same tendency towards asymmetry in the final member:

> He has put on the strong armour of sickness, he is wrapped in the callous hide of suffering, he keeps his sympathy, like some curious vintage, under trusty lock and key, for his own use only (Lamb, "The Convalescent").

> Speak as you think, be what you are, pay your debts of all kinds (Emerson, "Illusions").

In Emerson, all three clauses speak imperatively, building a unified aphorism for right living. The identical verb forms reinforce the overall parallelism, as do the repetitions of the initial pronoun subject in Lamb; this sort of emphatic parallelism by initial repetition (*anaphora*) is a favorite device of rhetorical connection (see also the Bacon passage just cited).

Two nice variations of parallelism with parataxis can be observed in these two passages from modern writers:

> Malaria was endemic, typhus never absent, bubonic plague a regular visitor, dysentery, without benefit of plumbing, a commonplace (Huxley, "Hyperion to a Satyr").

> The Ordinary lets us live out our humanity; it doesn't scare us; it doesn't excite us; it doesn't distract us—it brings us the safe return of the school bus every day, it lets us eat one meal after another, put one foot in front of the other (Ozick, "The Riddle of the Ordinary").

Huxley's four-part parallelism (with lengthened final member) omits the verb "was" after the first clause, a good device of concision when all clauses share the same implicit verb. Ozick creates a contrastive set of parallel sentences ("it doesn't" vs. "it brings") beautifully curtailed, rather than lengthened, in the last member by omitting the subject + verb + complement structure ("it lets us") established in the two preceding clauses.

A special case of parallelism with unusually strong connective force is *balance:* the pairing of syntactic elements whose similar *form* expresses similar or associated *ideas*, as in the following:

> Their characters are respectable; their motives, I am willing to believe, were laudable (Macaulay, "On the Royal Society of Literature").

> The gaiety and frolic of a bottle companion improves with him into a solid friendship: and the ardor of a youthful appetite becomes an elegant passion (Hume, "Of the Delicacy of Taste and Passion").

Macaulay sets two clauses side by side without grammatical connection. The first subject, "their characters," balances the structurally identical and semantically associated second subject, "their motives"; the verb "are" is balanced by the verb "were"; the parenthetic clause, "I am willing to believe," in the second member creates a pleasing asymmetry. In the more subtle Hume excerpt, two grammatically compounded clauses achieve an easy forward movement of thought along two balanced parts.

A skillful variation of balance is *chiasmus:* the inverted or crossed parallel. Here are two straightforward examples (members of the chiasmus in italics):

> In the poetical quarter, I found there were *poets who had no monuments*, and *monuments which had no poets* (Addison, *Spectator* No. 26).

> But this act of comparison means that our attitude has changed; we are no longer the friends of the writer, but his judges; and just as *we cannot be too sympathetic as friends*, so *as judges we cannot be too severe* (Woolf, "How Should One Read a Book?")

In Addison, the sequence "poets . . . monuments" is reversed as "monuments . . . poets"; what was subject in the first clause becomes complement in the second, and vice versa. In the Woolf passage, the clause "we cannot be too sympathetic" precedes its modifying phrase "as friends"; the second, balancing member, reverses this order. Chiasmus may take in larger patterns beyond the single sentence, as in this passage from King's "Letter from Birmingham Jail":

> But even if the church does not come to the aid of justice, I have no despair about the future. I have no fear about the outcome of our struggle in Birmingham, even if our motives are at present misunderstood.

In the first sentence, the subordinate "even if . . ." clause *precedes* the main clause; in the second, it *follows*. Try undoing this reversal to produce a conventional parallelism—something is lost, some sense of climax, and, more subtly, more elusively, some sense of the mind reckoning with itself, grappling with the composition of an idea rather than laying it out in a smoothly predetermined parallel syntax.

Perhaps the most elegant variant of parallelism is *balance* with *antithesis:* similarity (even identity) of syntactic *form* with difference (even opposition) of *meaning*. The expressive economy of this device is difficult to overstate; a closely wrought balanced syntax with antithesis of sense adheres so tightly, so forcibly, one would have a hard time prying the sense apart from the syntax—that is, to "translate" such a passage into a less architectonic style. Certain writers (Bacon, Macaulay, King among them) are particularly fond of this device, though nearly all essayists attempt it whenever striking and emphatic compression of ideas is called for. Here is a simple example from Franklin's "The Ephemera":

> Alas, art is long, and life is short.

Clause balances clause, permitting the play of antithesis between art/life, long/short. A similar design from Cowley:

> The truth of it is, that a man in much business must either make himself a knave, or else the world will make him a fool . . . ("The Dangers of an Honest Man in Much Company").

Fielding, in his next example, balances a whole row of nouns with finely different connotations against each other:

> For instance, when mistaking certain things called gravity, canting, blustering, ostentation, pomp, and the like, for wisdom, piety, magnanimity, charity, true greatness, etc., we give to the former the honour and reverence due to the latter ("An Essay on Nothing").

The preceding selections offer a mere glimpse of the stylistic wealth afforded by the connective power of parallelism in its many forms. To close, here are three memorable longer passages showing intricate designs of parallelism with antithesis, both within clauses and across whole sentence patterns. These designs are so economical they compose entire arguments in a very small space; beyond that, their finely wrought logic encapsulates the whole moral vision of their respective essays.

From Thoreau's "Life Without Principle":

> Do we call this the land of the free? What is it to be free from King George and continue the slaves of King Prejudice? What is it to be born free and not live free? What is the value of any political freedom, but as a means to moral freedom? Is it a freedom to be slaves, or a freedom to be free, of which we boast?

From King's "Letter from Birmingham Jail":

> An unjust law is a code that a numerical or power majority group compels a minority group to obey but does not make binding on itself. This is difference made legal. By the same token, a just law is a code that a majority compels a minority to follow and that it is willing to follow itself. This is sameness made legal.

From Dickens's "Night Walks":

> Are not the sane and the insane equal at night as the sane lie dreaming? Are not all of us outside this hospital, who dream, more or less in the condition of those inside it, every night of our lives? Are we not nightly persuaded, as they daily are, that we associate preposterously with kings and queens, emperors and empresses, and notabilities of all sorts? Do we not nightly jumble events and personages and times and places, as these do daily? Are we not sometimes troubled by our own sleeping inconsistencies, and do we not vexedly try to account for them or excuse them, just as these do sometimes in respect to their waking delusions? . . . I wonder that the great master who knew everything, when he called Sleep the death of each day's life, did not call Dreams the insanity of each day's sanity.

* * *

At different moments in the history of English prose, certain ways of shaping sentences have counted as more "natural" than others, less "artificial." Written styles based on what are assumed to be the spontaneous usages of talk have tended to count as the most "natural." Yet speech habits themselves have been and are so varied, so rich (and, to some extent, shaped by writing), that the notion of a speech-based prose becomes moot. Whose speech? In what situation, to what audience, for what end? Listen to people around you and you discover that few of them talk in the kinds of paratactic strings often believed to be most "natural," most speech-like. Quite obviously, talk is not limited to patterns such as "I sat down, I yawned, I wondered what to do next." How is this any more speech-like, more "natural," than "I sat down and yawned and wondered what to do next," or "After I sat down I yawned, wondering what to do next"? Speakers of all kinds, all ages and stations, tend to run on, wrap thoughts inside other thoughts (not always as neatly as writing can do), hook ideas onto and around and under other ideas, and so on.

Whether in speaking or writing, syntax constantly opens paths of choice and, thus, creates inevitable pressures to select and arrange—craft—our utterances as we need to and wish to. The difference between speaking and writing is that, in the latter, the crafting can go on at greater leisure and more purposively; and, of course, the options we reject in writing are invisible in the final product, the text, whereas in speech, all that is said stands for better or worse, however modified or qualified in the stream of talk. In the sense that all utterance is more or less consciously crafted, all style is "artificial"—or, more to the point, artful. Like the words we choose, the ways in which we arrange them "ring true"—sound "natural"—to the extent that they harmonize with our chosen material and our sense of who we are and how we want to exist in the world through the discourses of our making.

The preceding discussion of style owes much to other writers on the subject, both specialists and generalists, whose work I have used and assimilated over many years in the classroom. The main ones are:

Abrams, M. H. *A Glossary of Literary Terms.* New York: Holt, Rinehart and Winston, Inc., 1971.

Bennett, James R., ed. *Prose Style: A Historical Approach Through Studies.* San Francisco: Chandler Publishing Company, 1971.

Gordon, Ian A. *The Movement of English Prose.* London: Longmans, Green and Co. Ltd., 1966.

Lanham, Richard A. *Analyzing Prose.* New York: Charles Scribner's Sons, 1983.

Patrick, J. Max, Robert O. Evans, John M. Wallace, and R. J. Schoeck, eds. *Style, Rhetoric, and Rhythm: Essays by Morris W. Croll.* Princeton, NJ: Princeton University Press, 1966.

Preminger, Alex, Frank J. Warnke, and O. B. Hardison, Jr., eds. *Princeton Encyclopedia of Poetry and Poetics.* Princeton, NJ: Princeton University Press, 1974.

Smith Charles Kay. *Styles and Structure: Alternative Approaches to Writing*. New York: W. W. Norton and Company, Inc., 1974.

Tufte, Virginia. *Grammar as Style*. New York: Holt, Rinehart and Winston, Inc., 1971.

Williams, Joseph M. *Origins of the English Language: A Social and Linguistic History*. New York: The Free Press, 1975.

———. *Style: Ten Lessons in Clarity & Grace*. Glenview, IL: Scott, Foresman and Company, 1981.

Author / Title Index

Absence of Windows (Selzer), An, 430-434
Achebe, Chinua, Language and the Destiny of Man, 471-478
Addison, Joseph, The Royal Exchange, 51-53
The Tombs at Westminster Abbey, 49-51
Apology for Idlers, An (Stevenson), 182-189
Atwood, Margaret, Happy Endings, 555-558

Bacon, Sir Francis, Of Boldness, 24-25
Of Studies, 22-23
Bad Time, A (Mitford), 306-316
Baker, Russell, The Flag, 381-385
Baldwin, James, Equal in Paris, 367-379
Barthelme, Donald, Not-Knowing, 485-497
Beerbohm, Max, A Relic, 206-211
Belloc, Hilaire, The Mowing of a Field, 199-205
Blackwood, Caroline, Portrait of the Beatnik, 499-506
Bly, Carol, Getting Tired, 480-483
Bowen, Elizabeth, Out of a Book, 278-282

City by the Sea, The (Naipaul), 615-630
City Walking (Hoagland), 519-520
Convalescent, The (Lamb), 87-91
Corn-pone Opinions (Twain), 173-176
Cornwallis, Sir William, Of Entertainment, 30-31
Cowardice (Theroux), 570-577
Cowley, Abraham, The Dangers of an Honest Man in Much Company, 35-39

Dangers of an Honest Man in Much Company, The (Cowley), 35-39
Death of the Everglades, The (Rhodes), 535-553
Death of the Moth, The (Woolf), 231-233
De Quincy, Thomas, On the Knocking at the Gate in *Macbeth*, 116-120
Detractor, A (Earle), 32-33
Dickens, Charles, Night Walks, 147-154
Didion, Joan, On Going Home, 525-527
On Morality, 522-525
Dillard, Annie, Life on the Rocks: The Galápagos, 601-613
Doing Time in the Thirteenth Chair (Sanders), 632-647
Donne, John, I Sleep Not Day Nor Night, 28-29
The Physician is Sent For, 26-28
Drugstore in Winter, A (Ozick), 423-428
Du Bois, W. E. B., On Being Black, 191-195
The Guilt of the Cane, 195-197

Earle, John, A Detractor, 32-33
Paul's Walk, 34
Earnest Proposal, An (Thomas), 334-336
Ehrlich, Gretel, The Smooth Skull of Winter, 649-651
Eiseley, Loren, The Winter of Man, 318-321
Eliot, T. S., Tradition and the Individual Talent, 245-251
Emerson, Ralph Waldo, Illusions, 129-136
Ephemera, The (Franklin), 54-56
Equal in Paris (Baldwin), 367-379
Essay on Nothing, An (Fielding), 57-65

Fielding, Henry, An Essay on Nothing, 57-65
Fisher, M. F. K., Moment of Wisdom, 322-326
Flag, The (Baker), 381-385
Foot-prints on the Sea-shore (Hawthorne), 138-145
Forster, E. M., What I Believe, 213-220

Franklin, Benjamin, The Ephemera, 54-56
Fun City: Las Vegas, U.S.A. (Morris), 396-407

Getting Tired (Bly), 480-483
Goldsmith, Oliver, National Prejudices, 77-80
Gould, Stephen Jay, Of Wasps and WASPs, 560-568
Grace Before Meat (Lamb), 81-87
Guilt of the Cane, The (Du Bois), 195-197

Happy Endings (Atwood), 555-558
Hawthorne, Nathaniel, Foot-prints on the Sea-shore, 138-145
Hazlitt, William, On the Feeling of Immortality in Youth, 101-109
On Going a Journey, 93-101
Hoagland, Edward, City Walking, 519-520
What I Think, What I Am, 690–692
How It Feels to Be Colored Me (Hurston), 293-296
How Should One Read a Book? (Woolf), 222-230
Hume, David, On the Delicacy of Taste and Passion, 73-76
Hurston, Zora Neale, How It Feels to Be Colored Me, 293-296
Huxley, Aldous, Hyperion to a Satyr, 264-276
Hyperion to a Satyr (Huxley), 264-276

Illusions (Emerson), 129-136
In Praise of Chekhov (McConkey), 345-355
In Pursuit of Fame (Johnson), 70-72
Irving, Washington, The Voyage, 111-115
I Sleep Not Day Nor Night (Donne), 28-29

Johnson, Samuel, In Pursuit of Fame, 70-72
On Spring, 66-69

Kind of Survivor, A (Steiner), 457-469
King, Martin Luther, Jr., Letter from Birmingham Jail, 441-455

Lamb, Charles, The Convalescent, 87-91
Grace Before Meat, 81-87
Language and the Destiny of Man (Achebe), 471-478
Laurence, Margaret, The Very Best Intentions, 387-394
Lawrence, D. H., Whistling of Birds, 235-238
Leopold, Aldo, Marshland Elegy, 239-243
Lessing, Doris, My Father, 337-344
Letter from Birmingham Jail (King), 441-455
Life on the Rocks: The Galápagos (Dillard), 601-613
Life Without Principle (Thoreau), 156-171
Looking for Zora (Walker), 584-599

Macaulay, Thomas, On the Royal Society of Literature, 122-127
McClane, Kenneth, Walls: A Journey to Auburn, 659-670
McConkey, James, In Praise of Chekhov, 345-355
McPhee, John, The Search for Marvin Gardens, 508-517
Madness of Nature, A (Russell), 408-414
Manchester, William, Okinawa: The Bloodiest Battle of All, 357-365
Marshland Elegy (Leopold), 239-243
Meynell, Alice, Solitudes, 177-180
Mitford, Nancy, A Bad Time, 306-316
Modest Proposal, A (Swift), 41-47
Momaday, N. Scott, The Way to Rainy Mountain, 529-533
Moment of Wisdom (Fisher), 322-326
Montaigne, Michel de, Of Practice, 679–688
Morris, Jan, Fun City: Las Vegas, U.S.A., 396-407
Mowing of a Field, The (Belloc), 199-205
My Father (Lessing), 337-344

Naipaul, Shiva, The City by the Sea, 615-630
National Prejudices (Goldsmith), 77-80

Night Walks (Dickens), 147-154
Not-Knowing (Barthelme), 485-497

Of Boldness (Bacon), 24-25
Of Entertainment (Cornwallis), 30-31
Of Practice (Montaigne), 679–688
Of Studies (Bacon), 22-23
Of Wasps and WASPs (Gould), 560-568
Okinawa: The Bloodiest Battle of All (Manchester), 357-365
On Being Black (Du Bois), 191-195
On Going a Journey (Hazlitt), 93-101
On Going Home (Didion), 525-527
On Morality (Didion), 522-525
On Spring (Johnson), 66-69
On the Delicacy of Taste and Passion (Hume), 73-76
On the Feeling of Immortality in Youth (Hazlitt), 101-109
On the Knocking at the Gate in *Macbeth* (De Quincey), 116-120
On the Royal Society of Literature (Macaulay), 122-127
Orwell, George, Reflections on Gandhi, 298-304
Out of a Book (Bowen), 278-282
Ozick, Cynthia, A Drugstore in Winter, 423-428
  The Riddle of the Ordinary, 416-423

Paul's Walk (Earle), 34
Physician is Sent For, The (Donne), 26-28
Porter, Katherine Anne, St. Augustine and the Bullfight, 253-262
Portrait of the Beatnik (Blackwood), 499-506

Quammen, David, Thinking About Earthworms, 653-657

Reflections on Gandhi (Orwell), 298-304
Relic, A (Beerbohm), 206-211
Rhodes, Richard, The Death of the Everglades, 535-553
Riddle of the Ordinary, The (Ozick), 416-423
Rose, Phyllis, Tools of Torture: An Essay on Beauty and Pain, 579-582
Royal Exchange, The (Addison), 51-53
Russell, Franklin, A Madness of Nature, 408-414

Sanders, Scott Russell, Doing Time in the Thirteenth Chair, 632-647
Search for Marvin Gardens, The (McPhee), 508-517
Selzer, Richard, An Absence of Windows, 430-434
  A Worm from My Notebook, 434-439
Slight Sound at Evening, A (White), 284-291
Smooth Skull of Winter, The (Ehrlich), 649-651
Solitudes (Meynell), 177-180
St. Augustine and the Bullfight (Porter), 253-262
Steiner, George, A Kind of Survivor, 457-469
Stevenson, Robert Louis, An Apology for Idlers, 182-189
Sweet Devouring, A (Welty), 328-332
Swift, Jonathan, A Modest Proposal, 41-47

Theroux, Paul, Cowardice, 570-577
Thinking About Earthworms (Quammen), 653-657
Thomas, Lewis, An Earnest Proposal, 334-336
Thoreau, Henry David, Life Without Principle, 156-171
Tombs at Westminster Abbey, The (Addison), 49-51
Tools of Torture: An Essay on Beauty and Pain (Rose), 579-582
Tradition and the Individual Talent (Eliot), 245-251
Twain, Mark, Corn-pone Opinions, 173-176

Very Best Intentions, The (Laurence), 387-394
Voyage, The (Irving), 111-115

Walker, Alice, Looking for Zora, 584-599
Walls: A Journey to Auburn (McClane), 659-670
Way to Rainy Mountain, The (Momaday), 529-533

Welty, Eudora, A Sweet Devouring, 328-332
What I Believe (Forster), 213-220
What I Think, What I Am (Hoagland), 690–692
Whistling of Birds (Lawrence), 235-238
White, E. B., A Slight Sound at Evening, 284-291
Winter of Man, The (Eiseley), 318-321
Woolf, Virginia, The Death of the Moth, 231-233
How Should One Read a Book?, 222-230
Worm from My Notebook, A (Selzer), 434-439

ACKNOWLEDGMENTS
(*continued from p. iv*)

Russell Baker. "The Flag." Reprinted from "So This is Depravity" © 1980 by Russell Baker. Reprinted with arrangement from Congdon & Weed, Chicago.

James Baldwin. "Equal in Paris." From *Notes of a Native Son* by James Baldwin. Copyright © 1955, renewed 1983, by James Baldwin. Reprinted by permission of Beacon Press.

Donald Barthelme. "Not-Knowing." Copyright © 1985 by Donald Barthelme.

Max Beerbohm. "A Relic" by Max Beerbohm. Reprinted by kind permission of Mrs. Eva Reichmann.

Uli Beier. "How the World Was Created from a Drop of Milk" from *The Origin of Life and Death* by Uli Beier in Chinua Achebe's essay "Language and the Destiny of Man." Reprinted by permission of Heinemann Publishers (Oxford) Ltd.

Hilaire Belloc. "The Mowing of a Field." Reprinted with permission of Charles Scribner's Sons, an imprint of Macmillan Publishing Company from "The Mowing of a Field" in *Hills and the Sea* by Hilaire Belloc. Copyright 1917 by Hilaire Belloc; copyright renewed.

Caroline Blackwood. "Portrait of a Beatnik" from *All That I Found There.* Copyright © 1973 by Caroline Blackwood. Reprinted by permission of George Braziller, Inc.

Carol Bly. "Getting Tired" from *Letters From the Country* by Carol Bly. Copyright © 1981 by Carol Bly. Reprinted by permission of Harper & Row, Publishers, Inc.

Elizabeth Bowen. "Out of a Book" from *Collected Impressions.* Reprinted by permission of Curtis Brown Ltd. Copyright © 1950 by Elizabeth Bowen.

Sir William Cornwallis. "Of Entertainment" from *Essayes by Sir William Cornwallis the Younger*, D. C. Allen, ed. Reprinted by permission of the Johns Hopkins University Press.

Abraham Cowley. "The Dangers of an Honest Man in Much Company" by Abraham Cowley from *Abraham Cowley, Poetry and Prose*, L. C. Martin, ed., Oxford University Press, 1949. Reprinted by permission of the Oxford University Press.

Joan Didion. "On Going Home" and "On Morality" from *Slouching Towards Bethlehem* by Joan Didion. Copyright © 1965, 1967, 1968 by Joan Didion. Reprinted by permission of Farrar, Straus and Giroux, Inc.

Annie Dillard. "Life in the Galápagos" from *Teaching a Stone to Talk* by Annie Dillard. Copyright © 1982 by Annie Dillard. Reprinted by permission of Harper & Row, Publishers, Inc.

John Donne. "The Physician is Sent For: Meditation No. 4" and "I Sleep Not Day Nor Night: Meditation No. 15." From *Devotions Upon Emergent Occasions* by John Donne, Anthony Raspa., ed. Reprinted by permission of McGill-Queen's University Press.

W. E. B. Du Bois. "On Being Black" from *W. E. B. DuBois: A Reader* edited by Meyer Weinberg. Copyright © 1970 by Meyer Weinberg. Reprinted by permission of Harper & Row, Publishers, Inc. "The Guilt of the Cane" from *W. E. B. DuBois: A Reader* edited by Meyer Weinberg. Copyright © 1970 by Meyer Weinberg. Reprinted by permission of Harper & Row, Publishers, Inc.

Gretel Ehrlich. "The Smooth Skull of Winter." From *The Solace of Open Spaces* by Gretel Ehrlich. Copyright © 1985 by Gretel Ehrlich. Reprinted by permission of the publisher, Viking Penguin, a division of Penguin Books USA Inc.

Loren Eiseley. "The Winter of Man." Copyright © 1972 by The New York Times Company. Reprinted by permission.

T. S. Eliot. "Tradition and the Individual Talent" from *Selected Essays* by T. S. Eliot, copyright © 1950 by Harcourt Brace Jovanovich, Inc. and renewed 1978 by Esme Valerie Eliot, reprinted by permission of the publisher. "Tradition and the Individual Talent" in *The Sacred Wood* by T. S. Eliot. Reprinted by permission of Methuen & Co. Excerpt from "Little Gidding." Reprinted by permission of Faber and Faber Ltd from *Collected Poems 1909–1962* by T. S. Eliot. Excerpt from "Little Gidding" in *Four Quartets*, copyright 1943 by T. S. Eliot and renewed 1971 by Esme Valerie Eliot, reprinted by permission of Harcourt Brace Jovanovich, Inc.

Edward Field. The poem "Magic Words" in Chinua Achebe's essay "Language and the Destiny of Man" is a passage from Edward Field's adaptation of Inuit material in the Rasmussen Archives. From *Eskimo Songs and Stories*, Delacourte Press, 1973. Reprinted by permission of the author.

M. F. K. Fisher. "Moment of Wisdom." From *Sister Age* by M. F. K. Fisher. Copyright © 1983 by M. F. K. Fisher. Reprinted by permission of Alfred A. Knopf Inc.

E. M. Forster. "What I Believe" from *Two Cheers for Democracy*, copyright 1939 and renewed 1967 by E. M. Forster, reprinted by permission of Harcourt Brace Jovanovich, Inc. "What I Believe" from *Two Cheers for Democracy*, by E. M. Forster. Reprinted by permission of Edward Arnold (the Educational, Academic and Medical Publishing Division of Hodder & Stoughton), London.

Stephen Jay Gould. "Of Wasps and WASPs" is reprinted from *The Flamingo's Smile, Reflections in Natural History*, by Stephen Jay Gould, by permission of W. W. Norton & Company, Inc. Copyright © 1985 by Stephen Jay Gould.

Nathaniel Hawthorne. "Foot-prints on the Sea-shore" by Nathaniel Hawthorne, from *Twice-told Tales*, Vol. IX of the Centenary Edition of the Works of Nathaniel Hawthorne, William Charvat, Roy Harvey Pearce, and Claude M. Simpson, eds., is reprinted by permission. © 1974 by the Ohio State University Press. All rights reserved.

Robert Hemenway. Selections from "Zora Neale Hurston and the Eatonville Anthropology" from *The Harlem Renaissance Remembered* in Alice Walker's essay "Looking for Zora." Reprinted by permission of the author.

Edward Hoagland. "City Walking" by Edward Hoagland. Copyright © 1975 by Edward Hoagland. "What I Think, What I Am." From *The Tugman's Passage* by Edward Hoagland. Copyright © 1976, 1977, 1978, 1979, 1980, 1982 by Edward Hoagland. Reprinted by permission of Random House, Inc.

Zora Neale Hurston. "How It Feels to be Colored Me" from *I Love Myself When I Am Laughing . . . And Then Again When I Am Looking Mean and Impressive.* Reprinted by permission of the Zora Neale Hurston Estate.

Aldous Huxley. "Hyperion to a Satyr" from *Tomorrow and Tomorrow and Tomorrow and Other Stories* by Aldous Huxley. Copyright © 1956 by Aldous Huxley. Reprinted by permission of Harper & Row, Publishers, Inc.

Alfred C. Kinsey. Material quoted from Alfred C. Kinsey's *Sexual Behavior in the Human Male* in Stephen Jay Gould's essay "Of Wasps and WASPs." Reprinted by permission of The Kinsey Institute for Research in Sex, Gender, and Reproduction, Inc.

Martin Luther King, Jr. "Letter from Birmingham Jail" from *Why We Can't Wait* by Martin Luther King, Jr. Copyright 1963, 1964 by Martin Luther King, Jr. Reprinted by permission of Harper & Row, Publishers, Inc.

Margaret Laurence. "The Very Best Intentions" from *Heart of a Stranger.* By permission of the estate of Margaret Laurence.

D. H. Lawrence. "Whistling of Birds" from *Phoenix: The Posthumous Papers* by D. H. Lawrence, ed. Edward D. McDonald. Copyright 1936 by Frieda Lawrence, renewed © 1964 by the Estate of the late Frieda Lawrence Ravagli. Reprinted by permission of the publisher, Viking Penguin, a division of Penguin Books USA Inc.

Doris Lessing. "My Father," from *A Small Personal Voice.* © 1963 Doris Lessing. Reprinted by permission of Johnathan Clowes Ltd., London, on behalf of Doris Lessing.

Aldo Leopold. "Marshland Elegy." From *A Sand County Almanac, With Other Essays on Conservation from Round River* by Aldo Leopold. Copyright © 1949, 1953, 1966, renewed 1977, 1981 by Oxford University Press, Inc. Reprinted by permission.

Kenneth McClane. "Walls: A Journey to Auburn." Reprinted by permission of Transaction Publishers from *Community Review,* Vol. VII, No. 2. Copyright © 1987 by the City University of New York.

James McConkey. "In Praise of Chekhov." Originally published in *The Hudson Review,* Autumn, 1967, Vol. XX, No. 3, and reprinted in *Court of Memory,* E. P. Dutton, copyright 1983 by James McConkey.

John McPhee. "The Search for Marvin Gardens" from *Pieces of the Frame* by John McPhee. Copyright © 1972, 1975 by John McPhee. Reprinted by permission of Farrar, Straus and Giroux, Inc.

William Manchester. "Okinawa: The Bloodiest Battle of All." Reprinted by permission of Don Congdon Associates, Inc. Copyright © 1987 by William Manchester.

Alice Meynell. "Solitudes" from *Prose and Poetry*. Reprinted by the Estate of Alice Meynell and Jonathan Cape Publishers.

Nancy Mitford. "A Bad Time" from *The Water Beetle*. Reprinted by permission of the Peters Fraser & Dunlop Group Ltd.

N. Scott Momaday. "The Way to Rainy Mountain." First published in *The Reporter*, 26 January 1967. Reprinted from *The Way to Rainy Mountain*, © 1969, The University of New Mexico Press.

Michel de Montaigne. "Of Practice." Reprinted from *The Complete Essays of Montaigne*, translated by Donald M. Frame with the permission of the publishers, Stanford University Press, © 1958 by the Board of Trustees of the Leland Stanford Junior University.

Jan Morris. "Fun City: Las Vegas, U.S.A." From *Journeys* by Jan Morris. Copyright © 1984 by Jan Morris. Reprinted by permission of Oxford University Press, Inc.

Shiva Naipaul. "The City by the Sea" from *Beyond the Dragon's Mouth: Stories and Pieces*. Copyright © 1984 by Shiva Naipaul. Reprinted by permission of the publisher, Viking Penguin, a division of Penguin Books USA Inc.

George Orwell. "Reflections on Gandhi" from *Shooting an Elephant and Other Essays* by George Orwell, copyright 1950 by Sonia Brownell Orwell and renewed 1978 by Sonia Pitt-Rivers, reprinted by permission of Harcourt Brace Jovanovich, Inc. "Reflections on Gandhi" in *Shooting an Elephant and Other Essays*. Reprinted by permission of the estate of the late Sonia Brownell Orwell and Martin Secker & Warburg Ltd.

Cynthia Ozick. "The Riddle of the Ordinary" and "A Drugstore in Winter." From *Art and Ardor* by Cynthia Ozick. Copyright © 1983 by Cynthia Ozick. Reprinted by permission of Alfred A. Knopf Inc.

Katherine Anne Porter. "St. Augustine and the Bullfight" from *The Collected Essays and Occasional Writings of Katherine Anne Porter*. Copyright © 1970 by Katherine Anne Porter. Reprinted by permission of Houghton Mifflin Co./Seymour Lawrence.

David Quammen. "Thinking About Earthworms: An Unpopular Meditation on Darwin's Silent Choir" from *Flight of the Iguana* by David Quammen, copyright © 1988 by David Quammen. Used by permission of Dell Books, a division of Bantam, Doubleday, Dell Publishing Group, Inc.

Richard Rhodes. "The Death of the Everglades." Excerpt(s) from *Looking For America* by Richard Rhodes, copyright © 1979 by Richard Rhodes. Used by permission of Doubleday, a division of Bantam Doubleday Dell Publishing Group, Inc. "The Death of the Everglades" is here reprinted in its entirety.

Phyllis Rose. "Tools of Torture: An Essay on Beauty and Pain." Reprinted by permission of Georges Borchardt, Inc. for the author. Copyright © 1986 by Phyllis Rose. First published in *The Atlantic Monthly*.

Franklin Russell. "A Madness of Nature." Reprinted by permission of Curtis Brown, Ltd. Copyright © 1968 by Franklin Russell.

Scott Russell Sanders. "Doing Time in the Thirteenth Chair" from *The Paradise of Bombs*. Copyright © 1987 by Scott Russell Sanders; reprinted by permission of the author and the author's agent, Virginia Kidd.

Richard Selzer. "A Worm from My Notebook." Copyright © 1986 by Richard Selzer. By permission of William Morrow & Co., Inc. "An Absence of Windows." Copyright © 1979 by David Goldman and Janet Selzer, Trustees. By permission of William Morrow & Co.

George Steiner. "A Kind of Survivor." Reprinted with permission of Atheneum Publishers, an imprint of Macmillan Publishing Company from *Language and Silence* by George Steiner. Copyright © 1963, 1967 by George Steiner.

Jonathan Swift. "A Modest Proposal" by Jonathan Swift from *Prose Works of Jonathan Swift* (Vol. XII, *The Irish Tracts*), Herbert Davis, ed. Oxford University Press, 1955. Reprinted by permission of Oxford University Press.

Paul Theroux. "Cowardice" from *Sunrise with Seamonsters: Travels and Discoveries* by Paul Theroux. Copyright © 1985 by Cape Cod Scriveners Company.

Lewis Thomas. "An Earnest Proposal." From *The Lives of a Cell* by Lewis Thomas. Copyright © 1974 by Lewis Thomas. Originally appeared in the *New England Journal of Medicine*. Reprinted by permission of Viking Penguin, a division of Penguin Books USA Inc.

Henry David Thoreau. "Life Without Principle" from *The Selected Works of Thoreau*. Walter Harding, ed. Published by Houghton Mifflin Co.

Mark Twain. "Corn-pone Opinions" from *Europe and Elsewhere* by Mark Twain. Copyright 1923 by the Mark Twain Company; copyright renewed 1951 by the Mark Twain Company. Reprinted by permission of HarperCollins Publishers Inc.

Alice Walker. "Looking for Zora" from *In Search of Our Mothers' Gardens*, copyright © 1975 by Alice Walker, reprinted by permission of Harcourt Brace Jovanovich, Inc.

Eudora Welty. "A Sweet Devouring." From *The Eye of the Story: Selected Essays and Reviews* by Eudora Welty. Copyright © 1978 by Eudora Welty. Reprinted by permission of Random House, Inc.

E. B. White. "A Slight Sound at Evening" from *Essays of E. B. White* by E. B. White. Copyright 1954 by E. B. White. Reprinted by permission of Harper & Row, Publishers, Inc.

Virginia Woolf. "The Death of the Moth" from *The Death of the Moth and Other Essays.* Reprinted by permission of the Executors of the Virginia Woolf Estate and the Hogarth Press. "How Should One Read a Book?" from *The Second Common Reader.* Reprinted by permission of the Executors of the Virginia Woolf Estate and The Hogarth Press. "How Should One Read a Book?" from *The Second Common Reader* by Virginia Woolf, copyright 1932 by Harcourt Brace Jovanovich, Inc. and renewed 1960 by Leonard Woolf, reprinted by permission of the publisher. "The Death of the Moth" from *The Death of the Moth and Other Essays* by Virginia Woolf, copyright 1942 by Harcourt Brace Jovanovich, Inc. and renewed 1970 by Marjorie T. Parsons, Executrix, reprinted by permission of the publisher.

W. B. Yeats. "The Choice" in Cynthia Ozick's "The Riddle of the Ordinary." Reprinted with permission of Macmillan Publishing Company from *The Poems of W. B. Yeats: A New Edition*, edited by Richard J. Finneran. Copyright 1933 by Macmillan Publishing Company, renewed 1961 by Bertha Georgie Yeats.